CRIMINAL EVIDENCE

CRIMINAL EVIDENCE

Principles and Cases

SEVENTH EDITION

Thomas J. Gardner
Attorney at Law and
former Assistant District Attorney

Terry M. Anderson
Creighton University School of Law

WADSWORTH
CENGAGE Learning

Australia • Brazil • Japan • Korea • Mexico • Singapore • Spain • United Kingdom • United States

WADSWORTH
CENGAGE Learning™

**Criminal Evidence: Principles and Cases,
Seventh Edition**
Thomas J. Gardner and Terry M. Anderson

Senior Acquisitions Editor: Carolyn Henderson Meier

Development Editor: Meaghan Banks

Assistant Editor: Meaghan Banks

Editorial Assistant: John Chell

Technology Project Manager: Bessie Weiss

Marketing Manager: Michelle Williams

Marketing Assistant: Jillian Myers

Marketing Communications Manager: Tami Strang

Project Managers, Editorial Production:
   Jennie Redwitz, Cheri Palmer

Creative Director: Rob Hugel

Art Director: Maria Epes

Print Buyer: Rebecca Cross

Permissions Editor: Bob Kauser and Robin Young

Production Service: Scratchgravel Publishing Services

Photo Researcher: Kim Adams Cox

Copy Editor: Carol Reitz

Illustrator: Scratchgravel Publishing Services

Chapter-Opening Image: © Ashley Cooper/Corbis

Cover Designer: Christopher Harris, RHDG

Cover Image: Peter Dazeley/Getty Images

Compositor: Pre-PressPMG

For product information and technology assistance, contact us at
Cengage Learning Customer & Sales Support, 1-800-354-9706
For permission to use material from this text or product,
submit all requests online at **www.cengage.com/permissions**
Further permissions questions can be e-mailed to
permissionrequest@cengage.com

Library of Congress Control Number: 2008940667

ISBN-13: 978-0-495-59924-1

ISBN-10: 0-495-59924-7

Wadsworth
10 Davis Drive
Belmont, CA, 94002-3098
USA

Cengage Learning is a leading provider of customized learning
solutions with office locations around the globe, including
Singapore, the United Kingdom, Australia, Mexico, Brazil, and Japan.
Locate your local office at **www.cengage.com/global.**

Cengage Learning products are represented in Canada by
Nelson Education, Ltd.

To learn more about Wadsworth, visit **www.cengage.com/wadsworth**

Purchase any of our products at your local college store or at our preferred
online store **www.ichapters.com**.

Printed in the United States of America
1 2 3 4 5 6 7 12 11 10 09

To high schoolers everywhere and especially
Alex and Nick Anderson, Brian and David Demet, Brenie Collins,
and Eli Feldman. Enjoy this great time of your life,
and may you live in a peaceful and prosperous world.

———————

ABOUT THE AUTHORS

Thomas J. Gardner, after earning a Bachelor of Science degree in economics, served three years as a naval officer in the South Pacific during and immediately after World War II. He then attended and graduated from Marquette Law School with a Juris Doctor degree in 1949 and earned a Master of Arts degree in political science. During the Korean War he worked in procurement for the Air Material Command. His long association with the criminal justice system began as a criminal defense lawyer. Gardner has also worked as a prosecutor, a police legal adviser, and in police in-service training. For 28 years he taught courses in Criminal Law, Criminal Evidence, and Arrest, Search, and Seizure at the Milwaukee Area Technical College complex of campuses. He lives in Milwaukee, Wisconsin.

Terry M. Anderson is a Professor of Law at Creighton University School of Law in Omaha, Nebraska. He received his Bachelor of Arts degree in 1968 and Juris Doctor degree in 1971 from the University of North Dakota, where he was a member of the Order of the Coif and the Case Editor of the *North Dakota Law Review*. After earning a Master of Laws degree from Harvard Law School in 1972, he joined the Creighton Law School faculty. He has also been a Visiting Professor of Law at the University of New Mexico and the Denver University College of Law. He teaches Contracts, Insurance, and Secured Transactions in Personal Property.

Brief Contents

CONTENTS

PART 3 | WHEN EVIDENCE CANNOT BE USED BECAUSE OF POLICE MISTAKES OR MISCONDUCT

CHAPTER 9 THE EXCLUSIONARY RULE 179

CHAPTER 10 WHERE THE EXCLUSIONARY RULE DOES NOT APPLY 193

PART 4 | CRIME-SCENE, DOCUMENTARY, AND SCIENTIFIC EVIDENCE

Introducing the Wadsworth Cengage Learning Criminal Justice Advisory Board

The entire Criminal Justice team at Wadsworth Cengage Learning wishes to express its sincere gratitude to the hardworking members of our Criminal Justice Advisory Board. This group of skilled, experienced instructors comes together once a year to further their driving mission, which can be summed up as follows:

> *This collaborative group of publishing professionals and instructors from traditional and nontraditional educational institutions is designed to foster development of exceptional educational and career opportunities in the field of criminal justice by providing direction and assistance to the faculty and administrators charged with training tomorrow's criminal justice professionals. The Advisory Board offers peer support and advice, consults from both the academic and publishing communities, and serves as a forum for creating and evolving best practices in the building of successful criminal justice programs.*

The members of our Advisory Board have the wisdom, expertise, and vision to set goals that empower students, setting them up to capitalize on the field's tremendous growth and expanding job opportunities. According to the U.S. Bureau of Labor Statistics, employment for correctional officers, law enforcement officers, investigators, and security officers is projected to increase at a rate of 9–26% over the next eight years. Add to that the growing number of jobs available in other parts of the criminal justice system—case officer, youth specialist, social services, and more—and one can begin to get a true sense of the vast employment opportunity in the field. Helping today's students unlock the door to exciting and secure futures is the ultimate goal of everyone associated with the Wadsworth Cengage Learning Criminal Justice Advisory Board.

Included on the board are faculty and administrators from schools such as:

- Brown College
- Florida Metropolitan University

- Globe University/Minnesota School of Business
- Hesser College
- Kaplan University
- Keiser University
- John Jay College of Criminal Justice
- Rasmussen College
- South University
- Western Career College
- Western Carolina University
- Westwood College

Again, the Wadsworth Cengage Learning Criminal Justice Team would like to extend our personal and professional thanks for all that the Advisory Board has enabled us to accomplish over the past few years. We look forward to continuing our successful collaboration in the years ahead.

We are always looking to add like-minded instructors to the Advisory Board. If you would like to be considered for inclusion on the Board, please contact Michelle Williams (michelle.williams@cengage.com).

Preparing Students for a Lifetime of Service

PREFACE

In 1791, just four years after the writing of the U.S. Constitution, representatives from the original thirteen states ratified the first ten amendments to the Constitution. These amendments, collectively called the Bill of Rights, reflect concerns of the Founding Fathers that the strong, central federal government would usurp rights then enjoyed in the American states. Although the first American Congress considered more than 145 proposed amendments to the Constitution, the ten that were adopted established the core of basic individual rights in the United States. Relevant selections from the Constitution and the Bill of Rights appear in Appendix A.

The Bill of Rights, as interpreted by the U.S. Supreme Court and state courts, has historically been the basis for the rules of evidence used in criminal trials in the United States. The federal government has promulgated the Federal Rules of Evidence (see Appendix B), which most states have adopted outright or used as a pattern for their rules of evidence. These rules incorporate more than 200 years of judicial and legislative debate on the proper evidentiary rules to be used in court trials in the United States. Today, as in 1791, the Bill of Rights continues to be the beginning point for an understanding of the rules of evidence in criminal trials.

In criminal trials, rules of evidence have as a primary goal securing a defendant's constitutional right to a fair trial. What is meant by a "fair trial" has varied over the years. What was considered a fair trial in the witchcraft trials in Salem, Massachusetts, in 1692 would not be regarded as such in any democratic nation in the world today. Most of the evidence introduced in those trials, as a result of which nineteen people were executed, would not be admissible today under the Bill of Rights and the Federal Rules of Evidence.

Rules of evidence are not only important for the protection of the fundamental rights of persons accused of crimes, but also are necessary in seeking to secure the interests of the American public in an efficient and effective criminal justice system.

To accomplish those goals, a necessary trade-off must be made between the protection of individual rights and judicial efficiency. Understanding this trade-off adds greatly to the student's appreciation of the dynamics of the criminal justice system. As in previous editions, we continue in this edition to try to identify this trade-off between the legitimate requirements of an efficient criminal justice system and individual rights.

ORGANIZATION OF THE BOOK

This book is divided into eighteen chapters and organized into four parts. Part 1, which includes Chapters 1–4, focuses on the historical basis for the American criminal justice system and evidentiary rules. Part 2 (Chapters 5–8) examines in detail the role of witnesses in that system. In Part 3 (Chapters 9–15) we discuss some of the many facets of the exclusionary rule and related issues, such as the use of confessions, the legal requirements for searches and seizures, and the "special needs" rules. In Part 4 (Chapters 16–18) we concentrate on the techniques used in gathering evidence for use in criminal trials and the legal rules to which those techniques must conform.

NEW TO THIS EDITION

In the seventh edition we strive to present the key rules of evidence, the rationale behind these rules, and the applicability of these rules in criminal prosecutions in a manner that is not encyclopedic or overwhelming to the student. We hope the text's clear explanations, accessible writing style, coverage of current issues, and numerous pedagogical aids combine to help students understand and be engaged by complex legal topics. Toward this same end, we use interesting, news-based examples wherever possible to help students understand and retain concepts. Boxes and charts are extensively incorporated to illustrate new and important developments in the rules of criminal evidence. Case discussions such as *Fry v. Pliler*, new to Chapter 2, detail the judicial decision-making process. Learning how laws evolve helps students to understand the laws themselves.

Large-scale changes to this edition of *Criminal Evidence* include Learning Objectives, which will help professors and students target specific subjects, and a new appendix explaining how to brief cases. The text addresses up-to-the-minute topics such as obtaining evidence from computers and the latest decisions and trends in DNA evidence collection and use. The topic of search and seizure has been expanded, and historical coverage has been streamlined throughout the text. Subjects that have traditionally been confusing, such as the discussion of husband–wife privilege, have been retooled to be as clear to students as possible.

In addition to the above enhancements, the seventh edition also features the following chapter-by-chapter changes:

- In Chapter 1 we added a box on habeas corpus and detainees at the Guantanamo Bay Naval Base, including discussion of the U.S. Supreme Court's decision in *Boumediene v. Bush*. We also expanded the discussion of the section on basic constitutional rights, including a new box on the "promptness rule" for the speedy trial requirement and the U.S. Supreme Court opinion in *Uttecht v. Brown* on selecting impartial juries in capital murder cases.

- In Chapter 2 we discuss the federal government's jurisdiction under the commerce clause to pass criminal laws, with examples of recent cases after the U.S. Supreme Court's opinion in *Gonzales v. Raich*. We expanded our discussion of reliable evidence, including a close look at the U.S. Supreme Court's opinion in *Fry v. Pliler*.

- In Chapters 3 and 4 we updated many of the sections and boxes, including in Chapter 4 the section on the use of the Internet in child pornography. We include a discussion of the PROTECT Act and child pornography and the U.S. Supreme Court's decision in *United States v. Williams* upholding the constitutionality of key provisions of that act.

- Chapters 5 and 6 have been updated, with substantial new material in Chapter 6, including: expansion of the judicial notice section; a new box on the meaning of "any criminal case" for the application of the Fifth Amendment rights; new boxes on how a client can lose the attorney–client privilege, and the crime-fraud exception to that privilege; and a new case applying the psychotherapist–patient privilege in federal courts that might preview a limit to that privilege. The sections on the husband–wife privilege have been expanded to show the limits of that privilege, in particular when one spouse is charged with a crime of violence against a person residing in the same household.

- We continue to modify the manner in which we present the hearsay materials, being mindful of the complexity of those materials. We made some changes in Chapter 7 to better explain the nature of hearsay. In Chapter 8 we made substantial updates in the Confrontation Clause–hearsay exceptions area. These include discussions of the U.S. Supreme Court's decision in *Davis v. Washington* on the meaning of "testimonial" evidence, and the Court's decision in *Giles v. California* on the relationship of the "forfeiture by wrongdoing" doctrine and the Confrontation Clause in a new section on that doctrine. We reorganized the U.S. Supreme Court's older decisions on "indicia of reliability," and attempted to put those decisions in the proper place in the light of *Crawford* and *Davis*. As part of that attempt, we added a new introduction to the "firmly rooted exceptions" section, which we hope will assist students in understanding the current law on the relationship between the Confrontation Clause and hearsay exceptions.

- Chapters 9 and 10 have been updated to reflect developments in the exclusionary rule. The U.S. Supreme Court's decision in *Hudson v. Michigan* on when evidence should be suppressed is discussed in detail in Chapter 9, and we include a new box that asks the question, "Should the exclusionary rule be limited?" In Chapter 10 we have substantially expanded the treatment of areas where the exclusionary rule has no application, such as in private searches. We added a section on consent searches, including the U.S. Supreme Court's decision in *Georgia v. Randolph* on when consent by a co-occupant of a residence is sufficient. We also expanded the discussion of the good faith exception, with new cases on how that doctrine is to be given effect.

- In Chapter 11 we added recent cases that considered whether the "special needs" doctrine justified suspicionless searches at border crossings or at entrances to public housing projects. We also discuss the U.S. Supreme Court's decision in *Samson v. California* in a new section on the expectation of privacy available to persons on parole.

- We made major changes in and additions to Chapter 12. They include: a new discussion of the "trustworthiness" doctrine for corroboration of confessions; recent applications of the "totality of the circumstances" for determining if a confession is voluntary; a new box on the interrogation tactic of "question first, warn later"; a new section on when a criminal prosecution commences for the purpose of the Sixth Amendment's right to counsel, including a discussion of the U.S. Supreme Court's decision in *Rothgery v. Gillespie County*; and finally a new section on "silence, *Miranda*, and impeachment."

- We have reorganized the first parts of Chapter 13 to focus on the problems associated with eyewitness identifications and procedures designed to minimize those problems. We include a 2008 study on the frequency of conviction of innocent persons, usually by faulty identifications. We also include recent examples of courts coping with eyewitness identification problems. We have updated the materials on surveillance and cell phone cameras and added a new box on biometrics.

- Chapter 14 has been extensively updated. The discussion of reasonable suspicion in *Terry* stops has been expanded, and includes the U.S. Supreme Court's decision in *Hiibel v. Sixth Judicial Court of Nevada* on the validity of state "stop and identify" laws. Several aspects of searches or arrests incident to vehicle stops have been expanded, such as the use of so-called "pretextual stops." The U.S. Supreme Court's decisions in *Brendlin v. California* and *Virginia v. Moore* on a passenger's rights after an illegal traffic stop and the arrest of a driver after a routine traffic stop are discussed. We also highlight the Supreme Court's decision in *Brigham City v. Stuart* on the scope of the emergency doctrine as a justification for police entry into private premises.

- We have expanded the section on obtaining evidence from computers in Chapter 15, adding new sections on obtaining evidence from the Internet and obtaining evidence from other kinds of electronic storage devices. Nighttime search warrants in illegal drug cases are considered in a recent Court of Appeals case, and the U.S. Supreme Court's decision in *United States v. Grubbs* on the constitutionality of anticipatory search warrants is discussed. The materials on wiretapping, tape recordings, and other kinds of electronic surveillance have been updated where possible.

- We added three new sections in Chapter 16: when can police search premises they have lawfully entered, with recent cases on "protective sweeps"; the use of "scent evidence" in criminal investigations and trials; and obtaining evidence by use of tracking devices under amendments to federal rules.

- In Chapter 18 we expanded the discussion of DNA evidence, with new boxes on cases where DNA evidence was insufficient, and other ways DNA evidence can be used to identify suspects. We expanded the materials on determining the time of death, and also added recent developments in the science of identifying weapons used in crimes.

PEDAGOGY

In this book, we explain the leading principles of criminal evidence, referring to sources such as constitutional provisions, legislative acts, and court decisions. These sources are presented in charts, boxes, case extracts, and studies in addition to the body of the text. We explain the foundation of each principle of criminal evidence, using cases to highlight important historical moments in those principles' development.

As in all our previous editions, we include extracts from important court opinions. As a supplement to those extracts, we have expanded the Case Analysis section at the end of each chapter. Every student now has access to court opinions through the Internet, and we believe reading and analyzing court opinions helps students better understand the concepts we present in the text. By using the free FindLaw website provided by Thomson Reuters, students can quickly and easily access the cases cited in the Case Analysis section and incorporate them into the assigned textual materials.

We have included in Appendix B a guide to using the FindLaw system, as well as a guide on how to analyze cases. We expect this appendix to foster critical thinking on the part of students. The expansion of the Case Analysis section provides the subject matter for analysis, while the information provided in Appendix B will help students take the first steps toward critical thought.

While many of the problems that appeared in the chapter-ending materials in the sixth edition have been deleted, we have retained some problems we believe will promote students' understanding of the chapter's materials. Finally, as we did in the tenth edition of our *Criminal Law* book, we have added a list of learning objectives to each chapter in this edition of *Criminal Evidence*.

ANCILLARIES FOR THE INSTRUCTOR

INSTRUCTOR'S RESOURCE MANUAL WITH TEST BANK

An improved and completely updated *Instructor's Resource Manual with Test Bank* has been developed by Sharon Tracy of Georgia Southern University. The manual includes learning objectives, detailed chapter outlines and summaries, key terms, and Internet resources. Each chapter's test bank contains questions in multiple-choice, true/false, fill-in-the-blank, and essay formats, with a full answer key. The test bank is coded to the learning objectives that appear in the main text and includes the page numbers in the main text where the answers can be found. Finally, each question in the test bank has been carefully reviewed by experienced criminal justice instructors for quality, accuracy, and content coverage. Our *Instructor Approved* seal, which appears on the front cover, is our assurance that you are working with an assessment and grading resource of the highest caliber.

POWERPOINT LECTURE SLIDES

These handy Microsoft® PowerPoint® slides, which outline the chapters of the main text in a classroom-ready presentation, will help you in making your lectures engaging and in reaching your visually oriented students. The presentations are available for download on the password-protected website and can also be obtained by e-mailing your local Cengage Learning representative.

EXAMVIEW® COMPUTERIZED TESTING

The comprehensive *Instructor's Resource Manual* described above is backed up by ExamView, a computerized test bank available for PC and Macintosh computers. With ExamView you can create, deliver, and customize tests and study guides (both print and online) in minutes. You can easily edit and import your own questions and graphics, change test layouts, and reorganize questions. And using ExamView's complete word-processing capabilities, you can enter an unlimited number of new questions or edit existing questions.

COMPANION WEBSITE

The book-specific website at www.cengage.com/criminaljustice/gardner offers students a variety of study tools and useful resources such as quizzing, weblinks, Internet exercises, glossary, flashcards, and more.

THE WADSWORTH CRIMINAL JUSTICE VIDEO LIBRARY

So many exciting, new videos—so many great ways to enrich your lectures and spark discussion of the material in this text. View our full video offerings and download clip lists with running times at www.cj.wadsworth.com/videos. Your Cengage Learning representative will be happy to provide details on our video policy by adoption size. The library includes these selections and many others:

- *ABC Videos:* ABC videos feature short, high-interest clips from current news events as well as historic raw footage going back forty years. Perfect for discussion starters or to enrich your lectures and spark interest in the material in the text, these brief videos provide students with a new lens through which to view the past and present, one that will greatly enhance their knowledge and understanding of significant events and open up to them new dimensions in learning. Clips are drawn from such programs as *World News Tonight*, *Good Morning America*, *This Week*, *PrimeTime Live*, *20/20*, and *Nightline*, as well as numerous ABC News specials and material from the Associated Press Television News and British Movietone News collections. Your Cengage Learning representative will be happy to provide a complete listing of videos and policies.
- *The Wadsworth Custom Videos for Criminal Justice:* Produced by Wadsworth and Films for the Humanities, these videos include short five- to ten-minute segments that encourage classroom discussion. Topics include white-collar crime, domestic violence, forensics, suicide and the police officer, the court process, the history of corrections, prison society, and juvenile justice.
- *Oral History Project:* Developed in association with the American Society of Criminology, the Academy of Criminal Justice Society, and the National Institute of Justice, these videos will help you introduce students to the scholars who have developed the criminal justice discipline. Compiled over the last several years, each video features a set of Guest Lecturers—scholars whose thinking has helped build the foundation of present ideas in the discipline. Vol. 1: Moments in Time; Vol. 2: Great Moments in Criminological Theory; Vol. 3: Research Methods.

- *Court TV Videos:* One-hour videos presenting seminal and high-profile cases such as the interrogation of Michael Crowe and serial killer Ted Bundy, as well as crucial and current issues such as cybercrime, double jeopardy, and the management of the prison on Riker's Island.
- *A&E American Justice:* Forty videos on topics such as deadly force, women on death row, juvenile justice, strange defenses, and Alcatraz.
- *Films for the Humanities:* Nearly 200 videos on a variety of topics such as elder abuse, supermax prisons, suicide and the police officer, the making of an FBI agent, domestic violence, and more.

ANCILLARIES FOR THE STUDENT

CURRENT PERSPECTIVES: READINGS FROM INFOTRAC® COLLEGE EDITION

These readers, designed to give students a deeper taste of special topics in criminal justice, include free access to InfoTrac College Edition. The timely articles are selected by experts in each topic from within InfoTrac College Edition. They are available for free when bundled with the text and include the following titles:

- *Cybercrime*
- *Victimology*
- *Juvenile Justice*
- *Racial Profiling*
- *White-Collar Crime*
- *Terrorism and Homeland Security*
- *Public Policy and Criminal Justice*
- *New Technologies and Criminal Justice*
- *Ethics in Criminal Justice*
- *Forensics and Criminal Investigation*

TERRORISM: AN INTERDISCIPLINARY PERSPECTIVE

Available for bundling with each copy of *Criminal Evidence*, Seventh Edition, this 80-page booklet (with companion website) discusses terrorism in general and the issues surrounding the events of September 11, 2001. This information-packed booklet examines the origins of terrorism in the Middle East, focusing on Osama bin Laden in particular, as well as issues involving bioterrorism, the specific role played by religion in Middle Eastern terrorism, globalization as it relates to terrorism, and the reactions and repercussions of terrorist attacks.

CRIME SCENES: AN INTERACTIVE CRIMINAL JUSTICE CD-ROM, VERSION 2.0

Recipient of several *New Media Magazine* Invision Awards, this interactive CD-ROM allows students to take on the roles of investigating officer, lawyer, parole officer, and judge in excitingly realistic scenarios. Available *free* when bundled with every copy of *Criminal Evidence,* Seventh Edition. An instructor's manual for the CD-ROM is also available.

INTERNET GUIDE FOR CRIMINAL JUSTICE, SECOND EDITION

Internet beginners will appreciate this helpful booklet. With explanations and the vocabulary necessary for navigating the web, it features customized information on criminal justice—related websites and presents Internet project ideas.

INTERNET ACTIVITIES FOR CRIMINAL JUSTICE, SECOND EDITION

This completely revised 96-page booklet shows how to best utilize the Internet for research through searches and activities.

ACKNOWLEDGMENTS

We would like to thank the many reviewers of the seventh and previous editions for their thoughtful suggestions and gracious comments on the organization and subject matter of our book. They are: Tim Bragg, Mississippi County Community College; Marjie Britz, The Citadel; Harry Bruno, Thomas College; Tod W. Burke, Radford University; Jean Comley, Ball State University; Michael Goodwin, Solano Community College; Craig Hemmens, Boise State University; Taiping Ho, Ball State University; David Jones, University of Wisconsin, Oshkosh; Raymond Kessler, Sul Ross State University; David Kotajarvi, Lakeshore Technical College; Walter Lewis, St. Louis Community College at Meramec; Jerry Maynard, Cuyahoga Community College; Michael Meyer, University of North Dakota; Tom O'Connor, North Carolina Wesleyan College; Anita Sedillo, Virginia Commonwealth University; Sandy Self, Hardin-Simmons University; Steven Sondergaard, Defiance College; Kelli Styron, Tarleton State University; Carroll T. Wagner, Harrisburg Area Community College; and Jack Williams, Western New England College.

We also would like to thank the staff at Cengage Learning, in particular Carolyn Henderson Meier and Meaghan Banks, as well as the production service editor for this edition, Anne Draus of Scratchgravel Publishing Services. As always, the publishing part of this endeavor has played a vital role in the book's progress.

Tom Gardner and Terry Anderson would like to thank their families for their patience and understanding while they worked on this edition of *Criminal Evidence.*

Terry Anderson would also like to thank Creighton Law School for the logistical support given him while he worked on this edition.

Thomas J. Gardner

Terry M. Anderson

CRIMINAL EVIDENCE

HISTORY AND DEVELOPMENT OF THE LAW OF CRIMINAL EVIDENCE

CHAPTER 1

LEARNING OBJECTIVES

In this chapter we provide a summary of the history of the use of evidence in criminal trials, with a special focus on criminal defendants' rights contained in the United States Constitution. The learning objectives for this chapter are:

- Explain the importance of the Magna Carta.
- Explain the function of the writ of habeas corpus.
- Identify how the U.S. Supreme Court made the Bill of Rights applicable in state court criminal cases.
- List the rights identified and made available to a criminal defendant under the U.S. Constitution.

CHAPTER CONTENTS

History of the Rules of Evidence

Early Methods of Determining Guilt or Innocence

Magna Carta and Habeas Corpus

The American Declaration of Independence

The U.S. Constitution and the American Bill of Rights

Basic Rights Under the U.S. Constitution Today

The Presumption of Innocence Until Proven Guilty

The Right to a Speedy and Public Trial

The Right to an Indictment

The Right to a Fair (Not Perfect) Trial

The Right to Assistance of Counsel

The Right to Be Informed of Charges

The Right of the Defendant to Compel Witnesses

The Right of the Defendant to Testify or Not Testify

The Right of the Defendant to Confront and Cross-Examine Witnesses

The Right to Be Free of Unreasonable Searches and Seizures

The Right to an Impartial Jury

1

HISTORY OF THE RULES OF EVIDENCE

One cannot understand the rules of evidence applicable in criminal trials today without some appreciation of the historical development of those rules. Evidentiary rules are the gates through which information flows into our criminal courtrooms; the size and shape of the gate have varied over the life of the United States and other English-speaking nations.

The United States and England share a common judicial heritage. Most of the early rules of evidence were made by English courts, and some were made by English parliaments. These early rules of evidence were brought to the American colonies and used by the first English settlers. The same rules were used by other English-speaking colonies, such as Canada and Australia, and were known as common-law rules of evidence.[1] Because of this common heritage, many similarities exist even today in the laws of evidence used in English-speaking countries. The following account of the first murder trial in the American colonies would also describe the court proceedings used in other English colonies:

> The first reported murder in the American colonies occurred in 1630. John Billington, one of the original band of 102 Pilgrims to sail on the Mayflower, waylaid a neighbor and killed the man by shooting him with his blunderbuss. As the colonies had no written criminal laws, Billington was charged with the English common-law crime of murder and tried using the English common-law rules of evidence and criminal procedure. After a prompt trial and conviction, Billington was sentenced to death and hanged.[2]

Rules of evidence are an important part of all criminal justice systems, just as rules are important in baseball, football, and basketball games. In a democracy, rules of evidence are important not only to safeguard the rights of accused persons in a fair trial but also to ensure the interests of the public in the proper functioning of the criminal justice system. Some rules of evidence are highly controversial and cause arguments over what would best serve the overall needs of society.

EARLY METHODS OF DETERMINING GUILT OR INNOCENCE

Today, persons charged with criminal offenses are presumed innocent until proven guilty. Defendants may admit or deny a criminal charge, and if the charge is denied, place the burden of proof on the government to come forward with sufficient, credible, and admissible evidence proving guilt beyond a reasonable doubt.

But the rights we enjoy today did not always exist. They developed slowly over the centuries, were incorporated into the common law, and many were made part of the U.S. Constitution by our Founding Fathers.

ordeals A medieval method of proof that was an appeal to God to determine guilt or innocence.

At the time the Normans conquered England in 1066, the use of **ordeals** to determine guilt or innocence was a common practice. A titled person or one of noble birth could demand trial by battle to determine his guilt or innocence. Winning a sword fight would prove innocence, whereas losing would show guilt. Since the loser would often be killed or seriously injured, the case would ordinarily be disposed of by the outcome of the battle.

The guilt or innocence of a common person was determined by other types of ordeals. The nineteenth-century English judge Sir James Stephens described these ordeals in his *History of the Criminal Law of England*:

> It is unnecessary to give a minute account of the ceremonial of the ordeals. They were of various kinds. The general nature of all was the same. They were appeals to God to work a miracle in attestation of the innocence of the accused person. The handling of hot iron, plunging the hand or arm into boiling water unhurt, were the commonest. The ordeal of water was a very singular institution. Sinking was the sign of innocence, floating the sign of guilt. As any one would sink unless he understood how to float, and intentionally did so, it is difficult to see how anyone could ever be convicted by this means. Is it possible that this ordeal may have been an honourable form of suicide, like the Japanese happy despatch? In nearly every case the accused would sink. This would prove his innocence, indeed, but there would be no need to take him out. He would thus die honourably. If by accident he floated, he would be put to death disgracefully.[3]

The ordeals adjudicated guilt by appeals to God (or the supernatural). People living in the Middle Ages believed in frequent divine intervention in human affairs and thus were content to leave questions of guilt or innocence to such intervention.

All this changed in England, however, at the Lateran Council of 1215, when clergy were prohibited from taking part in ordeals. Without the clergy, one could not be sure God had ordained the result of the ordeal. Indeed, in the reign of King John (1199–1216), the ordeal went from being the standard of proof to completely nonexistent.

In its place came the oath and oath-helpers. Although still an appeal to divine guidance, the oath, in which the accused swore before God his innocence, began the journey toward trial by jury. To support his oath, the accused gathered oath-helpers to swear to his innocence. Over time, these oath-helpers began to swear not to the ultimate guilt or innocence of the accused but to facts relevant to his guilt or innocence. They became witnesses.

presentment juries English forerunners to grand juries; gave information that crimes had been committed.

At the same time, itinerant justices holding court around England began to impanel groups of local residents into **presentment juries**, whose purpose was to inform the justices of crimes committed by other residents. The accused then put himself "on the oath" of his fellow residents, rather than producing his own oath-helpers. Over time, it came to be realized that those serving on the presentment jury should not serve on the smaller petit jury. By the fourteenth century, the origins of our grand jury and trial jury system were firmly established in English law.

As the use of presentment and petit juries became widespread in England, rules developed to control and direct the tasks of those juries. Then, as now, the presentment jury had few evidentiary limitations. The petit jury, however, became charged not only with determining the guilt or innocence of the accused but also with finding the facts upon which its determination depended. Once the jury was established as a fact-finding body, rules of evidence controlling how facts could be presented to the jury began to develop.

In the long period between the fourteenth century and today, rules governing the introduction of facts into criminal trials developed slowly and inconsistently. For example, even though hearsay evidence was regarded as unreliable even in the

WHEN EVIDENCE OF WITCHCRAFT WAS PERMITTED IN THE COURTS OF THE AMERICAN COLONIES

Not too many years prior to the signing of the American Declaration of Independence, evidence of the crime of witchcraft was permitted in the criminal courts of some of the American colonies. Massachusetts, Connecticut, and Virginia permitted prosecutions for the crime of witchcraft based on superstition and ignorance.

Witchcraft was first prosecuted as a crime in the Roman Empire. Over the years, thousands of people in Europe were tried, convicted, and put to death for being witches or practicing witchcraft. For example, in 1431 Joan of Arc was convicted in France of being a witch and burned at the stake by a tribunal under the direction of English invaders. The English used the accusation of witchcraft as a convenient way of eliminating a very effective French military opponent.

A crop failure, a sickness, or an epidemic within a community could lead to accusations that a local person was a witch and the cause of the problems. The Salem, Massachusetts, witchcraft trials of 1692 resulted in the execution of 19 people and the imprisonment of over 150 others. Arthur Miller's famous play *The Crucible* is a contemporary dramatization of the Salem witchcraft trials. In Miller's play, the accusations were not of crop failure or an epidemic but of sexual improprieties made by teenaged girls. The book form of Miller's play contains commentary by the author. Miller observes in the introduction to his play that after the accusations by the teenaged girls were made, "long-held hatreds of neighbors could now be openly expressed … one could cry witch against one's neighbors … old scores could be settled … and any envy of the miserable toward the happy could and did burst out in the general revenge."[a]

A crucible is a severe test and is a most appropriate title for Miller's play because the Salem witch trials severely tested not only the town and the colony of Massachusetts, but also the new nation coming into existence in 1788. Under the U.S. Constitution, and the Bill of Rights ratified in 1791, evidence of crime has to be relevant, reliable, and competent before it can be admissible in criminal trials. The evidence used in the Salem witch trials was none of these and could never again be used to convict a person of witchcraft. The crime of witchcraft no longer exists, and under the American criminal justice system could never exist again.

[a]Arthur Miller, *The Crucible* (New York: Viking Press, 1953).

early thirteenth century,[4] such evidence was still widely permitted in the American colonies. Other nonjudicial forces helped move the nature of criminal trials and rules of evidence forward.

MAGNA CARTA AND HABEAS CORPUS

In twelfth-century England, people could be jailed based on anonymous accusations of wrongdoing, or they could be seized on mere suspicion or on the whim of a government official. English kings suppressed political opposition by jailing anyone who dared criticize the Crown or the government. Absolute loyalty was compelled by the arrest of those suspected of antigovernment sentiments or statements.

Because of these abuses by English kings, the great barons of England revolted against the Crown. After many years of fighting, King John met with the barons in 1215 at a field in Runnymede, England. An agreement between the

Magna Carta The Great Charter signed by King John of England and his barons in 1215; created the first standards for arresting and imprisoning those accused of crimes.

custody Under police control, whether or not physically constrained.

probable cause The quantum (amount) of evidence required by the Fourth Amendment to make an arrest or to issue a search warrant; greater than reasonable suspicion but can be less than proof or reasonable doubt.

habeas corpus Latin name of the writ used to compel a government official, such as a prison warden, to show cause why the official is holding a person in custody.

parties to stop the fighting resulted in the king and the barons signing a document called **Magna Carta,** or the Great Charter. Among other clauses, Magna Carta stated that there would be no criminal "trial upon … simple accusation without producing credible witnesses to the truth therein" and that "no freeman shall be taken, imprisoned … except by lawful judgment of his peers or the law of the land." Magna Carta was a historic first step toward democracy and the establishment of minimum standards for arresting and imprisoning people accused of crimes. Under this new concept of law, no one could be taken into **custody** on mere suspicion, on whim, or without substantial good cause. Magna Carta began the development of the concept in law that there had to be **probable cause**, or "reasonable grounds to believe," to justify arresting or holding a person in custody.

Magna Carta deeply affected the drafters of the American Declaration of Independence:

> The event became the rallying cry of individual liberty in England during the 17th century, and so influenced the Founding Fathers of our country that the Seal of the Magna Carta was emblazoned on the cover of the *Journal of the Proceedings of the First Continental Congress*, held in Philadelphia on September 5, 1774, where our forefathers laid the foundation stone of individual liberty in the United States.[5]

Another important milestone in the protection of personal liberties was the development of the Writ of Habeas Corpus. This famous writ is believed to date to the fourteenth and fifteenth centuries. The Writ of Habeas Corpus was and is a safeguard against the illegal or improper holding of a person against his or her will. The word *writ* means a "writing," and *habeas corpus* is a Latin term meaning "have the body." This writ, when signed by a judge, is served upon the government official who has custody of a person and orders that official to appear before the court and show cause for holding the person.

Magna Carta and habeas corpus not only are very important legal concepts in the English-speaking world but also have had an important impact worldwide. Magna Carta first expressed the idea that a person should not be jailed or held without just cause. The Writ of Habeas Corpus was the earliest legal procedure by which illegal or improper jailing or detention could be challenged in a court of law. If a person is being held without just cause and legal authority, the judge presiding at the habeas corpus hearing must order his or her release.

The American Founding Fathers guaranteed the right of habeas corpus in the U.S. Constitution. ARTICLE I, SECTION 9 of the U.S. Constitution provides that "The privilege of the Writ of Habeas Corpus shall not be suspended, unless when in Cases of Rebellion or Invasion the public Safety may require it." The original thirteen states, and all those that subsequently joined the union, did the same. Some states strengthened the constitutional guarantee by statutes, such as Wisconsin statute 782.09, which provides that "any judge who refuses to grant a writ of habeas corpus, when legally applied for, is liable to the prisoner in the sum of $1,000." Other statutes impose penalties for "refusing papers" ($200), "concealing" or "transferring" the prisoner ($1,000 or six months imprisonment), and "reimprisoning party discharged" ($1,250 and misdemeanor violation).

The famous English writer Sir William Blackstone wrote that habeas corpus is "the most celebrated writ in the English law." Chief Justice Marshall of the U.S.

HABEAS CORPUS AND ENEMY COMBATANTS

Since 2001, the U.S. military has detained alien, enemy combatants at Guantanamo Navel Base in Cuba. Some of these detainees sought to obtain review of their detentions by use of the habeas corpus writ. The U.S. government initially contended that federal courts had no jurisdiction over the navel base, but in *Rasul v. Bush* [542 U.S. 466 (2004)], the U.S. Supreme Court held that under existing jurisdictional statutes, federal courts did have jurisdiction over the navel base.

In response to that decision, Congress passed the Military Commissions Act of 2006 [28 U.S.C. § 2241(e)], which contained a clause stating that federal courts had no jurisdiction to hear habeas corpus claims made by alien, enemy combatants detained at military installations. Several detainees appealed dismissal of their habeas corpus petitions, and on review the Supreme Court held that enemy combatants detained at military installations had the constitutional right to bring habeas corpus petitions, and as a result section 2241(e) was an unconstitutional violation of the Suspension Clause [Art. I, § 9, cl. 2], which prohibits the suspension of the writ except in cases of "Rebellion or Invasion." See *Boumediene v. Bush* [128 S.Ct. 2229 (2008)].

Supreme Court called the writ a "great constitutional privilege," and the U.S. Supreme Court has stated a number of times that "there is no higher duty than to maintain it unimpaired."

THE AMERICAN DECLARATION OF INDEPENDENCE

When students are asked where their personal freedoms come from, they will often answer that personal freedoms come from government. This answer was correct hundreds of years ago, when it was believed that kings received their authority to rule from God. What few personal rights the ordinary person had in those days came from the ruler. This was known as the divine right of kings. Generally accepted and promoted throughout the world in the Middle Ages, this doctrine stated that monarchs received absolute authority to govern from God and that their subjects had only such personal freedoms as fit their status under their sovereign. This theory, actively promoted by those in power, helped monarchs rule and maintain control over their subjects.

Early American documents show that the American colonies did not accept the European concept of the divine right of kings. The 1641 Massachusetts Body of Liberties commenced by discussing the "free fruition of such liberties, Immunities and privileges ... as due every man."[6] The 1765 Declaration of Rights spoke of "inherent rights and liberties," "freedom of a people," and "the undoubted rights of Englishmen."[7]

The American Declaration of Independence of 1776 specifically repudiated the doctrine of the divine right of kings, pointing out that personal freedoms do not

SOME ABUSES LEADING TO THE SIGNING OF THE DECLARATION OF INDEPENDENCE

The American Declaration of Independence, celebrated each year on the Fourth of July, lists more than twenty-five abuses by the "King of Great Britain" against the American colonies. It was these abuses that caused the colonies to declare their independence from Great Britain. About two-thirds of the abuses concerned the English mercantile system, which Great Britain forced upon the American colonies. Under this system, Americans had to buy only English products and goods at prices set by the English. The system was enforced against the colonies by military force and heavy taxation, which led to the famous cry "No taxation without representation" and incidents like the Boston Tea Party. The famous Scottish economist Adam Smith, who wrote the *Wealth of Nations* in 1776 and opposed the English policy of mercantilism, became known as the father of the American economic system. The following is a brief summary of the remaining one-third of the abuses listed in the Declaration of Independence:

Abuses Concerning Liberty, Freedom, and the Judiciary	Correction of the Abuse in the U.S. Constitution
"He has made Judges dependent on his will alone ..."	ARTICLE III, creating an independent judiciary
"He has kept among us in times of peace Standing Armies ... [and] has quartered large bodies of armed troops among us."	Third Amendment to the Bill of Rights
He "... protect[s] [the armed troops], by a mock trial, from punishment for any Murders which they should commit on the Inhabitants ..."	The establishment of an independent judiciary, an elected president and Congress, and grand juries
"... depriving us in many cases, of the benefits of Trial by Jury."	"... the accused shall enjoy the right of a ... trial ... by an impartial jury" (Sixth Amendment)
He "... transport[s] us beyond the Seas to be tried for pretended offenses."	The right to an "indictment by a Grand Jury" and the right to be tried in "the State and district where the crime shall have been committed ..." (Fifth and Sixth Amendments)
"He has plundered our seas, ravaged our Coasts, burnt our towns, and destroyed the lives of our people."	The establishment of an independent judiciary, an elected Congress and president, and grand juries
"He is at this time transporting large Armies of foreign Mercenaries to compleat the work of death, desolation and tyranny ..."	Limiting the powers of the president and the Congress to those specifically set forth in ARTICLE I and II, and the protection of the Third Amendment

come from government or kings. Every Fourth of July, we celebrate the signing of the document that established the following propositions:

- That the United States is independent from Great Britain, detailing the "history of repeated injuries and usurpations" of the king of Great Britain, who sought to establish "an absolute Tyranny over these States"

- That "Governments are instituted among Men, deriving their just powers from the consent of the governed"
- That "all men are created equal, that they are endowed by their Creator with certain unalienable Rights, that among these are Life, Liberty, and the pursuit of Happiness"

THE U.S. CONSTITUTION AND THE AMERICAN BILL OF RIGHTS

When the American Founding Fathers met in Philadelphia in 1787, many of the wrongs of the past had been eliminated. For example, trial for witchcraft had been abolished, and people accused of crimes no longer had to prove their innocence by ordeal or battle. The delegates set about writing a constitution for the new American democracy that would embody the spirit of the Declaration of Independence and create a workable, practical government to serve the people. They stated their goals in the preamble to the new U.S. Constitution:

> We the People of the United States, in order to form a more perfect Union, establish justice, insure domestic Tranquility, provide for the common defense, promote the general Welfare, and secure the Blessings of Liberty to ourselves and our Posterity, do ordain and establish this Constitution for the United States of America.

The U.S. Constitution sought to protect the privilege of habeas corpus and prohibited such abuses as the passing of bills of attainder and ex post facto laws. The right of trial by jury was protected, and *corruption of blood* (punishing a family for the criminal acts of another family member) was forbidden. The drafters of the Constitution knew that such abuses had occurred in England and were determined that they would not occur in the new American nation.

The delegates to the Constitutional Convention set about writing a constitution that would embody the spirit of the Declaration of Independence, create a working, practical government to serve the people, and protect the people from abuses by government.

© Bettmann/Corbis

ANCIENT WRONGS THAT INFLUENCED THE AMERICAN CRIMINAL JUSTICE SYSTEM

Wrong	Resulted In	Led to the Following Development	U.S. Constitution
The practice of English kings jailing persons for no good reason, on mere suspicion or on simple accusation by another.	The English civil war of the late 1100s and early 1200s, which was settled by King John signing Magna Carta in 1215, abolished this practie.	Magna Carta provides that there will be no criminal "trial upon … simple accusation without producing credible witnesses to the truth therein." Magna Carta led to the development of the great English Writ of Habeas Corpus, which requires law officers to show probable cause to a court in order to hold a person in custody.	The Fourth Amendment requires probable cause to arrest and to issue a search warrant. Habeas corpus is guaranteed by ARTICLE I, SECTION 9 of the Constitution.
The use of torture and coercion to obtain confessions.	The English Parliament abolished the inquisitorial court, the Star Chamber, in 1640s. [See *Miranda v. Arizona*, 384 U.S. 436 (1966).]	The development was the privilege against self-incrimination and the right to remain silent while in police custody.	The Fifth Amendment contains privilege against self-incrimination, and the Sixth Amendment the right to an attorney.
The use of general warrants, which gave British officials power to search anywhere and anything they wished.	The practice was discontinued in England but continued to "bedevil" the American colonies.	The continued practice of the British to search "where they pleased" was the "most prominent event" that led to the Declaration of Independence and the American Revolutionary War. [*Stanford v. State of Texas*, 85 S.Ct. 506, 510 (1965).]	The Fourth Amendment forbids "unreasonable searches and seizures" and requires probable cause and search warrants.
The practice of English courts of convicting persons on hearsay and written statements or testimony by persons who did not appear in court and who were not identified to the accused.	This practice was used to "frame" Sir Walter Raleigh in 1603 and send him to prison for treason.	The hearsay rules were developed, along with the requirement that the government prove criminal charges with witnesses who testified in court in the presence of the accused.	The Sixth Amendment makes it a requirement that "… the accused shall enjoy the right to be confronted with the witnesses against him …" ARTICLE II, SECTION 3 of the Constitution prohibits conviction for treason except on "the testimony of two witnesses."
Charging a person with a trumped-up criminal charge and then putting pressure on the jury to convict the person.	William Penn was charged in this manner in 1670. When an English jury would not convict him, the jury was held for two days without food, water, or toilet facilities.	When the jury would not give in to the pressures of the judge and the king, they were fined for their conduct. This case was important in the development of a system of independent juries. William Penn left England and founded the state of Pennsylvania.	Persons charged with crimes have a right to "an impartial jury" (Sixth Amendment) and "due process of law" (fundamental fairness requirement of the Fourteenth Amendment).

As a further protection, the Constitution provided that all federal officials, including the president of the United States, could be removed upon "Impeachment for, and Conviction of, Treason, Bribery, or other high Crimes and Misdemeanors" (ART. II, SEC. 4).

When the Constitution was presented to the states for ratification, it was criticized as not going far enough to protect the people from possible abuses by the new federal government. The people understood their state governments and believed they could control them, but they were suspicious of the new central government. As a result, prior to ratification of the new Constitution, it was agreed that additional protections would immediately be added to the Constitution. The U.S. Constitution was ratified in 1788, and ten amendments, now known as the **Bill of Rights**, were added in 1791.

Bill of Rights The first ten amendments to the U.S. Constitution.

In a 1991 U.S. Supreme Court opinion, Justice Scalia pointed out that "most of the procedural protections of the federal Bill of Rights simply codified traditional common-law privileges (that) had been widely adopted by the states." Justice Scalia used the following quote from 1878: "the law is perfectly well settled that the first ten amendments to the Constitution ... were not intended to lay down any novel principles of government, but simply to embody certain guarantees and immunities which we had inherited from our English ancestors."[8]

The Bill of Rights (see Appendix A) originally applied only to the federal government. Beginning in 1961, however, the U.S. Supreme Court began to make the Bill of Rights applicable to the states through the Fourteenth Amendment. (See the case of *Mapp v. Ohio* and the material in Chapter 9 on the use of the American exclusionary rule.)

BASIC RIGHTS UNDER THE U.S. CONSTITUTION TODAY

The United States celebrated the 200th anniversary of the U.S. Constitution in 1988. This remarkable document, which includes the Bill of Rights, has received worldwide attention and has been a model for many countries. It sets forth the foundation and requirements for the law of criminal evidence used throughout the United States.

The people of the United States may change, abolish, or modify any part of the Constitution; polls show, however, that the great majority of Americans want to keep the Constitution and the Bill of Rights intact. Although individual rights in criminal prosecutions are articulated in various parts of the Constitution and Bill of Rights, the Fifth and Sixth Amendments contain an extensive list of those rights. The Fifth Amendment states:

> No person shall be held to answer for a capital, or otherwise infamous crime, unless on a presentment or indictment of a Grand Jury, except in cases arising in the land or naval forces, or in the Militia, when in actual service in time of War or public danger; nor shall any person be subject for the same offence to be twice put in jeopardy of life or limb; nor shall be compelled in any criminal case to be a witness against himself, nor be deprived of life, liberty, or property, without due process of law; nor shall private property be taken for public use, without just compensation.

THE 48-HOUR REQUIREMENT OF A PROBABLE CAUSE HEARING (THE "PROMPTNESS RULE")

When an arrest warrant is issued, there has already been a determination that probable cause exists for the arrest. However, when an arrest occurs without a warrant, no such determination is made before the arrest. In *County of Riverside v. McLaughlin* [500 U.S. 44 (1991)], the U.S. Supreme Court held that a suspect arrested without an arrest warrant must have a probable cause hearing before a judge or magistrate "promptly," within 48 hours of the arrest, including weekends and holidays. If such a hearing is held within 48 hours, the jurisdiction will "as a general matter, comply with the promptness requirement." However, even a hearing held within a 48-hour period can be unreasonable if the delay was "for the purpose of gathering additional evidence to justify the arrest [or] motivated by ill will against the arrested individual, or delay for delay's sake."

If the probable cause hearing is delayed beyond the 48-hour period, the burden is on the government "to demonstrate the existence of a bona fide emergency or otherwise extraordinary circumstance."

Because of the "promptness" rule, writs of habeas corpus are generally not needed to secure the release of persons arrested without a warrant.

The Sixth Amendment states:

> In all criminal prosecutions, the accused shall enjoy the right to a speedy and public trial, by an impartial jury of the State and district wherein the crime shall have been committed, which district shall have been previously ascertained by law, and to be informed of the nature and cause of the accusation; to be confronted with the witnesses against him; to have compulsory process for obtaining witnesses in his favour, and have Assistance of Counsel for his defence.

The following sections summarize some of the most basic rights protected or created by the Bill of Rights. Many of these rights will be discussed more fully in later chapters of this book.

THE PRESUMPTION OF INNOCENCE UNTIL PROVEN GUILTY

beyond a reasonable doubt The burden that the prosecution must meet in proving guilt in criminal cases; applies to every element of the crime charged.

One of the most deeply rooted traditions of modern Anglo-Saxon law is that an accused is innocent until proven guilty **beyond a reasonable doubt**.[9] In *Estelle v. Williams*,[10] the U.S. Supreme Court stated: "The presumption of innocence, though not articulated in the Constitution, is a basic component of a fair trial under our system of criminal justice." A violation of this right can occur when the jury is not properly instructed on the presumption of innocence and the burden of the prosecution to overcome the presumption by competent evidence. In *Taylor v. Kentucky*,[11] the Supreme Court held that the failure of the trial court to give a requested instruction on the presumption of innocence was, under the facts of that case, a violation of the right to a fair trial.

presumption of innocence The legal presumption required in all criminal courts that the defendant is innocent until sufficient credible evidence is produced to carry the burden of proving guilt beyond a reasonable doubt.

A violation can also occur through statements made by the prosecution. For example, in *Pagano v. Allard*,[12] the court held that, after a prosecutor referred to the presumption of innocence as a "cloak" that protected a defendant, the prosecutor's statement in closing argument to the jury that "… now that cloak comes off" violated the right to a fair trial.

Besides the **presumption of innocence** until proven guilty, the United States uses an accusatorial system of justice. In 1961, the U.S. Supreme Court stated that "ours is an accusatorial and not an inquisitorial system—a system in which the State must establish guilt by evidence independently and freely secured and may not by coercion prove its charge against an accused out of his mouth."[13]

THE RIGHT TO A SPEEDY AND PUBLIC TRIAL

The Sixth Amendment provides that "the accused shall enjoy the right to a speedy and public trial." A defendant may waive the right to a speedy trial with the permission of the court. The federal government and many states have enacted statutes that state the time within which a trial must be held. The federal government requires a trial within seventy days for a felony and within sixty days for a misdemeanor, unless the requirement for a speedy trial is waived.[14]

THE RIGHT TO AN INDICTMENT

About half of the states follow the system imposed upon the federal government by the Fifth Amendment requiring a grand jury indictment for a "capital, or otherwise infamous crime." In the other states, elected prosecutors (district attorneys or state attorneys) make the decisions about whether to charge and what crimes to charge. Defendants charged by a district or state attorney have the right to a preliminary hearing if they are charged with a felony.

In the case of separate trials of multiple defendants, many courts have held that the prosecution cannot charge each defendant with the same criminal act. For example, in the trial of *A*, the prosecutor cannot allege that *A* pulled the trigger on the murder weapon, and then in the trial of *B* allege that *B* did so. In 2004, a federal circuit court of appeals held that doing so violated the Due Process Clause.[15] In 2005, the U.S. Supreme Court reversed,[16] holding that the use of inconsistent charges did not prejudice the defendant because he could have been convicted under the state aiding and abetting statute. (This aspect of this decision is discussed in the guilty plea section in Chapter 3.) The Supreme Court remanded the case to determine whether the use of inconsistent charges prejudiced the defendant in the sentencing process, where he was given the death sentence.

THE RIGHT TO A FAIR (NOT PERFECT) TRIAL

In any trial, mistakes can be made. The U.S. Supreme Court and state courts have repeatedly held that under the Due Process clauses of the Fifth and Fourteenth Amendments "the law does not require that a defendant receive a perfect

PEREMPTORY CHALLENGES AND DISCRIMINATION

In jury trials, the parties are generally entitled to strike a limited number of potential jury members without giving a reason for the decision to strike. The prosecutor often uses this "peremptory challenge" to exclude a potential juror who might be reluctant, for one reason or another, to find the defendant guilty of the crime charged. In most instances, the prosecution does not have to explain the reasons for exercising the challenge. In one area at least, the U.S. Supreme Court has said the prosecution cannot use peremptory strikes to exclude potential jurors. In *Batson v. Kentucky* [476 U.S. 79 (1986)], the Court held that if a defendant in a criminal case makes a prima facie case showing that jurors were excluded because of their race, the prosecution must provide "race-neutral" reasons justifying the challenges. In a 2005 decision (*Johnson v. California*, [545 U.S. 162]), the Court reversed the murder conviction of a black male because the prosecution used its peremptory challenges to exclude the only three black prospective jurors. The Court said that all the defendant needed to produce to force the state to show a race-neutral reason for the challenges was evidence that supports the inference of a discriminatory purpose. The California Supreme Court, like many other state courts, had interpreted *Batson* to require the defendant to show discriminatory purpose by a preponderance of the evidence. The Supreme Court rejected that interpretation.

The U.S. Supreme Court has not extended *Batson* to include peremptory strikes based on other factors, such as the religious affiliation of a prospective juror. Some lower federal courts have approved the use of such strikes where the religious views of the juror would hamper the ability of the juror to sit in judgment of others. [See *United States v. Brown*, 352 F.3d 654 (2d Cir. 2003).] Some state courts have held that peremptory challenges based on religious affiliation are prohibited. [See *Thorson v. State*, 721 So.2d 590 (Miss. 1998).]

trial, only a fair one."[17] As a result, a defendant convicted in a trial where harmless error has occurred has received a fair trial, though not a perfect trial. However, if the error was harmful, reversible, or plain, the defendant has not received a fair trial and is entitled to a new trial or to have the criminal charges dropped.

A defendant is not entitled to a new trial if it is shown that the error was harmless beyond a reasonable doubt. An error is harmless if it did not in any meaningful way contribute to the defendant's conviction. Where the error is the improper admission of evidence, the U.S. Supreme Court has held that "the test for harmfulness is whether there is a reasonable possibility that the improperly admitted evidence contributed to the conviction."[18] For example, the use of a confession obtained by force would be reversible (harmful or plain) error when the conviction rests only on this evidence. But if the crime charged is bank robbery, and ten eyewitnesses testified and the bank's video also showed the defendant robbing the bank, an appellate court could hold that the use of the coerced confession was harmless error.

THE RIGHT TO ASSISTANCE OF COUNSEL

Persons charged with a state or federal crime (or juveniles where a delinquency petition has been filed against them) have the Sixth Amendment right to counsel. If the defendant (or juvenile) cannot afford an attorney, one will be provided by the state or federal government.[19]

THE RIGHT TO BE INFORMED OF CHARGES

A defendant charged with a crime has a right to be informed of what he or she is alleged to have done and what specific crime or crimes are being charged. The Sixth Amendment provides that "the accused shall enjoy the right … to be informed of the nature and cause of the accusation." This right may become an issue where a guilty plea has been given by a defendant but is later sought to be retracted because it was not "voluntary and intelligent." In *Bousley v. United States*,[20] the Supreme Court stated that a guilty plea is constitutionally valid only if it is made voluntarily and intelligently. That requires that the defendant be realistically informed of the charges against him. The Court stated that while giving the defendant a copy of the indictment creates a presumption that the defendant has been informed of the charges against him, if the circumstances indicate the defendant was misinformed by the court or the prosecutor, the plea is invalid.

THE RIGHT OF THE DEFENDANT TO COMPEL WITNESSES

The Sixth Amendment provides that "the accused shall enjoy the right … to have compulsory process for obtaining witnesses in his favor… ." If there are witnesses who can help a defendant's case, the accused may compel their appearance by use of subpoenas. Such witnesses, however, could be very uncooperative. They could make efforts to avoid service by a subpoena, fail to appear in court, or state that they do not remember or did not see or hear the incident. They could also use the Fifth Amendment privilege against self-incrimination.

THE RIGHT OF THE DEFENDANT TO TESTIFY OR NOT TESTIFY

In criminal cases the burden is on the government to come forward with sufficient credible evidence to prove guilt beyond a reasonable doubt. It is the choice of the defendant to take the witness stand and testify in his or her own defense. Most defendants, however, do not testify for various tactical reasons. The most important of these reasons is that a defendant who testifies is then subject to cross-examination, which could be disastrous to the defendant's case. Therefore, many defense lawyers do not want their clients to take this risk.[21]

THE RIGHT OF THE DEFENDANT TO CONFRONT AND CROSS-EXAMINE WITNESSES

The Sixth Amendment's Confrontation Clause provides that "the accused shall enjoy the right ... to be confronted with the witnesses against him." The U.S. Supreme Court pointed out that the famous London trial of Sir Walter Raleigh in 1603 was one of the reasons the Confrontation Clause was included in the Sixth Amendment of the Bill of Rights.[22] (See the discussion in Chapter 7.)

THE RIGHT TO BE FREE OF UNREASONABLE SEARCHES AND SEIZURES

The Fourth Amendment forbids unreasonable searches and seizures by officers of the federal and state governments. Therefore, law officers must have a search warrant or must show that a search or seizure is justified by an exception to the search warrant requirements.

The historic roots of the Fourth Amendment go back to Magna Carta and the development over the centuries of the probable cause requirement. In 1965, the U.S. Supreme Court traced the events that led to the American Revolution against British rule:

> Vivid in the memory of the newly formed independent Americans were those general warrants known as writs of assistance under which officers of the Crown had so bedeviled the Colonists. The hated writs of assistance had given customs officials blanket authority to search where they pleased for goods imported in violation of British tax laws. They were denounced by James Otis as "the worst instrument of arbitrary power, the most destructive of English liberty, and the fundamental principles of law, that ever was found in an English law book" because they placed "the liberty of every man in the hands of every petty officer." The historic occasion of that denunciation in 1761 at Boston has been characterized as "perhaps the most prominent event which inaugurated the resistance of the colonies to the oppressions of the mother country." "Then and there," said John Adams, "was the first scene of the first act of opposition to the arbitrary claims of Great Britain. Then and there the child Independence was born."[23]

THE RIGHT TO AN IMPARTIAL JURY

The Sixth Amendment of the U.S. Constitution guarantees defendants the right to "an impartial jury of the State and district wherein the crime shall have been committed...." Juror challenges, either for cause or peremptory, are a procedural device designed to help ensure that the jury is impartial. However, the challenges themselves are not of constitutional dimension. Thus, in *United States v. Martinez-Salazar*,[24] the Supreme Court held that a wrongful refusal by a trial judge to excuse a juror for cause, forcing the defendant to use a peremptory challenge, was not by itself a constitutional violation, so long as the jury actually chosen was impartial.

Excusing jurors for cause has long been an issue in death penalty cases. A defendant can persuasively argue that excusing any juror who expresses doubt about capital punishment denies him an "impartial jury" because the resulting jury will consist only of those who favor capital punishment. The prosecution's response is that a jury made up of those opposed to capital punishment would be unwilling to apply the law correctly because of the possible death sentence for a guilty verdict.

In the 2007 case of *Uttecht v. Brown*,[25] the U.S. Supreme Court reversed the Ninth Circuit Court of Appeals, which had overturned the conviction of a defendant charged with murder because a prospective jury member had been excused for cause based on his statements about the death penalty. In holding that the juror had been properly excused by the trial court judge, the Supreme Court stated that four principles must be used to determine whether a juror has been properly excused for cause in capital cases:

1. The defendant has a right to have a jury that is not tilted in favor of capital punishment, which means the prosecution may not challenge for cause any juror who expresses doubt about capital punishment.
2. The state has a legitimate interest in having jurors who are willing to apply capital punishment where the law so permits.
3. Unless a juror is "substantially impaired" in his ability to impose the death sentence, his excusal for cause is improper.
4. The trial judge is entitled to deference in the determination of when a prospective juror is "substantially impaired."

SUMMARY

Rules of evidence are the gates through which information flows into courtrooms in both civil and criminal cases. Guilt or innocence in criminal cases was determined a thousand years ago by trial by battle for the titled and the nobility, or by ordeals for commoners.

In the 1692 Salem, Massachusetts, witchcraft trials, nineteen people were convicted of being witches and were put to death on evidence that would not be permitted in the courtrooms of any democracy today.

Original copies of Magna Carta are on display in the National Archives in Washington, DC, and in the British Museum in London. This "Great Charter" signed in 1215 and the writ of habeas corpus were among the first steps taken toward democracy in the English-speaking world in the thirteenth and fourteenth centuries. The American Declaration of Independence, the U.S. Constitution, and the American Bill of Rights were strongly influenced by both Magna Carta and the writ of habeas corpus.

PROBLEMS

Refer to Appendix A, which contains the Bill of Rights and applicable sections of the U.S. Constitution, and answer the questions about rights and privileges in the United States by choosing one of the following available answers. You may also have to use the index for further information on a few of the questions.

Available Answers

a. This is a right or privilege protected by the U.S. Constitution.
b. This is not a right or privilege protected by the U.S. Constitution.

A Person Charged with a Crime Has a Right To:

1. A perfect trial.
2. A speedy trial.
3. A private (not public) trial.
4. The assistance of a lawyer for his or her defense.
5. Compel witnesses to appear in his or her defense.
6. Not be tried more than once for the same offense and the same conduct.
7. Due process of law (fundamental fairness).
8. An impartial jury.
9. Not take the witness stand in his or her criminal trial (right to remain silent).
10. Make false statements in court under oath.
11. See and hear witnesses as they testify in court.
12. Cross-examine witnesses.
13. Be informed of the charge or charges.
14. Be tried in the county in which the crime was committed.
15. An unbiased judge.
16. A defense lawyer who believes the defendant to be innocent.
17. Reasonable bail if bail is set.

All Persons Have the Following Rights or Freedoms (Answer True or False):

18. Freedom to say, print, or write anything and everything they wish (absolute freedom of speech).
19. Freedom from any and all government searches.
20. The right to have *Miranda* warnings given when in police custody.
21. The right to a habeas corpus hearing if held illegally or improperly.
22. Freedom of movement without interference by a government official unless there is lawful authority.
23. The right to remain silent when a person is an important material witness to a serious felony and is not incriminating himself.
24. Freedom to move from one state to another or from one city to another.
25. The right to block sidewalks or streets as part of a protest.

CASE ANALYSIS

Read Appendix B, Finding and Analyzing Cases (p. 427). With these guidelines in mind, please continue with the Case Analysis selections for Chapter 1.

1. Read the Maryland Court of Appeals decision in *Brogden v. State* [866 A.2d 129 (2005)] [Case No. 55/04]. In this chapter, we stated that criminal defendants are entitled to a "Fair (Not Perfect) Trial." This means that sometimes mistakes can be made in a criminal trial, but the trial is nonetheless "fair." What mistake did the trial judge make in the *Brogden* trial, and why did the mistake make the trial unfair?
2. Read the Hawaii Supreme Court decision in *State v. Maluia* [108 P.3d 974 (2005)] [Case No. 25689]. What mistake did the prosecutor make in *Maluia,* and why didn't it make the trial unfair?
3. Read the U.S. Supreme Court's opinion in *Shirro v. Landrigan* [127 S.Ct. 1933 (2007)]. How does the Court interpret the "Assistance of Counsel" language of the Sixth Amendment? How, if at all, does the fact that the case was in the federal court system under the habeas corpus jurisdiction affect the decision?
4. Read the U.S. Supreme Court's opinion in *United States v. Gonzalez-Lopez* [548 U.S. 140 (2006)], another assistance of counsel case. How does it differ from the *Shirro* case discussed above? How did this difference affect the outcome?

Notes

1. Common law is sometimes referred to as "un-written law." In early England and during American colonial times, legislatures did not meet often to enact statutory law. Courts made most of the laws, usually based on the custom and usage of the community. This judge-made law became known as "common law." Since printing presses were rare and few people could read and write, law for the most part in those days was unwritten and carried in the minds of judges, lawyers, and government officials. Today, written law is recorded in statutes enacted by legislative bodies, and common law is found in court reports, court transcripts, and other written material.

2. See *Bloodletters and Sudmen: A Narrative Encyclopedia of American Criminals from the Pilgrims to the Present* by Jay Robert Nash (New York: M. Evans & Co., 1974).

3. *A History of the Criminal Law of England*, vol. 1, p. 73 (London: MacMillan & Co., 1883).

4. F. Pollack and F. W. Maitland, *History of English Law*, 2nd ed., vol. 2, p. 622 (Cambridge, U.K.: Cambridge University Press, 1968).

5. J. Few, *In Defense of Trial by Jury*, vol. 1, p. 1 (Greenville, SC: American Jury Trial Foundation, 1993).

6. See *The Harvard Classics*, vol. 43, p. 70 (Boston: Collier & Son, 1910).

7. See *The Harvard Classics*, vol. 43, p. 70 (Boston: Collier & Son, 1910).

8. *Pacific Mutual Life Ins. Co. v. Haslip*, 499 U.S. 1, 111 S.Ct. 1032 (1991).

9. T. Cooley, *Constitutional Limitations*, chap. 10 (4th ed., 1878). Abraham's widely used text makes the statement that all democracies use the presumption of innocence until proven guilty. See Abraham, *The Judicial Process*, 2nd ed., p. 101 (New York: Oxford University Press, 1968).

10. 425 U.S. 501, 503 (1976).

11. 436 U.S. 478 (1978).

12. 218 F.Supp.2d 26 (D. Mass. 2002).

13. *Rogers v. Richmond*, 365 U.S. 534 at 540–41, 81 S.Ct. 735 at 737–40 (1961).

14. 18 U.S.C. § 3161.

15. *Stumpf v. Mitchell*, 367 F.3d 594 (6th Cir. 2004).

16. *Bradshaw v. Stumpf*, 125 S.Ct. 2398 (2005).

17. *Lutwak v. United States*, 344 U.S. 604, at 619, 73 S.Ct. 481, at 490 (1953).

18. *Chapman v. California*, 386 U.S. 18, 87 S.Ct. 824 (1967), *rehearing denied*, 386 U.S. 987, 87 S.Ct 1283; *State v. Jones*, 575 A.2d 216 (Conn. 1990); and *Schneble v. Florida*, 405 U.S. 427, 92 S.Ct. 1056 (1972).

19. In the 1975 case of *Faretta v. California* [422 U.S. 806, 95 S.Ct. 2525], the U.S. Supreme Court recognized the right of a criminal defendant under the Sixth Amendment to act as his or her own attorney. Denial of this constitutional right of self-representation is reversible error unless it is shown that (1) the request was untimely, (2) the defendant abused the right of self-representation, (3) the request was made solely for the purposes of delay, (4) the case is so complex that it requires the assistance of a lawyer, or (5) the defendant is unable to voluntarily and intelligently waive her right to a lawyer. See also *McKaskle v. Wiggins* [465 U.S. 168, 177 n.8, 104 S.Ct. 944, 950 n.8 (1984)].

    A convicted defendant who claims he was represented by an inadequate or ineffective lawyer must prove that (1) the lawyer's defense fell below an objective standard of reasonableness and (2) a reasonable probability exists that, but for the lawyer's unprofessional errors, the results would have been different [*Strickland v. Washington*, 466 U.S. 668, 104 S.Ct. 2052 (1984)].

    When the state is paying the attorney fee, the right to choose one's own attorney is limited in most states and is balanced with the public's need for the efficient and effective administration of criminal justice. The annual cost to taxpayers in a state of 5 or 6 million people for public defense attorneys is more than $30 million. For a discussion of the right to pick an attorney to be paid with public funds, see *People v. Phelps* [557 N.E.2d 235 (App. 1990)].

    When a criminal case is receiving considerable public attention, experienced lawyers either volunteer their services or accept the public fee for their services. The publicity in the 1992 *Dahmer* case in Wisconsin was worldwide (Dahmer was the bizarre confessed killer of seventeen young men). Many experienced criminal lawyers were interested in handling the case because of the extensive publicity.

20. 523 U.S. 614, 619 (1998).

21. Witnesses and prosecutors cannot comment on the fact that a defendant in a criminal case has exercised the constitutional right to remain silent. Such comments or statements would in most instances be reversible error should the defendant be convicted. Such comments could also be grounds for charging the lawyer before a bar association.

    In 1993 the U.S. Supreme Court held that "defendant's right to testify does not include a right to commit perjury." However, a defendant who only enters a not guilty plea does not commit perjury if the defendant is found guilty after a trial (see Chapter 6). [See *United States v. Dunnigan*, 507 U.S. 87, 113 S.Ct. 1111(1993). Also see *United States v. Havens*, 446 U.S. 620 at 626, 100 S.Ct. 1912 at 1918 (1980).]

22. *California v. Green*, 399 U.S. 149 (1970).

23. *Stanford v. Texas*, 379 U.S. 476, 85 S.Ct. 506 (1965).

24. 528 U.S. 304 (2000).

25. 127 S.Ct. 2218, 2224.

IMPORTANT ASPECTS OF THE AMERICAN CRIMINAL JUSTICE SYSTEM

CHAPTER **2**

LEARNING OBJECTIVES

In this chapter we discuss some aspects of the American criminal justice system, specifically the notion of federalism and the adversary system. The learning objectives for this chapter are:

- Know the meaning of *federalism* as it applies to criminal justice.
- Identify the constitutional basis for the exercise of federal criminal jurisdiction.
- Identify the limits of federal criminal jurisdiction under the Interstate Commerce Clause.
- Know the meaning of reliable, relevant, and competent evidence.
- List some differences between accusatorial and inquisitional systems.
- State the requirements of the *Brady* rule.
- State the requirements of the U.S. Supreme Court's rule for lost or destroyed evidence.

FEDERALISM IN THE UNITED STATES

federalism
Division of power between state governments and the federal government, in which the federal government has specified powers delegated to it, with the remaining powers vested in the states.

The United States uses a form of government based on a division of powers called **federalism,** which was first presented to the original states at the 1787 Constitutional Convention in Philadelphia. Federalism is generally regarded as a compromise between the competing ideas of a strong central government and independently run state governments. The people of the original thirteen states thought of themselves as being primarily citizens of their state. They were familiar with the political and civic leaders of their local community but knew little of the leaders of the proposed central government. They were thus reluctant to grant complete authority to a national government; however, they needed a strong central government to provide for national defense, to create a national currency and central banking system, to establish a postal system, to regulate trade with foreign nations, and to establish a taxation system to pay the expenses of the new national government.

The United States was the first country in the world to use a federal form of government.[1] Under a federal system, the central government has the power and authority to handle national problems, while the states have the power to regulate local needs and problems. Federalism provides diversity and flexibility at both the state and local levels of government. The needs and problems of states such as Maine or Colorado differ from those of New York, California, or Illinois. Under American federalism, states are primarily responsible for public safety and can enact laws that they believe are most effective in providing for public order and an efficient, effective criminal justice system.

FEDERALISM AND THE LAW OF EVIDENCE

The keystone of American federalism is the U.S. Constitution. ARTICLE VI of the Constitution provides that "This Constitution...shall be the supreme Law of the Land; and the Judges in every State shall be bound thereby...." The powers of the U.S. Congress, the president, and the U.S. Supreme Court are limited to those powers granted in the Constitution. The Tenth Amendment provides that "The powers not delegated to the United States by the Constitution...are reserved to the States ... or to the people."

Each state is sovereign, and the officials of each state have the powers granted to them by the constitution of that state. Each state has its own criminal codes, and each has enacted a code of criminal procedure and evidence. These codes and the rulings of state courts must conform to the requirements of the U.S. Constitution. However, state laws and state court rulings may provide additional rights to the people of the state and to criminal defendants within that state, beyond those extended by the Constitution.

Federal Rules of Evidence
Codification in 1975 of common-law rules of evidence; applicable only in federal courts but the model for most state evidence codes.

In 1975 Congress enacted the **Federal Rules of Evidence** (see Appendix C). Since that time, most states have adopted rules of evidence almost identical to the Federal Rules, with local modifications. However, each state retains the power to interpret and modify those rules of evidence. Thus, the meaning and application of the Federal Rules of Evidence can vary between federal courts and state courts and between the states.

The Federal Rules of Evidence and most state rules of evidence apply in both civil and criminal trials. However, some rules or parts of rules may apply differently in criminal cases.[2]

STATE AND FEDERAL JURISDICTION OVER CRIMES IN THE UNITED STATES

The great majority of crimes committed in the United States are violations of state criminal codes. Some crimes are federal offenses in violation of the federal criminal code. A small percentage of criminal offenses are violations of both the federal criminal code and a state criminal code.

Because each state is sovereign and has the power and authority granted to it by its residents, it may enforce its criminal laws against anyone who violates them.[3] The federal government is also sovereign, having the power and authority to enforce violations of federal law.

The U.S. Constitution does not grant to the federal government a general police power, nor has there ever been federal criminal common law. All federal crimes therefore have to be statutory crimes enacted by Congress.[4] States have general police power in providing for domestic tranquility. Common law, both civil and criminal, has always been part of the legal systems of the states. **Common law,** or unwritten law, is the rules developed over many years by courts and judges. Common-law crimes and common-law rules of evidence were used for years during the early history of the United States. Today, criminal codes and rules of evidence are enacted by state legislatures and are found in the codified laws of each state.

common law Legal rules that evolved over many years in English and American court opinions.

To enact federal criminal law, the U.S. Congress must act within the powers granted to it by the U.S. Constitution. Criminal laws may be enacted by the federal government in the following areas:

- To protect itself, its officials and employees, its property, and the administration of its authorized functions
- To regulate interstate and foreign commerce
- To protect civil rights
- To enact criminal laws for places beyond the jurisdiction of any state, such as the District of Columbia, federal territories, and federal enclaves such as military bases and national parks

Defendants in prosecutions for violations of federal criminal law sometimes attack the jurisdiction of the federal government to make their conduct criminal— in particular, when the basis of that jurisdiction is the Commerce Clause. The 2005 U.S. Supreme Court case of *Gonzales v. Raich* raised the issue of the constitutionality of a federal criminal statute passed under the Interstate Commerce Clause.

The scope of federal criminal jurisdiction under the Commerce Clause continues to be contentious after the *Gonzales v. Raich* decision. For example, in 2008 two federal district courts reached different conclusions on the power of Congress to enact certain provisions of the Sex Offender Registration and Notification Act (SORNA), 18 U.S.C. 2250(a), and sex offender registration requirements set out in 42 U.S.C. 16913.

Gonzales v. Raich

United States Supreme Court, 125 S.Ct. 2195 (2005)

Raich and other users and growers of marijuana for medical purposes brought an action to declare the federal Controlled Substances Act (CSA) unconstitutional. The CSA regulates the production, sale, and use of various controlled substances, including marijuana. Violation of the CSA's provisions is a federal crime. Raich and other California residents produced and used marijuana pursuant to a California statute, the California Compassionate Use Act. This act permitted the production and use of marijuana where the user has a medical condition that may be made less burdensome by the use of marijuana and a physician has prescribed the use of the drug. Federal agents seized and destroyed marijuana plants grown by persons claiming coverage under the California Compassionate Use Act, and they sought an injunction against further federal actions, including criminal prosecutions under the CSA. The Ninth Circuit Court of Appeals granted the injunction, but the U.S. Supreme Court reversed the Ninth Circuit, holding that the Commerce Clause permitted Congress to regulate even purely intrastate production of marijuana.

Marijuana is a Schedule I substance, and under the CSA all use or production of the substance is prohibited. Raich did not contend that Congress could not regulate or prohibit the interstate commerce in a Schedule I controlled substance such as marijuana. However, she did contend that Congress had no jurisdiction under the Commerce Clause to make purely intrastate production or use of the substance illegal. She argued that since the marijuana was only for her personal use under a physician's care, she could not affect interstate commerce.

The Supreme Court disagreed. It held that Congress could reasonably conclude that the presence of a permitted local market for a Schedule I substance would adversely affect efforts to totally eradicate the interstate market for marijuana, and that under established case law the Commerce Clause permits Congress to regulate activity that "substantially affects" interstate commerce. Among other things, the Court said that producers of marijuana for medical purposes might be induced by higher prices to re-route their product to the interstate market, thus frustrating the congressional goal of total eradication of the substance.

The Supreme Court held that the reasonable possibility of such an effect gives Congress the authority to make the CSA applicable to those who use or produce marijuana under the California Compassionate Use Act.

Under section 16913, all persons convicted under state sex offender laws are required to register in the state where they were convicted and any state to which they travel. Section 2250(a) then makes it a federal crime for a sex offender to travel to another state and fail to register as a sex offender in the arrival state. In both of the cases that came before a federal district court, a sex offender who was required to register in one state traveled to another state and failed to register on that state's sex offender list. Both were charged with violation of section 2250(a).

In *United States v. Waybright*,[5] the federal district court held that, although the Interstate Commerce Clause supports federal jurisdiction to make an activity a crime where the person charged actually travels in interstate commerce, the clause does not give the federal government the power to require every convicted sex offender to register on a state's sex offender list. The *Waybright* court then reasoned that a person could be convicted under section 2250(a) only because section 16913 mandated sex offender registration in the first place, and since sex offenses are purely local crimes with no interstate economic impact, Congress lacked the power to require sex offenders to register. That being so, Congress could not make it a crime to travel from state to state and fail to do some act that Congress lacked the power to mandate.

In *United States v. Thomas*,[6] the court agreed that section 16913 involved conduct that did not affect interstate commerce unless a sex offender in fact traveled to another state. However, the court concluded that Congress had the power under the Necessary and Proper Clause, which authorizes Congress to pass laws necessary to obtain the object of permissible legislation, to pass section 16913 as a legitimate method to identify sex offenders who travel between states and conceal their sex offender status.

These and similar cases will likely be appealed to one of the federal courts of appeal and may even end up in the U.S. Supreme Court for a resolution of this issue.

Law Enforcement in the American Federal System

There are more than 17,000 law enforcement agencies in the United States. Most of these are at the local levels of government (cities, counties, towns, and so on). All fifty states have law enforcement agencies working at the state level of government. At the federal level are the federal law enforcement agencies created by Congress to enforce specific federal laws.

Local law enforcement agencies such as police and sheriff departments enforce city and county ordinances in addition to the criminal laws of their state. They bring their cases to city attorneys and state attorneys (district attorneys) for charging and prosecution. Municipal police officers often spend more time in municipal courts on ordinance violations than they spend in state courts appearing in criminal cases. Both municipal and state courts use state rules of evidence.

Law enforcement agencies working at the state level of government are generally created by state law to enforce state criminal laws or to enforce hunting, fishing, health, sanitation, fire, and other state codes. Typical state law enforcement officers are state troopers; state traffic patrol; game wardens; and health, sanitation, and fire inspectors.

Federal law enforcement officers work in the many federal law agencies created by Congress. They enforce specific federal laws assigned to their agencies and take most of their cases to federal prosecutors for trial in the federal court system. Some of the many federal law enforcement agencies are the Federal Bureau of Investigation (FBI), the Drug Enforcement Agency (DEA), Immigration and Customs Enforcement (ICE), the Secret Service, the U.S. Marshals Service, and the U.S. Postal Inspection Service. ICE is the newest of the large federal law enforcement agencies and runs the Criminal Alien Program. In 2007 that program identified 164,000 criminals who were in this country illegally and were serving time in jails and prisons in the United States.

COURTS AND TRIALS IN THE UNITED STATES

In 2001, the National Crime Victimization Survey (NCVS) reported that 24.2 million violent and felonious property crimes were known to more than 16,000 law enforcement agencies in the United States (see Figure 2.1). This number does not include misdemeanors and offenses charged as ordinance violations throughout the United States, such as shoplifting and traffic violations.

These criminal cases are tried in the following manner:

Federal and State Courts	Military Courts	Military Commissions
(handling about 95% of all criminal trials in the United States)	(for members of the U.S. Armed Forces)	(established in 2004 for "enemy combatants" held by the U.S. military)[a]
Trial: Can be held by jurors selected at random	Before a panel of military personnel appointed by the military authority	Before an appointed military officer
Presiding Official: Independent judges either elected or appointed	Appointed military officer	Appointed military officer
Appeals: Independent legal courts	Military appellant courts	Panel appointed by U.S. Secretary of Defense
Hearsay: Federal or state rules apply	Federal Rules of Evidence apply	Hearsay evidence allowed
Exclusionary Rule: Federal and state rules apply	Only federal rules apply	Most federal rules do not apply
Exculpatory Evidence Proving Innocence: In both federal and state courts, must be provided to defense	Same	May be withheld if deemed classified
Right to Confront Witnesses: Defendants in all criminal trials have right to confront witnesses against them	Same	Not guaranteed to enemy combatants
Right to Speedy Trial: Sixth Amendment guarantees this right, and state and federal courts have speedy trial rules	Same	Enemy combatants may be held until end of war without trial
Right to Habeas Corpus Hearings: U.S. Constitution and most state constitutions protect the right to habeas corpus	Same	In 2008 the U.S. Supreme Court held that alien enemy combatants had the right to habeas corpus and that federal courts had jurisdiction to hear their claims[b]

[a]Prisoners of war are protected under the Geneva Convention Treaties signed by the United States and over one hundred other nations. Prisoners of war are entitled to the basic levels of humane treatment and may refuse to answer questions other than name, rank, and serial number. If POWs violate the laws of war, they can be tried for criminal violations.

[b]In one of the first hearings brought by one of the 270 detainees held for 6 years at the Guantanamo Navel Base, a federal court of appeals held that a military tribunal had improperly classified a detainee as an enemy combatant. (See "U.S. Court, in a First, Voids Finding by Military Tribunal," *The New York Times,* June 24, 2008.)

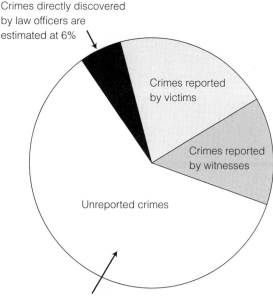

Crimes directly discovered by law officers are estimated at 6%

Crimes reported by victims

Crimes reported by witnesses

Unreported crimes

Over 50% of crimes are estimated to be unreported. NCVS reports that only about half of violent crimes and only 37% of property crimes were reported to police in 2001. In addition, high percentages of many other crimes are unreported. (See NCJ report 194610 of September 2002.)

FIGURE 2.1 | ESTIMATES OF REPORTED CRIMES IN THE UNITED STATES

THE AMERICAN ADVERSARY SYSTEM

In the American court system, the function of a criminal trial is to provide a venue for determining the facts upon which the guilt or innocence of the accused is based.

The main actors at the trial are the judge, the jury, the prosecutor, and the defense attorney. Each has a well-defined role to play in the trial. In the American **adversary system,** the prosecutor and the defense attorney assume adversarial roles; that is, they do not seek to establish the facts in cooperation with each other, but in opposition. Each side has two goals: to present the facts most advantageous to their position, and to seek to prevent and make it difficult for their opponent to do the same. (See Figure 2.2.)

This system—which "sets the parties fighting," in the words of former U.S. Supreme Court Justice Jackson—gives the adversaries clearly defined roles. The prosecutor, though obligated to "seek justice, not merely to convict," attempts to have the defendant "found guilty beyond a reasonable doubt by a unanimous jury."[7] The defense counsel's duty is "to represent his client (the defendant) zealously within the bounds of the law."[8]

adversary system The judicial system in which opposing parties present evidence, and an impartial judge or jury weighs the evidence; contrasts with the inquisitorial system, where the judge actively questions the accused and witnesses.

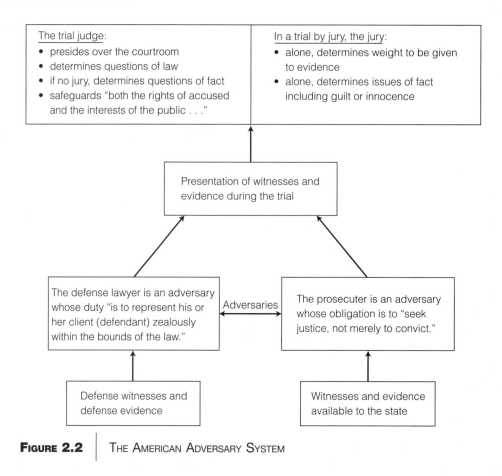

The trial judge:
- presides over the courtroom
- determines questions of law
- if no jury, determines questions of fact
- safeguards "both the rights of accused and the interests of the public . . ."

In a trial by jury, the jury:
- alone, determines weight to be given to evidence
- alone, determines issues of fact including guilt or innocence

Presentation of witnesses and evidence during the trial

The defense lawyer is an adversary whose duty "is to represent his or her client (defendant) zealously within the bounds of the law."

Adversaries

The prosecuter is an adversary whose obligation is to "seek justice, not merely to convict."

Defense witnesses and defense evidence

Witnesses and evidence available to the state

FIGURE 2.2 | THE AMERICAN ADVERSARY SYSTEM

Note: In most civil and criminal jury trials, the names and addresses of jurors are available from public records for people with the interest and knowledge of how to go about obtaining them. It does not occur to most people sitting on juror panels that this could be a problem. However, jurors sitting on criminal cases where defendants are potentially dangerous or retaliatory should have some concerns for their families and themselves.

Trial courts can restrict the disclosure of juror information if the court determines that jurors need protection. Courts have held that factors that could justify restricting jury information include "... but are not limited to: (1) the defendant's involvement in organized crime; (2) the defendant's participation in a group with the capacity to harm jurors; (3) the defendant's past attempts to interfere with the judicial process; and (4) extensive publicity that could enhance the possibility that jurors' names would become public and expose them to intimidation or harassment." See *United States v. Darden* [70 F.3d 1507, 1532 (8th Cir. 1995)] and *United States v. Ross* [33 F.3d 1507 at 1520 (11th Cir. 1994)].

The two adversaries (the prosecutor and the defense lawyer) approach the facts in the case from entirely different perspectives. Each advocate comes to the trial prepared to present evidence and arguments. The trial judge and the jury come to the trial uncommitted. Within the framework of the rules of evidence and the rules of court procedure, witnesses and evidence are presented. Witnesses are cross-examined and evidence is challenged.

The trial judge presides neutrally at the criminal trial and

has the responsibility for safeguarding both the rights of the accused and the interests of the public in the administration of criminal justice. The adversary nature of the proceedings does not relieve the trial judge of the obligation of raising, on his own initiative, at all appropriate times and in an appropriate manner, matters which may significantly promote a just determination of the trial. The only purpose of a criminal trial is to determine whether the prosecution has established the guilt of the accused as required by law, and the trial judge should not allow the proceedings to be used for any other purpose.[9]

Because a criminal trial "is in the end basically a fact-finding process,"[10] questions of fact must be determined in all contested criminal cases.[11] The Supreme Court stated in the case of *Tehan v. U.S. ex rel. Shott*[12] that "(t)he basic purpose of a trial is the determination of truth." Therefore, after the adversaries have presented all their evidence and made all their motions and arguments, the trier of fact must make the determination as to whether the government has carried the burden of proving the defendant guilty beyond reasonable doubt.

The determination of truth is the function of the jury. Because the jury must determine that truth based only on the often-conflicting versions presented by the adversaries, however, the system has elaborate rules to control how those versions of the truth are presented. The purpose of the rules of evidence is to ensure that each adversary's version of the truth is put before the jury by relevant, reliable, and competent evidence.

THE ADVERSARY SYSTEM AND BATTLES OVER WHAT IS RELEVANT, RELIABLE, AND COMPETENT EVIDENCE

Each adversary (prosecution and defense) seeks to present the facts that are most advantageous to its position. Each adversary also seeks to prevent and make it difficult for the opponent to do the same.

The parties often battle over what is relevant, reliable, and competent evidence. To be admissible, evidence must be relevant, reliable, and competent. If evidence is not relevant, or not reliable, or not competent, it is not admissible and cannot be used in a trial.

RELEVANT EVIDENCE

relevant evidence Evidence that has a tendency to make a material issue that is before the court more or less probable; see Chapter 5.

Relevant evidence is direct or circumstantial evidence[13] that has "any tendency to make the existence of any fact that is of consequence to the determination of the action more probative or less probative than it would be without the evidence."[14] Nonrelevant evidence is inadmissible (see Federal Rule of Evidence 402 in Appendix C).

Examples
- To show that the defendant was benefiting from illegal drug operations, evidence that he purchased expensive cars and jewelry and that his assets (net worth) far exceeded his wages from legitimate employment was relevant.[15]

In the American adversary system, the prosecutor and the defense attorney assume adversarial roles; that is, they seek to establish the facts not in cooperation with each other, but in opposition. Each side has two goals: first, to present the facts most advantageous to their position, and second, to seek to prevent and make it difficult for their opponent to do the same.

© Michael Newman/Photo Edit

- To show that the defendant knew illegal drugs were in his rental truck, evidence that the defendant traveled with his wife in prior drug transportations was relevant and admissible. But evidence that the defendant's children had been involved in illegal drug operations was held not relevant and not admissible evidence.[16]
- In a charge of sexual assault, evidence that the defendant operates an X-rated movie theater is not relevant because, even if true, the evidence has no logical basis as tending to increase the probability that the defendant did any acts constituting the sexual assault.
- In a charge of transporting stolen property, evidence that the defendant has a gambling addiction is not relevant to that charge. Addiction does not logically support the inference that the defendant lacked the ability to refrain from nongambling crimes.[17]

However, under Rule 403 (see Appendix C) relevant evidence may be excluded and held not admissible if the evidence may (1) unfairly prejudice a party, (2) confuse the jury, or (3) waste the court's time. Trial judges are generally given great discretion in striking the balance between the evidence's probative value and its likely prejudicial or confusing potential.

Examples
- In child pornography prosecutions, photographs of the child pornography are highly probative and outweigh prejudicial effects on the jury that views such photographs.[18]
- If the admissible child pornography pictures that were the basis of the criminal charge did not show violent and gruesome sexual practices, then sexually explicit narratives in the defendant's possession that described the violent and gruesome practices were not admissible because of the prejudicial effect that such narratives had.[19]

- In a prosecution for making false statements on a passport application, evidence of the defendant's marriage to a Japanese citizen were held inadmissible because such evidence was likely to confuse the jury and create sympathy for the defendant, who sought a passport to return to his wife in Japan.[20]

RELIABLE EVIDENCE

reliable evidence Evidence that possesses a sufficient degree of likelihood that it is true and accurate.

Reliable evidence is evidence that possesses a sufficient degree of believability—that is, a likelihood that the evidence is true and accurate. An adult witness' testimony about what he actually saw or heard is generally reliable. A statement by a witness about what another person said she saw or heard is generally unreliable. (This is the hearsay rule, discussed in detail in Chapters 7 and Appendix 8.) Unreliable evidence is inadmissible.

Example

A witness to a robbery who testified at a defendant's trial for robbery identified her as the driver of the getaway car. Earlier, the witness had identified the defendant in a photograph array (see Chapter 13) that was subsequently found to be improperly suggestive. Because the prosecution failed to independently prove the reliability of the witness' in-court identification by establishing the conditions prevailing when the witness saw the robbery and the accuracy of her descriptions of the perpetrator, her identification was determined to be unreliable, and the defendant's conviction was overturned.[21]

Reliable and admissible evidence is needed to justify charging a person with a crime. The U.S. Supreme Court pointed out in the 1986 case of *Holbrook v. Flynn*[22] that central to the right to a fair trial, guaranteed by the Sixth and Fourteenth Amendments, is the principle that "one accused of a crime is entitled to have his guilt or innocence determined solely on the basis of the evidence introduced at trial, and not on grounds of official suspicion, indictment, continued custody, or other circumstances not adduced as proof at trial."[23]

Each state has authority to commence a criminal prosecution if sufficient evidence is available to justify the criminal charge. The U.S. Supreme Court pointed out that the authorities of the states "derive from separate and independent sources of power and authority originally belonging to them before the admission to the Union and preserved to them by the Tenth Amendment."[24]

Each state also "has the power, inherent in any sovereign, independently to determine what shall be an offense against its authority and to punish such offenses, and in doing so each 'is exercising its own sovereignty, not that of the other.'"[25]

Under the American federal system, each state has its own constitution, court system, and other governmental units. States have the principal responsibility of maintaining public order within their boundaries.

COMPETENT EVIDENCE

competent evidence Any evidence that is relevant and reliable and not otherwise excludable. See Chapter 5.

Competent evidence is a catch-all term that includes relevant, reliable evidence that is not otherwise rendered inadmissible. Relevant, reliable evidence may also be incompetent.

Fry v. Pliler

United States Supreme
Court, 127 S.Ct. 2321
(2007)

It is not uncommon for a defendant in a criminal case to attempt to present evidence that a third person committed the crime of which he is charged. The prosecution often seeks to exclude such evidence because, to the extent the jury believes the evidence is credible, it is less likely to convict the defendant even if strong evidence of his guilt exists. Ultimately, a trial court must determine whether such evidence is admissible based on its relevance and reliability. In this case, the Supreme Court considered important questions raised when a trial court excludes such evidence: How are decisions excluding such evidence to be reviewed in appellate courts? Should that review be the same for direct review and review under habeas corpus?

After two mistrials ended in hung juries, the defendant Fry was convicted of two counts of murder by a third jury. At his trial he introduced the testimony of several witnesses that a third person had committed the murders. However, the trial court excluded the testimony of one witness, holding that the defendant had not provided sufficient evidence linking the excluded testimony to the murders. The California Supreme Court affirmed the conviction, and the defendant filed a petition for habeas corpus in the federal courts. The district court denied the petition, and the Ninth Circuit Court of Appeals affirmed. The U.S. Supreme Court granted certiorari to consider the scope of review of constitutional error in habeas corpus cases.

In *Holmes v. South Carolina* [547 U.S. 319 (2006)], a defendant was charged with murder. He attempted to introduce evidence that a third party had committed the murder, and offered witnesses who were prepared to testify that the third party told them he had killed the victim. The trial court excluded the testimony, based on a court-made rule that evidence that another person committed the crime should be excluded if it creates a "bare suspicion" and the case against the defendant is strong. Holmes was convicted of murder and sentenced to death; his conviction was affirmed by the South Carolina Supreme Court.

On review, the U.S. Supreme Court held that Holmes was deprived of his constitutional right to "a meaningful opportunity to present a complete defense," and the Court reversed his conviction. The Court reasoned that while evidence of a third party's involvement may be excluded if it bears little logical connection to the crime, the South Carolina rule went much further than this. It operated to exclude evidence that might have a logical connection to the crime if the jury doubted the credibility of the prosecution's evidence, which in effect made the decision to exclude the evidence depend on the strength of the prosecution's case. The Court held that this was a violation of Holmes's constitutional right to present a complete defense.

The *Fry* court concluded that even if the testimony of the witness was wrongly excluded by the trial court in habeas corpus cases, unlike cases of direct review as in *Holmes*, where the "harmless beyond a reasonable doubt" rule of *Chapman v. California* applies (see Chapter 1), a trial judge's decision to exclude evidence would be overturned, even if wrongful, only if it had a "substantial and injurious effect" on the jury verdict. The court of appeals had concluded that even if the witness should have been permitted to testify, her evidence was merely "cumulative" because other witnesses had been permitted to testify about the same facts, and thus the exclusion of her testimony could not have had an adverse effect on the jury's decision. The Supreme Court affirmed the lower courts' holdings denying habeas relief.

COMPARING THE U.S. CRIMINAL JUSTICE SYSTEM WITH THOSE OF OTHER INDUSTRIAL DEMOCRACIES

The United States

Uses a guilty plea and a plea-bargaining system to dispose of the vast majority of criminal cases.

Has 70 percent of the world's lawyers. "Let's ask ourselves: Does America need 70 percent of the world's lawyers?" (Vice President Dan Quayle to the American Bar Association in 1991)

Uses a system of political appointment or election of judges.

Places a great amount of discretion and responsibility in the hands of public prosecutors. (The American prosecutor is unique in the world and is not part of the system that came to the United States from the old English common-law system.)

Has created rules that make it difficult to obtain confessions and admissions to use as evidence.

Has adopted the American exclusionary rule.

Has the highest crime rate and illegal drug use of the industrial democracies, which places heavy loads on the criminal justice system. More than two million persons are in American jails and prisons.

Has elections of judges in most states. Special-interest groups now pour large amounts of money into judicial elections and often use "slash and burn" election tactics. Retired U.S. Supreme Court Justice Sandra Day O'Connor publicly criticized the practice, stating "... you are not going to get fair and impartial judges that way." A scathing article entitled "Gutter Politics and the Wisconsin Supreme Court" in *Wisconsin Lawyer Magazine* (May 2008) condemned such election tactics in a Wisconsin Supreme Court election, as did the article "Rendering Justice, with One Eye on Re-Election" in *The New York Times* (May 25, 2008).

Other Industrial Democracies

Use guilty pleas more often, especially in European and Asian criminal cases, probably because confessions and incriminating statements are more easily introduced as evidence.

Do not rely on plea bargaining to the extent that it is used in the United States.

Israel has the next highest number of lawyers; the rest of the world shares the remaining 20–25 percent.

Use career magistrates. Other legal systems are less political and less adversarial generally than the U.S. legal system.

Do not place as much discretion and responsibility in the hands of prosecutors.

Rely more heavily on obtaining confessions and admissions for use as evidence in criminal trials.

Have not adopted the strict American exclusionary rules; therefore, some evidence that cannot be used in the United States can be used in their criminal trials.

Do not have such high crime rates or as much illegal drug use. Do not use prison as a punishment to the extent that the United States does.

Have a high degree of confidence in their courts and the police, especially in European countries, and particularly England. Judges generally are selected on a merit basis either by a comprehensive written and oral examination process (France), or by appointment by nonpolitical commissions of experts appointed by the Crown (England). European judges are sometimes viewed as umpires calling balls and strikes, which is the model the current Supreme Court Chief Justice, Justice Roberts, made reference to in his confirmation hearing before the Senate Judiciary Committee in 2006.

Examples

- Evidence that a defendant in an armed robbery told the treating physician that the injury occurred during the robbery is inadmissible. Though clearly relevant and reliable, the communication between patient and treating physician is privileged.[26]
- Evidence seized in violation of the Fourth Amendment's probable cause requirement, though relevant and reliable, is inadmissible under the exclusionary rule adopted by the U.S. Supreme Court to promote the purposes of the Fourth Amendment.[27]

The rules of evidence discussed in the balance of this book are thus designed as complements to the adversary system. Though the system encourages the prosecutor and the defense attorney to "fight it out," it limits the tactics in that fight by rules of evidence. By doing so, the jury will see and hear only that evidence that properly should influence its deliberations.

THE AMERICAN ACCUSATORIAL SYSTEM

The United States and most of the English-speaking democracies in the world use the accusatorial system in criminal investigations and in criminal trials. The U.S. Supreme Court stated in the case of *Rogers v. Richmond*[28] that

> ours is an accusatorial and not an inquisitorial system—a system in which the State must establish guilt by evidence independently and freely secured and may not by coercion prove its charge against an accused out of his own mouth.

Under the accusatorial system, suspects and defendants have an absolute right to remain silent about matters that could incriminate them. If a defendant chooses to remain silent, the state must carry the burden of proving guilt beyond a reasonable doubt—using evidence obtained elsewhere in a manner that did not violate the rights of the suspect.

Most European countries and other democracies of the world do not use the accusatorial system but use instead an inquisitorial system. Under the inquisitorial system, defendants do not have an absolute right to remain silent. In some European countries, special judges become responsible for investigating serious crimes and question witnesses and suspects.

Although countries that use the inquisitorial system rely more heavily on obtaining confessions to solve crimes, the U.S. Supreme Court expressed a different philosophy in the 1964 case of *Escobedo v. Illinois*[29] and the 1966 case of *Miranda v. Arizona*.[30]

Some of the ways that the American criminal justice system differs from the criminal justice systems of other industrial democracies are pointed out in the boxed material on page 33.

DISCLOSING INFORMATION IN THE ADVERSARY SYSTEM

When a criminal charge has been made (see Chapter 3 for a discussion of the charging process), the prosecution and the defense begin separate investigations of the facts. As adversaries, neither the prosecution nor the defense is inclined to share information with the other side. However, the U.S. Supreme Court has placed limits on this unwillingness to share:

> The adversary system of trial is hardly an end in itself, it is not yet a poker game in which players enjoy an absolute right always to conceal their cards until played.[31]

Many of the rules that compel disclosure apply to the prosecution, but some compel a defendant to disclose information to the prosecution.

NOTICE OF ALIBI STATUTES

In using the alibi defense, a defendant is alleging that he or she physically could not have committed the crime that is charged because the defendant was at another place at the time the crime was committed.

Example

X is charged with robbing a liquor store and has been identified by two witnesses and an employee of the store as the man who robbed the store. X uses the defense of alibi and states that at the time of robbery, he was at his mother's home 100 miles away. X's wife and mother corroborate X's story, stating that they were with X at the time of the robbery.

Because an alibi can easily be fabricated, it must be carefully investigated. Most states have notice of alibi statutes that require defendants who plan to use an alibi defense to serve notice on the prosecutor before trial. These statutes are meant to safeguard against the wrongful use of alibis and to give law enforcement agencies and prosecutors necessary notice and time to investigate the merits of the proposed alibi.

Notice of alibi statutes require a defendant to disclose the place where the defendant claims to have been at the time the crime was committed and the names and addresses of witnesses to the alibi, if known. In the 1973 case of *Wardius v. Oregon*,[32] the U.S. Supreme Court held that if a defendant is compelled to disclose information, then the state must also make similar disclosures so that discovery is a "two-way street." The Court held in the *Wardius* case that:

> [In] the absence of a strong showing of state interests to the contrary, discovery must be a two-way street. The State may not insist that trials be run as a "search for truth" so far as defense witnesses are concerned, while maintaining "poker game" secrecy for its own witnesses. It is fundamentally unfair to require a defendant to divulge the details of his own case while at the same time subjecting him to the hazard of surprise concerning refutation of the very pieces of evidence which he disclosed to the State.

THE DUTY TO DISCLOSE EVIDENCE TENDING TO SHOW THE INNOCENCE OF AN ACCUSED (THE *BRADY* RULE)

Brady rule The rule that requires the prosecution to disclose upon request evidence favorable to the accused.

Exculpatory evidence is evidence that tends to show innocence. The following cases establish the well-recognized rule that a prosecutor has a duty to disclose evidence favorable to an accused upon request, where the evidence is material to guilt or innocence (the **Brady** rule). Where such evidence is in the exclusive possession of the prosecution, it must be disclosed even when there is no request for disclosure by the defense if such evidence is "clearly supportive of a claim of innocence."[33] For discovery purposes, it has been held that law enforcement officers are part of the prosecution and also have a duty of disclosure.

In *Steckler v. Greene*,[34] the U.S. Supreme Court reviewed its decisions after *Brady* and stated that (1) the duty to disclose exists even if the defense makes no request for disclosure, (2) the duty includes evidence useful in impeachment as well as exculpatory evidence, and (3) evidence is material if there is a reasonable probability that, if the evidence were known to the defendant, the result in the trial might have been different.

In the 2004 case of *Banks v. Dretke*,[35] a capital murder case, the U.S. Supreme Court held that the failure of the prosecutor to inform the defense that a key witness was a paid informant violated the *Brady* rule. The prosecution told the defense that it would not have to ask for exculpatory information, as the prosecution would give them everything they had. Nonetheless, a paid informant testified against the defendant, and, when asked whether he had any agreements with the prosecution, he stated he did not. The prosecution permitted that false testimony to stand. The Court said those actions violated the *Brady* rule and ordered a new hearing to determine whether the defendant should have a new trial.

Brady v. Maryland

United States Supreme Court, 373 U.S. 83, 83 S.Ct. 1194 (1963)

The defendant testified that he had participated in the robbery charged but stated that his accomplice had killed the victim. Despite a request for exculpatory evidence from the defense lawyer, the prosecutor withheld a statement by the accomplice admitting the killing but claiming that the defendant had wanted to strangle the victim, whereas the accomplice had wanted to shoot him. After a jury sentenced the defendant to death, the case was remanded for retrial on the question of punishment, but not on the question of guilt. The Supreme Court quoted the Maryland Court of Appeals as saying that there was "considerable doubt" about how much good the undisclosed statement would have done the defendant, but that it was "too dogmatic" to say that the jury would not have attached "any significance" to the evidence. The Court held that

> the suppression by the prosecution of evidence favorable to an accused upon request violates due process where the evidence is material either to guilt or to punishment, irrespective of the good faith or bad faith of the prosecution.

Since the 1963 *Brady* case, all states have enacted statutes providing for the discovery of information and evidence by defense lawyers. Although an accused does not have a right to all information available to the prosecutor, he or she does have the right to information as provided by the statutes of the state and to information required under the *Brady* rule.

LOST, MISPLACED, AND DESTROYED EVIDENCE

Hundreds of thousands of criminal cases are handled every year by thousands of law officers. Sometimes evidence is lost, misplaced, or accidentally destroyed. In the investigation of a violent crime, an item of clothing or other potential evidence can be overlooked in the concern to render medical assistance to the victim or to apprehend the offender. These problems have occurred over the years and raise

A SUMMARY OF THE *BRADY* RULE BY THE NATIONAL INSTITUTE OF JUSTICE

The following is the summary of the *Brady* rule presented by the National Institute of Justice in a May 2002 publication (NCJ 191717):

- Under the *Brady* rule, the state is required to turn over any and all exculpatory evidence to the defense.
- In most states, "missing" evidence or failure to turn over evidence violates the *Brady* rule only if it is found to have been done in bad faith, which requires a showing that it was known that (a) the evidence was exculpatory and (b) the evidence was intentionally withheld.
- Potentially useful but not conclusively exculpatory information does not necessarily need to be turned over.
- To prevail on a *Brady* claim, the defendant must prove a conscious effort to suppress exculpatory evidence.

Law enforcement officers are part of the prosecution and have a duty of disclosure, as does the prosecutor.

the question of the government's duty to collect and preserve evidence that might assist a defense lawyer in defending a client.

In the 1984 case of *California v. Trombetta*[36] and the 1988 case of *Arizona v. Youngblood*,[37] the U.S. Supreme Court established rules concerning the government's duty to preserve evidence. In the *Trombetta* case, California law officers followed routine procedure in not saving the breath samples of persons charged with driving while intoxicated where the chances were very low that the samples would have helped defense lawyers. In the *Youngblood* case, Arizona law officers did not properly refrigerate evidence of a sexual assault. The Supreme Court held that a violation of **due process** has not occurred unless the following is shown:

due process The minimum procedural protections courts must afford those charged with crimes; guaranteed by the Fifth and Fourteenth Amendments to the U.S. Constitution.

- *Bad faith on the part of the police or other law enforcement official:* The Court held that "unless a criminal defendant can show bad faith on the part of the police, failure to preserve potentially useful evidence does not constitute a denial of due process of law."[38]
- *The evidence also would be of likely significance to the defendant's defense:* The Court held that "[the] evidence must both possess an exculpatory value that was apparent before the evidence was destroyed, and be of such a nature that the defendant would be unable to obtain comparable evidence by other reasonably available means."[39]

In both the *Trombetta* and the *Youngblood* cases, the Supreme Court held that there was no bad faith on the part of the law officers and that both convictions were based on other strong, credible evidence.

If a *Brady* violation occurs, the penalty will be more severe and there will probably be a new trial or a complete dismissal of the criminal charges. A *Brady* violation occurred in *Ouimette v. Moran*,[40] where a state prosecutor's chief witness had an extensive criminal record and the state failed to disclose that record, which the defense lawyer needed for cross-examination. A new trial was ordered. A new trial was also ordered where, because of the improper handling of a murder weapon, blood and fingerprint evidence was lost.[41]

Other lesser penalties could include forbidding the state to use some of its evidence, warning the state in court, or filing a complaint with the employer of the person causing the problem.

USE OF FALSE OR PERJURED EVIDENCE

The deliberate use of false or perjured evidence in an attempt to obtain a criminal conviction is a crime in itself. Such conduct could also be the basis for a civil lawsuit in which large compensatory and punitive damages could be awarded. The following U.S. Supreme Court cases illustrate misconduct by prosecutors.

In a 2007 case, the Ninth Circuit Court of Appeals held that a prosecutor's obligation to reveal known perjury by a state witness to the defense applied to allegations that a state witness committed perjury. In *Morris v. Ylst*,[42] a defendant appealed his murder conviction based on a report made available to the prosecution in which a legal assistant in the prosecution office stated that a co-defendant perjured herself at the defendant's trial. The circuit court held that the state had a duty to investigate an allegation of perjury, and the failure to do so could be a violation of a defendant's rights. Here, however, the court concluded that the defendant did not show that correcting any falsehood would have changed the result at his trial. The defendant's murder conviction was affirmed.

Mooney v. Holohan

United States Supreme Court, 294 U.S. 103, 55 S.Ct. 340 (1935)

The Supreme Court made it very clear that a conviction obtained by the knowing use of false testimony or false evidence is a denial of due process of law and will be reversed. The Court held that:

> if a state has contrived a conviction through the pretense of a trial which in truth is but used as a means of depriving a defendant of liberty through a deliberate deception of court and jury by the presentation of testimony known to be perjured. Such a contrivance by a state to procure the conviction and imprisonment of a defendant is as inconsistent with the rudimentary demands of justice as is the obtaining of a like result by intimidation.

Miller v. Pate

United States Supreme Court, 386 U.S. 1, 87 S.Ct. 785 (1967)

The Supreme Court reversed and remanded the defendant's murder and rape conviction. The prosecutor referred to and exhibited to the jury a pair of "blood-stained shorts" that were an important link in the chain of the circumstantial evidence case against the defendant. The prosecutor knew but did not tell the jury or the defense lawyer that the reddish-brown stains on the shorts were not blood, but paint. The Court held that the prosecution "deliberately misrepresented the truth" and that:

> More than 30 years ago this Court held that the Fourteenth Amendment cannot tolerate a state criminal conviction obtained by the knowing use of false evidence.... There has been no deviation from that established principle.... There can be no retreat from that principle here.

SUMMARY

The United States uses the federal system of government because it is made up of many different states with many different needs.

The United States uses an adversary system, in which the prosecutor and the defense attorney present facts (evidence) that are most advantageous to their position. Each of the parties seeks to prevent and make it difficult for the other to do the same. Under the adversary system, there is an almost constant fight over what is relevant, reliable, and competent evidence.

The United States uses an accusatorial system under which a person accused of a crime has an absolute right to remain silent. Most European countries use inquisitorial systems where the right to remain silent is not total.

Federal and state governments have disclosure statutes whereby parties to a criminal or civil proceeding are required to disclose information to the other party. Prosecutors (including law officers) must disclose exculpatory evidence, and defense lawyers generally must give notice if they are going to use an alibi defense.

PROBLEMS

Finish each sentence using one of the available answers provided.

Available Answers (Problems 1–6)

a. An accusatorial system
b. An inquisitorial system
c. A totalitarian system
d. All of the above are correct.
e. None of the above is correct.

1. The United States uses
2. Most European countries use
3. Defendants charged with a crime have an absolute right to remain silent under
4. Defendants charged with crimes do not have an absolute right to remain silent under
5. More confessions are obtained and used as evidence under
6. Confessions and incriminating statements cannot be used as evidence under

Available Answers (Problems 7–13)

a. Relevant evidence
b. Reliable evidence
c. Competent evidence
d. All of the above are correct.
e. None of the above is correct.

7. To be admissible, evidence must be
8. Most hearsay is not admissible because it is not
9. Testimony that the defendant's son has a long criminal record is not admissible because it is not
10. Evidence obtained by a police burglary of the defendant's home is not admissible because it is not
11. A voluntary confession is not ordinarily admissible because it is not
12. An eyewitness who saw X commit the armed robbery he or she is charged with cannot testify as to what the witness saw because it is not
13. Testimony of a defendant's wife about a confession to the crime charged is not admissible because it is not

CASE ANALYSIS

Read Appendix B, Finding and Analyzing Cases (p. 427). With these guidelines in mind, please continue with the Case Analysis selections for Chapter 2.

1. In *People v. Braunthal* [31 P.3d 167 (Colo. 2001)], the Colorado Supreme Court refused to suppress the testimony of witnesses who viewed a videotape that was subsequently destroyed and thus was unavailable at the defendant's trial. In *Roberson v. State* [766 N.E.2d 1185 (Ind. App. 2002)] [Case No. 48A02–0108-CR-504], the Indiana Court of Appeals reversed a trial court's decision that refused to dismiss a charge of possession of dangerous material by an inmate based on the state's failure to preserve evidence of a deadly weapon. Why did these courts reach different results? Did they rely on the same rule in reaching their results?

2. In *Com. v. Laquer* [863 N.E.2d 46 (Mass. 2007)], the prosecution failed to disclose the report of an investigation that discovered four sets of fingerprints on a telephone in the victim's apartment, none of which matched the fingerprints of the defendant. The court concluded that this failure did not constitute a *Brady* violation. Why not?

3. Notice of alibi statutes require a defendant who intends to present such a defense to give notice to the prosecution so that the prosecution can investigate the alibi. What if a defendant files such a notice but then doesn't produce the witnesses listed in the notice whose testimony would provide the alibi? May the prosecution use the alibi notice in its case? See *State v. O'Neal* [176 P.3d 1169 (N.M. App. 2007)].

4. Many states have discovery rules in criminal cases that go beyond the rules established by *Brady* (disclosure) and *Youngblood v. Arizona* (lost evidence). Two examples of such rules are in *State v. Harris* [680 N.W.2d 737 (Wis. 2004)] and *State v. Steger* [158 P.3d 280 (Haw. App. 2006)]. The Hawaii court discussed the reasons the Supreme Court gave for a different rule in *Brady* cases as opposed to lost evidence cases. What were those reasons? Are you convinced?

Notes

1. Since the invention of federalism more than 200 years ago, other democratic countries also adopted forms of federalism, including Canada, Mexico, Australia, and the Federal German Republic. Democratic nations also use two other forms of government: (a) The *unitary form*—used by England, France, Ireland, Norway, and other countries—has one center of power (the central government), which creates smaller units, such as cities and provinces, to provide services. Countries that use unitary forms of government are generally small in both size and population. (b) The *confederate form* of government, which Switzerland has used for more than 700 years, bands together provinces and states in a loose organization called a confederacy. The United States used this form of government after the American Revolution until 1791. Because it was not working, the Constitutional Convention was convened in Philadelphia in 1787 to draft a new constitution and to invent a workable system of government acceptable to all thirteen states.

2. See, e.g., Federal Rules of Evidence 201(g) and 404(b).

3. In the 1985 case of *Heath v. Alabama* [474 U.S. 82, 106 S.Ct. 433], the U.S. Supreme Court ruled that under the dual sovereignty doctrine, a defendant who "in a single act violates the 'peace and dignity' of two sovereigns by breaking the laws of each . . . has committed two distinct 'offenses.'"

   In the *Heath* case, the defendant confessed that he hired two men in Georgia to kidnap his pregnant wife from their Alabama home and kill her. After his wife was murdered in Alabama, the defendant (and the men) was convicted of crimes in both Alabama and Georgia. The Supreme Court affirmed the criminal convictions under the dual sovereignty doctrine, holding that "(t)o deny a State its power to enforce its criminal laws because another state has won the race to the courthouse 'would be a shocking . . . deprivation of the historic right and obligation of the States to maintain peace and order within their confines.'"

Dual sovereignty also applies when criminal acts violate both state and federal laws. The 1993 trial of four Los Angeles police officers for beating Rodney King is an example. When federal prosecutors were not satisfied with the outcome of the California trial (the officers' acquittals resulted in a large-scale riot in Los Angeles), criminal indictments were sought under federal law, and the officers were tried again in a federal court for the same conduct. The second trial resulted in conviction of two of the officers and acquittal of the other two.

Some states, however, have enacted statutes that forbid criminal prosecution for a criminal act (or acts) already prosecuted in another state or in the federal courts. Wisconsin Statute 939.71 is such an example.

4. See the 1812 U.S. Supreme Court case *United States v. Hudson and Goodwin* [11 U.S. (7 Cranch) 32] and the 1949 Supreme Court case *Krulewitch v. United States* [336 U.S. 440, 69 S.Ct. 16], where Justice Jackson stated, "It is well and wisely settled that there can be no judge-made offense against the United States and that every federal prosecution must be sustained by statutory authority."

5. 561 F.Supp.2d 1154 (D. Mont. 2008).

6. 534 F.Supp.2d 912 (N.D. Iowa 2008).

7. American Bar Association (ABA) Standards Relating to the Prosecution Function and the Defense Function, 1.1(c).

8. ABA Code EC 7–1.

9. *General Responsibility of the Trial Judge*, p. 167, ABA Standards Relating to the Administration of Criminal Justice.

10. *Herring v. New York*, 422 U.S. 853, 95 S.Ct. 2550 (1975).

11. Questions of fact are determined by the fact finder. The fact finder is a jury in a jury trial or the trial judge when a case is tried without a jury. Questions of law are always determined by the trial judge.

12. 382 U.S. 406, 416, 86 S.Ct. 459, 465 (1966).

13. See Chapter 4 for definitions of *direct* and *circumstantial*.

14. Federal Rules of Evidence, sec. 401. Evidence, even though relevant, may be excluded under evidentiary rules like Rule 403 of the Federal Rules if it is unduly prejudicial or may tend to mislead the jury. This is sometimes referred to as the "legally relevant" test.

15. *United States v. Burgos*, 254 F.3d 8 (1st Cir. 2001).

16. *United States v. Espinoza*, 244 F.3d 1234 (10th Cir. 2001).

17. *United States v. Garcia*, 94 F.3d 57 (2d Cir. 1996).

18. *United States v. Becht*, 267 F.3d 767 (8th Cir. 2001).

19. *United States v. Grimes*, 244 F.3d 375 (5th Cir. 2001).

20. *United States v. George*, 266 F.3d 52 (2d Cir. 2001).

21. *Hull v. State*, 607 So.2d 369 (Ct. Crim. App. Ala. 1992).

22. 475 U.S. 560, 106 S.Ct. 1340.

23. *Taylor v. Kentucky*, 436 U.S. 478, 485 (1978).

24. *Heath v. Alabama*, 474 U.S. 82 (1985).

25. *Id.*

26. See Chapter 6 for a discussion of privileged communications.

27. See Chapter 9 for a discussion of the Fourth Amendment exclusionary rule.

28. 365 U.S. 534, 540–41, 81 S.Ct. 735, 739–40 (1961).

29. 378 U.S. 478, 84 S.Ct. 1758.

30. 384 U.S. 436, 86 S.Ct. 1602.

31. *Williams v. Florida*, 399 U.S. 78, 90 S.Ct. 1893, 1896 (1970).

32. 93 S. T. 2208 (1973). See also *Williams v. Florida* [399 U.S. 78 (1970)] and *Taylor v. Illinois* [484 U.S. 400 (1988)].

33. *Brady v. Maryland*, 83 S.Ct. 1194.

34. 527 U.S. 263 (1999).

35. 540 U.S. 668 (2004).

36. 467 U.S. 479, 104 S.Ct. 2528.

37. 488 U.S. 51, 109 S.Ct. 333.

38. 488 U.S. 58, 109 S.Ct. 337.

39. 467 U.S. 489, 104 S.Ct. 2534.

40. 942 F.2d 1 (1st Cir. 1991).

41. *Sanburn v. State*, 812 P.2d 1279 (Nev. 1991).

42. 447 F.3d 735 (9th Cir. 2007), *cert. denied*, 127 S.Ct. 957 (2007).

Using Evidence to Determine Guilt or Innocence

CHAPTER 3

LEARNING OBJECTIVES

In this chapter we discuss pleas and plea bargaining in criminal prosecutions. The learning objectives for this chapter are:

- Outline the criminal court process.
- List the pleas a defendant may enter to a criminal charge.
- Evaluate the pros and cons of plea bargaining.
- Compare the use of evidence at various stages of a criminal trial.

CHAPTER CONTENTS

EVALUATION AND REVIEW OF EVIDENCE

The rules of evidence ultimately decide what evidence will be presented to the judge and jury for evaluation and what evidence will not. However, at various stages of the investigatory and criminal court process, evidence may be evaluated in a variety of settings. In many of these settings, the rules of evidence do not apply. Consider the stages in a shoplifting case:

1. Store employees or security personnel are usually the first to evaluate and judge the information and evidence available to them before detaining a person for shoplifting. Probable cause based on firsthand information by a reliable adult employee is the standard required. Store employees are told, "If you did not see it, it did not happen" and "When in doubt, let him go."
2. After a suspect is detained for shoplifting and the police are called, the officer evaluates the available evidence before proceeding. If the evidence is insufficient, the suspect is immediately released.
3. Evaluations made in stages 1 and 2 are often reviewed immediately by superiors (store managers and police sergeants).
4. If the case is presented to a prosecutor (a city attorney or a district attorney), the prosecutor reviews the available evidence to determine whether further proceedings are warranted.
5. If a charge or citation is issued, a defense lawyer often reviews the evidence, looking for weaknesses in the case. Insufficient or questionable evidence, use of improper procedure, or lack of probable cause based on firsthand information are some of the weaknesses for which a defense lawyer would look.
6. A **motion to suppress evidence** and dismiss could bring the matter before a judge. To rule on the motion, the judge must review the evidence.
7. If the defense motion is denied, the case may be tried before a jury, which evaluates the evidence and determines guilt or innocence.
8. A convicted defendant can appeal the case and argue to an appellate court that the evidence was not sufficient to support a finding or a judgment of guilt. The appellate court then reviews the evidence.

motion to suppress evidence A written or oral request to a judge to keep out evidence at a trial or hearing, often made when a party believes the evidence was unlawfully obtained.

The defendant in the 1984 case of *Lee v. State*[1] did not argue insufficient evidence, but in his appeal argued instead that a shoplifter had to leave a store in order to be convicted of larceny (theft). The Maryland Court of Special Appeals, however, affirmed the defendant's conviction, holding that it was not necessary for a state to show that a defendant left a store to be convicted of shoplifting. Stating that they found no court decision holding otherwise, the court held that once "a customer goes beyond the mere removal of goods from the shelf and crosses the threshold into the realm of behavior inconsistent with the owner's expectations, the circumstances may be such that a larcenous intent can be inferred."

In the process of review and evaluation of evidence, weaker cases are filtered out of the system or lesser charges are used. Not all cases go to court and trial. A merchant might recover the stolen merchandise from a shoplifter and, after warning the person, take no further action. A police officer might take a teenaged shoplifter home to his or her parents. After the parents have been informed of the incident, the matter may be dropped.

TEAM EVIDENCE REVIEWS AND CLEARANCE RATES

In the investigation of both major and minor crimes, a determination must be made about whether sufficient evidence exists to obtain a conviction or more investigation is needed. A February 2008 *FBI Law Enforcement Bulletin* article, "Homicide Investigations: Identifying Best Practices," points out that almost 40 percent of criminal homicides committed in the United States are not cleared. Police departments that use the practice of team review of evidence within a short time after the discovery of major crimes have a higher clearance rate than the national average, the article concludes.

Team reviews allow for better communication and exchange of information between officers involved in an investigation, who might work different shifts. Whether done informally or pursuant to established department policy, evidence reviews can increase the efficiency of investigations and lead to higher clearance rates. The following list suggests some of the methods and questions that are raised in a team review (most of these topics are developed more fully in this book):

1. What physical evidence is available?

DNA	Documents
Latent prints	Videos or photos
Weapons	Sexual assault evidence
Ballistics	Illegal drugs evidence
Stolen property	Test results

2. Was the physical evidence obtained in a manner that may be seriously attacked or suppressed under the exclusionary or derivative evidence rule? Are there problems with the chain of custody of the evidence?

3. What witnesses are available, and how reliable and dependable are the witnesses? Have the witnesses listed below been evaluated (on a scale from Excellent to Poor, or unknown) on their reliability, dependability, credibility, willingness to testify, and importance of their testimony, as well as their age and appearance?

   Eyewitnesses

   Victim(s)

   Other civilian witnesses

   Police/sheriff/law enforcement personnel

   Expert witnesses (qualifications?)

4. What are some likely ways the witnesses may be attacked on cross-examination? What evidence is available to corroborate statements made by witnesses, especially eyewitnesses?

5. Is there a suspect or suspects? What are the reasons for targeting the suspect? Are any persons related to the case in police custody? If so, on what charges? Are charges for an offense other than the crime under investigation? If so, are the offenses related? Is there an opportunity for multiple clearances?

6. Are confessions or incriminating statements available as evidence? If so:

   Where and when were the statements made?

GOALS OF THE CRIMINAL JUSTICE SYSTEM

The most basic function of any government is to provide for the security of the individual and her or his property [U.S. Supreme Court in *Lanzetta v. New Jersey*, 306 U.S. 451, 455, 59 S.Ct. 618 (1939)]. The generally recognized overall goals of the criminal justice system are:

- To discourage and to deter people from committing crimes
- To protect society from dangerous and harmful people
- To punish people who have committed crimes
- To rehabilitate and reform people who have committed crimes

Were they taped or on a video? If so, by whom?
Can they be seriously attacked as made involuntarily?
Are there omissions, false statements, or inaccuracies in the statements?
Are there any violations of the *Miranda, Massiah,* or *Bruton* rules?
Were departmental or state standards for taking confessions followed?

THE CRIMINAL COURT PROCESS

criminal complaint The formal charge made by the prosecution against a defendant, which begins criminal proceedings.

In this text, we study the rules of evidence as they apply in formal judicial proceedings, principally jury trials. Included here is a short discussion of the criminal court process. In misdemeanor cases, the process typically begins with the filing of a **criminal complaint** with a magistrate or other judicial official. The complaint can come before or after the defendant is placed under arrest. The magistrate determines only whether probable cause exists to believe that a crime has been committed and that the named defendant committed the crime.

initial appearance The first appearance by an accused before a judge or magistrate; a plea is entered and bail is set at this hearing.

Following the issuance of the complaint, a warrant could be issued for the defendant's arrest, if he or she is not already in custody. The **initial appearance** before the magistrate is then promptly held. At this appearance, the charges are read to the defendant, a plea is entered, and bail is set.

preliminary hearing Full adversarial hearing with a lawyer present.

If a felony is charged, the next step is the **preliminary hearing** in states that do not use the indictment system. This is a full adversarial hearing where lawyers are present, evidence is heard, and a judge makes the determination whether probable cause exists to believe the defendant committed the crime charged. Although this hearing is more detailed than the initial appearance, it is not a full trial. At this juncture, however, a judge may dismiss the charges if the prosecution's case is weak. If sufficient evidence is introduced to show probable cause, the defendant is bound over for trial.

Federal and many state courts use the indictment system for felonies instead of public prosecutors issuing criminal complaints. In some states, such as Texas,

criminal indictment The formal charge issued by a grand jury, listing crimes believed to have been committed by the named defendant.

the prosecutor issues a criminal complaint and then proceeds through the indictment process. A **criminal indictment** is a list of criminal charges issued by a **grand jury**, which has heard evidence presented by the federal attorney or state prosecuting attorney. The grand jury proceedings are held in secret, are not adversarial, and include only evidence presented by the prosecution.

In states that do not use the grand jury system, a criminal case can begin with the filing of an *information,* which is a statement by the prosecution detailing the basis on which it is believed the defendant committed a crime.

grand jury A jury that hears evidence presented by the prosecution and determines whether to charge persons with crimes; used in federal and many state criminal proceedings.

After an indictment or information has been issued, the defendant is *arraigned.* At the **arraignment**, the defendant enters a plea and the case is bound over to the appropriate criminal court for trial.

During the period between arraignment, or preliminary hearing, and full trial, the defendant may reevaluate the evidence and either change a simple not guilty plea or begin plea bargaining. Because of the prevalence of such practices, the following section discusses the plea and plea-bargaining process in greater detail.

PLEAS A DEFENDANT MAY ENTER TO A CRIMINAL CHARGE

arraignment The formal proceeding following the indictment or information, where a plea is entered and the case is bound over for trial.

After a defendant has been charged with a criminal offense, the defendant and the attorney must evaluate the evidence available to the state to support its criminal charge. Their evaluation of the evidence could determine what defenses they will or will not use and what plea they will enter. The following pleas are available to defendants:

- *Not guilty plea.*
- *Guilty plea:* This may be a regular guilty plea or an Alford guilty plea in states that permit the Alford plea.
- *An insanity plea (or defense):* The usual insanity plea is not guilty by reason of mental disease or defect. This plea may be joined with a plea of not guilty. If it is not joined with a not guilty plea, the defendant then admits committing the offense but pleads a lack of mental capacity.

A jury or a judge may, if the evidence permits, find a defendant guilty but mentally ill under the statutes of eight states.[2] Such a person is not legally insane but at the time of the offense had serious mental or emotional problems. Under this verdict, prison authorities must provide necessary psychiatric or psychological treatment to restore the offender's mental and emotional health in an appropriate treatment setting.

- *No contest (nolo contendere) plea:* This plea is permitted if the statutes of a state allow it, subject to the approval of the court. A defendant who uses this plea seeks to avoid admitting guilt in the hope of successfully denying the truth of the charges in a subsequent civil lawsuit.
- *Standing mute or refusing to enter a plea:* This plea ordinarily causes the court to direct that a plea of not guilty be entered on behalf of the defendant.

PURPOSES OF RULES OF EVIDENCE

- *Rules of evidence that are designed to be of assistance to the judge or jury in the search for the truth*

    Examples are rules that exclude and keep evidence out of court:

    i. Rules requiring that evidence be relevant, reliable, and competent

    ii. The *opinion evidence* rule

    iii. The hearsay rules

    } These rules of evidence guard against unreliable evidence that could be prejudicial, misleading, inaccurate, or distracting.

- *Rules of evidence that expedite trials and move them along without unnecessary delays*

    i. Rules concerning *judicial notice* that relieve parties to a trial of proving uncontested facts that are of common knowledge to the community or are available in a reliable text or other publication

    ii. Rules concerning presumptions and inferences that give directions to judges and juries and also determine in criminal and civil trials which of the parties has the burden of proof and the burden of coming forward with evidence

- *Rules of evidence that are not designed to be of assistance in the search for the truth but have other purposes; they often actually hinder the search for the truth.*

    i. Testimonial privilege rules that have been created to protect relationships and interests, such as husband–wife, attorney–client, and physician–patient. These relationships have been determined to be of sufficient importance to justify sacrificing what might be reliable evidence from being used in criminal and civil trials.

    ii. The rule of the exclusion of evidence (the *exclusionary rule*) that is used to discourage and deter law enforcement officers from improper or illegal conduct or procedure. This form of "policing the police" sometimes prevents reliable evidence from being used in criminal trials.

THE NOT GUILTY PLEA

All defendants in criminal cases are presumed innocent until proven guilty through the use of evidence and witnesses presented during a trial. The burden of proof is always on the state or government to prove the elements of the crime charged.

The level of proof required in criminal cases is proof beyond a reasonable doubt. This is the highest level of proof the law requires in any kind of case. It means that the evidence presented during the trial must convince the fact finder (jury or judge) of the defendant's guilt to a moral certitude. It does not mean that the evidence must show that the defendant is guilty beyond *any* doubt, nor does it require evidence of absolute certainty of the defendant's guilt. The burden on the state is to prove the defendant guilty beyond any *reasonable* doubt.

Because of the constitutional presumption of innocence, the system of justice used in the United States is an accusatorial system. The accuser must bear the entire burden of proving the charge by the use of competent evidence. The defendant does not have to do anything. The burden is on the state to come forward with sufficient evidence to carry the burden of proof beyond reasonable doubt.

The defendant can remain silent and inactive. Or the defendant can appear as a witness on his or her own behalf and may present evidence showing or tending to show his or her innocence. The defense may also actively attack or seek to hinder and minimize the state's evidence and case by the use of motions before, during, or after the trial.

The defendant can deny performing the acts charged or assert an affirmative defense. In an affirmative defense, a defendant in effect admits to performing the acts charged but claims that he or she had a lawful excuse for doing so and thus is not guilty of the crime charged. To assert an affirmative defense, the defendant must come forward with evidence showing a basis for it, and in some states must prove the affirmative defense by a preponderance of evidence.

An example of an affirmative defense is the claim of entrapment. Many states require that a defendant using an entrapment defense admit that he or she committed the criminal act or acts. The defense is that law enforcement officers used excessive or improper inducements that caused the defendant to violate the law. Other affirmative defenses are outrageous government conduct, frame-up, and coercion or duress ("I was forced to do it"). [For an explanation of affirmative defenses, see Chapter 6 of T. Gardner and T. Anderson, *Criminal Law: Principles and Cases*, 10th ed. (Thomson Wadsworth, 2009).]

THE GUILTY PLEA

In the United States, well over 70 percent of the people charged with felonies plead guilty.[3] The U.S. Supreme Court held in the 1969 case of *Boykin v. Alabama*[4] that "[a] plea of guilty is more than a confession which admits that the accused did various acts; it is itself a conviction; nothing remains but to give judgment and determine punishment."

Most guilty pleas are entered because defendants realize that the evidence that the state or government has against them will result in a conviction. Defendants therefore enter the guilty plea because of the standard practice of rewarding a defendant who acknowledges guilt in open court with a lighter sentence.[5]

The U.S. Supreme Court has held that the foundations of a valid guilty plea are the defendant's voluntary admission in open court that he committed the acts charged and the defendant's knowing consent to the judgment of guilt without a trial. Because the defendant stands before the court as a witness against himself in entering a guilty plea, the admission of guilt cannot be compelled but must be a voluntary expression of his own choice. And because a defendant's consent to judgment without trial constitutes a waiver of the constitutional rights attending a trial, his consent must be made with knowledge of the waiver of those rights.[6]

The defendant who offers a guilty plea must admit that he committed the crime charged. In the 2005 case of *Bradshaw v. Stumpf*,[7] the U.S. Supreme Court held that a guilty plea in an aggravated murder case was valid even with the defendant's "steadfast assertion" that he had not shot the victim. The Court stated that because under Ohio statutes one who aids and abets a murder can be charged the same as the person who actually does the killing, the defendant's admission that he did aid and abet satisfied the requirement that he admit a specific intent to cause death.

It must be shown that a defendant entered a guilty plea voluntarily and intelligently.[8] The trial judge must be convinced by the evidence presented that the defendant did in fact commit the criminal act of which she is charged. There is no constitutional right to plead guilty, but a state may create a statutory right to do so.[9]

In *Boykin v. Alabama*,[10] the Court held that the following rights are waived by a guilty plea:

> Several federal constitutional rights are involved in a waiver that takes place when a plea of guilty is entered in a state criminal trial. First, is the privilege against compulsory self-incrimination guaranteed by the Fifth Amendment and applicable to the States by reason of the Fourteenth....
> Second, is the right to trial by jury....
> Third, is the right to confront one's accusers....
> We cannot presume a waiver of these three important federal rights from a silent record.

The Alford Guilty Plea   In the case of *North Carolina v. Alford*,[11] the U.S. Supreme Court held that a defendant "may voluntarily, knowingly, and understandingly consent to the imposition of a prison sentence even if he is unwilling or unable to admit his participation in the acts constituting the crime." The **Alford guilty plea** permits a defendant to enter a guilty plea while at the same time protesting his innocence. The Alford plea is not mandatory for states, but most states have adopted it. State judges, however, are generally not obligated to accept an Alford plea. Most judges do accept it because the sentence given is the same as the sentence given for a regular guilty plea under the state sentencing guidelines.

Alford guilty plea A guilty plea that permits the accused to maintain innocence.

Most state courts hold that an Alford plea is the "functional equivalent" of a regular plea of guilty.[12] Therefore, a defendant who enters a guilty plea, whether an Alford plea or a regular guilty plea, has lost almost all rights to appeal. Most courts hold that the only issues applicable are the voluntary and intelligent nature of the plea and the jurisdiction of the court.

Defendants seek to use an Alford plea when they want to avoid the greater sentence they generally face if they take their case to trial and lose. In the 1991 case *State v. Hansen*,[13] the defendant entered an Alford plea to a second-degree murder charge of killing her husband during one of their many domestic disputes. She acknowledged that there was sufficient evidence to convict her but denied she intended to kill her husband. At the sentencing hearing, she sought to withdraw her Alford plea. The judge refused her motion to withdraw her plea and sentenced her to fifteen years in prison. On appeal, the sentence was affirmed.

The No Contest or Nolo Contendere Plea   Most (if not all) states also have statutes permitting the **no contest or nolo contendere plea**. In most states and in the federal court system, the plea may be made only with the consent of the trial judge. Some states limit the plea to misdemeanors and ordinance violations.

no contest or nolo contendere plea A plea in which the accused neither contests nor admits the charges against him; treated as a guilty plea.

The no contest plea has been called a troublesome legal creature. In 1974 the advisory committee writing a proposed code of federal criminal procedure noted that the "defendant who asserts his innocence while pleading guilty or nolo contendere is often difficult to deal with in a correctional setting."[14]

GUILTY PLEAS

The majority of criminal cases that come before courts in the United States end with the defendant entering a guilty plea in open court. All states and the federal government have different forms of guilty pleas, including the following:

- The *regular guilty plea* is made in open court upon a showing that the defendant did in fact commit the criminal act or acts with which he or she is charged and upon a showing that the defendant voluntarily and intelligently is entering the guilty plea and waiving the right to a trial.

  In this guilty plea and all other guilty pleas, the defendant is subject to the statutory penalties of the state. However, it is a common practice in the United States to reward the defendant who enters a guilty plea with a lesser sentence under the sentencing guidelines and practices of the state.

- The *Alford guilty plea* permits a defendant to enter a guilty plea without admitting guilt.

- The *no contest* or *nolo contendere plea* allows the defendant not to contest the criminal charge or charges against her. Defendants who believe they will be sued in a civil court for their criminal conduct sometimes seek to use this plea.

- The *conditional guilty plea* is used when a defendant seeks to preserve the right to appeal a ruling of the trial judge. A defendant who enters any of the other guilty pleas loses practically all rights to appeal many aspects of the case.

In the 1991 case of *State v. Smith*,[15] the defendant elected not to contest the state's case against him and entered a plea of nolo contendere. The Utah Court of Appeals found that the defendant's failure to admit his guilt "also prevented rehabilitative efforts [while he was on probation] and ultimately resulted in his incarceration." The trial judge stated that this is "the first and last no contest plea … that … I will receive."

The Conditional Guilty Plea Defendants do not have a constitutional right to plead guilty and may be forced to go to trial. But because forcing a defendant to stand trial rarely serves a useful purpose, all states have statutes and case law setting the procedure for accepting guilty pleas. Nor does a criminal defendant "have an absolute right under the Constitution to have his guilty plea accepted by the court."[16] Trial judges have the discretion under the laws of all states to refuse to accept a plea of guilty.

Defendants who enter a guilty plea in any form to a criminal charge lose most of their right to appeal. The U.S. Supreme Court ruled in 1973 that "[w]hen a criminal defendant has solemnly admitted in open court that he is in fact guilty of the offense with which he is charged, he may not thereafter raise independent claims relating to the deprivation of constitutional rights that occurred prior to the entry of the guilty plea."[17]

To preserve the right to appeal on any issue before a trial court, defense lawyers sometimes use the conditional guilty plea. They might do this, for example, after the defense has failed in a motion to suppress evidence, after an attack on the validity of a search warrant, or following a defense attack on the validity of an arrest. The defendant can enter a guilty plea conditioned upon the defendant's right to appeal the trial judge's ruling.

THE INSANITY PLEA

insanity plea A plea to a criminal charge of not guilty because of mental disease or defect.

The plea of not guilty because of mental disease or defect (the **insanity plea**) is found in the criminal codes of most states. At least three states (Idaho, Utah, and Montana) have abolished the insanity defense. If a defendant enters an insanity plea in a minor criminal matter, the state may agree and join the defendant in requesting the court to find the defendant legally insane. The defendant probably will then be held for mental observation and treatment for a much longer period than would have been the case had he or she been convicted of the crime charged.

plea bargaining Agreement to enter a guilty plea in return for a reduction in the charge or sentence. For example, first-offense shoplifters are often given the opportunity to plea to disorderly conduct in a municipal court instead of going to trial for a theft charge. First-offense drunk drivers are often permitted to enter a guilty plea in return for the dropping of one of the three or four criminal charges that they face.

Therefore, the insanity plea is used by defendants primarily in murder cases, for which sentences are severe. In using the insanity defense, most defendants also enter a not guilty plea. The trial is then bifurcated, with the first part of the trial determining guilt or innocence of the charge and the second part determining whether the defendant was legally insane when the criminal act was committed.

Because there is a legal inference that all people are sane and normal, most states place the burden on a defendant using the insanity plea to come forward with evidence showing that he or she was so mentally diseased or defective that he or she was unable to formulate the mental intent to commit the crime charged.

In 1981 John Hinckley, Jr., was charged with attempting to kill President Ronald Reagan. In a wild shooting spree in Washington, DC, Hinckley seriously wounded the president and three others. At the time of the Hinckley trial, federal courts required the government to carry the burden of proving that the defendant was sane and normal. The government could not produce evidence showing that Hinckley was sane and normal and therefore, under the rule used then, Hinckley was found not guilty because of insanity.

In 1984 Congress passed legislation providing that the federal courts rejoin most of the state courts in requiring defendants using the insanity plea to prove by clear and convincing evidence that the defendant was insane at the time of the crime.

PLEA BARGAINING OR SENTENCE BARGAINING

Multiple criminal charges are often issued in criminal or ordinance violations. Defendants who agree to plead guilty in return for the dropping of one or more of the charges are **plea bargaining**. In plea bargains, defendants sometimes agree to help law officers or to appear as a witness in return for concessions from the government.

Sentence bargains are agreements on the sentence a defendant will receive. All sentence or plea bargains are subject to the approval of the trial judge, who may refuse to accept them if the judge concludes the plea agreement is not in the best interests of the public.

In 1967 the President's Commission on Law Enforcement and Administration of Justice stated that "[w]hen a decision is made to prosecute, it is estimated that in many courts as many as 90 percent of all convictions are obtained by guilty pleas."[18]

In appraising the amount and quality of the evidence against a client, the American defense lawyer often turns to plea bargaining if the government has a strong case. The defense lawyer usually informs the client that there is a strong likelihood of conviction and advises "copping a plea." Not all guilty pleas are plea bargained, however. Many guilty pleas are entered every day in U.S. courts without

Is the Insanity Defense an Effective Defense?

There has long been controversy about the insanity defense. Some of that controversy may be the result of the public's perception that significant numbers of criminal defendants use the defense, are found not guilty by reason of insanity (NGRI), and are released to prey on the public. However, virtually all the empirical studies done on this subject show that is not the case. Here are some results of these studies:

- The defense is used in only about 1 percent of the felony cases prosecuted and has a success rate of just over 20 percent. That means that for every 1,000 felony defendants, only 2 or 3 are found NGRI.[a]
- The defense is risky. Unsuccessful defendants who assert the defense but are found guilty go to prison for a period 22 percent longer than similar defendants charged with the same crime.[b]
- For those defendants who are successful in raising the defense, only 1 percent are released after being found NGRI. Four percent are placed on conditional release, and 90 percent are hospitalized for a substantial period.[c]
- For defendants found NGRI in violent crimes other than murder, the period of confinement in a mental hospital or similar institution is twice as

long as the confinement of a defendant convicted of a similar crime. For nonviolent crimes, the confinement period is ten times the sentence given defendants convicted of similar crimes.[d]

These studies suggest that the defense of insanity is really the last resort for most defendants; even if the defense is successful, it does not often result in the release of the defendant. Nonetheless, dissatisfaction with the defense continues, and some states—including Idaho, Montana, and Utah—have abolished the defense.[e]

[a]Lisa A. Callahan et al., *The Volume and Characteristics of Insanity Defense: An Eight-State Study*, 19 Bull. Am. Acad. Psychiatry & L. 331 (1991).
[b]Joseph H. Rodriguez et al., *The Insanity Defense Under Siege: Legislative Assaults and Legal Rejoinders*, 14 Rutgers L. J. 397 (1983). The authors of this article suggest that the reason for longer sentences for the unsuccessful defendant asserting the insanity defense is the defense's obstacle to plea bargains.
[c]H. Steadman et al., *Before and After Hinckley: Evaluating Insanity Defense Reform* (Guilford Press, 1993), p. 58.
[d]*Id.*
[e]See T. Gardner and T. Anderson, *Criminal Law: Principles and Cases*, 10th ed. (Thomson Wadsworth, 2009), chap. 4, p. 90.

any assurance from a prosecutor concerning the penalty. Plea bargaining, or sentence bargaining, implies a situation in which a defendant receives (or is assured of) a consideration in return for a guilty plea. The following circumstances could cause a defendant to plead guilty:

- The defendant receives an agreed-upon sentence or penalty instead of running the risk of a more severe sentence.
- An agreement is reached in a case having multiple charges to drop one or more of the charges, which in most situations are then "read into the record" in court for sentencing consideration.[19]
- The defendant is permitted to plead guilty to a lesser charge.
- The court receives a recommendation that the defendant receive probation or a suspended sentence.
- The prosecutor agrees to drop charges against another person.

- Charges are reduced or dropped when the defendant agrees to testify as a state's witness (such as a burglar turning state's evidence against a "fence").
- The defendant receives reduced charges, probation, or a suspended sentence when he agrees to compensate the victim for damages or injuries that occurred.
- The defendant receives probation or a suspended sentence when she agrees to undergo psychiatric, drug, or alcohol treatment when the criminal conduct was caused by any of these conditions. (In some of these situations, the defendant agrees to commit herself to an institution for such treatment.)

Prosecutors list the following reasons why plea bargaining, negotiated pleas, and sentence pleading have become standard practice in most American communities:

- It clears the court calendar of that case with a rapid trial and punishment.
- Defendants participate and admit their guilt to the charges to which they plead guilty.
- The practice eliminates many appeals.
- It provides a certainty of adjudication.
- A guilty plea could be the first step toward genuine rehabilitation.

The President's Commission commented in the 1967 report entitled "The Challenge of Crime in a Free Society":

> Many overburdened courts have come to rely upon these informal procedures to deal with overpowering caseloads, and some cases that are dropped might have been prosecuted had sufficient resources been available. But it would be an oversimplification to tie the use of early disposition solely to the problem of volume, for some courts appear to be able to deal with their workloads without recourse to such procedures....

The main danger in the present system of nontrial dispositions is that it is so informal and invisible that it gives rise to fears that it does not operate fairly or that it does not accurately identify those who should be prosecuted and what disposition should be made in their cases. Often important decisions are made without adequate information, without sound policy guidance or rules, and without basic procedural protections for the defendant, such as counsel or judicial consideration of the issues. Because these dispositions are reached at an early stage, often little factual material is available about the offense, the offender, and the treatment alternatives.

No record reveals the participants, their positions, or the reason for or facts underlying the disposition. When the disposition involves the dismissal of filed charges or the entry of a guilty plea, the case is likely to reach court, but only the end product is visible and that view often is misleading. There are disturbing opportunities for coercion and overreaching, as well as for undue leniency. The informality and flexibility of the procedures are sources of both potential usefulness and abuse.

Debates about plea bargaining have been going on for years. The practice was denounced as early as 1875.[20] Over the years, plea negotiation has continued, however. Some states have enacted statutes regulating the practice.

FAST-TRACK TRIALS AND FAST-TRACK PLEA BARGAINS

For years, many states and the federal government have had policies of putting criminal trials that have high public concern on a "fast track." Defendants in these cases must then prepare for a speedy trial or have the choice of "fast-tracking" plea bargaining.

Conferences between defense lawyers and prosecutors are held to accelerate cases that can be settled through plea or sentence agreements. In such a conference, federal prosecutors in California included an additional requirement in a criminal proceeding against defendant Ruiz. Ruiz had to waive his right to receive impeachment information relating to any informant witness or other prosecution witnesses, and also possible evidence that could have helped Ruiz establish an affirmative defense. Prosecutors were obligated to provide Ruiz with any exculpatory evidence (tending to prove innocence) as required under the Brady rule.

Ruiz refused the fast-track plea agreement that was offered to him. The government then withdrew the offer and indicted Ruiz. Despite the absence of an agreement, Ruiz pleaded guilty and at the sentencing hearing asked for the reduced sentence offered in the plea agreement. The trial court refused and sentenced Ruiz to the maximum penalty permitted.

On appeal, the United States Court of Appeals held that the fast-track plea agreement was unconstitutional because it required the defendant to waive the right to receive impeachment and affirmative defense information. In the case of *United States v. Ruiz* [122 S.Ct. 2450 (2002)], the U.S. Supreme Court reversed and held that a guilty plea can be voluntary even if the defendant is not aware of all the information known to the prosecution. Exculpatory information must be disclosed under the *Brady* rule, but the prosecution need not disclose impeachment and affirmative defense information.

AN OFFER TO PLEAD GUILTY CANNOT BE USED AS EVIDENCE IF THE OFFER IS LATER WITHDRAWN

Both public policy and the judicial system encourage voluntary, intelligent guilty pleas. By admitting guilt in open court, the defendant acknowledges the wrongful conduct, which is the first step in rehabilitation. Guilty pleas also help to keep court calendars current.

To encourage guilty pleas, the federal government and many states have statutes such as Rule 410 of the Federal Rules of Evidence and Rule 11(6) of the Federal Rules of Criminal Procedure, which forbid the use of any of the following as evidence:

> evidence of a plea of guilty, later withdrawn, or a plea of nolo contendere, or of an offer to plead guilty or nolo contendere to the crime charged or any other crime, or of statements made in connection with any of the foregoing pleas or offers.

States with similar statutes also prohibit evidence of pleas offered in plea negotiations, including incriminating statements made in the offer, as the following cases illustrate:

- After a sex crime had occurred, Muniz (the defendant) offered to pay some of the victim's medical expenses. The State of California then charged Muniz with the sex crime. Because Muniz's statements were not part of an offer to plead guilty, his statements were held to be admissible as an admission against interest.[21]

USE OF EVIDENCE AT A BAIL HEARING

The purpose of bail is to assure the defendant's appearance at trial. Bail hearings can become hotly contested—angry confrontations with defense lawyers arguing that high bail punishes a defendant and that defendants can be punished only after trial and conviction.

Another argument of defense lawyers is that high bail can be used as preventive detention, to unlawfully detain a defendant based on only the possibility that the defendant may be a threat to others. In most states, preventive detention in this sense is not regarded as a legitimate basis for setting bail.

In asking for high bail, prosecutors generally stress the seriousness of the crime, the viciousness of the criminal act, and the strength of the evidence against the defendant. Because the likelihood of flight by a defendant goes up with the probability of a long prison term, very high bail is often set in murder and other violent crime cases.

Although the past criminal record of the defendant is not admissible evidence during a trial, it is admissible evidence during both bail hearings and sentencing hearings. The prosecution must provide defense lawyers with the defendant's known criminal record (or lack of criminal record) prior to the bail hearing.

In bail headings, both sides may present evidence of a defendant's roots in the community, such as whether the defendant has a family, close relatives, a good job, and a home, as well as his or her age and marital status.

The Eighth Amendment of the U.S. Constitution states that "Excessive bail shall not be required...." Therefore, either the defense or the prosecutor could immediately appeal a bail ruling by a lower court and present arguments to a higher court seeking a different bail ruling.

Historically, about 60 percent of persons charged with felony crimes are released on bail. Of those released, about half are released on signature bonds, frequently with the requirement that the person report to authorities on a daily or weekly basis. The other half are released on bail bonds, either bonds from commercial bail bondsmen or full cash or property bonds. Bench warrants end up being issued in about one-fourth of the cases of persons released on bail because of their failure to appear in court for their trials.

Source: Bureau of Justice Statistics Report NCJ 14994, November 2007.

- When a plea-bargain agreement was not carried out due to a failure on both sides, the state sought to use incriminating statements the defendant had made during the negotiations. The Supreme Court of Louisiana held that the statements could not be used as evidence against the defendant on the basis of "equitable immunity."[22]
- During the sentencing hearing where the state was seeking the death penalty, the state sought to use as evidence the fact that the defendant offered to plea bargain to avoid the death penalty. It was held that such evidence was inadmissible. (The defendant was nevertheless sentenced to death for murder and robbery by force.)[23]
- Before going to trial, a drug-trafficking defendant wrote a letter to the prosecutor offering to plead guilty in return for sentencing concessions. The letter was held to be inadmissible against the defendant at trial.[24]

THE TRIAL

The vast majority of criminal charges result in guilty pleas after plea bargaining. Only about 8 percent of criminal cases in the United States actually go to trial. Of those, about 20 percent are tried before a judge, and 80 percent are tried before a jury.

discovery
Formal procedures used by prosecution and defense attorneys to gather documents, witnesses, and other evidence.

Prior to the trial, the parties undertake **discovery**. In the discovery process in most states, both the prosecution and the defense gather evidence through formal questions put to the other side, depositions of witnesses, and examination of documents and records.

As a result of discovery, the parties can file various *motions*, such as to compel discovery, to dismiss for lack of jurisdiction or evidence, or to exclude evidence obtained in violation of a defendant's rights, such as violations of the defendant's Fourth Amendment rights. At this time or at any other time during the trial, the defendant may agree to enter a guilty plea ending the trial. The guilty plea may be based on a sentence or plea agreement, which would be subject to the approval of the trial judge.

If the trial goes forward, jurors are summoned and selected, and subpoenas are issued to compel witnesses to attend and testify at the trial. Jurors are selected from the community in which the court sits (the *venue*) from lists maintained by the court, such as registered voters. The jury may consist of six to twelve people, depending on the seriousness of the crime charged and state rules.[25]

prima facie case
A civil or criminal case that is so strong that the opponent must respond with rebutting evidence to avoid losing the case.

The prosecution presents evidence first and must establish a **prima facie case**; that is, the evidence must be sufficient to permit a reasonable jury to believe the defendant was guilty beyond a reasonable doubt. A defendant may move for a judgment of acquittal after the close of the prosecution's case. If the judge concludes that the evidence is insufficient to support a reasonable jury verdict of guilty beyond a reasonable doubt, the case will be dismissed without going to the jury.

affirmative defense A defense that admits the defendant committed the crime charged but asserts that the defendant should not be convicted.

If the case is not dismissed, the defendant may present evidence either to cast doubt on the prosecution's case or to prove an **affirmative defense**. Affirmative defenses include insanity, immunity, entrapment, and double jeopardy. The defendant carries the burden of proving any affirmative defense raised, and the prosecution may offer *rebuttal* evidence to such defense and other new matters brought out in the defendant's case.

After all evidence is in and both sides have delivered closing arguments to the jury, the trial judge issues *jury instructions*. These instructions are the judge's explanation of the relevant law that governs the case. Following the trial judge's instructions, the jury begins its deliberations. Jury members weigh the evidence presented to them during the trial and vote on the issue of guilt or innocence of the defendant.

judgment NOV
A posttrial judgment made by a judge changing or reversing the jury decision; literally, *non obstante veredicto* ("notwithstanding the verdict").

If the jury reaches a verdict of not guilty, the case is over and the defendant is discharged from custody. If the verdict is guilty, the defendant may file posttrial motions in the trial court. These motions include motions for *judgment notwithstanding the verdict* (sometimes called **judgment NOV**) and motions for a new trial. Motions for judgment NOV are rarely granted because the trial judge has usually already heard motions for a *directed verdict* after the close of the prosecution and

USE OF EVIDENCE IN THE STAGES OF THE CRIMINAL PROCESS

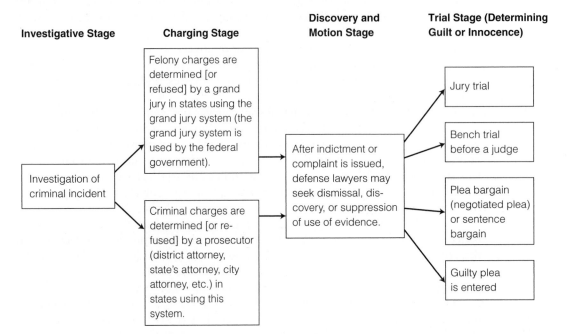

| Investigative Stage | Charging Stage | Discovery and Motion Stage | Trial Stage (Determining Guilt or Innocence) |

Investigation of criminal incident

Felony charges are determined [or refused] by a grand jury in states using the grand jury system (the grand jury system is used by the federal government).

Criminal charges are determined [or refused] by a prosecutor (district attorney, state's attorney, city attorney, etc.) in states using this system.

After indictment or complaint is issued, defense lawyers may seek dismissal, discovery, or suppression of use of evidence.

Jury trial

Bench trial before a judge

Plea bargain (negotiated plea) or sentence bargain

Guilty plea is entered

If it is known (or suspected) that a crime or offense has been committed, law enforcement officers or private persons and investigators seek evidence of the offense. If competent evidence exists amounting to probable cause to believe that

- a crime (or offense) has been committed, and
- a specific person (persons) committed the offense

then the matter can be taken to a prosecutor.

If it is determined that probable cause exists to prove

- corpus delicti (a crime has been committed), and
- the suspect was a party to the crime[a]

then a criminal charge or indictment can be issued.

The defense lawyer seeks to discover and obtain evidence helpful to his client. He may also make some or all of the following motions[b] before the court:

- Motion to dismiss because of insufficient evidence, etc.
- Motion to dismiss because of improper procedure, constitutionality of statute, etc.
- Motion to suppress evidence (statements, physical evidence, identification evidence, or procedure, etc.)
- Motion for discovery of evidence

The defense's decision on whether to try the case before a jury or a judge is generally based on the evaluation of the case and the evidence. Because weaker cases are filtered out of the system or charged as lesser offenses, most cases that reach the trial stage are strong governmental cases. In these cases, the defense may attempt to plea bargain or may enter a guilty plea. If the state has a weakness in its case at this stage, the state may attempt to plea bargain.

---

[a]A party to a crime may be (1) the person (or persons) who actually committed the crime; (2) a conspirator who hired, procured, planned, or counseled the crime; or (3) a person (or persons) who aided and abetted in the commission of the crime. Different evidence is required to carry the burden of proving each of the different categories of parties to a crime.

[b]A *motion* means an application for an order from that judge or other court.

Following deliberations, the jury members vote on the guilt or innocence of the defendant. A head or presiding juror, sometimes called the foreman, then presents the verdict to the court.

© Bill Fritsch/Brand X/Corbis

defense cases. Motions for a new trial meet with better success because the trial judge may have a better opportunity following the trial to consider errors that occurred during the trial.

If the defendant's motions are overruled, the defendant may appeal the criminal conviction and/or the sentence imposed upon the defendant. In state cases, the defendant's initial appeals go through the state appellate process, which frequently includes an intermediate court called a *court of appeals* and a final court called a *state supreme court.*

reversible errors
Errors that occur in a trial court that might have a bearing on the outcome of the trial; an error is not sufficient for reversal if the outcome would have been the same without the error.

The state appellate court does not conduct a new trial. Rather, it looks at the evidence to see whether it supports the conviction and determines whether the judge made any **reversible errors**—such as permitting the use of damaging, inadmissible evidence. The state appellate court also rules on other claims the defendant may make, such as a constitutional violation.

After the defendant has exhausted his or her state court appeals, the defendant may seek review in the federal courts but only for violation of federal constitutional rights. The defendant may file for a writ of certiorari in the U.S. Supreme Court or a writ of habeas corpus in U.S. district courts.

REVIEW OF SENTENCING

Sentencing authority is granted to the trial judge (or jury) by the law defining the crime and by other statutes in the state or federal criminal code. The sentencing judge may be further guided by sentencing guidelines enacted by that state's legislature. Imposed sentences may be reviewed by the following authorities:

- *Trial judge:* On a motion by the defense attorney, the trial judge reviews his or her sentence of a particular defendant and may modify the sentence after hearing arguments presented by both the defense lawyer and the prosecutor.
- *Appellate courts (including the U.S. Supreme Court and state supreme courts):* On appeal, an appellate court may find that a particular sentence was not within the statutory authority of the trial judge to impose, or that the sentence violated the Eighth Amendment's Cruel and Unusual Punishment Clause.
- *Federal courts:* A state prisoner ordinarily uses a writ of habeas corpus in attempting to get his or her case into the federal courts. To do this, a violation of a right under the U.S. Constitution must be shown. Because there are very few

violations (or errors) of this type, few habeas corpus hearings are granted.

- *State parole board or parole authorities:* Parole authority is granted by a statute of that state. State statutes might provide that parole eligibility for murder does not commence until after sixteen years—or after twenty or twenty-five years. Whether the convicted person is released on parole (and the conditions of parole) is then determined by the parole board.
- *The president of the United States and state governors:* The president and state governors have broad power to pardon, grant amnesty, or commute a sentence. Such authority is constitutional, with additional statutory power often provided. ARTICLE II of the U.S. Constitution provides that the president "shall have Power to grant Reprieves and Pardons for Offenses against the United States, except in Cases of Impeachment."[a]

---

[a]See the case of *Murphy v. Ford* [390 F.Supp. 1372 (W.D. Mich. 1975)], in which a federal district court found that President Gerald R. Ford had the constitutional authority to grant a pardon to former President Richard M. Nixon before Nixon was charged with a crime.

---

writs of certiorari Formal notice by the U.S. Supreme Court to a lower federal or state court that a case will be reviewed by the Supreme Court.

Writs of certiorari are limited to a review of state court rulings that violate the defendant's rights under the Constitution, such as the right to counsel, fair trial, confrontation of witnesses, and so on. Writs of certiorari are very rarely granted.

Habeas corpus writs, filed with a federal district court, ask that court to determine whether the defendant is being held in violation of his constitutional rights. Frequently, constitutional issues not reviewed by the Supreme Court under the certiorari power are raised in habeas corpus writs. The denial of a writ is itself appealable by the defendant through the federal appellate system.

In theory, the habeas corpus writ is the final stop in the criminal process. Filing successive habeas corpus writs is possible, however, so it is not accurate to say the process is ever truly complete.

NOTABLE CASES WHERE INSUFFICIENT EVIDENCE HAS RESULTED IN UNCLEARED CRIMES

Criminal Incident	Disposition
Deadly anthrax spores sent through the mails in 2001 killed five people and injured seventeen others.	Early suspicion directed at a research scientist failed to produce incriminating evidence, and a subsequent civil suit brought by the scientist against federal agencies was settled in 2008 by a payment to the scientist of $4.6 million. The FBI investigation subsequently focused on another scientist, Bruce Ivins, but Ivins commited suicide in 2008 before he could be charged with the crime. No other suspects have been identified by the FBI. It has been reported that some members of Congress are not convinced Ivins acted alone. See the September 18, 2008, *New York Times* article, "Senator, Target of Anthrax Letter, Challenges F.B.I. Finding."
The most followed murder trial of the 1990s was the charge against O. J. Simpson of murdering his wife and Ron Goldman.	Simpson was acquitted despite DNA evidence showing his blood was found at the crime scene. The Goldman family brought a civil lawsuit against Simpson, and the same evidence was used to acquire a judgment of $34 million; little of that judgment has been paid. The police have not identified any other person as a suspect in the murders.
The 1996 murder of 6-year-old JonBenet Ramsey in Boulder, Colorado, remains a mystery, reminding us that 40% of murder cases go unsolved.	In July 2008 DNA evidence was found to exclude JonBenet's parents as suspects. Despite extensive efforts by law enforcement agencies, no charges or indictments have been made.
No eyewitnesses to the 1963 assassination of President John F. Kennedy have ever been identified, and for some time after the incident there was confusion about where the gunfire originated. Strong circumstantial evidence established that Lee Harvey Oswald was the lone shooter; he was subsequently shot and killed in the basement of the Dallas Police Department.	No criminal trial was ever held; however, a fact-finding commission headed by then U.S. Supreme Court Chief Justice Earl Warren reviewed all the evidence available and concluded Oswald was the sole assassin. The conclusion remains controversial, however, and a book written by former prosecutor Vincent Bugliosi in 2007 will be made into a 10-hour HBO miniseries starring Tom Hanks in 2009.

SUMMARY

Many people evaluate and review evidence in suspected or known criminal incidents, and for that reason, they all should have a working knowledge of the law of criminal evidence.

Public prosecutors review evidence in cases presented to them and decide based on the evidence whether to seek or to issue criminal charges. Defense lawyers review the evidence to determine what possible defenses are available.

The plea that a defendant or a defense lawyer enters in court is based on the evidence that exists. Pleas that may be entered are: not guilty, guilty, Alford, no contest (with the permission of the court), conditionally guilty, and insanity.

If the government has a strong case, defense lawyers often attempt to plea bargain. When the evidence against a defendant is weak, prosecutors are likely to charge a lesser crime or offer a negotiated plea.

Studies show that the majority of criminal cases in the United States result in either a guilty plea without plea bargaining or a guilty plea based on a plea agreement. The trial judge can reject a prior plea agreement and set a date for the case to go to trial.

Only about 8 percent of criminal cases in the United States go to trial. Twenty percent of these are tried before a judge, and 80 percent are tried before a jury. For example, thousands of drunk-driving cases come before judges every month in the United States. Because the evidence against the average defendant in these cases is so strong, most defendants enter guilty pleas.

PROBLEMS

Finish each sentence using one of the available answers provided.

Available Answers

a. Not guilty plea
b. Guilty plea
c. Alford plea
d. Insanity plea
e. Only a and d

1. Most felony cases in the United States are concluded when the defendant enters a
2. When a defendant refuses to enter a plea or stands mute, the court enters a
3. A defendant who has evidence supporting a strong defense is likely to enter a
4. In most states defendants have the burden of producing evidence to prove a
5. The plea that is a not guilty plea is a
6. A defendant who acknowledges that sufficient evidence exists to convict but denies guilt might seek to enter a
7. All but three states are reported to have statutorized a
8. In drunk-driving cases, there is a very high percentage of
9. The defense is likely to seek an expert witness to support a
10. Defendants entering a ___ have the right to a jury trial in most states.

CASE ANALYSIS

Read Appendix B, Finding and Analyzing Cases (p. 427). With these guidelines in mind, please continue with the Case Analysis selections for Chapter 3.

1. When a plea agreement is made, the defendant commonly makes statements about the crime that might otherwise not be made voluntarily. What effect, if any, does the rescission of the plea by the prosecution have on the admissibility of these statements? Should it make a difference if the plea agreement was rescinded because the defendant did not keep his part of the bargain? That was the case in *Pitt v. State*

[832 A.2d 267 (Md. App. 2003)] [Case No. 199/01]. What did the Maryland Court of Appeals conclude should happen?

2. Can a guilty plea be withdrawn? If so, must the defendant have some good reason for requesting a withdrawal? Why did the Seventh Circuit Court of Appeals decide that the defendant in *United States v. Gomez-Orozoco* [188 F.3d 422 (1999)] [Docket No. 98–4274] should have been permitted to withdraw his guilty plea? What rule did the court apply? Why didn't the Second Circuit Court of Appeals in *United States v. Gregory* [245 F.3d 160 (2001)] let the defendant withdraw his guilty plea?

3. The prosecution may not use evidence of an offer to plead guilty against the defendant in a criminal trial. May the defendant introduce such evidence at either the guilt or penalty phase of a trial? What about evidence that defendants in other cases received lighter sentences when they pleaded guilty? Read the opinion in *State v. Dixon* [805 N.E.2d 1042 (Ohio 2004), *cert. denied*, 543 U.S. 1060 (2005)], and consider the court's reasoning.

4. How is evidence used in a bail hearing? What are the burdens of proof on the prosecution? See *Simpson v. Owens* [85 P.3d 478 (Ariz. App. 2004)].

Notes

1. 59 Md. App., 28, 474 A.2d 537, 35 CrL 2147 (1984).

2. The states that use the verdict of guilty but mentally ill are Michigan, Indiana, Illinois, Georgia, Kentucky, New Mexico, Delaware, and Alaska.

3. Cities studied by the Department of Justice in 1988 that have a high ratio of guilty pleas to felony charges are Bakersfield (93%), Brooklyn (80%), Dallas (80%), Los Angeles (84%), Manhattan (81%), Miami (82%), Queens (82%), Riverside (90%), St. Louis (83%), and San Diego (92%) (February 1992, NCJ 130914).

4. U.S. 238, 242, 89 S.Ct. 1709, 1711–12 (1969).

5. For many years, courts have encouraged guilty pleas by rewarding a guilty plea with a shorter sentence. Court time is saved, court calendars are not so overloaded, witnesses are not required to come to court more than once, and the interests of justice are served.

   In the 1992 case of *United States v. Jones* [973 F.2d 928 (D.C. Cir.)], the defendant received an additional six-month sentence when he took his case to trial instead of entering a guilty plea. The Federal Court of Appeals held that the procedure did not unconstitutionally burden the defendant's right to stand trial. The present federal sentencing guidelines (U.S.S.G. sec. 3 E 1.1) provide that a sentence may be reduced by two levels "if the defendant clearly demonstrates a recognition and affirmative acceptance of personal responsibility for his criminal conduct."

Guilty pleas are particularly common in misdemeanor offenses such as drunk driving. The evidence in most drunk-driving cases is strong, and conviction rates in these cases are high. Many drunk drivers feel genuine remorse for what they have done and admit their guilt to get the matter settled quickly. Some drunk-driving defendants have said, "Why waste money on a lawyer? I'll save money by going into court and pleading guilty."

Many prosecutors have established standard pleading and sentencing practices, which are explained to people charged with misdemeanor or ordinance violations. For example, people charged for the first time with shoplifting or soliciting for prostitution might be told that it is standard office procedure to permit first-time offenders to plead to a lesser charge, such as disorderly conduct, if they enter a guilty plea. Those who wish to go to trial are charged with the more serious offense.

People charged with ordinance or misdemeanor offenses are also told the standard sentences if they enter a guilty plea. Another standard procedure is the practice of issuing multiple charges to an offense such as drunk driving. In return for pleading guilty to the drunk-driving charge and receiving the standard court sentence, the additional charge or charges are dropped.

6. Federal Rule 11c (3) of the Federal Rules of Criminal Procedure requires the judge accepting a guilty plea to inform the defendant of her

constitutional rights at the time such plea is taken. Most states have a similar rule. In *United States v. Vonn* [535 U.S. 55 (2002)], the Supreme Court held that failure to give a defendant such advice permits withdrawal of a guilty plea only if the record as a whole shows the defendant was not informed of those rights. Thus, even though such advice was not given at the plea proceeding, the fact that the defendant was informed of her rights at the first arraignment showed that the defendant was aware of her rights when she entered her plea.

The rule that guilty pleas be voluntary does not require the trial judge to inform the defendant of all the consequences of the plea. For example, in *Irala v. Connecticut* [792 A.2d 109 (Conn. App. Ct. 2002)], a defendant entered a nolo contendere plea to a charge that, under federal law, would result in deportation upon conviction. The trial judge informed the defendant only that conviction of the state crime might have deportation consequences. The defendant subsequently sought to withdraw the plea, but her request was denied. On appeal, the court held that the "voluntary" requirement does not require a judge to inform the defendant of all the "collateral" consequences of a plea.

7. 125 S.Ct. 2398.
8. *Irala v. Connecticut, supra.*
9. *United States v. Jackson,* 390 U.S. 570, 584, 88 S.Ct. 1209, 1217 (1968); *North Carolina v. Alford,* 400 U.S. 25, 38 n.11, 91 S.Ct. 160, 168 n.11 (1970).
10. 395 U.S. 238, 89 S.Ct. 1709 (1969).
11. 400 U.S. 25, 37, 91 S.Ct. 160, 167 (1970).
12. *Ward v. State,* 575 A.2d 771 (Md. App. 1990).
13. 815 P.2d 484 (Idaho App. 1991).
14. Fed. R. Crim. P 11(b), Advisory Committee's Note to 1974 Amendment.
15. 812 P.2d 470 (Utah App. 1991).
16. *North Carolina v. Alford,* 400 U.S. 25, 38 n.11, 91 S.Ct. 160, 168, n.11 (1970).
17. *Tollett v. Henderson,* 411 U.S. 258, 93 S.Ct. 1602 (1973).
18. "Task Force Report: The Courts," p. 4, President's Commission on Law Enforcement and Administration of Justice (Government Printing Office, 1967).
19. *Read-in* plea bargains are used most often in property offenses such as burglary and forgery when there is repetitious conduct on the part of the defendant. An example of a read-in plea bargain occurred in Milwaukee. A woman was charged with forging ten checks. She pleaded guilty to two of the charges. The other eight charges were dismissed, and information that she had forged 628 checks was read into the record. The judge sentenced her to the maximum twenty years. Because the woman had young children, she stayed in prison long enough to cause the parole board to believe that she would not go back to forging checks again before they placed her on parole with the warning that any further violation would send her back to prison.
20. *Golden v. State,* 49 Ind. 424, 427 (1875), in which the Supreme Court of Indiana labeled a plea arrangement a "corrupt agreement" and compared the procedure to "corrupt purchasing of an indulgence."
21. *People v. Muniz,* 262 Cal. Rptr. 473 (Calif. App. 1989).
22. *State v. Lewis,* 539 So.2d 1199 (La. 1989).
23. *Thomas v. State,* 811 P.2d 1337 (Okla. Crim. App. 1991).
24. *Russell v. State,* 614 So.2d 605 (Fla. App. 1993).
25. Either the defense attorney or the prosecutor may challenge a member of the jury panel for cause and disqualify the person. Challenge for cause could be because the panel member is a friend or relative of one of the attorneys or because an answer to a question in voir dire disclosed prejudice in favor of or against a party. The parties are also allowed a limited number of *peremptory challenges,* in which a prospective juror is excused without cause. In *Batson v. Kentucky* [476 U.S. 79 (1986)], the Supreme Court held that the prosecution could not use these peremptory challenges in a discriminatory manner. An example of a prima facie case showing such discrimination is *Roe v. Fernandez* [286 F.3d 1190 (2001)], where the prosecution used most of its peremptory challenges to strike Hispanic and African American members of the jury.

Direct and Circumstantial Evidence and the Use of Inferences

CHAPTER 4

LEARNING OBJECTIVES

In this chapter we discuss the framework in which evidence, both direct and circumstantial, is used in criminal prosecutions. The learning objectives for this chapter are:

- Distinguish between the burden of production and the burden of persuasion.
- Give a constitutionally acceptable definition of *reasonable doubt.*
- Distinguish between direct evidence and circumstantial evidence.
- List some examples of inferences that may be drawn from facts proved.
- List some inferences that may not be drawn.
- Define *presumption*, and state how a presumption may be used in a criminal prosecution.

EVIDENCE AND PROOF

WHAT IS EVIDENCE?

evidence The means of establishing the truth or untruth of any fact that is alleged.

Evidence is ordinarily defined as the means of establishing and proving the truth or untruth of any fact that is alleged. Evidence can be the testimony of witnesses, physical objects, documents, records, fingerprints, photographs, and so on. The famous English lawyer and writer Sir William Blackstone defined evidence in the 1760s as "that which demonstrates, makes clear or ascertains the truth of the very fact or point in issue, either on the one side or other." When the quality and quantity of the evidence presented are so convincing and are sufficient to prove the existence of the fact sought to be proved or disproved, the result is *proof* of the fact.

proof The result of evidence; evidence is the means of attaining proof.

Proof is therefore the result of evidence, and evidence is the means of attaining proof. Whether a fact has been proved is determined by the trier of the facts (jury or judge).

In trials, the parties introduce evidence to satisfy the *burdens of proof* assigned to them. The burden-of-proof requirement is actually two burdens: the burden of production and the burden of persuasion. The **burden of production** requires the party with the burden on a factual issue to introduce sufficient relevant evidence to prove the fact at issue. Failure to do so means the fact has not been proved, which usually means the person with the burden loses. The **burden of persuasion** requires the party with the burden to produce sufficient evidence to persuade the fact finder that a fact exists.

burden of production That part of the burden of proof that requires a party to produce sufficient evidence to establish the fact at issue.

In criminal trials, both the burden of production and the burden of persuasion rest on the prosecution:

burden of persuasion That part of the burden of proof that requires a party to persuade the jury that a fact exists.

> The Due Process Clause protects the accused against conviction except upon proof beyond a reasonable doubt of every fact necessary to constitute the crime with which he is charged.[1]

Thus, for every element of an offense, the prosecution must produce evidence sufficient to establish the element and also to persuade the jury that no reasonable doubt exists about the fact's existence, based on the evidence produced. In most states, the defendant bears the burden of proof for an affirmative defense.

THE REASONABLE DOUBT STANDARD

reasonable doubt standard The standard for evidence that fact finders (juries or judges) must use in criminal cases to find a defendant guilty of the crime charged.

Every essential element of the crime charged must be proved by the government beyond **reasonable doubt** in order to convict and punish a defendant for the crime charged. The requirement of "proof beyond a reasonable doubt" is one of the most familiar legal standards in our society. However, courts and legal scholars have not reached a consensus on the exact definition of that important term. As a result, the instructions trial judges give juries on the standard of proof they must apply to the evidence in order to convict a defendant in a criminal case varies from state to state, and even from court to court within a state. These differences in instructions have caused the U.S. Supreme Court in several cases to consider whether the Due Process Clause has been satisfied by a "reasonable doubt" instruction. Those cases, and the history of the reasonable doubt standard, help to explain the standard's meaning today.

As far back as the seventeenth century, English courts recognized that, in many cases, a criminal defendant's guilt could never be known with absolute certainty. That is, a jury could not be sure of a defendant's guilt beyond any doubt because a chance always existed, no matter how unlikely, that the defendant was innocent. English courts thus instructed juries to find guilt if they were morally certain of that guilt.

In the United States, influenced by decisions like Chief Justice Shaw's of the Supreme Judicial Court of Massachusetts in 1850, judges began instructing juries to find guilt by use of a reasonable doubt standard. Shaw said the following about what constitutes reasonable doubt:

> What is reasonable doubt? ... It is not mere possible doubt; because everything relating to human affairs, and depending on moral evidence, is open to some possible or imaginary doubt.[2]

In 1970, the U.S. Supreme Court held in *In re Winship*[3] that the Due Process Clause requires that the prosecution prove each element of a crime beyond a reasonable doubt. However, the Court did not in *Winship* mandate any particular jury instruction on the exact meaning of *reasonable doubt*. In the 1994 case of *Victor v. Nebraska*,[4] the Supreme Court held that while jury instructions may attempt to define reasonable doubt, they need not do so; all the Constitution requires is that "taken as a whole, the instructions properly convey the concept of reasonable doubt."

The jury must be instructed to judge the guilt of the defendant according to a high degree of certainty. The Supreme Court has identified certain language in jury instructions that does not properly convey the concept of reasonable doubt. In *Cage v. Louisiana*,[5] the trial court instructed the jury that reasonable doubt meant "such doubt as would give rise to a grave uncertainty" and "an actual substantial doubt." The Supreme Court held that the instruction suggested to the jury that it must find a greater degree of doubt than the reasonable doubt standard requires.

The U.S. Supreme Court has also upheld definitions of reasonable doubt that spoke to the degree of doubt. In *Sandoval v. California*,[6] the Court upheld a jury instruction that defined reasonable doubt as "not a mere possible doubt." Thus, from these cases it can be said that reasonable doubt is less than "actual substantial doubt" but more than "a mere possible doubt." Jurors should not find a defendant guilty because they did not have "substantial doubt" about the defendant's guilt. However, they should not refuse to find that same defendant guilty simply because a "mere possible doubt" exists about the defendant's guilt.

The reasonable doubt jury instruction proposed by the Federal Judicial Center, and that Justice Ginsburg cited with approval in *Victor v. Nebraska*,[7] has been praised by several commentators.[8] That instruction has the advantage of clearly identifying the quantity of doubt the jury must possess, as well as informing the jury that the standard of reasonable doubt is stricter than the standard of proof used in civil cases. That instruction reads:

> The government has the burden of proving the defendant guilty beyond a reasonable doubt. Some of you may have served as jurors in civil cases, where you were told that it is only necessary to prove that a fact is more likely than not true. In criminal cases,

the government's proof must be more powerful than that. It must be beyond a reasonable doubt.

Proof beyond a reasonable doubt is proof that leaves you firmly convinced of the defendant's guilt. There are very few things in this world that we know with absolute certainty, and in criminal cases the law does not require proof that overcomes every possible doubt. If, based on your consideration of the evidence, you are firmly convinced that the defendant is guilty of the crime charged, you must find him guilty. If on the other hand, you think there is a real possibility that he is not guilty, you must give him the benefit of the doubt and find him not guilty.[9]

DIRECT EVIDENCE AND CIRCUMSTANTIAL EVIDENCE

direct evidence
Evidence that proves or disproves a fact in question with no need for inferences.

The U.S. Constitution requires that in all criminal cases the state or the federal government prove each and every essential element of a crime beyond reasonable doubt. This can be done by the use of either **direct evidence** or **circumstantial** (indirect) **evidence** or, as occurs in most criminal cases, by a combination of both direct and circumstantial evidence.

Example of Direct Evidence

A witness testifies that he or she saw the defendant commit the crime. Further questioning shows that the witness has good eyesight, the witness was close enough to observe the incident, the lighting was good, and the witness accurately described the defendant to the police and in the courtroom identified the defendant without any doubt. This is an example of strong direct credible evidence that would be sufficient to convict unless the defense can produce evidence sufficient to impeach the credibility of the witness.

circumstantial evidence
Evidence from which proof of the fact in question may be inferred.

Circumstantial evidence is evidence that indirectly proves a fact in issue. Testimony that the defendant was at the scene of the crime and ran from the scene with a pistol in his or her hand is circumstantial, or indirect evidence. Inferences have to be drawn for indirect evidence. If it were shown that no one other than the defendant had an opportunity to commit the crime and that the defendant and the victim were heard arguing angrily, the circumstantial evidence against the defendant would be stronger.

While direct evidence can be used to directly prove facts, circumstantial evidence requires the fact finder to draw inferences. An inference is a conclusion that can be drawn from a fact.

Direct and circumstantial evidence are used not only to prove criminal conduct but also to prove mental elements that are required essential factors in many crimes.[10] Mental elements that must be proved in many crimes of violence include intent, recklessness, and criminal negligence.

In the case of *Commonwealth v. Lee*,[11] the defendant testified that he did not intend to take the victim's life when he pointed a gun directly at the victim and pulled the trigger. In affirming the defendant's conviction, the Pennsylvania Superior Court held:

[I]t is well settled that the intentional use of a deadly weapon on a vital part of the body raises a permissible inference of malice....

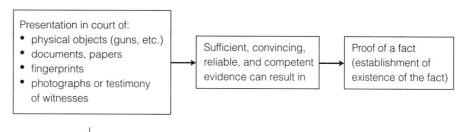

FIGURE 4.1 | USE OF EVIDENCE TO PROVE A FACT

The finder of fact is not required to ignore this inference merely because the defendant testifies that he did not intend to take a person's life....

...The law infers ... from the use of a deadly weapon, in the absence of circumstances of explanation or mitigation, the existence of the mental element—intent, malice, design, premeditation, or whatever term may be used to express it—which is essential as culpable homicide. [See generally 40 Am. Jur. 2d *Homicide* § 265 (1968).]

THE INFERENCE THAT PEOPLE INTEND THE NATURAL AND PROBABLE CONSEQUENCES OF THEIR DELIBERATE ACTS

In the proof of intent, recklessness, malice, or negligence, the law infers that people intend the reasonable, foreseeable consequences of their intentional and deliberate acts.[12] Such inferences must flow rationally from the evidence presented in court. The United States Court of Appeals, in the 1992 case of *United States v. Ortiz*,[13] pointed out that "jurors are neither required to divorce themselves from their common sense nor to abandon the dictate of mature experience.... [A] criminal jury [does not have] to ignore that which is perfectly obvious."

Attempted murder and assault with intent to cause serious bodily harm or death are examples of crimes that require proof of the defendant's intent. This intent can be inferred from the defendant's conduct and from the "deadly weapon" doctrine if the defendant uses an object likely to cause death or great bodily harm. A fist could be a deadly weapon if it is used in a way that could cause death or great bodily harm to the victim.

What are the natural and probable consequences of the conduct in the following examples? What commonsense conclusions could a fact finder draw about intent or malice?

- A man drops a 20-pound cement block from a highway overpass, hitting the windshield of a car traveling 60 miles per hour.
- An angry 70-year-old woman hits a 200-pound man with a folded newspaper.
- A strong young man in a rage hits a baby hard in the face with his fist.
- Two men of about equal strength are involved in a fistfight. One of the men hits the other as hard as he can in the face.

DIRECT AND CIRCUMSTANTIAL EVIDENCE

Direct evidence is that evidence that proves or disproves a fact in issue without the fact finder having to draw upon any reasoning or inferences. *Circumstantial evidence* is that evidence that indirectly proves or disproves a fact in issue. The fact finder must reason or draw an inference from circumstantial evidence.

Types of Evidence	Direct Evidence	Circumstantial Evidence
Statements by a suspect or defendant	A full or partial confession by a suspect	A statement that the suspect was with the victim a short time before the murder (an incriminating statement, but neither a full nor a partial confession)
Testimony of witnesses or the victim	Identification of the suspect as the person who committed the crime	Evidence that links the suspect to the crime or that shows motive, means, or opportunity for the suspect to commit the crime (e.g., suspect seen fleeing from the crime scene)
Physical evidence	Contraband (drugs, stolen property, concealed weapons, etc.) when a suspect is charged with possession	Other physical evidence (fingerprints, blood stains, weapons used to commit the crime, bite marks, etc.)
Evidence obtained as a result of wiretapping or electronic surveillance	Statements directly showing who committed the crime	Statements that incriminate but do not directly show who committed the crime

Scientific evidence such as DNA and fingerprints are generally circumstantial evidence (see Chapter 18).

WHEN CIRCUMSTANTIAL EVIDENCE ALONE IS USED TO OBTAIN A CRIMINAL CONVICTION

In many criminal investigations, direct evidence is unavailable. One common reason for that unavailability is that the suspect controls the direct evidence. This has long been a problem for prosecutions for income tax evasion because often only the defendant has access to records that show total income. As a result, prosecutors use circumstantial evidence called the "net worth method." In that method, a defendant's net worth is calculated at some beginning point, and then for each succeeding year under investigation the defendant's net worth is recalculated to determine whether it increased in an amount greater than declared income. The increase in net worth is then used by the prosecution to prove the income tax evaded.

In 1954 the U.S. Supreme Court decided the case of *Holland v. United States*.[14] In that case, the federal government prosecuted a taxpayer for tax evasion and used the net worth method of proof as evidence of tax evasion. The defendant contended that evidence introduced to show growth of his net worth was inadmissible because other sources of funds besides income could explain the increase. The defendant argued that the prosecution was required to introduce evidence negating all the other possible ways the defendant could have increased his net worth.

The Supreme Court disagreed and affirmed the defendant's conviction under the net worth method, stating:

> Circumstantial evidence in this respect is intrinsically no different from testimonial evidence. Admittedly, circumstantial evidence may in some cases point to a wholly incorrect result. Yet this is equally true of testimonial evidence. In both instances, a jury is asked to weigh the chances that the evidence correctly points to guilt against the possibility of inaccuracy or ambiguous inference. In both, the jury must use its experience with people and events in weighing the probabilities. If the jury is convinced beyond a reasonable doubt, we can require no more.

In most criminal cases, the government uses a combination of direct evidence and circumstantial evidence to obtain convictions. However, in some cases, circumstantial evidence alone is used. When only circumstantial evidence is used, many states do not follow the federal rule stated in the *Holland* decision and add requirements like those in the following jury instruction used in California:

> However, a finding of guilt as to any crime may not be based on circumstantial evidence unless the proved circumstances are not only (1) consistent with the theory that the defendant is guilty of the crime, but (2) cannot be reconciled with any other rational conclusion....
>
> Also, if the circumstantial evidence [as to any particular count] is susceptible of two reasonable interpretations, one of which points to the defendant's guilt and the other to [his] [her] innocence, you must adopt that interpretation which points to the defendant's innocence, and reject that interpretation which points to [his] [her] guilt.
>
> If, on the other hand, one interpretation of such evidence appears to you to be reasonable and the other interpretation to be unreasonable, you must accept the reasonable interpretation and reject the unreasonable. [1 *California Jury Instructions: Criminal* (5 Ed. 1988) 23, section 2.01]

In a few crimes, prosecutors are limited to direct evidence in proving the offenses. For example, ARTICLE III, SECTION 3, CLAUSE 1 of the U.S. Constitution states that "No person shall be convicted of Treason unless on the Testimony of Two Witnesses to the same overt Act, or on Confession in open Court."

MEANS—OPPORTUNITY—MOTIVE AS CIRCUMSTANTIAL EVIDENCE

When eyewitness evidence is not available, it has often been stated that investigators and officers should ask, as guidelines in investigating crimes, these questions:

- Who had the *means* of committing the crime?
- Who had the *opportunity* to commit the crime?
- Who had the *motive* to commit the crime?

Evidence that a person satisfied one or all of these circumstances could make that person a suspect, justifying further investigation. For example, when President John F. Kennedy was killed in Dallas in 1963, strong circumstantial evidence pointed to Lee Harvey Oswald as the assassin. The facts that Oswald fled and then later killed a Dallas police officer were strong circumstantial evidence that Oswald killed Kennedy. There was no direct evidence linking Oswald to the Kennedy killing.

CONDUCT THAT HAS BEEN USED AS CIRCUMSTANTIAL EVIDENCE TO PROVE A DEFENDANT'S CONSCIOUSNESS OF GUILT

General Conduct	Specific Conduct and Cases
Flight and furtive action	The U.S. Supreme Court held in 1968 that "deliberate furtive actions and flight at the approach of strangers or law officers are strong indicia of mens rea (guilty mind)" [*Peters v. New York,* 392 U.S. 40, 88 S.Ct. 1889].
Threats directed at a witness in an attempt to discourage cooperation with the police	The Supreme Court of Wisconsin held that "the [defendant's] threat is circumstantial evidence of consciousness of guilt and, hence, of guilt itself" [*Price v. State,* 154 N.W.2d 222 (1967), *review denied,* 391 U.S. 908, 88 S.Ct. 1662 (1968); see also *State v. Canaday,* 392 S.E.2d 457 (N.C. App. 1990)].
Interference with police investigation	Examples are refusal to take a blood test or other test when arrested for drunk driving [*South Dakota v. Neville,* 459 U.S. 553, 103 S.Ct. 916 (1983)]; refusal of fingerprinting [*Myers v. State,* 427 A.2d 1061 (Md. App. 1981)]; eating and destroying evidence [*Sewell v. State,* 368 A.2d 1111 (Md. App. 1977)]; refusal to provide voice or handwriting sample as ordered by the court (*United States v. Franks,* 511 F.2d 25 (6th Cir. 1975)]; rape suspect in jail shaved pubic hair to prevent sample being taken [*Marshall v. State,* 583 A.2d 1109 (Md. App. 1991)]; refusal to take test to determine firing of a gun [*Commonwealth v. Monaba,* 44 CrL 1031 (Pa. Super. 1988)]; false and evasive answers [*Player v. State,* 568 So.2d 370 (Ala. App. 1990)], *Commonwealth v. Lavalley,* 574 N.E. 1000 (Mass. 1991); use of aliases [*Cabrera v. State,* 576 So.2d 1358 (Fla. App. 1991)]; attempted suicide and flight [*State v. Mann,* 582 A.2d 1048 (N.J. Super. 1990)]; possession of gun and flight [*Hope v. Commonwealth,* 392 S.E.2d 830 (Va. App. 1990)]; and hiding to avoid arrest [*United States v. Pallais,* 921 F.2d 684 (7th Cir. 1990)].
Behavior after a crime is committed that is used as evidence to prove consciousness of guilt	Examples are spending spree and high living after a theft [*United States v. Ewings,* 936 F.2d 903 (7th Cir. 1991)]; "attempt to lick blood" off shirt in murder case [*State v. Arlt,* 833 P.2d 902 (Haw. App. 1992)]; and failure to appear for trial [*Langborne v. Commonwealth,* 409 S.E.2d 476 (Va. App. 1991)].

Other cases include the 1896 Supreme Court case of *Allen v. United States* [164 U.S. 492, 17 S.Ct. 154] (flight and concealment); *Hickory v. United States* [160 U.S. 408, 16 S.Ct. 327 (1896)] (destruction of evidence); *Wright v. State* [541 A.2d 988 (Md. 1988)] (concealment of identity); and *Hunt v. State* [540 A.2d 1125 (Md. 1988)] (escape or attempt to escape).

Motive evidence is generally not required to be introduced by the prosecution. Motive is seldom an element of a crime, and courts usually reject claims by defendants that failure to introduce proof of motive makes other circumstantial evidence insufficient.[15]

Evidence tending to establish a defendant's motive can take a variety of forms. Some are common, such as financial benefit a defendant receives as a result of the crime or personal animosity against a victim. In other cases, motive may be

EVIDENCE OF MOTIVE IS A TWO-WAY STREET

Prosecutors may use evidence of motive: "[Motive] is evidence of the commission of any crime" [*United States v. Bradshaw*, 690 F.2d 704, 708 (1982), *review denied*, U.S. Supreme Court, 463 U.S. 1210, 103 S.Ct. 3543 (1983)].

Defendants may also use the lack of motive as evidence: "[T]he absence of motive tends to support the presumption of innocence; it is a fact to be reckoned [with] on the side of innocence" [Supreme Court of California in the 1945 case of *People v. Weatherford*, 164 P.2d 753, 765 (Calif.); see also *Martin v. United States*, 606 A.2d 120 (D.C. App. 1991)].

established in more unusual ways. For example, in a 2002 Wisconsin case,[16] the prosecution was permitted to introduce testimony establishing a cultural heritage that members of a Korean family would place family loyalty above other interests. The prosecution argued that the defendant, a Korean American, burned down his father's financially troubled business at his father's request out of loyalty to his father. The cultural tradition was thus used by the prosecution as evidence to show the son's motive.

If the prosecution does not introduce evidence of motive, defendants can argue to the jury that the failure to do so creates reasonable doubt. In *State v. Caruolo*,[17] the Rhode Island Supreme Court said a defendant is not entitled to a jury instruction that absence of motive evidence is a circumstance that shows innocence.

Defendants may also use circumstantial evidence. A defendant might show that she was 200 hundred miles away at the time the crime was committed, a fact from which a strong inference of innocence could be drawn. Some crimes require a great deal of skill, strength, or physical agility; therefore, a defendant lacking such traits has presented circumstantial evidence tending to prove innocence.

FINGERPRINTS AND SHOE PRINTS AS CIRCUMSTANTIAL EVIDENCE

Fingerprints and shoe prints are circumstantial evidence, and inferences can be drawn from their presence at a crime scene.

Example

Your home or apartment is burglarized. Fingerprints of a stranger are found at the site of the forced entry. The prints match those of a person with a long history of committing burglaries. A search warrant for his home results in the police seizure of many items taken from your home. The presence of the stolen articles supports the inference that the fingerprints were made during the crime.

In the 1992 case of *Commonwealth v. Hall*,[18] the Massachusetts Court of Appeals affirmed the conviction of the defendant for burglary, holding:

The presence of a fingerprint at a crime scene is insufficient by itself to support a guilty finding. "The prosecution must couple the [fingerprint] with evidence which reasonably excludes the hypothesis that the [fingerprint] [was] impressed at a time other than

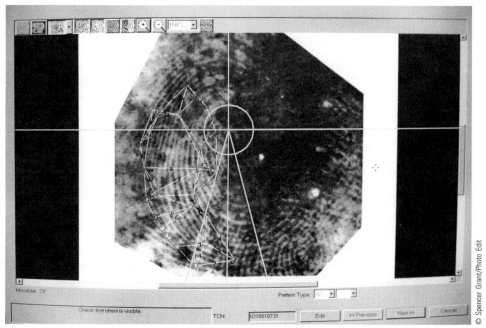

This close-up of a numerical mapping technique links similarities between fingerprints on a computer monitor in a forensic crime lab. The software enables the identification of the owner of the fingerprints. The circumstantial evidence of fingerprints at a crime scene can lead to the inference that the fingerprint owner was involved in the crime.

© Spencer Grant/Photo Edit

when the crime was being committed." *Commonwealth v. Fazzino,* 27 Mass. App. Ct. 485, 487, 539 N.E.2d 1060 (1989). We conclude that the evidence submitted in this case supports a reasonable inference that the defendant placed his fingerprint on the doorknob at the time of the crime.

Circumstantial evidence may produce inferences, and these inferences "need only be reasonable and possible, … not necessary or inescapable." [*Commonwealth v. Merola,* 405 Mass. 529, 533, 542 N.E.2d 249 (1989), quoting from *Commonwealth v. Beckett,* 373 Mass. 329, 341, 366 N.E.2d 1252 (1977)]

permissible inference Inferences made from proof of facts that a fact finder may, but need not, draw.

Although inferences "need only be reasonable and possible," as the court in the above case observed, this means only that the jury may use such a **permissible inference** to reach a conclusion. The prosecution retains the duty to persuade the jury to make the inference.

Fingerprints were also used as circumstantial evidence to obtain convictions in the 1992 burglary case *Brown v. State* and in the 1991 Georgia auto theft case *In the Interest of N.R.*[19] The Georgia court held that "[t]here was no evidence of any other explanation of how defendant's fingerprints came to be on the [car window] other than that they were put there during the course of the [theft]."

Shoe prints differ from fingerprints because, unlike fingers, shoes are not part of the human body. It must be shown that the shoes belonged to the defendant and the defendant was wearing them at the time the crime was committed. An inference of use by the defendant could be drawn from this showing. The Supreme Court of Illinois affirmed the conviction of the defendant for burglary in the 1992 case of *People v. Campbell,*[20] based on a clear and distinctive shoe print found in the burglarized home. The court held that this evidence, plus flight and a showing that the defendant had an opportunity to commit the crime, was sufficient to prove guilt:

> While flight by itself is not sufficient to establish guilt, it may be a circumstance to be considered with other factors tending to establish guilt....
>
> This evidence, along with the shoeprint evidence and evidence of opportunity, could properly have been considered as tending to establish defendant as the perpetrator of the charged offense. Again, we note that the weight to be given all the evidence was for the trier of fact to determine.

Conclusion

The trial court made a reasoned decision based upon all of the evidence presented at trial. The court properly weighed the evidence, giving full cognizance to its infirmities and the inferences to be drawn therefrom. While we might have weighed the evidence differently, we have neither the authority nor the duty to substitute our judgment. The evidence here, while not of the strongest caliber, does not seem to us so unreasonable as to support a reversal of defendant's conviction for residential burglary.

INFERENCES DRAWN FROM OTHER BAD ACTS OR OTHER CONVICTIONS OF DEFENDANTS

A defendant charged with a crime must answer for only that crime at his trial. Evidence of prior crimes or other bad acts is generally held to be inadmissible because of the prejudice it could cause in the minds of the jury or fact finder. In the 1988 case of *Thompson v. United States*,[21] the court pointed out that "the jury may condemn the defendant because of his prior criminal behavior and not because he is guilty of the offense charged."

Example

The 1991 rape trial of William Kennedy Smith (nephew of Senator Edward Kennedy) received nationwide news coverage. A critical point in the trial was a hearing before the trial judge as to whether three women (a doctor, a medical student, and a law student) would be permitted to testify that Smith had either raped or tried to rape them. The testimony of the three women could have been devastating and could have changed the outcome of the trial. Trial Judge Mary E. Lupo ruled against the state and would not permit the testimony of the three women. Smith was acquitted.

However, there are exceptions to the rule forbidding evidence of prior crimes or bad acts. Most states have statutes similar to the federal "Other crimes, wrongs, or acts" statute (Federal Rule of Evidence 404[b]), which provides:

> *Other crimes, wrongs, or acts.* Evidence of other crimes, wrongs, or acts is not admissible to prove the character of a person in order to show that he acted in conformity therewith. It may, however, be admissible for other purposes, such as proof of motive, opportunity, intent, preparation, plan, knowledge, identity, or absence of mistake or accident....

An example of evidence admissible under Rule 404(b) appears in the 2005 case of *United States v. Brand.*[22] There, the government was permitted to introduce images of child pornography seized from the defendant's computer at the defendant's trial for attempting to entice a minor to engage in sexual activity. The images were held admissible under Rule 404(b) because they tended to show the intent of

EVERYDAY USE OF INFERENCES AND DEDUCTIONS

We all draw inferences from observations in our everyday life. From observations you may conclude that a friend is angry or upset, that it is going to rain, that a motorist is driving recklessly, or that a pet is getting old or is sick. Consider the following example of an inference: You awake one morning to see snow falling in your backyard. In the newly fallen snow are animal tracks across your yard. From your observations and past experiences, you could conclude:

- A large dog crossed your yard a few minutes earlier.
- The dog was moving slowly from east to west.
- The dog probably belongs to your neighbor to the east, who lets his dog out every morning.

If you had seen the dog cross your yard, you would have direct information regarding the dog. But because you did not see or hear the dog, you made your deductions or conclusions based on the circumstantial facts available to you. Further investigation could either affirm or rebut the conclusions you have made.

---

the defendant to use computers for illicit purposes, thus serving as rebuttal evidence to the defendant's claim that he had no criminal intent.

In 1994, Congress passed the Violent Crime Control and Law Enforcement Act.[23] As part of its provisions, this law amended the Federal Rules of Evidence by adding Rules 413, 414, and 415. These rules make admissible in criminal cases evidence of prior sexual assaults (Rule 413) and child molestations (Rule 414) by a defendant charged with those crimes. Unlike the limited use of evidence of "bad acts" under Rule 404(b), evidence introduced under Rule 413 or 414 "may be considered for its bearing on any matter to which it is relevant."[24]

Example

Evidence that the defendant had committed child molestation acts twenty years before the crime charged was admissible in the present sexual abuse prosecution. The earlier acts were similar to the acts charged, involved the same form of abuse, and both victims were 6- or 7-year-old girls related to the defendant.

In some circumstances, the defendant may introduce evidence of past violent acts by the victim. In *People v. Harris*,[25] the Michigan Supreme Court reversed a conviction for manslaughter because the trial court excluded evidence of the victim's reputation for violence. The court held that such evidence is relevant to create the inference that the victim initiated violence, a fact that would have some bearing on the culpability of the actions taken by the defendant. Moreover, the court held that the defendant need not have knowledge of that violent reputation because such evidence tends only to prove the likelihood of the victim's violent acts. The court also stated, however, that if the defendant offers evidence of the victim's past violence as part of a self-defense claim, the defendant must show he was aware of the victim's reputation.

SOME INFERENCES SHOULD NOT BE DRAWN

impermissible inference An inference a fact finder may not draw; an example is inferring guilt because the defendant does not testify.

In the following situations, courts have ruled that certain inferences are **impermissible**, and no inference of guilt or the victim's role in the crime may be drawn from them.

When a Defendant Exercises the Privilege Against Self-Incrimination   An inference of guilt should not be drawn when a defendant or suspect asserts the Fifth Amendment privilege against self-incrimination. This includes situations where defendants do not take the witness stand to defend themselves against criminal charges made against them. It also includes situations such as the assertion of rights after *Miranda* warnings are given.

In the 1990 case of *United States v. Rocha*,[26] the United States Court of Appeals held that "[t]he Fifth Amendment prohibits a trial judge, a prosecutor or a witness from commenting upon a defendant's failure to testify in a criminal trial."

When police officers appear as witnesses, they should not comment on a defendant's use of the right to remain silent and not answer questions. In the 1989 case of *State v. Marple*,[27] the Oregon appellate court held that "[h]ere, defendant invoked his right to remain silent when he refused to answer the officer's question, and his refusal cannot be used as evidence against him."

The prosecution is also prohibited from using the fact that the defendant remained silent after receiving the *Miranda* warnings for purposes of either its case-in-chief or impeachment.[28]

The U.S. Supreme Court has held that the prosecution can use post-arrest, pre-warning silence for impeachment purposes.[29] It has not decided the question of the use of such pre-warning silence by the prosecution in its case-in-chief. In a 2005 case,[30] the Eighth Circuit Court of Appeals held that the prosecution could use as evidence the fact that the defendant remained silent and did not show surprise after drugs were found in the car he was driving and he was arrested. At trial, the defendant contended that he was driving the car for a friend and knew nothing about the drugs. The arresting officer was permitted to testify that the defendant said nothing and showed no surprise when he was arrested. The court of appeals held that because this silence occurred before the *Miranda* warning had been given, the use of it by the prosecution did not violate the defendant's Fifth Amendment rights. At least one other circuit court of appeals has reached the opposite conclusion. In *United States v. Velarde-Gomez*,[31] the court held that the prosecution could not use post-arrest, pre-warning silence in its case-in-chief.

In some states, the prosecution may not use or comment on the fact that a defendant remained silent after arrest, whether or not *Miranda* warnings have been given. For example, see *State v. Mainaaupo*.[32]

When the Information Is Protected by the Rape Shield Law   Before the enactment of rape shield laws, defense lawyers in rape cases questioned victims about their past sex life in hopes that the jury and judge would draw the inference that the woman was sexually promiscuous and likely to consent to sex.

In the 1990 case of *Commonwealth v. Nieves*,[33] the Pennsylvania Superior Court pointed out that "[r]ape shield laws were intended to end the abuses … by limiting the harassing and embarrassing inquiries of defense counsel into irrelevant prior sexual conduct of sexual assault complainants."

Rape shield laws enacted by the federal government and probably all states contain exceptions. Federal Rule of Evidence 412 (found in Appendix C of this book) contains the federal exceptions to the relevance of evidence as to the "alleged victim's past sexual behavior or alleged sexual predisposition."

When Courts Rule Both Ways on the Cessation of Signature Crimes After a Suspect's Arrest   *Signature crimes* are crimes that are so similar that they bear the mark of a common pattern. Many cities and communities have faced the terrible problem of serial crimes. If a suspect is arrested and the serial, or signature, crimes stop, can this be used as evidence?

Although some courts may rule otherwise, the Pennsylvania Superior Court held that such evidence is inherently unreliable. In the 1992 case of *Commonwealth v. Foy*,[34] the court pointed out that there are many reasons why reports of signature crimes could stop:

> Further signature crimes may have been committed but never reported to the police. The true culprit may have died, or left the community, or been incarcerated on unrelated charges about the time of the defendant's arrest. Or perhaps the true culprit has decided to refrain from further acts of violence in order to shift suspicion onto the defendant and thereby escape detection.

When a Suspect Seeks to Contact a Lawyer   The United States Court of Appeals held in the 1984 case of *United States v. Daoud*[35] that "[t]he right to counsel is included in the *Miranda* warnings, and as such is covered by the implicit assurance that invocation of the right will carry no penalty."

In seeking legal advice and the assistance of a lawyer, the person may well believe that he or she is guilty of a crime. But an innocent person may also seek legal advice to assist in proving that he or she has not committed a crime. Or the person may be involved in only a minor way in the crime being investigated. The most likely purpose for seeking legal advice or representation is to be informed about the person's status and what possible exposure may be involved.

Attempting to use evidence that a defendant sought to contact a lawyer is forbidden by most (if not all) courts. The Maryland Court of Appeals held in the 1990 case of *Hunter v. State*[36] that:

> Where the request for ... counsel arises in some other circumstance, as in the case at bar, comment on it has been condemned under principles enunciated in *Griffin v. California*, 380 U.S. 609, 85 S.Ct. 1229, 14 L.Ed.2d 106 (1965). One of the earliest expressions of this rule came in *United States ex rel. Macon v. Yeager*, 476 F.2d 613 (3rd Cir. 1973).

USING DIRECT AND CIRCUMSTANTIAL EVIDENCE

In most criminal cases, both direct and circumstantial evidence is used. Following are some examples.

FINDING ILLEGAL DRUGS IN A MOTOR VEHICLE

Illegal drugs are found in motor vehicles in a variety of situations. In a lawful stop of a vehicle, a law officer may see or smell illegal drugs. An informant or other source might provide probable cause to believe drugs are in the vehicle.

If the illegal drugs are in an open position in the vehicle and only the driver is in the car, the inference of knowledge and possession of drugs is easy. When more than one person is in the car, the inference of illegal possession is strongest against the owner and driver of the vehicle. It would be more difficult to convict a passenger in the vehicle because the inferences of knowledge and possession are weaker. However, the location of the drugs in the vehicle, the amount of illegal drugs found, the criminal record of the passenger, and the passenger's relationship to the driver and owner would all be circumstantial factors in determining whether or not to charge the passenger.

The United States Court of Appeals, in the 1992 case of *United States v. Gibson*,[37] made the following observations in affirming the conviction of the defendant:

> It is well established in this circuit that in cases involving hidden compartments, reliance may not be placed solely on the defendant's control of the vehicle. In such an instance, possession can be inferred only if knowledge is indicated by additional factors, such as circumstances evidencing a consciousness of guilt on the part of the defendant. Inconsistent stories may constitute substantive evidence of a defendant's guilty knowledge. Circumstantial factors also include lack of knowledge of the name of the true owner and implausible explanations for one's travels. [... "nervousness, in certain instances, may also be a factor."]

PROVING THE CRIME OF POSSESSION OF ILLEGAL DRUGS WITH INTENT TO DELIVER

A defendant apprehended in the act of selling illegal drugs usually can easily be convicted of the offense because strong direct evidence exists to prove selling, transferring, or delivering of the drugs.

When the crime of possession with intent to deliver is charged, the defendant usually has a large quantity of illegal drugs in his or her possession. State and federal governments argue that sufficient circumstantial evidence exists to prove that the defendant had the intent to sell, transfer, or deliver the illegal drugs to others and did not intend all of the drugs for personal use. The crime of possession with intent to deliver has higher penalties than mere possession.[38]

In the 1991 case of *State v. Morgan*,[39] the Supreme Court of North Carolina listed the following cases and circumstances where intent to deliver was inferred from circumstantial evidence:

> A jury can reasonably infer from the amount of the controlled substance found within a defendant's constructive or actual possession and from the manner of its packaging an intent to transfer, sell, or deliver that substance. *See, e.g., State v. Williams*, 307 N.C. 452, 298 S.E.2d 372 (1983) (presence of material normally used for packaging); *State v. Baxter*, 285 N.C. 735, 208 S.E.2d 696 (1974) (amount of marijuana found, its packaging, and presence of packaging materials); *State v. Rich*, 87 N.C. App. 380, 361 S.E.2d 321 (1987) (twenty grams cocaine plus packaging paraphernalia); *State v. Casey*,

59 N.C. App. 99, 296 S.E.2d 473 (1982) (possession of over 25,000 individually wrapped dosage units of LSD); *State v. Mitchell,* 27 N.C. App. 313, 219 S.E.2d 295 (1975), *cert. denied,* 289 N.C. 301, 222 S.E.2d 701 (1976) (possession of considerable inventory of marijuana plus other seized, "suspicious" items). *See also State v. James,* 81 N.C. App. 91, 344 S.E.2d 77 (1986) (cocaine of small quantity packaged in multiple envelopes); *State v. Williams,* 71 N.C. App. 136, 321 S.E.2d 561 (1984) (less than one ounce marijuana packaged in seventeen small bags); *State v. Francum,* 39 N.C. App. 429, 250 S.E.2d 705 (1979) (quantity of LSD unspecified, but found in plastic bags inside larger plastic bags).

Other circumstantial evidence used to prove intent to deliver is mentioned in the 1991 case of *United States v. Solis,*[40] where drugs were found in Solis's luggage:

As counsel for Ms. Solis conceded on appeal, her intent to distribute the cocaine found in her luggage was at issue. The government had to establish that intent through circumstantial evidence. Evidence of Ms. Solis' actions and of the other articles in her possession was therefore relevant on the issue of whether she intended to distribute the contraband. For instance, evidence of repeated trips to Anchorage, paid for in cash by or on behalf of a woman living on Social Security, certainly provides important pieces to the government's evidentiary puzzle. The simultaneous presence of beeper numbers helps complete the picture—*if* the trier of fact is aware of the role that beepers often play in the conduct of illegal drug trade. The government was entitled to demonstrate through the use of expert testimony that someone traveling with two kilograms of cocaine under the conditions we have described would find access to beepers a useful means of effectuating the transportation and eventual distribution of her deadly cargo.

In addition to beepers, guns are tools of drug traffickers and can be used as circumstantial evidence from which fact finders can infer intent to deliver. The federal court in the 1989 case of *United States v. Carstens*[41] held that "courts have recognized that any gun is a 'tool of the trade' for drug traffickers. The presence of weapons is evidence of … intent to distribute controlled substances."

In the 1991 crack house case *United States v. Bruce,*[42] the court described the crack house scenario as follows:

If guns are strewn around a "crack house" in which drugs are stored, it might be inferred that the guns are there to protect the occupant's "possession." In such a case, the guns are "used" in relation to the drug trafficking crime of possession with intent to distribute because they are intended to protect the stash of drugs that will subsequently be distributed. And although actual distribution is a separate crime, courts have treated evidence of the use of guns in such a house for protection of the distribution function as equivalent to protection of possession.

PROVING USE OF THE INTERNET IN CHILD PORNOGRAPHY

Although possession of child pornography is both a federal and a state crime, federal prosecutors have more resources for prosecutions.[43] If a defendant is found to possess child pornography, the government must prove he received the images over the Internet to obtain a federal conviction (an interstate violation).

Internet use must often be proved by circumstantial evidence. An example of how circumstantial evidence can be used for such a conviction is *United States v. Dodds.*[44]

The defendant was charged under 18 U.S.C. section 1462 after being found with more than 3,400 images of child pornography in his possession. The prosecution proved that the images were taken from the Internet by the following circumstantial evidence:

- The photographs were shown to be available on the Internet and traded there.
- Some of the children pictured were shown to live in states other than the defendant's.
- There was no evidence the defendant traveled to those other states.
- The defendant was shown to be familiar with using the Internet.

The court of appeals held that this evidence was sufficient and affirmed the defendant's conviction.

Congress has passed several acts designed to protect children from sexual exploitation on the Internet, but many of these acts have been held unconstitutional by the U.S. Supreme Court. [For a discussion of these cases, see T. Gardner and T. Anderson, *Criminal Law: Principles and Cases,* 10th ed. (Thomson Wadsworth, 2009), p. 307.] In the 2008 case of *United States v. Williams,*[45] the Supreme Court reversed the Eleventh Circuit Court of Appeals and held the PROTECT Act[46] constitutional. The PROTECT Act makes it a crime for a person to distribute information on the Internet in a manner that "reflects a belief" or is "intended to make another believe" the person was distributing child pornography.

Charges of distributing child pornography over the Internet can be difficult to prove because the U.S. Supreme Court had held that persons distributing pictures alleged to contain images of actual children in sexual poses, but who are in reality young-looking actors or computer-created animations, cannot be prosecuted as child pornographers. As a result, it is difficult for a prosecution to prove that images depicted in an Internet posting are actual children. The PROTECT Act alleviates this problem by making it a violation to post images in such a manner that suggests the person posting the image either believes it to be of an actual child or posts it in a manner designed to make others believe the images are real children. The Supreme Court upheld the statute, stating it narrowly prohibited conduct that relates to the depiction of sexual poses involving actual children, and did not operate to prohibit conduct that does not involve actual children.

Proving Physical and Sexual Abuse of Children

Many child abuse cases must be proved using circumstantial evidence because direct evidence is not available. In many instances, the child is unable to tell what happened, and the offender does not ordinarily disclose the truth. Inferences are therefore very important in proving child abuse cases.

When an adult has sole custody of a child and it is shown that the injury was not accidental or self-inflicted, a jury may infer that the adult inflicted the injury. In the 1989 case of *Commonwealth v. Earnest,*[47] the Superior Court of Pennsylvania relied on this rule, allowing:

> [A]n inference of guilt where a child suffers a fatal injury while an adult has sole custody of the child. *Commonwealth v. Nissly,* 379 Pa. Super. 86, 549 A.2d 918 (1988). In *Nissly,* the defendant was not the only adult in the house when the fatal injury was inflicted, but the inference of guilt was still applicable as the defendant was the only

© Mary Demet

Large billboards such as this one were seen in Florida during 2007. The state of Florida paid for these billboards in a public awareness campaign on the dangers of shaking a baby, which can cause serious crippling injuries and death. Felony criminal charges can be brought against a person who intentionally, recklessly, or negligently causes such injury or death. What type of circumstantial evidence would be needed when an accused in such a case denies liability?

adult with the child when the injury had to have occurred. As in the instant case, the fact finder found the injury was not accidental or self-inflicted, therefore, the evidence was sufficient for the conviction, as we find it is here.

In the 1991 case of *Campbell v. Commonwealth*,[48] the victim was a 3-year-old child. The court of appeals held that:

> [T]he trial judge could have inferred from all the facts and circumstances that the defendant intended to do exactly what he did—beat the child with such force that it left his back and side extensively marked and bruised. Further, the trial judge could have found that the probable and natural consequence of this act, given the force with which the blows were applied and the location of the marks near Cecil's spinal column and right kidney, was disfigurement or disablement of the child....
>
> A three-year-old child with no way to defend himself, except by screaming and crying, received a brutal beating from the much stronger defendant. We conclude that the trial judge could have inferred from all the evidence that this beating was delivered with the intent to disfigure or disable the child.
>
> For the foregoing reasons, therefore, we affirm the defendant's conviction of malicious wounding.

Some sexual abuse statutes require proof of *forcible compulsion*. When the victim is a child, the child often submits to the advances of adults who have parental or similar authority over the child.

The highest courts in Pennsylvania, North Carolina, and Alabama permit an inference of forcible compulsion where sexual intercourse or abuse is shown even if no physical force was used and no threats were uttered by the adult. In adopting this inference in the 1991 case of *Powe v. State*,[49] the Supreme Court of Alabama held:

> We note that our holding is limited to cases involving the sexual assault of children by adults with whom the children are in a relationship of trust. The reason for the distinction between cases involving children as victims and those involving adults as victims is the great influence and control that an adult who plays a dominant role in a child's life may exert over the child. When a defendant who plays an authoritative role in a child's world instructs the child to submit to certain acts, an implied threat of some sort of disciplinary action accompanies the instruction. If the victim is young, inexperienced, and perhaps ignorant of the "wrongness" of the conduct, the child may submit to the acts because the child assumes the conduct is acceptable or because the child does not have the capacity to refuse. Moreover, fear of the parent resulting from love or respect may play a role as great or greater than that played by fear of threats of serious bodily harm in coercing a child to submit to a sexual act.

PROVING THE DEFENDANT WAS THE DRIVER OF A MOTOR VEHICLE

Thousands of drivers on American highways have had their driver's license suspended or revoked. Many others do not have a valid driver's license or are driving under the influence of drugs or alcohol. In 2001 alone, 17,448 people were killed and half a million people were injured as the result of drunk or drugged driving. Experts state that four out of five people killed on highways and streets are killed by drunk or drugged drivers.

Proof beyond reasonable doubt that the defendant was driving the vehicle is required and is central to the conviction of the defendant in many moving vehicle trials. The following cases illustrate only a few of those that come before American courts every year, where inferences drawn from circumstantial evidence are used to determine who was driving the vehicle in question.

Mirro v. United States

Unpublished Fourth Circuit Court of Appeals, *review denied*, U.S. Supreme Court, 44 CrL 4005 (1988)

When a truck was stopped, a military police officer testified that he saw the defendant climb out of the driver's seat of the truck while another person took his place. This testimony was held sufficient to support the inference that the defendant was the driver of the truck. The defendant was convicted of drunk driving. The Supreme Court refused review.

State v. McGlone

Supreme Court of Ohio, 570 N.E.2d 1115 (1991)

An intoxicated person found in the driver's seat of a motor vehicle parked on private or public property with the key in the ignition is "operating" the vehicle and can be convicted of drunk driving.

State v. Mills

Iowa Court of Appeals, 458 N.W.2d 395 (1990)

After police officers determined that a vehicle's owner had a suspended driver's license, they made the inference that the owner was driving the vehicle illegally. It was held that they had reasonable suspicion to make a stop of the vehicle in the absence of evidence showing that someone else was driving the car. A substantial amount of cocaine was found in a plastic bag at the defendant's feet after a pat-down for weapons.

The defendant was convicted of possession of cocaine with intent to deliver. His conviction was affirmed in view of the large amount of cocaine and a large amount of money found in his sock and in his shoe.

PROVING CORPUS DELICTI BY DIRECT OR CIRCUMSTANTIAL EVIDENCE

corpus delicti
The body of the crime; the requirement that the government must prove that the crime charged has been committed.

In all criminal cases, the state or government must prove that (1) a crime has been committed by someone (**corpus delicti**) and (2) the defendant(s) committed the offense. Most states have adopted a definition of *corpus delicti* similar to that used by the Supreme Court of California in the 1991 case of *People v. Jennings:*[50] "The corpus delicti of a crime consists of two elements, the fact of the injury or loss or harm, and the existence of a criminal agency as its cause."

The corpus delicti of most crimes is ordinarily proved by direct evidence, as when the victim or a witness tells the police of the crime. The corpus delicti of other crimes is proved by physical evidence; for example, the corpus delicti of a burglary is shown by a broken window and missing valuables. The corpus delicti of a murder could be proved by a dead body with a knife in the chest. The following examples illustrate common corpus delicti problems.

Examples
- A suspicious fire destroys a building housing a business that was in serious financial trouble. Investigators suspect arson but cannot prove corpus delicti (that the fire was deliberately started). The insurance company is unhappy because of the large amount of insurance. It can be shown that the owner of the building and business had the means, opportunity, and motive for "torching" the building, but if the state cannot prove corpus delicti, it cannot charge the owner with a criminal offense.
- All cities in the United States have "missing persons." Some of these people may be living elsewhere and may have deliberately cut all ties with their family and friends. Families and friends of a missing person may believe the missing person has been murdered. Before criminal charges can be filed, however, corpus delicti must be proved.

As a general rule, corpus delicti must be established beyond a reasonable doubt.[51] Corpus delicti may be proved by a combination of direct and circumstantial evidence or by either alone. When an attempt is made to prove corpus delicti by circumstantial evidence, the general rule is that the evidence must be so conclusive as to eliminate all reasonable doubt in concluding that a crime was committed. The following case illustrates.

Epperly v.
Commonwealth

Supreme Court of
Virginia, 224 Va. 214,
294 S.E.2d 882 (1982)

An 18-year-old college girl (Gina Hall) was last seen leaving a dance with the defendant. Her body was never found to prove conclusively that she was murdered, but her blood-soaked clothing was found. Her car was also found, and there was evidence of a violent struggle at a house on Claytor Lake where the defendant was seen after the dance. Dog-tracking evidence was admitted at the defendant's trial, corroborating some of the allegations of the state about her whereabouts after the dance. The defendant also made incriminating statements that were admitted as evidence. In holding that the state carried the burden of proving corpus delicti, the Supreme Court of Virginia affirmed the defendant's conviction, ruling that:

> The court instructed the jury that the Commonwealth must first prove that Gina was dead and that her death was caused by criminal violence. The instruction told the jury that these elements might be proved "either by direct evidence or by proof so strong as to produce the full assurance of moral certainty." Defendant agrees that this instruction correctly states the law, but argues that the evidence was insufficient to warrant the jury's finding the existence of the corpus delicti....
>
> In homicide cases, the corpus delicti must consist of proof (1) of the victim's death and (2) that it resulted from the criminal act or agency of another.... Although this is the first such case to come to this Court in which the victim's body was not found, we have long held that the corpus delicti may be proven by circumstantial evidence.
>
> We think the evidence was sufficient to warrant the jury in finding, to the full assurance of moral certainty, that Gina Hall was dead as the result of the criminal act of another person. The jury was entitled to take into account, in this connection, her sudden disappearance, her character and personal relationships, her physical and mental health, the evidence of a violent struggle at the house on Claytor Lake, her hidden, blood-soaked clothing, and the defendant's incriminating statements— particularly his reference to "the body" before it was generally thought she was dead.

In 1990 the Supreme Court of North Carolina affirmed the first-degree murder conviction of the defendant in the case of *State v. Franklin,*[52] holding that:

> [When a] body is found with marks of violence upon it, as was the case here, such evidence establishes *corpus delicti.*
>
> Evidence of *corpus delicti* coupled with the testimony of a cell mate [Woolard] relating inculpatory statements made by the defendant is sufficient to support a conviction.
>
> In this case, according to Woolard, defendant said that he had killed a girl, had been questioned about it, and had gotten away with it. He further told Woolard that the reason he had killed the girl was because she owed him money. The evidence shows that defendant had previously been questioned about Jean Sherman's disappearance but had not been charged with her murder. The evidence further conclusively shows that Jean Sherman owed defendant money for the cocaine she had stolen on the night before her disappearance. All of this evidence, taken as a whole, is sufficient to take the case to the jury, which was then entitled to evaluate its weight. We conclude that the State's evidence, when viewed in the light most favorable to the State, is sufficient to withstand defendant's motion to dismiss. This assignment of error is overruled.

THE SUFFICIENCY-OF-EVIDENCE REQUIREMENT TO JUSTIFY A VERDICT OR FINDING OF GUILT

sufficiency-of-evidence requirement
The demand for a reasonably substantial foundation of evidence to support a verdict or finding.

One of the most common grounds for appeal of a jury verdict or a judge's finding of guilty is insufficiency of evidence (**sufficiency-of-evidence requirement**). In this appeal, the defense argues that there was not sufficient evidence to support the verdict or finding of guilt beyond a reasonable doubt.

A jury's verdict or a judge's finding must be supported and based on legal and substantial evidence. Mere possibilities, suspicion, or conjecture will not support a verdict or finding of guilt. If the evidence is inherently incredible or is contrary to common knowledge and experience or established physical facts, it will not support a finding of guilt.

Either direct or circumstantial evidence will support a finding of guilt if the evidence is legally sufficient to prove all of the essential elements of the crime charged. The Court of Special Appeals of Maryland held in the case of *Metz v. State*[53] that "we feel that the test for sufficiency is the same whether the evidence be direct, circumstantial, or provided by rational inferences therefrom." The following cases illustrate sufficiency-of-evidence issues that have come before appellate courts.

Burkhart v. State

Supreme Court of Nevada, 107 Nev. 797, 820 P.2d 757 (1991)

The defendant was convicted after a jury trial of the crime of kidnapping based on the following conduct: The defendant approached a child (Mathew) who was standing near his parents in a Nevada gambling casino. The defendant touched the child twice and then "it appears that (defendant) may have momentarily grabbed a jacket that Mathew was wearing." After the third contact, Mathew's parents, who saw and heard all that happened, notified casino security. This evidence was permitted to go to a jury, and the jury inferred that the evidence justified a conviction of kidnapping. The Supreme Court of Nevada reversed the conviction, holding that:

> [T]here was no testimony which would have allowed the jury to infer what appellant intended to do with Mathew. The undisputed evidence showed that appellant ceased his final contact with Mathew as soon as Mathew indicated that he did not wish to go with appellant. Further, all of the contacts took place in the hallway of a public facility, within easy view of Mathew's parents.
>
> The first two contacts were innocuous enough that Mathew's parents made no effort to intervene. Even after Mathew's parents called security, appellant calmly remained in the casino.
>
> Finally, it appears that appellant had no ready means available to take Mathew away from the casino, unless it is to be argued that appellant intended to ride away with Mathew on appellant's bicycle. No rational juror could have inferred from this evidence that appellant seized Mathew with the specific intent to detain him against his will. Any inference as to appellant's specific intent must have been based on unbridled speculation.

In re Woods

Illinois Court of Appeals, 20 Ill.App.3d 641, 314 N. E.2d 606 (1974)

Identification evidence of the defendant's involvement in a robbery was suppressed and could not be used because of improper procedures. The only remaining evidence that could be used was his presence at the scene of the crime and the fact that he ran away. In holding that this evidence was insufficient to support the defendant's conviction, the court ruled that:

> [M]ere presence at the scene of the crime is insufficient to establish accountability ..., and we believe that presence at the scene together with flight, in the absence of other circumstances indicating a common design to do an unlawful act, does not establish accountability.

THE USE OF PRESUMPTIONS AND INFERENCES

PRESUMPTIONS

McCormick on Evidence (West Publishing, 1992) writes that the term "presumption is the slipperiest member of the family of legal terms." This is because *presumption* is used in so many ways by different courts.

The following is an example of a jury instruction that must be given to juries in criminal cases. The presumption stated in the jury instruction is ordinarily referred to as the "presumption of innocence." However, some writers and McCormick prefer the term "assumption of innocence."

> The law presumes every person charged with the commission of an offense to be innocent. This presumption attends the defendant throughout the trial and prevails at its close unless overcome by evidence which satisfy the jury of his (or her) guilt beyond a reasonable doubt. The defendant is not required to prove his (or her) innocence.

Is the above presumption "rebuttable" (meaning that it can be "overcome" by evidence showing otherwise)? Yes, it can, but the state must carry this burden "throughout the trial."

Is the above presumption "mandatory" (meaning that the jury must "presume" or "assume" the innocence of the defendant "unless overcome by evidence which satisfy the jury of ... guilt beyond a reasonable doubt")? Yes, it is mandatory.

The terms *conclusive* and *irrebuttable presumptions* are used and defined in different ways by different writers and different courts. The old common-law presumption that a child under age 7 is incapable of committing a crime can be called an irrebuttable or conclusive presumption because it cannot be overcome by evidence showing otherwise. A state could statutorize this presumption as a law, but most states leave the concept in its common-law form.

The Supreme Court of Pennsylvania[54] and the Supreme Court of Indiana[55] defined the legal significance and nature of a presumption as follows:

> [A] presumption of law is not evidence nor should it be weighed by the fact finder as though it had evidentiary value. Rather, a presumption is a rule of law enabling the party in whose favor it operates to take his case to the jury without presenting evidence of the fact presumed. It serves as a challenge for proof and indicates the party from whom such proof must be forthcoming. When the opponent of the presumption has met the burden of production thus imposed, however, the office of the presumption has been performed; the presumption is of no further effect and drops from the case.

CLASSIFICATIONS OF EVIDENCE

Corroborative evidence

Corroborative evidence is evidence that adds weight or **credibility** to a case. In many instances, corroborative evidence is important in carrying the burden of persuasion in the mind of the fact finder. For example, in rape cases, corroborative evidence is important to reinforce the testimony of the victim.

Prima facie evidence

The term *prima facie* is Latin for "at first sight" or "on the face of it." Prima facie evidence is that amount of evidence or that quality of evidence that is sufficient in itself to prove a case. When the state presents a prima facie case, the defense must respond or accept a serious risk of conviction. A prima facie case is a very strong case with sufficient evidence to obtain a conviction.

Conclusive evidence and conflicting evidence

Conclusive evidence is evidence from which only one reasonable conclusion may be drawn. The term *conclusive evidence* is sometimes used in statutes where the legislature requires evidence so strong as to conclusively prove the fact or issue. The term *conflicting evidence* is usually used to indicate a situation where evidence both proving and disproving a fact or issue has been presented, and, depending on the weight and credibility accorded the evidence, the fact finder could find either way.

Cumulative evidence

Cumulative evidence is additional evidence of the same kind that proves the same point as evidence already presented. However, evidence from a different source or evidence of a different kind is not cumulative even though it tends to prove or disprove the same fact or issue. (See the U.S. Supreme Court case of *Hamling v. United States* [418 U.S. 87, 94 S.Ct. 2887] discussing cumulative evidence.)

Positive and negative evidence

Most evidence is positive evidence in that it is presented in positive terms. Some evidence, however, is presented in negative terms and is referred to as negative evidence. For example, a motorist testifying that he saw a "Construction Ahead" sign on the road is positive evidence. However, another motorist testifying that he did not see any signs is negative evidence. The sign may have been there, but the motorist did not see it. (See 32 C.J.S. Evidence 1079 for discussion and case citations.)

Parole and testimonial evidence

Oral or verbal evidence is parole evidence. If a confession is only verbal, it is a parole confession. Testimonial evidence is the statement of a witness in court, under oath.

Real, tangible, or mere evidence

Tangible, or physical, evidence is evidence such as weapons, illegal drugs, or shoplifted items. Real evidence can be physically brought into court, as in the case of small items, or, in the case of large items like stolen vehicles, can be stored with authorities and photographs or videos of the large items can be brought into court. Clothing worn by the defendant, such as ski masks, sunglasses, hats, or jackets, can be used to link the defendant to the crime. In rape cases, the victim's clothing is often used as evidence.

Other evidence

See Chapters 7 and 8 for *secondhand evidence* and *hearsay;* see Chapter 16 for *trace evidence* and *demonstrative evidence;* see Chapter 17 for the *best evidence* or *original document rule;* and see Chapter 18 for *scientific evidence.*

Res Ipsa Loquitur as an Inference

The phrase, doctrine, or rule *res ipsa loquitur* ("the thing speaks for itself") is used in both civil and criminal law. *McCormick on Evidence* (West Publishing, 1972) points out that this doctrine is an inference that is permissible but does not require a jury to draw a conclusion.

Example
In a sexual or physical assault case where the victim has been terribly injured, photographs of the battered victim are introduced into evidence and a medical person who attended the victim verifies the accuracy of the photographs.

Whether or not the photographs are contested by the defense, the prosecutor can argue that the photographs speak for themselves in presenting strong evidence proving that the criminal harm and wrong charged in the criminal action did occur (proof of corpus delicti).

The only issue then remaining before the court and jury is the identity of the perpetrator. The defense lawyer could agree that corpus delicti has been proved and take the position "Yes, a terrible crime has occurred, but my client did not commit the crime and is innocent."

INFERENCES

credibility
Believability.

inferences Conclusions that may be drawn from facts.

Inferences are reasonable conclusions or deductions that fact finders (juries or judges) *may* draw from the evidence presented to them. Fact finders should use common sense and their knowledge of everyday life in their reasoning process.

Whereas a *presumption* is an assumption that the law expressly directs that the trier of fact *must* make, an *inference* is a conclusion that a jury or judge *may* make based on the evidence presented.

Persons charged with a crime have a constitutional right to a jury trial. Juries in criminal trials, therefore, must decide all issues of fact presented by evidence in the trial. If a jury instruction interferes or infringes upon the jury's obligation to determine and decide issues of fact, a violation of the defendant's right to jury has occurred.

The defendant's right to a jury was violated in the case of *Sandstrom v. Montana*.[56] The U.S. Supreme Court held that an instruction to a jury that "the law presumes that a person intends the ordinary consequences of his voluntary acts" shifted the burden of proof in Sandstrom's criminal case to the defendant. Because the state must prove all essential elements of the crime charged, the burden-shifting presumption as to the intent of the defendant violated his due process rights.

Juries may infer that a defendant intended "the ordinary consequences of his or her voluntary act," but they cannot be told by a judge in a jury instruction that they have to presume this.

SUMMARY

In criminal trials, both prosecutors and defense lawyers use evidence to either prove or disprove facts that are in issue. The prosecution always has the burden of production of evidence and the burden of persuasion to prove the defendant guilty beyond reasonable doubt.

Direct evidence (if available) may be used to either prove or disprove facts in issue. Circumstantial evidence may also be used. Circumstantial evidence requires the fact finder to draw inferences from evidence that is presented. For example, the fact that a person has child pornography stored on his computer may lead to the permissible inference that he used his computer for illicit purposes.

In most criminal cases, both direct and circumstantial evidence are used. However, a defendant may be convicted on circumstantial evidence alone. Circumstantial evidence is most often used to prove the mental elements, which are essential to many crimes. For example, the requirement of specific intent in the crime of murder is most often proved by inferences drawn from the proven conduct of the defendant.

Inferences are conclusions or deductions that a jury or a judge as the fact finder may draw from the evidence presented. Legal presumptions are rules of law that establish which party has the burden of proof in the production of evidence and the burden of persuasion.

PROBLEMS

1. A New York state trooper saw a car traveling at an excessive rate of speed on the New York Thruway. The officer overtook the speeding vehicle and stopped it. Four men were in the vehicle, two in the front seat and two in the back seat. While the officer was asking the driver for his license and vehicle registration, the officer smelled burning marijuana. The officer then saw an envelope marked "Supergold" lying on the floor of the car between the two men in the front seat.

   The evidence that was available to the officer permitted him to draw an inference about which of the men possessed the marijuana. Did the evidence and the inference drawn from the evidence establish probable cause to arrest the driver? The two men in the front seat? Can it be inferred from the evidence that probable cause existed to arrest all four men? Explain. [*New York v. Belton,* 453 U.S. 454, 101 S.Ct. 2860 (1981)]

2. A guard at the state prison in Walpole, Massachusetts, heard loud voices coming from a walkway. The officer immediately opened the door to the walkway and saw "an inmate named Stephens bleeding from the mouth and suffering from a swollen eye. Dirt was strewn about the walkway, which the officer viewed to be further evidence of a scuffle." The officer saw three inmates, including an inmate named Hill, jogging away together down the walkway. There were no other inmates in the area, which was enclosed by a chain-link fence. The officer concluded that the three men acted as a group in assaulting Stephens. There was no evidence as to who actually beat Stephens. Was there sufficient evidence to punish Hill as one of the three men involved in the assault by taking away his good-time credits? Explain. [*Superintendent, Mass. Correctional Institution, Walpole v. Hill,* 472 U.S. 445, 105 S.Ct. 2768, 37 CrL 3108 (1985)]

3. Kent Hansen was sitting on a public park bench close to a man who was smoking a marijuana cigarette. When an officer in plain clothes saw the marijuana cigarette and smelled burning marijuana, he arrested both men. The officer did not see Hansen holding or smoking the marijuana cigarette. Could the officer properly infer from the information he had that Hansen was an active participant in the use or possession of the marijuana? Should Hansen's conviction be affirmed? Give reasons

for your answer. [*State of Arizona v. Hansen,* 573 P.2d 896 (Ariz. App. 1977)]

4. An experienced law enforcement officer used the following incident as an example for classes. The officer's wife was babysitting for their 3-year-old grandson while the parents were away. No one else was in the house when the grandmother put the child to bed for an afternoon nap. A short time later, while the grandmother was in the basement, she heard a crash and ran back upstairs. When she entered the child's room, she saw the window drapes lying across the bed and on the floor. Because the child had the means and opportunity of pulling the drapes down, the grandmother said to the child, "Why did you pull the drapes down?" The child looked his grandmother in the eye and replied, "You didn't see me do it, and you can't prove that I did it." List the evidence available to the grandmother that caused her to conclude that the child pulled the drapes down. Indicate whether this evidence was direct or circumstantial.

If this situation was presented to a jury, would they be justified in drawing the same conclusion that the grandmother did? Would a jury's verdict of guilty be sustained by the trial court and the appellate court in that there was sufficient evidence to sustain the jury's finding?

5. A young woman wakes up in a bed in a hotel. Her state of dress appears to have been altered from that of the previous evening. The man who took her to the hotel had a bottle of Rohypnol, the "date rape" drug, in his possession. Experts testified that the woman had been drugged with Rohypnol. The woman has no memory of being raped, and there is no physical evidence of sexual intercourse. The man states that he simply watched the woman sleep. Is the evidence sufficient to convict the man of rape? If not, what other evidence might you look for? [See *Sera v. Norris,* 400 F.3d 538 (8th Cir. 2005).]

CASE ANALYSIS

Read Appendix B, Finding and Analyzing Cases (p. 427). With these guidelines in mind, please continue with the Case Analysis selections for Chapter 4.

1. Proving sexual abuse of children frequently involves only circumstantial evidence because the child is often unable to give direct testimony about the abuse. In *State v. Schoommaker* [105 P.3d 302 (2005)], the New Mexico court affirmed a conviction of a defendant for negligent child abuse. What circumstantial evidence was deemed sufficient there? What did the defendant contend?

2. In *State v. Kelbel* [648 N.W.2d 690 (2002)], the Minnesota Supreme Court upheld the conviction of a defendant charged with child abuse. What role did circumstantial evidence play in that conviction, and why did the prosecution need that evidence?

3. In *State v. Surratt* [932 So.2d 736 (La. App. 2006), *cert. denied,* 957 So.2d 165 (La. 2007)], the prosecution used fingerprints to prove that the defendants committed two murders. How were the fingerprints tied to the crimes? What problems did the prosecution confront in making that connection?

4. In many criminal prosecutions, convicting a defendant of the crime charged also entitles the prosecution to seize money used in or derived from the crime. The prosecution must first find the money and then prove, usually by circumstantial evidence, the connection of the money to the crime. The case of *State v. Forty Three Thousand Dollars* [591 S.W.2d 208 (W.V. 2003)] illustrates how a prosecutor can prove that connection.

Notes

1. *In re Winship*, 397 U.S. 358, 364 (1970).
2. *Commonwealth v. Webster*, 59 Mass. 295, 320 (1850). In *Apodaca v. Oregon* [406 U.S. 404, 412 (1972)], the Supreme Court noted that following *Webster*, courts in the United States began using the "reasonable doubt" standard in criminal cases.
3. *In re Winship*, *supra*.
4. *Victor v. Nebraska*, 511 U.S. 1 (1994).
5. *Cage v. Louisiana*, 498 U.S. 39, 40 (1990).
6. *Sandoval v. California*, 511 U.S. 1, 6 (1994).
7. *Victor v. Nebraska*, *supra*, at 23 (Justice Ginsburg concurring).
8. Elisabeth Stoffelmayr and Shari S. Diamond, *The Conflict Between Precision and Flexibility in Explaining "Beyond a Reasonable Doubt,"* 6 Psychol. Pub. Pol'y & L. 769 (2000).
9. Federal Judicial Center, *Pattern Criminal Jury Instructions* (1988), p. 21.
10. The Supreme Court of Louisiana pointed out that "[s]pecific intent to kill or inflict great bodily harm can easily be inferred where an individual discharges a firearm pointed directly at a victim from a short distance" [*State v. Noble*, 425 So.2d 734 (La. 1983)]. The Supreme Court of Indiana approved of the following jury instruction in the case of *Henderson v. State* [544 N.E.2d 507 (1989)], where intent to steal had to be proved to convict Henderson of burglary:

    [Y]ou may infer that a person is presumed to intend the natural and probable acts, unless the circumstances are such to indicate the absence of such intent. When an unlawful act, however, is proved to be knowingly done, no further proof is needed on the part of the state in the absence of justifying or excusing facts.

    The Supreme Court of North Carolina affirmed the first-degree murder conviction of the defendant in the 1990 case of *State v. Porter* [391 S.E.2d 144]. To prove intent to kill, the defendant's statement "I meant to kill the s-of-a-b-" (direct evidence) was used, as was the fact that he "pumped three rounds into the body" of his girlfriend (circumstantial evidence of intent).

    State of mind in attempted murder or assault in the first degree can be shown by circumstantial evidence, as was done in the 1991 case of *State v.*

Turner [587 A.2d 1050], where the Connecticut Appellate Court held:

    "The intent of the actor is a question for the trier of fact, and the conclusion of the trier in this regard should stand unless it is an unreasonable one." *State v. Avcollie*, 178 Conn. 450, 466, 423 A.2d 118 (1979), *cert. denied*, 444 U.S. 1015, 100 S.Ct. 667, 62 L.Ed.2d 645 (1980).

    The jury was free to credit the testimony that the defendant pointed the loaded gun at Russell, pulled the trigger, and that the gun clicked but did not fire. Crediting this testimony, we cannot say that an inference that the defendant intended to inflict serious physical injury on Russell was either unreasonable or illogical. "It was within the province of the [trier] to draw reasonable and logical inferences from the facts proven." *State v. Avcollie*, *supra*, 178 Conn. at 470, 423 A.2d 118. Also, the jury can draw an inference from the facts they found as the result of other inferences. Thus, the evidence presented at trial amply supported the existence of the requisite intent.

    In the 1991 case of *Commonwealth v. Chester* [587 A.2d 1367], the Supreme Court of Pennsylvania held that slashing a victim's throat was sufficient evidence to support a jury's finding that the killing was intentional.

    The crime of theft requires proof of a specific intent to steal, which is almost always proven by inferences drawn from the defendant's conduct. In the case of *Morissette v. United States* [72 S.Ct. 240 (1952)], Morissette took rusted bomb casings that had been lying for years in a wooded area. For all his hard work, Morissette made $84. He was charged with theft and argued that he honestly believed the junk to be abandoned, unwanted, and of no value to the government. The trial judge instructed the jury that the government did not have to prove criminal intent for this crime and refused to allow Morissette's defense of honest mistake of fact. The U.S. Supreme Court reversed the trial judge, ruling that the specific intent to steal must be proven beyond a reasonable doubt and that juries must be properly instructed as to the law.
11. 626 A.2d 1238 (Pa. Super. 1993).

12. The inference that a person who has possession of recently stolen property is the thief is not used in many states. The validity of this inference, however, was tested in the U.S. Supreme Court in 1992. In the case of *Wright v. West* [112 S.Ct. 2482], the defendant was charged with grand larceny for the possession in his home of many household items stolen from another home two to four weeks earlier.

   The defendant was convicted under a Virginia law that permits "an inference that a person who fails to explain, or falsely explains, his exclusive possession of recently stolen property is the thief." The court affirmed the defendant's conviction, holding that the evidence was sufficient to justify the conviction.

   In the 1991 case of *Buchannon v. State* [405 S.E.2d 583 (Ga. App.)], the police stopped the defendant while he was driving a stolen car. The defendant and his passenger both gave false names to the police and had an explanation of the defendant's possession of the stolen car. The Georgia jury did not believe the defendant and convicted him of theft of the car.

   Many prosecutors would not have charged theft in the *West* and *Buchannon* cases. Under the law of most states, crimes such as possession (receiving or concealing) of stolen property and operating a motor vehicle without the consent of the owner are charged because they are much easier to prove.

13. 966 F.2d 707 (1st Cir.).

14. 348 U.S. 121, 139, 75 S.Ct. 127, 137.

15. See, for example, *Cantrell v. Commonwealth*, 329 S.E.2d 22 (Va. S.Ct. 1985).

16. *CHV v. Wisconsin*, 643 N.W.2d 878 (2002), *cert. denied*, 123 S.Ct. 443 (2002).

17. 524 A.2d 575 (R.I. S.Ct. 1987).

18. 590 N.E.2d 1177 (Mass. App.).

19. *Brown v. State*, 837 S.W.2d 457 (Ark.); *In the Interest of N.R.*, 402 S.E.2d 120 (Ga. App.).

20. 586 N.E.2d 1261.

21. 546 A.2d at 419 (D.C. App.).

22. 66 Fd. R. Evid. Serv. 242 (S.D. N.Y. 2005).

23. P.L. 103–322.

24. Federal Rules of Evidence 413(a) and 414(a).

25. 583 N.W.2d 680 (Mich. 1998).

26. 916 F.2d 219 (5th Cir.), *cert. denied*, 500 U.S. 934, 111 S.Ct. 2057 (1991).

27. 780 P.2d 772.

28. *Wainwright v. Greenfield*, 474 U.S. 284 (1986).

29. *Fletcher v. Weir*, 455 U.S. 603 (1982).

30. *United States v. Fruzier*, 408 F.3d 1102 (8th Cir. 2005).

31. 269 F.3d 1023 (9th Cir. 2001).

32. 178 P.3d 1 (Haw. 2008).

33. 582 A.2d 341.

34. 612 A.2d 1349, 52 CrL 1014.

35. 741 F.2d 478 (1st Cir.).

36. 573 A.2d 85.

37. 963 F.2d 708 (5th Cir.).

38. The crime of transfer of an illegal drug also has a higher penalty than the crime of possession of the illegal drug. In the case of *Meek v. Mississippi* [806 So.2d 236 (2002), *cert. denied*, U.S. Supreme Court], it was held that the inference that the defendant knew that marijuana was in a toilet kit he transferred was reasonable and proper. In the *Meek* case, the defendant was injured in a car crash. A passing motorist attempted to help the defendant, and in the course of doing so, the defendant handed the motorist a shaving kit and asked him to "get rid of it." When the police arrived, the motorist gave the kit to them. When the kit was discovered to contain marijuana, the defendant was charged with the crime of transfer of marijuana. The court held that the evidence was sufficient to prove the defendant knew the kit contained illegal drugs when he transferred it to the motorist.

39. 406 S.E.2d 833.

40. 923 F.2d 548 (7th Cir.).

41. 747 F. Supp. 528 (N.D. Iowa).

42. 939 F.2d 1053 (D.C. Cir.).

43. See 18 U.S.C. 1462.

44. 347 F.3d 893 (11th Cir. 2003).

45. 128 S.Ct. 1830 (2008).

46. 18 U.S.C. 2252(A)(a)(3)(B).

47. 563 A.2d 158.

48. 405 S.E.2d 1 (Va. App.).

49. 597 So.2d 721, 50 CrL 1342.

50. 807 P.2d 1009.

51. See 23 CJS, Criminal Law, 917.

52. 393 S.E.2d 781.

53. 262 A.2d 331, 335 (Md. App. 1970).

54. *Commonwealth v. Vogel*, 268 A.2d 89, 102 (Pa. 1970).

55. *Sumpter v. State*, 261 Ind. 471, 306 N.E.2d 95 (1974).

56. 442 U.S. 510, 99 S.Ct. 2450.

WITNESSES AND THE TESTIMONY OF WITNESSES

CHAPTER **5**

QUALIFICATIONS NECESSARY TO BE A WITNESS

witness Person who appears and testifies under oath or affirmation before civil and criminal courts and other hearings.

Witnesses are essential in all cases. Without witnesses, neither civil nor criminal cases could commence.[1] In order to be a **witness**, a person must satisfy the following requirements:

- *Requirement of personal knowledge:* The witness must have some personal knowledge of the matter before the court. If the governor of a state was in a bank at the time it was robbed, he or she could have enough personal knowledge to be subpoenaed if needed as a witness by either the state or the defense. If it is shown that the governor has no personal knowledge of the robbery, however, the governor should not be permitted to testify.
- *Requirement to declare that testimony is truthful:* Most witnesses take an oath swearing that they will tell the truth. However, the Federal Rules of Evidence (Rule 602) and the Uniform Rules of Evidence also provide for an *affirmation*, which, like the oath, requires "every witness ... to declare that he will testify truthfully."

competency The fitness or ability of an individual to participate in legal proceedings.

- *Requirement of competency:* The usual modern standard for determining the **competency** of a witness is: "Competency depends upon the witness' capacity to observe, remember and narrate as well as an understanding of the duty to tell the truth."[2]

THE GENERAL PRESUMPTION THAT ADULTS ARE COMPETENT TO BE WITNESSES

Because the law presumes that adults are competent, most adult witnesses take the witness stand and testify without being challenged. The competency of a witness may be challenged, but the opposing attorney would have the burden of showing that the witness lacked one or more of the required qualifications.

Competency of witnesses can relate both to the ability of the witnesses to testify about the particular event they witnessed and to circumstances that cast doubt on the credibility of that testimony. Thus, a witness whose mental state renders her incapable of comprehending the event about which she seeks to testify can be judged incompetent. An example of this kind of incompetence is a witness who was so intoxicated at the time the witnessed event occurred that the witness lacked the capacity to properly observe and remember the event. Where the witness possessed the capacity to accurately observe the event but subsequently lost the mental faculties necessary to remember and testify about the event, the witness lacks the competence to testify. This could happen where the witness becomes mentally unstable or where some physical condition affects the memory of the witness.

A witness is not normally judged incompetent based on circumstances that affect only the credibility of the witness. Thus, in *United States v. Bedonie*,[3] a witness was not found incompetent to testify simply because the witness had previously made several prior inconsistent statements. Also, in cases where the prosecutor presents testimony by paid informants, the fact that the informant was paid to testify does not usually render the witness incompetent (*United States v. Cresta*[4]). In these cases, the jury can decide what effect, if any, the circumstances should have on the credibility of the testimony given by the witness.

CHILDREN AS WITNESSES

If a young child is called as a witness, the trial judge first questions (voir dire—see below) the child to determine whether the child is competent to testify. The child must be able to remember what occurred, tell about the events, and know that he or she must be truthful. The trial judge then rules on the child's competence as a witness. The judge has broad discretion, and a court of appeals will not disturb the judge's ruling unless there was a clear abuse of that discretion.[5]

The Supreme Court of Arizona traced the history of child witnesses in the 1985 case of *State v. Schossow*,[6] where it was held that four children (aged 7 to 9) were competent to testify:

> At common law no child under fourteen years of age was eligible to testify as a witness. Annot., 81 A.L.R.2d 386, 389–90 (1962). It was not until 1779 that the law renounced the rule of absolute disqualification. In *Rex v. Brasier,* 1 Leach 199, 168 Eng. Rep. 202 (1779), the court held that a child less than seven years old was competent to testify "*provided* such infant appears, *on strict examination by the court,* to possess a sufficient knowledge of the nature and consequences of an oath...." The United States Supreme Court followed the *Brasier* rule in *Wheeler v. United States,* 159 U.S. 523, 16 S.Ct. 93, 40 L.Ed. 244 (1895), and held that a five-year-old child was competent to testify in a criminal trial for murder. The Court stated that the decision of this question rests primarily with the trial judge, who sees the proposed witness, notices his manner, his apparent possession or lack of intelligence, and *may resort to any examination* which will tend to disclose his capacity and intelligence.

The age of the child is important but not determinative. For example, in *Commonwealth v. Monzon,*[7] a 5-year-old child was judged competent to testify in a criminal case, but her 6-year-old sister was not. The older child told the judge she did not know the difference between telling the truth and lying, whereas the younger child was able to make that distinction. Today most states have statutes or court rules that enable children as young as 3 years old to appear as witnesses.

VOIR DIRE

voir dire The preliminary examination of a prospective juror or a child who is going to be a witness to determine qualifications.

The phrase *voir dire* comes from medieval French and roughly means "to speak the truth." The term describes the preliminary examination used to determine whether a witness or juror is competent or qualified.

The voir dire of a young child whom one of the parties seeks to use as a witness is a series of questions to determine whether the child has the perception, memory, and ability to testify as a witness in that case. The voir dire of an expert witness consists of questions to determine whether that person qualifies as an expert. The voir dire of jurors consists of questions to determine whether they are competent and what their interests and biases are. For example, an old friend of the arresting officer or the neighbor of the defendant would not qualify to sit on the jury.

Questioning during the voir dire is often done by the trial judge. However, depending on the law or practice within a state, the questioning may be done by the attorneys.

PROTECTING AND HELPING CHILD VICTIMS AND WITNESSES

Being the victim of a crime is a terrible experience, but the crime itself may be just the beginning of the trauma. The child victim is often grilled repeatedly about the crime by a succession of total strangers (police officers, social workers, lawyers, and others). Court appearances could make the nightmare worse, especially for children who are victims of sex offenses. To protect children and minimize emotional damage, states have enacted statutes to help children in the following ways:

- *Testimony by closed-circuit television:* When a "child [is] suffering serious emotional distress," closed-circuit testimony was allowed by the U.S. Supreme Court in the 1990 case of *Maryland v. Craig* [497 U.S. 836, 842, 110 S.Ct. 3157, 3162], where this procedure was approved under a Maryland statute. The trial court found that the child witnesses were so traumatized that they could not "reasonably communicate." The Supreme Court held in *Craig* that the face-to-face right to confront an accusing witness is not absolute and "must occasionally give way to considerations of public policy and the necessities of the case." More than thirty states have statutes permitting this procedure when it is shown to be needed.
- *Videotaped testimony:* In criminal child abuse proceedings, videotapes are used in more than thirty-five states.
- *Statutes making it easier for children to be found competent to testify:* Such statutes have been enacted in all states to enable children as young as 3 years of age to appear as witnesses.
- *Special hearsay exceptions for child victims and child witnesses:* These have been enacted by more than thirty states. Such statutes and the regular hearsay exceptions (see Chapter 8) make it easier for adults such as teachers, neighbors, and parents to testify about

statements made by child victims. However, the Supreme Court's decision in *Washington v. Crawford*, discussed in Chapter 8 of this book, may limit the admissibility of some child hearsay. In *State v. Hopkins* [154 P.3d 250 (Wash. App. 2007)], the court concluded that a 3-year-old's statements to relatives could be admitted but that her statements to a social worker were inadmissible.

Other statutes that seek to help and protect children include the following:

- *Use of anatomical dolls in criminal child abuse cases:* These dolls make it easier for child witnesses because they can point to body parts as they testify. Some states have statutes, while others use the practice as part of accepted court procedure.
- *Closing the courtroom to all but necessary parties:* Fewer people in the courtroom make a child victim or witness feel more comfortable while testifying. Many judges have this power; some states have statutes.
- *Use of leading questions with child witnesses:* Most state judges can permit this, and a few states now have statutes authorizing it.
- *Limiting the length of time a child is on the witness stand:* A few states have statutes, but judges in all states may limit cross-examination under their broad discretion in the conduct of criminal and civil trials.
- *Limiting the number of interviews with child victims:* In 1992 a California grand jury reported that some child victims were interviewed as many as thirty-two times. California and other states now have statutes limiting the number of interviews.
- *Statutes requiring speedy handling of cases involving child victims:* These have been enacted by more than half of the states.

FALSE MEMORY OR "TAINT"

When children testify as victims in criminal trials, particularly in sexual offenses, the defendant sometimes challenges the child's competency to testify based on a theory called "false memory" or "taint." (The related false memory syndrome is discussed in note 57 of this chapter.) The basis of a taint claim was stated by the Pennsylvania Supreme Court in *Commonwealth v. Delbridge* [855 A.2d 27, 35 (2003)] as follows:

> Taint is the implantation of false memories or the distortion of real memories caused by interview techniques of law enforcement, social service personnel, and other interested adults, that are so unduly suggestive and coercive as to infect the memory of the child, rendering that child incompetent to testify.

Defendants asserting the taint claim attempt to exclude a child's testimony based on these factors, claiming the taint results in the child testifying not to what actually happened but to what was suggested to the child. Some courts permit a defendant to subject a child witness to a competency hearing to explore the taint claim,[a] while others do not, on the theory that taint goes only to credibility, not competency.[b]

Where taint hearings are permitted, additional questions arise about the admissibility of expert testimony and about whether a child witness has or has not been "tainted" by interrogation techniques. Some courts exclude expert testimony on taint, finding that there is inadequate scientific foundation to support the theory (see Chapter 18). Other courts exclude it because the expert testimony improperly enhances the child's testimony—called "vouching"—or addresses the credibility of the testimony, which should be the function of the jury.

[a]See, for example, *State v. Michaels*, 642 A.2d 1372 (N.J. 1992).
[b]For example, *Pendleton v. Kentucky*, 83 S.W.3d 522 (Ky. 2002).

CREDIBILITY OF WITNESSES

METHODS USED TO KEEP WITNESSES HONEST

Witnesses have a serious responsibility to tell the truth. To encourage witnesses to tell the truth and to bring before the court and the jury the facts pertaining to the issues of the case, the following procedures are used:

- Witnesses must take an oath or affirmation that they will tell the truth.
- Witnesses must be personally present at the trial (the defendant's Sixth Amendment right to confront witnesses must be ensured).[8]
- Witnesses are subject to cross-examination.

In addition, witnesses who do not tell the truth run the risk of being charged with *perjury*. If they refuse to testify or refuse to answer questions that are not privileged, they could be found in *contempt of court* and punished.

CREDIBILITY AND THE WEIGHT OF EVIDENCE

It is up to a judge or jury, as the trier of fact, to determine whether statements made by witnesses are to be believed and what weight to give them. In determining the credibility and the weight to be given to the testimony of witnesses, the following factors should be considered:

- *Perception:* Did the witness perceive (see, hear, smell, and so on) accurately? Did the witness have an opportunity to observe and perceive?
- *Memory:* Has the witness retained an accurate impression of what the witness saw, heard, smelled, and so on? Is the witness' memory of the events accurate?
- *Narration by the witness:* Do the testimony of the witness and the language used accurately describe the events?

In determining the weight and the credit to be given to the testimony of each witness, juries and judges as the triers of fact also use their knowledge and experience. Witness statements that are incredible or contrary to commonly known facts do not have to be accepted. The *incontrovertible physical facts rule* (also known as the *physical facts rule*) holds that the fact-finding body will give no weight to witness statements that are inherently incredible, unbelievable, and contrary to physical facts, known physical laws, general knowledge, or human experience.[9]

The reasonableness of witnesses' testimony, their interest or lack of interest in the results of the trial, their bias or prejudice (if any is shown), their clearness or lack of clearness of recollection, and the overall impression obtained by the jury are factors used in determining the weight and credit to be given to the testimony of a witness.

In a jury trial, the jury is the sole judge of the credibility of all witnesses, including the defendant if he or she takes the witness stand. The jury evaluates the weight and credibility of testimony, free from the influence of the trial judge.

EYEWITNESS TESTIMONY

The testimony of an eyewitness to a crime is usually important to both the prosecution and the defendant. If the testimony is credible, the jury is likely to give it great weight. Because eyewitnesses can, and often do, make a mistaken identification (see Chapter 13), though, state and federal courts have developed standards for evaluating eyewitness testimony. In the federal courts, the case of *Neil v. Biggers*,[10] discussed in Chapter 13, states that the test is the likelihood of "irreparable misidentification." The *Neil* court said that factors to be considered when evaluating the likelihood of misidentification are the opportunity of the witness to view the criminal at the time of the crime, the witness' degree of attention, the accuracy of the witness' prior description of the criminal, the witness' level of certainty, and the length of time between the identification and the crime.

Many states have adopted similar rules. For example, in *State v. Hollen*,[11] the Utah Supreme Court held that the eyewitness testimony of four victims of a robbery at an amusement park was reliable and admissible. The court stated that under the Utah Constitution, unreliable eyewitness testimony is not admissible. Reliability of an eyewitness identification depends on five factors, the court stated:

1. The opportunity of the witness to view the actor during the event

THE JURY TRIAL OF WILLIAM PENN

An important case in the historical development of the power and authority of the jury to independently determine the credibility of witnesses and the weight to be given to their testimony occurred in London in 1670. William Penn (the founder of Pennsylvania) was a peaceful and nonviolent man who was charged with preaching to an unlawful assembly. The basis for the charge was that Penn had addressed his religious group in an orderly church meeting in London. Penn was not of the same religious faith as the king of England. After the trial, the jury refused to convict Penn. They were ordered to reconsider their finding but continued to refuse to convict. The jury was held for two days without food, water, or other accommodations (a fire and a chamber pot, which they had requested). When this did not break them, they were finally released, after being fined for holding to their verdict of not guilty. A plaque can be found today in the Old Bailey (the central criminal justice building in London) commemorating the "courage and endurance" of that jury. An appellate court sustained Penn and the jury in a writ of habeas corpus, holding that juries were not to be punished for failing to make findings as ordered by the trial court.

The Right to and the Purpose of a Jury Today

The Sixth Amendment of the U.S. Constitution provides that: "In all criminal prosecutions, the accused shall enjoy the right to ... an impartial jury of the State and district wherein the crime shall have been committed...."

> The purpose of a jury is to make available the commonsense judgment of the community as a hedge against the overzealous or mistaken prosecutor [*Taylor v. Louisiana* (1975), 419 U.S. 522, 530].... It is the jury's duty to assess the credibility of witnesses and to weigh the evidence in determining a defendant's guilt or innocence. [See, e.g., *Glasser v. United States* (1942), 315 U.S. 60, 80.]

2. The witness' degree of attention to the actor at the time of the event
3. The witness' capacity to observe the event, including his or her physical and mental acuity
4. Whether the witness' identification was made spontaneously and remained consistent thereafter, or whether it was the product of suggestion
5. The nature of the event being observed and the likelihood that the witness would perceive, remember, and relate it correctly

DEMEANOR AS EVIDENCE IN DETERMINING WITNESS CREDIBILITY

Not only are the words of the witness evidence in a trial, but the demeanor of the witness also has been held to be evidence that may be used in determining credibility. In everyday life, we judge other people not only by what they say but also to some extent by their appearances and their conduct. Judge Learned Hand's ruling in the 1952 case of *Dyer v. MacDougall*[12] is sometimes quoted by other courts:

It is true that the carriage, behavior, bearing, manner and appearance of a witness—in short, his "demeanor"—is a part of the evidence. The words used are by no means all that we rely on in making up our minds about the truth of a question that arises in our ordinary affairs, and it is abundantly settled that a jury is as little confined to them as we are. They may, and indeed they should, take into consideration the whole nexus of sense impressions which they get from a witness....

In the 1991 case of *Michigan v. Sammons*,[13] a Michigan court of appeals held that permitting an informant to wear a ski mask at a hearing on whether entrapment occurred violated the defendant's Sixth Amendment right to confront the witness. The court held that the mask prevented the judge from observing the informer's demeanor and adequately assessing his credibility. The U.S. Supreme Court denied review of the case.[14] In the 2004 Texas case of *Romero v. State*,[15] the court reversed a defendant's assault conviction because a key witness was permitted to testify with sunglasses, a baseball hat, and an upturned coat collar. The witness told prosecutors he was frightened to testify in the defendant's presence and would do so only if permitted to wear a disguise. The court of appeals held that the disguise attached improper drama and emphasis to the testimony and forced the defendant to ask the witness why he was wearing a disguise, thereby prejudicing the jury against the defendant.

CONSTITUTIONAL RIGHTS OF DEFENDANTS REGARDING WITNESSES

THE RIGHT TO COMPEL THE ATTENDANCE OF WITNESSES

The Sixth Amendment of the U.S. Constitution provides that "In all criminal prosecutions, the accused shall enjoy the right ... to have compulsory process for obtaining witnesses in his favor." To ensure the attendance of a witness, a subpoena must be issued. A **subpoena** is a command to the person to whom it is directed to appear on a specified date at a given time and place for the purpose of testifying. In addition, the person may be required to bring documents or other materials that are expected to be useful in the proceedings. A **subpoena duces tecum** describes the material that the witness is to bring.

subpoena An order compelling a person to appear as a witness; defense lawyers and prosecutors may have subpoenas issued for witnesses needed in either criminal or civil cases.

The right to the compulsory process to obtain the attendance of witnesses does not mean that the defendant can subpoena anyone at all in order to delay the case and to make the trial a cumbersome process. Only competent witnesses who have a personal knowledge of facts relevant to the case may be subpoenaed.

THE RIGHT TO CONFRONT AND CROSS-EXAMINE WITNESSES

subpoena duces tecum A subpoena that not only requires the appearance of a witness but also requires the witness to bring relevant and competent documents or writings that may be in his or her possession.

The Sixth Amendment also provides that "The accused shall enjoy the right ... to be confronted with the witnesses against him." The witness not only testifies in open court in the presence of the accused but is also subject to cross-examination by the opposing party.

The U.S. Supreme Court has pointed out that for centuries cross-examination has been considered to be one of the safeguards of the accuracy and completeness of testimony by a witness. The Court held in the 1974 case of *Davis v. Alaska*[16] that:

Cross-examination is the principal means by which the believability of a witness and the truth of his testimony are tested. Subject always to the broad discretion of a trial judge to preclude repetitive and unduly harassing interrogation, the cross-examiner is not only permitted to delve into the witness' story to test the witness' perceptions and memory, but the cross-examiner has traditionally been allowed to impeach, i.e., discredit, the witness. One way of discrediting the witness is to introduce evidence of a prior criminal conviction of that witness. By so doing the cross-examiner intends to afford the jury a basis to infer that the witness' character is such that he would be less likely than the average trustworthy citizen to be truthful in his testimony. The introduction of evidence of a prior crime is thus a general attack on the credibility of the witness. A more particular attack on the witness' credibility is effected by means of cross-examination directed toward revealing possible biases, prejudices, or ulterior motives of the witness as they may relate directly to issues or personalities in the case at hand. The partiality of a witness is subject to exploration at trial.... We have recognized that the exposure of a witness' motivation in testifying is a proper and important function of the constitutionally protected right of cross-examination.

There are situations where the right of cross-examination has been limited—for example, when the child victim of a sexual assault is called to testify, discussed earlier in this chapter. When a defendant elects to exercise his Sixth Amendment right to represent himself in a criminal trial,[17] trial courts have sometimes limited his cross-examination rights, as the following case illustrates.

THE DEFENDANT'S RIGHT TO TESTIFY IN HIS OR HER DEFENSE

Defendants have a right to testify in their own behalf. As the U.S. Supreme Court pointed out in the 1987 case of *Rock v. Arkansas*,[18] this right is derived from the Sixth and Fourteenth Amendments. The Supreme Court held that the right "is essential to due process of law in a fair adversary process."

Under the old common law, defendants in criminal cases were not considered competent to appear as witnesses in their own trial.[19] Today all defendants are considered competent to take the witness stand in their own behalf.

Partin v. Commonwealth

Supreme Court of Kentucky, 2005 WL 1183158 (2005)

A defendant was charged with kidnapping and other acts of domestic violence against his wife and children. The defendant elected to conduct his own defense, and the court appointed "stand-by counsel" to assist the defendant. During the trial the defendant's family members were called upon by the prosecution to testify concerning the defendant's actions. The defendant attempted to cross-examine the family witnesses, but the trial court refused to permit him to do so, because a victim's advocacy group advised the court that the wife and children were terrified of the defendant and would be afraid to testify if he confronted them. The court directed the stand-by counsel to conduct the cross-examination, using questions prepared by the defendant. The defendant was convicted and appealed, claiming his Sixth Amendment right to defend himself was violated.

On appeal, the Kentucky Supreme Court affirmed the conviction. It held that as long as the defendant had the opportunity to conduct his own defense in his own way, the Sixth Amendment was satisfied. Where evidence supported the trial court's belief that the defendant's intimidating presence during questioning would adversely affect the witnesses, requiring the defendant to ask his questions through the stand-by counsel did not deprive him of that opportunity, the court held. The dissent argued that though other courts have limited the right of a defendant personally to cross-examine witnesses [for example, *Fields v. Murray*, 49 F.3d 1024 (4th Cir. 1995)], those cases all involved child witnesses who were victims of child abuse. Limiting cross-examination in those cases is justified for the well-being of the child. However, the dissent said, such a limitation should not be applied in other settings.

However, defendants who take the witness stand to testify in their behalf waive their right to remain silent and must answer questions on cross-examination. Because of the danger of cross-examination and the risk of impeachment, defense lawyers in most instances strongly urge their clients not to risk testifying in their own defense, pointing out the additional danger that a defendant's testimony may "open the door to otherwise inadmissible evidence which is damaging to the case."[20]

In the 1993 case of *United States v. Dunnigan*,[21] the U.S. Supreme Court unanimously and bluntly held that "a defendant's right to testify does not include a right to commit perjury." It is not perjury for a defendant to enter a not guilty plea and then be found guilty. But it is perjury for a defendant to take the witness stand and lie in a material way. The Supreme Court stated in the *Dunnigan* case that a "defendant who commits a crime and perjures herself in an unlawful attempt to avoid responsibility is more threatening to society and less deserving of leniency than a defendant who does not defy the trial process."[22]

TYPES OF WITNESSES AND OPINION EVIDENCE

ORDINARY WITNESSES AND EXPERT WITNESSES

ordinary witnesses
Witnesses who have firsthand information about a fact gained by personal observation.

Most witnesses are **ordinary** (or **lay**) **witnesses** who are called to testify about the firsthand information they have regarding the case before the court. Their testimony is typically limited to what they have seen, heard (although hearsay is in most instances excluded), smelled, felt, and, on rare occasions, tasted. Law enforcement officers appear in most instances as ordinary witnesses, although some officers also appear as expert witnesses when they qualify, testifying about fingerprinting, traffic matters, weapons, and so on.

expert witness
A witness who has special knowledge or training in a specialized area.

An **expert witness** is a person who has had special training, education, or experience. Because of this experience and background, the expert witness may be able to assist the jury and the court in resolving the issues before them. The party that offers a witness as an expert must lay a foundation (that is, ask a series of questions) establishing the witness as an expert in the field in which the expert will testify and offer opinions.

Three questions are presented to a trial court when one of the parties seeks to introduce an expert witness:

- Is the subject on which the expert witness will testify one for which the court can receive the opinion of an expert?
- What qualifications are necessary to qualify the witness as an expert?
- Does the witness meet these qualifications?

When there is a subject on which an expert witness may testify, the trial judge has to determine whether the expert testimony is reliable enough to admit into evidence. The trial judge is given a great deal of latitude and discretion in determining whether a witness qualifies as an expert witness.

In recent years the U.S. Supreme Court has adopted new standards to be used in federal courts for the admissibility of scientific evidence and supporting expert testimony. These standards are discussed extensively in Chapter 18 of this book.

Terry Joe Franklin, a forensic science supervisor for the Washington State Patrol Crime Lab in Tacoma, Washington, identified a .45 SIG-Sauer pistol during his testimony as an expert witness in the penalty phase of the trial of convicted sniper John Allen Muhammad. Muhammad was convicted of capital murder for his role as organizer of a two-man sniper team that killed 10 people and terrorized the Washington, D.C., area.

© Dave Ellis/Pool/Corbis

To qualify as an expert in some fields (such as a medical expert) requires years of formal education, training, and a license. Other subjects, such as fingerprinting or handwriting analysis, require other qualifications. Rule 702 of the Federal Rules of Evidence provides that:

> If scientific, technical, or other specialized knowledge will assist the trier of fact to understand the evidence or to determine a fact in issue, a witness qualified as an expert by knowledge, skill, experience, training, or education, may testify thereto in the form of an opinion or otherwise, if (1) the testimony is based upon sufficient facts or data, (2) the testimony is the product of reliable principles and methods, and (3) the witness has applied the principles and methods reliably to the facts of the case.[23]

In discussing the qualifications necessary to be a handwriting expert, the court in the 1938 case of *First Galesburg National Bank & Trust Company v. Federal Reserve Bank*[24] stated that:

> There is no test by which it can be determined with mathematical certainty how much experience or knowledge of handwriting a witness must have in order to qualify as an expert for comparison.... In order that a witness be competent as an expert in respect to handwriting, it is not necessary that he should belong to any particular calling or profession; it is only necessary that the business opportunities and intelligence of the witness should be such as to enable him to have reasonable skill in judging of handwriting.

In the 1973 case of *Miller v. California*,[25] the U.S. Supreme Court held that a police officer qualified as an expert witness to "community standards" in an obscenity case, stating that:

> The record simply does not support appellant's contention, belatedly raised on appeal, that the State's expert was unqualified to give evidence on California "community standards." The expert, a police officer with many years of specialization in obscenity offenses, had conducted an extensive statewide survey and had given expert evidence on 26 occasions in the year prior to this trial. Allowing such expert testimony was certainly not constitutional error.

It is the fact finder (jury or judge) who determines the weight and credibility to be given to the testimony of both expert and ordinary witnesses.

OPINION EVIDENCE BY ORDINARY WITNESSES

An ordinary witness is qualified to testify because of firsthand knowledge of an issue before the court. The expert witness has something different to contribute in assisting the trier of fact. Neither type of witness is permitted to give an opinion as to whether the defendant is guilty or innocent. This determination is made by the fact finder, based on the evidence presented.

The testimony of ordinary witnesses usually consists of statements about the facts in a case that have been observed firsthand but may also include opinions and conclusions about common things that are within the knowledge of the average person. An opinion that the defendant was intoxicated or angry, for example, or as to the value of his property that was stolen or destroyed would be allowed. Rule 701 of the Federal Rules of Evidence provides that:

> If the witness is not testifying as an expert, his testimony in the form of opinions or inferences is limited to those opinions or inferences which are (a) rationally based on the perception of the witness and (b) helpful to a clear understanding of his testimony or the determination of a fact in issue.

A witness' knowledge of the defendant can support an opinion. In the 2008 case of *Dawson v. State*,[26] an ordinary witness was allowed to give his opinion about the identity of a suspected murderer captured on a video surveillance camera. Because the witness knew the defendant at the time the video was made, and because the defendant had changed his physical characteristics between that time and the time of trial, the witness was allowed to give his opinion that based on gestures and manner of speaking, the defendant was the person in the video. Similarly, if it is shown that an ordinary witness is well acquainted with a defendant's or another person's handwriting, that witness could be qualified to testify regarding the handwriting.[27]

Ordinary witnesses who are drug users, or who are well acquainted with drugs or guns, could be held qualified by a trial court to testify about the identity of drugs[28] or guns and ammunition.[29] Where there was sufficient foundation to justify a deputy sheriff's opinion about the cause of a snowmobile accident, the judgment in the civil case of *Cline v. Durden*[30] was affirmed in 1990.

The Federal Rules of Evidence provide that an ordinary witness may express an opinion that is "rationally based on the perception of the witness" (Rule 701). Under this type of rule, ordinary witnesses expressed opinions concerning in-

WITNESSES AND THEIR TESTIMONY

In order to qualify as a witness, a person:

- Must have relevant information
- Must be competent
- Must declare that he or she will testify truthfully

To be competent, a witness:

- Must be able to remember and tell what happened
- Must be able to distinguish fact from fantasy
- Must know that he or she must tell the truth

In evaluating a witness' testimony, the fact finder should consider:

- Accuracy of perception
- Accuracy of memory and recall
- Accuracy of narration

Anglo-Saxon law seeks to keep witnesses honest by having them testify:

- Under oath or affirmation
- In the presence of the fact finder and the accused
- Subject to cross-examination
- Subject to possible perjury charges for failure to tell the truth

Methods used to help forgetful witnesses include:

- Jogging the memory by questions such as What else happened at this point?
- Handing reports, notes, files, and so on to the witness to refresh his or her memory
- Introducing the documents as evidence if refreshing memory does not work and documents exist

---

sanity,[31] intoxication,[32] drug impairment,[33] the speed of a vehicle,[34] the time of death (testified to by a lieutenant in a fire department),[35] and the difficulty in interviewing a child witness (testified to by a police officer).[36]

When a witness testifies that the defendant was drunk, or looked surprised, or "seemed like he was trying to break my neck," the witness is using a "shorthand way" of collecting facts and expressing opinions about what the witness saw or experienced. Trial courts have considerable discretion and generally will permit such opinions.[37]

For example, in the 2001 case of *United States v. Bogan*,[38] the Seventh Circuit Court of Appeals permitted a lay witness to testify that based on his perception of the nature of an assault, he believed the defendants were trying to kill the victim. The defendants were convicted of assault with intent to commit serious bodily harm based on this and other evidence.

Here is another example of a court decision approving the use of opinion evidence by an ordinary witness.

Haycraft v. State

Indiana Court of Appeals, 760 N.E.2d 203 (2002), *trans. denied* (2003)

During the summer of 2000, a 12-year-old boy and his 8-year-old brother stayed at the home of their grandfather, the defendant. The defendant resided at his home with another man, his life partner. The defendant's ex-wife believed the defendant was abusing the boys and contacted the police. A police detective, Charles Scarber, investigated the case, and ultimately the defendant was charged with four counts of felony child molesting.

At the defendant's trial, Scarber testified that child molesters "groom" their intended victims by gradually introducing them to sexually explicit materials and sexual contact before having sex with them, all actions taken by the defendant in this case. Based on this evidence and testimony by the victims, as well as the defendant's own statements, the defendant was convicted of child molestation and sentenced to 190 years in prison. The defendant appealed, contending among other things that the trial court erred by permitting the police detective to testify about the "grooming" habits of child molesters. The appeals court disagreed, stating that under Rule 701 of the Indiana Rules of Evidence (the same rule as Rule 701 of the Federal Rules of Evidence) the detective's opinion was based on his own perceptions and was one that a reasonable person could reach on the perceived facts and was thus admissible. The court affirmed the conviction, though it reduced the sentence to 150 years.

DIRECT EXAMINATION OF WITNESSES

In criminal cases, the government has the burden of proving the charges made against the defendant beyond a reasonable doubt. The state also has the burden of coming forward first with evidence showing that the defendant committed the offenses with which she is charged. Therefore, the first witnesses to appear in criminal cases are government witnesses called by the prosecutor to support the state's case.

In most instances, the government's case is presented by testimony about the chronological order of events as they occurred. Usually an attempt is made to let the witness tell his or her story first with as few interruptions as possible, by using such questions as:

- Where were you on the night of June 23?
- Will you tell the court and jury what you saw and heard at that time?

direct examination Questioning of a witness by the lawyer who subpoenaed the witness.

The question-and-answer method is used in American courtrooms so that the opposing lawyer may object to the question before the answer is in evidence. However, by the use of short general questions `such as What did you see?, What did you do?, and What happened next?, the witness is able to tell the story and at the same time is kept to the point. After the witness has presented a general account of the facts as known to the witness, through **direct examination**, the prosecutor may go back and fill in or emphasize details with more specific questions.

CROSS-EXAMINATION OF WITNESSES

cross-examined Re-examination of a witness by the opposing attorney following the direct examination of the witness.

After the direct examination, the witness may be **cross-examined** by the opposing attorney. For centuries, cross-examination has been considered one of the essential safeguards of the accuracy and completeness of testimony given by a witness. The U.S. Supreme Court held in the 1974 case of *Davis v. Alaska*[39] that:

Cross-examination is the principal means by which the believability of a witness and the truth of his testimony are tested. Subject always to the broad discretion of a trial judge to preclude repetitive and unduly harassing interrogation, the cross-examiner is not only permitted to delve into the witness' story to test the witness' perceptions and

THE USE OF FALSEHOODS TO IMPEACH KEY WITNESSES IN CRIMINAL TRIALS

In both civil and criminal cases, lawyers look for ways to impeach key witnesses who testify against their clients. Law enforcement officers are often important key witnesses in criminal cases, and efforts by the defense are sometimes made to obtain material that could be used to embarrass or impeach the officer.

In the 1959 case of *Napue v. Illinois* [360 U.S. 264], the U.S. Supreme Court held that "... guilt or innocence of an accused may turn on the credibility of witnesses at their trial ... (therefore) due process requires the government to disclose to a defendant information regarding witness credibility prior to trial."

A November 2003 *FBI Law Enforcement Bulletin* article, "The Discovery Process and Personnel File Information," discussed this aspect of discovery, and noted that "a single lie can taint an officer's credibility forever and render the officer virtually useless as a witness." The article used the following case examples to illustrate penalties that might follow from a failure to make the necessary disclosures:

Case or Incident	Failure to Disclose	Resulting Action
Conviction of 38 defendants for drug violations in Tulia, Texas, as reported in the *Washington Post,* June 17, 2003	The prosecutor failed to disclose that the lead investigator had previously "falsified reports (that) ... misidentified various defendants during his investigation."	All 38 convictions were vacated.
U.S. Supreme Court case of *Napue v. Illinois* [360 U.S. 264 (1959)]	A witness falsely testified at trial that he had not received any consideration for his testimony. The prosecution did nothing to correct the falsehood.	The defendant's murder conviction was reversed. The Court held that the use of false evidence violated due process.
U.S. Supreme Court case of *Giglio v. United States* [405 U.S. 150 (1972)]	A key witness testified at trial that he received nothing for his testimony against the defendant, even though he had been promised leniency by another attorney in the federal prosecutor's office.	The Court held that the earlier promise should have been disclosed to the defendant.

memory, but the cross-examiner has traditionally been allowed to impeach, i.e., discredit, the witness.

The most effective defense to cross-examination is for a witness to testify truthfully and simply in answering all questions, even though the answers may sometimes be embarrassing or harmful. The purposes of cross-examination are:

- To test the "believability of a witness and the truth of his testimony" (the U.S. Supreme Court in *Davis v. Alaska*)
- To bring out facts that support the cross-examiner's case
- To impeach (discredit) the witness (which also is a means of testing the "believability of a witness and the truth of his testimony")

If a witness has not hurt the opposing party's case, there usually is no reason to cross-examine unless there is a possibility of bringing out facts that might help the case of the cross-examiner.

Cross-examination is often exploratory, and for that reason it is risky: Facts uncovered in cross-examination could hurt the cross-examiner's case. In the 1931 case of *Alford v. United States*,[40] the U.S. Supreme Court stated that:

> Counsel often cannot know in advance what pertinent facts may be elicited on cross-examination. For that reason it is necessarily exploratory; and the rule that the examiner must indicate the purpose of his inquiry does not, in general, apply. It is the essence of a fair trial that reasonable latitude be given the cross-examiner, even though he is unable to state to the court what facts a reasonable cross-examination might develop. Prejudice ensues from a denial of the opportunity to place the witness in his proper setting and put the weight of his testimony and his credibility to a test, without which the jury cannot fairly appraise them.

impeachment
Calling into question the truth or accuracy of direct testimony by cross-examination or introduction of contradictory evidence.

Impeachment is another aspect of cross-examination, and in criminal cases it is probably the most effective cross-examination technique. By using impeachment, "the cross-examiner intends to afford the jury a basis to infer that the witness' character is such that he would be less likely than the average trustworthy citizen to be truthful in his testimony."[41] Impeachment may be accomplished by cross-examination and also by the introduction of other evidence. The functions of impeachment may be classified as follows:

1. To attack the witness' credibility and qualifications to testify truthfully because of prior criminal conviction (and in some jurisdictions and some instances, a showing of prior bad conduct). Rule 609 of the Federal Rules of Evidence limits evidence of prior criminal convictions to crimes with a penalty in excess of one year of imprisonment, or crimes involving dishonesty or false statement, regardless of the punishment.

   Examples

   - Evidence of a witness' conviction of assault was admissible to attack the witness' credibility, where the punishment was more than one year in prison.[42]
   - Evidence of a witness' conviction of a misdemeanor offense of receiving stolen property was not admissible because the punishment was less than one year imprisonment, and the crime of receiving stolen property does not automatically involve dishonesty or false statement.[43]

2. To attack the testimony given by the witness on direct examination by a showing of prior inconsistent statements.

   Example

   In a prosecution related to a defendant's alleged spousal abuse, prior inconsistent statements made by the witness (defendant's wife) about the nature of the abuse were admissible on the witness' credibility.[44]

3. To attack the witness' credibility by showing bias, prejudice, or ulterior motives of the witness.

Rule 611(a) of the Federal Rules of Evidence states that the "court shall exercise reasonable control over the mode and order of interrogating witnesses and presenting evidence so as to ... avoid needless consumption of time, and ... protect witnesses from harassment or undue embarrassment." In the 1988 case of *Olden v. Kentucky*,[45] the U.S. Supreme Court again pointed out that trial judges

AN EXAMPLE OF EFFECTIVE CROSS-EXAMINATION

In 1984 former car maker John DeLorean was indicted for drug trafficking. In his California trial, which lasted five months, DeLorean did not take the witness stand in his own defense. It was through lengthy cross-examination of government witnesses that evidence supporting DeLorean's defense of entrapment was made part of the trial record. Through cross-examination, lawyers for DeLorean were able to show that potential evidence was destroyed, that investigative guidelines of the government agency were violated, and that government agents failed to keep a proper rein on their paid informant. When DeLorean backed out of the drug deal because of a lack of cash, it was government agents who called him back, suggesting the use of collateral. When the government's chief prosecutor and the drug agents had drinks together, the defense presented the meeting as a boozy celebration of DeLorean's imminent arrest. On cross-examination, government agents admitted that they speculated about whether they would make the cover of *Time* magazine.

With this evidence on the trial record as the result of cross-examination, the jury found DeLorean not guilty of all eight criminal charges after seven days of deliberation. The decision to not put DeLorean on the witness stand and subject him to lengthy cross-examination was probably not made until after the defense saw how successful their cross-examinations had been.

have "broad discretion … to preclude repetitive and unduly harassing interrogation." In the 1987 case of *Kentucky v. Stincer*,[46] the Supreme Court held that the "Confrontation Clause guarantees only 'an *opportunity* for effective cross-examination, not cross-examination that is effective in whatever way, and to whatever extent, the defense might wish.'"

OBJECTIONS TO QUESTIONS

objections Formal statements made by attorneys during trials, objecting to the form or substance of a question or to the answer given by a witness to a question.

Under the adversary system, **objections** to questions are the first line of defense against statements the opposing party seeks to use. It is the lawyers who must object, not the judge. Failure to object, in most instances, waives the grounds for an appeal to a higher court.

The trial judge has considerable discretion in ruling on objections and in determining what is relevant, material, and competent. The trial judge will not be overruled by a higher court unless there is an abuse of discretion or plain error.

Objections are classified as follows:

- *Objections to the substance of the question:* These objections concern the answer called for by the question. Usual objections in this area are irrelevant, immaterial, incompetent, and hearsay.
- *Objections to the form of the question:* These objections concern the manner in which the question is worded. In most instances, the question may be rephrased and asked again in a form in which both the question and answer are

OBJECTIONS TO QUESTIONS

Objections to the Form of the Question

- Leading question (suggests the answer that is wanted)
- Calls for speculation
- Argumentative
- Misstates facts in evidence
- Assumes facts not in evidence
- Vague and ambiguous
- Repetitive or cumulative
- Misleading

Objections to the Substance of the Question

- Irrelevant
- Immaterial

- Incompetent
- Calls for hearsay
- Insufficient foundation
- Calls for inadmissible opinion answer
- Beyond the scope of the direct examination

Objections to the Answer

- Unresponsive
- Inadmissible opinion
- Inadmissible hearsay statement

admissible. Usual objections to the form of a question are that the question is leading, argumentative, calls for speculation, or misstates a fact in evidence.

- *Objections to the answer:* If an attorney is slow in objecting, the attorney usually pays the penalty and is told to object faster. In this situation and others, a lawyer can object to an answer and ask that the answer be stricken from the record because: (1) the answer is unresponsive to the question (most often when the witness volunteers additional information beyond the scope of the question asked), (2) the answer contains an inadmissible opinion, or (3) the answer includes inadmissible hearsay statements.

THE REQUIREMENTS OF RELEVANCY, MATERIALITY, AND COMPETENCY

Criminal and civil trials would be much longer if there were no controls on the testimony and information allowed. Unrelated evidence would cause confusion and clutter the fact-finding process. To minimize confusion and to make trials manageable, all evidence must be **relevant, material, and competent**. Therefore, to introduce facts, testimony, or a physical object as evidence, it must be shown that:

relevant, material, and competent Evidence that will affect the result of a trial.

- The evidence addresses a material fact.
- The evidence is relevant to that fact.
- The evidence is able to affect the probable truth or falsity of that fact by being competent.

A fact is *material* if it will affect the result of a trial. For example, a defendant is charged with a crime committed in a tavern at ten o'clock at night. State witnesses testifying that they saw the defendant in a tavern at that time are relevant and material. Defense witnesses testifying that the defendant was at another place five miles away are also relevant and material to the fact in issue.

Evidence is *relevant* if it has a tendency to make a material fact more or less probable. Testimony by a witness that he saw the defendant in the tavern at ten o'clock is relevant evidence. However, testimony that the tavern was hit by lightning and burned down a week later is not relevant because the fire is not material to the case. These questions must be asked:

- Is the fact material to the dispute?
- If so, does the proposed evidence make the material evidence more or less probable (relevant)?

After our hypothetical witness has testified that the defendant was in the tavern at the time the crime was committed, the questioning continues:

Q: Were you in the tavern that night?

A: No, I wasn't.

Q: How do you know the defendant was in the tavern?

A: John told me.

The testimony is relevant to the material issue in dispute, but it is not *competent* because the personal knowledge foundation required by Federal Rule of Evidence 602 has not been satisfied. However, changing the example slightly makes the testimony competent:

Q: How do you know the defendant was in the tavern?

A: The defendant told me he was in the tavern.

Since the defendant is the opposing party in the criminal action, the matter about which the witness has personal knowledge is the defendant's incriminating admission. The testimony is now competent, relevant, and material. It is not forbidden by the hearsay rule.

REDIRECT EXAMINATION AND RECROSS-EXAMINATION

After the cross-examination, the lawyer who produced the witness may conduct a redirect examination of the witness. Questions on redirect examination are generally limited to new matters drawn out during cross-examination and in refuting and explaining impeachment issues. The purposes of redirect examination are as follows:

- To restore the credibility of a witness who has been impeached on cross-examination by explanations of matters on which the cross-examiner sought to impeach the witness. Questions such as these may be asked: Officer Smith, why did you ...? and Officer Smith, what did you mean when you stated ...?
- To restore the credibility of a witness by pointing out prior consistent statements when the impeachment was made by means of prior inconsistent statements.

During the redirect examination, additional witnesses may be used to rebut the cross-examination and assist in rehabilitation. New evidence may also be presented if the cross-examiner has opened the door to new matters.

Recross-examination is the fourth and usually the last stage of the examination of the witness. With many witnesses, the questioning is completed before reaching this stage. The recross-examination is usually confined to matters covered in the redirect examination.

THE ROLE OF THE TRIAL JUDGE

The trial judge manages the courtroom and the trial and rules on questions of law. The judge rules on motions and objections made by attorneys before and during a trial and gives instructions to the jury. The trial judge has an obligation to safeguard both the rights of the accused and the interests of the public in the efficient and effective administration of criminal and civil justice.

In the great majority of jurisdictions in the United States, the trial judge may not comment on the weight of the evidence. Juries are usually instructed on the manner in which they may determine the weight of the evidence—that is, the credibility of witnesses and the weight that they may give to physical evidence. In only a very few jurisdictions in the United States may the trial judge comment on the weight of the evidence presented in a trial.

Virtually all states follow Federal Rule of Evidence 614(b). Rule 614(b) states that the *court* (the term as used here refers to the trial judge) "may interrogate witnesses, whether called by itself or by a party." In a few jurisdictions, jurors are permitted to question witnesses indirectly through the trial judge.

Because the trial judge must remain impartial, he or she must be careful in the use of leading questions in those jurisdictions that forbid the judge from commenting on the weight of the evidence. The improper use of leading questions could suggest to the jury that the judge believed the witness was lying, which violates the rule against commenting on the evidence. In the 1972 case of *Commonwealth v. Butler*,[47] the Supreme Court of Pennsylvania disapproved of a trial judge's practice of questioning only the witnesses he suspected of untruthfulness, while not questioning other witnesses. The court held:

> If a judge followed the practice which this judge advocated here, a practice of questioning every witness whom the judge did not believe to be telling the truth, while questioning no other witnesses, it would be tantamount to telling the jury his views of which witnesses were to be believed. Credibility is solely for the jury. Just as a trial judge is not permitted to indicate to the jury his views on the verdict that they should reach in a criminal case, ... similarly he is not permitted to indicate to a jury his views on whether particular witnesses are telling the truth.

Virtually all federal courts permit jurors to ask questions of witnesses by submitting the questions to the judge.[48] Many state courts also permit this practice,[49] and at least two states, Arizona and Florida, do so by statute.[50] As with questions posed by the judge, the parties may object to these questions on the same grounds as questions asked by one of the parties. However, the routine practice of allowing questions by jurors is generally discouraged. The court in *United States v. Collins*[51] suggested that juror questions be limited to cases where the trial is long and complicated, the parties are not properly questioning witnesses, or the witness becomes difficult or confused.

CAN A PERSON WHO HAS BEEN HYPNOTIZED TESTIFY AS A WITNESS?

hypnosis The induction of a sleeplike condition in which a subject obeys many of the suggestions and orders of the hypnotizer.

Studies of **hypnosis** began more than 200 years ago, but to date there is no single explanation of the phenomenon that satisfies most scientists. Hundreds of cases involving hypnotized witnesses have come before American courts.[52] In the 1987 case of *Rock v. Arkansas*,[53] the U.S. Supreme Court identified the following three problems in the use of a witness whose testimony has been hypnotically refreshed:

> [T]he subject becomes "suggestible" and may try to please the hypnotist with answers the subject thinks will be met with approval; the subject is likely to "confabulate," that is, to fill in details from the imagination, in order to make an answer more coherent and complete; and, the subject experiences "memory hardening," which gives him great confidence in both true and false memories, making effective cross-examination more difficult.

Because of these and other problems, some states do not permit the use of hypnotically refreshed testimony as evidence. Other states have established guidelines for the use of hypnotically refreshed testimony, such as those in New Jersey[54] and New Mexico.[55] Such safeguards seek to ensure the accuracy and reliability of hypnotically refreshed testimony. The facts in the case of *Rock v. Arkansas* and the ruling of the U.S. Supreme Court follow.

Rock v. Arkansas

United States Supreme Court, 483 U.S. 44, 107 S.Ct. 2704 (1987)

The defendant was charged with manslaughter in the killing of her husband during an argument. Because she could not remember precise details of the shooting, her attorney suggested hypnosis to refresh her memory. After the defendant underwent hypnosis, the trial court permitted her to testify only about what she had been able to remember before hypnosis.

After her conviction for manslaughter, she appealed to the U.S. Supreme Court on the issue that she had the constitutional right to testify in her own behalf. The Supreme Court vacated the conviction and ordered a new trial, stating:

> The more traditional means of assessing accuracy of testimony also remain applicable in the case of a previously hypnotized defendant. Certain information recalled as a result of hypnosis may be verified as highly accurate by corroborating evidence. Cross-examination, even in the face of a confident defendant, is an effective tool for revealing inconsistencies. Moreover, a jury can be educated to the risks of hypnosis through expert testimony and cautionary instructions. Indeed, it is probably to a defendant's advantage to establish carefully the extent of his memory prior to hypnosis, in order to minimize the decrease in credibility the procedure might introduce.
>
> ... We are not now prepared to endorse without qualifications the use of hypnosis as an investigative tool; scientific understanding of the phenomenon and of the means to control the effects of hypnosis is still in its infancy. Arkansas, however, has not justified the exclusion of all of a defendant's testimony that the defendant is unable to prove to be the product of prehypnosis memory. A State's legitimate interest in barring unreliable evidence does not extend to per se exclusions that may be reliable in an individual case. Wholesale inadmissibility of a defendant's testimony is an arbitrary restriction on the right to testify in the absence of clear evidence by the

THE FUNCTIONS OF THE TRIAL JUDGE AND THE JURY

The Trial Judge Determines:

- Whether a witness is qualified
- The competence of a witness
- Questions of law:
  - Rules on motions
  - Rules on objections by attorneys
  - Instruction of the jury
  - Running the courtroom and trial
  - Safeguarding both the rights of the accused and the interests of the public in the administration of criminal justice

As Fact Finders, the Jury Alone:

- Determines the credibility of the testimony of all witnesses. The fact finders may believe one witness as against many.
- Passes on and resolves conflicts in the testimony of witnesses.
- Determines the weight to be given all evidence (statements of witnesses, physical evidence, and so on).
- Determines whether sufficient evidence exists to justify a verdict of guilty. (A guilty verdict is subject to review by the trial judge and appellate courts, however, who determine as a matter of law whether sufficient evidence exists to sustain the guilty verdict.)

State repudiating the validity of all posthypnosis recollections. The State would be well within its powers if it established guidelines to aid trial courts in the evaluation of posthypnosis testimony and it may be able to show that testimony in a particular case is so unreliable that exclusion is justified. But it has not shown that hypnotically enhanced testimony is always so untrustworthy and so immune to the traditional means of evaluating credibility that it should disable a defendant from presenting her version of the events for which she is on trial.

In the *Rock* case it was the defendant who wished to testify after hypnosis, and the Supreme Court held that the defendant had a constitutional right to testify in her own behalf. As a result, the Supreme Court held that the Arkansas *per se* inadmissibility rule was unconstitutional. Where a witness who is not a defendant wishes to testify after hypnosis, courts have held that a *per se* rule of inadmissibility is permitted.[56]

Another problem area commonly associated with hypnotically refreshed memory is "repressed memories." Accusations of sexual assaults that occurred years prior to the accusation could be based on a repressed memory that has been hypnotically or clinically refreshed.[57]

SUMMARY

To appear as a witness in a civil or criminal case, a person must have personal knowledge of an issue before the court. A witness must also be competent and declare (or swear) that he or she will testify truthfully.

Today, children as young as 3 years of age may qualify to testify as witnesses. Because of the trauma that a child victim or witness may experience when appearing as a witness, all of the states and courts have statutes and procedures that attempt to help child witnesses.

Defendants have the right to compel witnesses to appear in court to testify for the defense. The Sixth Amendment right of a defendant to confront and cross-examine witnesses against the defendant is probably the most important tool of defense lawyers in defending their clients in criminal cases.

Witnesses may be either ordinary witnesses or expert witnesses. Both ordinary and expert witnesses may testify as to opinions within the rules of evidence of their state. (See Appendix C for Federal Rules of Evidence 701, 703, 704, and 705.)

All witnesses testify under oath or affirmation and may be cross-examined by the opposing attorney. Witnesses may also be questioned on redirect and recross-examination.

CASE ANALYSIS

Read Appendix B, Finding and Analyzing Cases (p. 427). With these guidelines in mind, please continue with the Case Analysis selections for Chapter 5.

1. Rule 701 of the Federal Rules of Evidence governs the admissibility of lay opinion testimony. Rule 702 governs the admissibility of expert opinion testimony. Most states have adopted rules similar to the federal rules. How do Rules 701 and 702 differ? What must be shown to permit the admission of lay opinions? What must be shown for expert opinions? When a police officer gives his opinion that an illegal drug transaction has taken place, based on the policeman's years of training and experience, is his opinion a lay opinion or an expert opinion? What answer did the Maryland Court of Appeals give in *Ragland v. State* [870 A.2d 609 (Md. App. 2005)] [Case No. 52/04]? Why did it matter in the case? Why did the court reverse its earlier decision on this question?

2. If a police officer's opinion based on years of experience and training is classified as expert testimony, how does the prosecution satisfy the burden imposed by Rule 702 that the officer is "qualified" as an expert? Why was it important to the prosecution in *People v. Clifton* [750 N.E.2d 686 (Ill. App. 2001)] [Case No. 1982126] to offer expert testimony on the workings of the internal leadership of the Gangster Disciples gang? Do you agree with the court's reasoning and decision?

3. In *Wright v. State* [178 S.W.2d 905 (Tex. App. 2005)], a detective gave testimony in a defendant's murder trial in which the detective stated his theory on how the defendant killed her husband. The defendant objected to the testimony on the grounds that the detective was not testifying based on personal knowledge. What must the prosecution show to satisfy the personal knowledge requirement?

4. What factors should courts look for when a child's testimony is alleged to be a "false memory"? See *Com. v. Davis* [939 A.2d 905 (Pa. Super. 2007)].

Notes

1. Most witnesses will cooperate in performing their civic duty, but unfortunately some witnesses will not. The following reasons are commonly given for some witnesses not cooperating: (a) *Threats:* One experienced official estimated that half of all criminal cases dismissed are dropped because of witnesses' concerns for their safety. (b) *Financial losses:* Most states pay up to $30 per day as witness fees, which means that many witnesses lose money or have to take vacation time from their job to appear as a witness. (c) *Too many court delays and adjournments:* The National Advisory Committee on Criminal Justice Standards and Goals recognized that "delays are an accepted defense practice for wearing down the witness. Not infrequently, the financial and emotional

costs become too much for the victim, and [he or] she asks to withdraw" (Report of the Task Force on Criminal Research and Development).

2. See *United States v. Benn*, 476 F.2d 1127 (D.C. Cir. 1972); *State v. Manning*, 291 A.2d 750 (Conn. 1972).

3. 913 F.2d 782 (10th Cir. 1990).

4. 825 F.2d 538 (1st Cir. 1987).

5. See 24A Corpus Juris Secundum 1869.

6. 703 P.2d 448.

7. 744 N.E.2d 1131 (Mass. App. Ct. 2001).

8. See Appendix A for the Sixth Amendment, which states in part: "In all criminal prosecutions, the accused shall enjoy the right ... to be confronted with the witnesses against him; to have compulsory process for obtaining witnesses in his favor...."

9. See 32A Corpus Juris Secundum, Evidence 1031, and the case of *Chapman v. State* [230 N.W.2d 824 (Wis. 1975)]. In the *Chapman* case, a witness testified that the defendant stated that he participated in the crime charged and complained that he did not receive any of the proceeds of the joint criminal venture. The jury believed the testimony of the witness and convicted the defendant. The Wisconsin Supreme Court affirmed the conviction, holding: "This court will not upset a jury's determination of credibility ... unless the fact relied upon is inherently or patently incredible. To be incredible as a matter of law, evidence must be ... in conflict with the uniform course of nature or with fully established or conceded facts.... There is nothing inherently incredible about a participant in a crime telling others what he did. This is particularly so where his expressed complaint is that he received none of the proceeds of the joint criminal venture. The determination of this witness' credibility and the weight to be given his testimony was ... properly a function of the trier of facts."

10. 409 U.S. 188 (1972).

11. 44 P.3d 794, 798 (Utah 2002).

12. 201 F.2d 265 (2d Cir. 1952).

13. 478 N.W.2d 901, *review denied*, U.S. Supreme Court, 112 S.Ct. 3015 (1991).

14. 112 S.Ct. 3015.

15. 136 S.W.3d 680.

16. In the case of *Davis v. Alaska* [94 S.Ct. 1105], the defendant was convicted of burglary and grand larceny. A crucial witness for the prosecution (Richard Green) was a 6-year-old who was on probation for burglarizing two cabins. The state obtained a protective order forbidding the disclosure of Green's juvenile record during his testimony in the trial of Davis. In reversing and remanding Davis's conviction for a new trial, the U.S. Supreme Court held that: "The State's policy interest in protecting the confidentiality of a juvenile offender's record cannot require yielding of so vital a constitutional right as the effective cross-examination for bias of an adverse witness. The State could have protected Green from exposure of his juvenile adjudication in these circumstances by refraining from using him to make out its case; the State cannot, consistent with the right of confrontation, require the petitioner to bear the full burden of vindicating the State's interest in the secrecy of juvenile criminal records. The judgment affirming petitioner's convictions of burglary and grand larceny is reversed, and the case is remanded for further proceedings not inconsistent with this opinion."

17. See *Faretta v. California*, 422 U.S. 806 (1975).

18. 483 U.S. 44, 107 S.Ct. 2704.

19. In 1972, the case of *Brooks v. Tennessee* [406 U.S. 605, 92 S.Ct. 1891] was before the U.S. Supreme Court. In that case, the defendant wanted to testify in his own behalf, but a Tennessee statute required a defendant "to testify before any other testimony for the defense is heard by the court trying the case." In holding that the defendant "was deprived of his constitutional rights when the trial court excluded him from the stand for failing to testify first," the Supreme Court stated that: "Although a defendant will usually have some idea of the strength of his evidence, he cannot be absolutely certain that his witnesses will testify as expected or that they will be effective on the stand. They may collapse under skillful and persistent cross-examination, and through no fault of their own they may fail to impress the jury as honest and reliable witnesses. In addition, a defendant is sometimes compelled to call a hostile prosecution witness as his own. Unless the State provides for discovery depositions of prosecution witnesses, which Tennessee apparently does not, the defendant is unlikely to know whether this testimony will prove entirely favorable."

20. U.S. Supreme Court in *McGautha v. California*, 91 S.Ct. 1454 (1971).

21. 113 S.Ct. 1111.

22. The term *perjury trap* was defined as follows in the case of *United States v. Chen* [933 F.2d 793 (9th Cir. 1991)]: A "perjury trap is created when the government calls a witness before the grand jury for the primary purpose of obtaining testimony from him in order to prosecute him later for perjury. *United States v. Simone* [627 F.Supp. 1264, 1268 (D. N.J. 1986)] (perjury trap involves 'the deliberate use of a judicial proceeding to secure perjured testimony, a concept in itself abhorrent'). It involves the government's use of its investigatory powers to secure a perjury indictment on matters which are neither material nor germane to a legitimate ongoing investigation of the grand jury."

    Knowingly making a material false statement to a federal investigator can be charged as a crime under the federal False Statement Act. The U.S. Supreme Court affirmed a criminal conviction under this act in the 1998 case of *Brogan v. United States* [118 S.Ct. 805], when Brogan denied to federal investigators that he had received illegal cash or gifts in the incidents being investigated.

23. Rule 702 was amended in 2000 in response to the decisions of the U.S. Supreme Court in *Daubert v. Merrill Dow Pharmaceuticals Co.* [509 U.S. 579 (1993)] and *Kumho Tire Co. v. Carmichael* [119 S.Ct. 1167 (1999)]. In those cases the Court established new standards for determining when a witness may be permitted to testify concerning scientific and technical knowledge. (*Daubert* and *Kumho,* and their influence on state court expert testimony rules, are discussed in more detail in Chapter 18 of this book.)

    Rule 702 and its counterparts in state evidence rules relate both to the qualification of a witness as an expert and to the nature of the testimony given by a witness, assuming he or she is an expert. As to the qualification aspect of Rule 702, a court usually looks at the witness' training, education, and experience to make the determination on the witness' qualification to be an expert. In the following cases, courts considered the qualifications necessary to give expert testimony.

    In the 2001 case of *United States v. Watson* [260 F.3d 301 (3d Cir. 2001)], the Third Circuit Court of Appeals held that narcotics officers with extensive experience in narcotics trafficking could give expert testimony about the meaning of behavior of persons involved in illegal narcotics possession or distribution. There, the narcotics expert testified that the presence of crack cocaine, together with several hundred small plastic baggies used by sellers of crack, was generally a sign that the holder of the crack was part of a distribution scheme, rather than holding the crack for personal use. The narcotics agent also testified, based on more than 200 arrests in bus stations, that bus trips between cities with brief layovers by persons in possession of crack and plastic bags were generally a sign of participation in a drug distribution system. The defendant, who was arrested on a bus trip to Philadelphia with a 4-hour layover, had in his possession small amounts of crack cocaine and several hundred plastic baggies of the type used in the sale of crack. He was convicted in the district court of possession with intent to distribute crack cocaine.

    In the 2001 case of *United States v. Havvard* [260 F.3d 597 (7th Cir. 2001)], the Seventh Circuit Court of Appeals held that an FBI agent who had studied the success rates of fingerprint comparisons in numerous national cases, and who had a detailed process that he used to establish such comparisons, could give expert testimony that the latent fingerprint found on a firearm matched the fingerprint of the defendant. The defendant was found guilty of illegal possession of a firearm.

    The second aspect of Rule 702 goes to the reliability of the testimony of the expert after the witness has been qualified as an expert. If the basis for the expert's opinion does not meet the Rule 702 and *Daubert* reliability tests, the expert may not testify. For example, in *United States v. Lea* [249 F.3d 632 (7th Cir. 2001)], a 2001 decision of the Seventh Circuit Court of Appeals, the defense sought to introduce evidence from a polygraph test administered by a Food and Drug Administration (FDA) agent to another person the defendant contended was the guilty party. Although the agent was qualified as an expert on administering and interpreting polygraph tests, he was not permitted to testify because his opinion that the person taking the test was not telling the truth was unreliable. The FDA agent could not say exactly which question was answered untruthfully and also had no statistical support for the accuracy of the testing methods used in the polygraph test administered. (The question of the reliability and admissibility of polygraph and voice spectrography is discussed more fully in Chapter 12.)

It is the fact finder (jury or judge) who determines the weight and credibility to be given to the testimony of both expert and ordinary witnesses. To promote this, most states have a rule similar to Federal Rule of Evidence 704(b), which states that in a criminal case an expert may not give an opinion that the defendant had or did not have the mental state constituting an element of the crime. That question must be decided by the jury. In *United States v. Watson*, discussed previously, even though the narcotics agents were qualified as experts, the trial court erred in permitting the agents to give their opinion that Watson, the defendant, had the intent to distribute the cocaine in his possession. The agents could testify generally about common behavior observed by them in drug distribution activities, but the jury must decide whether a given defendant exhibiting such behavior possesses the required intent to distribute. In *Watson,* the court of appeals reversed the defendant's conviction because of the expert's opinions on Watson's intent.

24. 15 N.E.2d 337 (Ill. App.).

25. 413 U.S. 15, 93 S.Ct. 2607, n.12.

26. 658 S.E.2d 755 (Ga. 2008).

27. *United States v. Tipton,* 964 F.2d 650 (7th Cir. 1992).

28. *United States v. Paiva,* 892 F.2d 148 (1st Cir. 1989).

29. *Waddell v. State,* 582 A.2d 260 (Md. App. 1990).

30. 803 P.2d 1077 (Mont.).

31. *United States v. Anthony,* 944 F.2d 780 (Okla. 1991).

32. *State v. Lamme,* 563 A.2d 1372 (Conn. App. 1989).

33. 1991 WL 263246.

34. *Commonwealth v. Cohen,* 605 A.2d 814 (Pa. Super. 1992).

35. *State v. Mallett,* 600 A.2d 273 (R.I. 1991).

36. *Kosbruk v. State,* 820 P.2d 1082 (Alaska App. 1991).

37. See the 1990 case of *Dysart v. State,* 581 So.2d 541 (Ala. Crim. App.).

38. 267 F.3d 614 (7th Cir. 2001).

39. 94 S.Ct. 1105.

40. 51 S.Ct. 218.

41. *Id.*

42. *Loehr v. Walton,* 242 F.3d 834 (8th Cir. 2001).

43. *United States v. Foster,* 227 F.3d 1096 (9th Cir. 2000).

44. *Udemba v. Nicoli,* 237 F.3d 8 (1st Cir. 2001).

45. 488 U.S. 277, 109 S.Ct. 480.

46. 482 U.S. 730, 107 S.Ct. 2658.

47. 291 A.2d 9 (Pa.).

48. *United States v. Richardson,* 233 F.3d 1285, 1288 (11th Cir. 2000).

49. *Id.*

50. Ariz. R. Ct. 39(b)(10); Fla. St. ch. 40.50(3).

51. 226 F.3d 457 (6th Cir. 2000).

52. Law enforcement officers have used hypnosis to assist an eyewitness in recalling a vehicle license plate number, the description of a fleeing offender, or a person seen in the vicinity of serious crime. Hypnosis was instrumental in apprehending offenders in the case of *State v. Joubert* [603 A.2d 861 (Me. 1992)] and in rescuing twenty-six children and their school bus driver in Chowchilla, California, when they were kidnapped in 1975. The school bus with all of its occupants had been buried in the ground to prevent the escape of the children and the bus driver.

53. 483 U.S. 44, 107 S.Ct. 2704.

54. *State v. Hurd,* 432 A.2d 86 (1989).

55. *State v. Varela,* 817 P.2d 731 (1991).

56. See *Stokes v. State,* 548 So.2d 188 (Fla. 1989).

57. More than 1,000 families in the United States belong to an organization known as the False Memory Syndrome Foundation. (The problem of false memories first became known more than 100 years ago when Sigmund Freud began treating patients. Freud was amazed at the number of hypnotized women who told of being raped by their fathers. Years later, Freud concluded that most of these women were fantasizing and that their memories were false. The problem of false memory syndrome is commonly associated with hypnotic therapy.) Most of these families struggle with the problem of a family member who has made accusations of sexual assault against another family member based on what might be a "false memory." Such accusations, whether true or false, affect whole families. The FMS Foundation (3401 Market Street, Philadelphia, PA 19104) tries to assist such families.

JUDICIAL NOTICE, PRIVILEGES OF WITNESSES, AND SHIELD LAWS

CHAPTER **6**

LEARNING OBJECTIVES

In this chapter we discuss the practice of judicial notice in criminal trials and the privileges that may be used to exclude the testimony of some witnesses. The learning objectives for this chapter are:

- State the basis for and the limits of the judicial notice doctrine.
- For each of the privileges discussed, state (1) the privilege, (2) the limits on the privilege, and (3) who may invoke the privilege.
- Define the "crime fraud" exception to the attorney–client privilege.
- List the "privileges" available to the government and government officers.

JUDICIAL NOTICE IN GENERAL

If the parties to criminal and civil trials had to prove every fact of common knowledge and define every term they use, trials would be unreasonably long. Court calendars would back up, and delays in getting a case to trial would increase considerably.

judicial notice
The doctrine that evidence of well-accepted facts may be introduced in court without proof; a judicial shortcut.

To avoid unnecessary delays, courts have developed the commonsense doctrine of **judicial notice**. This notice relieves parties in criminal and civil trials from the duty of introducing witnesses, documents, and other evidence to prove uncontroverted facts. For example, in 1919 the California Supreme Court held that: "Judicial notice is a judicial short cut, a doing away ... with formal necessity of evidence because there is no real necessity for it."[1]

All states have statutes or court rules that authorize the use of a judicial notice doctrine. Many state statutes that permit this use are similar to the Federal Rules of Evidence, Rule 201, found in Appendix C of this book. For example, Rule 201 of the New Hampshire Rules of Evidence states:

> [a] court may take judicial notice of a fact. A judicially noticed fact must be one not subject to reasonable dispute in that it is either (1) generally known within the territorial jurisdiction of the court or (2) capable of accurate and ready determination by resort to sources whose accuracy cannot reasonably be questioned.

JUDICIAL NOTICE OF MATTERS OF GENERAL KNOWLEDGE

Judicial notice of matters generally known within the community or state is probably the oldest application of the doctrine of judicial notice.[2] This aspect of the doctrine permits judges and jurors to recognize facts commonly known to them without formal evidence proving those facts. In this way, judicial notice shortens and simplifies trials. The Supreme Court of California gave the following explanation of the "general knowledge" rule in a 1970 case:

> Judicial notice may not be taken of any matter unless authorized or required by law (Evid. Code, § 452). This court is compelled to take judicial notice only of facts and propositions of generalized knowledge that are so universally known that they cannot reasonably be the subject of dispute (Evid. Code, § 451). If there is any doubt whatever either as to the fact itself or as to its being a matter of common knowledge, evidence should be required.[3]

The following are common examples of the use of judicial notice to prove matters of general knowledge:

- *Establishing the meaning of words, phrases, or abbreviations commonly used "on the street"*: The street terms *fix* in drug cases and *turning a trick* in prostitution cases might be established by judicial notice. The parties may also establish the terms by asking a law enforcement witness to define them.
- *Establishing the sex of a witness or defendant*: For example, the Supreme Court of Indiana held that: "The sex of a human being is generally its most obvious characteristic. We can look at another human being and, with a very high degree of certainty, ascertain his or her sex. Therefore, why couldn't a presiding judge take judicial notice of a defendant's sex? We believe he can and should."[4]

- *Establishing the location of well-known sections of a city or well-known streets and buildings:* Another example is determining the distances to well-known cities and the interstates or highways used to drive to those cities.
- *Establishing well-known habits:* For example, in the 1991 case of *State v. Mundell*,[5] the Court of Appeals of Hawaii held: "We take judicial notice that drug dealers and traffickers rarely carry 'large' amounts of drugs on their person. Their supplies are generally secreted in their homes, in their luggage, or in other such places where they may be accessible for sale. Drug dealers often use other people to transport large quantities of drugs for them."

However, a court may not take judicial notice of a fact solely because the fact is well known to the trial judge. For example, in the 2002 case of *United States v. Mariscal*, the Ninth Circuit Court of Appeals held that a trial judge could not take judicial notice of traffic conditions at a local intersection, when knowledge of those conditions arose only from the judge's personal driving experience. Narcotics agents made an investigative stop of a vehicle in which the defendant was present, and the prosecution attempted to justify the stop using evidence that the driver of the vehicle made an unsignaled right turn. This court ruled that an unsignaled turn is illegal only if traffic is present at the intersection where the turn occurred. The prosecution failed to offer evidence of such traffic, but the trial court filled that gap by taking judicial notice that the intersection was one of the busiest in the city. The court of appeals found the investigative stop unlawful because the agents had no reasonable belief that a law had been broken.

Judicial Notice of Facts Obtained from Sources, Such as Records, Books, and Newspapers

A court may properly take judicial notice of facts cited in recognized reports, learned treatises, or dictionaries, or simple data printed in newspapers, such as dates and temperatures. Such facts are not in controversy but may be very important to one of the parties in the trial.

The following examples illustrate the use of judicial notice in this area:

- In 1921, the U.S. Supreme Court held that judicial notice could be taken of the date on which a state ratified a proposed constitutional amendment because this information could be easily obtained from records or books.[6]
- Courts could take judicial notice of dates, days, or time because this information is readily available in almanacs, newspapers, and the like (such as, that the Fourth of July fell on a Friday in the year 2008, at what hour the sun set on a given day, or whether it rained or snowed on a given day).
- Courts may take notice of statutes of other states, court records of your state or other states, and ordinances of counties and cities within your state. In the 1992 case of *People v. Hardy*,[7] the Supreme Court of California pointed out that California Evidence Code, section 452, provides that "Judicial notice may be taken … (of the) records of … any court of record of the United States." As an example of when this may be used, in the 1991 case of *In the Matter of Breedlove*,[8] the West Virginia Supreme Court held that it was proper to take judicial notice of a previous drunk-driving conviction in ordering a ten-year revocation of the driver's license.

Courts must be careful how they take judicial notice. In *State v. Gagnon,*[9] a defendant was convicted of negligent driving when he sped on the paved surface surrounding a fire station. The negligent driving statute applied to driving on a public "way," which under New Hampshire law means (a) a public road or (b) a private road maintained by the state through the use of state funds. The trial judge took judicial notice of the fact that the paved surface around the fire station was a "way," and the defendant was convicted. On appeal, the New Hampshire Supreme Court held that it was not "generally known" that public funds were appropriated for maintaining the fire station's paved surfaces, which makes the first part of the New Hampshire judicial notice statute inapplicable. Because the trial court did not specify which source would provide the "accurate and ready determination" that state funds were so used, the court also held that the second part of the statute was not satisfied. The defendant's conviction was reversed.

SCIENTIFIC AND TECHNOLOGICAL FACTS RECOGNIZED BY JUDICIAL NOTICE

Judicial notice can be taken of a court ruling that a scientific technique is reliable; for example, after a state or federal court establishes that DNA fingerprinting is a reliable scientific technique, there is no need to bring in expert witnesses again and again in every case to prove that DNA fingerprinting is reliable and accurate. (This issue is discussed in more detail in Chapter 18.)

Examples
- In the 1993 case of *United States v. Jacobetz,*[10] DNA fingerprinting was used to identify the defendant as the man who abducted a woman in Vermont, repeatedly raped her, and released her in New York. The court held that "in future cases with a similar evidentiary issue, a court could properly take judicial notice of the general acceptability of the general theory and the use of these specific techniques."
- An Ohio Court of Appeals held in the 1973 case of *State v. Brock*[11] that "courts may take judicial notice of any scientific fact that may be ascertained by reference to a standard dictionary or is of such general knowledge that it is known by any judicial officer. In the instant case, the trial court was correct in taking judicial notice of the fact that heroin is a narcotic drug and is habit forming."

THE PRIVILEGE AGAINST SELF-INCRIMINATION

privilege
A benefit or right enjoyed by a person; for example, the privilege of a witness not to answer a question might be based on the privilege against self-incrimination or the marital privilege.

In tracing the origins of the Fifth Amendment's right to remain silent, the U.S. Supreme Court pointed out in the case of *Miranda v. Arizona* that the privilege's "roots go back into ancient times" and probably has origins in the Bible.[12]

The Fifth Amendment **privilege** against self-incrimination is the only privilege that has been incorporated into the U.S. Constitution and many state constitutions. All other privileges exist only in statutory or common law. The Fifth Amendment of the U.S. Constitution provides that: "No person ... shall be compelled in any criminal case to be a witness against himself...."

This privilege "protects a person ... against being incriminated by his own compelled testimonial communications."[13] Because statements made by a person in any civil hearing or questioning might later be used against that person in a criminal proceeding, the U.S. Supreme Court has repeatedly held that the privilege "can be asserted in any proceeding, civil or criminal, administrative or judicial, investigatory or adjudicatory."[14] The privilege has thus been invoked, for example, in divorce and tax cases as well as in criminal cases and questioning by law enforcement officers.[15]

The U.S. Supreme Court has held that the privilege against self-incrimination "reflects many of our fundamental values and noble aspirations."[16] Because this privilege is "the essential mainstay of our adversary system," the U.S. Constitution requires "that the government seeking to punish an individual produce the evidence against him by its own independent labor rather than by the cruel, simple expedient of compelling it from his own mouth."[17]

AREAS WHERE THE FIFTH AMENDMENT PRIVILEGE AGAINST SELF-INCRIMINATION DOES NOT APPLY

The Fifth Amendment privilege against self-incrimination applies only to evidence of a communicative or testimonial nature. It does not apply when only physical evidence is sought and obtained. Seizure of physical evidence is controlled by the Fourth Amendment to the U.S. Constitution. Thus, the privilege against self-incrimination does not extend to the following circumstances:

- Withdrawing blood and using it as evidence to show that the defendant was driving a vehicle while intoxicated (*Schmerber v. California*).[18]
- Using a handwriting exemplar, or sample, which was held to be controlled by the Fourth Amendment (*Gilbert v. California*).[19]
- Compelling the accused to exhibit his person for observation, as in a lineup or showup (*United States v. Wade*).[20]
- Making a voice exemplar, or sample (*United States v. Dionisio*).[21]
- Federal Courts of Appeals have held that no Fifth Amendment violation occurred when, for identification purposes, the defendant was compelled to wear a false goatee (*United States v. Hammond*),[22] to wear a wig (*United States v. Murray*),[23] to shave for identification purposes (*United States v. Valenzuela*),[24] to put on a stocking mask at trial to permit a witness to testify as to similarity to the masked robber (*United States v. Roberts*),[25] or to dye her or his hair to the color it was at the time of the offense (*United States v. Brown*).[26]
- Testimony of a witness that the defendant was compelled to put on a shirt, or other item of clothing, and that the item fit the defendant (*Holt v. United States*).[27]
- Where immunity has been granted and the person is compelled to testify or agrees to testify as part of a plea agreement. An example of a person agreeing to the grant of immunity is Monica Lewinsky, who received immunity as part of a plea agreement. In the Iran–Contra scandal, Colonel Oliver North (a presidential advisor) and Admiral John Poindexter (North's boss) were both granted limited immunity to compel them to answer questions before congressional committees in 1986.[28]

THE MEANING OF "ANY CRIMINAL CASE"

The Fifth Amendment privilege applies to a prosecution or the possibility of a prosecution "in any criminal case." As a result, it has always been held that the privilege does not apply to a refusal to answer a question because it might subject the witness to civil liability. The nature of the prospective criminal prosecution has been controversial, however. Initially, courts held that a witness in a federal court could be forced to answer an incriminating question if given immunity from federal prosecution, even though the statement might subject him to state criminal prosecution. In *Murphy v. Waterfront Comm.* [378 U.S. 52 (1964)], the U.S. Supreme Court held that the possibility of criminal prosecution by either the federal or state governments made the privilege available.

In *United States v. Balsys* [524 U.S. 666 (1998)], the Supreme Court considered whether the possibility of criminal prosecution in a foreign jurisdiction based on incriminating statements enabled a witness to plead the Fifth Amendment privilege. There, a resident alien was called by a government agency to give testimony about the alien's actions during World War II. The agency suspected the witness was guilty of war crimes and, if so, planned to deport him. The alien's answers to questions about his wartime actions created no possibility of federal or state prosecution. Nonetheless, the witness refused to answer questions, claiming protection under the Fifth Amendment.

The Court first stated that the possibility of deportation was not a "criminal case," so the only justification for invoking the privilege was the likely prosecution by foreign jurisdictions. The Court then stated that the issue was the meaning of "any criminal case" in the Fifth Amendment. It held that "criminal case" did not include prosecution by a foreign jurisdiction:

> [w]e read the Clause contextually as apparently providing a witness with the right against compelled self-incrimination when reasonably fearing prosecution by the government whose power the Clause limits, but not otherwise. 524 U.S. at 673.

The Court reasoned that because no state or federal court could know whether the foreign jurisdiction would itself compel the witness to testify, even if the privilege was recognized or the witness was given immunity, recognizing the privilege would not afford any protection to the witness but would result in harm to the government. As a result, the witness could be compelled to answer questions about his wartime activities.

- The U.S. Supreme Court has repeatedly ruled that the Fifth Amendment privilege applies only to people and not to corporations, labor unions, and other organizations. Corporations and unincorporated unions and other organizations cannot claim the privilege against self-incrimination.[29]
- Where the incrimination is of others and is not self-incrimination.[30]
- Where the public interest in protecting children from abuse outweighs the Fifth Amendment privilege. After a small child had received numerous physical injuries and the child's mother was seen abusing the child, the mother was ordered to disclose the location of the child. The mother was jailed on

contempt when she would not do so. The U.S. Supreme Court affirmed the contempt sentence in the 1990 case of *Baltimore Department of Social Services v. Bouknight*.[31]

- U.S. military personnel and law enforcement officers are obligated to report illegal conduct of their fellow officers and military associates. The U.S. Supreme Court upheld this service requirement as not being in violation of the Fifth Amendment privilege. It was held that the defense of fear of retaliation could not be used against the offense of failure to report the illegal conduct of others.[32] However, the Fifth Amendment privilege would apply if the military service person or law enforcement officer had also been a party to the crime, such as drug use.[33]

- Where there has been a voluntary, intelligent waiver of the privilege.

RECENT EXAMPLES WHERE THE FIFTH AMENDMENT PRIVILEGE AGAINST SELF-INCRIMINATION DOES APPLY

The Fifth Amendment privilege against self-incrimination has been found to apply in the circumstances of these recent cases:

- A witness may raise the Fifth Amendment privilege even where the witness insists she is innocent of any crime. In *Ohio v. Reiner*,[34] the U.S. Supreme Court held that a babysitter called to testify in the prosecution of a father for the death of his infant son could assert the privilege, even though she professed her complete innocence of any relation to the crime.

- A taxpayer may invoke the privilege to refuse to answer specific questions on a tax return but may not refuse to file a return altogether (*United States v. Sabino*).[35]

- The privilege is available when a person is questioned by a probation officer, so long as the officer makes it clear that answers to the question are mandatory, not optional. Answers could lead to violations of probation, which is a form of incrimination (*United States v. Davis*).[36]

- Where a defendant remains silent under questioning, the Fifth Amendment prohibits the prosecution from introducing evidence of that silence at trial. The fact that the defendant remained silent may lead one to conclude that the defendant admitted the accuracy of the questions, and the silence is thus incriminatory (*United States v. Velarde-Gomez*).[37]

THE ATTORNEY–CLIENT PRIVILEGE

As the U.S. Supreme Court pointed out in the 1981 case of *Upjohn Company et al. v. United States et al.*, "the attorney–client privilege is the oldest of the privileges for confidential communications known to the common law."[38] In that case the Supreme Court held that communications by Upjohn employees to corporate lawyers about illegal payments made to foreign government officials were covered by the **attorney–client privilege.** The Court stated that the purpose of the privilege was

attorney–client privilege
The oldest of the privileges.

to encourage full and frank communication between attorneys and their clients and thereby promote broader public interests in the observance of law and administration of justice. The privilege recognizes that sound legal advice or advocacy serves public ends and that such advice or advocacy depends upon the lawyer being fully informed by the client. As we stated last Term in *Trammel v. United States,* 445 U.S. 40, 51 (1980), "The attorney–client privilege rests on the need for the advocate and counselor to know all that relates to the client's reasons for seeking representation if the professional mission is to be carried out." ... Admittedly complications in the application of the privilege arise when the client is a corporation, which in theory is an artificial creature of the law, and not an individual; but this Court has assumed that the privilege applies when the client is a corporation, and the Government does not contest the general proposition.

Many states have statutes regulating the attorney–client privilege. Other states, like the federal government, use the *principles of common law.* For example, Rule 501 of the Federal Rules of Evidence (see Appendix C) provides that the "common law as ... interpreted by the courts of the United States in light of reason and experience" is to be used for all of the communicative privileges.

REQUIREMENTS OF THE ATTORNEY–CLIENT PRIVILEGE

For the attorney–client privilege to exist, both state and federal governments require that certain conditions be met. The client must seek the professional legal services of an attorney and have the intention of establishing an attorney–client relationship. Consulting with an attorney for nonlegal services has been held not to fall within the privilege. Situations in which one informally seeks free legal advice from an attorney, such as at a chance meeting with the attorney, do not create the privilege. Additionally, it is generally held that the privilege applies only to confidential communications made within the attorney–client relationship. Talking about legal matters with an attorney at a social function, for example, would probably not fall within the privilege.

However, the necessary presence of the attorney's secretary, law clerk, or other employee during a conference in the attorney's office would not cause a court to hold that the communications were not privileged. The privilege would also probably hold for most situations in which the client brought another person with her to the attorney's office for a conference. The presence of a parent or spouse in a conference just before a trial or hearing is not uncommon, and there is every reason to believe that the privilege would apply to such communications.

The Supreme Court has held that where the client is a corporation, not only are communications between officers of the corporation and corporate counsel privileged, but also communications of employees giving information to counsel at the request of their superiors.[39] Federal courts have reached different conclusions about whether the common-law attorney–client privilege applies to a government lawyer. Government lawyers frequently raise the attorney–client privilege when subpoenaed to testify before a federal grand jury. Some courts have held that the privilege may not be asserted by a government lawyer.[40] In a 2005 case, the Second Circuit Court of Appeals held that the privilege could be asserted by a government lawyer. In *In re Grand Jury Investigation (United States v. Doe),*[41] a federal grand jury was investigating alleged corruption in the office of John Rowland, the governor of Connecticut. The federal prosecutors called an attorney who worked in the governor's office before the grand jury and asked her questions pertaining to the alleged corruption. She asserted the attorney–client privilege on

crime-fraud exception
The exception made to attorney–client privilege when a client consults with an attorney for the purpose of committing a future crime such as perjury; communication and documents relating to this fraud are not protected.

LOSING THE ATTORNEY–CLIENT PRIVILEGE

Privileges are rights that normally must be invoked by the person who is protected by the privilege. Like other rights, though, they can be lost, usually through actions that courts call waiver. This happens with some frequency in the case of the attorney–client privilege. Because the attorney–client privilege often involves documents or other written materials, how these written materials are managed by the attorney or the client can result in a waiver of the privilege. Two examples illustrate some risks associated with the privilege.

- *United States v. Ary*, 518 F.3d 775 (D.C. Cir. 2008): The government seized materials from a defendant during a theft-of-government-property investigation. Among the items seized was a box filled with documents. The defendant's lawyer attended a discovery meeting with the U.S. attorney prosecuting the case, and inspected the documents in the boxes, making photocopies of them but not reviewing them at that time. More than six weeks later the defendant moved to exclude some of the documents, claiming they were covered by his attorney–client privilege. The trial court denied the motion, holding that the failure of the attorney to review the documents and claim the privilege at the discovery meeting resulted in a waiver of the privilege. The defendant appealed his conviction, and the court of appeals affirmed the trial court's ruling.

  The court concluded that in the case of the involuntary disclosure of documents, the defendant must (1) specify the documents covered by the privilege, (2) inform the government that it seized protected material, and (3) do so promptly. Here, waiting six weeks to identify the covered material and inform the government was not timely, and as a result the privilege was waived.

- *In re Grand Jury (Attorney-Client Privilege)*, 527 F.3d 200 (D.C. Cir. 2008): A psychiatrist was under investigation for Medicare fraud. As part of his defense, his attorney showed patient records to the U.S. attorney investigating the case. Subsequently the government subpoenaed the originals of the records for inspection by an ink expert to determine whether they were created later than the date that appeared on the records. The defendant moved to quash the subpoena, invoking his attorney–client privilege. The trial court denied the motion, holding that when the attorney showed the records to the government, any privilege associated with the records was lost. The court of appeals affirmed the denial of the motion to quash, holding that the attorney's voluntary sharing of the records waived the attorney–client privilege. The court also held that the doctor could claim no Fifth Amendment privilege with respect to the documents because they were not in his possession, and thus he was not personally compelled to produce them.

behalf of her client, the governor, stating that she advised the governor on matters involved in the investigation. The district court ordered her to testify, but the court of appeals reversed, stating that the same purposes served when the privilege is asserted by private individuals required the privilege to be available to a lawyer whose client is the government. The court also specifically noted that the **crime-fraud exception** would apply to government lawyers who become involved in any illegal conduct with their client.

LIMITS OF THE ATTORNEY–CLIENT PRIVILEGE

The U.S. Supreme Court pointed out in the 1989 case of *United States v. Zolin*[42] that since "the privilege has the effect of withholding relevant information from the fact finder, it applies only where necessary to achieve its purpose." There are therefore limits to the attorney–client privilege:

- The privilege applies when a client discloses past wrongdoing to the attorney, but the privilege does not protect disclosures about future wrongdoing. An attorney becomes part of a criminal conspiracy when he or she advises a client on how to best commit a crime or fraud. Quoting a lower court, the Supreme Court ruled in the *Zolin* case that:

  > It is the purpose of the crime-fraud exception to assure that "the seal of secrecy" be-tween lawyer and client does not extend to communications "made for the purpose of getting advice for commission of a fraud" or crime.

- Most courts hold that an attorney has a legal and ethical obligation to deliver physical evidence of a crime to the police. The Maryland Court of Appeals (the highest court of Maryland) reviewed cases from other state courts addressing this question in the 1992 case of *Rubin v. State*,[43] stating that:

  > ("[D]efense counsel may not retain physical evidence pertaining to the crime charged."); *Commonwealth v. Stenhach*, 356 Pa. Super. 5, 16, 514 A.2d 114, 119 (1986), *appeal denied*, 517 Pa. 589, 534 A.2d 769 (1987) ("[T]he overwhelming majority of states ... hold that physical evidence of crime in the possession of a criminal defense attorney is not subject to a privilege but must be delivered to the prosecution.")...

- The general rule is that the attorney–client privilege does not protect the name and identity of a client and the amount of the attorney fee.[44] This rule was stated as follows by the Fourth Circuit Court of Appeals:

  > the identity of a client is a matter not normally within the privilege ... nor are mat-ters involving the receipt of fees from a client usually privileged. *United States v. (Under Seal)*, 774 F.2d 624, 628 (4th Cir. 1985), *review denied*, 475 U.S. 1108, 106 S.Ct. 1514 (1986).

THE HUSBAND–WIFE PRIVILEGE

To foster marital harmony and to encourage a bond of confidentiality between wife and husband, English courts began in the early 1600s to use the rule that a spouse could not be forced to testify against the other spouse. Today, all states and the federal government use the husband–wife privilege (also known as the *marital privilege*), which originated before the United States became a nation.

The U.S. Supreme Court pointed out in the 1980 case of *Trammel v. United States*[45] that when the husband–wife privilege came into use, women were "re-garded as chattel or demeaned by denial of a separate legal identity and dignity as-sociated with recognition as a whole human being." The Supreme Court stated that because the "ancient foundations for so sweeping a privilege have long since disap-peared," many changes have been made in the laws of states regarding the privi-lege. Today, the husband–wife privilege varies somewhat from state to state. The

SHOULD STATES MAKE MINOR CHANGES TO THEIR ATTORNEY–CLIENT PRIVILEGE LAWS TO PERMIT AN ATTORNEY TO DISCLOSE CLIENT COMMUNICATIONS THAT MAY EXCULPATE A PERSON WRONGLY CONVICTED OF A CRIME?

If a client confesses a crime to his or her attorney, the confession is inadmissible under most circumstances. What the limits should be on that inadmissibility is illustrated by the case of Andrew Wilson. In 1982 Wilson killed a security guard in a robbery of a McDonald's restaurant. Wilson subsequently confessed to the killing to his lawyers, two Chicago public defenders. Further investigation by the attorneys produced additional evidence that corroborated the confession.

Later another man, Alton Logan, was wrongly convicted of the murder and was sentenced to life in prison in an Illinois penitentiary. The public defenders knew their evidence could free Logan, but only if they divulged statements made to them by their client, Wilson. Although most state privilege laws permit attorneys to reveal confidences to prevent a death, serious bodily harm, or criminal fraud, the public defenders found, after consulting legal scholars, experts on legal ethics, and a bar association, that no Illinois exception to the attorney–client privilege permitted them to disclose the Wilson confession. As a result, the evidence that could have freed Logan remained in a locked box, while Logan remained in prison.

The lawyers were able to convince Wilson to agree to release the confession after his death. Wilson died in prison in 2008, while he was serving time for the murders of two Illinois police officers. After the confession and supporting evidence were given to an Illinois court, Logan was freed. The incident, which received widespread news media coverage, raised the question of whether states should amend their privilege laws to prevent similar problems in the future. (See the *Chicago Tribune* article of April 21, 2008, entitled "After 26 years, a taste of freedom.")

requirements that must exist to use the privilege in federal courts are stated in the 1992 case of *United States v. Evans*:[46]

1. ... The marital confidential communications privilege prohibits testimony regarding private intra-spousal communications.... The privilege extends only to words or acts that are intended as a communication to the other spouse.
2. ... The communication must also occur during a time when the marriage is valid under state law and the couple is not permanently separated.[47]
3. ... Finally, the communication must be made in confidence; in other words, it cannot be made in the presence of a third party, and the communicating spouse cannot intend for it to be passed on to others.... Once these three prerequisites are met, a defendant may invoke the privilege to prevent his spouse from testifying as to the content of the protected communication. See 2 *Weinstein's Evidence* § 505[04] (1991). This privilege continues even after the marriage has ended.

THE CRIME-FRAUD EXCEPTION TO THE ATTORNEY–CLIENT PRIVILEGE

In 1997, Monica Lewinsky signed an affidavit under oath that her attorney had prepared after consulting with her on the matter. The affidavit, which was filed with a court, stated that Lewinsky "never had a sexual relationship with the president [former President Bill Clinton]." The U.S. Court of Appeals found that her false statement made under oath was "material" under federal law. The court of appeals agreed with the federal district court's conclusion that Lewinsky had consulted with her attorney "for the purpose of committing perjury" and therefore the *crime-fraud exemption* was properly applied. Because it was held that the crime-fraud exception applied, the independent counsel was permitted to subpoena and examine the records of Lewinsky's attorney on this matter [*In re Sealed Case,* 162 F.3d 670 (D.C. Cir. 1998)].

In *In re Grand Jury Subpoena* [445 F.3d 266 (2d Cir. 2006)], the court refused to quash a subpoena in which the government demanded notes an attorney made after a discussion with a target of the grand jury investigation. Because the target in those discussions with her attorney asked specific questions about the kinds of information the grand jury was looking for, including e-mail messages, and then used that information to delete certain e-mail messages, the court held the crime-fraud exception applicable. It also held that the exception applied even if the attorney didn't know the client was seeking advice about committing a crime, so long as that was the client's intent.

PARTNERSHIP-IN-CRIME EXCEPTION TO THE HUSBAND–WIFE PRIVILEGE

The husband–wife privilege does not extend to situations where the wife and the husband are committing a crime (or crimes) together. Examples of the **partner-in-crime exception** or the *joint-criminal-participation exception* to the husband–wife privilege follow:

partner-in-crime exception
The exception to the marital privilege if a husband and wife commit a crime together.

- Both the wife and husband were involved in growing marijuana. In holding that the marital privilege did not apply, the U.S. Court of Appeals held that "the interests of justice outweigh the goal of fostering marital harmony."[48]
- The husband–wife privilege was held not to apply where both spouses were involved in trafficking cocaine.[49]
- When the husband ran off with his secretary, the angry wife provided the Internal Revenue Service with information of criminal tax evasion. The husband argued the marital privilege when the wife appeared as a prosecution witness against him at his criminal trial. The court held that the privilege would ordinarily be available to prevent the wife's testimony, but that in this case the wife was also guilty of the criminal conduct and the partnership-in-crime exception applied. It did not matter, the court held, that the wife was not prosecuted in return for her cooperation. The husband's conviction based on the testimony of his ex-wife was affirmed.

The husband–wife privilege is directed at privileged communications, but not necessarily the fact that a communication occurred, as illustrated in the 2008 case of *Humphrey v. State.*[50] There, a husband was charged with murder. The state offered as evidence cell phone records obtained from the husband's cell phone provider. These records showed numerous calls between the defendant and his wife, which identified the time of each call and the location of the cell phone when the call was made. These records placed the cell phone outside the victim's workplace in the hours preceding the murder, and also at the murder scene at about the time the murder occurred. The trial court admitted the records over the husband's privilege claim, and the husband was convicted of murder. On appeal, the court upheld the trial court's decision admitting the cell phone records, stating that the husband–wife privilege went only to the contents of the conversations between the husband and wife, not the fact that such conversations occurred. The murder conviction was affirmed.

WHEN ONE SPOUSE COMMITS CRIMES AGAINST THE OTHER SPOUSE OR CHILDREN

If a husband were to beat his wife or children and his wife could not testify against him in a criminal or divorce court because of the husband–wife privilege, the law would not make sense. Spouses can testify in criminal courts and divorce courts about beating and other violence against either the spouse or children. The husband–wife privilege does not forbid the testimony in such cases of the victim spouse against the offending spouse.[51]

However, some states limit this exception to personal violence committed against the victim spouse. In the 1992 case of *State v. Webb,*[52] the husband destroyed his wife's property, and the wife could not testify against her husband because the crime was not a crime of personal violence against her. But in the 1992 case of *State v. Delaney,*[53] the defendant's ex-wife could testify about the husband's sexual assaults against their child and the wife's two younger sisters, which occurred during the marriage.

At least one state has held that the violence against spouse exception also applies to persons outside the immediate family of the accused. In *Lynch v. Com.,*[54] the court held that the Kentucky exception to the marital privilege for harm to a person who was a "resident" of the household of the accused, Kentucky Rule of Evidence 504(c), applied to a third person living with the husband who invoked the privilege. The defendant and his wife were having marital problems, mainly due to the husband's jealously of his wife's earlier romantic arrangement with a former boyfriend, the eventual murder victim, and his wife moved out of the house. "Oddly enough," the court observed, the former boyfriend moved in with the husband after the wife left. The husband then murdered the former boyfriend as he slept one evening, and subsequently confessed the killing to his wife. The state called her as a witness, and the husband moved to exclude her testimony about his confession under the marital privilege statute. The trial court held that the former boyfriend qualified as a "person residing" in the defendant's household, and as a result the marital privilege did not extend to the wife's testimony about harm done to the former boyfriend. The defendant's murder conviction was affirmed.

THE PHYSICIAN–PATIENT PRIVILEGE

physician–patient privilege
The privilege created, not by common law, but by state law for state courts; belongs to the patient and may be waived by the patient.

The **physician–patient privilege** did not exist at common law and therefore exists only in states that have created such a privilege by statutes. The state statutes define the extent and the limitations of the privilege. In the absence of a statute, there would be no privilege to information obtained by a nurse, a dentist, a druggist, an orthopedist, a chiropractor, a Christian Science practitioner, or a veterinary surgeon. All these professions, however, have codes of ethics and would ordinarily be reluctant to reveal information obtained in a professional relationship unless compelled to do so.[55]

Because state statutes control the privilege, if it does exist, physicians have to comply with the statutory requirements of their state. If the statutes of the state require that physicians report persons treated for gunshot wounds, physicians must comply with this requirement. If the statutes require physicians to report persons treated for venereal disease, this requirement must also be met.

The physician–patient privilege is considered a very limited privilege, subject to the interpretation of the statutes of each state. The privilege, where it does exist, is for the protection of the patient, not the physician. Where the privilege does exist, it may be waived by the patient or a representative of the patient. Whether the privilege exists after the death of the patient depends on each state's laws and court rulings. The attending physician must file a death certificate, however, and all states have laws that permit public officials with statutory authority to order autopsies and coroner's inquests.

REQUIREMENTS OF THE PHYSICIAN–PATIENT PRIVILEGE

For the physician–patient privilege to exist, the patient must have consulted the physician for treatment or diagnosis for possible treatment. Where such conditions exist, it is immaterial who employs or pays the physician. If the physician under these circumstances calls in other medical doctors to aid in the treatment or diagnosis, any disclosures made to any of the physicians are also privileged.

The general rule is that a physician–patient privilege does not exist when a suspect or a defendant is being examined at the request of a court, a law enforcement agency, or a prosecutor. Such examinations may be requested or ordered when a court or prosecutor wants to determine whether a defendant is competent to stand trial or whether commitment proceedings should be commenced instead of filing criminal charges. When probable cause exists to believe a person has been driving a vehicle under the influence, a law enforcement agency might request medical testing to determine whether a crime has been committed. The results of such tests are normally excluded from the physician–patient privilege.

State v. Poetschke

Minnesota Court of
Appeals, 750 N.W.2d
301 (2008)

The defendant was involved in a single-vehicle automobile accident. The police officer at the scene suspected that the defendant had been drinking and informed her of the Minnesota implied consent law. The defendant then agreed to submit to blood tests. Because she was injured, the defendant was taken to the emergency room of a hospital for treatment. Her treating physician ordered blood tests for diagnostic purposes, and blood was taken from the defendant's arm. After the defendant was treated in the emergency room, the officer again asked whether she consented to an alcohol test, and she agreed. However, hospital technicians summoned to take a blood sample were unable to do so because of the condition of the defendant's veins.

Subsequently, the state obtained copies of the defendant's medical records, including the results of the blood tests conducted by the hospital. She was then charged with third-degree DWI, and at her trial the state introduced, over her claim of physician–patient privilege, the medical records containing her blood test results. She was convicted of DWI and sentenced to 365 days in jail.

On appeal, the Minnesota Court of Appeals reversed her conviction, holding that the physician–patient privilege applied to the medical records containing her blood test results. The court noted that the privilege applies to medical records about treatment as well as communications with a medical professional. Because the privilege applied to the medical records, the court framed the issue as whether the defendant's consent to tests waived the privilege.

The court first held that under the Minnesota implied consent statute, the only testing "impliedly consented to by a driver is one administered at the direction of a peace officer."[56] This distinguishes the Minnesota statute from the implied consent statutes in those states that permit the results of any blood test, once consent has been given. The court noted as an example that the Wisconsin physician–patient statute, section 905.04(4)(d) of the Wisconsin Statutes, states that there is no privilege concerning the results of any chemical tests for intoxication.[57]

The prosecution argued that the defendant's consent to blood tests waived her physician–patient privilege, but the court disagreed, holding that neither the state-implied consent statute nor the physician–patient privilege statute could be read to mean that consent to a state-administered blood test was also consent to release the results of blood tests done as part of her medical treatment. The defendant's conviction for DWI was reversed.

THE PSYCHOTHERAPIST–PATIENT PRIVILEGE

**psychotherapist–
patient privilege**
A privilege created
by statute in many
states.

Although no **psychotherapist–patient privilege** existed in common law, many states have created this privilege by statute. For a patient to qualify for this privilege, the patient must seek the treatment or diagnosis of a licensed psychotherapist for treatment of mental or emotional conditions, including drug addiction. Those professionals defined as psychotherapists ordinarily include licensed physicians and psychologists, or persons reasonably believed by the patient to be so licensed. The conditions and limitations of this privilege are ordinarily similar to those of the physician–patient privilege.

Under Rule 501 of the Federal Rules of Evidence, U.S. courts are responsible for formulating privileges. The federal courts have generally recognized those privileges that are available in state courts. In *Jaffee v. Redmond*,[58] the U.S. Supreme Court recognized the psychotherapist–patient privilege: "confidential communications between a licensed psychotherapist and his or her patients in the course of diagnosis and treatment are protected from compelled disclosure under Rule 501 of the Federal Rules of Evidence." The *Jaffee* court observed that all fifty states had enacted some form of psychotherapist privilege.

The psychotherapist privilege can be avoided in some kinds of cases. For example, in *United States v. Butrum*,[59] the court held that the privilege was not available where the patient was charged with child sexual abuse. The court permitted evidence of communications and records of psychiatric treatment the defendant received following the sexual abuse incidents.

THE DANGEROUS PATIENT EXCEPTION TO THE PSYCHOTHERAPIST–PATIENT PRIVILEGE

Beginning with the 1976 case of *Tarasoff v. Regents of the University of California*,[60] states begin adopting a "duty to protect" rule. Under this rule, once a psychotherapist discovers that a patient poses a serious threat to a third person, the psychotherapist must exercise reasonable efforts to protect that person. Many states have codified this duty. (See, for example, Tenn. Code Ann. 33-10-302.) California has adopted as part of its Evidence Code an exception to the psychotherapist–patient privilege that communications by a dangerous patient are not privileged. (See West's Cal. Evid. Code 1024.)

One federal court has adopted a "dangerous patient" exception to the psychotherapist privilege. In *United States v. Glass*,[61] the court held that a psychotherapist could testify in a criminal case about otherwise privileged communications only if no other alternative to disclosure of threats made by the patient against a third party existed to avert harm to that person. The defendant was charged with threats to kill the president of the United States, a federal crime. Testimony of the psychotherapist to whom the threats were made was the only evidence of the threats, upon which the defendant's conditional guilty plea based. Although the *Glass* court found that the evidence did not support the government's position that disclosure by the psychotherapist was the only way to protect the president, and therefore vacated the guilty plea, it found that under the proper circumstances the privilege could be lost. The *Glass* court based its decision on a footnote in *Jaffee,* where the Supreme Court said: "[W]e do not doubt that there are situations in which the privilege must give way, for example, if a serious threat of harm to the patient or to others can be averted only by means of a disclosure by a therapist."[62]

One other federal court has refused to adopt the dangerous patient exception. In *United States v. Hayes*,[63] the court held that grafting such an exception onto the psychotherapist privilege would have a serious chilling effect on patients' willingness to seek treatment. It concluded that while the "duty to protect" might permit a psychotherapist to inform authorities about a patient's threats, that duty did not require that the psychotherapist be compelled or permitted over the patient's objection to testify at a criminal trial based on those threats.

In the 2008 case of *United States v. Auster*,[64] the Fifth Circuit Court of Appeals refused to follow the *Hayes* decision. The *Auster* court observed that it was now common practice for psychotherapists to inform dangerous patients in advance that a *Tarasoff* letter would be sent to persons threatened by the patient during a psychotherapy session. As a result, the patient would know in advance that not all his communications would be confidential. The *Auster* court thus concluded that the negative impact on the patient's willingness to confide in the psychotherapist would be minimal if the psychotherapist was compelled to testify about the threats, and the court held that the privilege did not apply.

THE SEXUAL ASSAULT COUNSELOR'S PRIVILEGE AND PRIVILEGES COVERING OTHER COUNSELORS

sexual assault counselor's privilege
The privilege for counselors of victims of sexual assault and crimes of violence; also applies to records and testimony by counselors without the consent of the victim or patient.

Victims of sexual assaults and other crimes of violence often need and are provided with counseling. Drug and alcohol rehabilitation counseling is also available in all states. Counselors are available in schools at all levels of education. Families under stress often receive counseling.

Many states have statutes that protect the private communications of persons receiving counseling. In the 1992 case of *Commonwealth v. Wilson*,[65] the Supreme Court of Pennsylvania held that the Pennsylvania sexual assault privilege statute provided an absolute privilege protecting not only testimony but also the production of documents covering the history of persons protected by the privilege. The defendants in this case were charged with sex crimes and sought records of their victims in the files of the sexual assault counselor to use in their defense. The court held that the **sexual assault counselor's privilege** prevented the production of the counselor's files.

THE CLERGY–PENITENT PRIVILEGE

About two-thirds of the states have statutes defining the clergy–penitent privilege, with a few other states recognizing the privilege by court decisions. No clear-cut privilege emerged from the old common law protecting confidential communications with clergy.

Statutes ordinarily define clergy as a minister, priest, rabbi, or other similar functionary of a religious organization, or a person reasonably believed to be so by the penitent consulting him or her. A clergyperson does not have to be engaged full time in the profession, but the definitions are not so broad as to include all self-denominated "ministers."

Because of moral and ethical reasons, ministers, priests, and rabbis would not ordinarily reveal confessions and confidential disclosures made to them. The privilege establishes a legal protection against being forced to testify on a witness stand about confidential disclosures made to them.

Do Privileges Prevent Law Officers from Talking to a Wife, Husband, or Others?

Privileges apply only to prevent the use of testimony in a judicial proceeding (in-court). [*United States v. Kaprelian,* 768 F.2d 893 (7th Cir. 1985), *cert. denied,* 474 U.S. 1008, 106 S.Ct. 533 (1985)]

Therefore, law officers can talk to and question spouses, children, and other persons. Whether a willing spouse can testify in a courtroom against the spouse in a criminal trial depends on the privilege law in that state.

The case of *People v. Ward* [604 N.Y.S.2d 320 (A.D. 1993)] illustrates. The defendant, Ward, confessed to a clergyman that he had committed a murder. The clergyman called the police, and the defendant then confessed to the police. The New York clergy–penitent privilege did not apply to this situation because privileges are evidentiary rules having to do with testimony in a courtroom. Ward's conviction for murder was affirmed because the police had probable cause to arrest him after his confession.

THE NEWS REPORTER'S PRIVILEGE NOT TO REVEAL THE SOURCE OF THE INFORMATION

Does the Constitution Give News Reporters a Privilege Not to Reveal the Source of Their Information?

news reporter's privilege
A privilege that does not exist in common law; created by statutes in many states.

We have all read stories about the newsperson who is sent to jail for contempt of court for refusing to disclose the source of a story or article. The newsperson usually contends that the **news reporter's privilege**, based on the First Amendment, provides a privilege against such disclosure. Does such a right exist? In the 1972 case of *Branzburg v. Hayes,*[66] the U.S. Supreme Court held it did not:

[T]he great weight of authority is that newsmen are not exempt from the normal duty of appearing before a grand jury and answering questions relevant to a criminal investigation. At common law, courts consistently refused to recognize the existence of any privilege authorizing a newsman to refuse to reveal confidential information to a grand jury.

Common law did not generally recognize journalist privilege, but most states have enacted a news reporter shield law or have established protections for news reporters.[67] These laws generally have exceptions, such as when a life is at risk or in a situation that concerns an emergency within the community such as a terrorist attack. The smorgasbord of different laws sometimes leaves journalists uncertain about the legal protections they can rely on.

Unless a state has a statute creating the privilege, news reporters have no general First Amendment privilege and right not to reveal sources of news articles when ordered by a court.[68] In the 2005 case of *In re Grand Jury Investigation-Judith Miller,*[69] the court of appeals held that the First Amendment does not create a privilege for a reporter to refuse to divulge the identity of a confidential source. It also stated that if there were a federal common-law privilege, it did not apply to grand jury proceedings involved in that case. In 2007 the House of Representatives passed a media shield bill. The Senate version, called the Free Flow of Information Act, had not been enacted as of August 2008.

THE PROBLEM OF LEAKING GOVERNMENT INFORMATION TO THE PRESS, OR SHOULD LEAKING BE ENCOURAGED?

Newspeople and other media representatives frequently contend that they need to rely on government employees as sources for information about things like fraud and corruption in federal, state, and local governments. They argue that newsperson shield laws are very important in helping them obtain information that governments might otherwise seek to hide.

This is particularly important in the case of the federal government, which because of its greater size and more tax money to spend, has power and influence in many different areas, which can increase the need for outside inspection.

Two recent examples illustrate the importance of leaks by federal government employees to news organizations:

- In 2005, thirty years after the Watergate scandal, it was disclosed that W. Mark Felt, the number-two man at the FBI at the time, was the informant known as "Deep Throat." Felt leaked sensitive, classified information to news reporters in the 1970s, gleaned from ongoing FBI investigations, which is a crime under federal law. Newspaper stories about the White House cover-up of the burglary of the Democratic headquarters in the Watergate office building led to an extensive congressional investigation of the role of the White House in the burglary and resulting cover-up. As a result of that investigation, impeachment proceedings against President Richard Nixon were begun, and ultimately President Nixon resigned and Vice President Gerald Ford became president.
- In 2003 newspaper columnist Robert Novak identified a prominent Washington, DC, woman as an undercover CIA operative in a news column. Novak also stated that two senior Bush administration officials had "leaked" the information that the woman was an "agent operative." After an FBI investigation and an extensive grand jury hearing, in 2007 Irv Lewis "Scooter" Libby, chief of staff to Vice President Dick Cheney, was convicted of lying to investigators about the CIA leak and sentenced to 30 months in prison. President George W. Bush commuted the sentence almost immediately and Libby was required to pay a $250,000 fine.

Not all leaks for good news stories come from government employees. For example, Linda Tripp taped the telephone conversations she had with her friend Monica Lewinski, in which Lewinski told of her sexual trysts with President Bill Clinton in the White House offices. This bit of gossip fell into the hands of newspapers and came to the attention of members of Congress. President Clinton was impeached—that is, charges were brought against him—but the Senate refused to convict him after a dramatic public trial. Criminal charges were brought against

Former CIA analyst Valerie Plame is sworn in on Capitol Hill in Washington, Friday, March 16, 2007, prior to testifying before the House Oversight and Government Reform Committee. Plame resigned after her identity as a classified, covert CIA operative was compromised when *Washington Post* columnist Robert Novak named her as "an agency operative on weapons of mass destruction."

© AP Photo/Dennis Cook

Tripp for violating Maryland's law that forbids taping a telephone conversation without the consent of all parties to the conversation. Tripp's charges were settled with a plea bargain.

IS THERE A PARENT–CHILD PRIVILEGE?

Can a parent be compelled to testify against a child? Could a child be compelled to testify against a parent? Or could either voluntarily testify in a criminal case against the other?

The question of whether a privilege exists based solely on the parent–child relationship has come before many courts in recent years. The Seventh Circuit Court of Appeals reviewed these cases and found that only one federal trial court and one state appellate court have recognized some type of parent–child privilege.[70] Most courts have refused to recognize a parent–child privilege. In rejecting the rulings of the two courts that recognized a parent–child privilege, the court of appeals in the following case refused to recognize the privilege.

United States v. Davies and Kaprelian

Seventh Circuit Court of Appeals, 768 F.2d 893 (1985), *review denied*, 474 U.S. 1008, 106 S.Ct. 533, 38 CrL 4105

While a jewelry salesman was paying for gasoline at a self-service station, another man got into his Cadillac and drove away with the car and sample cases filled with jewelry. The Cadillac was driven to another state, where a witness and other information led the FBI to believe that a man named Kaprelian was involved in the theft. While FBI agents had Kaprelian's house under surveillance, Kaprelian's teenaged daughter left the house. FBI agents questioned the daughter and learned that Kaprelian was living with Ms. Davies. FBI agents obtained Davies's telephone number from Kaprelian's daughter and were able to arrest Davies as she was transporting the jewelry in a tote bag. In rejecting Kaprelian's claim of parent–child privilege, the court held:

> Even were there some substantial support for the defendant's proposition that there is a parent–child privilege, this case would not be one in which it could be applied. Privileges apply only to prevent the use of testimony in a judicial proceeding. Kaprelian's daughter gave the F.B.I. agent his telephone number during the F.B.I.'s investigation of the jewel robbery. As the Supreme Court has noted, "... [neither the husband–wife privilege] nor any other privilege, prevents the Government from enlisting one spouse to give information concerning the other to aid in the other's apprehension." *Trammel,* 445 U.S. at 52 n.12, 100 S.Ct. at 913 n.12. Kaprelian makes no assertion that the government ever intended to call his daughter at the trial; his assertions of privilege are based solely on her questioning during the investigation. Thus neither this phone number nor any other evidence obtained through this critical investigative lead are subject to suppression by the district court.
>
> We thus reject Kaprelian's claim that there exists a privilege for communications between parents and their children in criminal cases and find no error in the admission of evidence developed as a result of obtaining Kaprelian's telephone number from his daughter.

THE PRIVILEGE CONCERNING THE IDENTITY OF INFORMANTS

informants
Persons who provide information to law officers.

Law enforcement agencies and government have always realized that information from private citizens and paid **informants** is needed for effective law enforcement. When a major crime occurs, law enforcement agencies often need information to head their investigations in the right direction. Most information that law officers receive from private citizens and informers is of little value in solving major crimes, but some information identifies wrongdoers or provides important clues about crimes.

To encourage people to provide information, governments must be able to assure those people that their identity will not be disclosed, whether it is a private citizen voluntarily providing the information or a person providing information for money or other consideration.

Common law has always recognized the informant's privilege as an essential aid to law enforcement. Today, many states have enacted statutes defining the privilege, while other states and the federal government use the privilege in its common-law form.

In the 1957 case of *Roviaro v. United States*,[71] the U.S. Supreme Court commented as follows regarding the informant's privilege:

> What is usually referred to as the informer's privilege is in reality the Government's privilege to withhold from disclosure the identity of persons who furnish information of violations of law to officers charged with the enforcement of that law.... The purpose of the privilege is the furtherance and protection of the public interest in effective law enforcement.

THE LIMITS TO THE INFORMANT'S PRIVILEGE

The informant's privilege is not an absolute privilege and must give way when there is a compelling need to protect the rights of the accused. In the *Roviaro* case,[72] the Supreme Court held that the limits of the privilege arise from

> fundamental requirements of fairness. Where the disclosure of an informer's identity, or of the contents of his communication, is relevant and helpful to the defense of the accused, or is essential to the fair determination of a cause, the privilege must give way. In these situations the trial court may require disclosure.

Defendants in criminal trials have the right to know the names of people who were at the scene of the alleged crime or persons who were participants in the crime that is alleged. These people could be important material witnesses for the defense, and their testimony could be relevant. The courts have held that defense lawyers should have access to these people as potential witnesses. If the informant was at the scene of the crime or participated in the crime, courts hold that the informant's identity must be disclosed to the defense lawyer.

It is unlikely that a court will order the disclosure of the identity of an informant unless the informant was present at the scene of the crime charged, participated in the crime charged, or was at the scene of the arrest. Because the informant could be an undercover police officer, informants should be kept away from the scene of a crime or an arrest, if possible.

The question of an informant's identity is frequently raised in drug prosecutions. Search warrants used to search for illegal drugs are often based on tips from confidential informants. When drugs are found and the defendants charged, the name of the informant may be demanded to better judge the accuracy of the search warrant. Since the informant does not testify at the trial and has no direct evidence of the crime, his or her identity is not "material to the determination of the case," and the privilege applies.[73]

When a suspect could be charged for multiple drug transactions, prosecutors can avoid problems by not charging crimes where an informant was present at the scene of the crime or participated in the crime. If the court orders the identity of an informant, two options are available:

1. Drop the criminal charge against the defendant, which means that the defense has won its case because this is what the defense lawyer seeks.
2. Disclose the identity of the informant if this is practical and go to trial, possibly using the informant as a witness.

THE GOVERNMENT'S PRIVILEGE NOT TO REVEAL GOVERNMENT SECRETS

THE PRIVILEGE NOT TO DISCLOSE MILITARY OR DIPLOMATIC SECRETS VITAL TO NATIONAL SECURITY

The U.S. Congress enacted the Classified Information Procedures Act (18 U.S.C.A. App. 1), which recognizes the power of the executive branch of the federal government to determine whether classified information should be disclosed in criminal or civil trials.

The use of the government's privilege was before the U.S. Supreme Court in the 1953 case of *United States v. Reynolds.*[74] Widows of civilians killed in the crash of a U.S. Air Force plane attempted to obtain the accident report for use in their civil lawsuit. The secretary of the Air Force wrote to the trial judge stating that the report contained information on secret electronic devices, so it was against the public interest to make the accident report public. In holding that the government had a privilege not to reveal such information, the Supreme Court held:

> In the instant case we cannot escape judicial notice that this is a time of vigorous preparation for national defense. Experience in the past war has made it common knowledge that air power is one of the most potent weapons in our scheme of defense, and that newly developing electronic devices have greatly enhanced the effective use of air power. It is equally apparent that these electronic devices must be kept secret if their full military advantage is to be exploited in the national interests. On the record before the trial court it appeared that this accident occurred to a military plane which had gone aloft to test secret electronic equipment. Certainly there was a reasonable danger that the accident investigation report would contain references to the secret electronic equipment which was the primary concern of the mission.
>
> [W]hen the formal claim of privilege was filed by the Secretary of the Air Force, under circumstances indicating a reasonable possibility that military secrets were involved, there was certainly a sufficient showing of privilege to cut off further demand for the document on the showing of necessity for its compulsion that had then been made.

THE PRESIDENT'S PRIVILEGE OF CONFIDENTIALITY

In holding that the president of the United States has a privilege of confidentiality of his conversations and correspondence, the U.S. Supreme Court held in the 1974 case of *United States v. Nixon*[75] that:

> There is nothing novel about governmental confidentiality. The meetings of the Constitutional Convention in 1787 were conducted in complete privacy.... Moreover, all records of those meetings were sealed for more than 30 years after the Convention.... Most of the Framers acknowledge that without secrecy no constitution of the kind that was developed could have been written. 418 U.S. at 705, 94 S.Ct. at 3106, n.15.

The Supreme Court gave these reasons for the privilege that protects confidential communications between the president and the president's immediate advisors:

> A President and those who assist him must be free to explore alternatives in the process of shaping policies and making decisions and to do so in a way many would be unwilling to express except privately. These are the considerations justifying a

WITNESS PRIVILEGES, SHIELD LAWS, AND IMMUNITY

The following summarizes some of the privileges and immunity rules discussed in this chapter, as well as related topics.

Witness privileges	• Only one, the privilege against self-incrimination, is constitutional. All others are created by statute or common law.
	• The privilege in most cases belongs to the client, patient, or other defendant.
	• The privilege applies only to testimony in court, judicial proceedings, or testimony before legislative bodies.
Shield laws	• Rape shield laws in most states prohibit evidence in sexual assault trials that is believed to be prejudicial or harassing to the victim in the case.
	• Journalist shield laws give news reporters the privilege to protect a news source. The privilege is not a constitutional right, and therefore the desire for a free press must be balanced with the need of government to uncover information of criminal activity.
Immunity laws, granting civil and criminal immunity	• Witness immunity may be granted to key witnesses, and they may then be compelled under power of contempt to testify.
	• Government officials have immunity where provided by statute. Under 42 U.S.C.A. section 1983, federal officers are immune from lawsuits based on actions taken within their authority. Most states have similar laws. Judges and prosecutors have absolute immunity for actions done in the performance of their duties [see *Mireles v. Waco*, 502 U.S. 9 (1991)]. Law enforcement officers, corrections officers, and most other public officials are entitled to only qualified immunity under section 1983 [see *Harlow v. Fitzgerald*, 457 U.S. 800 (1982)].
	• Heads of state have sovereign immunity, which under international law provides that they are not subject to the jurisdiction of foreign courts [see *United States v. Noriega*, 117 F.3d 1206 (11th Cir. 1997), *cert. denied*, 118 S.Ct. 1389 (1998)].

presumptive privilege for Presidential communications. The privilege is fundamental to the operation of Government and inextricably rooted in the separation of powers under the Constitution. 418 U.S. at 708, 94 S.Ct. at 3107.

The Court held, however, that the privilege is a qualified privilege and would give way should a party to a legal action show a great need for relevant evidence that is protected by the privilege.[76]

THE SECRECY OF GRAND JURY PROCEEDINGS AS A PRIVILEGE

The federal government and some states use grand juries to criminally indict, or charge, persons. Probably all states and the federal government also use grand juries to investigate situations where criminal activities may be occurring.

The use of grand juries goes back in English history more than a hundred years before the American Revolution. The Framers of the Constitution included in the Fifth Amendment the requirement that the federal government use a grand jury of private citizens for indicting persons with federal felonies (see Appendix A). States do not have to follow this requirement.

Citizens who serve on a grand jury are required to take an ancient oath that binds them to keep secret "the King's counsel, your fellows' and your own." The Federal Rules of Criminal Procedure forbid disclosure of "matters occurring before ... [a] grand jury" and provide that violations can be punished as contempt of court [Rule 6(e)].

grand jury secrecy requirements
The mandates that persons serving on grand juries will not to disclose "matters occurring before" the grand jury on which they serve.

According to the **grand jury secrecy requirements**, people who serve on a grand jury, therefore, cannot disclose proceedings and deliberations by that body. They have a privilege not to answer questions requiring disclosure of such matters unless they fall within exceptions listed in Federal Rule of Criminal Procedure 6(e).

Some of the reasons for the historic use of secrecy regarding deliberations and evidence considered by grand juries are to encourage and protect the independence and freedom of grand jury deliberations, to protect the reputations of people who are not indicted for criminal offenses but were considered, to prevent people who will be indicted from fleeing because they had information of the coming criminal charges, to encourage witnesses to testify freely, and to encourage members of the grand jury to deliberate freely knowing that what is said will not be made public.

SUMMARY

Judicial notice statutes in every state function to avoid unnecessary delays in courts. Trial judges may take judicial notice of facts known to the community that are not subject to reasonable disputes and to other information listed in the statutes of the state. This saves time and effort in helping to move both criminal and civil cases along.

Testimonial privileges are rules of evidence. The privilege against self-incrimination is a constitutional requirement that protects suspects from becoming witnesses against themselves unless they voluntarily waive this privilege.

Other testimonial privileges were created to protect relationships and interests, such as husband–wife, attorney–client, and physician–patient. These relationships have been determined to be of sufficient importance so as to justify sacrificing what might be reliable evidence from being used in criminal and civil trials.

Privileges apply only to prevent the use of testimony in criminal trials and other judicial proceedings. In investigating criminal matters, law officers may talk to spouses, children, and others who will cooperate. Whether a spouse can testify against the other spouse depends on whether the evidence falls within the spousal privilege and whether the other spouse asserts the privilege.

CASE ANALYSIS

Read Appendix B, Finding and Analyzing Cases (p. 427). With these guidelines in mind, please continue with the Case Analysis selections for Chapter 6.

1. The husband–wife privilege does not apply to situations in which both spouses are charged with a crime. In such cases, one spouse is permitted to testify against the other spouse

over that spouse's invoking of the privilege. The same is often true where one spouse commits a crime against the other spouse while in the process of committing a crime against a third person. In such a case, the injured spouse may testify against the other spouse over his or her objection. Wisconsin has by statute created such an exception. Can you think of the reason for the exception? Consider the case of *State v. Richard G. B.* [656 N.W.2d 469 (Wis. App. 2002)] [Case No. 02-1302], *review denied* (2003). In that case, the wife of the defendant was permitted over his privilege claim to testify about a private conversation between the couple. Should the Wisconsin exception apply? Why or why not? What crime was committed against the spouse during the crime against the third person?

2. How broad is the crime-fraud exception to the attorney–client privilege? If a client asks his lawyer for advice on how to best persuade the client's girlfriend to convince a grand jury that she, not the defendant, a convicted felon, owned a firearm, may the attorney be compelled to testify concerning all the communications between the attorney and the client? If not, which communications are privileged, and which are not? Can you fashion a sensible rule for these situations? Read *In re Grand Jury Subpoena* [419 F.3d 329 (5th Cir. 2005)] [Docket No. 04–30508] for that court's ruling.

3. Can a judge take judicial notice of a letter sent to the judge by the defendant, stating facts that were different from those given in the defendant's subsequent testimony? For what purpose might a judge take such judicial notice? See *Sanders v. State* [782 N.E.2d 1036 (Ind. App. 2003)].

4. In many cases, affidavits given by the police to show probable cause for the issuance of a search warrant contain information about confidential informants, including the informant's identity. It is therefore common to seal the parts of the affidavit that contain such information. In *Franks v. Delaware* [438 U.S. 1541 (1978)], the U.S. Supreme Court held that the Fourth Amendment gives defendants the right to challenge the validity of information in such affidavits. Called a *Franks* hearing, a defendant must make some initial showing that some basis exists to believe the affidavit is false. Can a defendant in a *Franks* hearing get the sealed part of an affidavit unsealed based on his claim that he needs the informant's information to satisfy the *Franks* requirements? See *United States v. Napier* [436 F.3d 1133 (9th Cir. 2006)].

Notes

1. *Varcoe v. Lee*, 181, pp. 223, 226.
2. Either party to a civil or criminal action may challenge a ruling by a judge who takes judicial notice of a fact. Many states have statutes similar to Federal Rule of Evidence 201(b), which provides that a "judicially noticed fact must be one not subject to reasonable dispute…." In the case of *Palmer v. Mitchell* [206 N.E.2d 776 (Ill. App. 1965)], a finding of judicial notice was reversed because the information was within the personal knowledge of the judge but was not a matter of common and general knowledge of the community.
3. *Barreiro v. State Bar of California*, 88 Cal. Rptr. 192, 471 P.2d 992 (1970).
4. *Sumpter v. State*, 306 N.E.2d 95 (1974).
5. 822 P.2d 23.
6. *Dillon v. Gloss*, 256 U.S. 368, 41 S.Ct. 510.
7. 825 P.2d 781.
8. 412 S.E.2d 473.
9. 924 A.2d 384 (N.H. 2007).
10. 955 F.2d 799 (2d Cir.).
11. 296 N.E.2d 837.
12. Footnote 27 of the *Miranda* decision [384 U.S. at 458, 86 S.Ct. 1619] states: "Thirteenth century commentators found an analogue to the privilege grounded in the Bible. 'To sum up the matter, the principle that no man is to be declared guilty on his own admission is a divine decree.'"

Maimonides, Mishneh Torah (Code of Jewish Law), Book of Judges, Laws of the Sanhedrin, c. 18, 6. III Yale Judaica Series 52–53. See also Lamm, *The Fifth Amendment and Its Equivalent in the Halakhah,* 5 Judaism 53 (Winter 1956).

13. *Fisher v. United States,* 425 U.S. 391, 409, 96 S.Ct. 1569, 1580 (1976).

14. *Kastigar v. United States,* 406 U.S. 441, 444, 92 S.Ct. 1653, 1656 (1972).

15. The problem of determining whether a person is properly using the privilege against self-incrimination and whether the person's answer will subject the person to criminal prosecution is complex. The U.S. Supreme Court stated in the 1953 case of *United States v. Reynolds* [73 S.Ct. 528] that:

> Too much judicial inquiry into the claim of privilege would force disclosure of the thing the privilege was meant to protect, while a complete abandonment of judicial control would lead to intolerable abuses. Indeed, in the earlier stages of judicial experience with the problem, both extremes were advocated, some saying that the bare assertion by the witness must be taken as conclusive, and others saying that the witness should be required to reveal the matter behind his claim of privilege to the judge for verification. Neither extreme prevailed, and a sound formula of compromise was developed. This formula received authoritative expression in this country as early as the Burr trial. There are differences in phraseology, but in substance it is agreed that the court must be satisfied from all the evidence and circumstances, and "from the implications of the question, in the setting in which it is asked, that a responsive answer to the question or an explanation of why it cannot be answered might be dangerous because injurious exposure could result." *Hoffman v. United States,* 341 U.S. 479, 486–487, 71 S.Ct. 814, 818 (1951). If the court is so satisfied, the claim of the privilege will be accepted without requiring further disclosure.

16. *Murphy v. Waterfront Comm.,* 378 U.S. 52, 55, 84 S.Ct. 1594, 1596 (1964).

17. *Miranda v. Arizona,* 384 U.S. 436, 460, 86 S.Ct. 1602, 1620 (1966).

18. *Schmerber v. California,* 384 U.S. 757, 86 S.Ct. 1826 (1966).

19. *Gilbert v. California,* 388 U.S. 263, 87 S.Ct. 1951 (1967).

20. *United States v. Wade,* 388 U.S. 218, 87 S.Ct 1926 (1967).

21. *United States v. Dionisio,* 410 U.S. 1, 93 S.Ct. 764 (1973).

22. *United States v. Hammond,* 419 F.2d 166, 168 (4th Cir. 1969), *cert. denied,* 397 U.S. 1068, 90 S.Ct. 1508 (1970).

23. *United States v. Murray,* 523 F.2d 489, 492 (8th Cir. 1975).

24. *United States v. Valenzuela,* 722 F.2d 1431, 1433 (9th Cir. 1983).

25. *United States v. Roberts,* 481 F.2d 892 (5th Cir. 1973).

26. *United States v. Brown,* 920 F.2d 1212 (5th Cir. 1991).

27. *Holt v. United States,* 218 U.S. 245, 31 S.Ct. 2 (1910).

28. Granting immunity has always been a means used by states and the federal government for obtaining information. Immunity can be either complete or limited. *Use and fruits* is a limited immunity; it differs from *transactional immunity,* which is referred to as an *immunity bath.* The Fourth Circuit Court of Appeals defined each in the 1992 case of *United States v. Harris* [973 F.2d 333, 336] as follows:

> The Supreme Court in *Kastigar v. United States,* 406 U.S. 441, 92 S.Ct. 1653, 32 L.Ed.2d 212 (1972), approved the government's grant of "use" immunity under 18 U.S.C. § 6002 to compel a witness' self-incriminating testimony. Because the government, under the statute, cannot use the immunized testimony or any evidence derived from it either directly or indirectly, the Court held that use immunity is "coextensive with the scope of the privilege against self-incrimination, and therefore is sufficient to compel testimony over a claim of the privilege." Id. at 453, 92 S.Ct. at 1661. The Court in *Kastigar* distinguished between use and the broader concept of transactional immunity. Transactional immunity protects an individual against prosecution for anything concerning the substance of compelled testimony. Use immunity, on the other hand, only protects against the government's use of compulsory testimony as a source of evidence, leaving the government free to use any other evidence to prosecute.

29. *George Campbell Painting Corp. v. Reid,* 392 U.S. 286, 88 S.Ct. 1978 (1968); *United States v. Doe,* 465 U.S. 605, 104 S.Ct. 1237 (1984); *United States v. White,* 322 U.S. 694, 64 S.Ct. 1248 (1944).

30. *Bursey v. United States,* 466 F.2d 1059 (9th Cir. 1972).

31. The U.S. Supreme Court held in the *Bouknight* case that:

> In *New York v. Quarles,* 467 US 649 ... (1984), we recognized a public safety exception to the usual Fifth

Amendment rights afforded by *Miranda v. Arizona*, 384 US 436 ... (1966), so that police could recover a firearm which otherwise would have remained in a public area. In the present case, a citation for civil contempt in order to obtain the production of a child such as Maurice M., or knowledge about his whereabouts, is not essentially criminal in nature and aims primarily to securing the safety of the child. Protecting infants from child abuse seems to me to rank in order of social importance with the regulation and prevention of traffic accidents.

32. *United States v. Medley*, 33 M.J. 75 (1991), *review denied*, U.S. Supreme Court, 112 S.Ct. 1473, 50 CrL 3199 (1992).

33. *United States v. Heyward*, 22 M.J. 35 (C.M.A. 1986).

34. 532 U.S. 17 (2001).

35. 274 F.3d 1053 (6th Cir. 2001).

36. 242 F.3d 49 (1st Cir. 2001).

37. 269 F.3d 1023 (9th Cir. 2001).

38. The "work–product" doctrine is closely related to the attorney–client privilege. The U.S. Supreme Court stated in *Upjohn Co. v. United States* [449 U.S. 383, 101 S.Ct. 677 (1981)] that:

This doctrine was announced by the Court over 30 years ago in *Hickman v. Taylor*, 329 U.S. 495 (1947). In that case the Court rejected "an attempt, without purported necessity or justification, to secure written statements, private memoranda, and personal recollections prepared or formed by an adverse party's counsel in the course of his legal duties." *Id.*, at 510. The Court noted that "it is essential that a lawyer work with a certain degree of privacy" and reasoned that if discovery of the material sought were permitted, "much of what is now put down in writing would remain unwritten. An attorney's thoughts, heretofore inviolate, would not be his own. Inefficiency, unfairness and sharp practices would inevitably develop in the giving of legal advice and in the preparation of cases for trial. The effect on the legal profession would be demoralizing. And the interests of the clients and the cause of justice would be poorly served." *Id.*, at 511.

39. *Upjohn Co. v. United States*, 449 U.S. 383 (1981).

40. *In Re: A Witness Before the Special Grand Jury*, 288 F.3d 289 (7th Cir. 2002).

41. 399 F.3d 527.

42. 109 S.Ct. 2619.

43. 602 A.2d 677, 687.

44. Many courts have adopted what is called the *last link doctrine* or *legal advice rule*: Where a client goes to an attorney for legal advice and where revealing the client's identity would be the last link in information needed to convict the client of a crime, the client's name is privileged. Examples of such rare situations where the last link doctrine apply are: (a) In 1960 the Internal Revenue Service received a letter from an attorney stating that a check enclosed of $12,706.85 was forwarded for additional taxes owed by undisclosed taxpayers. The attorney refused to disclose any names, citing the attorney–client privilege. When the matter was appealed, the U.S. Court of Appeals, applying California law, upheld the privilege holding that disclosing the clients' names would amount to an acknowledgement of guilt by the clients of the very matter for which legal advice was sought [*Baird v. Koerner*, 279 F.2d 623 (9th Cir. 1960)]. (b) In a federal drug conspiracy prosecution, prosecutors sought to compel the defense lawyer to disclose the name of the unknown person who paid the defense lawyer's fees. Claiming his client was also involved in the drug conspiracy and that disclosing his client's name would disclose a confidential communication, the defense lawyer was successful in asserting the attorney–client privilege [*Matter of Grand Jury Proceeding*, 898 F.2d 565 (7th Cir. 1990)].

The last link or legal advice rule is not applicable if a lawyer is hired to further illegal activity. For example, this could occur where legal advice is sought for the operation of an illegal drug operation or to provide tax advice for illegal activities. See *In re Grand Jury Investigation* [723 F.2d 447 (6th Cir. 1983), *review denied*, U.S. Supreme Court, 467 U.S. 1246, 104 S.Ct. 3524 (1984)].

45. 445 U.S. 40, 100 S.Ct. 906.

46. 966 F.2d 398 (8th Cir.).

47. See 260 F.3d 1295 (11th Cir. 2001). Probably no state extends the husband–wife privilege to people living together but not married. See the 1991 case of *Montanez v. State* [592 So.2d 650 (Ala. Crim. App.)], where the court held that the defendant's communications with his "paramour" were not protected by the marital communications privilege. In that case, the woman was granted use immunity and testified against the defendant. In addition, she was a joint participant in the drug trafficking and came under the partners-in-crime exception.

Most states have abolished common-law marriages, but the husband–wife privilege may generally be invoked not only in states that recognize common-law marriages but also in other states where common-law married couples have moved. See the 1998 case of *People v. Schmidt* [1998 WL 101837], where Michigan extended the privilege to a couple who had entered into a valid common-law marriage in Alabama and then moved to Michigan.

48. *United States v. Evans,* 966 F.2d 398 (8th Cir. 1992).

49. *United States v. Hill,* 967 F.2d 902 (3d Cir. 1992).

50. 979 So.2d 283 (Fla. App. 2008).

51. *United States v. Marashi,* 913 F.2d 724 (9th Cir. 1990).

52. 824 P. 1257 (Wash. App.).

53. 417 S.E.2d 903 (W. Va.).

54. 74 S.W.3d 711 (Ky. 2002).

55. For an extensive discussion of the physician–patient relationship, see Chapter 12 of *McCormick on Evidence,* 4th ed. (West Publishing, 1992).

56. 750 N.W.2d at 306.

57. *Id.*

58. 518 U.S. 1, 15 (1996).

59. 17 F.3d 1299 (10th Cir. 1993), *review denied,* 513 U.S. 863.

60. 551 P.2d 334 (Cal. 1976).

61. 133 F.3d 1356 (10th Cir. 1998).

62. 518 U.S. 1, 18.

63. 227 F.3d 578 (6th Cir. 2000).

64. 517 F.3d 312 (5th Cir.).

65. 602 A.2d 1290.

66. 408 U.S. 665, 92 S.Ct. 2646.

67. See, for example, Nebraska Rev. Stat. 20–146 (reissue 1991).

68. If the general public is excluded from a crime scene or an area where a disaster has occurred, do newspersons have rights and privileges that the general public does not have? The U.S. Supreme Court addressed this question in the 1972 case of *Branzburg v. Hayes* [92 S.Ct. 2646], stating: "Newsmen have no constitutional right of access to the scenes of crime or disaster when the general public is excluded, and they may be prohibited from attending or publishing information about trials if such restrictions are necessary to assure a defendant a fair trial before an impartial tribunal...." In 1989 a Milwaukee news reporter refused to leave the scene of the crash of a commercial airline. The site was sealed off so that emergency equipment and personnel could assist the injured and dying. The newsman was arrested because he insisted that he had a right to photograph and view the scene. The Wisconsin Supreme Court affirmed his conviction for disorderly conduct in *City of Oak Creek v. King* [436 N.W.2d 285].

69. 397 F.3d 964 (D.C. Cir. 2005), *cert. denied,* 125 S.Ct. 2977 (2005).

70. The courts and cases holding that a parent–child privilege exists are *In re Agosto* [553 F.Supp. 1298 (D. Nev. 1983)] and *In re Application of A & M* [403 N.Y.S.2d 375 (App. Div. 1975)].

71. 353 U.S. 53, 77 S.Ct. 623.

72. 353 U.S. 60, 77 S.Ct. 628.

73. See *United States v. Hollis,* 245 F.3d 671 (8th Cir. 2001).

74. 345 U.S. 1, 73 S.Ct. 528.

75. 418 U.S. 683, 94 S.Ct. 3090.

76. Members of the U.S. Congress also have a privilege referred to as a "nondisclosure privilege." In 2006 search warrants were issued to obtain criminal evidence in the investigation of Congressman William Jefferson, who was later charged with sixteen counts of money laundering and other offenses. Jefferson filed motions to have the evidence seized from his congressional office returned to him, claiming the information was privileged. In *United States v. Rayburn House Office Building, Room 2113* [497 F.3d 654 (D.C. Cir. 2007), *cert. denied,* 128 S.Ct. 1738 (2008)], the court of appeals held that all privileged evidence must be returned to Jefferson under the Speech or Debate Clause of ARTICLE I of the U.S. Constitution. That clause provides that the speech of a member of Congress "shall not be questioned in any other place ... for any speech or debate in either House."

The Use of Hearsay in the Courtroom

CHAPTER 7

LEARNING OBJECTIVES

In this chapter we define hearsay and examine its boundaries. The learning objectives for this chapter are:

- State why hearsay raises questions of reliability.
- Define an *assertive statement*.
- Explain why the statement "He said he would kill me" might not be hearsay.
- State the co-conspirator rule.
- Identify when a prior statement by a witness is not hearsay.

CHAPTER CONTENTS

WITNESSES AND THE HEARSAY RULE

Central to the nature of criminal prosecutions in the United States is the role of witnesses. It is through the testimony of witnesses that the facts are presented to the jury and upon which the guilt or innocence of the accused is determined.

When witnesses give their testimony, the subject matter is typically some event that they observed in some manner and then they subsequently recollect it in the courtroom. This testimony generally presents four risks relative to its truthfulness: the accuracy of the witness' perception, the memory of the witness, the meaning of the testimony, and the sincerity of the witness.

The principal means courts use to guard against these risks are the requirements that the witness testify under oath, which helps ensure sincerity, and that the witness be available for cross-examination, which can be used to test recollection, narration, and perception.

Imagine that a witness in an arson trial gives the testimony: "I saw the defendant throw something through the window of the building, and then the building caught fire." The truth of this statement carries the risks identified above: Is the witness sincere? Is his memory of the event clear? Were his perceptions of the event accurate? Did the event mean what he said it meant?

These risks can be tested by cross-examination, where the witness is available to explain his perceptions or demonstrate the clarity of his memory. Questions about the witness' eyesight, the time of day or night, his distance from the defendant, and so forth can test the accuracy of his perceptions. Similar questions can assess his memory and narration of the event.

But what if the witness testifies: "Fred told me he saw the defendant throw something through the window of the building, and then the building caught fire." It is possible, but very unlikely, that the witness may have questioned Fred to determine the accuracy of this statement. If not, the defendant will not be able to do so because Fred is not at the trial.

The witness' statement about what Fred said is, of course, hearsay and in most federal and state criminal proceedings is inadmissible under the relevant hearsay rule. Unfortunately, identifying what is and is not hearsay is considerably more complex than this simple example. Moreover, even if something is hearsay, the rule excluding its admissibility is subject to numerous exceptions: The hearsay rule in the Federal Rules of Evidence has two exemptions and twenty-eight exceptions. Finally, in criminal trials, the Confrontation Clause of the Sixth Amendment to the U.S. Constitution imposes a constitutional restriction on out-of-court testimony by witnesses.

In this chapter we explore the basic elements of hearsay evidence, giving examples of what is and is not hearsay. In Chapter 8 we discuss the Confrontation Clause and the exceptions to the hearsay rule.

THE HISTORY OF THE HEARSAY RULE

As we observed in Chapter 1, as far back as the thirteenth century hearsay evidence was regarded as unreliable. Yet, between the thirteenth and seventeenth centuries, English criminal courts continued to convict defendants based on "anonymous accusers and absentee witnesses."[1]

While English common law in criminal cases was based on an accusatorial principle—that is, live testimony by witnesses in open court—during this period English courts adopted some procedures from the European, inquisitorial, civil law system, discussed in Chapter 2. Among these practices was the private examination of witnesses by justices of the peace or other government officials, with the testimony used in a subsequent criminal trial.

This practice was particularly prevalent in the infamous Star Chamber trials of the Elizabethan period in England, during the reign of Queen Elizabeth I (1558–1603) and her successor, King James I (1603–1625). The monarch used the Star Chamber, consisting of royal officers, to control political enemies. Such persons were often charged with treason and tried in the Star Chamber rather than in the usual courts. In such trials the evidence frequently consisted of testimonial statements made by witnesses to court or government officers and then read into the record at the trial. The witnesses were not available for cross-examination by the accused.

These abuses were condemned by many of Elizabeth's subjects, among them William Shakespeare. In his play *Richard II*, written in 1595, Shakespeare's fictional king sets the following procedure for trial—so unlike the standard the actual sovereign, Queen Elizabeth, was using: "Then call them into our presence—face to face, and frowning brow to brow, ourselves will hear the accuser and the accused freely speak ..." (Act I, Scene I).

THE 1603 TRIAL OF SIR WALTER RALEIGH

More than any other case, the trial of Sir Walter Raleigh in 1603 illustrates the abuses that occurred in English criminal trials before hearsay rules were introduced. As a soldier and explorer, Sir Walter Raleigh was a colorful member of the English court of Queen Elizabeth.[2] Raleigh enjoyed the patronage and protection of Queen Elizabeth during her lifetime, but he had powerful enemies in the English court.

Upon Queen Elizabeth's death in 1603, the new king, James I, feared Raleigh and had him seized and thrown into the Tower of London in July 1603. In November 1603, Raleigh was tried for treason against the king. He was convicted based on statements made before the Privy Council by his alleged accomplice, Lord Cobham, who did not appear as a witness at the trial. These statements implicated Raleigh in a **conspiracy** to commit treason and, along with a letter Cobham wrote to officials, were read to the jury.

conspiracy An agreement by two or more people to commit an illegal act.

In the years following the trial of Sir Walter Raleigh, the English courts began to develop hearsay rules, and by 1690, it is reported that English courts were using hearsay rules to prevent the kind of abuses that occurred during that period.

After the 1670 trial of William Penn (see Chapter 5), the historic development of the concept of an impartial jury continued along with the development of the hearsay rule. Wigmore (5 Wigmore, Evidence Sec. 1364) called the hearsay rule "the greatest contribution of the [English] legal system ... next to the jury trial."

HEARSAY RULES AND THE USE OF INDEPENDENT JURIES IN THE AMERICAN COLONIES/STATES

English settlers brought the concepts of impartial, independent juries and hearsay rules to the American colonies as part of the English common-law system.

However, trials in Admiralty Courts followed the civil law methods of private judicial examinations of witnesses. The infamous English Stamp Act, which was one of the English actions found most objectionable by the American colonies, was used to expand the jurisdiction of the Admiralty Courts and was strongly contested on that basis.

After the American Revolutionary War, both the right to an impartial jury and the use of hearsay rules were made part of the American legal system. The former colonists were determined that the new federal government would not resort to the same civil-law procedures that the English Crown had attempted to use in America. The result was the adoption of the Sixth Amendment's Confrontation Clause, which was made part of the American Bill of Rights in 1791: "In all criminal prosecutions, the accused shall enjoy the right ... to be confronted with witnesses against him...."[3]

The U.S. Supreme Court has observed that the rule against hearsay is closely related to the constitutional right of confrontation, as both "stem from the same roots" and that "... hearsay rules and the Confrontation Clause are generally designed to protect similar values...."[4]

WHAT IS HEARSAY?

hearsay Secondhand testimony; reports by one person about what another person said.

Rule 801(c) of the Federal Rules of Evidence defines **hearsay**: "'Hearsay' is a statement, other than one made by the declarant while testifying at the trial or hearing, offered in evidence to prove the truth of the matter asserted." The **declarant** is the person who makes the statement. That statement is *offered* into evidence by some other person, usually one to whom the declarant made the statement or who overheard (or observed[5]) the statement.

WHAT IS AN ASSERTIVE STATEMENT?

declarant A person who makes a statement, either in or out of court.

assertive statement A statement by which a person intends to communicate a thought or belief.

To fall within the hearsay rule, a declarant's statement must be an **assertive statement** offered as proof that the subject matter of the statement is true.[6] An assertive statement is one in which the declarant intends to communicate his or her thoughts or beliefs.

Examples
- Witness W testifies: "My brother (X) told me that he shot my dad because he thought my dad was planning to kill him." This is hearsay and not admissible because it is an assertive statement. There is no opportunity to test the accuracy of this statement by cross-examination unless the brother is brought into court. If the brother is the defendant in this trial, however, this would be an incriminating statement that would be admissible under Federal Rule of Evidence 801(d)(2) (see Appendix C).
- Witness W testifies: "I heard my brother (X) mutter 'I killed my dad' in his sleep." This is not hearsay because X, while sleeping, did not intend to communicate.[7] It is not hearsay if X is a defendant in this action charged with killing his dad. See Federal Rule of Evidence 801(d)(2).

NONVERBAL COMMUNICATIONS CAN BE ASSERTIVE

nonverbal communication Acts that do not involve words or speech but that may be assertive and therefore hearsay.

Nonverbal acts can be used to communicate. If the purpose of the nonverbal act is to communicate and the communication is assertive, it is then hearsay.

Examples

- The witness testifies that when she asked X where his drug dealer lived, X pointed to the defendant's house. This is hearsay because it is an assertion that cannot be tested by cross-examination. X should be brought in as a witness if he is available.
- The witness testifies that she requested the victim of a mugging to draw a sketch of the mugger. This is hearsay because it is assertive conduct that cannot be tested by cross-examination. The victim must be brought in as a witness.

CONDUCT THAT IS NOT MEANT TO COMMUNICATE

If a person is engaging in conduct that is not meant to communicate, this would generally not be treated as hearsay because there is no attempt to be assertive.[8]

Example

A police officer testifies: "I showed Ms. __ (rape victim) a display of seven photographs. When she saw the picture of X (the defendant), she gasped and began to cry." This is not hearsay because the rape victim's conduct is not meant as a communication even though it creates the indirect inference that she believes the defendant was the person who raped her.[9]

THE HEARSAY RULE FORBIDS ONLY STATEMENTS OFFERED TO PROVE THE TRUTH OF THAT STATEMENT

truth of the matter asserted The subject to be proved in an assertive statement.

If an attorney can convince a judge that a statement offered for use in evidence is meant to prove something other than the truth of that statement, the judge will rule that it is admissible for evidence. The hearsay rule forbids only statements offered to prove the **truth of the matter asserted**. The hearsay rule does not forbid evidence offered to prove something other than the truth of that statement.

McCormick on Evidence[10] points out that there are "an almost infinite variety of other purposes" to take a statement out of the hearsay rule and permit it to be used as evidence. The following examples illustrate only a few of the numerous other purposes that take an out-of-court statement out of the hearsay classification:

- *Knowledge:* William Witness testifies that Fred Firebug told him that a can of gasoline was in the attic of the house the day before the fire occurred. Witness' testimony would *not* be admissible to prove that there was gasoline in the attic the day before the fire. It would be admissible to show that Firebug *knew* that there was gasoline in the attic before the fire.
- *Feelings or state of mind:* William Witness testifies that Fred Firebug had said, "Bobby Burnout took my money, stole my girl, and wrecked my car on the

night of the senior prom." This testimony would not be admissible to show that Burnout had taken Firebug's money, or stolen his girlfriend, or wrecked his car. It would be admissible to demonstrate Firebug's feelings or state of mind about Burnout.

- *Insanity:* William Witness testifies that Charles Crazy had said, "I am Napoleon Bonaparte, Emperor of All France." Witness' testimony would not be admissible to show that Crazy was in fact a person named Napoleon Bonaparte. It would, however, be admissible to show circumstantially that Crazy was insane.

- *Effect on hearer:* William Witness testifies that he heard Bill Bully say to Tom Timid, "No one better mess with me. I am carrying a loaded 38." The testimony would not be admissible to show that Bully was carrying a gun. It would be admissible to show the effect on Timid's state of mind.

The trial judge should instruct the jury that it must consider the evidence only for the allowable purpose. This would work well in the above Charles Crazy example. The jury would view the statement as bearing on Crazy's state of mind and would not conclude that Crazy might indeed be Napoleon Bonaparte.

But as Professor McCormick points out, "such … instructions may not always be effective," and there are situations in which juries misuse the evidence or become unduly confused by the judge's instructions.

Statements that would otherwise be testimonial and require that the defendant have the right of cross-examination under the rule of *Crawford v. Washington*[11] (discussed in Chapter 8) can be admitted without such right of cross-examination if they are not intended to prove the truth of their contents. An example of this principle is the 2004 decision of the California Supreme Court in *People v. Combs.*[12] California's evidence code has a provision called "adoptive admissions." Under this rule, an out-of-court statement is not hearsay if the defendant has manifested "by words or other conduct" that he or she adopts the truth of those statements. In *Combs*, the defendant and an accomplice reenacted the killing of a victim. The police filmed the reenactment. In the video, the accomplice made statements that were damaging to the defendant. The video captured the defendant's expressions while these statements were made, and he made no effort to object to the statements when they were made. When the video was offered in evidence, the defendant objected, alleging the statements were testimonial hearsay and inadmissible under *Crawford*. The California Supreme Court held that the video was offered not to prove the truth of the statements but to show that the defendant had adopted those statements. As a result, the statements were not hearsay and were admissible.

WHAT IS NOT HEARSAY? FEDERAL RULES OF EVIDENCE 801(D)(1), 801(D)(2), AND 801(D)(2)(E)

Besides being limited to assertions offered to establish proof of the assertion, the hearsay rule does not apply to various out-of-court statements that would otherwise literally fall within the definition of hearsay. These statements are described in Rule 801(d)(1) and (2) of the Federal Rules of Evidence.

PRIOR STATEMENT BY A WITNESS

If a witness testifies at a trial and is cross-examined concerning an earlier statement made by the witness, the statement is not hearsay if:

1. The statement is inconsistent and was given under oath at a previous trial, hearing, or deposition.

   ### Example

   At D's murder trial, W testifies that he saw D in the victim's car on the night the victim was killed. In a deposition taken prior to the trial, where D's attorney was present and able to cross-examine W, W stated that D was not in the victim's car. W's earlier statement is not hearsay.

2. The statement is consistent and is offered to rebut a charge that the witness' present testimony is a recent fabrication or stems from an improper motive.

   ### Example

   The witness, who is the defendant's employee, testifies that he saw the defendant in Cleveland on the date a robbery occurred in Denver. On cross-examination, the prosecutor suggests the witness' motive is to protect his employer. A similar, consistent statement made by the witness to a police officer investigating the robbery, made before the witness was employed by the defendant, is not hearsay.

ADMISSION BY A PARTY-OPPONENT

Where the statement sought to be admitted is an out-of-court statement made by the defendant (a "party" in the trial) or someone acting on his or her behalf, Federal Rule of Evidence 801(d)(2) provides that the statement is not hearsay.[13]

Different reasons are given as the basis for the rule, but as Professor McCormick points out, the hearsay rule never forbids admissions by a party-opponent (the defendant in a criminal case).

Examples
- Witness W testifies in D's trial for possession of stolen property that shortly after a burglary D stated, "I have the jewels stolen from the Johnson house." The statement is not hearsay.
- Witness W testifies at D's trial for assault against V that, in the presence of D, V stated, "Last night after work, D beat me up," and D said nothing. D's silence can be seen as adoption or belief in the statement and prevents the statement from being hearsay.
- Witness W testifies at D's trial for illegal bookmaking that E, a person who worked for D by picking up betting slips, stated, "These are markers in D's sports book." The statement is not hearsay.

THE CO-CONSPIRATOR RULE

Federal Rule of Evidence 801(d)(2)(E) provides that statements made by a co-conspirator during and in furtherance of the conspiracy are not hearsay.[14] The justification for this rule is that parties in a conspiracy are essentially partners, and an admission by one partner is fairly attributable to the other partners. The U.S. Supreme Court has said that statements by a co-conspirator "provide evidence of the conspiracy's context that cannot be replicated, even if the [co-conspirator] testifies to the same matters in court." The Court also noted that "simply calling the [co-conspirator] in hopes of having him repeat his prior out-of-court statements is a poor substitute for the full … significance that flow[s] from statements made when the conspiracy is operating in full force"[15] (co-conspirator rule).

Example

A and *B* are engaged in a conspiracy to import and sell illegal drugs. While acting in furtherance of the conspiracy, *A* states to *C*, "*B* sold the cocaine from the last shipment." *A*'s statement is not hearsay as an admission of a co-conspirator and is admissible in *B*'s prosecution.

SUMMARY

It is reported that the word *hearsay* is a contraction of the old English phrase, "I heard it said." When a witness at a criminal trial is asked to repeat in court a statement made out of court, the following questions should be asked to determine whether that testimony is inadmissible hearsay:

1. Is the statement (verbal or nonverbal conduct) an assertion?
2. Is the statement offered to prove the truth of the assertion?
3. Was the statement made under oath and subject to cross-examination at a prior trial, hearing, or deposition?

4. Was the admission (or statement) made by a party-opponent in a civil case or the defendant in a criminal case?

Even if a statement ends up being hearsay, in many circumstances hearsay testimony is admissible under one of the exceptions to the hearsay rule. Many of these exceptions, and their relationship to the Confrontation Clause, are considered in Chapter 8.

CASE ANALYSIS

Read Appendix B, Finding and Analyzing Cases (p. 427). With these guidelines in mind, please continue with the Case Analysis selections for Chapter 7.

In this chapter we distinguished between hearsay statements and statements that are not offered to prove the truth of the statement. Applying this distinction to statements offered at trial may be difficult, as can be seen in the first two cases described next. The first case shows a common battleground for hearsay fights: One party files a pretrial motion, called a "motion *in limine*," to ask the trial judge to admit or exclude testimony

proposed to be offered at trial. The trial judge must decide whether to admit or exclude the evidence if it is subsequently offered at trial. If it is so offered, the losing party at the motion would object again to its admission or exclusion.

1. In *Primeaux v. State* [88 P.3d 893 (Ok. App. 2004)], a defendant sought to have the out-of-court statements of a co-suspect in a killing admitted at the defendant's trial. The co-suspect was unavailable because he would invoke his Fifth Amendment rights and refuse to testify. The defendant argued that the

statements were not offered to prove the truth of the statements and thus were not hearsay. The court disagreed. Why?

2. When a police officer testifies at a criminal trial resulting from a criminal investigation of the defendant, the officer is often asked to describe how the officer became aware of the possibility that the defendant was engaged in criminal activity. If the officer gained that information from a confidential informant, courts have permitted the officer to testify as much. To what extent, if at all, may the officer be permitted to testify about specific statements made by the informant? Will those statements be hearsay, or can the prosecution contend they are not? *United States v. Becker* [230 F.3d 1224 (10th Cir. 2000)] [Docket No. 98–3361] is an example of a court ruling on such a contention. What happened at the trial, in addition to the admission of the statements attributed to the informant,

to convince the court of appeals that the statements were hearsay?

3. In prosecutions of crimes such as theft of property like checks, the state hopes to introduce bank accounts, cashed checks, and signatures on checks. What are the hearsay implications for the introduction of such evidence? See *State v. Beele* [931 A.2d 1258 (N.H. 2007)].

4. Charged with the rape of a child, the defendant sought to admit out-of-court statements made by the victim to her father for the purpose of rebutting the state's proof of oral penetration. Are the child's statements "assertive statements" and thus covered by hearsay rules? Are they prior inconsistent statements, and not hearsay, because the witness testified at trial that oral penetration did occur? Are the statements "admissions by a party-opponent" and not hearsay? See *State v. Flood* [219 S.W.2d 307 (Tenn. 2007)].

Notes

1. See Chapter 8 (pp. 162, 164)—*White v. Illinois* [502 U.S. 346 (1992)]—for a discussion of the development of Confrontation Clause law.

2. Sir Walter Raleigh established a reputation as a ruthless fighter and is said to have come to the attention of Queen Elizabeth by spreading his coat over a mud puddle so that the queen could walk on his coat. Raleigh's later conviction for treason put him in the Tower of London for twelve years, where he lived comfortably with his family and servants. Upon his release, he violated the king's order not to invade Spanish territory in South America and was sentenced to death.

3. Justices Thomas and Scalia state in the 1992 case of *White v. Illinois* [502 U.S. 346, 112 S.Ct. 736, 744, 50 CrL 2036] that there "is virtually no evidence of what the drafters of the Confrontation Clause intended it to mean." They quote Justice Harlan's concurring opinion in the 1970 case of *Dutton v. Evans* [400 U.S. 74, 94, 91 S.Ct. 210, 222]: "From the scant information available it may tentatively be concluded that the Confrontation Clause was meant to constitutionalize a barrier against flagrant abuses, trials by anonymous accusers, and absentee witnesses."

The famous English Judge, Sir James Stephens, stated in his 1883 book, *A History of the Criminal Law of England* (Macmillan, 1883), that early English judges questioned the prisoner, accomplices, and others prior to criminal trials and that the "prisoner had no right to be, and probably never was, present." At the trial itself, "proof was usually given by reading depositions, confession of accomplices, letters, and the like; and this occasioned frequent demands by the prisoner to have his 'accusers,' i.e., the witnesses against him, brought before him face to face" (vol. 1, p. 326, *A History of the Criminal Law of England*).

4. *Dutton v. Evans*, 400 U.S. 74, 86, 91 S.Ct. 210, 218 (1970).

5. A statement need not be verbal. It can be in writing, or it can be a nonverbal act intended as an assertion. See Federal Rule of Evidence 801(a).

6. See *Martinez v. McCaughtry* [951 F.2d 130 (7th Cir. 1991)]. Statements by the declarant that "you're a dead man" made to the accused are not hearsay because they are not assertions. Many courts use the kind of sentence made by the declarant as a guide to whether the statement is

assertive. Sentences that are questions (interrogative) or commands (imperative) are not assertions. Only indicative or declaratory sentences can be assertions. See, for example, *Holland v. State* [713 A.2d 364 (Md. App. 1998)].

7. See, for example, *State v. Tate* [817 S.W.2d 578 (Mo. App. 1991)].

8. The Advisory Committee on Rules of Evidence, which drafted Rule 801 of the Federal Rules, made this comment about nonassertive conduct:

   Subdivision (a). The definition of "statement" assumes importance because the term is used in the definition of hearsay in subdivision (c). The effect of the definition of "statement" is to exclude from the operation of the hearsay rule all evidence of conduct, verbal or nonverbal, not intended as an assertion. The key to the definition is that nothing is an assertion unless intended to be one. [Cited in *People v. Jones*, 579 N.W.2d 82, 92 (Mich. App. 1998).]

9. Federal Rule of Evidence 801(d)(1)(C) also permits prior out-of-court identifications by a witness available for cross-examination at the trial. See *Gilbert v. California* [388 U.S. 263 (1967)].

10. *McCormick on Evidence*, 4th ed. (West, 1992).

11. 541 U.S. 36 (2004).

12. 22 Cal. Rptr. 3d 61.

13. However, under the *Bruton* rule (see Chapter 12), the confession of an accomplice may not ordinarily be introduced at a joint trial of persons who commit a crime together if the confession incriminates the other defendant or defendants. Such a confession could be admissible, however, (a) if the person making the confession takes the witness stand, (b) if the confession does not incriminate other defendants, or (c) if all defendants confess and the confessions are significantly interlocking to rebut the presumption of unreliability.

14. Federal Rule of Evidence 801(d)(2)(E) provides that the co-conspirator's statement, while relevant to the question, cannot alone establish that the person against whom the statement is offered was a party to the conspiracy. Most courts require some independent proof of that fact, and if such proof is not available, the co-conspirator's statement is inadmissible. See *United States v. Tellier* [83 F.3d 578 (2d Cir. 1996), *cert. denied*, 117 S.Ct. 373 (1996)].

15. 475 U.S. 307 (1985).

EXCEPTIONS TO THE HEARSAY RULE

CHAPTER 8

LEARNING OBJECTIVES

In this chapter we consider exceptions to the hearsay rule and the role of the Confrontation Clause in admitting hearsay evidence. The learning objectives for this chapter are:

- State the pre-*Crawford* test for admissibility of hearsay evidence.
- State the rule of *Crawford v. Washington.*
- Define a *testimonial statement.*
- State when a testimonial out-of-court statement may be admitted as evidence.
- Identify hearsay exceptions in child sexual abuse cases.

HEARSAY AND THE CONFRONTATION CLAUSE

Confrontation Clause The clause in the U.S. Constitution that entitles a defendant in a criminal case to demand witnesses to testify against him in his presence.

In criminal trials, the admission of out-of-court statements presents not only issues under relevant hearsay rules but also potential conflict with the Sixth Amendment's **Confrontation Clause**. That clause states: "In all criminal prosecutions, the accused shall enjoy the right ... to be confronted with the witnesses against him...." The implications of hearsay evidence for the Confrontation Clause are clear: If an out-of-court statement is admitted as evidence against the accused, the person making that statement is a "witness"[1] who is not "confronting" the accused.

Prior to 1965 few cases discussed the relationships among the hearsay rule, hearsay exceptions, and the Confrontation Clause. This was because the Confrontation Clause had not been extended to state criminal cases and applied only to federal criminal trials. In those trials, admissibility tended to be determined by reference only to federal evidentiary rules.[2]

In the 1965 case of *Pointer v. Texas*,[3] the U.S. Supreme Court held that the Fourteenth Amendment Due Process Clause made the Confrontation Clause binding in state criminal trials. Because state evidentiary rules differed widely from federal evidence rules and from one another, the Supreme Court was forced to consider the admissibility of hearsay evidence as a Confrontation Clause problem. A state might, for example, have an evidentiary rule that permits admissibility of hearsay evidence in criminal cases for reasons unique to that state's evidentiary system. In such a case, the state's justification for admission of the hearsay evidence must pass the Confrontation Clause test.

In the early cases decided after *Pointer v. Texas*, the Supreme Court noted that "hearsay rules and the Confrontation Clause are generally designed to protect similar values."[4] They both recognize the importance of face-to-face contact between witness and accused and the crucial role of cross-examination, "the greatest legal engine ever invented for the discovery of truth."[5] Although the Court has always been careful not to equate the Confrontation Clause with the hearsay rule,[6] the early Confrontation Clause cases looked to the hearsay exceptions as appropriate "indicia of reliability" for admission in criminal trials of out-of-court statements. A discussion of those early cases is in the box on page 163.

THE INDICIA OF RELIABILITY REQUIREMENT

indicia of reliability Characteristics of a statement, otherwise inadmissible as hearsay, that courts believe sufficiently establish the statement's reliability so that cross-examination is not required.

Hearsay ("I heard it said") is not admissible as evidence unless there is a showing of substantial reliability for the statement. One of the ways reliability is shown in criminal trials is by reference to exceptions to the hearsay rule developed in the common law. If there is a long-recognized exception to the hearsay rule, courts feel confident in concluding that the hearsay statements possess the required reliability.

This chapter presents the major exceptions to the hearsay rule. Each exception has conditions and circumstances that the courts and legislative bodies have determined create sufficient reliability and trustworthiness to allow the hearsay statements to be used as evidence. The showing of reliability and trustworthiness necessary to use the statements as evidence is known as **indicia of reliability**. State and federal law provide that several exceptions to the hearsay rule, such as those

Hearsay and Unavailable Witnesses

The U.S. Supreme Court cases listed below deal with the question of whether the prosecutor had a burden to show "unavailability" of the declarant and "reliability" of the statement before that person's statements could be used as evidence. Although the Confrontation Clause aspect of these cases has been modified by the Supreme Court in *Crawford v. Washington* [541 U.S. 36 (2004)], discussed in the next section, to the extent that "unavailability" may still be required for applying a hearsay exception under state or federal law, the cases raise questions about "unavailability" and hearsay exceptions.

Case	Circumstances	Question Before the Supreme Court
Ohio v. Roberts, 448 U.S. 56 (1980)	Roberts was convicted of forgery and receiving stolen checks and credit cards. His defense was that the daughter of the owner of the cards gave him permission to use the cards and checks. Although the daughter testified at the preliminary hearing that she did not give him permission, after five subpoenas failed to find her, she did not testify at Roberts's trial. Instead, her testimony at the preliminary hearing was placed into evidence.	Did the prosecutor prove that the daughter was "unavailable"? The records showed that the defense lawyer questioned the daughter at the preliminary hearing using leading questions and challenging her veracity. Was this sufficient to indicate the reliability of the daughter's evidence?[a]
White v. Illinois, 502 U.S. 346 (1992)	A 4-year-old victim of sexual assault sat in the courtroom while a babysitter, her mother, an emergency room nurse, a law enforcement officer, and a doctor all testified about statements the child made to them that implicated White as the person who assaulted her. Defense counsel objected to the testimony, which was admitted under the Illinois hearsay exceptions for spontaneous declarations and statements made in the course of medical treatment. No attempt was made to show that the child was unavailable.	Is the opportunity to cross-examine the witness enough, or must the state show that the witness was unavailable?[b]
United States v. Inadi, 475 U.S. 387 (1985)	Taped conversations between the defendant and others involved in the manufacture and sale of methamphetamines were used at the defendant's trial pursuant to Rule 801(d)(2)(E) of the Federal Rules of Evidence. No showing of unavailability was made.	Should the prosecutor be obligated to prove that the witnesses were unavailable?[c]
Lily v. Virginia, 527 U.S. 116 (1999)	Three men were arrested after a two-day crime spree that resulted in the kidnapping and killing of a man. Under police questioning, defendant Mark Lily admitted to other crimes but stated that his brother and a third man killed the victim. At their murder trial, Mark Lily was called as a witness but invoked his Fifth Amendment privilege against self-incrimination. His statements to the police were admitted as evidence of an unavailable witness made against his penal interest, and the defendants were convicted of murder.	Should the response to a police interrogation made by an intoxicated, frightened person who might be charged with murder be a substitute for cross-examination at trial?[d]

[a]The Supreme Court affirmed the conviction, stating that the daughter was "constitutionally" unavailable and that the cross-examination at the preliminary hearing made the testimony sufficiently reliable.

[b]No showing of unavailability was required because statements made under well-recognized exceptions to the hearsay rule, such as excited utterances, or made during medical treatment were sufficiently reliable, the Court held.

[c]The Court held that no showing of unavailability was required for a co-conspirator's statements because such statements have reliability based on the circumstances in which they were made.

[d]The Court held that although Mark Lily was unavailable, his statements were not made under circumstances where there was a sufficient showing of reliability.

listed in Rule 804 of the Federal Rules of Evidence, require a showing that the declarant (the speaker) is unavailable as a witness at the trial. If the state or federal law requires a showing of "unavailability" for an exception, then this burden must be carried before the statement (or statements) can be used as evidence.

forfeiture by wrongdoing A rule permitting the admission of hearsay evidence as a penalty against a defendant who wrongfully made the declarant unavailable; often used in murder cases.

In addition to the hearsay exceptions, most states have adopted some form of a doctrine called **forfeiture by wrongdoing**, a doctrine specifically accepted by the Supreme Court in *Crawford v. Washington*.[7] Under this doctrine, a person who has wrongfully made the declarant unavailable for the purpose of preventing his or her testimony has waived the right to object to the declarant's out-of-court statements as hearsay. In the 2004 case of *State v. Meeks*,[8] the Kansas Supreme Court held that the defendant waived his confrontation rights to object to the victim's statements by murdering the victim and thus making him unavailable to testify. Other courts have held the opposite. In the 2005 case of *United States v. Jordan*,[9] a Colorado district court said that the forfeiture by wrongdoing doctrine requires an intent to make the declarant unavailable to testify, not just acts that in fact have that result. Thus, the court held that a defendant accused of murdering the declarant did not forfeit his confrontation rights by killing the declarant. In the 2008 case *Giles v. California*, discussed later in this chapter, the U.S. Supreme Court rejected the line of cases that made the forfeiture by wrongdoing rule depend only on the fact of a defendant making a witness unavailable, and adopted the rule that requires a showing of intent to do so.

The Federal Rules of Evidence divide the hearsay exceptions into two groups: Rule 803 exceptions and Rule 804 exceptions. Many states have a similar division. Most states and the federal government provide that a showing of "unavailability" of a declarant is not required for hearsay exceptions like those listed in Federal Rule of Evidence 803. Federal Rule of Evidence 804 deals with exceptions that require a showing that the declarant is unavailable to testify in person. Rule 804 defines "unavailability" and also lists some kinds of hearsay that are not excluded even if the declarant is unavailable as a witness.

THE 2004 U.S. SUPREME COURT CASE OF *CRAWFORD V. WASHINGTON* ON TESTIMONIAL HEARSAY

Many testimonial statements are statements made by a witness in court, while under oath, and subject to cross-examination. If the witness is testifying to events that the witness saw or knew from firsthand experience, then the testimony is not hearsay. If the witness is not testifying from firsthand knowledge, however, the testimony is generally hearsay and inadmissible unless an exception to the hearsay rule applies. (See the discussion of the hearsay exceptions in this chapter.)

In the 2004 landmark case of *Crawford v. Washington*, the U.S. Supreme Court adopted a new "bright-line" rule for the introduction of "testimonial" evidence. The Court held that the Sixth Amendment Confrontation Clause requires that a defendant in a criminal case have an opportunity to cross-examine the person who made the statement, and if the person is unavailable to testify at the trial, the statement is inadmissible. This is true, the Court held, even if the statement meets the indicia of reliability requirement established in *Ohio v. Roberts* or is covered by a "firmly rooted" exception to the hearsay rule. Thus, the rule of cases like *Ohio v. Roberts* on the admissibility of hearsay evidence in criminal trials is no longer applicable to "testimonial" hearsay.

In the *Crawford* case, Michael Crawford was convicted of assault after he stabbed a man who Crawford believed had tried to rape his wife, Sylvia. Crawford claimed self-defense and asserted that the victim had a weapon and was going to use it against him. At Crawford's trial, the prosecution introduced a tape recording of answers given by Sylvia to police officers shortly after the stabbing occurred. Some of her statements cast doubt on Crawford's claim that the victim had a weapon. Sylvia's statements were testimonial and hearsay, but because Crawford invoked his marital privilege to prevent Sylvia from testifying, Sylvia was "unavailable" as a witness and could not be cross-examined.

The prosecution successfully argued in the trial court that because Sylvia had facilitated the assault and had her own criminal responsibility, at the time she made her statements they were "against her penal interests" and admissible under that exception to the hearsay rule. The statements were admitted, and Crawford was convicted of the assault. The Washington Court of Appeals reversed his conviction, but the Washington Supreme Court held that the statements were admissible and reversed the appeals court.

The U.S. Supreme Court reversed the Washington Supreme Court, holding that where "testimonial" hearsay is offered and the person who made the statement is unavailable to testify, the Confrontation Clause prohibits the introduction of the statement unless the defendant has an opportunity to cross-examine the person who made the statement. Because Sylvia was "unavailable" to testify and thus could not be cross-examined, her "testimonial" hearsay statements were inadmissible.

A difficult question left open in *Crawford* is the meaning of "testimonial" statements. On this issue the Court said: "We leave for another day any effort to spell out a comprehensive definition of 'testimonial.'"[10] The Court did list some examples of statements that are "testimonial": "What ever else that term covers, it applies at a minimum to prior testimony at a preliminary hearing, before a grand jury, or at a former trial; and to police interrogations."[11]

Davis v. Washington

United States Supreme Court, 547 U.S. 813 (2006)

In *Davis* and a companion case, *Hammon v. Indiana*, the U.S. Supreme Court answered the question left open in *Crawford*, and announced a test to be used to determine whether an out-of-court statement was "testimonial" and thus subject to *Crawford*'s holding that the statement could not be admitted unless the declarant was unavailable and the defendant had an opportunity to cross-examine the declarant.

In *Davis* the defendant was charged with a domestic battery offense, in which his spouse was the victim. She did not appear to testify at the defendant's trial, so the prosecution introduced a 911 tape that included the spouse's statements describing the domestic abuse. The defendant was convicted and appealed.

In *Hammon* the defendant was also charged with a domestic violence offense in which his wife was the victim. The spouse did not appear at the trial, so the prosecution introduced notes taken by a police officer who interrogated the spouse shortly after the abuse incident. These statements described the abuse for which the defendant was charged. The defendant was convicted and appealed. The appeals were consolidated in the U.S. Supreme Court.

The Court held that the statements were testimonial in *Hammon* but nontestimonial in *Davis.* As a result, the conviction in *Hammon* was reversed because the Confrontation Clause requirements set forth in *Crawford* had not been satisfied. Because the Confrontation Clause did not apply to the nontestimonial statements in *Davis*, however, the statements were properly admitted and the conviction was affirmed.

The Court established the following test for distinguishing between testimonial and nontestimonial out-of-court statements:

> Statements are nontestimonial when made in the course of police interrogation under circumstances objectively indicating that the primary purpose of the interrogation is to enable police assistance to meet an ongoing emergency. They are testimonial when the circumstances objectively indicate that there is no such ongoing emergency, and that the primary purpose of the interrogation is to establish or prove past events potentially relevant to later criminal prosecution. 547 U.S. at 822.

In *Davis*, the questions asked and answered during the 911 call, the Court said, were clearly intended to deal with the domestic crisis that was occurring during the call. As a result, the statements made by the victim were more in the nature of an excited utterance. Since the statements were not testimonial under the rule just announced, the Court stated that the Confrontation Clause did not apply to the statements.

Conversely, the statements made by the victim in *Hammon* to the officer who came to the scene were made after the emergency was over and were specifically obtained by the officer, he testified, "to establish events that have occurred previously." *Id.* at 832. As a result, they were testimonial, and the Confrontation Clause requirements were applicable.

The Court was careful to limit the breadth of its holding in *Davis*. The Court stated:

> Although we necessarily reject the Indiana Supreme Court's implication that virtually any "initial inquiries" at the crime scene will not be testimonial, (citation omitted) we do not hold the opposite—that no questions at the scene will yield nontestimonial answers. *Id* at 832.

Furthermore, the Court said:

> This is not to say that a conversation which begins as an interrogation to determine the need for emergency assistance cannot, as the Indiana Supreme Court put it, "evolve into testimonial statements (citation omitted), once that purpose has been achieved. *Id* at 828.

After the decision in *Davis,* statements made as a result of interrogation by officers will be testimonial unless they were made in response to questions that were asked only to identify and control an emergency. Even interrogations begun as such can develop another purpose, the preservation of statements for subsequent use, and when they do, the statements become testimonial and the Confrontation Rules must be met.

Finally, in both *Davis* and *Hammon* the state argued that domestic abuse cases needed a relaxed Confrontation Clause analysis, because the defendants in such cases have considerable power over their victims, and can often prevent them from testifying through threats of future harm. The Court rejected that argument, stating that in cases where the state could prove such intimidation, the common-law rule of "forfeiture by wrongdoing" could be used to find a waiver of Confrontation Clause rights.

FORFEITURE BY WRONGDOING

In 2008 the Supreme Court settled any questions about the required relationship between a "forfeiture by wrongdoing" rule and the Confrontation Clause. In *Giles v. California*,[12] the Court held that in order for the doctrine to be used to obviate the need for Confrontation Clause protections, the state must show that the defendant committed the acts that prevented the victim from testifying with the intent to make the witness unavailable. It rejected the California court's holding that a defendant who murdered his girlfriend forfeited his Confrontation Clause rights concerning earlier statements the victim made to a police officer, whether or not his purpose in murdering the victim was to keep her from testifying.

"FIRMLY ROOTED" EXCEPTIONS TO THE HEARSAY RULE[13]

Hearsay rules and the right of a defendant to view and confront witnesses against him or her were "designed to protect similar values."[14] The U.S. Supreme Court has pointed out that they have been "careful not to equate the Confrontation Clause's prohibitions with the general rule prohibiting the admission of hearsay statements."[15]

The Supreme Court has refused many times the requests of defense lawyers to interpret the Sixth Amendment Confrontation Clause so strictly that it would eliminate virtually every hearsay exception. The Supreme Court has stated that this is "a result long rejected as unintended and too extreme."[16] Even in *Crawford,* the Court did not rule out the possibility that a recognized hearsay exception would make nontestimonial hearsay statements admissible.

Thus, even though the Court in *Crawford* held that exceptions to the hearsay rule cannot suffice to satisfy the Confrontation Clause's requirements for cross-examination for testimonial statements, those exceptions may still be used by some courts for determining the admissibility of nontestimonial hearsay statements.

For nontestimonial hearsay the "reliability" test from *Ohio v. Roberts* may or may not continue to have meaning. Because the Supreme Court in *Davis v. Washington* (see above) held that the Confrontation Clause does not apply to nontestimonial hearsay, some courts have held that the "reliability" test has no further role in admissibility of nontestimonial hearsay: All the prosecution must show is that any hearsay fits within one of that jurisdiction's exceptions to the hearsay rule.[17] Other courts continue to apply the "reliability" test to nontestimonial hearsay, although it is not clear exactly what the test controls.[18] It is possible that courts might use the "reliability" test as a supplement or addition to one of the recognized hearsay exceptions.

In the materials that follow, we discuss the "firmly rooted" exceptions to the hearsay rule.

The hearsay rule and its exceptions developed over a 300-year history in English and American law. The rule developed by English and American courts has now been made a part of federal and state law. The present Federal Rules of Evidence, which most states follow, list twenty-eight specific, "firmly rooted" exceptions.

In enacting these exceptions into statutory law, the U.S. Congress and state legislatures have concluded that these exceptions have sufficient guarantees of reliability to be classified as "firmly rooted" hearsay exceptions. Some of the most widely used exceptions, which are part of federal law and the laws of most states, are described in the remaining sections of this chapter.[19]

EXCITED UTTERANCE EXCEPTION[20]

Federal Rule of Evidence 803(2), excited utterance: "A statement relating to a startling event or condition made while the declarant was under the stress of excitement caused by the event or condition."

Reason for the Exception   Many crimes are "startling events" that cause victims and witnesses to make excited statements during or immediately after the event. If such statements are in response to the startling event, the trustworthiness of such statements comes from the fact that the victim or witness had no time to reflect and possibly fabricate the statements.

Examples
- Statements by witnesses and victims during or immediately after shootings, stabbings, or robberies are almost always made "under the stress of excitement" caused by the startling event of the crime of violence.[21]
- Statements of rape victims immediately after the crime.[22]
- Recorded 911 calls and other telephone calls where courts held that the caller was speaking under the stress of excitement and permitted the recording to be used as evidence.[23]
- Many courts hold that there can be more of a time lapse between the startling event and statements when crimes such as sex crimes are reported by children or mentally retarded persons.[24]

THEN EXISTING MENTAL, EMOTIONAL, OR PHYSICAL CONDITION EXCEPTION

then existing mental, emotional, or physical condition The exception defined by Rule 803(3); for example, testimony that the victim stated that she was going to visit her boyfriend is admissible under this exception to show intent.

Federal Rule of Evidence 803(3), **then existing mental, emotional, or physical condition**: "A statement of the declarant's then existing state of mind, emotion, sensation, or physical condition (such as intent, plan, motive, design, mental feeling, pain, and bodily health)."

Reason for the Exception   Hearsay is defined by statute as a statement "offered in evidence to prove the truth of the matter asserted." If a statement is not offered to prove the truth of the matter asserted, courts almost always hold that such statements are not hearsay and are admissible as evidence.

Examples
- *Motive of the offender can be shown:* Prior to death, murder victims sometimes make statements to other persons about why they are afraid of the killer. The statement is offered not to show that the defendant committed the murder but to

show motive or state of mind. In the 1990 case of *State v. Alvarez*,[25] the victim owed the defendant money for cocaine; in the 1992 case of *Parker v. State*,[26] a woman victim was afraid of the defendant because she had been with another man.

- *Intent can be shown:* In a murder case, the victim had stated to a friend that she was going to visit the defendant (her boyfriend) and then go skating. The victim was then found strangled and beaten to death. The state-of-mind statement was allowed in evidence to show the victim's present purpose and intent at the time the statement was made.[27]
- *Insanity or mental illness can be shown:* Witness *A* testifies that *X* repeatedly said that he heard voices and that he believed he was Napoleon. The testimony is offered not to prove that *X* was Napoleon but to prove that *X* had serious mental problems.
- *State of mind can be shown:* In 1962 a bigamy case, *People v. Marsh*,[28] came before the Supreme Court of California. The defendant was charged with being married to two women at the same time. It was held that statements supporting the defendant's defense of his reasonable belief that he was free to remarry were admissible to prove his state of mind at that time.

Horton v. Allen

First Circuit Court of Appeals, 370 F.3d 75 (2004), *cert. denied*, 125 S.Ct. 971 (2005)

The defendant, Horton, was convicted of robbery and murder in a Massachusetts state court. At his trial, the out-of-court statements of another participant in the robbery, Christian, were admitted over Horton's objection. A witness testified that on the day of the robbery Christian told him that he needed money for drugs, that a drug dealer named Desir would not give him drugs on credit, and that he knew Desir carried a sizable amount of money. Desir was subsequently robbed, and persons with him were murdered.

After the Massachusetts appellate court upheld Horton's conviction, he filed a writ of habeas corpus in federal district court. He alleged that admission of Christian's hearsay statements violated his Confrontation Clause right. The district court denied his petition, and he appealed to the U.S. Court of Appeals. While his appeal was pending, the U.S. Supreme Court decided the *Crawford* case (discussed previously). The court of appeals affirmed the denial of the writ, holding that the statements made by Christian were admitted only to show Christian's state of mind and were admissible under the Massachusetts state-of-mind exception to the hearsay rule:

> Under Massachusetts law, the state-of-mind exception permits the admission of statements that demonstrate the declarant's intent to perform some future act. (Citation omitted.) The [Massachusetts Appellate Court] determined that Christian's statements that he needed money and that Desir would not give him drugs on credit suggested his intent to subsequently rob Desir, and the statements were admissible to show this intent.[29]

The court concluded that Christian's statements were not "testimonial" because they were made to a casual acquaintance, not to someone who would be expected to use the statements in a criminal trial. As a result, the court held that *Crawford* did not apply, and the statements were properly admitted as a "firmly rooted" hearsay exception under the rule in *Ohio v. Roberts* (discussed previously).

STATEMENTS FOR PURPOSES OF MEDICAL DIAGNOSIS OR TREATMENT EXCEPTION

statements for purposes of medical diagnosis or treatment exception The exception defined by Rule 803(4); for example, statements by doctors and nurses are admissible in child abuse cases.

Federal Rule of Evidence 803(4): "**statements for purposes of medical diagnosis or treatment.**"

Use of the Exception in Criminal Trials Because the physician–patient privilege forbids medical doctors from disclosing information regarding their patients, few cases involve adult defendants. Most of the cases concern child victims of sexual abuse. If the child reasonably understands the need to be truthful to his or her physician and the identification of the assailant is reasonably necessary to his or her medical diagnosis and treatment, the exception would apply and the physician could testify about statements the child made under such circumstances.

> ### Example
> In the 1992 case of *White v. Illinois*,[30] the U.S. Supreme Court held that the testimony of an emergency room nurse and a medical doctor about statements made to them by a 4-year-old child concerning sexual abuse by the defendant were admissible under the Illinois medical-treatment hearsay exception and did not violate the Sixth Amendment's Confrontation Clause. At the criminal trial, the state attempted on two occasions to call the child as a witness, but in both instances the child left without testifying because of emotional difficulty. The defense made no attempt to call the child as a witness. The defendant's convictions were affirmed.[31]

REGULARLY KEPT RECORDS EXCEPTION

regularly kept records exception The exception defined by Rule 803, which allows the use of regularly kept business records and public, religious, and family records.

Regularly kept business records, public records, records of religious organizations, and family records are admissible under certain federal rules (**regularly kept records exception**).

The following records are admissible under Rule 803 of the Federal Rules of Evidence:

- 803(6) Records of regularly conducted (business) activity
- 803(8) Public records and reports
- 803(9) Records of vital statistics
- 803(11) Records of religious organizations (marriage, baptism, and so on)
- 803(13) Family records (personal and family history)
- 803(16) Statements in ancient documents (more than twenty years old)
- 803(18) Learned treatises (history, medicine, or other science established as a reliable authority)

Reason for the Exception The regularly kept records exception (shop books) goes back to the 1600s in England and was adopted by the American states. The exception refers to usually accurate records that can be attacked by the opposing party. The fact finder (jury or judge) always determines the credibility and weight to be given to such evidence.

Dying Declaration Exception[32]

dying declaration exception The exception defined by Rule 804(b)(2), making admissible statements made by a victim or other person under the belief of impending death.

Federal Rule of Evidence 804(b)(2) is about a statement under belief of impending death (**dying declaration**). "In a prosecution for homicide or in a civil action or proceeding, a statement made by a declarant while believing that the declarant's death was imminent, concerning the cause or circumstances of what the declarant believed to be impending death."

Reason for the Exception   The use of dying declarations as evidence goes back to the 1500s in England. The practice became an exception to the hearsay rules by the 1700s. In the 1789 King's Bench case of *Rex v. Woodcock*,[33] the English court stated the reason for the exception:

> [T]hey are declarations made in extremity, when the party is at the point of death, and when every hope of this world is gone, when every motive to falsehood is silenced, and the mind is induced by the most powerful considerations to speak the truth. A situation so solemn and so awful is considered by the law as creating an obligation equal to that which is imposed by an oath administered in court. Woodcock's case, I Leach, 502.

In the 1990 case of *State v. Weir*,[34] the Florida Appellate Court held that:

> Admission of dying declarations is justified on the grounds of public necessity, manifest justice and the sense that impending death makes a false statement by the decedent improbable. § 90.804, Law Revision Council Note–1976.

Examples

- To use a dying declaration as evidence, the person must have died or otherwise become unavailable (lack of memory, in a coma, and so forth). The Supreme Court of Minnesota stated the requirement for use of the exception in the 1990 case of *State v. Bergeron*:[35]

  > To make a dying declaration admissible, something more is required than that declarant realize the seriousness of his condition and the possibility of death. The testimony offered as a dying declaration ... must have been spoken without hope of recovery and in the shadow of impending death. This state of mind must be exhibited in the evidence and not left to conjecture.

- The Supreme Court of Florida held in the 1991 case of *Henry v. State*[36] that:

  > It is not required that the declarant make "express utterances ... that he knew he was going to die, or could not live, or would never recover." *Lester v. State*, 37 Fla. 382, 385, 20 So. 232, 233 (1896). Rather, the court should satisfy itself, on the totality of the circumstances, "that the deceased knew and appreciated his condition as being that of an approach to certain and immediate death." *Id.*, 20 So. at 233.

Because killings are startling events, statements made immediately after a fatal shooting or knifing could be found to be admissible under both the excited utterance exception and the dying declaration exception to the hearsay rule. Two cases where statements were admissible under both exceptions are *Lyons v. United States*[37] and *State v. Griffin*.[38]

STATEMENT AGAINST-PENAL-INTEREST EXCEPTION

statement against-penal-interest exception The exception defined by Rule 804(b)(3) making admissible a statement that exposes the speaker to criminal liability.

Federal Rule of Evidence 804(b)(3), **statement against-penal-interest:** "A statement which was at the time of its making so far contrary to the declarant's pecuniary or proprietary interest or so far tended to subject the declarant to civil or criminal liability ... that a reasonable person in the declarant's position would not have made the statement unless believing it to be true...."

Reason for the Exception Persons who admit they have committed a crime or were involved in criminal activity are making a statement against penal interest. Such incriminating admissions or confessions ordinarily are considered to have a reliable basis. The U.S. Supreme Court pointed out in the 1971 case of *United States v. Harris*[39] that: "People do not lightly admit a crime and place critical evidence in the hands of the police in the form of their own admissions."

In the *Harris* case, the statement against penal interest was made by a known informant. The Supreme Court held that the statement against penal interest plus other evidence established the trustworthiness of the informant's statement.

Examples
- In the 1973 U.S. Supreme Court case of *Chambers v. Mississippi*,[40] the defendant was charged with a murder, but another person had admitted to committing that murder and had signed a number of confessions. Mississippi's hearsay rules prevented Chambers from introducing any of the confessions or statements into evidence in his defense. The Supreme Court held that a state may not use the hearsay rule to deprive defendants in criminal cases of reliable and important evidence.
- In the *Chambers* case, there was sufficient corroborating evidence that "clearly" supported the "trustworthiness of the statement [confession]." Two cases in which trial courts held there was insufficient evidence to support the trustworthiness of confessions are *State v. Rosado*[41] and *Lee v. McCaughtry*.[42] In these cases, the defendants were convicted (one of murder and the other of drug trafficking) when evidence that other people had confessed to the crimes was not allowed because of a lack of supporting evidence.[43]

THE FRESH COMPLAINT AND THE OUTCRY RULE

Hundreds of years ago, the victim of a crime was expected to raise an immediate *hue and cry*, or *outcry*. The failure to do so frequently resulted in the victim losing the right to charge the perpetrator with the crime in a later trial. The requirement of raising the outcry was imposed as a method of marshaling the neighborhood defenses to catch the assailant. It also served to negate the inference that the victim somehow was in complicity with the defendant. The requirement that one make an outcry was dropped from the law many years ago, but a vestige of the requirement survives in the fresh complaint and outcry rule.

In the nineteenth century and well into the twentieth century, the common law assumed that only those victims who immediately complained of rape were actually raped, whereas those persons who remained silent somehow consented to the sexual assault.

THE DEFENSE THAT SOMEONE ELSE COMMITTED THE CRIME

When the state has a strong case against a defendant, the defense that someone else committed the crime is sometimes offered as evidence, usually through testimony of persons to whom incriminating statements were made by a third party. These statements are admissible as "statements against interest" under Federal Rule of Evidence 804(b)(3), but only if it can be shown that "corroborating circumstances clearly indicate the trustworthiness of the statement" [Federal Rule of Evidence 804(b)(3)].

Example

In *Guinn v. Kemna* [489 F.3d 351 (8th Cir. 2007), *cert. denied*, 128 S.Ct. 1716 (2008)], a defendant accused of assault attempted to introduce testimony of witnesses who claimed that a third person had told them he committed the assault for which the defendant was being tried. The trial court refused to permit the testimony, and on appeal the court of appeals upheld the trial court's decision. The court stated that the witnesses' proposed testimony lacked sufficient trustworthiness to be admitted as a statement against the interest of the third person. Among other problems with the proposed hearsay testimony, the court stated that the witnesses who proposed to testify that they heard the third-party confession were not people to whom such a confession might be made, that the alleged confession was made in response to a specific question by one of the witnesses, and that no corroborating evidence was offered to show a connection between the third party and the crime.

Today, modern courts reject the concept that there was no rape if there was no immediate, or fresh, complaint. However, a long delay in reporting a sexual assault could be a factor considered by a jury in determining whether there was consent to the sexual act. Delay could also cause the loss of important physical evidence of the crime of sexual assault.

Some states continue to use the old common-law exception to the hearsay rule known as the "fresh complaint exception." In 1990 the Maryland Court of Special Appeals pointed out that a victim's timely complaint of a sexual assault is admissible as follows:

> In prosecution for sex offenses, evidence of the victim's complaint, coupled with the circumstances of the complaint is admissible as part of the prosecution's case if the complaint was made in a recent period of time after the complaint.[44]

Among the states that use the fresh complaint rule are California,[45] New Jersey,[46] Oregon,[47] Maryland,[48] Massachusetts,[49] and Florida.[50] Texas uses the outcry rule.[51]

In other states, the excited reporting of a rape or other crimes, which are startling events, while under the stress of excitement could be admissible under the excited utterance exception to the hearsay rule.

MODERN HEARSAY EXCEPTIONS IN CHILD SEXUAL ABUSE CASES

Statements by children reporting crimes are often admitted as evidence under the excited utterance hearsay exception. Statements children make to physicians and nurses often qualify as evidence under the medical diagnosis and treatment exception of the hearsay rule. These and other exceptions are often relaxed for children so that juries and judges may determine the reliability and weight that should be given to such evidence in child sexual abuse cases.

Not only have existing hearsay rules been relaxed for children in response to the increasing number of child sexual abuse cases reported in every city throughout the United States, but new state laws have also been enacted in more than thirty states. The new child hearsay statutes permit more out-of-court statements by children to be used as evidence in child sexual abuse cases.

Because these new state hearsay exceptions are not "firmly rooted" hearsay exceptions that go back hundreds of years in the law, the reliability of such statements cannot be inferred. Therefore, prosecutors must show that statements by children have "particularized guarantees of trustworthiness."

The U.S. Supreme Court held in the 1990 case of *Idaho v. Wright*[52] that for a child's out-of-court statement to be admissible, the child's truthfulness must be "so clear from the surrounding circumstances that the test of cross-examination would be of marginal utility." The Supreme Court listed the following factors that it thought "properly relate to whether hearsay statements made by a child witness in child sexual abuse cases are reliable:"[53]

1. "spontaneity and consistent repetition"[54]
2. "mental state of the declarant [child]"[55]
3. "use of terminology unexpected of a child of similar age"[56]
4. "lack of motive to fabricate"[57]

The U.S. Supreme Court added that these "factors are ... not exclusive, and courts have considerable leeway in their consideration of appropriate factors."[58]

HAVE INNOCENT PEOPLE BEEN CHARGED OR CONVICTED IN CHILD SEXUAL ABUSE CASES?

Sexual abuse of children does occur in the United States, and the frequency of child sexual abuse is shocking. Courts have responded to the problems of very young children as victims by relaxing hearsay rules so that more adults can testify about out-of-court statements made by children.

The new state child hearsay statutes permit additional use of out-of-court statements by children as evidence in criminal trials. Such statements may be used to corroborate the testimony of children concerning sexual abuse or may be sufficient to present a case without the child testifying where it is shown that the child has been traumatized or is otherwise unable to testify—due to loss of memory, for example.

After years of prosecutions in the 1980s and 1990s and thousands of cases where accusations of child sexual abuse were made against child-care workers, babysitters, family members, and others, however, it has become clear that many problems exist. The following child day-care cases have received national attention:

- In 1990 the California *McMartin* trial ended with no criminal convictions against a 62-year-old woman and her 30-year-old son who ran a child day-care center. The two were charged with 321 criminal counts of child molestation. The trial was the longest and probably the most expensive criminal trial in the United States, costing more than $13 million. The son spent more than five years in jail because bail was set so high.[59]
- In 1993 the Supreme Court of Nevada threw out numerous sexual assault convictions against day-care workers in the case of *Felix v. State*,[60] holding that "most of the claims of sexual assault could not have occurred as described by these girls."
- In 1993 the Superior Court of New Jersey reversed the convictions of a nursery school teacher of 115 counts of sexual offenses alleged to have been committed on very young children in the case of *State v. Michaels*.[61]

SUMMARY

The hearsay rules that we use today have developed over more than 300 years. If all hearsay was inadmissible as evidence, important relevant evidence would not be heard by juries and judges. If all hearsay was admitted as evidence, criminal and civil trials would be cluttered with unreliable evidence.

An accused in a criminal case has a Sixth Amendment right "to be confronted with the witnesses against him." Nontestimonial statements are not governed by the Confrontation Clause and may be admissible under state or federal hearsay exceptions. Testimonial statements cannot be admitted unless the defendant had an opportunity to cross-examine the declarant who made the statement, and the declarent is unavailable to testify in court.

Some of the "firmly rooted" exceptions developed years ago are the excited utterance exception; the then existing mental, emotional, or physical condition exception; statements for purposes of medical diagnosis or treatment exception; regularly kept records exception; dying declaration exception; and statements against-penal-interest exception.

CASE ANALYSIS

Read Appendix B, Finding and Analyzing Cases (p. 427). With these guidelines in mind, please continue with the Case Analysis selections for Chapter 8.

1. Is the U.S. Supreme Court's holding in *Davis* given retroactive effect and thus applicable in collateral review such as habeas corpus? What is the key to determining when new rules will apply to criminal convictions that were final before the new rule was announced? See *Whorten v. Bockting* [127 S.Ct. 1173 (2007)].

2. In *United States v. Arnold* [486 F.3d 177 (6th Cir. 2007)], a woman (a) called a 911 number and stated that the defendant had a gun and planned to kill her. She was in her car when she called the 911 operator, and when police arrived, she got out of her car and (b) made further statements about the defendant's plan to kill her and his possession of a gun. Finally, when the defendant approached the car, the woman said, (c) "That's him; that's the guy that pulled a gun on me...." Which, if any, of

these three statements was testimonial hearsay?

3. Is a police lab report testimonial, and thus inadmissible, if the person who prepared the report is unavailable to testify? Does either *Crawford* or *Davis* decide the question? See *State v. Caulfield* [722 N.W.2d 304 (Minn. 2006)].

4. The defendant and another man, Saunders, were charged with murder. Saunders made a plea agreement, and at his sentencing the state introduced facts to support his guilty plea, including a statement by Saunders to the prosecution that a third person, not the defendant, shot the victim. When the defendant was tried, he called Saunders to testify, and Saunders invoked his right to remain silent and refused to testify. The defendant then attempted to place Saunders's statements at his plea hearing into evidence, including a statement by the prosecutor that he believed Saunders was telling the truth in his statements. The trial court excluded the statements. Was the trial court correct? See *Bellamy v. State* [941 A.2d 1107 (Md. App. 2008)].

Notes

1. Some have contended that the term *witness* in the Confrontation Clause was originally intended to refer only to out-of-court statements directed solely at inculpating the defendant, such as affidavits, depositions, and confessions. Those were "particular abuses common in 16th and 17th century England: prosecuting a defendant through the presentation of ex parte affidavits without the affiants ever being produced at trial" [*White v. Illinois*, 502 U.S. 346, 352 (1992)]. The federal government—and Justice Thomas, concurring in *White v. Illinois*—argued that the Confrontation Clause "extends to any witness who actually testifies at trial, but the Confrontation Clause is implicated by extrajudicial statements only insofar as they are contained in formalized testimonial materials, such as affidavits, depositions, prior testimony, or confessions" [*White*, 502 U.S. 365 (J. Thomas, concurring) (1992)].

    The majority in *White* rejected this argument: "We think that the argument presented by the Government comes too late in the day to warrant reexamination of this approach" [*White*, 502 U.S. 353]. In *Lilly v. Virginia* [527 U.S. 116 (1999)], the Court again rejected this argument. See 119 S.Ct. at 1894. However, the decision in *Davis* comes close to taking this approach.

2. See Friedman, *Confrontation: The Search for Basic Principles*, 86 Geo. L.J. 1011, 1014 (1998).

3. 380 U.S. 400.

4. *California v. Green*, 399 U.S. 149, 155 (1970).

5. 399 U.S. at 158.

6. *Idaho v. Wright*, 497 U.S. 805 (1990).

7. 541 U.S. at 62.

8. 88 P.3d 789 (Kan. 2004).

9. 2005 Wl 513501 (D. Colo. 2005).

10. 541 U.S. 68.

11. *Id.*

12. 2008 WL 250298.

13. Almost by definition, the hearsay exceptions in Federal Rules of Evidence 803 and 804 are "firmly rooted" because most of them stem from federal common law or English law. Even if a hearsay exception is not of the "firmly rooted" variety, *Ohio v. Roberts* held that the evidence may still be admissible if there exist "particularized guarantees of trustworthiness." The Supreme Court in *Lilly* [119 S.Ct. 1887 (1900)] found that those guarantees did not exist in the case of Mark's statements.

14. *California v. Green*, 399 U.S. 155, 90 S.Ct. 1933 (1972).

15. *White v. Illinois*, 502 U.S. 346, 112 S.Ct. 741.

16. *Ohio v. Roberts*, 448 U.S. 56, 63, 100 S.Ct. 2531 (1980).

17. See, for example, *United States v. Williams* [506 F.3d 151(2d Cir. 2007), *cert. denied*, 128 S.Ct. 1329 (2008).

18. See, for example, *United States v. Thomas* [453 F.3d 838 (7th Cir. 2006)].

19. Many state evidence codes have adopted the language of the hearsay exceptions in the Federal Rules of Evidence.

20. Many years ago the excited utterance exception was lumped with other exceptions under a broad category known as the "res gestae exception" to the hearsay rule. A few states continue to use the res gestae exception.

Federal Rule of Evidence 803(1) states the hearsay exception called "present sense impression," which in some states is called the "spontaneous statement exception." The unexcited statement exception of present sense impressions is made part of the laws of many states. Rule 803 (1): "*Present sense impression*: A statement describing or explaining an event or condition made while the declarant was perceiving the event or condition, or immediately thereafter."

21. *Webb v. Lane*, 922 F.2d 390 (7th Cir. 1991); *State v. Farmer*, 408 S.E.2d 458 (W. Va. 1991); *State v. Anaya*, 799 P.2d 876 (1990); *State v. Baker*, 582 So.2d 1320 (La. App. 1991); *State v. Gibson*, 413 S.E.2d 120 (W. Va. 1991); *Russell v. State*, 815 S.W.2d 929 (Ark. 1991); *Royal v. Commonwealth*, 407 S.E.2d 346 (W. Va. 1991).

22. *State v. Reaves*, 596 So.2d 650 (La. App. 1990); *State v. Ferguson*, 540 So.2d 1116 (La. App. 1989); *Cole v. State*, 818 S.W.2d 573 (Ark. 1991).

23. *Ware v. State*, 596 So.2d 1200 (Fla. App. 1992); *State v. Edwards*, 485 N.W.2d 911 (Minn. 1992); *State v. Guizzotti*, 1991 WL 4995 (Wash. App. 1991).

24. *State v. Fox*, 585 N.E.2d 561 (Ohio 1990); *People v. Garcia*, 826 P.2d 1259 (Colo. 1992); *People v. Houghteling*, 455 N.W.2d 440 (Mich. App. 1990); *Cole v. State*, 818 S.W.2d 573 (Ark. 1991); *State v. Hy*, 458 N.W.2d 609 (Iowa 1990); *State v. Murphy*, 462 N.W.2d 715 (Iowa App. 1990); *Commonwealth v. Sanford*, 580 A.2d 784 (Pa. Super. 1990); *State v. Bryant*, 828 P.2d 1121 (Wash. App. 1992); *People v. Enoch*, 545 N.E.2d 429, 45 CrL 1059 (Ill. 1989).

25. 579 A.2d 515 (Conn.).

26. 606 So.2d 1132 (Miss.).

27. *State v. MacDonald*, 598 A.2d 1134 (Del. Super. 1991).

28. 376 P.2d 300.

29. 370 F.3d at 84.

30. 502 U.S. 346, 112 S.Ct. 736.

31. Other cases where it was held that physicians and other medical personnel could testify as to statements made by children while receiving medical treatment include statements that a 5-year-old made to the examining physician, *State v. Alvarez* [822 P.2d 1207 (Or. App. 1991)]; a 6-year-old child, *People v. Meeboer* [1992 WL 113254 (Mich. 1992)]; a 5-year-old child, *State v. Olesen*

[443 N.W.2d 8 (S.D. 1989)]; an 8-year-old's statements to pediatrician, psychologist, and social worker as to medical history and sexual abuse were admissible, *United States v. Balfany* [965 F.2d 575 (8th Cir. 1992)]; a 4-year-old's statements to a pediatrician and mental health therapist as to sexual abuse were admissible hearsay, *Fleming v. State* [819 S.W.2d 237 (Tex. App. 1991)].

32. The U.S. Supreme Court has previously held that the use of a dying declaration as evidence does not violate a defendant's Sixth Amendment right to confrontation and cross-examination. See *Mattox v. United States* [156 U.S. 237, 15 S.Ct. 337 (1895)]. The continued viability of the *Mattox* case is brought into question by the Court's decision in *Crawford*.

33. 168 Eng. Rep. 352.

34. 569 So.2d 897.

35. 452 N.W.2d 918, 922.

36. 586 So.2d 1033.

37. 606 A.2d 1354 (D.C. App. 1992).

38. 540 So.2d 1144 (La. App. 1989).

39. 403 U.S. 573, 91 S.Ct. 2075.

40. 410 U.S. 284, 93 S.Ct. 1038.

41. 588 A.2d 1066 (Conn. 1991).

42. 933 F.2d 536 (7th Cir. 1991).

43. There is some disagreement about the amount of corroboration needed for the admissibility of statements by people who assert they committed the crime being charged. More corroboration seems to be required for out-of-court confessions than for in-court confessions. For a discussion of some of the cases, see *McCormick on Evidence*, 4th ed. (West, 1992), vol. 2, pp. 340–43.

44. *Cole v. State*, 574 A.2d 326, 330 (Md. App. 1990).

45. *People v. Burton*, 359 P.2d 433 (1961).

46. *State v. Hill*, 578 A.2d 370 (1990).

47. *State v. Campbell*, 705 P.2d 694 (1985).

48. *Cole v. State*, 574 A.2d 326 (App. 1990).

49. *Commonwealth v. Licata*, 591 N.E.2d 672 (1992).

50. *McDonald v. State*, 578 So.2d 371 (1991).

51. *Anderson v. State*, 831 S.W.2d 50 (App. 1992).

52. 497 U.S. 805, 806, 110 S.Ct. 3139, 3142.

53. 497 U.S. 821, 110 S.Ct. 3150.

54. *State v. Robinson*, 735 P.2d 801 (Ariz. 1987).

55. *Morgan v. Foretich*, 846 F.2d 941 (4th Cir. 1988).

56. *State v. Sorenson*, 421 N.W.2d 77 (Wis. 1988).

57. *State v. Kuone*, 757 P.2d 289 (Kans. 1988).

58. 497 U.S. 822, 110 S.Ct. 3150.

59. The criminal proceedings in the *McMartin* case went on for more than five years, with the preliminary hearing alone lasting a year and a half. The trial and proceedings received national attention. All of the national talk shows covered the trial, in which there were many criminal charges of bizarre sex acts and naked children. Civil lawsuits by former defendants are discussed in *Satz v. Supreme Court (McMartin)* [275 Cal. Rptr. 710 (1990)] and *McMartin v. Children's Institute International* [261 Cal. Rptr. 437 (1989), *review denied*, 494 U.S. 1057, 110 S.Ct. 1526 (1990)].

60. The Supreme Court of Nevada noted that the *Felix* [849 P.2d 220] case was "the most extensive and costly criminal investigation and prosecution in Carson City [Nevada] history." It was alleged that as many as nineteen children had been sexually assaulted.

61. In the *Michaels* [625 A.2d 489] case, parents of very young children were permitted to testify as to out-of-court statements of their very young children under the New Jersey Child Hearsay Law without any showing that the hearsay "was probably trustworthy" as required by New Jersey statutes and also the U.S. Supreme Court [625 A.2d 517].

The New Jersey court also cited an unpublished Hawaii opinion that "each child had been subjected to layers and layers of interviews, questions, examinations, etc., which were fraught with textbook examples of poor interview techniques" [*State v. McKellar*, No. 85–0553 (Haw. Cir. Ct. Jan. 15, 1983)].

THE EXCLUSIONARY RULE

CHAPTER 9

LEARNING OBJECTIVES

In this chapter we examine the scope of the exclusionary rule, a court-created rule that, when invoked, results in the suppression of otherwise admissible evidence based on improper police conduct. The learning objectives for this chapter are:

- State the origin of the exclusionary rule.
- List some of the reasons an exclusionary rule is needed.
- Define the derivative evidence rule.
- List the exceptions to the exclusionary rule and what they entail.
- State the role of the exclusionary rule for evidence obtained by an improper search.
- State the role of the exclusionary rule for evidence obtained as a result of a violation of the *Miranda* rule.

CHAPTER CONTENTS

The Exclusionary Rule (or the Rule of the Exclusion of Evidence)

The Fruit of the Poisonous Tree Doctrine (or the Derivative Evidence Rule)

Exceptions to the Fruit of the Poisonous Tree Doctrine

The Independent Source Doctrine

The Inevitable Discovery Rule

The Attenuation, or Passage of Time, Rule

The *Miranda* Rule and the Fruit of the Poisonous Tree Doctrine

Many States Have Two Sets of Exclusionary Rules

THE EXCLUSIONARY RULE (OR THE RULE OF THE EXCLUSION OF EVIDENCE)

There are more than 17,000 police and sheriff departments in the United States, employing over 600,000 full-time officers with general arrest powers. Although these officers are charged with the responsibility of performing their duties within the limitations set by statutes, state constitutions, and the U.S. Constitution, they do not always do so. When that happens, the criminal justice system "polices the police."[1]

Just as football teams are penalized five or ten yards for a rule violation by an individual player, the **exclusionary rule** excludes (keeps out) evidence that was improperly or illegally obtained (see Figure 9.1). Like a football penalty, the exclusionary rule seeks to discourage improper or illegal investigative procedures by law enforcement officers.

Investigative conduct by law enforcement officers (both state and federal officers) can be improper for many reasons. Conduct might violate a police department rule, an FBI procedures handbook, or even a police union rule. These violations, which may have no real impact on a defendant, can be dealt with by internal police procedures.

Some law enforcement conduct is improper because it does adversely affect a criminal defendant's statutory or constitutional rights. The principal U.S. constitutional rights threatened by police misconduct are the Fifth Amendment's privilege against self-incrimination[2] and the Fourth Amendment's protection against unreasonable searches and seizures.[3] Other constitutional protections are secured for both federal and state defendants under the Due Process Clauses of the Fifth and Fourteenth Amendments.[4]

exclusionary rule A judicial rule that makes evidence obtained in violation of the U.S. Constitution, state or federal laws, or court rules inadmissible.

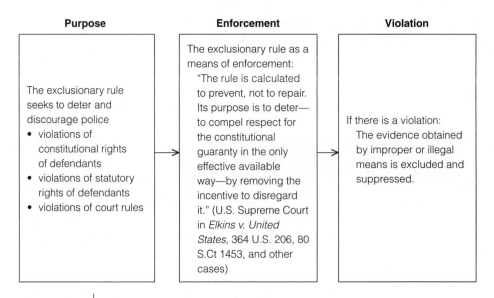

Purpose	Enforcement	Violation
The exclusionary rule seeks to deter and discourage police • violations of constitutional rights of defendants • violations of statutory rights of defendants • violations of court rules	The exclusionary rule as a means of enforcement: "The rule is calculated to prevent, not to repair. Its purpose is to deter—to compel respect for the constitutional guaranty in the only effective available way—by removing the incentive to disregard it." (U.S. Supreme Court in *Elkins v. United States,* 364 U.S. 206, 80 S.Ct 1453, and other cases)	If there is a violation: The evidence obtained by improper or illegal means is excluded and suppressed.

FIGURE 9.1 | THE FUNCTION OF THE EXCLUSIONARY RULE

For much of U.S. history, relevant and reliable evidence was admissible in criminal prosecutions even if it was obtained illegally. Beginning in 1914 in federal cases[5] and 1961 in state cases,[6] the U.S. Supreme Court required courts to exclude such evidence—that is, declare the evidence inadmissible to help prove the prosecution's case.

The U.S. Supreme Court has also used the exclusionary rule for violations of court-fashioned rules, like the famous *Miranda*[7] rule. In the *Miranda* case, the Supreme Court adopted a court rule[8] for determining the minimum safeguards that must be used by police before obtaining a confession or other incriminating statements. If these safeguards are not used, any resulting confession or incriminating statement is inadmissible.

The use of exclusionary rules to suppress otherwise reliable, relevant evidence has a cost to society because some clearly guilty defendants may go free if vital evidence is excluded from their trials. Defenders of exclusionary rules usually argue that such rules are necessary to deter official police misconduct and are the only practical alternatives available to achieve that deterrence.

Hudson v. Michigan

United States Supreme Court, 547 U.S. 586 (2006)

Defendants in criminal cases who move to suppress evidence obtained by improper police conduct do so by invoking the exclusionary rule, contending that the improper police conduct violated their constitutional rights (and in some instances statutory rights) and therefore the evidence must be suppressed. Logically, two questions are posed by such a contention: (1) Did the police conduct violate the defendant's rights? and (2) If so, is the suppression of evidence obtained the appropriate remedy? Although defendants might argue that an affirmative answer to the first question inevitably leads to the same answer to the second, the U.S. Supreme Court has long refused to accept such a broad reading of the rule. In *United States v. Leon*,[9] the Court said "whether the exclusion sanction is appropriately imposed in a particular case … is an 'issue separate from the question whether the Fourth Amendment rights of the party seeking to invoke the rule were violated by police conduct.'" In *Hudson v. Michigan* the Court reiterated that approach, and affirmed a Michigan appellate court's refusal to suppress evidence obtained after a violation of a "knock-and-announce" warrant.

The defendant was arrested and charged with possession of unlawful drugs and firearms under Michigan state law. At his trial, the prosecution sought to introduce evidence obtained when police searched the defendant's residence pursuant to a valid search warrant. When the police arrived at the defendant's residence, they knocked at his door, announced their presence, and after a three- to five-second wait opened the door and conducted a search. The search uncovered unlawful drugs and firearms.

The defendant moved to suppress the evidence based on his claim that the police failed to wait a sufficient time after announcing their presence. The trial court initially ordered the evidence suppressed, but after a Michigan appellate court reversed that decision, the evidence was admitted and the defendant convicted. He appealed to the Michigan Court of Appeals, which affirmed his conviction, and the Michigan Supreme Court refused review. The U.S. Supreme Court granted certiorari and affirmed the conviction.

The Supreme Court first noted that the only issue presented on appeal was the appropriateness of the exclusionary sanction. The State of Michigan conceded that the police violated the defendant's rights by failing to wait a sufficient time after announcing their presence.[10]

The Court then stated that under *Wilson v. Arkansas*,[11] announcing police presence is part of the Fourth Amendment requirements for a reasonable search, unless the police have some basis for believing that announcing would (1) allow evidence to be destroyed, (2) create a threat of violence against the officers about to enter the residence, or (3) be futile. The *Hudson* Court stressed, however, that in *Wilson* the Court specifically refused to determine whether the exclusionary rule applied to a knock-and-announce violation.[12]

The Court stated that the exclusionary rule is most appropriate in the case of warrantless searches because the Fourth Amendment clearly operates to protect citizens' right to "shield their persons, houses, papers and effects" from warrantless searches.[13] When there is no valid warrant, a citizen is entitled to keep his personal effects free from police inspection, and the exclusionary rule is appropriate to make sure that happens, the Court concluded.

When a valid warrant has been issued, it is inevitable that the citizen's right to keep his effects private will be lost because the police will at some time be able to inspect the private dwelling as provided in the search warrant. Thus, the Court reasoned, the real question was: What interests are protected by the knock-and-announce requirement? It concluded that the primary interests were the avoidance of a potential violent reaction to a surprise entrance, the protection against property damage occasioned by a forceful police entry, and the right of the citizen to prepare for police entry by getting dressed, getting out of bed, or arranging one's appearance. Beyond that, the Court said

> What the knock-and-announce rule has never protected, however, is one's interest in preventing the government from seeing or taking evidence described in a warrant. Since the interests that were violated in this case have nothing to do with the seizure of the evidence, the exclusionary rule is inapplicable. *Id.* at 594.

Thus, the Court reasoned, unlike cases where a search was invalid because the police did not have a valid warrant, here the questioned evidence was not discovered as a result of the violation. Whether or not the police properly announced their presence, they were going to discover the evidence. Although a defendant might suggest that a longer announcement period would have enabled him to hide the evidence, the defendant has no right to do so, the Court said. This eliminated the "but-for" causation that exists in warrantless searches, because "but for" the violation the police would not have discovered the evidence.

Moreover, the Court stated, in knock-and-announce cases application of the exclusionary rule would turn on extremely fine determinations of how long the police should have waited before entering under a valid search warrant. This makes the deterrent effect of the rule difficult to evaluate. Also, the Court said, professional police departments that obtain valid search warrants can be expected to follow reasonable rules about announcing their presence. For these additional reasons, the Court concluded, the exclusionary rule is inappropriate for knock-and-announce violations.

THE FRUIT OF THE POISONOUS TREE DOCTRINE (OR THE DERIVATIVE EVIDENCE RULE)

fruit of the poisonous tree Evidence obtained legally through the use of evidence obtained illegally.

derivative evidence rule Another term for the fruit of the poisonous tree doctrine.

The exclusionary rule applies not only to evidence obtained directly as a result of improper police conduct but also to evidence obtained indirectly from that improper conduct. Evidence derived from initial improper conduct is called **fruit of the poisonous tree.** For example, if the police wrongfully enter a house and find a key to a storage locker, the key is a direct result of the wrongful entry and is inadmissible. If the police then use the key to unlock the storage locker and find illegal drugs, the drugs are excluded as fruit of the initial wrongful entry. (The doctrine is also known as the **derivative evidence rule.**)

Example

Assume that either the police officers do not comply with the *Miranda* requirements or they beat a suspect until he confesses to a murder. In either example, the confession is a direct product of improper police conduct and cannot be used as evidence in an American criminal court.

Assume also that in his confession, the suspect told the police where the murder weapon is hidden. Even if the police obtain the weapon by lawful means, the weapon cannot be used as evidence to link the suspect to the crime under the fruit of the poisonous tree doctrine. The weapon is the indirect product of improper police conduct; that improper conduct is the "poisonous tree," and any evidence derived solely from that improper conduct is the "fruit."[14] Not only would the weapon in the example be suppressed ("thrown out"), but any evidence obtained from the weapon, such as fingerprints and ballistic tests, also would be excluded under the derivative evidence rule.

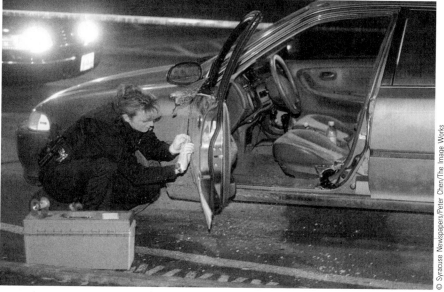

A police officer searches a car door for evidence of criminal activity. Evidence that she finds will be admissible only if the initial stop was made legally and if her search techniques follow legal procedures.

© Syracuse Newspapers/Peter Chen/The Image Works

The fruit of the poisonous tree doctrine is applicable if improperly or illegally obtained evidence is the basis for the discovery of:

- Other evidence that otherwise would not have been found
- A witness who otherwise might not have been found
- A confession or incriminating admission that would not have been made if the suspect or defendant had not been confronted with the tainted (soiled) evidence

The following U.S. Supreme Court case further illustrates the derivative evidence rule (fruit of the poisonous tree doctrine):

Fahy v. Connecticut

Supreme Court of the United States, 375 U.S. 85, 84 S.Ct. 229 (1963)

A police officer saw a car driving slowly in downtown Norwalk, Connecticut, at about 4:40 in the morning. The police officer lawfully stopped the car and questioned the two men in the car. In checking the car for weapons, the officer found a can of black paint and a paintbrush under the front seat. Fahy (the driver of the car) then drove his car home. A short time later, the police officer found that someone had painted swastikas on a Jewish synagogue a short distance from where he had stopped Fahy's car.

The officer went to Fahy's home and, without a search warrant or consent from Fahy, entered Fahy's garage and removed the paint and brush from Fahy's car. After determining that the paint and brush fit the markings on the synagogue, the officer obtained an arrest warrant. When arrested, Fahy made incriminating statements, and later, at the police station, Fahy made a full confession. All the evidence was used in obtaining a conviction of Fahy and his companion. In reversing, the U.S. Supreme Court held that:

> petitioner (Fahy) should have had a chance to show that his admissions were induced by being confronted with the illegally seized evidence.
>
> Nor can we ignore the cumulative prejudicial effect of this evidence upon the conduct of the defense at trial. It was only after admission of the paint and brush and only after their subsequent use to corroborate other state's evidence and only after introduction of the confession that the defendants took the stand, admitted their acts, and tried to establish that the nature of those acts was not within the scope of the felony statute under which the defendants had been charged. We do not mean to suggest that petitioner has presented any valid claim based on the privilege against self-incrimination. We merely note this course of events as another indication of the prejudicial effect of erroneously admitted evidence.

EXCEPTIONS TO THE FRUIT OF THE POISONOUS TREE DOCTRINE

The *derivative evidence rule* as the name suggests, applies only if the challenged evidence is directly and exclusively derived from improper police conduct. The U.S. Supreme Court has developed three exceptions to the doctrine in those situations where the police misconduct has not "tainted" the challenged evidence.

THE INDEPENDENT SOURCE DOCTRINE

Improper police conduct may lead to the discovery of evidence while at the same time another proper source leads to the same evidence. If the second, proper source of the evidence is independent—that is, not tainted by the improper conduct—the evidence is admissible.[15]

Murray v. United States

United States Supreme Court, 487 U.S. 533 (1988)

Federal agents made an unlawful entry into a warehouse where they saw bales of marijuana. The federal agents later applied for a search warrant without making reference to the unlawful entry. The U.S. Supreme Court sent the case back to the trial court "for determination whether the [search authorized by the warrant] was an independent source of the challenged evidence ..." stating:

> Knowledge that the marijuana was in the warehouse was assuredly acquired at the time of the unlawful entry. But it was also acquired at the time of entry pursuant to the warrant, and if that later acquisition was not the result of the earlier entry there is no reason why the independent source doctrine should not apply. Invoking the exclusionary rule would put the police (and society) not in the same position they would have occupied if no violation occurred, but in a *worse* one....

THE INEVITABLE DISCOVERY RULE

inevitable discovery rule An exception to the exclusionary rule where illegally discovered evidence would certainly have been discovered legally.

If police error or police misconduct has tainted some evidence, then that evidence and also derivative evidence are suppressed and cannot be used in a criminal trial. If it can be shown that the challenged derivative evidence would have certainly been discovered by legitimate police efforts, however, it is admissible under the **inevitable discovery rule**. The U.S. Supreme Court adopted the inevitable discovery rule in the following case and explains its relationship to the independent source test.

Nix v. Williams

United States Supreme Court, 467 U.S. 431 (1984)

A 10-year-old Iowa girl was reported missing, and a massive search involving hundreds of police officers and volunteers was organized. During the search, Williams was arrested, based on reports that he had been seen carrying a small girl near the place and at the time she was reported missing. During questioning, the police violated the *Massiah* rule[16] by questioning Williams about the location of the girl's body without the consent or presence of his attorney. Based on Williams's statements, the girl's body was found and the search suspended.

Williams's statements to police were declared inadmissible, but the prosecution sought to introduce evidence of the condition of the body, articles of clothing found, and results of medical tests on the body. The defense contended that this evidence was the "fruit" of the "poisonous" questioning. In upholding the admissibility of this evidence, the Supreme Court concluded that the inevitable discovery rule has the same justification as the independent source rule:

> [The] core rationale consistently advanced by this Court for extending the Exclusionary Rule to evidence that is the fruit of unlawful police conduct has been that this admittedly drastic and socially costly course is needed to deter police from violations of constitutional and statutory protections. [On] this rationale, the prosecution is not to be put in a better position than it would have been in if no illegality had transpired.

By contrast, the derivative evidence analysis ensures that the prosecution is not put in a worse position simply because of some earlier police error or misconduct. The independent source doctrine allows admission of evidence that has been discovered by means wholly independent of any constitutional violation. That doctrine, although closely related to the inevitable discovery doctrine, does not apply here: Williams' statements to Learning [police officer] indeed led police to the child's body, but that is not the whole story. The independent source doctrine teaches us that the interest of society in deterring unlawful police conduct and the public interest in having juries receive all probative evidence of a crime are properly balanced by putting the police in the same, not a worse, position than they would have been in if no police error or misconduct had occurred. When the challenged evidence has an independent source, exclusion of such evidence would put the police in a worse position than they would have been in absent any error or violation. There is a functional similarity between these two doctrines in that exclusion of evidence that would inevitably have been discovered would also put the government in a worse position, because the police would have obtained that evidence if no misconduct had taken place. Thus, while the independent source exception would not justify admission of evidence in this case, its rationale is wholly consistent with and justifies our adoption of the ultimate or inevitable discovery exception to the Exclusionary Rule....

The U.S. Supreme Court concluded that the search parties, which were systematically searching the area where the body was found, would have found the body in a short time without Williams's directions, and thus the evidence found on or near the body would have been found at the same time.

THE ATTENUATION, OR PASSAGE OF TIME, RULE

passage of time rule (attenuation) An exception to the exclusionary rule where the "taint" from the improper conduct is dissipated over a significant period of time after the improper conduct.

Where improper police conduct occurs and shortly thereafter that conduct leads to the discovery of other evidence, the fruit of the poisonous tree doctrine reasonably concludes that a connection exists between the improper conduct and the other evidence. Where, however, a significant period of time goes by between the improper conduct and the new evidence, the U.S. Supreme Court has long held that the "taint" from the improper conduct can be dissipated. This is termed the **passage of time rule,** or **attenuation.**

Wong Sun v. United States

United States Supreme Court, 371 U.S. 471 (1963)

Federal narcotics agents illegally broke into a suspect's laundry and pressured him to make statements that led to the arrest of Wong Sun on narcotics charges. After his arrest, Wong Sun was arraigned and released on his own recognizance. Several days later, Wong Sun voluntarily appeared at the San Francisco Narcotics Bureau and confessed to the illegal transportation and concealment of heroin.

At his trial, Wong Sun sought to exclude his confession as the fruit of the illegal entry. The Supreme Court found the evidence admissible because the connection between Wong Sun's illegal arrest and his confession "had became so attenuated as to dissipate the taint."

TYPES OF EVIDENCE CONTROLLED BY THE EXCLUSIONARY RULE

Type of Evidence	U.S. Constitutional Amendment That Controls the Evidence	Test of Admissibility for Use of Evidence
Physical evidence (drugs, weapons, contraband, clothing, fingerprints, etc.)	*Fourth Amendment:* "The right of the people to be secure ... against unreasonable searches and seizures shall not be violated."	The Fourth Amendment requires a search warrant if a right of privacy is involved. If a warrant is not used, the burden is on the officer to show that the search was authorized by one of the well-recognized exceptions to the requirement of a search warrant. (See Chapters 14 and 15.)
Confessions, incriminating admissions, and statements	*Fifth Amendment:* "No person ... shall be compelled ... to be a witness against himself." *Sixth Amendment:* "In all criminal prosecutions, the accused shall enjoy the right ... to have the assistance of counsel for his defense."	The voluntariness test applies to the use of all statements as evidence. The following tests may be applicable depending on the circumstances: *Miranda* requirements and test, *Massiah* test, and *Bruton* requirements. (See Chapter 12.)
Eyewitness and voice identification	*Fifth and Fourteenth Amendments:* "No person shall be ... deprived of life, liberty, or property, without due process of law." *Sixth Amendment:* "In all criminal prosecutions, the accused shall enjoy the right ... to have the assistance of counsel for his defense."	Were the procedures used so unnecessarily suggestive and conducive to irreparable mistaken identification as to be a denial of due process of law? (See Chapter 13.) Was the accused denied the assistance of counsel at an important and critical stage of the criminal proceedings? [See *Kirby v. Illinois*, 406 U.S. 682, 92 S.Ct. 1877 (1972).]
Evidence obtained as a result of wiretapping and electronic surveillance	Wiretapping and electronic surveillances are searches controlled by the Fourth Amendment. Wiretapping is also controlled by Title III, Federal Omnibus Crime Control and Safe Streets Act, and applicable statutes in every state.	

THE *MIRANDA* RULE AND THE FRUIT OF THE POISONOUS TREE DOCTRINE

The fruit of the poisonous tree doctrine places emphasis on the "poisonous tree"—that is, the improper police conduct. Where the improper conduct is an illegal search and seizure, the doctrine is justified by the reasons for having an exclusionary rule at all: The improper police conduct must be deterred in order to accomplish the purpose of the Fourth Amendment. Where the improper police conduct is failure to give a *Miranda* warning (see Chapter 12), courts have been uncertain about the applicability of the poisonous tree doctrine. An example of that uncertainty is the Wisconsin case of *State v. Knapp.*[17] There, a suspect in a murder case permitted a police officer into his home to wait while he got dressed to go to the police station and answer questions. Without giving a *Miranda* warning, the officer asked the defendant what he was wearing the night before, the night of the murder. The defendant pointed to a sweatshirt, and the officer seized it. Subsequent DNA tests established the presence of the victim's blood on the sweatshirt.

Based on that and other evidence, the defendant was charged with murder. He moved to suppress both his pre-*Miranda* warning statements made to the officer and the physical evidence (the sweatshirt) seized as a result of those statements. The prosecution conceded that the statements must be excluded but argued that the physical evidence was admissible.

The Wisconsin Supreme Court held that the physical evidence must be excluded as the fruit of a poisonous tree. The "poisonous tree" was the intentional failure to give the defendant *Miranda* warnings. Since the violation was intentional, the court concluded that the deterrent effect of the exclusionary rule required suppression of the evidence. Other courts have decided this issue differently. For example, in *United States v. Sterling*,[18] the Fourth Circuit Court of Appeals upheld the admission of a gun found as a result of statements made by the defendant without a *Miranda* warning. That court concluded that, so long as the statement was voluntary, physical evidence can never be the fruit of the poisonous tree. In the case of *United States v. Patane*,[19] the Tenth Circuit Court of Appeals went further than the Wisconsin court in the *Knapp* case when it held that physical evidence obtained by the police as a result of a negligent failure to give a defendant his *Miranda* warnings must be suppressed.

The U.S. Supreme Court granted certiorari in *Knapp* and *Patane*.[20] In 2004 in *United States v. Patane*,[21] the Court reversed the Tenth Circuit Court of Appeals, holding that the Fifth Amendment's Self-Incrimination Clause does not require the exclusion of physical evidence obtained as a result of a voluntary statement made without a *Miranda* warning:

> [T]he *Miranda* rule is a prophylactic employed to protect against violations of the Self-Incrimination Clause. The Self-Incrimination Clause, however, is not implicated by the admission into evidence of the physical fruit of a voluntary statement....
> The *Miranda* rule is not a code of police conduct, and police do not violate the Constitution (or even the *Miranda* rule, for that matter) by mere failure to warn. For this reason, the exclusionary rule articulated in cases such as *Wong Sun* does not apply.[22]

The Court stated that the Self-Incrimination Clause has only one, specific goal: to protect against compelled, self-incriminating statements. As a result, the Court said, the only exclusionary rule necessitated by the Fifth Amendment is the exclusion of unwarned statements:

> It follows that police do not violate a suspect's constitutional rights (or the *Miranda* rule) by negligent or even deliberate failures to provide the suspect with the full panoply of warnings prescribed by *Miranda*. Potential violations occur, if at all, only upon the admission of unwarned statements into evidence at trial. And, at that point, "[t]he exclusion of unwarned statements ... is a complete and sufficient remedy" for any perceived *Miranda* violation. (Citation omitted.)
>
> Thus, unlike unreasonable searches under the Fourth Amendment or actual violations of the Due Process Clause or the Self-Incrimination Clause, there is, with respect

to a mere failure to warn, nothing to deter. There is therefore no reason to apply the 'fruit of the poisonous tree' doctrine of *Wong Sun*." (Citation omitted.)

Following the decision in *Patane*, the decision of the Wisconsin Supreme Court in *Knapp* was vacated by the U.S. Supreme Court, and the case remanded to the Wisconsin Supreme Court. In 2005, that court on remand held that the physical evidence must be excluded under the Wisconsin State Constitution, ARTICLE I, SECTION 8, because it was the result of intentional police conduct.[23]

Patane by its terms applies only to physical evidence obtained as a result of a voluntary, unwarned statement. If the statement is involuntary, such physical evidence would likely be suppressed under the Due Process Clause. Moreover, if the original unwarned statement is repeated, after the proper *Miranda* warning has been given, the subsequent statement may be excluded. (See *Missouri v. Seibert*, discussed in Chapter 12.)

MANY STATES HAVE TWO SETS OF EXCLUSIONARY RULES

The federal exclusionary rule has become very complex since the 1961 *Mapp v. Ohio* case.[24] All states must follow the federal *Mapp* rule in determining the admissibility of evidence. However, it is not uncommon for state courts to impose additional requirements in interpreting that state's constitution or statutes. State statutes, by themselves, may alter the federal *Mapp* rule and impose a stricter standard in a given area of the law.

An example of such an alteration is in *State v. Eckel*,[25] where the New Jersey Supreme Court joined several other states that have rejected the U.S. Supreme Court's rule that the Fourth Amendment permits police to routinely search the passenger compartment of a vehicle incident to the arrest of a recent occupant. (See *New York v. Belton*,[26] discussed in Chapter 14.) The New Jersey court held that under the New Jersey Constitution police cannot search a passenger compartment of a vehicle without a warrant after the occupant has been removed from the vehicle, handcuffed, and placed in the police vehicle.

Therefore, many states have two sets of exclusionary rules. The federal rule is defined by the U.S. Supreme Court and other federal courts, while the state exclusionary rule is defined and required by the state supreme court (and sometimes by state statutes). State law enforcement officers are required to comply with the state requirements, which may be more stringent than those required by the federal *Mapp* rule. However, evidence to be used in criminal cases in federal courts in all states is judged by the federal *Mapp* rule. Because most crimes are violations of state criminal codes, however, most criminal cases go to state criminal courts.

Some states have simplified this situation by eliminating, to a large extent, their state exclusionary rule. California and Florida are among the states that have added sections to their state constitutions requiring state courts to determine the admissibility of evidence "in conformity with the 4th Amendment ... as interpreted by the U.S. Supreme Court" (Florida Constitution). (For the California change, see *In re Lance W.*[27])

SHOULD THERE BE CHANGES, MAJOR OR MINOR, IN THE AMERICAN EXCLUSIONARY RULE?

A front-page article in the July 19, 2008, edition of *The New York Times* is entitled "U.S. Stands Alone In Rejecting All Evidence When Police Err." The article reported on a case in the Canadian legal system in which a Canadian trial court and a Canadian court of appeals both refused to suppress evidence of illegal drugs found after the illegal search of a vehicle. The trial court found that police officers stopped the vehicle on a contrived or made-up reason and then conducted a search that uncovered more than 77 pounds of cocaine. Although the court described the officers' conduct as a "brazen and flagrant" violation of the rights of the vehicle's owner, it refused to suppress the evidence, and the owner was convicted of drug violations.

The court of appeals affirmed the conviction, refusing to suppress the illegal drugs found in the defendant's vehicle. The court stated:

> the exclusion [as evidence] of 77 pounds of cocaine with a street value of several millions of dollars and the potential to cause serious grief and misery to many, would bring the administration of justice into greater disrepute than would its admission.

The case is now before the Canadian Supreme Court and will likely be decided near the end of 2008 or early in 2009. Canada is an example of a country that has not adopted an exclusionary rule for evidence obtained in violation of citizens' rights. Even those countries that have some kind of exclusionary rule, such as Australia, make imposition of the rule dependent on the balance between the seriousness of the violation and the nature of the crime and evidence to be suppressed.

Some justices of the U.S. Supreme Court have expressed discontent with the present scope of the American exclusionary rule because it suppresses virtually all evidence obtained by police misconduct, whether the misconduct is slight or serious, and without regard to the seriousness of the crime or the value of the evidence. No other democratic nation in the world has a rule that requires automatic suppression of all evidence obtained by police misconduct.

As illustrated by the *Hudson v. Michigan* case discussed on page 181, a majority of the justices now sitting on the U.S. Supreme Court seem willing to reexamine the appropriateness of the exclusionary rule, and they might welcome a case with facts similar to the case before the Canadian Supreme Court. Because the exclusionary rule is a court-made rule, it could be changed by a majority of the Supreme Court. It is possible that such changes might occur, whether they are minor or major, if the Court is presented with the proper case.

After reviewing the material on the American exclusionary rule, what do you think should happen? Although complete revocation of the rule seems unlikely, should it be modified to permit fewer occasions for exclusion of important evidence? If so, should the Supreme Court determine the scope of an exclusionary rule, or should legislative bodies become involved? What is the status of the exclusionary rule under your state law? Does it go beyond the federal rule? Should it?

SUMMARY

Prior to 1914, practically all relevant and material evidence was admitted for use at criminal trials regardless of how law enforcement officers obtained the evidence. A federal exclusionary rule was established in 1914, and in 1961 an exclusionary rule was made binding on the states under the Due Process Clause of the Fourteenth Amendment. In addition, some states have established exclusionary rules in their state constitutions. These state exclusionary rules tend to be broader than the federal exclusionary rule.

The exclusionary rule or the rule of the exclusion of evidence suppresses, or throws out, evidence that a law enforcement officer has obtained in violation of the constitutional or statutory rights of a defendant. The rule is applicable to violations of both the Fourth Amendment's limitations on searches and seizures and the Fifth Amendment's privilege against self-incrimination, although the scope of the exclusionary rule differs depending on the right or privilege violated.

There are three exceptions to the fruit of the poisonous tree doctrine (or the derivative evidence rule):

1. The independent source doctrine, where evidence is discovered by or through a source different from and independent of the prohibited police conduct
2. The inevitable discovery rule, where it can be shown that the evidence would have been discovered even if the prohibited police conduct had not occurred
3. The attenuation, or passage of time, rule, where because of the amount of time that passed between the police misconduct and the discovery of the evidence, the connection between the violation and the discovery is broken

CASE ANALYSIS

Read Appendix B, Finding and Analyzing Cases (p. 427). With these guidelines in mind, please continue with the Case Analysis selections for Chapter 9.

1. The independent source doctrine comes into play when the police have discovered evidence through illegal means but contend that other legal means also lead to the discovery of the evidence. The key to the doctrine is the word *independent*; the legal means must not be connected to the illegal means. Determining whether this connection exists can be very difficult. In *United States v. Jenkins* [396 F.3d 751 (6th Cir. 2005)] [Docket No. 03–3989], the court concluded that although police officers initially conducted an illegal search and uncovered evidence of illegal drug transactions, a lawful search warrant subsequently obtained uncovered the same evidence, and the two searches were not connected. What arguments did the defendant make that the lawful search was connected to the unlawful search and thus was "tainted"? Do you agree with the argument?

2. *United States v. Johnson* [380 F.3d 1013 (7th Cir. 2004)] [Docket Nos. 03-3192, 03-3195] illustrates the complexity associated with applying the independent source doctrine and the inevitable discovery doctrine. Indeed, as the opinion's author, Judge Posner, admits, the court in *Johnson* is not sure which of theses doctrines actually applied to the case. When analyzing the case, keep this in mind. The search of the defendant's car trunk was clearly illegal from the driver's perspective. Had the police simply stopped the defendant and searched his car trunk, any evidence found in that search would have been inadmissible. What does the prosecution argue was the "independent source" of the evidence found in the car trunk? Why did the court reject this contention?

3. Can an airline passenger who has passed through an airport screening gate object to a subsequent secondary search and, if so, suppress evidence of illegal drugs discovered in that search? See *United States v. Aukai* [497 F.3d 955 (9th Cir. 2007)].

4. What must the police show under the "inevitable discovery" rule if they wish to have evidence admitted that was the result of an unlawful search? What did the police argue in *United States v. Heath* [455 F.3d 52 (2d Cir. 2006)]?

Notes

1. Former Chief Justice of the U.S. Supreme Court Warren Burger raised the question in his 1964 article, *Who Will Watch the Watchman?* (14 Am. U. L. Rev. 1), before he was appointed to the Court.

2. See Chapter 12 for material on Fifth Amendment rights.

3. See Chapter 14 for material on Fourth Amendment rights.

4. Early Supreme Court cases seem to have tied inadmissibility of involuntary confessions to the Fifth Amendment's privilege against self-incrimination. See *Bram v. United States* [168 U.S. 532 (1897)]. Since *Brown v. Mississippi* [297 U.S. 278 (1936)], the Due Process Clause has been regarded as the basis for the requirement that confession be voluntary.

5. The federal *Weeks* rule is named after the 1914 case of *Weeks v. United States* [34 S.Ct. 341], in which federal agents entered Weeks's home without consent and without a search warrant or any other authority. The agents seized evidence in Weeks's home, which was used to obtain Weeks's criminal conviction.

6. In *Mapp v. Ohio* [81 S.Ct. 1684 (1961)], police officers forced their way into Ms. Mapp's home without probable cause, consent, a search warrant, or any other authority. The officers suspected that a fugitive was hiding in the house. When they did not find a fugitive, they searched through drawers and boxes until they found evidence of pornography, which they used to convict Mapp of the crime of possession of pornography.

7. *Miranda v. Arizona*, 384 U.S. 436 (1966). The *Miranda* rule is discussed more fully in Chapter 12.

8. The *Miranda* warnings are: (a) the suspect has the right to remain silent, (b) any statements made can be used against the suspect, (c) the suspect has the right to have an attorney present, and (d) an attorney will be appointed if the suspect cannot afford one.

9. 468 U.S. 897, 906 (1984).

10. 547 U.S. at 590.

11. 514 U.S. 927 (1995).

12. *Id.*

13. *Id.* at 593.

14. It is clear that the murder weapon would be excluded if the police beat the confession out of the suspect. If the police "merely" failed to give the *Miranda* warning, however, and the suspect's inadmissible statements led to the discovery of physical evidence, the fruit of the poisonous tree doctrine may not apply. See *Oregon v. Elstad* [470 U.S. 298 (1985)]. Although *Elstad* is not explicit on this issue, lower federal and state courts seem to be admitting such physical violence. See Wollin, *Policing the Police: Should Miranda Violations Bear Fruit?* 53 Ohio St. L.J. 805, 835–36 (1992): "[F]ollowing *Elstad*, federal and state courts have almost uniformly ruled that the prosecution can introduce nontestimonial fruits of a *Miranda* violation in a criminal trial." *United States v. Patane* (see note 21) now establishes that the derivative evidence aspect of the exclusionary rule is not applicable to Fifth Amendment violations.

15. See *Silverthorne Lumber Co. v. United States* [251 U.S. 385 (1920)] and *Nardone v. United States* [308 U.S. 338 (1939)]. *Nardone* was the first case to use the fruit of the poisonous tree analogy.

16. See *Massiah v. United States* [377 U.S. 201 (1964)], discussed in Chapter 12. The rescue exception or the public safety exception to the *Miranda* rule might reasonably be applied to the *Massiah* doctrine in cases like *Williams*.

17. 666 N.W.2d 881 (2003).

18. 283 F.3d 216 (4th Cir. 2002), *cert. denied*, 536 U.S. 931 (2002).

19. 304 F.3d 1013 (10th Cir. 2002).

20. 123 S.Ct. 1788 (2003).

21. 124 S.Ct. 2620 (2004).

22. 124 S.Ct. at 2626.

23. *State v. Knapp*, 2005 WL 1639308 (Wis. July 14, 2005).

24. See note 6 for a summary of *Mapp v. Ohio*.

25. 888 A.2d 1266 (N.J. 2006).

26. 453 U.S. 454 (1981).

27. Cal. Rptr. 631, 694 P.2d 744 (1985).

WHERE THE EXCLUSIONARY RULE DOES NOT APPLY

CHAPTER 10

LEARNING OBJECTIVES

In this chapter we present some of the accepted situations where the exclusionary rule does *not* apply. The learning objectives for this chapter are:

- Define *standing* for Fourth Amendment purposes.
- Explain the role of "consent" in searches of persons or residences.
- State when property is abandoned for Fourth Amendment purposes.
- List the factors to be considered when the good faith test from *Leon* is applied to a search warrant.
- Distinguish "good faith" from "honest mistake."

CHAPTER CONTENTS

The exclusionary rule and its applications (discussed in Chapter 9) have been the subject of extensive criticism. The principal argument against the rule is that society pays a high cost to secure its benefits. The goal of the exclusionary rule is to deter improper police conduct, which in theory benefits all citizens, but in most cases the direct beneficiary of the rule is someone who would be convicted if the evidence were not excluded. The rule can thus result in dangerous criminals going free.

Mindful of this cost, the U.S. Supreme Court has repeatedly held that "the [exclusionary] rule has been [and is] restricted to those areas where its remedial objectives are thought most efficaciously served."

In this chapter we define the scope and extent of the exclusionary rule by examining its borders. In what areas of conduct, even improper or illegal conduct, should the exclusionary rule be inapplicable?

THE EXCLUSIONARY RULE DOES NOT APPLY TO EVIDENCE OBTAINED IN A PRIVATE SEARCH BY A PRIVATE PERSON

The Fourth Amendment to the U.S. Constitution prohibits unreasonable search and seizures. Evidence obtained in violation of the Fourth Amendment is generally inadmissible under the exclusionary rule.[1] This prohibition applies to mistakes or misconduct by the police and other officials in the executive branch of government. The exclusionary rule does not apply to private persons. Evidence obtained by private persons, even if the result of illegal conduct, is not subject to the exclusionary rule, as the Supreme Court held in the following case.

Burdeau v. McDowell

United States Supreme Court, 256 U.S. 465 (1921)

An unknown person or persons burglarized the defendant's office, breaking into his desk and private safe. The burglars took files and papers that implicated the defendant in criminal activity. These papers and files ended up in the possession of federal prosecutors, who showed "clean hands" and then used them in the indictment and conviction of the defendant.

The defendant argued that the evidence should have been excluded because it was obtained by an unlawful search and seizure. The Supreme Court rejected that argument, holding "the record clearly shows that no official of the federal government had anything to do with the wrongful seizure of the petitioner's property, or had any knowledge thereof until several months after the property had been taken from him."

In refusing to make the Fourth Amendment applicable to purely private conduct, the Supreme Court observed that the origin and history of that amendment "clearly shows that it was intended as a restraint upon the activities of sovereign authority and was not intended to be a limitation upon other than government agencies."[2]

A private search can be transformed into a government search if the government participates in the search, as the 2008 California case of *People v. Wilkinson*[3] illustrates. There, the defendant was charged with burglary when he entered the bedroom of a co-occupant of his residence and downloaded images from her computer showing her engaged in sexual acts with her boyfriend. At his trial, the defendant moved to suppress the computer discs he had made and kept in his room

WHEN IS A SEARCH PRIVATE?

If a search is **private** (conducted solely by a private person), the exclusionary rule does not apply. Courts have adopted the following requirements to determine whether a search is purely private:

	Held Not Private	**Held Private**
The evidence was obtained by a private person acting in a private capacity.[a]	*State v. Woods*, 790 S.W.2d 253 (Mo. App. 1990): An off-duty officer working as caretaker searched a cabin for drugs.	*State v. Castillo*, 697 P.2d 1219 (Idaho 1985): An off-duty police officer inadvertently opened a letter to his brother-in-law and found drugs.
The idea or initiative to obtain the evidence originated with the private person.	*United States v. Knoll*, 16 F.3d 1313 (2d Cir. 1994): The prosecutor knew the private person who burglarized the defendant's office, and the prosecutor said he needed more information, which the private party then inspected stolen papers to find.	*United States v. Jacobson*, 466 U.S. 109 (1984): A FedEx employee opened a package, found drugs, and called police, who then reopened the package. The court held that the search did not go beyond the initial private search.
The police or government agent did not participate in obtaining the evidence.	*People v. Aguilar*, 897 P.2d 84 (Colo. 1995): Police and a tow truck operator acted together to see whether an impounded vehicle held "anything suspicious."	*State v. Patch*, 702 A.2d 1278 (N.H. 1997): When police ordered a woman to leave the defendant's apartment, they had no duty to prevent the woman from taking the defendant's drugs with her and handing it over to police.

[a]State courts differ as to whether an off-duty police officer is a private person. The different rulings of the Missouri and Idaho courts illustrate this difference.

private search A search by a private person that is not subject to the exclusionary rule.

because the discs were taken from his room by the boyfriend in cooperation with police. The trial court denied his motion, and he was convicted of burglary. On appeal, the court of appeals reversed, holding that while the boyfriend's original entry into the defendant's room to find the discs was a purely private search, because the police only "passively" acquiesced in the search, after the police viewed the discs and urged the boyfriend to find some with more explicit sexual images, the search was "instigated" by the police and lost its private status. The evidence was suppressed.

THE EXCLUSIONARY RULE APPLIES ONLY IN CRIMINAL CASES

The exclusionary rule forbids the use of evidence tainted or soiled by improper or illegal police conduct in criminal cases. Such evidence, however, can be used in civil cases. For example, after O. J. Simpson was found not guilty of murder charges in 1995, a civil lawsuit was brought against him by the estates of the two homicide victims. Evidence that had been suppressed in Simpson's murder case was used against him in the civil lawsuit, which resulted in jury awards of more than $34 million against Simpson.

In the 1976 case of *United States v. Janis*,[4] evidence that had been suppressed in a criminal action against Janis for illegal wagering was turned over to the Internal Revenue Service. The evidence was used against Janis to obtain a civil judgment of tax fraud. The U.S. Supreme Court affirmed the judgment against Janis, holding that:

> Jurists and scholars uniformly have recognized that the exclusionary rule imposes a substantial cost on the societal interest in law enforcement by its proscription of what concededly is relevant evidence.... And alternatives that would be less costly to societal interests have been the subject of extensive discussion and exploration....
>
> ...We conclude that exclusion from federal civil proceedings of evidence unlawfully seized by a state criminal enforcement officer has not been shown to have a sufficient likelihood of deterring the conduct of the state police so that it outweighs the societal costs imposed by the exclusion. This Court, therefore, is not justified in so extending the exclusionary rule.

THE EXCLUSIONARY RULE DOES NOT APPLY TO EVIDENCE OBTAINED IN A CONSENT SEARCH

The U.S. Supreme Court has long held that a warrantless search of premises is permissible if undertaken with the valid consent of the person who occupies the premises.[5] As a July 2008 article in the *FBI Law Enforcement Bulletin* pointed out, "consent is a well-known and lawful tool police officers often rely on to conduct searches and seizures in a wide variety of situations and circumstances." In *United States v. Drayton*,[6] the Court said:

> police officers act in full accordance with the law when they ask citizens for consent. It reinforces the rule of law for the citizen to advise the police of his or her own wishes and for the police to act in reliance on that understanding. When this exchange takes place, it dispels inferences of coercion.

There are two requirements for the admissibility of evidence obtained in a consent search:

1. *Proof that consent was given voluntarily:* Law officers must prove that consent to enter premises or consent to search a person was given voluntarily and was not the product of duress or coercion. Whether consent is voluntary is a question of fact to be determined by the totality of the circumstances.[7] Factors to be considered under this test are the age of the person giving consent (very young or very old); the vulnerability of that person based on mental impairment, lack of education, intoxication, or other similar causes; and the use of threats, promises, deception, or trickery to obtain consent. Courts have held that consent is not necessarily rendered involuntary under the following circumstances:
   a. The person is not advised of the right to refuse to give consent. This advice is not required, but some officers give it.[8]
   b. Consent is given by a handcuffed person while officers had their weapons drawn.[9]
   c. Consent is given while a person was under the influence of drugs.[10]

2. *Proof that consent was obtained from a person with "actual or apparent authority" to grant the consent:* The person granting consent to search premises or a vehicle need not be the owner of the property. It is enough if the person giving consent has actual authority (authority to consent to the search is actually possessed by the consenting person) or apparent authority (authority that a reasonable person would believe the consenting person possesses). The driver of a car or a tenant in an apartment building could have actual or apparent authority to consent to a search. However, a co-tenant of an apartment may not give consent over the objection of the other co-tenant (see *Georgia v. Randolph* below), nor can a landlord or motel manager consent to a search of rented space.

The person giving consent may limit the area to be searched or, after giving consent, may revoke the consent. If the revocation is clear and specific, it is effective if done prior to the discovery of contraband evidence, even if in plain view. Revocation of consent is not permitted in two situations: (1) persons who present themselves and their belongings to security screening at airports and (2) persons visiting prisons. Such persons give their consent by entering restricted areas, and that consent may not be withdrawn.[11]

Finally, consent is not needed to enter premises if exigent circumstances require police officers to enter. Screams for help, fire, and gunshots are examples of circumstances that justify officers to enter premises without first obtaining consent.

Georgia v. Randolph

United States Supreme Court, 547 U.S. 103 (2006)

In *United States v. Matlock,*[12] the U.S. Supreme Court held that consent to search under the Fourth Amendment may be given by a person other than the defendant, if that person has "common authority" over the area searched. "Common authority," the *Matlock* Court said, is authority that rests on "mutual use of the property by persons generally having joint access or control for most purposes."[13] The *Matlock* Court then held that "the consent of one who possesses common authority over premises or effects is valid as against the absent, nonconsenting person with whom the authority is shared."[14]

The holding in *Matlock* was interpreted differently in lower courts presented with third-party consent cases. Some courts held that consent by one cohabitant was valid even if the other cohabitant was present and objected to a search. Others held that the risk assumed by choosing to live with another person is limited to the risk that person might give permission to search the residence in the other person's absence. In *Georgia v. Randolph*, the Supreme Court held that if a cohabitant is present when the other cohabitant gives consent to search, but objects to the search, the search is no longer consensual.

In *Randolph,* the defendant's estranged wife gave police permission to search their home for illegal drugs. The defendant was present when this occurred and unequivocally refused to give his consent to the search. The search proceeded, illegal drugs were found, and the defendant was convicted on drug charges. The Georgia Supreme Court reversed, holding that the drugs should have been suppressed because the search lacked a valid warrant, or consent. The state appealed to the U.S. Supreme Court, which affirmed the Georgia Supreme Court.

The U.S. Supreme Court said that the basis of third-party consent in *Matlock* was the reasonable expectation one cohabitant should have about the authority of another cohabitant to use the common premises. The Court concluded that there exists a common understanding that one cohabitant has the authority to, among other things, invite persons into the premises. However, the Court concluded that there is no common understanding that "one co-tenant generally has a right or authority to prevail over the express wishes of another, whether the issue is the color of the curtains or invitations to outsiders." As a result, the objection by the defendant meant the police officer had no more reason to assume entry was permitted than the officer would have had if there had been no consent at all, the Court held.

The *Randolph* Court noted that the line being drawn was very "fine." If the cohabitant is not asked for consent, even if present, and remains silent, then the consent remains valid, reaffirming the holding in *Illinois v. Rodriguez.*[15] Moreover, the Court refused to require police who have obtained consent from one cohabitant to take affirmative steps to obtain the other cohabitant's consent, so long as they did not remove the cohabitant from the premises for the purpose of obtaining the other's consent.

The response to *Randolph* has been to regard its holding as limited to the "fine line" drawn. For example, in *United States v. Groves,*[16] the Seventh Circuit Court of Appeals upheld the validity of a search under the consent of one cohabitant, even though police officers planned to arrive at the shared residence at a time the officers knew the defendant would be away from home.

THE EXCLUSIONARY RULE DOES NOT APPLY IF THE DEFENDANT DOES NOT HAVE STANDING OR IF NO RIGHT OF PRIVACY OF THE DEFENDANT HAS BEEN VIOLATED

standing Possession of the necessary relationship to an issue to be permitted to raise that issue in a court of law.

Evidence may be excluded under the exclusionary rule when the defendant makes a motion to suppress that evidence. To succeed in this motion, however, the defendant must show that his or her own rights were violated, not the rights of some other person. This concept is called **standing**, which means that the defendant is the proper person to challenge the police conduct because it violated the defendant's rights.

In the following cases, defendants argued that the police violated their Fourth Amendment rights. In Fourth Amendment cases, the right violated is often characterized as a "sufficient expectation of privacy." Those with such an expectation have standing; those without do not.

Alleged Improper or Illegal Police Conduct	Ruling	Case
The defendant placed a large amount of illegal drugs in the purse of a woman friend for safekeeping. When the police searched the woman's purse, the defendant admitted ownership of the drugs.	The defendant did not have standing to "challenge the legality of the search of [the woman's] purse … as he had no legitimate expectation of privacy in [the] purse at the time of the search."	*Rawlings v. Kentucky*, U.S. Supreme Court, 448 U.S. 98, 100 S.Ct. 2556 (1980)

The defendants were convicted of armed robbery and challenged the police search of the trunk of the car in which they were passengers. The owner of the car was driving the car at the time of the lawful stop of the car by the police.

The defendants "made no showing that they had any legitimate expectation of privacy in the glove compartment [or trunk] or area under the seat of the car in which they were merely passengers ... a passenger would not normally have a legitimate expectation of privacy." Mere lawful presence in a car is only a fact that a court will consider in determining the existence of a legitimate expectation of privacy.

Rakas v. Illinois, U.S. Supreme Court, 439 U.S. 128, 99 S.Ct. 421 (1978)

Evidence obtained from a home where the defendant was an overnight guest was used to charge and convict the defendant.

It was held that the overnight guest had a sufficient expectation of privacy in the home of the host to claim Fourth Amendment protection against unreasonable searches and seizures.

Minnesota v. Olson, U.S. Supreme Court, 495 U.S. 91 (1990)

Police looked through a window of an apartment after an informant stated that white powder was being packaged in small bags in the apartment. When two men left the apartment, police stopped their car. The men were arrested when a handgun was seen in the car. Cocaine was found in the car in the search incident to the arrest, and a search warrant was then obtained to search the apartment.

It was held that the defendants did not have a sufficient expectation of privacy in the apartment because (1) they were not overnight guests, (2) they were essentially in the apartment for a business transaction, and (3) they were in the apartment for only a few hours. The U.S. Supreme Court held that the men had no standing to challenge the evidence used for the car stop. The Court did not decide whether looking through the apartment window was a search because the defendants had no expectation of privacy while in the apartment.

Minnesota v. Carter, U.S. Supreme Court, 525 U.S. 83 (1998)

After a murder, the defendant hid the murder weapon in his cousin's house. Police seized the weapon when they searched the cousin's house. Evidence against the defendant was obtained in a search of the hotel room in which the defendant was sleeping.

The defendant lacked standing to challenge the police search of his cousin's house, and the defendant's conviction and death penalty were affirmed. Because the room was not registered in the defendant's name and it was 3 hours after checkout time, it was held that the defendant did not meet the burden of showing a legitimate right of privacy in a hotel room.

People v. McPeters, Supreme Court of California, 832 P.2d 146 (1992)
State v. Rhodes, Wisconsin Court of Appeals, 149 Wis.2d 722, 439 N.W.2d 630 (1989)

Alleged Improper or Illegal Police Conduct	Ruling	Case
Police gained entrance into an apartment building and obtained evidence against the defendant in the common hallway.	Courts held that there may be an "expectation of security" but there "can be no expectation of privacy in the [locked] common hallway."	*United States v. Eisler*, Eighth Circuit Court of Appeals, 567 F.2d 814 (1977)
Police stopped the defendant as he was driving a stolen vehicle. Evidence against the defendant was obtained in a search of the vehicle.	A defendant lacks standing to assert a Fourth Amendment right of privacy in stolen property. In a traffic stop, however, defendants can challenge the seizure (stop) of their person.	*Nelson v. State*, Supreme Court of Florida, 578 So.2d 694 (1991)
Police stopped the defendant as he was driving a vehicle that he said he had borrowed from his uncle.	Because the defendant was driving the vehicle with the owner's consent, he had a right of privacy in the vehicle and standing to challenge the police search of the car.	*United States v. Soto*, Tenth Circuit Court of Appeals, 988 F.2d 1548 (1993)

EVIDENCE OBTAINED FROM ABANDONED PROPERTY WILL NOT BE SUPPRESSED

abandoned property Property that a person has deserted or thrown away and thereby disclaims interest in it; may be used as evidence against the former owner.

If by conduct or words the defendant shows that he or she has relinquished the expectation of privacy in property, the object may be used as evidence. This legal concept of **abandoned property** was defined in the 1989 case of *United States v. Thomas*[17] as follows:

> The test for abandonment in the search and seizure context is distinct from the property notion of abandonment: it is possible for a person to retain a property interest in an item, but nonetheless to relinquish his or her reasonable expectation of privacy in the object.

The following sections present different forms of abandonment.

THROWAWAY AS A FORM OF ABANDONMENT

Persons who flee the police with illegal drugs or other contraband on their person often throw away what can be very incriminating evidence. If the throwaway is a voluntary abandonment of the object, courts allow the object to be used as evidence against the person. But if the throwaway is the direct or indirect product of an illegal police stop or other improper police conduct, courts generally forbid the use of the throwaway item as evidence. The following U.S. Supreme Court cases are examples of this kind of abandonment:

Privacy Defined

The Fourth Amendment protects the right of privacy of persons. The U.S. Supreme Court held in the case of *Katz v. United States* [88 S.Ct. 507 (1967)] that:

> The Fourth Amendment protects people, not places. What a person knowingly exposes to the public, even in his own home or office, is not a subject of Fourth Amendment protection.... But what he seeks to preserve as private, may be constitutionally protected.

A reasonable expectation of privacy exists *only* if:

- An individual actually expects privacy.
- His (or her) expectation is reasonable.

Therefore, a person who beats his spouse in the front room of their home and can be seen by police and other persons standing on a public sidewalk does not have a reasonable expectation of privacy.

A police search is an intrusion into a right of privacy. The U.S. Supreme Court stated in *United States v. Jacobson* [104 S.Ct. 1654 (1984)] that

"a search occurs when a expectation of privacy that society is prepared to consider reasonable is infringed." If the officer can show authority to make the search, the intrusion into privacy is lawful.

In *Mancusi v. DeForte* [392 U.S. 364 (1968)], the U.S. Supreme Court held that employees have a reasonable expectation of privacy in the workplace. The *Katz* principle stated above means that anything knowingly exposed to fellow workers or supervisors is not protected. However, an employee is protected in areas of the workplace used for the employee's private purposes. In the 2005 case of *People v. Galvadon* [103 P.2d 923], the Colorado Supreme Court held that a night manager of a liquor store had a reasonable expectation of privacy in the store's back room, which he used for his work and which was not open to the public, even though the store owner used video cameras to monitor the back room. The court held that knowledge of the video cameras was not the kind of "knowing exposure" contemplated by *Katz*.

California v. Hodari

United States Supreme Court, 499 U.S. 621, 111 S.Ct. 1547 (1991)

Police officers on patrol in an unmarked police car observed four or five youths huddled around a car parked at a curb. All the young men began to run at the approach of the officers' car, so one of the officers chased them on foot. The officer caught up with Hodari and tackled him. Just before he was tackled, Hodari threw to the ground what turned out to be crack cocaine. In holding that the cocaine could be used as evidence against Hodari, the Supreme Court held that:

> assuming that Pertoso's [policeman] pursuit in the present case constituted a "show of authority" enjoining Hodari to halt, since Hodari did not comply with that injunction he was not seized until he was tackled. The cocaine abandoned while he was running was in this case not the fruit of a seizure, and his motion to exclude evidence of it was properly denied.

Michigan v. Chesternut

United States Supreme Court, 486 U.S. 567, 108 S.Ct. 1975 (1988)

Chesternut was standing on a street corner in Detroit, and when he saw a police car approaching the corner, he began to run. The police, on routine patrol, followed Chesternut in their car "to see where he was going." As he ran, Chesternut began throwing objects away. A police officer picked up the packets and found they contained pills. Based on the officer's experience as a paramedic, he believed that the pills contained codeine. Chesternut was arrested, and in the search incident to the arrest, heroin and a hypodermic needle were found. The Supreme Court held that the defendant "was not unlawfully seized during the initial police pursuit" and affirmed the use of the pills, heroin, and needle as evidence, holding that:

> the police conduct here—a brief acceleration to catch up with respondent, followed by a short drive alongside him—was not "so intimidating" that respondent could reasonably have believed that he was not free to disregard the police presence and go about his business. The police therefore were not required to have "a particularized and objective basis for suspecting [respondent] of criminal activity," in order to pursue him.[18]

DENIAL OF OWNERSHIP AS A FORM OF ABANDONMENT

Persons who deny ownership of property to a law enforcement officer relinquish their right of privacy in the property and do not later have standing to challenge the use of evidence obtained from the property. The following are a few of the hundreds of denial cases that have come before criminal courts in recent years:

- Travelers' denial of ownership of luggage at airports. Because of their denials, the defendants could not later challenge searches of their luggage by law officers. Illegal drugs and other contraband found in the luggage were used as evidence against the defendants.[19]
- Train passenger's denial of a garment bag under his feet.[20]
- Denial of luggage in the trunk of the car.[21]
- Denial of a satchel that the defendant hid after a car accident.[22]
- Denial of ownership of an apartment.[23]

EVIDENCE OBTAINED FROM GARBAGE OR TRASH

The owners of trash receptacles kept in a home or a garage have Fourth Amendment constitutional protection while the receptacles are located in such places. Evidence obtained from these places without valid consent or a search warrant is suppressed and may not be used, even if it is proven that the trash was abandoned.

In *California v. Greenwood*[24] police asked the regular trash collector to turn trash collected at the curb in front of the Greenwood home over to them without commingling it with trash from other homes. Inspection of the Greenwood trash revealed evidence of drugs, which was used to obtain a search warrant of the Greenwood home. Greenwood was then charged and convicted of felony drug use. In affirming the drug convictions, the U.S. Supreme Court held that the defendants "could have no reasonable expectation of privacy in ... the plastic garbage bags left on or at the side of the public street."[25]

A few state courts, however, impose stricter standards, including New Jersey, Washington, and Vermont.[26] In the 2005 case of *Litchfield v. State*,[27] the Indiana Supreme Court held that the Indiana Constitution requires police to have an "articulable individualized suspicion" that a crime occurred, similar to that required for a *Terry* stop (see Chapter 14), before trash left outside a defendant's home for regular pickup can be searched.

POLICE SEARCHES OF TRASH BARRELS

A two-part article entitled "*Katz*[a] in the Trash Barrel" in the *FBI Law Enforcement Bulletin* (February and March 1979) presented these conclusions on the seizure of abandoned personal property:

> Criminals who dispose of contraband and other evidence of criminal offenses in their trash cans are unskilled practitioners. They assume the risk that their discards will be seized by, or turned over to, law enforcement officers for use against them. Such items can be used directly as evidence in a criminal prosecution, or indirectly by forming the basis for issuance of a search warrant.

The following conclusions also can be drawn from an analysis of federal and state trash search decisions:

- A search warrant is the best assurance that evidence seized from a trash container will not be challenged successfully on constitutional grounds.
- One who disposes of personal property in a trash receptacle placed at curbside for collection, or in a commonly used receptacle, or in a refuse pile accessible to the public generally is held to have abandoned the property.
- A former possessor retains no reasonable expectation of privacy in abandoned property, and thus has no standing to object to its seizure or inspection.
- Warrantless entry by police or their agents to a constitutionally protected area, such as the yard or garage, in order to gain access to trash, may taint the search or seizure, regardless of the intent of the possessor to abandon.
- Officers contemplating a warrantless trash inspection should be thoroughly familiar with state as well as federal principles governing the search or seizure of trash because state courts may impose under state constitutions more restrictive rules than those announced by federal courts.

[a]See the U.S. Supreme Court case of *Katz v. United States* in Chapter 15.

ABANDONED MOTOR VEHICLES

Abandoned and stolen vehicles are a problem in every American city and state. Many states have statutes that define when a vehicle is legally abandoned. For example, Section 342.40(i) of the Wisconsin Statutes provides that if a vehicle is left unattended on a public highway or on private or public property "under such circumstances as to cause the vehicle to reasonably appear to have been abandoned" for more than 48 hours, "the vehicle is deemed abandoned and constitutes a public nuisance."

In the following case, a court held that a suitcase in a vehicle was abandoned.

United States v. Oswald Sixth Circuit Court of Appeals, 783 F.2d 663 (1986)	The defendant was transporting $300,000 worth of cocaine north from Florida in a stolen car when the car caught on fire on an interstate highway. Oswald ran from the car in fear that the car would blow up. Oswald did not report the fire or the car on the highway because the car was stolen and had cocaine in a suitcase in the trunk. Local authorities put out the fire, which extensively damaged the vehicle. Before having the vehicle towed away, a deputy sheriff took the valuables out of the car. After attempting to determine the identity of the owner of the vehicle and why they had not reported the incident, the sheriff (more than an hour and a half later) began to go through the items he had taken from the car. When the sheriff pried open a metal suitcase, the cocaine in the suitcase cleared up the mystery of why no one had claimed the property.

In affirming Oswald's conviction, the trial court and the appellate court held that Oswald had abandoned the suitcase when he made no efforts to preserve his right of privacy in the metal suitcase.

EXPIRATION OF RENTAL AGREEMENTS FOR MOTELS AND LOCKERS AS A FORM OF ABANDONMENT

Many courts have held that the expiration of a motel room agreement or the expiration of the rental time for a storage locker constitutes abandonment. In those cases, courts held that defendants had no standing to challenge evidence obtained by police searches.

In the 1990 case of *United States v. Reyes*,[28] the evidence was obtained twelve days after the expiration of the rental of a bus terminal storage locker. The defendant did not remove the contraband used as evidence because he had been arrested and was in custody.

EVIDENCE DISCOVERED IN OPEN FIELDS WILL NOT BE SUPPRESSED

curtilage The area close to a home where persons have a right of privacy.

Curtilage is that area close to a home where persons assert a right of privacy. The protection of the Fourth Amendment extends to the home and to the curtilage. The U.S. Supreme Court defined *curtilage* as follows in 1984:[29]

> At common law, the curtilage is the area to which extends the intimate activity associated with the "sanctity of a man's home and the privacies of life," *Boyd v. United States*, 116 U.S. 616, 630, 6 S.Ct. 524, 532, 29 L.Ed. 746 (1886), and therefore has been considered part of the home itself for Fourth Amendment purposes. Thus, courts have extended Fourth Amendment protection to the curtilage; and they have defined the curtilage, as did the common law, by reference to the factors that determine whether an individual reasonably may expect that an area immediately adjacent to the home will remain private.

In 1987 in *United States v. Dunn*,[30] the U.S. Supreme Court held that curtilage questions should be resolved with particular reference to four factors:

1. The proximity of the area claimed to be curtilage to the home
2. Whether the area is included within an enclosure surrounding the home
3. The nature of the uses to which the area is put
4. The steps taken by the resident to protect the area from observation by people passing by

There is a high degree of privacy in the curtilage, or backyard, of a one-family dwelling that is fenced in so as to be protected from observation by people passing. The degree of privacy is much lower, however, in the curtilage of a fifty-unit apartment building because all occupants of the building can use the common area available to them.[31]

One frequent question raised about the extent of the curtilage involves driveways and walkways on the edge of a defendant's property. The following two cases are examples of courts applying the four factors identified by the Supreme Court, and discussed above, to such situations (see also Figure 10.1):

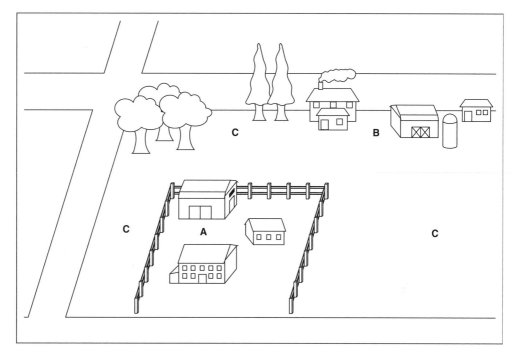

FIGURE 10.1 PERSONS LIVING IN SINGLE-FAMILY HOMES HAVE A GREATER EXPECTATION OF PRIVACY IN THEIR CURTILAGE (**A** AND **B**) THAN DO THOSE LIVING IN A LARGE APARTMENT BUILDING. OWNERS OR OTHER PERSONS HAVE NO PRIVACY RIGHTS IN OPEN FIELDS (**C**).

United States v. Diehl

First Circuit Court of Appeals, 276 F.3d 32 (2002), *cert. denied,* 537 U.S. 834 (2002)

Defendants were charged with conspiracy to manufacture and possess with intent to deliver marijuana in violation of federal drug laws. They entered a conditional guilty plea, subject to the appellate review of their claim that evidence seized from their property should have been suppressed, because the warrant under which the search was conducted was based on information gained by a police officer who unlawfully entered the defendants' curtilage. A police officer, suspecting that a building located on the defendants' rural premises was being used for illegal marijuana cultivation, walked onto a dirt driveway that was located on the defendants' premises and was connected to a county road. Standing there, the officer smelled a strong odor of growing marijuana coming from the property. Based on this odor and results obtained from a hand-held thermal imaging device, the officer obtained a search warrant for the property, where illegal drugs were subsequently found. The defendants moved to suppress the evidence, arguing that the officer was unlawfully in the curtilage when he smelled the marijuana, and that without evidence of that odor the search warrant would not have been based on probable cause. The trial court overruled their motion and held that the dirt driveway was not part of the curtilage.

On appeal, the court held that the driveway was part of the curtilage. The court applied the four factors identified by the Supreme Court in *Dunn*[32] and found that:

1. The proximity of the driveway to the buildings on the premises, about 82 feet away, did not indicate it was not in the curtilage.

2. The woods around the property and the driveway formed a natural enclosure, making the absence of an artificial enclosure less meaningful.
3. There was evidence of "intimate use" of the property where the officer stood when he smelled the marijuana, and the fact that winter snows prevented the officer from observing that evidence was irrelevant.
4. The defendants took steps to keep the public from observing that area, such as having mail delivered elsewhere and telling neighbors to stay away from the property.

These factors led the court to conclude that the driveway was within the curtilage and that as a result the intrusion by the officer was unlawful. (The court nonetheless affirmed the trial court's refusal to suppress the evidence, holding that the warrant was valid on its face, and that the good faith mistake of the officer in believing he was outside the curtilage made the warrant lawful under the good faith exception of *United States v. Leon*, discussed below.)

United States v. French

Seventh Circuit Court of Appeals, 291 F.3d 945 (2002)

The defendant was charged with various counts of attempting to manufacture methamphetamine and possession of a firearm in furtherance of a drug offense, based on evidence obtained by officers after a search of the defendant's property. The search was conducted under a search warrant obtained after a probation officer observed evidence of suspected illegal drug manufacture while standing on a walkway located on the defendant's property. The defendant moved to suppress the evidence obtained in the search on the theory that the warrant was itself based on evidence gained by the probation officer's unlawful entry onto the curtilage of the property. The trial court held that the curtilage did not extend to that part of the walkway upon which the officer was standing when he observed the illegal activity, and it refused to suppress the evidence seized. The defendant then pled guilty to one count of illegal drug manufacture and one count of illegal firearm possession, subject to appellate review of the curtilage claim.

On appeal, the U.S. Court of Appeals affirmed the conviction. It applied the four factors from *Dunn*[33] and concluded that the walkway was not in the curtilage. It concluded that although the spot where the officer was standing when he observed the illegal activity was within 20 feet of the defendant's residence, that fact alone did not make the walkway part of the curtilage. More significant, the court found, were the facts that no attempt was made to erect an enclosure around the walkway or the area near it, that no evidence of "intimate use" of the area by the defendant existed, that no "keep out" or "no trespassing" signs had been posted, and that clutter and debris in the area indicated the public was free to and often did use the walkway for various purposes. These facts, the court concluded, indicated that the defendant did not use the property for personal, private uses, and the surrounding area was not part of the curtilage. The defendant's conviction was affirmed.

plain view or open view doctrine The principle that if a law officer is where he or she has a right to be and sees evidence or contraband in plain view, then the evidence may be seized and used in a criminal trial.

Should Fourth Amendment protection extend beyond the curtilage to open fields? The U.S. Supreme Court noted in 1974 that the Supreme Court refused in the 1924 case of *Hester v. United States*[34] "to extend the Fourth Amendment to sights seen in the open fields."[35] In the *Hester* case, government agents were trespassing on the defendant's land when they observed the defendant running away

THE PLAIN VIEW OR OPEN VIEW DOCTRINE[a]

If a law enforcement officer is where he or she has a right to be and sees contraband or evidence of a crime in plain view, the evidence may be seized and will be admissible at a trial.

The **plain view or open view doctrine** was stated as follows in the case of *Texas v. Brown* [103 S.Ct. 1535 (1983)]:

> First, the police officer must lawfully make an "initial intrusion" or otherwise properly be in a position from which he can view a particular area.
>
> Second, the officer must discover incriminating evidence "inadvertently," which is to say, he may not "know in advance the location of ... evidence and intend to seize it," relying on the plain-view doctrine only as a pretext.
>
> Finally, it must be "immediately apparent" to the police that the items they observe may be evidence of a crime, contraband, or otherwise subject to seizure.

Plain View and the Five Human Senses

Most plain view cases occur when an officer, who is where he or she has a right to be, sees contraband or evidence of a crime. However, plain view is not limited to visual observations. Any of the five human senses may provide information that makes it "immediately apparent" to the police that the object is evidence of a crime.

- *Plain smell:* In 1948, the U.S. Supreme Court in *Johnson v. United States* [333 U.S. 10, 13, 68 S.Ct. 367, 368] held that odors may be "found to be evidence of the most persuasive character." [However, odor alone has been found to be not enough to support a search without a warrant. For example, in *People v. Michigan* [564 N.W.2d 24 (1997)], the Michigan Supreme Court held that evidence seized from an automobile after a police officer smelled marijuana in the vehicle was inadmissible. The court stated that smell differed from "plain view" and "plain touch" because odor alone does not

both identify the illegal contraband and show its location, as plain view and plain touch do.]

- *Plain hearing:* The "naked ear" or plain hearing rule applies to sounds that are heard without the use of any electronic or mechanical devices.[b]

- *Plain touch:* If police officers have made a lawful *Terry* stop (see Chapter 14) because a suspect has exhibited suspicious behavior, they may "pat down" the suspect to determine whether the suspect is armed. The purpose of the pat-down is not to search the suspect but to protect the officers. In *Minnesota v. Dickerson* [508 U.S. 366 (1993)] (also discussed in Chapter 14), the U.S. Supreme Court held that if the officers doing the pat-down discover an article whose nature is "immediately apparent from its tactile impression," the officers may seize the article without a search warrant. In *Dickerson* the officer conducting the pat-down felt a small object in the suspect's pocket and, by manipulating the object, concluded that it was crack cocaine. The Court held that the seizure violated the Fourth Amendment and the drugs were inadmissible because their identity as contraband was discernible only after the pat-down had already determined that the suspect was not armed. If the initial pat-down had made the drug's identity "immediately apparent," the seizure would have been lawful, the Court held.

- *Plain taste:* The sense of taste is rarely used to provide information to a law enforcement officer. No reported decisions can be found on this point.

---

[a]See the U.S. Supreme Court case of *Coolidge v. New Hampshire* [91 S.Ct. 2022 (1971)], where one justice stated that the terms *plain view* and *open view* differ. This distinction, however, has not been followed. *Plain view* is now the term used broadly without any distinction from *open view*.

[b]See *United States v. Agapito* [620 F.2d 324 (2d Cir. 1980)]; *United States v. Mankani* [738 F.2d 538 (2d Cir. 1984)]; *United States v. Lopez* [475 F.2d 537 (7th Cir. 1973)]; and *United States v. Fisch* [474 F.2d 1071 (9th Cir. 1973)].

from them and throwing contraband to the ground in open fields. In holding that the contraband could be used as evidence to obtain a conviction against the defendant, the U.S. Supreme Court ruled that:

> The special protection accorded by the Fourth Amendment to the people in their "persons, houses, papers and effects," is not extended to the open fields. The distinction between the latter and the house is as old as the common law. 4Bl.Comm. 223, 225, 226.

open field An unoccupied or undeveloped area outside of the curtilage; objects found there may be used as evidence.

In *Oliver v. United States*,[36] the Supreme Court defined "open fields":

> Open fields include any unoccupied or undeveloped area outside of the curtilage. An open field need be neither "open" nor a "field" as those terms are used in common speech.

An **open field** can consist of woods, swamps, meadows, or fields of farm crops.

EVIDENCE DISCOVERED IN GOOD FAITH OR BY HONEST MISTAKE WILL NOT BE SUPPRESSED

THE GOOD FAITH EXCEPTION

In the 1984 U.S. Supreme Court case of *United States v. Leon*,[37] police officers executed a search warrant that they believed to be valid but was defective. The evidence obtained under the defective warrant was ruled to be admissible because the police believed in good faith that the search warrant was valid. In holding that the evidence could be used, the Court held that "the exclusionary rule is designed to deter police misconduct rather than punish the errors of judges and magistrates."

good faith exception The exception that makes admissible evidence that is obtained under a search warrant that has a technical error unknown to the law officers executing the warrant.

The *Leon* **good faith exception** permits the use of evidence obtained through the use of a search warrant containing a technical error that does not violate a fundamental constitutional right of a suspect.[38] However, the warrant and affidavits given to obtain it must be sufficient so that an "objectively reasonable" officer would rely on the warrant that was issued. The following case is an example of a search warrant that did not satisfy this requirement.

State v. Laughton

Sixth Circuit Court of Appeals, 409 F.3d 744 (2005)

Following a tip from a confidential informant, police officers staked out and observed the informant making "controlled" purchases of illegal drugs from the defendant at his home. Based on these purchases, one of the officers prepared an affidavit seeking a search warrant for the defendant's residence. The warrant was issued even though the affidavit submitted did not state all the facts of the controlled purchases as they actually occurred and were known to the officer preparing the affidavit. As a result, the search warrant was a "bare bones" warrant and would not satisfy the probable cause requirement. The police argued that the good faith exception of *Leon* was applicable and justified the search because the officer who obtained the warrant had actual knowledge that probable cause existed, even though the affidavit and the warrant did not recite this knowledge.

The U.S. Court of Appeals held the good faith exception inapplicable. It stated that even though the officer who obtained the warrant possessed enough knowledge to support probable cause, neither the warrant nor the affidavit submitted to obtain it contained sufficient information to lead an "objectively reasonable" officer to believe the search was proper. If the personal knowledge of the officer who obtained the search warrant were relevant, the court said, every suppression hearing on a search warrant would require an inquiry into what the officer knew and when he knew it. This kind of subjectivity, the court reasoned, had consistently been rejected by the Supreme Court.

One area where courts disagree on the application of the good faith doctrine is illustrated by the case of *United States v. McClain*.[39] In that case, police conducted a warrantless search of premises that appeared to be vacant and discovered a marijuana-growing operation in the basement. They informed drug investigators, who conducted surveillance of the house and connected the defendant to the house. Using the information given them by the officers who first entered the house, the drug investigators obtained a warrant to search the house, and they found evidence used to charge the defendant with illegal drug crimes.

The defendant moved to suppress the evidence, contending that the initial entry into the house was a violation of the Fourth Amendment because the officers lacked probable cause to enter under the "exigent circumstances" exception to the warrant requirement. The trial court suppressed the evidence, but on appeal the court of appeals held that the good faith exception from *Leon* applied, even though in this case the warrant was not technically invalid because of a magistrate mistake, as was the case in *Leon*, but was itself the "fruit of the poisonous tree." The court agreed that the initial search was invalid but not so unreasonable that the officers who obtained the search warrant based on that illegal entry should clearly have known it was invalid. As a result, the court concluded that those officers could objectively and reasonably have believed the search warrant was valid, thus invoking the good faith exception. The court noted that other circuits had reached the opposite result.[40]

Not all states have adopted a good faith exception that permits the use of evidence because of a mistake by a judge, prosecutor, police dispatcher, or computer. In *State v. Eason*,[41] the Wisconsin Supreme Court held that a good faith exception existed under the Wisconsin Constitution. A dissenting judge noted that as of the date of that case, fourteen states had rejected the *Leon* good faith exception under their state constitutions.[42]

THE HONEST MISTAKE RULE

After an armed robbery, California police had probable cause to arrest Hill for the robbery. They obtained Hill's home address and his description. A man who "exactly fit [Hill's] description" answered the door to Hill's home but denied that he was Hill. Nevertheless, the police arrested the man, believing that he was Hill. In the search incident to the arrest of the man, the police found and seized evidence that incriminated Hill. The police later became aware that they had arrested the wrong man. They released the man and within a short time arrested Hill.

Because probable cause existed to arrest the man in Hill's home, the U.S. Supreme Court held in the 1971 case of *Hill v. California*[43] that the "arrest (of the wrong man) and subsequent search were reasonable and valid under the Fourth Amendment" and therefore the evidence could be used in the trial and conviction of Hill.

honest mistake rule The U.S. Supreme Court's ruling that courts must "allow some latitude for honest mistakes that are made by officers in the dangerous and difficult process of making arrests and executing search warrants."

In the 1987 U.S. Supreme Court case of *Maryland v. Garrison*,[44] a search warrant was issued to search a third-floor apartment. The police reasonably believed that only one apartment was on the third floor of the building and did not become aware of the second apartment, which belonged to Garrison, until after they found heroin, cash, and drug paraphernalia there. In holding that the evidence could be used to convict Garrison of drug violations, the Supreme Court pointed out that the Court has "recognized the need to allow some latitude for honest mistakes that are made by officers in the dangerous and difficult process of making arrests and executing search warrants." The result in *Garrison* would likely have been different had the police realized during their search that the dwelling contained a second apartment. The following case illustrates this limitation on the **honest mistake rule.**

United States v. Ritter

Third Circuit Court of Appeals, 2005 WL 1813268 (2005)

Based on aerial photographs of the defendants' property as well as on the informant's statements, federal officers obtained a search warrant to search that property. The warrant and supporting affidavits identified only one address as the property to be searched. When officers arrived at the property and entered a "common area" located on the property, they realized that more than one dwelling was located on the property shown in the aerial photographs and identified by the informant. The defendants resided in only one of the dwellings. The police searched all the buildings on the property and found illegal drugs. The defendants moved to suppress the evidence seized in the search, contending that the inaccurate description of the property as containing only one property rendered the search warrant invalid.

On appeal, the court of appeals held that the search warrant was not rendered invalid by the mistake and that any evidence found by the officers in the common area was admissible. After the officers discovered that more than one dwelling was located on the property, however, they were required to stop the search. The honest mistake rule did not apply to any evidence seized after the officers knew of the mistake, the court held. Because it was not clear when the illegal drugs were found, the case was remanded for a determination of this question.

OTHER AREAS WHERE THE EXCLUSIONARY RULE DOES NOT APPLY

Source of Evidence or Use of Evidence	Court Rulings
Common carriers (airlines, parcel services, truckers, railroads, and so on)	"Common carriers have a common-law right to inspect packages they accept for shipment, based on their duty to restrain from carrying contraband."[45]
U.S. Customs Service	"The U.S. Government has the undoubted right to inspect all incoming goods at a port of entry… [but like the common carriers] it would be impossible for customs officers to inspect every package."[46]
Grand jury proceedings	"… it is unrealistic to assume that application of the rule of grand jury proceedings would significantly further [the] goal of deterrence of police misconduct…. The grand jury's investigative power must be broad if its public responsibility is adequately to be discharged."[47]
Probation or parole revocation	"… the overwhelming number of reported hearings cases have held that the Fourth Amendment's 'exclusionary rule' was not applicable under the circumstances to probation revocation proceedings or qualitatively comparable proceedings to revoke parole…. The only reservation expressed by several courts in denying application of the 'exclusionary rule' to a revocation proceeding might occur in situations where police harassment of probationers is demonstrated."[48] In 1998 the U.S. Supreme Court followed the ruling of a state court in a parole revocation case.[49]
Searches by probation or parole officers	"… [A] probation agent who reasonably believes that a probationer is violating the terms of probation may conduct a warrantless search of a probationer's residence…. A probation agent has a duty to see that a probationer is complying with the terms of his probation."[50] In 1987 the U.S. Supreme Court affirmed the

Source of Evidence or Use of Evidence	Court Rulings
	conviction of a probationer, Griffin, for possession of a handgun discovered by a warrantless search of Griffin's home. The Court held that the "search of Griffin's home satisfied the demands of the Fourth Amendment because it was carried out pursuant to a regulation that itself satisfies the Fourth Amendment reasonableness requirement."[51] The U.S. Supreme Court affirmed another probation search in 2001 in *United States v. Knights*.[52] Knights was on probation and had signed a consent to search agreement to obtain the benefits of probation. Detectives had reasonable suspicion that Knights had started an arson fire. Without a search warrant, the detectives searched Knights's apartment, relying on the probation consent to search. The U.S. Supreme Court affirmed the use of the evidence obtained.
Military discharge proceedings	A military administrative discharge proceeding is a civil proceeding and not a military criminal proceeding. Illegally seized drugs may be used as evidence. The court held that to force the military to keep a serviceman who uses drugs "is a price which our society cannot afford to pay."[53]
Child protective proceedings	"... because a child protective proceeding ... is not punitive in nature ... the State's interest in protecting its children mandates the admissibility of relevant evidence seized during an illegal search."[54]
Civil tax proceedings and civil deportation proceedings	The U.S. Supreme Court refused to extend the exclusionary rule to civil tax proceedings[55] and to civil deportation proceedings.[56]
"Community caretaking functions" by police	During the thousands of traffic accidents that occur monthly, police are performing "community caretaking functions," such as moving a damaged vehicle to allow traffic to

move. If evidence or contraband is seen under such circumstances, it may be used as evidence as the plain view doctrine would apply. The U.S. Supreme Court pointed out that the conduct of law officers under these circumstances is "totally divorced from the detention, investigation or acquisition of evidence relating to the violation of a criminal statute."[57]

Evidence obtained in foreign countries by foreign officials

To deter the estimated $50-billion-a-year illegal drug industry in the United States, evidence seized in foreign countries by foreign officials is being used to prosecute both American and foreign citizens. Evidence obtained by a foreign official is admissible even if the search or seizure violated the suspect's rights under the U.S. Constitution. Two exceptions are: (1) The conduct of the foreign official was extremely inhumane or outrageous, or (2) there was substantial participation by an American law officer in the seizure.[58]

Important witness testimony against defendants

In seeking to apprehend a robber, police improperly took Crews into custody on mere suspicion. A photo taken of Crews while he was in custody led to a robbery victim identifying Crews as the offender. The woman was a witness at Crews's trial and again identified him as she had in the photo array and in a lineup. The U.S. Supreme Court affirmed Crews's conviction and the use of the in-court witness.[59] A case with some similarities was affirmed by the Illinois Supreme Court.[60]

Sentencing proceedings after a criminal conviction

Holding that evidence seized by the police in violation of the Fourth Amendment is not necessarily unreliable, courts have held that sentencing courts should consider all "reliable" evidence in doing so.[61]

SUMMARY

The exclusionary rule (or the rule of the exclusion of evidence) generally applies to law officers who improperly or illegally:

- Obtain physical and other evidence (Chapter 14)
- Obtain confessions and statements to be used as evidence (Chapter 12)
- Obtain evidence by use of search warrants, wiretapping, or trained dogs (Chapter 15)
- Obtain identification evidence (Chapter 13)
- Obtain fingerprints and DNA evidence (Chapters 16 and 18)
- Obtain evidence from the crime scene (Chapter 16)
- Obtain scientific evidence (Chapter 18)
- Obtain videotapes, photographs, documents, or writings for use as evidence (Chapter 17)

The exclusionary rule generally does *not* apply to:

- Evidence obtained by private persons lawfully or illegally
- Civil cases and proceedings; it applies only to criminal cases
- Searches made with the consent of the inhabitant or co-inhabitant of premises
- Situations where a defendant does not have standing or where no right of privacy of a defendant has been violated
- Abandoned property that is used as evidence against a defendant
- Evidence found in open fields or discovered in plain view

CASE ANALYSIS

Read Appendix B, Finding and Analyzing Cases (p. 427). With these guidelines in mind, please continue with the Case Analysis selections for Chapter 10.

1. Refer again to the *Johnson* case cited in the Chapter 9 Case Analysis section. Both the passengers and the driver of the car were subjected to illegal searches. The standing rule discussed in this chapter determines which person can object to which illegal search. Who had standing in that case, and for which illegal search? After making that determination, answer this question: Does a person who borrows a vehicle have standing to object to an illegal search of that vehicle? Read *State v. Crisp* [74 S.W.3d 474 (Tex. App. 2002)]. Did both the borrower of the car and the person she let drive the car have standing? Why was the search unlawful for each of them?

2. This chapter discussed the good faith exception to the exclusionary rule, which applies where the police in good faith believe a search warrant is valid. The *Laughton* case, included

in the section on the good faith exception, held that the reasonableness of the police officer's reliance on a search warrant was to be viewed from an objective perspective, which did not include facts known to the officer but not contained in the warrant or communicated to the magistrate who issued the warrant. In *United States v. Frazier* [423 F.3d 526 (6th Cir. 2005)], the same court that decided *Laughton* upheld the admissibility of evidence obtained under a defective search warrant under the good faith exception, because the police officer who obtained the warrant had knowledge that was not contained in the warrant but supported the finding of probable cause. How did the court distinguish *Laughton*? Do you agree with the basis of the distinction, or should *Laughton* simply be overruled?

3. When has property been abandoned for purposes of the Fourth Amendment? Is *abandonment* here used differently than in property law? See *State v. Rynhart* [125 P.3d 938 (Utah 2005)].

4. How "personal" is the personal computer you use at work? If your supervisor permits police to view your files and evidence of illegal activity is discovered, should that evidence be excluded? What are the issues presented here? Consent by a third party? Expectation of privacy based on use of the computer? See *State v. Young* [974 So.2d 601 (Fla. App. 2008)] and *United States v. Ziegler* [474 F.3d 1184 (9th Cir. 2007)].

Notes

1. Chapter 14 discusses the Fourth Amendment exclusionary rule in more detail.
2. Virtually all states follow the *Burdeau* rule. See N. Lafave, *Search and Seizure: A Treatise on the Fourth Amendment*, 3d ed. (West, 1996), sec. 1.8, note 16.
3. 78 Cal. Rptr. 3d 501.
4. 428 U.S. 433.
5. See *Schneckloth v. Bustamonte*, 412 U.S. 218 (1973).
6. 536 U.S. 194 (2002).
7. *Schneckloth*, 412 U.S. at 227.
8. 412 U.S. at 227.
9. *United States v. Wilkenson*, 926 F.2d 22 (1st Cir. 1991), *cert. denied*, 501 U.S. 1211 (1991).
10. *Id*.
11. See "Revoking Consent to Search," *FBI Law Enforcement Bulletin* (February 2005).
12. 415 U.S. 164 (1974).
13. 415 U.S. at 171, fn.7.
14. *Id*. at 171.
15. 497 U.S. 177 (1990).
16. 2008 WL 2550745.
17. 864 F.2d 843 (D.C. Cir.).
18. *United States v. Cortez*, 449 U.S 411.
19. *United States v. Tolbert*, 692 F.2d 1041 (6th Cir. 1982); *United States v. Sanders*, 719 F.2d 882 (6th Cir. 1983); *United States v. Roman*, 849 F.2d 920 (5th Cir. 1988).
20. *United States v. Carrasquillo*, 877 F.2d 73 (D.C. Cir. 1989).
21. *United States v. McBean*, 861 F.2d 1570 (11th Cir. 1988).
22. *Commonwealth v. Anderl*, 477 A.2d 1356 (Pa. Super. 1984).
23. *Hayes v. State*, 158 N.W.2d 545 (Wis. 1968).
24. 486 U.S. 35 (1988).
25. In the 1998 case of *Redmon v. United States* [138 F.3d 1109], the city of Urbana, Illinois, forbade leaving trash at the curb, so Redmon placed his cans for collection at the top of his 28-foot-long driveway. The cans were outside the attached two-car townhouse garage that Redmon shared with another townhouse. To reach the only approach to the front door of the townhouses, visitors had to walk up the driveway to a walkway that ran along the side of the garage. Walkways to and from a front door, though on private property, are generally regarded as open to the public. Because Redmon had no control over visitors to his neighbor's townhouse, the court pointed out that the area was open to the public.

   Drug enforcement agents had Redmon under surveillance and searched the garbage cans outside his garage, where they found evidence of cocaine that enabled the DEA agents to obtain a search warrant. The search of Redmon's townhouse resulted in additional evidence. On appeal to the Seventh Circuit Court of Appeals, the conviction was upheld in an eight-to-five vote.
26. New Jersey: *State v. Hempele*, 576 A.2d 793 (1990); Washington: *State v. Boland*, 48 CrL 1205 (1990); Vermont: *State v. Morris*, 1996 WL 135179 (1996).
27. 824 N.E.2d 356.
28. 908 F.2d 281 (8th Cir.).
29. *Oliver v. United States*, 466 U.S. 170, 104 S.Ct. 1735 (1984).
30. *United States v. Dunn*, 480 U.S. 294, 107 S.Ct. 1134 (1987), where the four factors were used to determine that the defendant's barn lay outside the curtilage of his ranch house.
31. In the case of *United States v. Acosta* [1992 WL 109641 (1992)], the Third Circuit Court of Appeals held that occupants of a three-story apartment building did not have any legitimate expectation of privacy in the backyard of the apartment building. Therefore, the defendant did not have standing and could not challenge the use of evidence thrown out of his bathroom window and picked up by law officers in the backyard of the apartment building.

32. *United States v. Dunn*, 480 U.S. 294, 107 S.Ct. 1134 (1987).

33. *Id.*

34. 265 U.S. 57, 44 S.Ct. 445.

35. *Air Pollution Variance Board of Colorado v. Western Alfalfa Corp.*, 416 U.S. 861, 94 S.Ct. 861 (1974).

36. 466 U.S. 170, 180, 104 S.Ct. 1735, 1742 n.11 (1984).

37. 104 S.Ct. 3405.

38. The U.S. Supreme Court followed the *Leon* case in the 1995 case of *Arizona v. Evans* [115 S.Ct. 1185]. Evans was stopped by Arizona police for a traffic violation. The officers checked their in-car computer and received information that there was an outstanding arrest warrant for Evans. The police then arrested Evans and, in the search incident to Evans's arrest, found marijuana. This evidence was used to convict Evans for the possession of marijuana. The use of the evidence was challenged because the warrant had been canceled seventeen days before Evans's arrest. The incorrect information was in the computer due to an error by a court clerk. Following *Leon*, the U.S. Supreme Court held that the evidence of the marijuana could be used because there had been a good faith reliance by the police on the incorrect information.

39. 444 F.3d 556 (6th Cir. 2005), *cert. denied*, 127 S.Ct. 580 (2006).

40. See, for example, *United States v. McGough*, 412 F.3d 1232 (11th Cir. 2005).

41. 629 N.W.2d 625 (Wis. 2001).

42. *Id.*, 629 N.W.2d at 660, fn.40 (Abrahamson, C.J., dissenting).

43. 91 S.Ct. 1106.

44. 107 S.Ct. 1013.

45. *Illinois v. Andreas*, 463 U.S. 765, 769 n.1, 103 S.Ct. 3319, 3323 n.1 (1983)

46. *Id.*

47. *United States v. Calandra*, 414 U.S. 338, 94 S.Ct. 613 (1974).

48. Supreme Court of Illinois in *People v. Dowery*, 340 N.E.2d 529 (Ill. 1975).

49. *Pennsylvania Board of Probation and Parole v. Scott*, 118 S.Ct. 2014.

50. *Wisconsin v. Griffin*, 107 S.Ct. 3164 (1987).

51. *Wisconsin v. Griffin*, 107 S.Ct. 3164, 3168.

52. 534 U.S. 112, and also see 483 U.S. 868.

53. *Garrett v. Lehman*, 751 F.2d 997 (9th Cir. 1985).

54. *In re Diane P.*, 494 N.Y.S.2d 881, 38 CrL 2168 (App. Div. 1985).

55. *United States v. Janis*, 96 S.Ct. 3021 (1976).

56. *INS v. Lopez-Lopez-Mendoza*, 104 S.Ct. 3479 (1984).

57. *Cady v. Dombrowski*, 93 S.Ct. 2523 (1971).

58. *United States v. Verdugo-Urquidez*, 112 S.Ct. 2986 (1992); *United States v. Alvarez-Machain*, 112 S.Ct. 2188 (1992).

59. *United States v. Crews*, 100 S.Ct. 1244 (1980).

60. *People v. Winsett*, 606 N.E.2d 1186 (1993).

61. *United States v. McCrory*, 930 F.2d 63 (D.C. Cir. 1991); *United States v. Lynch*, 934 F.2d 1226, 49 CrL 1361 (11th Cir. 1991).

EVIDENCE IS ADMISSIBLE IF OBTAINED DURING AN ADMINISTRATIVE FUNCTION UNDER THE "SPECIAL NEEDS" OF GOVERNMENT

CHAPTER **11**

LEARNING OBJECTIVES

In this chapter we identify various governmental administrative functions that have "special needs" and, as a result, fewer limits on searches and seizures. The learning objectives for this chapter are:

- In your own words, state the concept called "special needs."
- List some activities in which drug testing may be required without probable cause.
- State when roadblocks may not be justified under the "special needs" doctrine.
- What are the limits, if any, on the right of a border guard or customs agent to search the person or belongings of a person entering this country?
- State the limits, if any, on a state's right to search a person on parole or probation.

CHAPTER CONTENTS

Security Screening at Airports, Courthouses, and Other Public Buildings and Places

Fire, Health, and Housing Inspections

School Searches on Reasonable Suspicion

Drug Testing Without Probable Cause or a Search Warrant

Drug Testing of Law Officers and Other Persons in Critical Occupations

Drug Testing on Reasonable Suspicion

Random Drug Testing of Student Athletes

Random Drug Testing of Students Participating in Extracurricular Activities

Searches Without Probable Cause or Search Warrants of Closely Regulated Businesses

Work-Related Searches in Government Offices (the *Ortega* Rule)

Roadblocks or Vehicle Checkpoint Stops

Border Searches

Sham Roadblocks

Correctional Programs, Hearings, or Requirements That May Cause a Prison Inmate to Incriminate Himself

Do Inmates on Parole Have Privacy Expectations Protected by the Fourth Amendment?

Other Special Government Needs Where Neither Probable Cause nor Search Warrants Are Needed

administrative functions Functions such as screening at airports and courthouses and many fire, health, housing, and school services.

"special needs" of government The basic government requirements of safety, health, education, and concern for the well-being of the society as a whole.

In 1987, the U.S. Supreme Court held that "the probable cause standard is peculiarly related to criminal investigations" and "may be unhelpful in analyzing the reasonableness of routine administrative functions."[1]

Thousands of administrative searches and functions are conducted every day by local, state, and federal employees. The majority of these employees are not law enforcement officers. They are not conducting criminal investigations but are conducting **administrative functions** that are related to the **"special needs" of government** and the community.

The U.S. Supreme Court and hundreds of lower courts have held that neither probable cause nor search warrants are required to carry out most of these routine administrative functions. Evidence obtained as a result of the administrative function is admissible if the function is performed within the guidelines established by law.

SECURITY SCREENING AT AIRPORTS, COURTHOUSES, AND OTHER PUBLIC BUILDINGS AND PLACES

At U.S. airports alone, more than one billion security screenings of persons and personal belongings occur each year. Since 9/11, security screening has been extended to courthouses, public buildings, sporting events, rock concerts, and other public functions.

Thousands of illegal weapons and other illegal objects are confiscated as a result of these administrative security screenings. Many of the seized items are then used as evidence in U.S. courts. In ruling that the objects are admissible evidence, most courts hold that security screenings are administrative searches under the special government need for security. Other courts hold that such evidence is admissible because once individuals present their person and their property to a security checkpoint for screening, they have consented to the screening, and that consent cannot be withdrawn during the screening process.[2]

However, such evidence may be held inadmissible if a defense lawyer can establish that the "security officers looked to considerations other than safety in conducting the screening, such as when they are on the lookout for evidence of drug trafficking, the search loses its protective character."[3]

FIRE, HEALTH, AND HOUSING INSPECTIONS

All large cities have valid concerns for health and fire safety within their community. Health and fire concerns are even greater in areas of cities where buildings are crowded, old, and decaying. Efforts are always made to prevent fires, the collapse of buildings, and the infestation of rodents or insects, and to preserve the community in a safe and healthful condition. The U.S. Supreme Court held that fire, health, and housing inspection programs "touch at most upon the periphery of the important interests safeguarded by the Fourteenth Amendment's protection against official intrusion."[4]

Most property owners consent to inspections by health, fire, and housing inspectors. If a homeowner or the owner of commercial property refuses to allow an inspection, however, a search warrant must be obtained, and the owner of the property cannot be punished for refusal to consent to a search.

The U.S. Supreme Court set a much lower standard for obtaining a fire, health, or housing inspection search warrant in the case of *Camara v. Municipal Court*,[5] holding:

> The warrant procedure is designed to guarantee that a decision to search private property is justified by a reasonable governmental interest. But reasonableness is still the ultimate standard. If a valid public interest justifies the intrusion contemplated, then there is probable cause to issue a suitably restricted search warrant.

Some states have passed laws or have established procedures where area search warrants may be issued when health and sanitation risks exist. For example, if an area of a city is infested with rats, an area search warrant could be issued to find the source (or sources) of the problem and eliminate the health risk.

In the case of *See v. City of Seattle*,[6] the U.S. Supreme Court made it clear that a search warrant was not needed in an emergency situation such as seizure of contaminated food, compulsory smallpox vaccinations, health quarantines, or destruction of tubercular cattle.

SCHOOL SEARCHES ON REASONABLE SUSPICION

The U.S. Supreme Court has held that "the (search) warrant requirement ... is unsuitable to the school environment and requiring a teacher to obtain a warrant before searching a child suspected of infraction of school rules (or the criminal code) would unduly interfere with maintenance of the swift and informal disciplinary procedures needed in the schools."[7]

The general rule in the United States is to permit school officials in school and quasi-school settings to conduct searches of students on reasonable suspicion. In *Vernonia School District v.* Acton[8] (discussed on page 221), the Court stated that three factors must be considered when determining whether a search is reasonable:

1. The students' legitimate expectations of privacy
2. The intrusiveness of the search
3. The importance of the school's needs serving as the basis for the search

In the 2005 case of *Beard v. Whitmore Lake School District*,[9] the court held that strip searches of male and female high school students by school officials looking for money stolen from a student during gym class violated the Fourth Amendment. The court concluded that the students' "significant privacy interest in their unclothed bodies" outweighed the school's interest in recovering a student's lost money.

In regulating school property and student activities, schools can make it known to students and parents that school lockers and other storage areas are the property of the school and subject to random searches at any time. Schools in the city of Milwaukee followed this procedure, and when a handgun was found in the locker of a student, a trial court permitted the handgun to be used as evidence. The

Supreme Court of Wisconsin held that Milwaukee students have no right of privacy in school lockers in view of the written policy and notice given to students.

DRUG TESTING WITHOUT PROBABLE CAUSE OR A SEARCH WARRANT

DRUG TESTING OF LAW OFFICERS AND OTHER PERSONS IN CRITICAL OCCUPATIONS

Private businesses may conduct drug testing of employees without fear of Fourth Amendment rights because the Fourth Amendment does not apply to searches by private persons. However, the Fourth Amendment does apply to drug testing by government.

In 1989, the U.S. Supreme Court decided two cases involving drug testing of government employees. In the case of *National Treasury Employees Union v. Von Raab*,[10] the Supreme Court sustained a U.S. Customs requirement that employees seeking transfers or promotions must submit to a urinalysis. In *Skinner v. Railway Labor Executive's Association*,[11] a similar requirement was approved for workers involved in certain train accidents or incidents. In these cases the Supreme Court stated:

> ... where a Fourth Amendment intrusion serves special governmental needs, beyond the normal need for law enforcement, it is necessary to balance the individual's privacy expectations against the Government's interests to determine whether it is impractical to require a (search) warrant or some level of individualized suspicion in the particular context.[12]

The U.S. Supreme Court identified three governmental interests that are sufficiently compelling to justify drug testing where there is no information causing suspicion of drug abuse:

1. Ensuring that certain employees "have unimpeachable integrity and judgment"[13]
2. Enhancing public safety[14]
3. "Protecting truly sensitive information"[15]

Many federal, state, and local governmental agencies now require suspicionless drug testing of employees who have secret and top secret security clearance, detectives, police officers, guards, firefighters, fire protection specialists, nurses, employees who handle or inspect hazardous wastes, motor vehicle operators, heavy equipment operators, locomotive operators, brake-switching employees, employees required to carry firearms, and other employees with duties "fraught with such risks of injury to others that even a momentary lapse of attention can have disastrous consequences."[16] The courts have sustained random drug testing of persons within these groups by virtue of being a "heavily regulated industry."[17]

DRUG TESTING ON REASONABLE SUSPICION

The Supreme Court of Hawaii pointed out that law officers have a diminished expectation of privacy because of their employment and "must always be mentally and physically alert while driving motor vehicles, and must exercise good judgment

Invalid State Laws That Required Drug Testing Without Probable Cause

State statutes held void, where the statute authorized drug testing without probable cause because the purpose of the drug testing was to obtain evidence for criminal prosecution	Case
A Georgia law required candidates for public office to take a drug test and test negative.	*Chandler v. Miller*, 117 S.Ct. 1295, U.S. Supreme Court (1997)
Because of concerns for babies born with crack addiction, a South Carolina law required pregnant women being treated at a state hospital to submit to a urine test to determine whether they were using cocaine.	*Ferguson v. Charleston, S.C.*, 532 U.S. 67, U.S. Supreme Court (2001)
An Illinois law required drivers who caused accidents where there was personal injury to take chemical or breath testing.	*King v. Ryan*, No. 72392, Illinois Supreme Court (1992)

in the use of guns."[18] In the following cases, drug testing was held to be constitutionally based on reasonable suspicion:

- There was reasonable suspicion to believe that a police officer was using drugs.[19]
- An anonymous telephone call that an airman with Air Force flight operations had recently used marijuana was held to provide reasonable suspicion for a drug test.[20]

Random Drug Testing of Student Athletes

In the 1995 case of *Vernonia School District v. Acton*,[21] the U.S. Supreme Court upheld the random, suspicionless urinalysis testing of public school students participating in interscholastic sports. The school district had required this testing in its custodial capacity to combat growing drug use by students and to protect the health and safety of student athletes.

The U.S. Supreme Court held that the procedure was not an unreasonable search, citing "special needs, beyond the normal need for law enforcement (making) the warrant and probable cause requirement (of the Fourth Amendment) impractical." The Supreme Court listed the following considerations in approving the reasonableness of the procedure:

- Student athletes have a reduced expectation of privacy.
- The intrusion on the student athletes' privacy by urine collection was "negligible."
- The government (school authorities) had an important and compelling interest in curbing drug use by student athletes as part of the effort to curb drug use.

RANDOM DRUG TESTING OF STUDENTS PARTICIPATING IN EXTRACURRICULAR ACTIVITIES

The U.S. Supreme Court stated in the 1969 case of *Tinker v. Des Moines Independent School District*[22] that "children do not shed their constitutional rights ... at the schoolhouse gate." That statement remains true today, but under the "special needs" of government doctrine, elected school boards may, if they deem necessary, require random drug tests of not only student athletes but also students participating in any extracurricular activities. The Supreme Court concluded in the 2002 case of *Board of Education of Pottawatomie County v. Earls* (discussed below) that: "We find that testing students who participate in extracurricular activities is a reasonably effective means of addressing the school district's legitimate concerns in preventing, deterring and detecting drug use."

A federal court in the 1998 case of *Todd v. Rush County Schools*[23] held that school boards may require drug testing of any student who wanted to participate in any extracurricular activity. Without comment, the U.S. Supreme Court refused to hear the case and left standing the rule of the lower court. The following similar 2002 case was decided by the U.S. Supreme Court after oral arguments and many written briefs by interested parties.

Board of Education of Pottawatomie County v. Earls

United States Supreme Court, 122 S.Ct. 2559 (2002)

Petitioners were students at a public high school run by the respondent board of education. The board passed a rule that required all students participating in extracurricular activities to submit to a urinalysis test for illegal drugs and to submit to random testing during that participation. The petitioners objected to the drug testing rule, contending that it violated their Fourth Amendment rights because the tests were given without any level of "individualized suspicion." In rejecting that contention, the Supreme Court described the "special needs" exception to the "particularized suspicion" usually required by the Fourth Amendment in normal criminal investigations:

> It is true that we generally determine the reasonableness of a search by balancing the nature of the intrusion on the individual's privacy against the promotion of legitimate governmental interests.... But we have long held that "the Fourth Amendment imposes no irreducible requirement of [individualized] suspicion." "[I]n certain limited circumstances, the Government's need to discover such latent or hidden conditions, or to prevent their development, is sufficiently compelling to justify the intrusion on privacy entailed by conducting such searches without any measure of individualized suspicion." 122 S.Ct., at 2563–2564.

SEARCHES WITHOUT PROBABLE CAUSE OR SEARCH WARRANTS OF CLOSELY REGULATED BUSINESSES

The U.S. Supreme Court held that a "businessman, like the occupant of a residence, has a constitutional right to go about his business free from unreasonable official entries upon his private commercial property."[24] Search warrants, therefore, are generally required for the administrative searches of commercial properties.

closely regulated businesses
Businesses that are subject to careful oversight by laws and codes, such as liquor stores, firearms dealers, coal mines, and pharmacies.

Search warrants are not required for searches of **closely regulated businesses,** however, where courts have held that the owner's privacy interests are adequately protected by detailed state or federal laws that authorize inspections (searches) without warrants. The U.S. Supreme Court held in 1978 that "the closely regulated industry ... is the exception," and "when an entrepreneur embarks upon such a business, he has voluntarily chosen to subject himself to a full arsenal of governmental regulation."[25]

> States and the federal government can address major social problems both by way of an administrative scheme and through penal sanctions.... An administrative statute establishes how a particular business in a "closely regulated" industry should be operated, setting forth rules to guide an operator's conduct of the business and allowing government officials (sometimes the police) to ensure that these rules are followed. Such a regulatory approach contrasts with that of the (criminal) laws, a major emphasis of which is the punishment of individuals for specific acts of behavior. (The U.S. Supreme Court in the 1987 case of *New York v. Burger*, 482 U.S. 691, 107 S.Ct. 2636.)

In the *Burger* case, the U.S. Supreme Court established three requirements for authorizing inspections without search warrants of closely regulated businesses:

1. There must be a "substantial" government interest that informs the business operator of the "regulatory scheme" to which the inspection is to be made. For example, in the *Burger* case, the closely regulated industry was the junkyard business. These businesses are regulated because of the serious problem of stolen cars and stolen vehicle parts. Five police officers entered Burger's junkyard to inspect the junkyard as permitted by New York law. Burger stated that he did not have a license or records of vehicles he was required to have. The officers then found stolen cars and stolen vehicle parts. Burger was charged with the possession of stolen property. The New York law was found to be constitutional by the U.S. Supreme Court.

2. The inspection without a search warrant must be "necessary to further the regulatory scheme."

work-related searches A search of a worker's desk and work station for necessary records or equipment so that another employee can fill in for the absent worker or the employer can check for theft or fraud.

3. The regulatory law must perform the two basic functions of a search warrant:

   a. It must advise the business owner that a search is to be made pursuant to the law.

   b. The law must limit the discretion of the inspecting officers.

Examples of industries that have "such a history of government oversight that no reasonable expectation of privacy ... could exist for proprietors over the stock of such an enterprise"[26] include liquor,[27] firearms,[28] coal mines,[29] pharmacies,[30] horse racing,[31] taverns,[32] common carriers in trucking industry,[33] and other businesses and industries regulated by specific state or federal statutes.

WORK-RELATED SEARCHES IN GOVERNMENT OFFICES (THE *ORTEGA* RULE)

Private employers may make **work-related searches** of employees' desks, files, and company-owned computers as they wish. This could be done if an employee is sick and another person is filling in for the absent employee. Or, an employer could suspect that theft or fraud is occurring.

Should government supervisors have the same ability? In *O'Connor v. Ortega*, the U.S. Supreme Court held that to require "the Government to procure a warrant for every work-related intrusion would conflict with 'the common-sense realization' that government offices could not function if every decision became a constitutional matter."[34]

Public supervisors have wide latitude to search public employees' offices, desks, and files without search warrants or probable cause to believe that the search will uncover evidence of wrongdoing. However, the Court noted that it would require greater justification to search personal items such as "a piece of closed personal luggage, a handbag or a briefcase that happens to be within the employer's business address."

ROADBLOCKS OR VEHICLE CHECKPOINT STOPS

Roadblocks and vehicle stops were used during the October 2002 sniper shootings in the Washington, DC, area. Law officers aided by the military used roadblocks in attempts to apprehend the snipers who killed ten people before they were caught.

If challenged regarding the roadblocks, the government may point to the very specific goal and purpose of the roadblocks, which addressed the "special needs" of the emergency situation.

Highway checkpoints are used in the United States for many reasons. There are checkpoints to weigh and inspect trucks,[35] to detect illegal aliens,[36] to check driver's licenses,[37] to look for drunk drivers,[38] and for other public safety reasons.

Under the "special needs" rule, police can use roadblocks to stop vehicles for certain purposes, such as finding drunk drivers or illegal aliens.

© Bruce Chambers/Orange County Register/Corbis

IDENTIFICATION CHECKPOINTS IN PUBLIC HOUSING PROJECTS

Public housing projects in large cities have often been plagued by excessive illegal drug use and associated violence. More than any others, it is the law-abiding residents of the housing projects who suffer the consequences. In recent years, in an attempt to combat this problem, city governments have adopted programs that turn over the supervision of streets within the housing projects to the housing authority, which then employs officers to patrol the streets. These officers have the status of police officers. Many housing authorities set up an "identification checkpoint" at an entrance to the housing project. Housing authorities believe they can reduce drug crimes and violence by excluding persons who have no lawful purpose for entering the housing project's grounds. To accomplish this, the housing authorities issue identification badges to residents, and when persons entering the premises fail to produce a badge, checkpoint officers inquire into that person's reasons for entering the housing project's grounds.

Are these checkpoints lawful? If officers stop a person entering the housing project for this identification check and then discover illegal drugs or other crimes, can the evidence discovered be used in the prosecution of that person?

In *State v. Hayes* [188 S.W.3d 505 (Tenn. 2006)], the Tennessee Supreme Court joined a growing number of courts that have held that such checkpoints violate the Fourth Amendment. In *Hayes* a housing authority officer stopped a motorist as he turned onto a street leading into the project. The officer had no suspicion of criminal activity. When the officer asked for identification, the motorist showed him an expired driver's license, for which the motorist was subsequently charged under Tennessee's motor vehicles laws. The motorist moved to suppress the evidence seized at the checkpoint, contending that the checkpoint was unconstitutional under *Indianapolis v. Edmond*. The Tennessee Supreme Court agreed.

The housing authority sought to distinguish *Edmond* by arguing that the problem with the checkpoint in *Edmond* was that its only purpose was the "general interest in crime control" and it was aimed at identifying those already involved in illegal activity. Here, the authority contended, the purpose was to prevent illegal activity.

The Tennessee Supreme Court rejected that contention, holding that a purpose of preventing crime is nonetheless only a general interest in crime control, and no different than the situation in *Edmond*. Other courts have agreed with this conclusion. See, for example, *People v. Pope* [738 N.Y.S.2d 543 (N.Y. Sup.Ct. 2002), *appeal denied*, 793 N.E.2d 421 (N.Y. 2003)].

The U.S. Supreme Court affirmed the conviction and the use of evidence obtained in the drunk driver case of *Michigan State Police v. Sitz*,[39] holding that a "special government need" existed because "drunk drivers cause an annual death toll of over 25,000 and … nearly one million personal injuries and more than five billion dollars in property damage."

In the case of a roadblock to check driver's licenses (*Texas v. Brown*),[40] the officer shined a flashlight into Brown's car and bent down at an angle where the officer saw loose white powder in small plastic vials and a green party balloon with white powder. The U.S. Supreme Court affirmed the admission into evidence of the white powder, heroin, as evidence obtained in a plain view seizure and affirmed Brown's illegal drug conviction.

In the 2000 case of *City of Indianapolis v. Edmonds*,[41] the U.S. Supreme Court held that law officers may not simply set up roadblocks in high-crime neighborhoods as general crime-fighting procedures but must have an "immediate vehicle-bound threat to life and limb." The Supreme Court held that the stops were unconstitutional. The purpose of the checkpoint was not to deal with some special need like a particular hazard related to the checkpoint, such as drunk driving in the *Sitz* case, but rather the police's "general interest in crime control." The Court reasoned that if such checkpoints were permitted, then the police could set up a checkpoint to see if motorists were violating any criminal law.

In the 2004 case of *Illinois v. Lidster*,[42] the Court upheld a roadblock established by police to obtain information about a hit-and-run accident that occurred at the location where the roadblock was set up. The Court said the *Edmonds* rule did not apply where the purpose of the roadblock was not to check for criminal activity by the occupants of vehicles stopped, but only to acquire information from those occupants. It therefore upheld the conviction for drunk driving of a motorist stopped at this roadblock.

The Supreme Court has identified some circumstances where "special needs" justify suspicionless highway stops:

* Detecting drunk drivers
* Verifying driver's licenses and vehicle registration
* Intercepting illegal aliens on border highways
* Apprehending fleeing criminals
* Thwarting terrorist activity or attack

BORDER SEARCHES

Thousands of vehicles crossing borders to enter the United States are searched every day. Often the reason a particular vehicle is searched is the instincts and experience of the border agent responsible for the border checkpoint. As a result, a line of cases has developed in which the Fourth Amendment's reasonableness requirement was determined by the routine or nonroutine character of the search.

In the 2004 case of *United States v. Flores-Montano*,[43] however, the U.S. Supreme Court rejected a balancing test based on the routine–nonroutine nature of the search. The Court said that the reasonableness requirement does not require border agents to have any "particularized suspicion" before searching a vehicle. In *Flores-Montano*, agents removed and disassembled a vehicle's fuel tank looking for illegal drugs. The Court upheld the agents' actions, stating that the test for determining whether a search was unreasonable should be the "intrusiveness" of the search, not its routine or nonroutine character. The Court did state that a search of a vehicle could be so "destructive" that it became unreasonable.

In *United States v. Cortez-Rocha*,[44] the court upheld a border search of the spare tire in a vehicle attempting to cross the border at a checkpoint. Agents suspected that the tire on the vehicle might contain illegal drugs, and agents slashed the tire, finding 42 kilograms of marijuana. The court held that the tire slashing was not so "destructive" that the search was unreasonable because it did not hinder the operation of the vehicle or prevent the occupants from continuing their travels.

In the 2008 case of *United States v. Arnold*,[45] the Ninth Circuit Court of Appeals held that federal border agents did not need any "particularized suspicion" to view the files on a laptop computer brought into this country by a passenger on an international flight. The border agents required the passenger to turn on the laptop, and then the agents browsed through the files, finally discovering child pornography photographs. At the trial on child pornography charges, the district court suppressed the laptop photographs, and the government appealed. The court of appeals reversed.

The passenger argued that in *Flores-Montano* the Supreme Court had left open the question whether a suspicionless border search might be unreasonable "because of the particularly offensive manner in which it is carried out." Because so much personal information might be stored in a laptop, the passenger argued, the search by the border agents was "particularly offensive." The court disagreed, noting that in the many cases where suspicionless border searches of containers have been upheld, the Supreme Court never suggested that the capacity of the container had any bearing on the offensiveness of the search. The court also refused to create a special exception based on the potential for the presence of "expressive materials" protected by the First Amendment in the property searched, choosing instead to follow the decision of the Fourth Circuit Court of Appeals in *United States v. Ickes*.[46]

SHAM ROADBLOCKS

After the decision in *Indianapolis v. Edmonds*, police cannot set up roadblocks and stop vehicles for the purpose of searching them for illegal drugs or evidence of other criminal activity. May police set up so-called sham roadblocks by posting signs on a highway that there is a drug checkpoint ahead, in the belief that motorists who are carrying drugs will respond to the fake notice by discarding those drugs. In *United States v. Flynn*[47] and *People v. Roth*,[48] the courts upheld such sham roadblocks. In both cases, police erected signs on a highway stating that a drug checkpoint was set up ahead on the highway. In fact, no such checkpoint existed. After passing the signs, a motorist in each case was observed by police throwing something out of the vehicle. The vehicles were then stopped and searched, and illegal drugs were found. The subsequent convictions were upheld by both courts. The Tenth Circuit Court of Appeals in *Flynn* held that posting a fake sign was not illegal, and that the resulting actions by the motorist gave the police the necessary "particularized suspicion" to stop the vehicle.

CORRECTIONAL PROGRAMS, HEARINGS, OR REQUIREMENTS THAT MAY CAUSE A PRISON INMATE TO INCRIMINATE HIMSELF

In 2002 the U.S. Supreme Court wrote about the seriousness of sexual assaults in the United States:

> In 1995 an estimated 355,000 rapes and sexual assaults occurred nationwide ... imprisoned sex offenders (have) increased at a faster rate than for any other category of violent crime ... victims of sexual assault are most often juveniles ... (n)early 4 in 10 violent sex offenders said their victims were 12 or younger ... sex offenders (when released from prison) are much more likely than any other type of offender to be rearrested for a new rape or sexual assault.[49]

Because of the seriousness of this problem, Sexual Abuse Treatment Programs (SATPs) are in place in state and federal prisons. In these programs inmates must disclose and accept responsibility for "the crimes for which they have been sentenced" and also "all prior sexual activities," whether lawful or whether "the activities constitute uncharged criminal offenses." Inmates have challenged various aspects of these programs, contending that participation in the programs is in essence mandatory, and that participation requires the inmate to abandon constitutional rights like the right to remain silent. The states' response to these challenges has been to contend that the "special needs" doctrine justifies their actions. The following SATP cases have come before the U.S. Supreme Court:

Case	Hearing Requirements and Consequences, Including Punishment If Inmate Refused to Disclose Uncharged Crimes	Court Ruling
McKune v. Lile, 536 U.S. 24 (2002)	Lile was convicted of the rape and sexual assault of a high school student. As an inmate in a Kansas prison, he challenged the Kansas SATP. Punishment for failure to comply in Kansas would be reduction and curtailment of visitation rights, earnings, work opportunity, access to television, sending money to family, and purchases in the canteen. Lile would also be transferred to a potentially more dangerous maximum-security unit.	"Acceptance of responsibility is the beginning of rehabilitation...." "The Kansas SATP represents a sensible approach to reducing the serious danger that repeat offenders pose to many innocent persons, most often children." (The fact that Kansas does not offer legal immunity from prosecution for disclosures does not render the Kansas SATP invalid.)
Minnesota v. Murphy, 104 S.Ct. 1136 (1984)	As a condition of probation, the defendant agreed to be	Murphy obtained probation from prison

	truthful with his probation officer in all matters. Because the defendant feared being returned to prison for sixteen months if he remained silent, he confessed to a rape and murder. Murphy was tried and convicted for these crimes.	by agreeing in writing to be truthful with his probation officer. Convictions for rape and murder were affirmed.
Ohio Adult Parole Authority v. Woodard, 118 S.Ct. 1244 (1998)	A death row inmate at his voluntary clemency interview chose to incriminate himself rather than be silent and cause "the clemency board (to) construe that silence against him."	The defendant faced "a choice quite similar to the sorts of choices that a criminal defendant must make in the course of criminal proceedings, none of which has ever been held to violate the Fifth Amendment." The Court held it was not an unconstitutional compulsion.
Baxter v. Palmigiano, 96 S.Ct. 1551 (1976)	A state prisoner objected to the fact that his silence at a prison disciplinary hearing would be held against him. The prisoner faced thirty days in punitive segregation. The Supreme Court held that the disciplinary board could draw an inference of guilt from the prisoner's silence.	Prison disciplinary hearings "involve the correctional process and important state interests" and are unlike a criminal trial where a jury is forbidden from drawing an inference of guilt from a defendant's failure to testify.

Do Inmates on Parole Have Privacy Expectations Protected by the Fourth Amendment?

At various times the U.S. Supreme Court has addressed the question of whether a person who in some way is under the jurisdiction of a prison authority has the expectation of privacy protected by the Fourth Amendment. The privacy expectation varies because the extent of the prison authority's control differs for an inmate incarcerated in a prison population and for an inmate released on parole or probation. In the following case the Supreme Court discussed the relationship of the Fourth Amendment to prisoners and their expectations of privacy. It should be noted that, in reaching its decision, the Court was careful to state that it was not reaching that decision solely under the "special needs" doctrine.

Samson v. California

United States Supreme
Court, 547 U.S. 843
(2006)

In *United States v. Knights*,[50] the Supreme Court held that a person on probation had a "diminished privacy" interest that justified an officer to stop and search that person based only on "reasonable suspicion" that the person was engaged in criminal activity. The Court also noted that as a condition of probation in *Knights,* the probationer had to submit to a search at any time, with or without reasonable suspicion. The state has a legitimate interest in closely monitoring those on probation, the Court said, both to reintegrate the probationer into society and to prevent recidivism. Viewing these factors together, the Court said the search was reasonable in *Knights*. The Court specifically declined to answer the question "whether the search would have been reasonable under the Fourth Amendment had it been solely predicated upon the condition of probation."[51] *Samson* directly presented that question, the Court in that case stated, "albeit in the context of a parolee search."[52]

In concluding that the search was reasonable under general Fourth Amendment principles, the Court first placed parole on a "continuum of state-imposed punishments" that resulted in fewer expectations of privacy than in the case of persons on probation. Parole, the Court said, is closely akin to being a prisoner, since under California law a parolee remains under the legal custody of the Department of Corrections and must comply with all the conditions of parole. The totality of these conditions, the Court said, "… demonstrate that parolees like petitioner have severely diminished expectations of privacy by virtue of their status alone."[53]

Moreover, the Court noted, as in *Knights*, that parolees must sign an order in which they must submit to suspicionless searches by officers at any time. The Court held:

> Examining the totality of the circumstances pertaining to petitioner's status as a parolee, "an established variation on imprisonment," *Morrissey*, 408 U.S. at 477, 92 S.Ct. 2593, including the plain terms of the parole search condition, we conclude that petitioner did not have an expectation of privacy that society would recognize as legitimate. *Id.*

By comparison, the state's interest in searches of parolees is substantial, the Court said. It noted that in 2005 California had more than 130,000 released prisoners on parole, and that the parolee population has a 68–70 percent recidivism rate.[54] Closely monitoring parolees is clearly in the state's interest, the Court concluded, and suspicionless searches serve the state's interest in reducing recidivism.[55]

Judging suspicionless searches under these circumstances, the Court held that "the Fourth Amendment does not prohibit a police officer from conducting a suspicionless search of a parolee."[56]

The Court was careful to make it clear that its decision was based solely on "general Fourth Amendment" principles, and as a result it did not reach the issue of whether acceptance of the search condition constituted "consent" and thus operated as a complete waiver of Fourth Amendment rights. Nor, the Court said, did it base its decision on "special needs" rules.[57] Finally, the Court said its decision did not equate parolees with prisoners, who have no Fourth Amendment rights, as was held in *Hudson v. Palmer*.[58]

OTHER SPECIAL GOVERNMENT NEEDS WHERE NEITHER PROBABLE CAUSE NOR SEARCH WARRANTS ARE NEEDED

The need to supervise persons on probation and parole closely: *Griffin v. Wisconsin*, U.S. Supreme Court, 483 U.S. 868, 107 S.Ct. 3164 (1987)

The U.S. Supreme Court upheld the search by a probation officer under a Wisconsin statute that authorized such searches on the basis of reasonable suspicion. The Supreme Court held that the "special needs of the probation system requires the need to supervise persons on probation and parole closely."

Not only do many states have such statutes, but it is also a common practice to include consent to search sections in parole and probation agreements. Persons being placed on parole or probation must sign these agreements to receive such status.

Illegal aliens: *United States v. Martinez-Fuerte*, U.S. Supreme Court, 428 U.S. 543, 96 S.Ct. 3078 (1976)

In permitting checkpoints for illegal aliens, the U.S. Supreme Court held that "requiring particularized suspicion before routine stops on major highways near the Mexican border would be impractical because the flow of traffic tends to be too heavy to allow the particularized study of a given car that would enable it to be identified as a possible carrier of illegal aliens."[59]

Safety in jails and prisons: *Bell v. Wolfish*, U.S. Supreme Court, 441 U.S. 520, 99 S.Ct. 1861 (1979)

Since persons in jails and prisons have a reduced right to privacy, they are subject to random searches for weapons and contraband without any showing of suspicion. The U.S. Supreme Court held that visual body cavity searches may be made of inmates to find weapons and drugs and to maintain safety in jails and prisons.

OBTAINING EVIDENCE IN FOREIGN COUNTRIES

Sometimes evidence of serious crimes about to be committed (or being committed) in the United States becomes available in foreign countries (including Mexico or Canada). The following general rules for the admissibility of such evidence in U.S. courts are presented in an article in the *FBI Law Enforcement Bulletin* (July 2002) entitled "Investigating International Terrorism Overseas: Constitutional Considerations":

- When law officers in the foreign country acting alone and independently obtain the evidence: "Generally, American legal standards do not apply to the seizure of evidence ... where a foreign country is conducting the investigation independently and seizes evidence that is later introduced into an American court."[a]
- "If American investigators are acting alone in seeking to obtain evidence in a foreign country, they should always comply with the laws of that country and should conduct their investigation as if they were operating in the United States."
- "When American investigators are working jointly with foreign officials, they should remember that searches or interrogations ... will invoke (American) constitutional protections on the part of the subject (of the search or interrogation)."

Another way of obtaining evidence from foreign countries is through the use of Mutual Legal Assistance Treaties (MLAT), which the United States signed with thirty-four countries including Canada and Mexico. If an MLAT does not exist, authority may be requested from a federal court to ask officials in a foreign country to obtain evidence. This is called a "letter rogatory." Subpoenas may also be issued on persons or corporations in the United States who have constructive possession of evidence located in foreign countries.[b]

---

[a]American courts would refuse to use evidence obtained by foreign government officials if the conduct of the foreign officials in obtaining the evidence shocked the conscience of the U.S. court. See the case of *United States v. Callaway* [446 F.2d 753 (3d Cir. 1971)], where Canadian police who were not acting in connection or cooperation with American law enforcement officials obtained criminal evidence that was used to convict Callaway in a New Jersey court. Because the actions of the Canadian police were not so outrageous as to shock the conscience of the trial court, the evidence was admitted, and Callaway's conviction was affirmed.

[b]The U.S. Supreme Court ruled in the 1999 case of *Flippo v. West Virginia* [120 S.Ct. 7] that American courts do not have the authority to issue search warrants authorizing searches in foreign countries.

SUMMARY

Local, state, and federal governments provide many services that are not related to criminal investigations. Many of these are routine administrative functions. The U.S. Supreme Court and other courts have held that the Fourth Amendment requirement of "reasonableness" has to be viewed differently "when analyzing the reasonableness of routine administrative functions."[60]

Evidence that is obtained in any of the administrative functions presented in this chapter is admissible if the guidelines established by law or the courts have been complied with.

The "special needs" of government are needs of safety, health, education, and concern for the well-being of the society as a whole.

CASE ANALYSIS

Read Appendix B, Finding and Analyzing Cases (p. 427). With these guidelines in mind, please continue with the Case Analysis selections for Chapter 11.

1. The "special needs" rationale discussed in this chapter has routinely been used by courts to justify searches based only on reasonable suspicion of persons on probation or parole. In *Coleman v. Commonwealth* [100 S.W.3d 745 (2003)], the Kentucky Supreme Court refused to justify the search by a parole officer of the parolee's residence. The conditions of the defendant's parole included his permission to search his residence without any necessary suspicion. What effect on the court's decision did this provision have? Would the Supreme Court decision in *Samson v. California* (discussed previously) have changed the result?

2. As this chapter notes, school officials may conduct searches of students and school lockers based only on reasonable suspicion, not on probable cause. In *People v. Williams* [791 N.E.2d 608 (Ill. App. 2003)] [Docket No. 93573], a police officer was investigating a burglary during which a handgun had been stolen. The police officer was at the time also acting as the police advisor to a high school. School officials called the officer and told him that the gun might be in the trunk of a student's car parked in the school parking lot.

Does the "special needs" rule justify the officer's search of the parked car's trunk without probable cause?

3. Child welfare agencies are charged with the task of determining when a child has been subjected to abuse or neglect. In their investigations, they often interview the child or children whose care is being questioned. What are the Fourth Amendment implications of such interviews, if done without the consent of the parents or a judicial warrant? See *Doe v. Heck* [327 F.3d 492 (7th Cir. 2003)]. Did it matter in that case that the interviews were conducted at a private school?

4. Police entered a liquor store in pursuit of two suspicious characters. Even though the store's night manager instructed the two men not to go into the backroom, they did, and the police followed them. While in the backroom, the police discovered illegal drugs and charged the store manager with possession of illegal drugs. Were the store manager's Fourth Amendment rights violated? Did it matter that a video surveillance camera was stationed in the backroom? The state did not contend that "special needs" justified the police activity. Do you think it should have made that argument? See *People v. Galvadon* [103 P.3d 923 (Colo. 2005)].

Notes

1. *National Treasury Employee Union v. Von Raab*, 489 U.S. 656, 668, and *Colorado v. Bertine*, 479 U.S. 367, 371.
2. *People v. Heimel*, 812 P.2d 1177 (1991). For similar rulings, see *State v. Plante*, 594 A.2d 165 (N.H. 1991), and *United States v. Vigil*, 989 F.2d 337 (9th Cir. 1993).
3. *Klarfeld v. United States*, 962 F.2d 866 (9th Cir. 1992).
4. *Frank v. Maryland*, 359 U.S. 360.
5. *Camara v. Municipal Court*, 387 U.S. 523 (1967).
6. 387 U.S. 541 (1967).
7. *New Jersey v. T.L.O.*, 469 U.S. 340 at 340 (1985).
8. 515 U.S. 646 (1995).
9. 402 F.3d 598 (6th Cir. 2005).
10. 489 U.S. 656.
11. 489 U.S. 602.
12. *Von Raab*, 489 U.S. at 665; *Skinner*, 489 U.S. at 617–18.
13. 489 U.S. at 670.
14. 489 U.S. at 628.
15. 489 U.S. at 676.
16. 109 S.Ct. at 1419.

17. *Policemen's Benevolent Ass'n v. Township of Washington*, 850 F.2d 133 (3d Cir. 1988), *review denied*, 490 U.S. 1004, 109 S.Ct. 1637, 45 CrL 4002 (1989). Not all courts go along with the reasoning in the U.S. Supreme Court's *Von Raub* decision. In the 1991 case of *Guiney v. Police Commissioner of Boston* [582 N.E.2d 523], the Massachusetts Supreme Judicial Court held that "unannounced, warrantless, suspicionless, random" urinalysis testing of Boston police officers violated the Massachusetts Constitution even if permitted under the U.S. Constitution.

18. *McCloskey v. Honolulu Police Department*, 799 P.2d 953 (1990).

19. *Copeland v. Philadelphia Police Department*, 840 F.2d 1139 (3d Cir. 1988), *review denied*, 490 U.S. 1004, 109 S.Ct. 1636, 45 CrL 4001 (1989).

20. *United States v. Blair*, 32 M.J. 404 (1991), *review denied*, U.S. Supreme Court, 112 S.Ct. 438, 50 CrL, 3077 (1991).

21. 115 S.Ct. 2386 (1995).

22. 393 U.S. 503 (1969).

23. No. 97–2021 (1998).

24. *See v. City of Seattle*, 387 U.S. 541, 543, 87 S.Ct. 1737, 1739 (1967).

25. *Marshall v. Barlow's Inc.*, 436 U.S. 307 (1978).

26. *Marshall v. Barlow's Inc.*, 436 U.S. at 313, 98 S.Ct. at 1821.

27. *Colonnade Catering Corp. v. United States*, 397 U.S. 72, 90 S.Ct. 774 (1970).

28. *United States v. Biswell*, 406 U.S. 311, 92 S.Ct. 1593 (1972).

29. *Donovan v. Dewey*, 452 U.S. 594, 101 S.Ct. 2534 (1981).

30. *State v. Del City*, 947 F.2d 432 (10th Cir. 1991).

31. *State v. Williams*, 417 A.2d 1046 (N.J. 1980).

32. *State v. Rednor*, 497 A.2d 544 (N.J. 1985).

33. *United States v. Dominguez-Prieto*, 923 F.2d 464 (6th Cir. 1991).

34. 480 U.S. 709 (1987).

35. *Delaware v. Prouse*, 440 U.S. 648, 663 n.26, 99 S.Ct. 1391, 1401 n.26 (1979).

36. *United States v. Martinez-Fuerte*, 428 U.S. 543, 96 S.Ct. 3074 (1976).

37. *Texas v. Brown*, 460 U.S. 730, 103 S.Ct. 1535 (1983).

38. *Michigan State Police v. Sitz*, 496 U.S. 444, 110 S.Ct. 2481 (1990).

39. *Id.*

40. 460 U.S. 730 (1983).

41. 531 U.S. 32 (2000).

42. 540 U.S. 419 (2004).

43. 541 U.S. 149.

44. 383 F.3d 1093 (9th Cir. 2004).

45. 523 F.3d 941 (9th Cir. 2008), *rehearing denied*, 2008 WL 2675794.

46. 393 F.3d 501 (4th Cir. 2005).

47. 309 F.3d 736 (10th Cir. 2002).

48. 85 P.3d 571 (Colo. 2003).

49. *McKune v. Lile*, 153 L.Ed.2d at 56.

50. 534 U.S. 112 (2002).

51. 547 U.S. at 850.

52. *Id.*

53. *Id.* at 852.

54. *Id.* at 853.

55. *Id.* at 854.

56. *Id.* at 857.

57. *Id.* at 852, fn.3.

58. 468 U.S. 517 (1984). *Id.* at 850, fn.2.

59. 428 U.S. at 557, 96 S.Ct. at 3082, and 489 U.S. at 668, 109 S.Ct. at 1392.

60. 489 U.S. 656, 668.

Obtaining Statements and Confessions for Use as Evidence

A confession is like no other evidence. Indeed, the defendant's own confession is probably the most probative and damaging evidence that can be admitted against him.... [T]he admissions of a defendant come from the actor himself, the most knowledgeable and unimpeachable source of information about his past conduct.[1]

These words by U.S. Supreme Court Justice White underscore both the evidentiary value and the risk associated with confessions and incriminating statements. A **confession** is generally viewed as the same as a guilty plea in open court. An **incriminating statement** differs from a confession in that a confession directly acknowledges guilt, whereas an incriminating statement "is any statement or conduct from which guilt of the crime can be inferred."[2] Sometimes even silence can constitute an incriminating statement. In *Key-el v. State*,[3] the prosecution introduced evidence that the defendant had remained silent when his wife, in the presence of a police officer, accused him of battering. The evidence was held properly admissible under the tacit admission rule, and the defendant's conviction was affirmed.

If true, confessions are the best evidence of guilt. On the other hand, if untrue and given by the defendant because of coercion or pressure, confessions carry a high risk of misleading the jury. For those and other reasons, the law governing the use of confessions and incriminating statements in criminal trials has a long and complex history. In many respects, it is still developing. In this chapter we explore some of those developments.

confession A direct acknowledgment of guilt; generally viewed the same as a guilty plea in open court.

incriminating statement "Any statement or conduct from which guilt of the crime can be inferred" [*People v. Stanton*, 158 N.E.2d 47 (Ill. 1959)].

CAN A CONFESSION ALONE SUSTAIN A CRIMINAL CONVICTION?

THE CORPUS DELICTI RULE

Frank Connelly approached a police officer on a Denver street and confessed to a murder.[4] If the police could find no other evidence of the murder, could Connelly be charged and convicted of a murder solely on the basis of his confession? The answer is no, because a confession alone will not sustain a conviction.

When a confession is used as evidence, corroborating evidence must also be provided to prove corpus delicti (that the crime was committed). This requirement originated in England in the notorious 1660 *Perry's* case,[5] where a defendant was convicted of murder and executed solely on the basis of a confession, only to have the murder "victim" subsequently appear alive. As the Supreme Court of California pointed out in 1991, the rule was used "to protect the defendant against the possibility of fabricated testimony which might wrongfully establish the crime and the perpetrator."[6]

In the 1991 case of *People v. Jennings*, the defendant bragged to others about how he picked up prostitutes, paid them for sex, and then later killed them and took their money before burying the bodies. The State of California produced evidence corroborating the confessions to three murders and other felonies such as kidnapping and robberies of the women. In affirming the convictions and death penalty in the *Jennings* case, the Supreme Court of California quoted another court in sustaining the corpus delicti rule, holding:

As one court explained, "Today's judicial retention of the rule reflects the continued fear that confessions may be the result of either improper police activity or the mental instability of the accused, and the recognition that juries are likely to accept confessions uncritically." [*Jones v. Superior Court*, (1979) 96 Cal. App. 3d 390, 397, 157 Cal. Rptr. 809.]

Viewed with this in mind, the low threshold that must be met before a defendant's own statements can be admitted against him makes sense; so long as there is some indication that the charged crime actually happened, we are satisfied that the accused is not admitting to a crime that never occurred.

The federal courts and the courts of some states use a modified version of the corpus delicti rule called the "trustworthiness doctrine" first announced by the U.S. Supreme Court in *Opper v. United States*.[7] Under this rule, although an uncorabborated confession is not by itself sufficient to convict a defendant, the corroborating evidence need not independently establish the commission of the crime. Rather, the corroborating evidence must establish the "trustworthiness" of the confession. However, many courts that have adopted this rule continue to require some evidence that a crime occurred.[8]

The following examples illustrate the traditional rule that confessions must be corroborated by proof of corpus delicti:

- In 1988 Marty James appeared on the ABC *Nightline* show and admitted that he had helped a friend with AIDS commit suicide. After questioning by reporters a day later, James stated that he assisted at least eight men with AIDS commit suicide. Relatives of the men accused James of murder, but prosecutors stated that investigations did not turn up evidence to corroborate James's confessions. Because the corpus delicti rule could not be satisfied, criminal charges could not be filed against James. (James was suffering from AIDS himself and died of an overdose of sleeping pills in 1992.)[9]
- The defendant's conviction for first-degree sexual assault was reversed in *State v. Torwirt*.[10] The defendant stated in recorded phone conversations with a friend and with a police officer that she touched and placed her lips on the genital area of a 3-year-old child she was babysitting. Because no physical evidence of the touching could be shown and no other corroboration existed, the Nebraska Court of Appeals held in 2000 that the confession alone could not support conviction.
- Proof of corpus delicti was presented to sustain confessions in the following cases: armed robbery,[11] embezzlement,[12] drug use by military personnel,[13] and manslaughter.[14]

THE REQUIREMENT THAT CONFESSIONS AND INCRIMINATING STATEMENTS BE VOLUNTARY

In fifteenth-century England, courts and law officers often obtained confessions to crimes by torture and violence. These abuses led the English courts to create the concept that "no man is bound to accuse himself" (*nemo tenetur seipsum accusare*) and ultimately led to Parliament's abolition of the infamous Star Chamber. English courts used this maxim to hold that persons ought not to be put on trial for a crime and compelled to answer incriminating questions until after they had been properly accused by a grand jury.

voluntariness test The requirement that confessions, incriminating statements, and consent be voluntary and freely given and not obtained by means that overwhelmed the will of the accused or another person.

To protect against the historic abuses that occurred in England, Europe, and Colonial America, the Fifth Amendment of the U.S. Constitution, adopted in 1791, requires that no person "… shall be compelled in a criminal case to be a witness against himself, nor be deprived of life, liberty, or property, without due process of law…."

It has never been held that interrogations by police are *per se* unconstitutional. However, the **voluntariness test** used today requires that confessions and admissions by a suspect must be voluntarily and freely given. If the police or a prosecutor obtains a confession or an incriminating admission by means that overbear the will of the accused, that statement or confession cannot be used as evidence, on the grounds that it is a denial of the Fifth and Fourteenth Amendment requirements of due process of law.

USING VIOLENCE TO OBTAIN CONFESSIONS

Until 1936, each state established its own voluntariness test and determined for itself what "due process of law" meant within that state. In the following important U.S. Supreme Court case, the Court reversed murder convictions in the state of Mississippi and, in a strongly worded decision, held that the confessions used as evidence were involuntarily obtained.[15]

Brown v. Mississippi

United States Supreme Court, 297 U.S. 278, 56 S.Ct. 461 (1936)

When a murder occurred in Mississippi in 1934, the defendants, three black men, were taken into custody by law enforcement officers. By means of whippings, beatings, and the actual hanging of one of the defendants by a rope to the limb of a tree, confessions to the murder were obtained from the defendants. With practically no other evidence and with the rope mark "plainly visible" on the neck of the defendant who was hanged, the criminal trial charging the defendants with murder began. The defendants were convicted despite the fact that a state witness (a deputy sheriff) admitted that brutality and violence were used to obtain the confessions.

In reversing the convictions, the U.S. Supreme Court held that:

> The question in this case is whether convictions, which rest solely upon confessions shown to have been extorted by officers of the state by brutality and violence, are consistent with the due process of law required by the Fourteenth Amendment of the Constitution of the United States.
>
> … The rack and torture chamber may not be substituted for the witness stand….
> In the instant case, the trial court was fully advised by the undisputed evidence of the way in which the confessions had been procured. The trial court knew that there was no other evidence upon which conviction and sentence could be based. Yet it proceeded to permit conviction and to pronounce sentence. The conviction and sentence were void for want of the essential elements of due process, and the proceeding thus vitiated could be challenged in any appropriate manner.

THE TOTALITY OF THE CIRCUMSTANCES TEST TO DETERMINE WHETHER A CONFESSION OR STATEMENT IS VOLUNTARY

Confessions and statements can be involuntarily obtained from a suspect not only by torture and violence but also by many other means. For example, if a confession was obtained by withholding food, heat, clothing, or other essentials of life from a prisoner, courts would refuse to allow the confession to be used as evidence because it was involuntarily induced and was a violation of due process.

Defendants in criminal cases can be convicted only on reliable, relevant evidence. To be admissible as evidence, confessions and statements must be made voluntarily and freely. If the police obtain a confession or admission by means that overbear the will of the accused, the statement or confession will not be admitted for use as evidence on the grounds that a denial of due process of law occurred.

In determining whether a confession or statement may be used as evidence, courts use the **totality of the circumstances test**. When a court looks at the whole picture (totality of the circumstances), it considers all of the following factors:

totality of the circumstances test The test that looks at the whole picture—all factors—in determining whether a confession, incriminating statement, or consent was freely and voluntarily given.

- *Suspect vulnerabilities:* Age (very young or very old), education, mental impairment, or physical condition that could make the suspect vulnerable. Was the suspect an alcoholic or a drug addict, a chain smoker, someone in need of a drink, a fix, or a cigarette?
- *Interrogating factors:* Length of questioning; number of officers; time of day or night; denial of food, water, heat, sleep, or other basic necessities. Did the questioning overbear the will of the accused?
- *Place of questioning:* Was questioning done in an isolated area of a police station, or did it occur in the suspect's home or office or in a public place?
- *Other factors:* Were any threats, promises, deception, lies, or trickery used?

Hundreds of state and federal court cases address the question of when lies, threats, promises, deceits, or trickery could cause a confession to be held to be involuntary. Courts generally hold that deception or lies used to promote a confession do not automatically make the confession involuntary, but are merely factors in the totality of circumstances test. For example, in the 2004 case of *Lincoln v State*,[16] a confession was held to be given voluntarily even though the police showed the defendant fabricated documents that incriminated him in a murder.

Explicit promises of leniency in exchange for a confession generally result in the confession being treated as involuntary. Although it is permissible to offer "limited assurances" of lighter punishment if a defendant cooperates with investigators, more specific references to lighter punishment if a defendant confesses to a crime are commonly viewed as being unduly coercive. For example, in the 2006 case of *United States v. Lopez*,[17] the court held that a confession was given involuntarily where the investigators interrogating the defendant placed two slips of paper before him, one that said "mistake—6" and one that said "murder—60." The numbers were the likely years in prison for a confession that a killing was the result of a mistake and a conviction for murder.

The *FBI Law Enforcement Bulletin* has published many articles reviewing this area of the law. Examples are: "Magic Words to Obtain Confessions" and "Conducting Successful Interrogations" (October 1998); "Ensuring Officer Integrity and Accountability" (August 1998); and "Lies, Promises, or Threats: The Voluntariness of Confessions" (July 1993).

THE *MIRANDA* REQUIREMENTS

For many years, the voluntariness requirement was the only test used to determine the admissibility of confessions and statements as evidence. In 1966, the U.S. Supreme Court added an additional requirement.

APPLICATIONS OF THE TOTALITY OF THE CIRCUMSTANCES TEST IN JUVENILE CASES

When juveniles are questioned by police about crimes they might have committed, the totality of the circumstances test is used to determine whether the juveniles made their statements voluntarily and whether they voluntarily waived the right of the Self-Incrimination Clause following a *Miranda* warning. The presence or absence of the juveniles' parents during questioning is often an issue in these determinations. In *Fare v. Michael C.* [442 U.S. 707 (1979)], the U.S. Supreme Court held that the age and experience of the juvenile must be considered in reaching that decision, but that the denial of a juvenile's request to talk to his parents would not in every case make the resulting statements inadmissible. The following cases illustrate the totality of the circumstances test in juvenile cases:

- *In re Jerrell, C.J.* [699 N.W.2d 110 (2005)]: The Wisconsin Supreme Court held that the denial by police of a 14-year-old boy's repeated requests to call his parents during a 5-hour interrogation made his waiver of his *Miranda* rights involuntary. The totality of the circumstances test applied by the court included the age of the boy, his low IQ, and his limited previous contacts with the police. The court also held that the denial of a juvenile's request

to speak to his parents would be "strong evidence of coercive tactics" by the police. The court also in this case exercised its supervisory power over lower courts in Wisconsin to adopt a requirement that all interrogations of juveniles must be videotaped. Such a videotape would be extremely useful in making the totality of the circumstances determination, the court decided.

- *State v. Burrell* [697 N.W.2d 579 (2005)]: The Minnesota Supreme Court overturned the first-degree murder conviction of a 16-year-old boy. The boy's 3-hour interrogation was videotaped and shown to the jury at the boy's trial. During the interrogation the boy on three occasions prior to being given a *Miranda* warning asked to speak to his mother, and he asked ten times after the warning. In addition, the police conducting the interrogation misrepresented to the boy the content of witness' statements about his involvement in the killing. Because the boy was claiming he was with his mother when the crime occurred, the supreme court concluded that the requests to talk to his mother indicated the boy wanted advice before answering questions. Under the totality of the circumstances test, the court said the boy's waiver was involuntary and his statements could not be used against him.

In the 1966 case of *Miranda v. Arizona*,[18] the U.S. Supreme Court made the admissibility of confessions and statements turn not only on a finding of voluntariness but also on proof by a prosecutor that procedural safeguards were complied with. In the *Miranda* case, the Court ruled that:

> The prosecution may not use statements, whether exculpatory or inculpatory, stemming from custodial interrogation of the defendant unless it demonstrates the use of procedural safeguards effective to secure the privilege against self-incrimination.

Miranda requirements
The procedural safeguards established by the U.S. Supreme Court in 1966.

The well-known **Miranda requirements** were established by the U.S. Supreme Court as part of the procedural safeguards. There are four *Miranda* requirements:

1. The suspect must be told of his right to remain silent.
2. Anything he says may be used against him in a court of law.

In 1963 Ernest Miranda (shown here) was charged with rape and armed robbery. (He was not charged and convicted of kidnapping, although he should have been because he transported the victim some distance.) He confessed to the crimes during a police interrogation in which he was not informed that he had a right to have an attorney present or that anything he said could be used against him in court. Although subsequently convicted, he successfully appealed to the U.S. Supreme Court, which overturned his conviction and established the *Miranda* warning to guard a citizen's right to protection against self-incrimination.

© Bettmann/Corbis

3. He is entitled to the presence of an attorney.
4. If he cannot afford an attorney, one will be appointed to represent him.

The *Miranda* requirements do not have to be complied with unless the following two conditions exist:

- The suspect must be in custody (custody is defined as "the functional equivalent of formal arrest").
- A government official (police, sheriff, and so on) seeks to interrogate the suspect about his or her suspected criminal conduct ("questioning initiated by a law enforcement officer after a person has been taken into custody or otherwise deprived of his freedom of action in any significant way").

When a prosecutor seeks to use statements that are the product of custodial interrogation as evidence, the prosecutor must demonstrate the following procedural safeguards:

- Sufficient and adequate warnings were given to the suspect.
- The suspect understood the warnings.
- The suspect waived his or her rights to remain silent and to have an attorney present during the questioning.

MIRANDA WARNINGS: WAIVER, TIMING, AND INVOCATION OF THE RIGHT TO COUNSEL

The Fifth Amendment rights protected by the *Miranda* warnings often present issues for courts concerning when or if the rights have been invoked or waived.

- *Waiver:* A defendant, after being fully advised of his Fifth Amendment rights, can waive them and answer questions asked of him by the police. However, the waiver must be clear and voluntary. (See *Edwards v. Arizona*, 451 U.S. 477 (1981)). In the 2005 case of *Garvey v. State* [873 A.2d 291], the Delaware Supreme Court held that the defendant in a murder investigation gave such a waiver, which made his subsequent statements admissible. After being given the *Miranda* warnings, the defendant was asked whether he wished to answer questions. He replied, "Depends on what you ask me." The court concluded that this statement indicated that the defendant was prepared to selectively answer questions, which indicated he understood that he was entitled to refuse to answer questions at all. As a result, the court reasoned, the defendant waived his right to refuse to answer any questions.

- *Timing:* How often must the *Miranda* warnings be given if there is a break in the interrogation session? In the 2005 case of *United States v. Pruden* [398 F.3d 241 (3d Cir.)], the court held that a 20-hour break in the session did not require a new warning. In *Pruden* the defendant was arrested on suspicion of illegal purchases of handguns. After being given his *Miranda* warnings, the defendant waived his rights and answered questions, stating he had not asked two women to purchase handguns on his behalf. After about 30 minutes, the session ended, and the defendant was taken to a detention center where he spent the night. The next morning, without a new *Miranda* warning, the police asked him more questions, and the defendant admitted that he asked the women to procure the handguns for him. These statements were admitted, and the defendant was convicted. On appeal, the court upheld the conviction, stating that the voluntary waiver of rights made by the defendant continued into the morning questioning because nothing occurred during the 20-hour break to indicate that the defendant did not understand the nature of his rights and the effect of his earlier waiver.

- *Invocation of Fifth Amendment rights:* In *Davis v. United States* [512 U.S. 452 (1994)], the U.S. Supreme Court held that once a defendant has unambiguously invoked his Fifth Amendment rights, the police must cease to question him. What must a defendant do or say to invoke his rights? In the 2005 case of *United States v. Johnson* [400 F.3d 187 (4th Cir.)], a suspect was given a form with various questions and a "yes" or "no" box by each question. He checked the "no" box for the question "Would you like to make a statement without a lawyer?" A few minutes later, the police asked him again if he wanted to make a statement without a lawyer, and this time the defendant checked the "yes" box. He then made incriminating statements. The court of appeals held that the first box checked was an unambiguous invocation of his right to a lawyer, and once the defendant invoked that right, the police could not resume questioning unless the defendant initiated further communication.

- In *People v. Atkins* [113 P.2d 788 (2005)], the Colorado Supreme Court suppressed a confession of a defendant charged with sexual assault. When questioned by police and given his *Miranda* warning that "he was entitled to an attorney," the defendant interrupted the interrogator and asked, "How come I don't have one now?" The police ignored the statement and continued to question the defendant, and he ultimately confessed. The court held that the response by the defendant to the statement that he was entitled to have a lawyer present could only be understood by the police that he wanted representation before answering any questions. As a result, the failure of the police to cease questioning him made his subsequent confession inadmissible.

WHEN *MIRANDA* WARNINGS ARE NOT REQUIRED

1. *Miranda* warnings are not required if the person is not in custody, or if a suspect is in custody and there is no intention or effort by a law officer to interrogate the suspect about the crime for which the suspect has been arrested. Some police and sheriff departments require that *Miranda* warnings be given after every arrest. This, then, would be a requirement of that department or within that state, but the U.S. Supreme Court does not require *Miranda* warnings under these circumstances.

2. *Miranda* warnings are not required when a person volunteers information. The U.S. Supreme Court held that: "There is no requirement that police stop a person who enters a police station and states that he wishes to confess to a crime, or a person who calls the police to offer a confession or any other statement he desires to make. Volunteered statements of any kind are not barred by the Fifth Amendment and their admissibility is not affected by our holding today."[19] As an example, a deputy sheriff asked a prisoner awaiting trial, "How's it going, Ashford?" Ashford answered with a statement that incriminated himself. The court held that the deputy could testify about Ashford's incriminating statement.[20]

    Other examples of volunteered statements include cases in which the defendant surprised everyone by admitting while he was on the witness stand that he killed the victim,[21] the defendant walked into a police station and told the police that he had shot his wife,[22] and the defendant voluntarily stated that he had a gun under the front seat of his automobile.[23]

    The Maryland Court of Appeals pointed out that there is no privilege against inadvertent self-incrimination, or even stupid self-incrimination, but only against self-incrimination.[24] In that case, the defendant blurted out he had a lot of illegal drugs in his car.

3. "*General on-the-scene questioning* as to facts surrounding a crime or other general questioning of citizens in the fact-finding process is not affected by our holding. It is an act of responsible citizenship for individuals to give whatever information they may have to aid in law enforcement. In such situations the compelling atmosphere inherent in the process of in-custody interrogation is not necessarily present."[25] Consider the following examples:

    • When a deputy sheriff working in a jail saw one of two men held in a drunk tank lying on the floor in a pool of blood, he asked the other man sleeping on a wall bench, "What happened?" The man answered, "I killed the son of a bitch last night; he would not shut up." The Supreme Court of Utah held that the defendant's response was properly admitted in evidence.[26]

    • Minutes after a shooting occurred on a street, a police officer arrived at the scene. A young boy at the scene told the officer that the assailant had run away between two houses. The officer proceeded in that direction and saw a man step out of a doorway. The officer (who had his revolver out) asked the man if he had been involved in the shooting. The man answered, "Yeah, I shot him." After the man was arrested, the murder weapon was found in his pocket. The statement of the defendant and the weapon were held to be properly admitted in evidence by the Wisconsin Supreme Court.[27]

- In investigating crimes, peace officers are required to ask questions and talk to persons who are *material witnesses* to crimes. In some instances, the investigation could reveal that a material witness is the person who committed the crime. In the 1991 case of *Wallace v. State*,[28] it was held that an officer called to a store to investigate a forged check was not obligated to give *Miranda* warnings to Wallace, who was viewed as a material witness when questioned.

4. *Miranda* warnings are not required for investigative detentions (stop and inquiry) based on reasonable suspicion to believe that the person is committing, has committed, or is about to commit a crime. In the 1984 case of *Berkemer v. McCarty*,[29] the U.S. Supreme Court stated this rule as follows:

> Under the Fourth Amendment, we have held, a policeman who lacks probable cause but whose "observations lead him reasonably to suspect" that a particular person has committed, is committing, or is about to commit a crime, may detain that person briefly in order to "investigate the circumstances that provoke suspicion." *United States v. Brignoni-Ponce*, 422 U.S. 873, 881, 45 L.Ed.2d 607, 95 S.Ct. 2574 (1975). "[T]he stop and inquiry must be 'reasonably related in scope to the justification for their initiation.'" *Ibid.* [quoting *Terry v. Ohio, supra*, at 29, 20 L.Ed.2d 889, 88 S.Ct. 1868]. Typically, this means that the officer may ask the detainee a moderate number of questions to determine his identity and to try to obtain information confirming or dispelling the officer's suspicions. But the detainee is not obliged to respond. And, unless the detainee's answers provide the officer with probable cause to arrest him, he must then be released. The comparatively non-threatening character of detentions of this sort explains the absence of any suggestion in our opinions that Terry stops are subject to the dictates of *Miranda*.

5. *Miranda* warnings are not required in "ordinary traffic stops." The U.S. Supreme Court also ruled in *Berkemer v. McCarty*[30] that an investigative stop and a traffic stop are similar in that both have "noncoercive aspect(s)," with traffic stops usually being temporary, brief, and public. The Court ruled that "persons temporarily detained pursuant to (traffic) stops are not 'in custody' for the purposes of *Miranda*." The reasons for this ruling were explained as follows by the U.S. Supreme Court:

> Two features of an ordinary traffic stop mitigate the danger that a person questioned will be induced "to speak where he would not otherwise do so freely," *Miranda v. Arizona*. First, detention of a motorist pursuant to a traffic stop is presumptively temporary and brief. The vast majority of roadside detentions last only a few minutes. A motorist's expectations, when he sees a policeman's light flashing behind him, are that he will be obliged to spend a short period of time answering questions and waiting while the officer checks his license and registration, that he may then be given a citation, but that in the end he most likely will be allowed to continue on his way. In this respect, questioning incident to an ordinary traffic stop is quite different from stationhouse interrogation, which frequently is prolonged, and in which the detainee often is aware that questioning will continue until he provides his interrogators the answers they seek.

Second, circumstances associated with the typical traffic stop are not such that the motorist feels completely at the mercy of the police. To be sure, the aura of authority surrounding an armed, uniformed officer and the knowledge that the officer has some discretion in deciding whether to issue a citation, in combination, exert some pressure on the detainee to respond to questions. But other aspects of the situation substantially offset these forces. Perhaps most importantly, the typical traffic stop is public, at least to some degree. Passersby, on foot or in other cars, witness the interaction of officer and motorist. This exposure to public view both reduces the ability of an unscrupulous policeman to use illegitimate means to elicit self-incriminating statements and diminishes the motorist's fear that, if he does not cooperate, he will be subjected to abuse. The fact that the detained motorist typically is confronted by only one or at most two policemen further mutes his sense of vulnerability. In short, the atmosphere surrounding an ordinary traffic stop is substantially less "police dominated" than that surrounding the kinds of interrogation at issue in *Miranda* itself, and in the subsequent cases in which we have applied *Miranda*.

If a motorist (or a passenger in a vehicle) is arrested or taken into custody, however, *Miranda* becomes applicable. In the *Berkemer v. McCarty* case, the defendant should have been given the *Miranda* warnings after his arrest for drunken driving and before police interrogation after his arrest.

6. Routine booking questions are exempt from *Miranda*'s coverage. In the 1990 case of *Pennsylvania v. Muniz*,[31] the U.S. Supreme Court held that questions and answers as to "name, address, height, weight, eye color, date of birth, and current age—did not constitute custodial interrogation … (and) fall within a *routine booking question exception*, which exempts from *Miranda*'s coverage questions to secure the 'biographical data necessary to complete booking or pretrial service' 873 F.2d 180, 181 n.2." The U.S. Supreme Court pointed out with approval that the trial court in the *Muniz* case held that these questions were "requested for recordkeeping purposes only" and therefore "appear reasonably related to the police's administrative concerns."

   Booking questions about employment are also routinely asked and were sustained in the 1991 case of *People v. Abdelmassih*.[32] In the 1991 case of *State v. Mallozzi*,[33] the defendant made incriminating statements during the booking process after an FBI agent informed him of the charges against him. Because no questions other than routine booking questions were asked, the defendant's statements were admissible in evidence against him.

7. The *Miranda* warnings are not imposed on private persons who ask questions. For example, a family member asks, "Why did you do it, Joe?" Or an employer or other private person asks questions that could produce incriminating answers. Because *Miranda* is not required of private persons, any incriminating statement could be admitted as evidence in both civil and criminal cases. The following cases further illustrate:

   • A shoplifter made incriminating statements in response to questions from a store clerk. The Georgia Court of Appeals held that *Miranda* is applicable only to law enforcement officers; the store clerk was not required to give the *Miranda* warnings before questioning.[34]

   • A journalist gathering material for a book visited John Joubert in a Nebraska prison where Joubert was sentenced to death. Joubert made statements incriminating himself in the death of an 11-year-old boy in Maine. The Supreme Court of Maine held that the admissions were admissible because the journalist was not acting as an agent of the police. No *Miranda* warnings were given or required.[35]

- Most courts hold that private security officers do not come under the *Miranda* requirements. The state of New York courts held:

  To hold that the conduct of [a] private store detective was governed by *Miranda* would be an extravagant expansion of the intended scope of that decision, and would constitute an unnecessary and unauthorized interference with the right of a merchant to protect his property by lawful means. *Id.* at 287, 480 N.W.2d at 1068, 491 N.Y.S.2d at 285. The duty of giving "*Miranda* warnings" is limited to employees of governmental agencies whose function is to enforce the law, or to those acting for such law enforcement agencies by direction of the agencies; ...

- In also holding that *Miranda* does not apply to private security persons, the Virginia Court of Appeals reviewed state court cases with similar rulings in the 1991 case of *Mier v. Commonwealth.*[36]

8. *Miranda* warnings are not required when border agents question aliens seeking admission into this country. Although aliens being questioned at a border about their admission into this country are in "custody," most courts have held that official, routine questioning of the alien does not require a *Miranda* warning, even if that questioning results in incriminating statements from the alien.[37] In the 2006 case of *United States v. Kiam,*[38] the Third Circuit Court of Appeals concluded that the exception should be expanded beyond "routine" questioning and held that any questioning of aliens related to their admissibility did not require a *Miranda* warning. However, the court stated that when questioning is directed solely at a potential criminal investigation, the warning must be given.

9. The *Miranda* requirements have been held *not* to be applicable in the following cases:

- Offenders (sexual and other offenses) who are required by conditions of their probation or parole to participate in treatment programs and be truthful "in all matters" or risk revocation of their parole or probation do not have to get *Miranda* warnings. In the 1984 case of *Minnesota v. Murphy,*[39] Murphy was in such a program and confessed to an unsolved rape and murder. The U.S. Supreme Court held his admissions could be used to sustain his conviction.

- Undercover officers conducting investigations while not disclosing their true identity do not have to give *Miranda* warnings and do not have to identify themselves. See the 1990 case of *Illinois v. Perkins,*[40] where an undercover officer went into a prison cell, and the 1966 case of *Hoffa v. United States,*[41] where an undercover agent was obtaining information against former Teamsters Union President James Hoffa.

- When a probation or parole officer is doing a presentence interview on behalf of the trial court, it has been repeatedly held that *Miranda* is not applicable.[42]

CHALLENGES TO MIRANDA

Can the U.S. Congress Overturn Miranda?

Two years after the Miranda decision, opponents to the Miranda rule attached a provision to a bill that overturned Miranda when it became law. The 1968 enactment provided that if a confession or incriminating statement was voluntary, then the confession or statement should be admitted as evidence in federal criminal cases whether Miranda had been complied with or not.

U.S. presidents for more than thirty years have instructed the Justice Department to ignore this law [18 U.S.C. section 3501] until 1999, when a federal appeals court in Richmond, Virginia, ruled in the case of Dickerson v. United States that the U.S. Congress was free to overturn Miranda and had done so in section 3501.

In the Dickerson case, Dickerson's incriminating statements about his involvement in a bank robbery were suppressed because he had not received a Miranda warning. The U.S. Court of Appeals in Virginia ruled that because the statements were voluntary, they were admissible under section 3501. The U.S. Supreme Court reversed in Dickerson v. United States [530 U.S. 428 (2000)], holding that the statements were not admissible and that the Miranda doctrine could not be overruled by the U.S. Congress:

> Miranda has become embedded in routine police practices [in the United States] to the point where the warnings have become part of our national culture ... we conclude that Miranda announced a constitutional rule that Congress may not supersede legislatively.

Is a Question First/Warn Later Procedure Permissible Under Miranda?

In the 1985 case of Oregon v. Elstad [470 U.S. 298], police inadvertently failed to give the Miranda warnings. After the defendant confessed (the "cat was out of the bag"), the police complied with the Miranda rule, and the defendant confessed again. The U.S. Supreme Court held that because both confessions were made voluntarily, the second confession was admissible as evidence and affirmed the defendant's conviction.

In the 2004 case of Missouri v. Seibert [542 U.S. 600, 124 S.Ct. 2601], the U.S. Supreme Court held that the police's deliberate failure to give the Miranda warnings to a woman suspected of arson before questioning her made the resulting confession inadmissible. After Seibert confessed to the arson, the police turned on a tape recorder and complied with the Miranda rule, reminding the defendant of her incriminating statements.

Because the police admitted to routinely using this two-step interrogation technique in an effort to obtain confessions and incriminating statements, the Missouri Supreme Court reversed Seibert's conviction, calling the procedure an "end run" around Miranda.

The U.S. Supreme Court agreed and affirmed the Missouri Supreme Court, stating:

> Strategists dedicated to draining the substance out of Miranda cannot accomplish by training instructions what Dickerson held Congress could not do by statute. Because the question-first tactic effectively threatens to thwart Miranda's purpose of reducing the risk that a coerced confession would be admitted, and because the facts here do not reasonably support a conclusion that the warnings given could have served their purpose, Seibert's postwarning statements are inadmissible. 124 S.Ct. at 2613.

In the 2006 case of United States v. Gonzalez-Lauren [437 F.3d 1128 (11th Cir. 2006), cert. denied, 127 S.Ct. 146], the court held that investigators did not violate a defendant's Fifth Amendment rights when they intentionally delayed giving the Miranda warnings until they had shown the defendant all the evidence they had gathered connecting him to a murder. The investigators did not ask the defendant any questions designed to elicit incriminating statements, the court noted, which made the case different from Missouri v. Seibert. The defendant's subsequent waiver of his rights and confession after the Miranda warning were upheld.

THE PUBLIC SAFETY EXCEPTION AND THE RESCUE DOCTRINE AS EXCEPTIONS TO *MIRANDA* REQUIREMENTS

The *Miranda* requirements must be complied with if answers to police questions are to be admitted into evidence in criminal cases. Two exceptions permit police questioning before *Miranda* warnings are given.

The Public Safety Exception The U.S. Supreme Court established the *public safety exception* in the 1984 case of *New York v. Quarles.*[43] In that case, an armed rapist was fleeing police in New York City. The man fled to an A&P supermarket, carrying a gun. He hid the gun somewhere in the store before being captured by police officers. After the man was handcuffed, he was asked where the gun was without being given the *Miranda* warnings. The suspect (Quarles) nodded in the direction of some empty cartons and answered, "The gun is over there." In addition to rape, Quarles was convicted of criminal possession of a weapon. The weapon and the statement by Quarles were used as evidence against him. In affirming the convictions and creating the public safety exception to *Miranda*, the U.S. Supreme Court held:

> The exception will not be difficult for police officers to apply because in each case it will be circumscribed by the exigency which justifies it. We think police officers can and will distinguish almost instinctively between questions necessary to secure their own safety or the safety of the public and questions designed solely to elicit testimonial evidence from a suspect.
>
> The facts of this case clearly demonstrate that distinction and an officer's ability to recognize it. Officer Kraft asked only the question necessary to locate the missing gun before advising respondent of his rights. It was only after securing the loaded revolver and giving the warnings that he continued with investigatory questions about the ownership and place of purchase of the gun. The exception which we recognize today, far from complicating the thought processes and the on-the-scene judgments of police officers, will simply free them to follow their legitimate instincts when confronting situations presenting a danger to the public safety.

The public safety exception to *Miranda* has been used many times since it was created in 1984. Following are a few of the many cases where it was held that police questions before giving suspects *Miranda* warnings were prompted by a concern for public safety:

- A man suspected of stealing vials of freeze-dried bacteria that could cause bubonic plague was questioned about the location of the vials.[44]
- Prior to executing search warrants for illegal drugs, defendants were asked whether they had weapons.[45]
- Police arriving on an emergency call for help asked White what had happened. White stated that he cut his girlfriend's throat.[46]
- Other examples are police questions about the location of the defendant's gun,[47] questions about the location of a gun in a motel room that concerned only the safety of the police,[48] and questions about the location of a gun in a motel room out of concern for people in nearby rooms.[49]

WHEN DOES A PERSON HAVE A RIGHT TO AN ATTORNEY?

A person may hire an attorney at any time, and generally may have that attorney present when dealing with law enforcement officers. There are only two situations in which the government may not proceed unless a person either has an attorney or elects to waive the right to have an attorney present. Those two situations are listed below. In those situations, if the person is indigent and lacks the resources to hire a lawyer, the government must provide a lawyer at the government's expense. Some situations where an attorney may be present, though not required, are also listed.

A Person Has a Right to an Attorney

1. During a custodial interrogation, when a person is in custody and a government official seeks to question the person regarding a crime, the right to an attorney is guaranteed by the Fifth and Sixth Amendments.

(Note that if the person is not in custody and is free to leave the police presence, or if the person is in custody but there is no attempt to interrogate the person, there is no right to an attorney. See *Miranda v. Arizona*, 384 U.S. 436 (1966).)

2. "... [O]nce a criminal prosecution is commenced ... whether by formal charge, indictment, preliminary hearing, or arraignment," the defendant has a right to an attorney at all "critical stages" of the prosecution under the Sixth Amendment. See *Rothgery v. Gillespie County*, 128 S.Ct. 2578 (2008), discussed below.

No Right to an Attorney Exists, Although One May Be Present

During voluntary conversations between a law officer and a private citizen.

During a traffic stop (speeding, for example).

During an investigative detention based on reasonable suspicion or probable cause.

During identification proceedings (showups or photo viewing).

During routine booking procedures after arrest.

During appearances before a prosecuting attorney.

During an appearance before a grand jury or a "John Doe" jury.

When a person is ordered by either the police or the prosecutor to appear in the office of the prosecutor. (In many of these situations there is a high likelihood that the prosecutor will seek criminal charges.)

Practices Required by State Law, Court Decisions, or Established Procedure

By long, well-established practice, persons arrested are permitted to make a telephone call to inform family, friends, or an attorney of their arrest. Depending on the criminal charge, it may be possible to immediately post bail and obtain the arrested person's release. If the suspect is held on a serious charge, bail is generally not determined until after an initial appearance before a judge, magistrate, or court commissioner.

It is required practice to advise a suspect appearing in a lineup that he or she has the right to have an attorney or another observer present to observe the lineup and note any possible violations of the suspect's rights during the lineup.

Persons appearing before a prosecuting attorney for possible criminal charges often bring an attorney with them, as do witnesses appearing before grand juries or legislative committees. Attorneys are not permitted to appear in a grand jury hearing but must wait outside the chambers where the grand jury is sitting. Witnesses called before a grand jury are usually given ample time to consult with their attorney.

The California Rescue Doctrine   The *California rescue doctrine* was adopted in the 1965 case of *People v. Modesto.*[50] California officers asked questions of an arrested suspect because of their concern for the safety of a missing or kidnapped victim. The defendant's statements were admitted even though he had not been given the *Miranda* warnings.

Other states have adopted this exception. The 1978 California case of *People v. Riddle*[51] was appealed to the U.S. Supreme Court, where review was denied.[52] *People v. Riddle* holds that *Miranda* warnings are excused when the following conditions exist:

1. Urgency of need in that no other course of action promises relief
2. The possibility of saving human life by rescuing a person whose life is in danger
3. Rescue as the primary purpose and motive of the interrogators[53]

In the 1992 case of *State v. Provost,*[54] the defendant, who smelled of gasoline, walked into a police station and asked to be locked up because he had burned his wife. Officers were concerned about the safety of the woman and asked where she was. Because the defendant was not coherent, he was placed in handcuffs after he agreed to take the officers to his wife. His statements and evidence of the murder were held admissible by the Minnesota Supreme Court, which adopted the rescue doctrine, noting that it was similar to but not the same as the public safety exception to the *Miranda* requirements.

WHEN DOES A CRIMINAL PROSECUTION COMMENCE?

The right to an attorney guaranteed by the Sixth Amendment is tied to a "criminal prosecution." Prior to the commencement of a criminal prosecution, the right to an attorney is not guaranteed by the Sixth Amendment. It thus becomes important to determine precisely when a criminal case "commences" because it is at that moment that the right to an attorney is triggered. Case law from the U.S. Supreme Court had tied commencement of a criminal case to the point where the state has "committed" itself to the prosecution of the crime. Lower federal and state courts found this definition of "commenced" unclear, and in the following 2008 case the U.S. Supreme Court addressed that question.

Rothgery v. Gillespie County

United States Supreme Court, 128 S.Ct. 2578 (2008)

The right to counsel guranteed by the Sixth Amendment applies in any "criminal prosecution." If the defendant cannot afford counsel, the government must appoint counsel once a criminal prosecution is commenced. The U.S. Supreme Court has said that a criminal prosecution is commenced by the initiation of adversary criminal proceedings, whether by formal charge, indictment, preliminary hearing, or arraignment. It is at that point, the Court stated, that the state has committed itself to prosecuting an arrestee, and the person is "immersed in the intricacies of substantive and procedural criminal law."[55]

In *Rothgery* the Court was called upon to clarify what it meant in earlier holdings that tied the attachment of the Sixth Amendment right to counsel to the state's "commitment" to prosecute. In the *Rothgery* case Texas police mistakenly believed that an indigent person was a convicted felon, who was thus in violation of state gun laws. The person was arrested and brought before a magistrate to determine whether probable cause existed for the arrest. Finding that probable cause existed, the magistrate informed the defendant of the accusations made by the police officers and set bail for his release. Unable to make bail, the defendant was sent to jail. Some months later a grand jury indicted the defendant, at which time appointed counsel began representing him. The attorney quickly discovered that the police had mistaken the defendant for another person. The attorney got the defendant released and the indictment dismissed.

The defendant sued the county that employed the police officers who arrested him under the civil rights laws, contending that he should have been given appointed counsel after his appearance before the county magistrate, and that if he had, the attorney would have discovered the mistaken identity and he would not have spent several weeks in jail. The county contended that the Sixth Amendment did not apply to the appearance before the magistrate because the prosecution attorney did not participate in that hearing and was not aware of the officers' accusations. As a result, the county contended, the prosecution had not yet made a "commitment" to prosecute the defendant, and the right to counsel had not attached. The U.S. District Court agreed and dismissed the civil rights action, and the Fifth Circuit Court of Appeals affirmed the dismissal. The U.S. Supreme Court granted certiorari and reversed.

The Court rejected the county's argument that because the prosecutor did not participate in the initial hearing before the magistrate, the "commitment" to prosecute had not been made. The Court noted that in its prior decisions on attachment of the right to counsel, the prosecutor's involvement was never used as a relevant fact, much less a controlling one. Rather, the Court held, the government's commitment is sufficiently concrete when the accusations prompt an appearance before a judicial officer and constraints are placed on the person's liberty. Thus, even though the prosecution had made no decision to prosecute at the hearing before the magistrate, a criminal case "commenced" at that point and the Sixth Amendment right to counsel was triggered. At that point, the Court reasoned, the individual is faced with the prosecutorial forces of the state and is entitled to appointed counsel.

The Court also noted that the Texas procedure of appointing counsel only after a formal indictment was in the distinct minority, and that forty-three states appointed counsel after the initial hearing before a judicial officer, with or without formal changes being filed.[56] The Court thus reversed the lower courts and remanded the case to the district court for a trial on the civil rights claims.

SILENCE, *MIRANDA*, AND IMPEACHMENT

If a defendant elects to assert his Fifth Amendment right to remain silent, the prosecution cannot later use the fact of the defendant's silence as proof of substantive guilt or for purposes of impeachment. In *Doyle v. Ohio*,[57] the U.S. Supreme Court held that such use would violate the Due Process Clause. In *Anderson v. Charles*,[58] however, the Court refused to extend the rule in *Doyle* to a case where the defendant waived his *Miranda* rights and subsequently made a post-arrest statement that proved to be inconsistent with his trial testimony. The Court saw nothing wrong

EVIDENCE OBTAINED BY THREATS OF LOSS OF A JOB OR LICENSE

When complaints are filed against a law enforcement officer, lawyer, teacher, doctor, or another person with a license, it is common practice to request that a written response to the complaint be submitted. Failure to submit a written response could result in disciplinary action. Must police officers, lawyers, teachers, doctors, and others face disciplinary action or the loss of their licenses if they do not incriminate themselves?

This question was before the U.S. Supreme Court in the 1967 case of *Spevack v. Klein* [87 S.Ct. 625], where a lawyer lost his license to practice law. The Supreme Court held:

> Lawyers are not excepted from the words "No person ... shall be compelled in any criminal case to be a witness against himself"; and we can imply no exception. Like the school teacher in *Slochower v. Board of Higher Education of City of New York*, 350 U.S. 551, ... and the policemen in *Garrity v. State of New Jersey*, 87 S.Ct. 616, ... lawyers also enjoy first-class citizenship.

Law enforcement agencies, employers, and licensing agencies can obtain reports concerning job-related incidents by stating on the request for information that answers provided will not be used as evidence in criminal prosecutions [see the case of *Broderick v. Police Commissioner of Boston*, 330 N.E.2d 199 (Mass. 1975)].

CAN THE FAILURE TO GIVE *MIRANDA* WARNINGS BE THE BASIS FOR A CIVIL LAWSUIT?

The 2003 Case of *Chavez v. Martinez*, 123 S.Ct. 1994

Two police officers stopped Martinez while he was riding his bicycle at night. During a subsequent search, a struggle ensued. One officer shouted, "He's got my gun," and the other officer shot Martinez several times. Martinez was brought to a hospital, and while he was receiving emergency treatment, a police supervisor, Chavez, questioned him about the altercation, including questions that related to criminal actions Martinez may have taken. Martinez was not given his *Miranda* warnings.

No criminal charges were brought against Martinez, and his statements made to Chavez were never used in any prosecution against him. Martinez brought a civil action against Chavez under federal civil rights laws, alleging that Chavez violated his Fifth Amendment rights by questioning him without *Miranda* warnings. The Ninth Circuit Court of Appeals held that Martinez's Fifth Amendment rights had been violated.

The U.S. Supreme Court reversed, holding that no Fifth Amendment rights had been violated because the statements were never used in a criminal case brought against Martinez. Noting that the Fifth Amendment provides that "No person ... shall be compelled in any criminal case ..." to be a witness against himself, the Court concluded that in the absence of such a criminal case, the Fifth Amendment did not apply. Thus, the police interrogation violated neither the *Miranda* rule nor the Fifth Amendment. The Court also noted that if the police use torture or other abuse in questioning a suspect but never attempt to use the resulting statements in a criminal case, the Fourteenth Amendment would provide a remedy for the torture or other abuse inflicted on the suspect.

WHEN DOES A CONVERSATION WITH A DEFENDANT BECOME "INTERROGATION"?

It can sometimes be difficult to determine whether conversations with a defendant in custody constitute "interrogation" requiring a *Miranda* warning. For example, in *Drury v. State* [793 A.2d 567 (Md. Ct. App. 2002)], police took a defendant to the police station for questioning concerning a burglary. The door of a store was pried open with a tire iron, which was found near the crime scene. Before the defendant was advised of his *Miranda* rights, police showed the defendant the tire iron and some other articles found near the crime scene and told the defendant the items were to be sent out for fingerprints. The defendant then made incriminating statements, which were used against him at his trial. On appeal, the court held that showing the defendant the evidence found near the crime scene was the functional equivalent of interrogation, since the police should have known that it would evoke an incriminating response from the defendant.

Other courts have reached the opposite result. In *United States v. Allen* [247 F.3d 741 (8th Cir. 2001)], the court held that it was not interrogation to inform the defendant in custody that three of four witnesses identified the defendant as present at the scene of a crime; the court said that information was merely describing the state of the investigation.

---

with impeaching a defendant who made voluntary statements after receiving the *Miranda* warnings.

After *Anderson*, courts have permitted prosecutors to compare statements given by defendants after a *Miranda* waiver with their testimony at trial, and to comment on omissions in the post-*Miranda* statements. Prosecutors can use the fact that the original statement omitted details that were subsequently included in testimony at trial to impeach the credibility of the trial testimony.

In the 2008 case of *United States v. Caruto*,[59] however, the Ninth Circuit Court of Appeals determined that there was a limit on such impeachment use in any case where a defendant invokes the Fifth Amendment right to remain silent after he or she has waived *Miranda* rights and made an initial statement. In *Caruto*, the defendant was taken into custody when border agents found 75 pounds of cocaine in her vehicle. She initially waived her *Miranda* rights and gave a limited statement to the agents, in which she said she had been told by "someone" to drive the vehicle to Los Angeles. After a few minutes of questioning, she invoked her rights and the interrogation stopped. At her trial, her testimony identified in more detail the circumstances under which she claimed she was driving the vehicle. The prosecution was permitted to highlight the omission of such detail from her earlier, post-*Miranda* statements, and she was convicted of drug offenses.

On appeal, the Court concluded that due process was violated when the prosecution was permitted to highlight the omissions in the defendant's initial statement because the defendant could not explain why her early statement was less detailed than her trial testimony without disclosing that she had invoked her *Miranda* rights. That would invite the jury to "draw meaning from silence," which is not permitted, the Court concluded.

THE SIXTH AMENDMENT RIGHT TO COUNSEL
AND THE *MASSIAH* LIMITATION

Massiah limitation The holding that, after a person has been charged with a crime, law officers cannot question the person regarding that crime without the person's attorney present.

Until a person is formally charged with a crime, the only criteria used to determine whether a confession or incriminating statements can be used are the voluntariness test and the *Miranda* requirements. After a suspect is formally charged with a crime, it is "entirely proper [for law officers] to continue an investigation of the … criminal activities of the defendant and his alleged confederates."[60]

However, law enforcement officers must remember that "once adversary proceedings have commenced against an individual, he has a right to legal representation when the government interrogates him."[61] This is the *Massiah* limitation. Failure to observe a defendant's Sixth Amendment right to an attorney by questioning the defendant without the attorney present violates that amendment, as the following cases held:

Massiah v. United States

United States Supreme Court, 377 U.S. 201, 84 S.Ct. 1199 (1964)

The defendant (a merchant seaman) and a man named Colson were charged with importing, concealing, and facilitating the sale of cocaine. The defendants were indicted for these offenses and released on bail. A few days later, and without Massiah's knowledge, Colson agreed to cooperate with the federal agents and permitted a radio transmitter to be installed under the front seat of his automobile. Then, according to a prearranged plan, Colson carried on a lengthy conversation with Massiah while federal agents listened in another car a short distance away. At Massiah's trial, one of the federal agents testified as to the incriminating statements he overheard by means of the radio transmitter. Although this investigative technique and procedure are a permissible means of obtaining evidence before suspects are indicted or charged, the U.S. Supreme Court held that Massiah's Sixth Amendment rights were violated because he had already been indicted and was awaiting trial. In reversing Massiah's conviction, the Court held that:

> [T]he [defendant] was denied the basic protection of [the Sixth Amendment] when there was used against him at his trial evidence of his own incriminating words, which federal agents had deliberately elicited from him after he had been indicted and in the absence of his counsel.

Brewer v. Williams[62]

United States Supreme Court, 430 U.S. 387, 97 S.Ct. 1232 (1977)

Williams was arrested and charged in Davenport, Iowa, for the abduction of a 10-year-old girl. Because the crime was committed in Des Moines, Iowa, Williams had to be transported 160 miles back to Des Moines.

The police officers driving Williams to Des Moines were told by the lawyer appointed to represent Williams that they were not to question Williams without his presence. Williams had stated to the officers, "When I get to Des Moines … I will tell you the whole story." The officers, however, believed that the little girl was dead, and one of the officers persuaded Williams to tell the officers where he had buried the girl's body.

The trial court allowed all the evidence obtained during the automobile trip, holding that Williams had waived his Sixth Amendment right to an attorney. The U.S. Supreme Court held that it was error to use the evidence of how the girl's body was recovered. In ordering a new trial, the Supreme Court held:

> [T]he clear rule of *Massiah* is that once adversary proceedings have commenced against an individual, he has a right to legal representation when the government interrogates him. It thus requires no wooden or technical application of the *Massiah* doctrine to conclude that Williams was entitled to the assistance of counsel guaranteed to him by the Sixth and Fourteenth Amendments.

Texas v. Cobb

United States Supreme Court, 121 S.Ct. 1335 (2001)

While Cobb was under arrest for an unrelated offense, he confessed to a home burglary. But Cobb denied knowledge of the disappearance of a woman and a child from the home. He was indicted for the burglary, and a lawyer was appointed to represent him. Cobb later confessed to his father that he killed the woman and child. His father contacted the police, and the police questioned Cobb without the presence of his attorney but after obtaining a waiver to Cobb's *Miranda* rights. Cobb confessed to the double murder and was convicted of capital murder and was sentenced to death.

On appeal, Cobb contended that his Sixth Amendment rights were violated because his lawyer was not present during the police interrogation that led to his confession to the double murders.

The U.S. Supreme Court held that the Sixth Amendment right to counsel is "offense specific" (limited here to the burglary Cobb was charged with) and was not "factually related" (to the two murders related to the burglary). The Court ruled "burglary and capital murder are not the same offense.... The Sixth Amendment right to counsel did not bar police from interrogating (Cobb) regarding the murders, and (Cobb's) confession was therefore admissible."

Fellers v. United States

United States Supreme Court, 540 U.S. 519 (2004)

In this case the Supreme Court held that once the Sixth Amendment's right to counsel attached, statements made by the defendant must be excluded if police "deliberately elicit" incriminating information from the defendant. After the defendant was indicted on drug charges, police went to his house and mentioned the names of other people named in the indictment. The defendant then stated that he had used drugs with those people. The defendant also later executed a valid rights waiver. The Supreme Court held that because the police admittedly went to the defendant's house to "discuss" the indictment, they violated the "deliberate elicitation" rule, and the statements had to be excluded under the Sixth Amendment.

THE *BRUTON* RULE

Major crimes are often committed by more than one person. For example, three men commit an armed robbery. One of the men, X, is apprehended and makes statements incriminating himself and the other two men (Y and Z). On the basis of this information, arrest warrants and/or search warrants are obtained, and Y and Z are taken into custody.

If the victim and witnesses can identify all three men, the state now has a good case to go to trial. But if witnesses can identify only X and the state cannot otherwise incriminate Y and Z, a *Bruton* problem is going to occur when X's lawyer becomes aware of the situation.

X's confession and incriminating statements can be used as evidence against X but cannot be used against Y unless X takes the witness stand and incriminates Y. Y has a Sixth Amendment right to be confronted with the witness against him or her.

But X does not have to take the witness stand and cannot be forced to incriminate himself and his friend. His confession can be used only against him unless X

Bruton rule The rule that a criminal trial may not hear a confession or incriminating statement against a defendant that was made by another party to the crime without producing the speaker.

takes the witness stand. This is where the bargaining begins. To get around this *Bruton* rule, the prosecutor ordinarily has two options available:

1. Make concessions to *X* (lower or drop criminal charges or sentence concessions) to get him to become a state witness and incriminate himself and *Y* and *Z*.
2. If *X* will not cooperate or if it is decided that concessions should not be made, drop the criminal charges against *Y* and *Z* and proceed to trial against *X* (failure to cooperate could result in a greater sentence).

In situations where there is sufficient evidence to go to trial against *Y* and *Z*, two additional options are available:

1. Try the defendants in two trials, which would permit using *X*'s confession in the trial against him.
2. Redact (reduce or edit) *X*'s statements to eliminate any references to *Y* and *Z* and use the statements in a joint trial.[63]

The 1968 *Bruton* case, which established this rule of law, follows.

Bruton v. United States

United States Supreme Court, 391 U.S. 123, 88 S.Ct. 1620 (1968)

The defendant (Bruton) and a co-defendant (Evans) were tried together and convicted of armed postal robbery. Evans had confessed and admitted that he had an accomplice whom he would not name. The confession was used as evidence against Evans, and the trial judge "instructed the jury that although Evans' confession was competent evidence against Evans it was inadmissible hearsay against petitioner (Bruton) and therefore had to be disregarded in determining petitioner's (Bruton's) guilt or innocence."

In reversing Bruton's conviction, the Supreme Court held that:

> Here the introduction of Evans' confession posed a substantial threat to petitioner's right to confront the witnesses against him, and this is a hazard we cannot ignore. Despite the concededly clear instructions to the jury to disregard Evans' inadmissible hearsay evidence inculpating petitioner, in the context of a joint trial we cannot accept limiting instructions as an adequate substitute for petitioner's constitutional right of cross-examination. The effect is the same as if there had been no instruction at all....
> Reversed.

QUESTIONING PEOPLE IN JAIL OR PRISON, INCLUDING USING INFORMANTS AND UNDERCOVER AGENTS

There are more than 2 million inmates in U.S. prisons and jails. The presence of a career or violent criminal in a jail or prison presents an opportunity for law officers to investigate and attempt to obtain evidence about unsolved crimes or additional evidence about crimes for which the person is incarcerated. There now is a substantial body of federal and state case law detailing the application of the four major tests (discussed in the box on page 258) for evidence obtained from prisoners.

An article entitled "Constitutional Rights to Counsel During Interrogation" in the September 2002 *FBI Law Enforcement Bulletin* points out the similarity between questioning by an undercover law enforcement officer and questioning by a cell mate informant or an undercover law officer posing as a prisoner. *Miranda* warnings are not required in either situation because, as the article points out, "(as) the subjects of the questioning do not know that the government is interrogating them, they cannot feel the coerciveness *Miranda* was designed to protect against. Consequently, the practice of using cell mate informants does not contravene the *Miranda* rule." The following U.S. Supreme Court decisions are applications of this principle in cases involving informants, cell mates, and other prison questioning tactics.

Case	Type of Questioning	Ruling
Kuhlmann v. Wilson, 477 U.S. 436, 106 S.Ct. 2616 (1986)	An informant was placed in Wilson's jail cell and told only to listen and not to ask any questions. The informant complied with these directions.	"[T]he defendant must demonstrate that the police took some action, beyond merely listening, that was designed deliberately to elicit incriminating remarks."
United States v. Henry, 447 U.S. 264, 100 S.Ct. 2183 (1980)	Henry's cell mate deliberately elicited information about the bank robbery that Henry was charged with and for which he was awaiting trial.	The conviction was reversed because the testimony of the cell mate violated Henry's Sixth Amendment right to counsel (*Massiah* violation).
Illinois v. Perkins, 496 U.S. 292, 110 S.Ct. 2394 (1990)	Perkins was in prison for assault. An undercover agent was placed in his cell to gain information about an unsolved murder. Perkins bragged about committing the murder when asked if he had ever "done" anyone. It was held that *Miranda* warnings were not required.	The Court held that: "The use of undercover agents is a recognized law enforcement technique, often employed in the prison context to detect violence against correctional officials or inmates, as well as for the purposes served here. The interests protected by *Miranda* are not implicated in these cases, and the warnings are not required to safeguard the constitutional rights of inmates who make voluntary statements."
Arizona v. Fulminante, 499 U.S. 279, 111 S.Ct. 1246 (1991)	A paid informant promised to protect the defendant from other inmates in the prison if he confessed to a murder. The defendant admitted he killed his 11-year-old stepdaughter.	It was held that the confession was coerced because there was a threat of physical violence unless the defendant confessed. However, because of the amount of other incriminating evidence in the case, the use of the confession, even if improper, might have been harmless error.
Maine v. Moulton, 106 S.Ct. 477 (1985)	Moulton was in jail for burglary and theft. Incriminating statements of these crimes were obtained by recording his conversations with an undercover cell mate.	The state could intercept conversations of other uncharged offenses but not of the crime the defendant was in jail for because of Sixth Amendment violation of right to an attorney.

Case	Type of Questioning	Ruling
Bradley v. Ohio, 541 N.E.2d 78 (Ohio 1989), *review denied,* 497 U.S. 1011, 110 S.Ct. 3258 (1990)	After the murder of a prison employee, a strip search of inmates in the area began. Blood was seen on the defendant's clothes; he was questioned and admitted that he committed the murder. No *Miranda* warnings were given.	Ohio courts held that it was "on-the-scene questioning," and this ruling was let stand by the U.S. Supreme Court.
Mathis v. United States, 391 U.S. 1, 88 S.Ct. 1503 (1968)	After a prison inmate falsely obtained income tax refunds, IRS agents came into the prison and questioned the defendant, who made incriminating statements.	Statements of the defendant could not be used because no *Miranda* warnings and waiver of rights occurred.

THE FOUR MAJOR TESTS CONTROLLING THE USE OF CONFESSIONS

1. The *voluntariness test*, which is used at all times during the criminal proceeding, requires that confessions be freely and voluntarily given. Violations occur when the government obtains a confession by means that overbear the will of the accused. The resulting confession would be excluded as evidence on the grounds that there was denial of due process law.

2. The *Miranda test* is required when (a) a suspect is in custody and (b) a law officer seeks to obtain incriminating information through questioning. *Miranda* must be complied with if answers are to be used as evidence. *Miranda* requires that:

   - Warnings (cautions) be given.
   - Suspect states or acknowledges that he or she understands the warnings.
   - Suspect waives rights and answers some or all questions.

3. After a suspect is charged with a crime, his Sixth Amendment right to an attorney must be observed. A *Massiah* violation could occur if a defendant who has already been charged with a crime is questioned in regard to that crime in violation of the defendant's Sixth Amendment right to an attorney. (See the U.S. Supreme Court cases of *Massiah v. United States* and *Brewer v. Williams* above.)

4. A confession by one suspect cannot be used against another suspect unless the second suspect has an opportunity to cross-examine the source of the accusation against him or her. A *Bruton violation* could occur unless:

   - The first suspect agrees to take the witness stand and testify.
   - The suspects are tried in separate trials.
   - The suspects are tried in one trial with reference to the second suspect taken out of the confession.
   - If all else fails, charges against the second suspect are dropped.

POLYGRAPH TEST RESULTS AS EVIDENCE

Persons charged or suspected of a crime cannot be ordered to take a polygraph (lie detector) test because such compulsion would violate their Fifth Amendment privilege against self-incrimination.[64] Nor does a defendant charged with a crime have a right to take a polygraph test to prove his or her innocence.[65]

It is reported that more than a million polygraph tests are given each year in the United States, however. Many of these tests are given by private companies, and some are administered within the criminal justice system. Prosecutors or a law enforcement agency might ask persons to voluntarily take a lie detector test to affirm statements they have made or to demonstrate their innocence.

In 1998 the U.S. Supreme Court noted that "(m)ost states maintain *per se* rules excluding polygraph evidence" and pointed out that "New Mexico is unique in making polygraph evidence generally admissible without prior stipulation of the parties and without significant restriction."[66] The reasons generally given by states for forbidding polygraph evidence entirely, or for placing severe restrictions on the use of polygraph evidence in criminal or civil trials, are:

- A belief that polygraph results are not sufficiently reliable and trustworthy
- The tendency of juries to rely too heavily on the report of polygraph examiners who appear as "expert" witnesses in criminal or civil cases and testify whether persons taking lie detector tests were truthful or not truthful
- The inability of trial courts to judge the competency of polygraph examiners

THE CONTROVERSY OVER POLYGRAPH TESTING

Polygraph testing is very controversial.[67] Persons who oppose the use of lie detector tests refer to them as degrading and humiliating. The late U.S. Senator Sam Ervin called the tests "twentieth-century witchcraft." On the other hand, defense lawyer F. Lee Bailey testified before the U.S. Congress in 1986 that polygraph tests are "useful investigative tools" and that when "properly run in good hands, it is a good test."

After it was discovered in 2001 that a high-ranking FBI agent (Robert Hanssen) had been selling secret information to Russia for more than 15 years, the FBI was criticized for not giving more lie detector tests to key FBI agents.

In 2002, however, a panel of leading scientists confirmed a U.S. congressional study done in 1983, with both studies reporting that lie detector tests do a poor job of identifying spies or other national security risks and are likely in security screenings to produce false accusations about innocent people. The 1983 congressional report stated that spies "may well be the most motivated and perhaps the best trained to avoid detection" by developing skills necessary to deceive polygraph machines and operators.

The 2002 panel of scientists acknowledged that their report would cause much debate and would probably reduce some of the tens of thousands of security lie detector tests that were being given yearly. The panel noted, however, that there is a place for polygraphs in the investigation of specific crimes.

Most states have refused to permit polygraph evidence under the rule announced in *Daubert v. Merrill Dow Pharmaceuticals Inc.*,[68] discussed in Chapter 18.

OTHER U.S. SUPREME COURT CASES ON THE LAW OF CONFESSIONS

Miranda

- The U.S. Supreme Court has "never insisted that *Miranda* warnings be given in the exact form described ..." [*Duckworth v. Eagan*, 492 U.S. 195, 109 S.Ct. 2875 (1989), and *California v. Prysock*, 453 U.S. 355, 101 S.Ct. 2806 (1981)].
- A defendant who states that he or she is willing to make an oral statement but is unwilling to make a written statement without his attorney has waived the rights stated in the *Miranda* warnings [*Connecticut v. Barrett*, 479 U.S. 523, 107 S.Ct. 828 (1987)].
- Undercover law enforcement officers do not have to give *Miranda* warnings and do not have to disclose their true identity [an undercover officer was placed in Perkins's prison cell block: *Illinois v. Perkins*, 110 S.Ct. 2394 (1990); an undercover officer pretended to be a friend of James Hoffa: *Hoffa v. United States*, 385 U.S. 293, 87 S.Ct. 408 (1966)].
- Police do not have to tell a suspect being interrogated that a lawyer hired by someone else has agreed to represent the suspect and has offered to be present [the suspect was about to confess to the brutal slaying of a young woman: *Moran v. Burbine*, 475 U.S. 412, 106 S.Ct. 1135 (1986)].
- Police do not trick a suspect when they fail to inform him as to all the crimes he may be questioned about [instead of questioning about only stolen firearms, ATF agents also questioned Spring about a murder to which he confessed: *Colorado v. Spring*, 479 U.S. 564, 107 S.Ct. 851 (1987)].

- Custody for *Miranda*'s purposes is based on facts and circumstances known to the suspect and not on the uncommunicated suspicions of the police [*Stansbury v. California*, 114 S.Ct. 1526 (1994)].
- "Interrogation" by police is not limited to express questioning; the term also includes "any words or actions on the part of the police ... that the police should know are reasonably likely to elicit an incriminating response from the suspect" [*Rhode Island v. Innis*, 446 U.S. 291 (1980)].
- A person may assert his constitutional rights at any time; he may answer questions if he wishes, but he may stop at any time. [*Miranda v. Arizona*, 384 U.S. 436, 86 S.Ct. 1602, 16 L.Ed.2d 694 (1966)].
- After a suspect lets the "cat out of the bag" and admits his guilt, *Miranda* warnings may be given (if they were not already given) and a second admission of guilt taken: "The relevant inquiry is whether, in fact, the second statement was also voluntarily made" [*Oregon v. Elstad*, 470 U.S. 298, 105 S.Ct. 1285 (1985)].
- Juveniles have the same rights as adults and should be given *Miranda* warnings prior to interrogation while in custody [*Fare v. Michael C.*, 442 U.S. 707, 99 S.Ct. 2560 (1979)].

Involuntary Confessions

A federal court reviewing the use of a confession in a state court is not bound by a state court's finding and has a "duty to make an independent evaluation of the record" [*Mincey v. Arizona*, 437 U.S. 385, 98 S.Ct. 2408 (1978); *Miller v. Fenton*, 474 U.S. 104, 106 S.Ct. 445 (1985)].

These states conclude that the scientific reliability of polygraph tests has not been adequately established. At least one state, New Mexico, permits the use of polygraph results in criminal cases by statute.[69] In the 2004 case of *Lee v. Martinez*,[70] the New Mexico Supreme Court held that polygraph results using the "control method" of questioning were sufficiently reliable to be admitted in criminal trials. Under the "control method," the examiner asks the examinee questions designed to generate psychological and physical responses, which then can be used to compare responses to questions involving the criminal conduct in question.

POLYGRAPH TESTING IN THE AMERICAN CRIMINAL JUSTICE SYSTEM

Polygraph testing is occasionally used by law enforcement agencies from the FBI to local police and sheriff departments, primarily for investigative and advisory purposes. Some defense lawyers also use lie detector tests in efforts to establish defense positions or arguments for their clients. Most states forbid the use of lie detector evidence in civil and criminal trials, but some states allow such evidence upon prior stipulation of both parties. The following cases and material illustrate some of the other uses of polygraph testing:

- While working undercover for the U.S. Air Force, Scheffer was required to periodically take drug tests and polygraph tests. When a drug test revealed the presence of an illegal drug in the airman's urine, a polygraph test was given, and it supported Scheffer's statement that he did not knowingly take the illegal drug. At Sheffer's trial for wrongfully using methamphetamine, the trial court excluded the evidence of the polygraph test because the military has a *pro se* ban on the use of polygraph evidence. The U.S. Supreme Court affirmed the ban on evidence of polygraph testing imposed on military courts, holding that "(s)tate and federal governments ... have a legitimate interest in ensuring that reliable evidence is presented to the trier of fact in criminal trials."[71]
- In the 1995 case of *Wood v. Bartholomew*,[72] the U.S. Supreme Court sustained the state of Washington's ban on the use of polygraph evidence even for impeachment purposes. In that case, a prosecutor failed to disclose that a witness had failed a polygraph test. The Court held that this failure did not deprive the defendant of "material" evidence under the *Brady* rule.
- In the 1991 case of *People v. Suly*,[73] the Supreme Court of California approved the use of a required lie detector test in a plea-bargain agreement. The defendant in this case was convicted of six murders and sentenced to death. His alleged accomplice who testified against him was required by the plea agreement to pass a lie detector test showing that she had not herself committed any of the murders.
- Governors and the president of the United States have the power to pardon and commute criminal sentences (including the death sentence). In 1992 the governor of Virginia ordered a polygraph test for Roger Keith Coleman, who faced execution in Virginia's electric chair. Coleman failed a lie detector test and was executed. His case received wide public attention.
- Several states have established polygraph testing as a condition of probation. In agreeing to the conditions of probation, defendants would agree to periodic polygraph examinations. If the defendant failed the test, the sentencing judge would reassess the case and could revoke probation and place the defendant in jail. Such programs are used in several states for sexual offenders and child abusers.

- A few courts have held that the results of lie detector tests could be used for establishing probable cause for search warrants. Courts that have approved of such use of polygraph tests are the Fifth Circuit Court of Appeals,[74] the Court of Appeals of the State of Washington,[75] and an Oregon court.[76] However, the Court of Appeals of Maryland held that the results of polygraph examinations could not be used to establish probable cause to arrest or charge a suspect with a crime.[77]

- In some instances, people make incriminating admissions or confessions before, during, or after a polygraph test is given. The polygraph operator or examiner may testify as to these statements if (1) the statements were voluntarily made and (2) the *Miranda* warnings were given and a waiver obtained in situations where the polygraph operator is a law enforcement officer. The *Miranda* warnings should also be given by private polygraph examiners if the suspect is in police custody.

VOICE SPECTROGRAPHY EVIDENCE

There have been many attempts to use voiceprints (spectrographic voice identification) as evidence over the years. Most courts that use the old *Frye* test (see Chapter 18 for a discussion of the *Frye* test) have held that spectrographic voice identification was inadmissible. The stricter and higher standards for the admission of scientific evidence established by the U.S. Supreme Court in the 1993 *Daubert* case (see Chapter 18 on scientific evidence) make it more difficult to use voiceprints as evidence unless dramatic improvements are made in voiceprints.

In seeking to use voiceprints as evidence, a lawyer is attempting to identify a speaker on a tape or wiretap recording. The technique could be used to evaluate the voice (or voices) heard on taped conversations and compare the results to other taped conversations of an identified person.

Some courts have admitted voice spectrography evidence—for example, *United States v. Smith*[78] and *United States v. Love*.[79] Those decisions were reached before the *Daubert* decision and may not accurately represent the current approach to voice spectrography. In a 2000 decision, the Eighth Circuit Court of Appeals excluded voice spectrography evidence offered by a defendant to prove that his voice was not the voice heard on a federal wiretap. The court found that the expert testimony did not meet the *Daubert* standards for reliability.[80]

SUMMARY

To be admissible as evidence, confessions and incriminating statements must be relevant, not in violation of the hearsay rule, and obtained in a manner that does not violate the exclusionary rule.

In addition, a violation of any of the following could cause the confession or incriminating statement to be held inadmissible as evidence:

1. The voluntariness test must be met, which requires that the confession or statement be freely and voluntarily given. If the government used means to overbear the will of the accused, a violation of this test has occurred.

2. If the suspect is in custody and the government seeks to obtain incriminating statements, the

following procedural safeguards must be established in court:

a. *Miranda* warnings were given.
b. The suspect understood the warnings.
c. The suspect waived his or her rights and answered some or all of the questions.

3. Once a suspect has been charged or indicted for a crime, the suspect's Sixth Amendment right to an attorney commences. Questioning a defendant about the crime with which she or he has been charged without the presence of the defense attorney is a Sixth Amendment *Massiah* violation. In states that follow the *Cobb* rule, defendants can be questioned about other crimes but not the crime charged. (See *Texas v. Cobb* in this chapter.)

4. A *Bruton* violation occurs if a confession by one suspect is used against another suspect unless the second suspect has an opportunity to cross-examine the source of the accusation against him or her.

CASE ANALYSIS

Read Appendix B, Finding and Analyzing Cases (p. 427). With these guidelines in mind, please continue with the Case Analysis selections for Chapter 12.

1. The corpus delicti rule has been used to prohibit convictions based only on a confession, without corroborating evidence. Should this rule be retained? In *State v. Mauchley* [67 P.3d 477 (2003)] [Case No. 20010551], the Utah Supreme Court decided to reject that rule and instead use the "trustworthiness" standard followed in several other jurisdictions. What is that standard, and does it adequately protect the same interests the corpus delicti rule protects? Note that the Utah court decided to apply the new "trustworthiness" rule prospectively, which meant the defendant in the case was tried under the rejected corpus delicti rule. He thus could not be convicted of the crime to which he confessed, even if his confession was found to be "trustworthy." This result was required, the court said, because of the Ex Post Facto Clause in the U.S. Constitution.

2. As stated in this chapter, it is a fundamental truth under the Fifth Amendment that incriminating statements are not admissible if they are not given voluntarily. Statements can be "compelled" in a variety of ways. One way the government can compel an admission is by subjecting a person to a penalty if the admission is not given. In *United States v. Saechao* [418 F.3d 1073 (9th Cir. 2005)] [Docket No. 04–30156], the Ninth Circuit Court of Appeals held that a term in a defendant's probation order that required him to answer "promptly and truthfully" all reasonable questions put to him by his probation officer violated the Fifth Amendment. How did the Ninth Circuit Court of Appeals distinguish the Supreme Court's opinion in *Minnesota v. Murphy* [465 U.S. 420 (1984)] [Docket No. 82–827], which held that a similar clause in that case did not violate the Fifth Amendment? Are you persuaded by the distinction?

3. Is a confession made to a private person admissible in a subsequent criminal prosecution? If so, is the prosecution required to prove that the confession was "voluntary"? Why or why not? See *Com. v. Miller* [865 N.E.2d 825 (Mass. App. 2007)].

4. The Sixth Amendment right to counsel is "charge specific," meaning that even though a defendant cannot be questioned without an attorney on pending charges, the prosecution can continue to investigate other crimes, including obtaining information from the defendant, without the presence of an attorney. What if the crimes are related? For example, if a defendant who is charged with criminal fraud tries to entice witnesses in that case to give false testimony, may the government secretly tape conversations between the defendant and those witnesses? See *United States v. Mir* [525 F.3d 351 (4th Cir. 2008)].

Notes

1. U.S. Supreme Court case of *Arizona v. Fulminante*, 499 U.S. 279 (1991).
2. *People v. Stanton*, 158 N.E.2d 47 (Ill. 1959).
3. 709 A.2d 1305 (Md. 1999).
4. This occurred in the U.S. Supreme Court case of *Colorado v. Connelly* [479 U.S. 157, 107 S.Ct. 515 (1986)]. In the *Connelly* case, the defense lawyer argued that Connelly was suffering from a psychosis that prevented Connelly from understanding his rights and motivated his confession. Because the confession had been corroborated, it was held to be admissible evidence, and Connelly's conviction was affirmed.
5. 14 How. St. Tr. 1311 (1660).
6. *People v. Jennings*, 807 P.2d 1009.
7. 348 U.S. 147 (1954).
8. See, for example, *State v. Weisser*, 150 P.3d 1043 (N.M. App. 2006).
9. See the *New York Times* obituary of Marty James, January 16, 1992.
10. 9 Neb. App. 52 (2000).
11. *People v. Cotton et al.*, 478 N.W.2d 681 (Mich. App. 1991).
12. *United States v. Chimal*, 976 F.2d 608 (10th Cir. 1992).
13. *United States v. Maio*, 34 MJ 215 (U.S. CMA 1992).
14. *Thornburgh v. State*, 815 P.2d 186 (Okla. Crim. App. 1991).
15. In the 1953 case of *Stein v. New York* [346 U.S. 156, 73 S.Ct. 1077], the U.S. Supreme Court pointed out why confessions obtained by physical violence are considered involuntary and unreliable:

    Physical violence or threat of it by the custodian of a prisoner during detention serves no lawful purpose, invalidates confessions that otherwise would be convincing, and is universally condemned by the law. When present, there is no need to weigh or measure its effects on the will of the individual victim. The tendency of the innocent, as well as the guilty, to risk remote results of a false confession rather than suffer immediate pain is so strong that judges long ago found it necessary to guard against miscarriages of justice by treating any confession made concurrently with torture or threat of brutality as too untrustworthy

    to be received as evidence of guilt. *Stein*, 346 U.S. at 182, 73 S.Ct. at 1091.

16. 882 A.2d 944 (Md. App.).
17. 437 F.3d 1059 (10th Cir.).
18. 384 U.S. 436 (1966).
19. *Miranda v. Arizona*, 384 U.S. 436, 86 S.Ct 1602 (1966).
20. *People v. Ashford*, 71 Cal. Rptr. 619 (Cal. App. 1968).
21. *People v. Gonzales*, 554 N.E.2d 1269 (N.Y. 1990).
22. *State v. Jackson*, 600 So.2d 739 (La. App. 1992).
23. *Commonwealth v. Daniels*, 590 A.2d 778 (Pa. Super. 1991).
24. *Ciriago v. State*, 471 A.2d 320 (1984).
25. *Miranda v. Arizona*, 384 U.S. 477, 86 S.Ct. 1629 (1966).
26. *State v. Bennett*, 517 P.2d 1029 (Utah 1973).
27. *Britton v. State*, 170 N.W.2d 785 (Wis. 1969).
28. 813 S.W.2d 748 (Tex. App.).
29. 468 U.S. 420, 104 S.Ct. 3138 (1984).
30. *Id.*
31. 496 U.S. 582, 110 S.Ct. 2638.
32. 577 N.E.2d 861 (Ill. App.).
33. 588 A.2d 389 (N.J. Super.).
34. *Glean v. State*, 397 S.E.2d 459 (Ga. App. 1990).
35. *State of Maine v. Joubert*, 603 A.2d 861 (1992).
36. 407 S.E.2d 342.
37. See *United States v. Gupta*, 183 F.3d 615 (7th Cir. 1999).
38. 432 F.3d 524 (3d Cir. 2006), *cert. denied*, 546 U.S. 1223.
39. 465 U.S. 420, 104 S.Ct. 1136.
40. 496 U.S. 292, 110 S.Ct. 2394.
41. 385 U.S. 293, 87 S.Ct. 408.
42. *United States v. Rosengard*, 949 F.2d 905 (7th Cir. 1991); *United States v. Cortes*, 922 F.2d 123 (2d Cir. 1990).
43. 467 U.S. 649, 104 S.Ct. 2626.
44. *United States v. Harris*, 961 F.Supp. 1127 (S.D. Ohio 1997).
45. *People v. Simpson*, 76 Cal. Rptr. 2d 851 (Calif. App. 4th 1998); *State v. Harris*, 384 S.E.2d 50 (N.C. App. 1989).
46. *State v. White*, 619 A.2d 92 (Maine 1993).

47. *Commonwealth v. Bowers*, 583 A.2d 1165 (Pa. Super. 1990).

48. *State v. Trangucci*, 796 P.2d 606 (N.M. App. 1990).

49. *State v. McKessor*, 785 P.2d 1332 (Kans. 1990).

50. 42 Cal. Rptr. 417, 398 P.2d 753.

51. 148 Cal. Rptr. 170 (App.).

52. 440 U.S. 937, 99 S.Ct. 1283 (1979).

53. 148 Cal. Rptr. at 177.

54. 490 N.W.2d 93 (Minn.).

55. *McNeil v. Wisconsin*, 501 U.S. 171 (1991).

56. 128 S.Ct. at 2587.

57. 426 U.S. 610 (1976).

58. 447 U.S. 404 (1980).

59. 532 F.3d 822 (9th Cir.).

60. *Massiah v. United States*, 377 U.S. 201, 84 S.Ct. 1199 (1964).

61. *Brewer v. Williams*, 430 U.S. 387, 97 S.Ct. 1232 (1977).

62. This case was before the U.S. Supreme Court again in 1984 under the title of *Nix v. Williams* [467 U.S. 431, 104 S.Ct. 2501 (1984)], discussed in Chapter 9.

63. The U.S. Supreme Court has decided two redacting cases. In *Richardson v. Marsh* [481 U.S. 200 (1987)], the Court upheld a conviction in a joint murder trial of two defendants. One defendant, Williams, made a confession implicating the co-defendant, Marsh. This confession was introduced at Marsh and Williams's joint trial but was redacted to omit any reference to Marsh and also any reference to Marsh's existence. The Supreme Court held that this redaction took the case outside the *Bruton* rule. In *Gray v. Maryland* [523 U.S. 185, 118 S.Ct. 1151 (1998)], Bell and Gray were jointly tried for murder. Bell confessed, and this confession was introduced in the joint trial. It was redacted to delete any reference to Gray, but where Gray's name appeared in the confession the police officer reading the confession in court said "deleted." For example, the confession read "Question: Who was in the group that beat Stacey?" Answer: "Me, deleted, deleted, and a few other guys." The Supreme Court said keeping the "deleted" spaces in the confession invited the jury to tie the confession to Gray and held the *Bruton* rule applicable.

64. See the 1992 case of *Melvin v. State* [606 A.2d 69, 50 CrL 1575 (Del.)], where the State of Delaware produced evidence during the trial showing that the defendant was in possession of cocaine. After the evidence was presented, the trial judge stated that he was "going to give this (juvenile) an opportunity to prove me wrong" by taking a polygraph test about whether the cocaine belonged to the defendant. When the defendant refused to take the test, the judge found him guilty, stating, "I gave him an opportunity to clear himself."

The Supreme Court of Delaware reversed the conviction and ordered a new trial for the violation of the Fifth Amendment privilege against self-incrimination.

65. In the 1977 case of *Sandlin v. Oregon Women's Correctional Center* [28 Or. App. 519, 559 P.2d 1308], the defendant argued that she had a right to a polygraph test. However, a test was not given to her. In affirming the defendant's conviction, the court held that due process did not require the state to grant the defendant's request for a polygraph test.

66. *United States v. Scheffer*, 118 S.Ct. 1265 (1998).

67. After holding public hearings on the use of polygraph testing, the U.S. Congress enacted the Employee Polygraph Protection Act, which generally forbids employers engaged in interstate commerce from using lie detector tests either for employment screening (i.e., as part of a job application procedure) or during employment with certain exceptions. One of the exceptions permits polygraph testing when an investigation into a money loss or other theft is being conducted.

68. 509 U.S. 579 (1993).

69. See N.M.R. Evid. 11–707.

70. 96 P.3d 291 (2004).

71. *United States v. Scheffer*, 118 S.Ct. 1261 (1998).

72. 116 S.Ct. 7.

73. 812 P.2d 163.

74. *Bennett v. City of Grand Prairie*, 883 F.2d 400 (1989).

75. *State v. Cherry*, 810 P.2d 940 (1991).

76. *State v. Coffey*, 788 P.2d 424 (1990).

77. *Kairys v. Douglas Stereo, Inc.*, 577 A.2d 386 (1990).

78. 869 F.2d 348 (7th Cir. 1989).

79. 767 F.2d 1052 (4th Cir. 1985), *cert. denied*, 474 U.S. 1081 (1986).

80. *United States v. Bahena*, 223 F.3d 797 (8th Cir. 2000).

THE LAW GOVERNING IDENTIFICATION EVIDENCE

CHAPTER 13

LEARNING OBJECTIVES

In this chapter we discuss some of the ways evidence that is intended to identify an offender is gathered and admitted in criminal trials. The learning objectives for this chapter are:

- List the reasons for mistaken eyewitness identification.
- State the differences between a lineup and a showup.
- State the requirements for a nonsuggestive photo array.
- Define *sequential lineup*.
- When may a single photograph be used to identify a suspect?
- Define "totality of the circumstances" in the context of eyewitness identification.

CHAPTER CONTENTS

Evidence Needed for a Criminal Conviction

The Problem of Mistaken Eyewitness Identification

The 2008 Study of Innocent Persons Mistakenly Incarcerated

What Is Being Done About the Problem of Convicting Innocent Persons?

U.S. Supreme Court Cases on Showups

Determining the Reliability of Identification Evidence: The *Neil v. Biggers* Guidelines

The Use of Police Lineups: Changes from the 1960s to the Present

Using Photographs to Obtain Identification Evidence

Using a Single Photograph for Identification

Obtaining Identification Evidence by Other Means

Courtroom Identification of a Defendant

EVIDENCE NEEDED FOR A CRIMINAL CONVICTION

To convict a person of a crime, the government must prove:

1. That the crime charged did occur (proof of corpus delicti)
2. That the defendant committed or was a party to the crime charged

In all criminal cases, the defendant must be identified as the person who committed or was a party to the crime. This can be done by direct or circumstantial evidence, or a combination of both direct and circumstantial evidence. Identification evidence may consist of one or more of the following:

- Identification by the victim of the crime
- Identification by an eyewitness to the crime (In a July 2002 release, *NCJ* reported that bystanders are present in 70 percent of simple and aggravated assaults, 52 percent of robberies, and 29 percent of rapes/sexual assaults. See *NCJ* 189100.)
- Confessions, admissions, or incriminating statements by the defendant or his associates showing that the defendant committed the crime or was a party to the crime
- DNA fingerprints, regular fingerprints, tire tracks, and the like, which place the defendant at the scene of the crime
- Other physical evidence left at the scene of the crime or obtained later by the police that implicates the defendant as the perpetrator of the crime (for example, the gun that killed the victim is found in the defendant's possession the day after the crime was committed)
- Photos or videos from a surveillance camera or hand-held video taken as the defendant committed the crime
- Voice identification or, if admissible, voiceprint (spectrographic) evidence that identifies the defendant as the perpetrator of the crime or as a party to the crime

It is the trier of the facts (the jury or the judge) who determines whether the identification evidence is sufficient to carry the burden of proof beyond reasonable doubt.

Examples of cases with unusual identification evidence include *People v. Sutterland*,[1] where a shoeprint, found on the victim's back, and tire tracks were held to be sufficient evidence to sustain charges of kidnapping, sexual assault, and murder of a 10-year-old girl; *Culbreath v. State*,[2] where the victim's caller ID was used as evidence to sustain a stalking prosecution; *People v. Campbell*,[3] where clear and unique shoeprints plus flight from an officer three days after the crime were held to be sufficient; *Spence v. State*,[4] where bite mark evidence on the body of the victim was used to link the defendant to the crime; *State v. Faircloth*,[5] where hair evidence (most often used in rape and murder cases) was used in identifying the offender (the court pointed out that although hair—unlike DNA—cannot positively identify an offender, it can be relevant evidence for identification purposes); and *State v. Jells*,[6] where footprints (as distinguished from shoeprints) were used as evidence for a murder conviction and the use of the death penalty.

THE PROBLEM OF MISTAKEN EYEWITNESS IDENTIFICATION

In the 1960s, the International Association of Chiefs of Police recognized that eyewitness "identification and description is regarded as a most unreliable form of evidence and causes more miscarriages of justice than any other method of proof."[7] In a 2008 article that reviewed studies of the reliability of eyewitness testimony, the author concluded that more than 40 percent of wrongful convictions were the result of mistaken identifications, with the highest percentage attributable to "showup identifications."[8]

Mistaken eyewitness identification may lead to the accusation or conviction of an innocent person, and it may allow a guilty person to avoid identification and conviction. Experts in the field give the following reasons for mistaken identifications:

- Memory decays rapidly and can be tainted or changed by subsequent events.
- The mind does not work like a video recorder; sometimes what we expect to see affects what we perceive, and sometimes what we perceive is not what actually happened.
- Not everything we see is recorded in the brain, and the brain may fill in the gaps.
- A look-alike innocent person can be mistaken for the person who committed the crime.
- Studies indicate that eyewitness identifications are less reliable when the witness is of a different race than the person identified.

In the cases that follow, innocent persons were mistakenly charged or convicted of crimes they did not commit based on mistaken identifications:

- In 2005 Steven Avery was released from a Wisconsin prison where he had been held for eighteen years on a rape conviction. Avery was lucky because eighteen years after his conviction, one strand of the hair samples found at the crime scene was discovered to have enough root material to conduct DNA tests. These tests were used to identify another inmate at a Wisconsin prison as the person who committed the rape of which Avery was convicted. DNA evidence cleared Avery of the rape in 2005; however, in 2007 DNA evidence was used to convict Avery of the murder of a young reporter who came to Avery's property in hopes of writing a story about the earlier rape conviction.
- Father Bernard Pagano, a Roman Catholic priest, was accused of robbing six Delaware stores in 1979. All of the victims and witnesses to the robberies identified the balding priest as the robber based on a composite sketch shown to them by police. Before Pagano's trial, a man 14 years younger and 20 pounds lighter with a full head of hair came forward and confessed to the crime.
- William Jackson of Ohio served four and a half years in prison for two rapes until Dr. Edward Jackson, a prominent physician, was arrested and charged with thirty-six counts of rape. It was subsequently determined that Dr. Jackson, not related to William Jackson but bearing a close resemblance, was guilty of the rapes for which William Jackson was convicted.
- Douglas Forbes, a Tennessee mailman, was convicted of two rapes and served five years in prison, until a look-alike truck driver confessed to the rapes.

It is the duty of the defense lawyer to attack eyewitness identification evidence, pointing out to the court and the jury the possibility of error inherent in such identifications. The prosecution generally tries to offer additional evidence to corroborate the identifications, as illustrated by the following two examples:

Examples

- In the 1990 case of *State v. Skelton*,[9] a woman who was raped in a wooded rural area identified the defendant as her attacker. To corroborate the woman's identification, police took soil samples and vegetation from under the defendant's car and matched them by expert testimony to soil and vegetation from the crime scene.
- Immediately after a violent crime occurred, police investigators interviewed separately two witnesses who gave independent descriptions identifying the assailant. To corroborate the witnesses' subsequent identification of the defendant, the investigating officers testified at the trial, showing the similar descriptions given by the witnesses and stating that those descriptions matched the defendant's appearance.

THE 2008 STUDY OF INNOCENT PERSONS MISTAKENLY INCARCERATED

In April 2007 DNA evidence was used to clear the 200th innocent person mistakenly convicted of a crime. These innocent persons served an average of twelve years in prison for crimes they had not committed. A study of the circumstances surrounding the convictions of these 200 people was published in the 2008 issue of *Columbia Law Review* and titled "Judging Innocence." The results revealed that:

- The leading cause of the wrongful convictions was erroneous identification by eyewitnesses; this occurred in 79 percent of the cases.
- Faulty forensic evidence was used in 55 percent of the cases. This included undue weight placed on evidence of limited value, such as the fact that the defendant's blood type matched the blood found at the crime scene. The faulty evidence also included exaggerated or mistaken testimony of expert witnesses for the prosecution, often involving the analysis of blood or semen. Forty-two cases had expert testimony about hair characteristics, forensic evidence the author called "notoriously unreliable."
- In 18 percent of the cases police informants testified against the defendants. Not only was the informant's testimony unreliable, but in three of the cases DNA evidence showed that the informants themselves were guilty of the crime they sought to attribute to the defendant.
- False confessions were admitted in evidence in 16 percent of the cases. Two-thirds of the defendants who gave false confessions were juveniles, mentally retarded, or both.
- More than 90 percent of the persons exonerated by DNA evidence were convicted of rape, murder, or both. DNA evidence is often available in these crimes of violence unless the perpetrator takes measures to remove all hair, semen, blood, and other bodily fluids from the crime scene.

- DNA testing and evidence are available in fewer than 10 percent of violent crimes, typically rape and murder cases, where it is more likely the offender will leave skin tissue or bodily fluids that will yield DNA.

The conclusions in the *Columbia Law Review* study were based on violent crimes where DNA evidence was available. Because DNA evidence is not available in 90 percent of the violent crimes committed each year in this country, however, it is difficult to estimate how many innocent persons are wrongly convicted each year. The National Institute of Justice estimates that more than 75,000 persons a year are brought to trial in this country on criminal charges based primarily on eyewitness identification. How many of these persons will be wrongly convicted?

WHAT IS BEING DONE ABOUT THE PROBLEM OF CONVICTING INNOCENT PERSONS?

Not only is the conviction of innocent persons shocking, but it also means the guilty person is free to commit other crimes. For years, courts have been aware of the unreliability of eyewitness testimony used in criminal convictions, which has contributed greatly to wrongful convictions. In the 1967 case of *United States v. Wade*,[10] the U.S. Supreme Court stated:

> The vagaries of eyewitness identification are well-known: the annals of criminal law are rife with instances of mistaken identification. Mr. Justice Frankfurter once said: "What is the worth of identification testimony even when uncontradicted? The identity of strangers is proverbially untrustworthy. The hazards of such testimony are established by a formidable number of instances in the records of English and American trials."[11]

Because it is inevitable, and perhaps necessary, that eyewitness identifications will continue to be used as evidence in criminal prosecutions in the United States, many steps have been taken to lessen the likelihood of convictions of innocent persons. Some of those steps are listed here:

- Throughout the United States, judges, prosecutors, defense lawyers, and law enforcement officers are being made aware of, and instructed in, the hazards inherent in collecting, processing, and using eyewitness testimony in criminal prosecutions. Prosecutors are advised to screen cases more thoroughly when eyewitness identification is a principal part of the prosecution's case. At the same time, judges are more demanding about reliability issues, and defense attorneys are urged to cross-examine witnesses more vigorously. Judges, prosecutors, and juries are more skeptical and demand higher burdens of proof in cases where eyewitness identification is a major part of the prosecution's case. Juries are cautioned more extensively by both defense attorneys and prosecuting attorneys about the risks of eyewitness identifications in closing arguments, and judges are giving jury instructions to the same effect.[12]
- It is likely that courts will permit more expert testimony on the hazards of eyewitness identifications. In eyewitness identification cases, particularly where no corroborating evidence is available, courts are increasingly willing to permit expert testimony about the unreliability of eyewitness identifications.[13]

- Corroborating evidence is important in eyewitness identification cases, and law enforcement officers are working harder to obtain evidence bearing on the reliability (or unreliability) of eyewitness testimony. For example, in the 2006 case of *State v. Williams*,[14] the defendants were convicted after eyewitness identifications by the victims of a robbery. The appeals court upheld the convictions, noting that the eyewitnesses stated that one of the robbers was on crutches, one was wearing an Orlando Magic jacket, and one was wearing a dark sweatshirt, which was true in each case. Also, a gold necklace owned by one of the victims was found in the backseat of the cruiser in which one of the defendants was transported to police headquarters.
- Witnesses to crimes are often separated and interviewed alone by officers who are skilled in obtaining details about the crime the witnesses observed, thus avoiding suggestive questions or coaching in any way. The resulting independent descriptions of the offender or offenders can then be compared to determine whether the identification is accurate and dependable. If independent, uncontaminated descriptions by different witnesses match in sufficient detail, the investigating officer can testify at the trial as to the similarity of the identifications and their match of the defendant charged with the crime.

SOME PROCEDURES, AND THEIR LIMITATIONS, USED IN PRETRIAL IDENTIFICATIONS

More than 75,000 persons each year are charged with crimes based on eyewitness identification. These identifications result from a variety of identification procedures or situations. Listed here are some of the procedures and situations that result in identifications as well as the problems associated with those procedures.

When the Person Who Committed the Crime Is Unknown

Composite sketches can be used to identify the suspect.	Research has shown that none of the existing methods used to produce a composite sketch are reliable in real-world settings. The Wisconsin Department of Justice has observed that "... an inaccurate composite might taint an eyewitness's memory and lead to a misidentification.... Composite sketches can alter witnesses' memory and lead witnesses to pick out suspects who resemble the sketch rather than the actual perpetrator."

When the Police Lack Probable Cause for an Arrest or Exigent Circumstances Are Present

In a showup, a victim or witness is permitted to view a suspect detained by police singly rather than as part of a group.	Evidence obtained from an out-of-court showup is admissible if the procedure was necessary. A showup was necessary if the police lacked probable cause to make an arrest or, as a result of other exigent circumstances, could not have conducted a lineup or photo array. If the showup was not necessary, courts use that as an important factor in determining whether the identification is admissible.

(Continued)

When a Suspect Is In Custody or Has Been Charged with a Crime

Lineups are used to minimize suggestiveness and to increase the reliability of identification evidence.

In order to minimize suggestiveness, courts prohibit police from telling victims and witnesses that police have made an arrest and having the suspect appear as the only person shown in a lineup. Courts also require that only one person in a lineup be highlighted at a time, to only one witness at a time, by an officer who does not know who the real suspect is.

When Police Have Photographs of a Suspect or in Lineups

Photo arrays, consisting of several photographs of different people including a suspect, and lineups can be shown to witnesses.

Generally, the same requirements apply to both photo arrays and lineups: (1) six or more persons or photographs must be shown; (2) each person or photograph of a person must be alike in age, size, color, and dress, and none (other than the suspect) can be known to the witness; (3) the persons or photographs must be shown one at a time by an officer who does not know who the real suspect is; and (4) persons in lineups can be required to speak certain words or phrases or put on specific clothing, such as a hat, jacket, or gloves.

Other Circumstances Where Identification Might Occur

Inadvertent confrontations by a witness or the victim can lead to an identification of a suspect.

Where without police involvement a witness or victim encounters a suspect and identifies him or her, the identification can be admitted as evidence so long as the encounter was really inadvertent.

In-court identifications as part of a criminal trial are permitted.

These identifications continue to be used, even though they are the most suggestive type of showup possible. Because the in-court identification is made in the presence of the judge and jury, and is subject to immediate cross-examination, its reliability can be tested in the presence of the jury. If the in-court identification is the product of an invalid pretrial identification, however, it can be excluded.

U.S. SUPREME COURT CASES ON SHOWUPS

showups An identification procedure in which only one subject is shown to witnesses or the victim of a crime.

Showups differ from lineups; in showups law enforcement officers permit witnesses or the victim of a crime to view a person being detained singly instead of as part of a group. In 1967 the U.S. Supreme Court stated that "(t)he practice of showing suspects singly to persons for the purposes of identification and not as part of a lineup, has been widely condemned."[15]

Showups are highly suggestive, and courts generally hold that law enforcement officers should not use them unless they are necessary under the circumstances. However, suggestiveness alone would not justify a ruling by a court that there has been a violation of the defendant's due process rights. To rule that the defendant's due process rights have been violated, there must have been impermissible suggestiveness to such a degree as to make the identification unreliable as a matter of law and resulting in a possible miscarriage of justice.

The U.S. Supreme Court has repeatedly held that whether there has been a violation of the defendant's due process rights must be determined "on the totality of the circumstances."[16] In using the totality of the circumstances test, the Supreme Court and other courts have held that showups do not violate the due process rights of defendants under the following circumstances:

- *The showup is necessary, and police lack probable cause.* This kind of showup is most often held a short time after the crime was committed, in a scene-of-the-crime, on-the-spot, or short-detour confrontation and viewing. Courts have approved such showups because the memory of the witness is fresh, and officers can immediately determine whether they have taken the right person into custody.

  Example
  A woman's purse is snatched. Witnesses to the incident chase the purse-snatcher, a man, and after several blocks catch him. A police officer is summoned and places the man under investigative detention. The victim is brought to the spot where the man was stopped, and asked to identify him as the purse-snatcher. If not, he may be immediately released; if the victim identifies him, the police have probable cause for an arrest, and he can then be searched for property of the victim.

- *Necessary and exigent circumstances are present.* Although showups are generally held a short time after the crime and are generally held at or near the crime scene, they have also been approved by the U.S. Supreme Court when the victim or witness was in critical condition and could die at any time. In the case of *Stovall v. Denno*,[17] one of the victims of a criminal attack was dead, and his wife was in critical condition because of eleven stab wounds. Two days after the crime, Stovall was taken in handcuffs to the victim's hospital room, where she identified him as the perpetrator of the crime. In affirming Stovall's convictions and the use of this procedure, the U.S. Supreme Court quoted a lower court, holding that:

  Here was the only person in the world who could possibly exonerate Stovall. Her words and only her words, "He is not the man," could have resulted in freedom for Stovall.

- *A suspect is in possession of property recently stolen from the victim.* The defendant in the case of *Kirby v. Illinois*[18] was arrested in downtown Chicago with traveler's checks and a Social Security card taken from a man who had been robbed the day before. The holdup victim was driven to the police station, where he identified Kirby as one of the holdup men. In affirming Kirby's conviction and in holding that there is no right to an attorney during showups, the U.S. Supreme Court stated:

  In this case we are asked to import into a routine police investigation an absolute constitutional guarantee historically and rationally applicable only after the onset of formal prosecutional proceedings. We decline to do so.

It should be noted that many states would hold that the showup used in *Kirby* was improper because the police had probable cause and could have used a lineup or photo array. Indeed, it is likely that had the defense in *Kirby* argued against the showup rather than the right to an attorney, it would have succeeded.

- *The showup does not create a substantial likelihood of irreparable misidentification, and the suspect is in custody for another crime.* If the victim or witness knows the offender or has seen the offender on previous occasions, but the police are not sure they have the right person in custody, a showup to identify the person is permissible. Or, if the victim or witnesses to the crime give the police such a specific or unique description of the suspect that it clearly distinguishes the offender from other persons, then a showup is permissible, as occurred in the following U.S. Supreme Court case.

Neil v. Biggers
United States Supreme Court, 409 U.S. 188, 93 S.Ct. 375 (1972)

A nurse was assaulted in her home and then taken outside, where she was raped. The incident lasted between 15 and 30 minutes on a bright moonlit night. The victim gave the police a very specific description of her assailant. In the months that followed, she viewed many lineups and photo arrays but made no identification.

Seven months after the rape, the defendant was taken into police custody for another offense. When the police noticed the similarity of the defendant to the description given by the rape victim, the police attempted to make up a lineup but could find no one fitting the defendant's "unusual physical description."

When the rape victim arrived at the police station, a showup was used. After hearing the defendant repeat "Shut up or I'll kill you," the victim identified the defendant as her assailant. The defendant appealed his rape conviction, arguing that the identification evidence obtained in the station house showup was so suggestive that it violated due process. The Supreme Court held that the identification evidence was properly admitted, ruling that: "Weighing all the factors, we find no substantial likelihood of misidentification. The evidence was properly allowed to go to the jury."

DETERMINING THE RELIABILITY OF IDENTIFICATION EVIDENCE: THE *NEIL V. BIGGERS* GUIDELINES

The U.S. Supreme Court has ruled that: "It is the reliability of identification evidence that primarily determines its admissibility [as evidence in a trial]."[19]

The guidelines for determining the reliability of identification evidence were established by the U.S. Supreme Court in the case of *Neil v. Biggers*, discussed above. There, the Supreme Court pointed out that, when eyewitness identification evidence is presented, defense lawyers can "both cross-examine the identification witness and argue in summation as to factors causing doubts as to the accuracy of the identification...."[20]

To minimize the possibility that an innocent person will be identified as a criminal and sent to prison, the following questions are asked to determine whether the evidence is sufficiently accurate and reliable to present to a jury for their deliberation:[21]

- What opportunity did the witness have to observe the criminal at the time of the crime? Relevant factors are length of time of the encounter, distance

THE IMPORTANCE OF OBTAINING PRIOR DESCRIPTIONS OF OFFENDERS

After separating witnesses and interviewing them away from other persons, investigating officers should have witnesses provide as detailed a description of the offender as possible soon after the crime is reported. Officers should assist the victim and the witness in searching their memories (without being in any way suggestive) for details of physical appearances and clothing, no matter how insignificant such details may seem. Such prior descriptions are important for several reasons:

- They will authorize stops in the neighborhood and elsewhere for investigative detentions of persons who reasonably match these descriptions.
- The descriptions may be compared to descriptions given by victims and witnesses of other crimes and further aid in the apprehension of the offender.
- Detailed descriptions that match the defendants can significantly increase the reliability of identifications made later by victims and witnesses.
- Testimony by the investigating officers in court concerning prior descriptions is important evidence for juries and judges in determining the issue of guilt or innocence.

between the witness and the suspect, lighting conditions, whether the witness' view was unobstructed, and the witness' state of mind at the time.

- Was the witness a casual observer, or did the witness show a high degree of attention? A witness who observed someone hurry down a hall or a street might be a very casual observer and may not be able to accurately describe or identify that person a short time later. On the other hand, the victim of a rape or a robbery ordinarily has a very high degree of attention, which could result in a more accurate and more reliable identification of the perpetrator of the crime.
- How accurate was the witness' prior description of the criminal? How accurate was the description recorded by the investigating officers? Did the description include unusual features, such as scars, moles, birthmarks, tattoos, and distinctive clothing, which could establish an independent basis of identification and make the identification highly reliable? How well did the testimony of the witness in court stand up under cross-examination? Was the witness able to explain why she identified the defendant as the person who committed the crime? Any discrepancies between the prior identification and the actual appearance of the defendant is ordinarily brought out in cross-examination.
- What level of certainty did the witness demonstrate at the confrontation? Did the witness immediately identify the suspect? Was there hesitancy? Was there a misidentification?
- How much time elapsed between the commission of the crime and the identification of the suspect as the perpetrator of the crime? Did the identification occur ten minutes after the crime or ten hours, ten days, or ten months? This factor, when combined with the other factors, would determine the reliability

of the identification, which is the basis for the decision by the trial judge as to whether to submit the identification evidence to a jury.

Most states have adopted these guidelines from the *Neil* decision, although some states have added minor modifications, such as those used by the Utah Supreme Court in *State v. Hollen*.[22] In *State v. Hunt*,[23] the Kansas Supreme Court adopted the Utah guidelines for eyewitness identification evidence.

THE USE OF POLICE LINEUPS: CHANGES FROM THE 1960s TO THE PRESENT

lineups An identification procedure in which six or more persons are shown to witnesses or the victim of a crime.

Lineups should be used whenever practical and must be used in situations where show-ups would not be authorized. Lineups properly run not only minimize suggestiveness but also increase the reliability of the identification evidence.

The procedures that state and local law enforcement agencies follow in police lineups historically have varied greatly from state to state. Recognizing that mistaken identifications in lineups often lead to mistaken in-court identifications and wrongful convictions, in the 1960s the U.S. Supreme Court decided several cases where lineup procedures were called into question.

The following Supreme Court cases reflect lineup problems that existed during that period, and the Court's response to those problems.

United States v. Wade

United States Supreme Court, 388 U.S. 218, 87 S.Ct. 1926 (1967)

Wade was arrested for robbing a bank in Texas. A lineup was conducted in the courtroom of a local courthouse without first informing Wade's attorney. The Supreme Court ordered a new hearing before excluding the identification at the trial of Wade by the bank witnesses because of the failure to notify the lawyer. At the hearing, the government was given an opportunity to establish by clear and convincing evidence that the in-court identifications were based on observations of the suspect other than the lineup identification.

Gilbert v. California

United States Supreme Court, 388 U.S. 263, 87 S.Ct. 1951 (1967)

Gilbert was arrested for robbing a savings and loan association and murdering a police officer during the robbery. Gilbert was also charged with other robberies. A lineup was held without notifying Gilbert's lawyer. The lineup was held on a stage with "upwards of 100 persons in the audience," each an eyewitness to one of the robberies charged to Gilbert. Bright lights prevented the persons in the lineup from seeing the audience. Persons in the audience would call out the number of the man they could identify in the lineup. It is not known whether audience members talked to one another during the lineup, but they did talk to one another after the lineup. In holding that the lineup was illegal, the Court stated that:

> The admission of the in-court identifications without first determining that they were not tainted by the illegal lineup but were of independent origin was constitutional error. *United States v. Wade, supra.* We there held that a post-indictment pretrial lineup at which the accused is exhibited to identifying witnesses is a critical stage of the criminal prosecution; that police conduct of such a lineup without notice to and in the absence of his counsel denies the accused his Sixth Amendment right to counsel and calls in question the admissibility at trial of the in-court identifications of the accused by witnesses who attended the lineup.

Foster v. California

United States Supreme Court, 394 U.S. 440 (1969)

The defendant was a suspect in a robbery. He was brought to the police station and placed in a lineup with five other persons, each of whom was shorter than he was. The robbery victim viewed the lineup but could not identify the suspect. Subsequently, a second lineup was held, and the defendant was the only person from the first lineup who appeared in the second lineup. The victim identified the defendant as the robber and subsequently made an in-court identification of him. The defendant was convicted of robbery. On appeal, the Supreme Court held that the procedures followed in the two lineups made them so suggestive of the defendant's guilt that he was denied due process. The convictions were reversed.

Because so many wrongful convictions can be tied to misidentifications by eyewitnesses viewing lineups, states have considered modifications of the classic police lineup. Two procedures that have been recommended, and adopted in some states, are (1) the sequential lineup, in which a witness is shown one person at a time rather than all at once, and (2) the double-blind administrator, where the officer conducting the lineup has no involvement in the underlying case and no knowledge of which person in the lineup is the suspect.

Lineups should be conducted to test recognition in a manner that avoids suggestiveness. The National Council of Judges provides the following rules for the lineup procedure:[24]

- Reasonable notice of the proposed lineup shall be given to the suspect and his counsel, and both shall be informed that the suspect may have his attorney present at the lineup. If the suspect is not represented by counsel, he shall be advised of his right to have counsel assigned without charge. He may waive in writing the presence of his attorney.[25]
- The lineup should consist of at least six persons, approximately alike in age, size, color, and dress; and none of them, other than possibly the suspect, shall be known to the witness.
- Persons in the lineup may be requested to speak certain words, identical for each person, for purposes of voice identification.
- Neither directly nor indirectly shall any police officer indicate or allow anyone but the witness to indicate in any way any person in the lineup as the suspect or defendant. Any instructions shall be given to all as a group, not individually.
- The lineup shall be viewed by only one witness at a time, others being excluded from the room and not permitted to discuss the lineup or descriptions of the suspect.

USING PHOTOGRAPHS TO OBTAIN IDENTIFICATION EVIDENCE

Photographs are often used for identification purposes in criminal investigations. The Metropolitan Police Department of the District of Columbia (Washington, DC) issued the following instructions in regard to the use of photographs and the photographic array:

photographic array A group of photographs shown to witnesses or the victim of a crime for identification purposes.

1. The use of photographs for identification purposes prior to an arrest is permissible provided the suspect's photograph is grouped with at least eight[26] other photographs of the same general description.[27]
2. Adequate records of the photographs shown to each witness must be kept so that the exact group of photographs from which an identification is made can be

presented in court at a later date to counteract any claim of undue suggestion and enhance the reliability of the in-court identification. This information shall be recorded in the statement of facts of the case.

3. Each witness shall view the photographs independently, out of the immediate presence of the other witnesses.

As in the case of lineups, some states require that photographs be shown one at a time instead of all together, and that the person showing the photographs have no knowledge of which (if any) is the photograph of a suspect.

Failure to preserve the photographs used to make an identification creates serious problems. The court cannot then determine whether law officers complied with due process and whether identification was made without excessive suggestiveness. In the 1980 case of *Branch v. Estelle*, the Fifth Circuit Court of Appeals held that "in situations where the police fail to preserve the photographic array, there shall exist a presumption that the array is impermissibly suggestive."[28]

USING A SINGLE PHOTOGRAPH FOR IDENTIFICATION

In the 1989 case of *People v. Kelly*, the Illinois Court of Appeals pointed out that as "a rule, the use of a single-photograph display is unduly suggestive and gives rise to a substantial likelihood of irreparable misidentification if the totality of the circumstances surrounding the identification renders it unreliable."[29]

Single-photograph showings are suggestive; however, a prosecutor and the police could attempt to show by testimony or other evidence that the identification is sufficiently reliable. Reliability is determined by the factors established in the U.S. Supreme Court case of *Neil v. Biggers* (discussed above).

The following single-photograph case was decided by the U.S. Supreme Court in 1977:

Manson v. Brathwaite

U.S. Supreme Court, 432 U.S. 98 (1977)

Connecticut State Trooper Glover was working as an undercover officer in narcotics. He and an informer went to an apartment building in Hartford, where Glover knocked on the door of one of the apartments. A man (the defendant in this case) opened the door and in a 5- to 7-minute period sold $20 worth of heroin to Glover. Glover had never seen the defendant before and did not know the defendant's proper name. Upon leaving the building, Glover described the man to Officer D'Onofrio, who had been backing him up outside the building. From the description, D'Onofrio suspected that the seller was the defendant. D'Onofrio obtained a single photograph of the defendant and left the picture at Glover's office. Two days later, Glover viewed the single picture and identified the defendant as the man who sold him the heroin. Based on this information, the defendant was arrested. With no objection by the defense, the picture was used as evidence, and Glover made a positive in-court identification of the defendant.

Using the *Neil v. Biggers* factors, the Supreme Court affirmed the criminal conviction, holding that even though using only one photograph was suggestive, the identification evidence was sufficiently reliable and did not cause a substantial likelihood of irreparable misidentification.

OBTAINING IDENTIFICATION EVIDENCE BY OTHER MEANS

Other means of obtaining identification evidence include those listed here:

- *Surveillance cameras, cell phone cameras, and camcorders:* These devices seem to be everywhere. Many businesses, apartment buildings, schools, parking lots, and public places have surveillance cameras. Private citizens have ready access to cell phone cameras and camcorders, with almost instantaneous ability to record images. As a result, it is no longer unusual to have crime-scene photographs as evidence. In the case of *United States v. Gray*,[30] bank surveillance photographs and descriptions of the offender from bank employees led to Gray's arrest two weeks after he robbed a bank. In affirming his conviction, the court pointed out that "the reliability of these identification procedures is obvious."

- *Fingerprint and DNA banks:* Both the federal government and many states maintain these data banks, which store crime-scene evidence such as semen, saliva, and hair particles. Comparisons between a sample taken from a suspect and evidence maintained by these data banks can assist in the identification of criminals. Such evidence has also proved important in preventing wrongful convictions of innocent persons.

- *AMBER Alert Program:* This is a notification system to provide immediate information to the public about suspected child abductions. It is named after Amber Hagerman, a 9-year-old child who was abducted and murdered in Texas in 1996. More than forty-three states use the system, which has been credited with the recovery of many children and the apprehension of offenders. The U.S. Department of Justice AMBER Alert report for 2007 states that 316 AMBER Alerts were issued in 2006, and 214 resulted in the recovery of the child. Nine children were found deceased. In AMBER Alerts, highway signs and television and radio broadcasts flash a description of the child, the possible abductor, and the license plates of any suspected vehicle in which the child might be held. Within a short time, thousands of persons are alerted to look for the abducted child or a suspect's vehicle.

sketches Drawings by an artist or with an Identi-Kit for use in identification.

- *Sketches:* **Sketches** can be made by an artist or with an Identi-Kit with the assistance of one witness or the input of a number of witnesses. "Wanted" posters may be made from a sketch, or the sketch may be published in newspapers or shown on television. The Identi-Kit, invented by a police officer, has hundreds of facial components (noses, eyes, chins, hairlines, hair, and so on) that can be combined into the likeness of a person.[31]

The admissibility of composite sketches has sometimes been at issue. Prosecutors are aware that in-court identifications are frequently viewed with skepticism by the jury because the defendant is sitting apart from others in the courtroom, charged with the crime. As a result, prosecutors usually ask the witness who has made an in-court identification whether the witness has made a previous identification, such as in a lineup. Assuming the prior identification was made consistent with the defendant's due process rights, the prior identification is admissible. Initially, many courts excluded composite sketches as hearsay, but most now permit the witness to testify to a prior identification through a composite sketch for purposes of corroborating an in-court identification. Federal Rule of Evidence

801(d)(1) provides that prior statements of the witness that are identification of a person are not hearsay. Some courts permit the introduction of a composite sketch as substantive evidence of identification.[32]

- *Unusual features:* A description of such features as tattoos, scars, gold teeth or other dental features, hair, weight, and size can increase the reliability of an identification. Such unusual features can be exhibited in a courtroom as identification evidence.

- *Clothing:* Clothing is often included in descriptions given by victims or witnesses. Sometimes in rape cases an offender's clothing becomes torn, dirty, or stained in his struggle with the victim. Hats or other items of clothing are sometimes left behind or dropped in a hasty exit. Knowledgeable suspects sometimes change their clothing with others in an effort to avoid identification through a hat or jacket.

  The Supreme Court of California held that a defendant's refusal to don a jacket and cap during a showup at a police station can be used as evidence in the trial of the defendant,[33] as can a defendant's refusal to participate in a lineup.[34] Such evidence is not protected by the Fifth Amendment privilege against self-incrimination and can be compelled, with refusal by the defendants used as evidence against them.

  The robbery victim's identification of the defendant's hat and jacket was used as evidence to convict the defendant in the case of *Johnson v. Ross.*[35] The suspect's voice and clothes were used as aids in identification in the case of *State v. Holloman.*[36] The gun carried by one of the defendants was used in identification in the case of *Turner v. State.*[37] In the case of *Holder v. State,*[38] the defendant was required to stand in court and put on a jacket, mask, and cap worn by the robber and to say words spoken by the robber. To mitigate such evidence, the defense lawyer also put on the cap and the bandana, but the jury's finding of guilt was sustained by the appellate court.

- *Voice identification:* Voice identification has been admissible as evidence for years in the United States. In some cases, the victim has had previous contact with the defendant and recognizes the voice. In other cases, the offender is unknown to the victim, but the victim or other persons recall features of the offender's voice. A recording of the offender's voice may be available from a message-recording machine, voice mail, or other means. The defendant can be required to give a voice sample at trial, so that the victim can determine whether the voice matches that of the assailant.

  In the 2004 case of *Hubanks v. Frank,*[39] the defendant in a sexual assault case was ordered at his trial to speak the words the assailant used to determine whether the victim could recognize the voice. The defendant refused to speak. The trial judge subsequently instructed the jury that it could consider the fact that the defendant refused to give the voice sample in deciding his guilt. The defendant was convicted and appealed, contending that his Fifth Amendment rights were violated by the trial judge's order to speak and instructions to the jury. The court of appeals rejected these contentions, holding that because giving a voice sample is not testimonial, the Fifth Amendment does not apply, and the trial court was correct in ordering the sample and in instructing the jury about the consequences of the defendant's refusal to give the sample.

In crimes such as rape and robbery, most victims not only see the offenders but also hear their voices. In cases of telephone threats, telephone harassment, and stalking, however, voice identification alone can be used as evidence if the victim can identify the voice.[40] Victims can ordinarily testify that the voice "sounds like" the voice of the offender. The Supreme Court of Minnesota stated the rule of law for the admissibility of voice identification evidence:

> It is the rule in this state that the foundation for admission of testimony as to the identity of the voice of a telephone caller is sufficient when it appears that the witness to whom the telephone call is made testifies that he is reasonably certain as to the voice of such caller and can identify it.[41]

spectrograms or voiceprints
Voice graphs made on a spectrograph, which analyzes voice recordings based on intensity, frequency, and time gaps.

- *Spectrograms or voiceprints:* If voice recordings become available in such crimes as kidnapping, murder plots, bomb threats, or false alarms, **spectrograms or voiceprints** may be made in an effort to identify offenders. If a match is made with the voiceprint of a suspect, some state courts permit the spectrograms to be used as evidence in criminal trials. The highest court in Maryland described the operation of a spectrograph in the case of *Reed v. State*:[42]

> The process involves the use of a machine known as a spectrograph. This machine analyzes the acoustic energy of the human voice into three components—time, frequency, and intensity—and graphically displays these components by generating, through an electric stylus, a series of closely spaced light and dark lines, varying in position, on a sheet of electrically sensitive paper. The resulting graphic representation is what is called a spectrogram or "voiceprint." It reveals certain patterns or "formals" which correspond to the sounds which are analyzed.

Many courts have rejected the scientific reliability of voice spectrographic evidence and have refused to permit such evidence in criminal trials. For example, in *United States v. Angleton*,[43] a defendant charged with commissioning a murder for hire sought to introduce expert testimony based on a voice spectrograph to identify the speaker on a wiretap recording. The trial court refused to admit the expert testimony, finding that the science of voice spectrography lacked reliability and thus was inadmissible under Rule 702 of the Federal Rules of Evidence (see Chapter 18).

COURTROOM IDENTIFICATION OF A DEFENDANT

In criminal trials the state must carry the burden of identifying the defendant beyond a reasonable doubt as the person who committed the crime or as an aider and abettor or a conspirator to the crime. This task can be accomplished through any of the means discussed in this chapter.

During criminal trials, defendants may be required to try on such items as jackets, hats, and glasses to show whether such items fit the defendant. Defendants may also be required to speak or to display tattoos, scars, or a gold tooth.

Eyewitnesses or earwitnesses are asked by the prosecutor to describe the person who committed the crime or who was seen fleeing from the crime scene. The witness is then asked whether that person is in the courtroom. When the witness answers yes, the witness is asked to point out the person.

Using Biometrics for Identification and Authentication

It is important that persons who enter security areas or cross borders into the United States be accurately identified. Unfortunately, cleverly forged identification documents are available in many parts of the world, including the United States. Because of this, accurate, on-the-scene identification is needed not only in the areas just mentioned but also for cashing checks, collecting welfare benefits, using automatic teller machines (ATMs) as well as other crime prevention purposes.

One response to this need is called biometric identification, which is identification not from documents but by biological reference systems. Fingerprints and DNA analysis continue to be used at crime scenes in efforts to determine the identity of the person who committed the crime, and then later to identify with certainty the persons who have been arrested and charged with the crime. In the June 2000 issue of the *FBI Law Enforcement Bulletin*, the article entitled "Biometrics: Solving Cases of Mistaken Identity and More" identifies the following biometric systems:

- Iris-based systems, which in the future may equal or exceed fingerprint evidence in accuracy.
- Hand-geometry systems, which have better access and control and can be vital in prisons and jails where high levels of accuracy and security are required.
- Voice recognition, which is the least accurate but the most available way to verify identity over a telephone.
- Facial-recognition systems, which present opportunities to identify people unobtrusively and without their cooperation in video surveillance and other means.

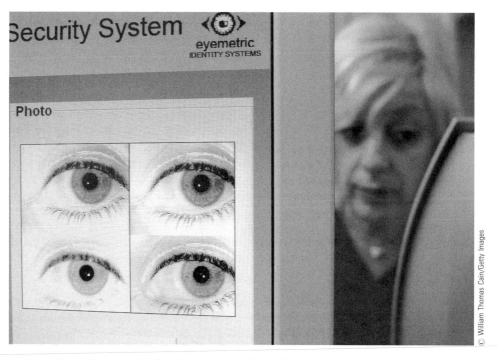

Teaching assistant Joann Lamaruggine has her iris recorded into the iris recognition system at Park Avenue Elementary School in Freehold, New Jersey. Iris recognition systems use a video camera to record the colored ring around the eye's pupil, matching the unique markings in the iris that identify each person.

TESTS THAT DETERMINE THE ADMISSIBILITY OF EYEWITNESS IDENTIFICATION EVIDENCE

- Were the defendant's Fifth Amendment due process rights violated by identification procedures that were so unnecessarily suggestive as to cause "a very substantial likelihood of irreparable misidentification"? [*Simmons v. United States*, 390 U.S. 377, 384, 88 S.Ct. 967, 974 (1968)]
- Was the defendant's Sixth Amendment right to an attorney observed during identification proceedings after the defendant was charged or indicted?

The One-on-One Showup

- Showups are suggestive but not necessarily in violation of the Fifth Amendment due process requirement.
- The propriety of a showup is determined by the "totality of the circumstances surrounding" the identification (U.S. Supreme Court in *Stovall v. Denno*).
- The suggestiveness inherent in the one-to-one showup can be outweighed by the following policy considerations:
    - The reliability due to the nearness in time of the identification to the crime committed and the need for immediate release of a person who is innocent.
    - The reliability of a witness, as demonstrated in *Neil v. Biggers*, in which the U.S. Supreme Court stated, "Her record for reliability was thus a good one, as she had previously resisted whatever suggestiveness inheres in a showup."
    - An emergency condition, such as in *Stovall v. Denno*, in which two days after a

murder, the only witness was in critical condition in a hospital. The U.S. Supreme Court held that an "immediate hospital confrontation was imperative."

Photographic Identification

- The propriety of pretrial photographic identification is determined by the "totality of the circumstances surrounding" the identification and will be set aside "only if the photographic identification was so impermissibly suggestive as to give rise to a very substantial likelihood of irreparable misidentification" [*Simmons v. United States*, 390 U.S. 377, 88 S.Ct. 967 (1968)]
- The suspect's photograph should be grouped with a sufficient number of other photographs of the same general description and shown to witnesses separately. The exact group of photographs should be preserved so it may be presented to the court at a later date to counteract any claim of undue suggestiveness and to enhance the reliability of the in-court identification.
- A suspect has no right to have an attorney present during a photographic identification proceeding [*United States v. Ash*, 413 U.S. 300, 93 S.Ct. 2568 (1973)], unless the state courts have held otherwise.
- A single-photograph identification procedure is suggestive but may not be impermissibly suggestive. The burden is on the state to show that the identification was sufficiently reliable to be used as evidence in view of the "totality of the circumstances surrounding" the identification procedure used.

Because the defendant is ordinarily seated next to his or her attorney at the defense table,[44] the witness points the person out to the court and the jury. To clearly establish that the witness has identified the defendant as the person who committed the crime, the witness is then ordinarily requested to further identify the defendant by one or more of the following methods:

- Asking the witness to describe what the defendant is wearing in court and to specifically describe where that person is sitting

- Asking the defendant to stand and asking the witness whether this is the person who committed the crime or was seen fleeing from the crime scene
- Requesting the witness to step down from the stand and to point to or to touch the person who committed the crime or who was seen fleeing from the crime scene

The prosecutor then requests that the court record show that the witness has identified the defendant as the person who was seen committing the crime or was seen fleeing from the crime scene.

courtroom identification A prescribed series of steps used during a trial to identify the defendant as the person who committed the crime or was a party to the crime charged.

Because many jurisdictions permit testimony by eyewitnesses regarding prior out-of-court identification, witnesses may then be asked whether they had previously identified the defendant as the person who assaulted them or committed the crime being charged. Such testimony can be technically considered hearsay, but it is important and meaningful because it gives the jury and judge a full picture of the identification process that was used. Such testimony also buttresses the ritualized **courtroom identification** against possible attack in cross-examination and shows to the jury and the judge the extent of the investigation and deliberation before the decision was made to bring the defendant to trial.

SUMMARY

Mistaken and inaccurate eyewitness identification continues to be a problem in criminal trials, as it has been for many years. In the 1960s, the English and American public became aware of serious problems in eyewitness identification evidence when twenty-two honest English citizens testified and falsely convicted a man for a crime he did not commit. The man served seven years in a penitentiary before other evidence showed he was innocent.

In the United States, thirty witnesses testified that the defendant in a forgery case had committed dozens of forgeries. The man was not convicted because he produced evidence showing that he was in jail at the time the forgeries were committed.

Reliable identification evidence is required to carry the burden of proving guilt beyond reasonable doubt to a jury or to a judge when the right to a jury has been waived.

The law governing identification evidence such as showups, lineups, and photo arrays is presented in this chapter.

CASE ANALYSIS

Read Appendix B, Finding and Analyzing Cases (p. 427). With these guidelines in mind, please continue with the Case Analysis selections for Chapter 13.

1. In *People v. Maldonado* [743 N.Y.S.2d 389 (2002)], the court held that a sketch made by a police artist of an assailant was inadmissible. How does this court treat such sketches, and what did the state try to argue to get around that treatment? Is New York in the majority or minority of courts on this issue, based on statements in the text?

2. Is it relevant that a witness had previously been shown a photograph of a person who resembled the defendant, and that the witness indicated it was not the perpetrator of the crime? Why would the prosecution want to introduce evidence of a non-identification? Should it be permitted to do so? An example of uncertainty on this issue is the murder trial and appeals in *People v. Tisdel*, an Illinois case. Tisdel was convicted of murder, based primarily on eyewitness testimony and identifications. The prosecution introduced

testimony that the witnesses who identified Tisdel had previously observed lineups with other persons and did not identify anyone as the perpetrator of the murder. In his first appeal, the Illinois Appellate Court reversed Tisdel's conviction because of the non-identification evidence [739 N.E.2d 31 (2000) (No. 1-98-0393)]. The state appealed, and the Illinois Supreme Court reversed the appellate court, holding that such testimony was admissible [775 N.E.2d 921 (2002) (No. 90480)]. On remand the appellate court affirmed Tisdel's murder conviction. Taken together, these cases illustrate both the complexity of eyewitness identification rules and how courts apply and sometimes change those rules.

3. In *State v. Herrera* [902 A.2d 177 (N.J. 2006)], the New Jersey Supreme Court found a showup to be impermissibly suggestive in the identification of the defendant who was convicted of carjacking. Why didn't the court reverse the conviction? What did the court say to the defendant's argument that an "exigent circumstances" rule should be adopted in showup cases?
4. If the victim identifies the defendant in a photo array, may the detective who conducted the array testify about the victim's demeanor during the array? For example, may the detective testify that the victim appeared "very positive" in her identification? See *State v. Lee* [873 So.2d 582 (Fla. App. 2004)].

Notes

1. 610 N.E.2d 1 (Ill. App. 1993).
2. 667 So.2d 156 (Ala. Crim. App. 1995).
3. 586 N.E.2d 1261 (App. 1992).
4. 47 CrL 1252 (Tex. Crim. App. 1990).
5. 394 S.E.2d 198 (N.C. App. 1990).
6. 559 N.E.2d 464 (Ohio 1990).
7. IACP Training Key #67 entitled "Witness Perception."
8. 86 Neb. L. Rev. 515 (2008).
9. *State v. Skelton*, 795 P.2d 349 (Kan. 1990).
10. 388 U.S. 218.
11. 388 U.S. at 228.
12. See generally *Eyewitness Identification: Science and Reform*, 29-Apr. Champ. 12 (2005).
13. See, for example, *State v. Palmer*, 715 N.W.2d 767 (Iowa App. 2007).
14. 2006 WL 337085 (Cal. App. 2006).
15. *Stovall v. Denno*, 388 U.S. 293, 87 S.Ct. 1967 (1967).
16. *Stovall v. Denno*; *Neil v. Biggers*, 409 U.S. 188, 93 S.Ct. 375 (1972).
17. 87 S.Ct. 1967 (1967).
18. 92 S.Ct. 1877 (1972).
19. *Manson v. Brathwaite*, 432 U.S. 98, 97 S.Ct. 2243 (1977).
20. *Watkins v. Sowders*, 449 U.S. 341, 101 S.Ct. 654 (1981).
21. These guidelines and factors for determining the accuracy and reliability of eyewitness identification were established by the U.S. Supreme Court in the case of *Neil v. Biggers*. Model Jury Instruction 52.20 is very similar to these guidelines and factors. This Model Jury Instruction can be found in *State v. Willis* [731 P.2d 287 (Kans. 1987)].
22. 44 P.3d 794 (2002).
23. 69 P.3d 571 (2003).
24. "Procedures for Obtaining Pretrial Eyewitness Identification," Series 304, No. 7.
25. In the 1992 case of *State v. Hoyte* [413 S.E.2d 806], the Supreme Court of South Carolina reversed the defendant's crack cocaine conviction because a showup without the defendant's attorney present was held five and a half months after the last drug sale and after the defendant's arrest. The court held that "there was no lineup; it was a one-man showup without notice to appointed counsel. While showups have been upheld by [this] Court, these situations usually involve either extenuating circumstances or are very close in time to the crime."
26. Courts have held that in view of the totality of circumstances less than eight photographs are sufficient. The Supreme Court of Nebraska held that five photographs constituted "a fair and adequate array when attempting to identify a single perpetrator" [*State v. Gibbs*, 470 N.W.2d 558 (Neb. 1991)]. In the case of *United States v. Sanchez* [24 F.3d 1259 (10th Cir. 1994)], it was held that six photos were not impermissibly suggestive when there was only a minor difference between the photos. In the *Sanchez* case, the

defendant's photo was the only photo depicting a person with his eyes closed. A major difference could consist of using photos depicting persons of different appearances (such as weight, lack of hair, age, sex, color, and dress) than the defendant.

27. Law enforcement agencies keep mug shots not only for citizen identification purposes but also to acquaint law enforcement officers with known suspects and persons who have criminal records. Mug shots should not be used as evidence, however, because they could easily cause jury members to believe that the defendant had a prior criminal record or prior trouble with the law; this could deny the defendant the right to a fair trial. Evidence of other offenses and prior trouble with the law is inadmissible as part of the government's case against a defendant. [See *Michelson v. United States*, 335 U.S. 469, 69 S.Ct. 213 (1948).]

28. 631 F.2d 1229 (5th Cir.).

29. Cases in which courts held that misidentification in single-photograph showings was a remote possibility due to "the totality of the circumstances" include *People v. Kelly* [540 N.E.2d 1125 (1989)], in which the victims were 5- and 7-year-old children; *United States v. Dring* [930 F.2d 687 (9th Cir. 1991)]; *State v. Barnett* [588 N.E.2d 887 (Ohio App. 1990)], in which the showing of only one photo was held to be "unnecessarily suggestive" but not "impermissibly suggestive"; and *State v. James* [592 So.2d 867 (La. App. 1991)], which held that an independent basis for identification existed in view of the *Manson* factors.

In the 1992 case of *State v. Martin* [595 So.2d 592], the Supreme Court of Louisiana held that a single-photograph showing was made under circumstances that resulted in substantial likelihood of irreparable misidentification and that there was no independent basis for the undercover police officer's in-court identification of the defendant. Another case in which a criminal conviction was reversed for a new trial was *Commonwealth v. Jarecki* [1992 WL 104524 (Pa. Super. 1992)], where a police officer permitted four witnesses to a store robbery to view a photographic array at the same time and talk among themselves in attempting to select the picture of the robber. In the 1991 case of *Hull v. State* [581 So.2d 1202], the Alabama Appellate Court reversed the conviction of Hull for a new trial because, in a photographic array of five pictures, only the defendant's picture was a black and white, whereas the other four photos were in color.

The court held that the in-court identification by a witness was not independently reliable.

30. 958 F.2d 9 (1st Cir. 1992).

31. In the 1992 case of *Sanders v. English et al.* [950 F.2d 1152 (5th Cir.)], Sanders was arrested as the result of a composite sketch of the "bicycle bandit" who repeatedly robbed at gunpoint. After Sanders was held in custody for fifty days, a grand jury refused to indict him after concluding that probable cause did not exist. In a civil lawsuit against the police officers involved, Sanders lost on the false arrest claims but was able to sue for the fifty days of illegal detention and malicious prosecution.

32. See, for example, *Commonwealth v. Weichell*, 453 N.E.2d 1038 (Mass. Sup. Jud. Ct. 1983).

33. *People v. Smith*, 91 Cal. Rptr. 786 (1970).

34. *People v. Johnson*, 842 P.2d 1 (Calif. 1992).

35. 955 F.2d 178 (2d Cir. 1992).

36. 837 P.2d 826 (Kan. App. 1992).

37. 803 P.2d 1152 (Okla. Crim. App. 1990).

38. 837 S.W.2d 802 (Tex. App. 1992).

39. 392 F.3d 926 (7th Cir. 2004).

40. It is a common practice to have persons in a lineup say words and sentences or to try on hats or clothing. Voice-only lineups could be held by having six or more persons repeat sentences or by tape-recording the voices stating the sentence or phrase for replay when necessary. Defense lawyers requested this procedure in the case *Evans v. Superior Court* [522 P.2d 681 (Calif. 1974)]. California trial judges have the authority to order voice-only lineups just as they have the authority to order physical lineups. [See *Garcia v. San Joaquin Superior Court*, 50 CrL 1312 (Calif. App. 1991).]

On-the-street and station-house voice identifications in rape cases were held not to be impermissibly suggestive in the cases of *State v. Jones* [587 N.E.2d 886 (Ohio App. 1990)] and *Jefferson v. State* [425 S.E.2d 915 (Ga. App. 1992)].

Voice exemplars, or recorded voice samples, were approved for use as evidence by the U.S. Supreme Court [*United States v. Wade*, 87 S.Ct. 1926 (1967), and *United States v. Dionisto*, 93 S.Ct. 764 (1973)]. Compelling a defendant or suspect to speak for the purposes of identification does not violate a suspect's Fifth Amendment privilege against self-incrimination.

41. *City of St. Paul v. Caulfield*, 94 N.W.2d 263 (Minn. 1959).

42. 391 A.2d 364 (1978).

43. 269 F.Supp.2d 892 (S.D. Tex. 2003).
44. In a few instances, defense lawyers have had persons who look similar to the defendant sit next to them at the defense table with the defendant sitting elsewhere in the courtroom during the trial. If the court is not informed of this situation, both the defense attorney and the look-alike could be charged with contempt. In the 1973 case of *Duke v. State* [298 N.E.2d 453 (Ind.)], the decoy sitting next to the defense lawyer was convicted and temporarily jailed in place of the defendant.

Other cases where defense lawyers were found in direct criminal contempt of court for not informing the trial court that the person sitting next to them was not the defendant include *United States v. Thoreen* [653 F.2d 1332 (9th Cir. 1981)], *People v. Simac* [603 N.E.2d 97, 52 CrL 1260 (Ill. App. 1992)], and *Miskovsky v. State ex rel. Jones* [586 P.2d 1104 (Okla. Crim. App. 1978)].

Obtaining Physical and Other Evidence

CHAPTER 14

LEARNING OBJECTIVES

In this chapter we focus on the methods employed to obtain physical evidence in the investigation of crimes. The learning objectives for this chapter are:

- Describe the level of evidence needed for an investigative detention.
- List searches that may be made without a search warrant.
- State what actions police may take in a routine traffic stop.
- Explain the "automobile exception."
- Define the "community caretaking" function and its impact on obtaining evidence of criminal conduct.

CHAPTER CONTENTS

physical evidence (real evidence) Physical objects, such as weapons, drugs, and clothing.

Physical evidence—or **real evidence**, as it is sometimes called—is important and even critical evidence in many criminal cases. Examples of physical evidence are weapons (guns, knives, and so on), illegal drugs, fingerprints, clothing, documents, footprints, hair, blood, grass marks or other stains on clothing, metal and wood fragments, and objects that were stolen, such as merchandise, money, and purses.

Investigators may obtain physical evidence in a variety of settings: in a public place where a crime has been committed, from the person of a suspect or the suspect's motor vehicle, or in a residence or other place. Real evidence might be obtained with lawful consent, it might be observed in plain view, or it might be obtained in a lawful search by a law enforcement officer. Depending on the location of the evidence or the circumstances under which it is obtained, limitations apply to the admissibility of physical evidence obtained by the police.

This chapter presents the legal rules that must be observed if physical evidence from constitutionally protected places is to be used in criminal trials.

OBTAINING PHYSICAL EVIDENCE FROM THE PERSON OF A SUSPECT

OBTAINING EVIDENCE AND INFORMATION BY MEANS OF VOLUNTARY CONVERSATIONS

There are three types of encounters between citizens and law enforcement officers:

Terry stop An investigative street detention named after the 1968 U.S. Supreme Court case of *Terry v. Ohio.*

1. The voluntary encounter or voluntary conversation
2. The investigative stop, or *Terry* stop, where the officer has reasonable suspicion to believe the suspect has committed, is committing, or is about to commit a crime
3. An arrest that is justified by probable cause to believe that the person has committed a crime

All persons in a democracy have a fundamental right to move freely about without unnecessary interference by the government. The U.S. Supreme Court pointed out that:

> No right is held more sacred, or is more carefully guarded, by the common law, than the right of every individual to the possession and control of their own person, free from all restraint or interference of others, unless by clear and unquestionable authority of law.[1]

free-to-leave test The test used to determine whether a conversation between a person and a law officer is voluntary; a reasonable person must believe he is free to leave.

Law enforcement officers may attempt to engage a person in a voluntary conversation in a public place, such as on a sidewalk or in an airport or train station.[2] The U.S. Supreme Court pointed out that:

> [T]he person approached ... need not answer any questions ... indeed, he may decline to listen to the questions at all and may go on his way.... He may not be detained even momentarily without reasonable objective grounds for doing so; and his refusal to listen, or answer does not, without more furnish these grounds....[3]

Most persons will engage in voluntary conversations with law enforcement officers. If at some point they wish to discontinue the conversation, they may do so.

City police officers question a man on a public sidewalk. Law enforcement officers may request a conversation with any person in a public place. The person can choose to respond or not.

© Chris McGrath/Getty Images

The test used by American courts to determine whether such situations are voluntary is the **free-to-leave test**, which was defined by the U.S. Supreme Court:[4]

> ... a person has been "seized" within the meaning of the Fourth Amendment only if in view of all the circumstances surrounding the incident, a reasonable person would have believed that he was not free to leave.[5]

AUTHORITY NEEDED TO MAKE AN INVESTIGATIVE DETENTION (*TERRY* STOP)

reasonable suspicion The amount of evidence a law enforcement officer needs to make an investigative stop (a *Terry* stop); less than probable cause but more than a hunch or mere suspicion.

That quantum (amount) of evidence known as **reasonable suspicion** is needed to authorize an investigative detention, or *Terry* stop. Reasonable suspicion is less than probable cause that would authorize an arrest. To make a temporary stop, the officer must be able to "point to specific and articulable facts which, taken together with rational inferences from those facts, reasonably warrant that intrusion."[6]

Reasonable suspicion is therefore more than a hunch, a gut reaction, or mere suspicion. Reasonable suspicion is that amount of evidence and facts that will cause a reasonable person to believe that the suspect has committed, is committing, or is about to commit a crime. The totality of the circumstances test is used to determine whether reasonable suspicion exists. That is, reasonable suspicion is determined by looking at the whole picture and all of the circumstances that existed. The following case illustrates the application of the totality of circumstances test.

THE 2002 U.S. SUPREME COURT CASE ON "FREE TO LEAVE"

Facts in the Case

In the case of *United States v. Drayton* [122 S.Ct. 2105 (2002)], passengers on a Greyhound bus disembarked at a scheduled stop in Tallahassee, Florida, while the bus was refueled and cleaned. Shortly after the passengers reboarded the bus, three plainclothes police officers boarded as part of a drug and weapons interdiction program. One officer knelt on the driver's seat facing the passengers, a second stood at the back of the bus, while the third walked down the aisle speaking with individual passengers, asking about their travel plans and trying to match them with luggage in the overhead bins. To avoid blocking the aisle, the officer stood next to, or behind, each passenger with whom he spoke. No general announcement was made about why the officers were on the bus, and the passengers were never told that they could refuse to consent to any search of their luggage.

An officer approached Drayton and his traveling companion, introduced himself, and told them he was looking for drugs and weapons. The officer asked whether the pair had any luggage. They responded that they shared a single bag located in the overhead bin. They gave the officer permission to search the bag, but no contraband was found. The officer then asked permission to frisk Drayton's

traveling companion. He consented to the frisk, and drug packages were found strapped to his inner thighs. He was arrested and escorted off the bus. Drayton was then asked to consent to a pat-down search. Drayton also consented, and similar packages were found in his possession. Drayton and his companion were charged with conspiracy to distribute cocaine and possession with intent to distribute cocaine.

Questions Before the Courts

1. Should the evidence be suppressed because the passengers were not free to leave the bus?
2. Were the officers obligated to inform the passengers that they could refuse to give consent to search?

Rulings of the Courts

- *Trial court:* The defense motion to suppress the evidence (drug packages) was denied.
- *Court of appeals:* The evidence was suppressed because the officers were obligated to inform the passengers of their right to refuse to give consent to search.

After considering the facts and the law in this case, you will find the U.S. Supreme Court ruling in note 64 of this chapter.

United States v. Arvizu

United States Supreme Court, 534 U.S. 266 (2002)

Arvizu was observed by a border patrol agent traveling in a remote area of Arizona on an unpaved road frequently used by smugglers. He was traveling in a minivan with a woman and three children. The position of the children in the back seat suggested to the agent that their legs were resting on some cargo on the floor. When Arvizu observed the agent, he immediately slowed the vehicle and avoided eye contact.

When the agent began following his vehicle, the children in the back seat began waving in an "abnormal pattern" as if they were following instructions. A registration check indicated that Arvizu's vehicle was registered to an address in an area that was notorious for alien and drug smuggling. The border patrol agent decided to stop the vehicle after noting that the route taken by Arvizu was designed to avoid area checkpoints and that he was traveling at a time when border patrol agents were changing shifts. Following the stop, Arvizu consented to a search of his vehicle, which resulted in the seizure of more than 128 pounds of marijuana.

Arvizu was charged with possession with intent to distribute a controlled substance. He moved to suppress the marijuana on the grounds that there was no reasonable suspicion to stop his vehicle as required by the Fourth Amendment.

The trial court concluded that the observations and inferences, viewed in their totality, drawn from the observations of the officer, did amount to reasonable suspicion and refused to suppress the evidence. The court of appeals considered each factor (observation) separately and concluded that a majority of the facts were susceptible to innocent explanations. It thus held that the vehicle stop was illegal because reasonable suspicion did not exist.

The U.S. Supreme Court reversed, holding that the officer did have sufficient grounds for reasonable suspicion. The Court stated that while any one factor by itself might be insufficient, the totality of the circumstances supported the officer's decision to stop the vehicle.[7]

The issue of reasonable suspicion arises frequently in suspected drug trafficking cases, where law enforcement officers make investigative stops based on circumstances they believe indicate signs of such trafficking. These stops have often been found to lack reasonable suspicion. For example, in *Reid v. Georgia*,[8] the U.S. Supreme Court held that no reasonable suspicion existed to justify an investigative detention based on the facts that the defendant (1) arrived at the Fort Lauderdale airport very early in the morning, (2) appeared to conceal that he was traveling with a companion, and (3) failed to check any luggage.

State and lower federal courts have done the same. In the following situations courts found that the officers lacked reasonable suspicion to make an investigative stop:

- A young man was driving a late-model car on an interstate highway in Florida at 4:15 A.M. *State v. Johnson*.[9]
- A nervous driver of a car with several visible air fresheners avoided eye contact with police officers.[10]
- A car known to be purchased from a dealer suspected of drug trafficking was registered in a common drug smuggling area and had a two-way antenna protruding from the trunk.[11]
- A nervous Hispanic-looking man was driving a car with out-of-state license plates, looking for work, but had no luggage in the car.[12]
- A man arriving on an early flight from San Francisco to Kansas was the first person to deplane, carried no luggage except a garment bag, was wearing a gold chain, and had paid cash for his airline ticket.[13]

THE IMPORTANCE OF "STOP AND IDENTIFY" LAWS

Many, but not all, states have statutes that require a person stopped to respond to an officer's request to identify himself or herself. In the 2004 case of *Hiibel v. Sixth Judicial District Court of Nevada*,[14] the U.S. Supreme Court considered the validity of these statutes.

In responding to a telephone call reporting an assault in a rural area, a Nevada deputy sheriff came upon a man, who appeared to be intoxicated, standing beside a truck on the side of a road. A young woman was sitting in the truck. The officer asked the man for identification, but the man refused to give any identification and instead asked why the officer wanted to see it. When the officer stated that he was conducting an investigation, the man became agitated and insisted he had done nothing wrong. The officer explained that he wanted to find out who the man was and what he was doing there. The officer asked for identification eleven times and was refused each time.

The man was then arrested under Nevada's "resisting, delaying or obstructing a public officer" law in failing to disclose his identity. The law specifically requires that the "person so detained shall identify himself, but may not be compelled to answer any other inquiry of any peace officer."[15]

The U.S. Supreme had held in three earlier cases that "an individual's refusal to answer or give a name does not give rise in and of itself to a reasonable suspicion that criminal activity is afoot."[16] Simply refusing to identify oneself is thus not a crime unless, like Nevada, a state has a "stop and identify" law. The question in *Hiibel* was whether a state could constitutionally pass such a law.

The U.S. Supreme Court held the Nevada law constitutional, stating:

> Asking questions is an essential part of police investigations. In the ordinary course a police officer is free to ask a person for identification without implicating the Fourth Amendment. "Interrogation relating to one's identity or a request for identification by the police does not, by itself, constitute a Fourth Amendment seizure."[17]

A search incident to the arrest in cases such as *Hiibel* often reveals the identity and other information about the person. If it does not, the person will not be released on bail but will be booked as a "John Doe" or an "unknown." Jailers delight in relating stories of conversations with lawyers who seek to see their client but either cannot or will not identify the client. Such persons are eventually identified through fingerprints or appearances before a very busy and impatient judge.

SEARCHES THAT CAN BE JUSTIFIED DURING AN INVESTIGATIVE DETENTION

Consent searches and protective searches (where the law officer has a valid safety concern) are the only searches that can be justified during an investigative detention.

Consent to search must be voluntarily and clearly given. Consent searches are then limited to the area or object consented to be searched. The consent to search could be of luggage, a parcel, a purse, a vehicle, or another object or place.

protective search A search limited to discovering threatening weapons.

A **protective search** can be made if an officer who has made a valid investigative stop has reasonable suspicion to believe that the suspect "may be armed and presently dangerous." The U.S. Supreme Court also pointed out that "it would be unreasonable to require that police officers take unnecessary risks in the performance of their duties. American criminals have a long tradition of armed violence, and every year in this country many law enforcement officers are killed in the line of duty and thousands more are wounded."[18]

The protective frisk is strictly limited to discovering threatening weapons. If the pat-down causes the officer to reasonably believe that an object detected in the frisk could be a weapon, the object may be removed and may be used as evidence if the object is a weapon or other illegal contraband.

In the 1993 U.S. Supreme Court case of *Minnesota v. Dickerson*,[19] a police officer making a lawful pat-down felt an object that he knew was not a weapon but suspected it was a lump of rock cocaine. The Supreme Court held that once it was immediately apparent that the object was not a weapon, no further search was permissible. If the nature of the unknown object is not immediately apparent and there is no probable cause to believe it is evidence of a crime, it cannot be seized and used as evidence.

In March 2000 the U.S. Supreme Court again considered the *Terry* rules in connection with anonymous tips. In *Florida v. J.L.*,[20] an anonymous caller told Miami–Dade police that a black male standing at a bus stop was carrying a concealed weapon. The caller identified the man as wearing a plaid shirt but gave no other basis for the caller's belief that the man was carrying a weapon. Police found J.L. at the bus stop and identified him by his plaid shirt. The police had no other basis for suspecting that J.L. was carrying a concealed weapon. They searched J.L. and found a concealed weapon.

The Supreme Court held that the tip alone did not justify the *Terry* stop. **Anonymous tips** require indicia of reliability—that is, corroborating information that the person giving the tip has "predictive information" about the suspect's behavior that allowed the police to judge the reliability of the anonymous tip. In *White v. Alabama*, for example, the tip included detailed information about the suspect's behavior, which the Court there said indicated the tipster had inside information about the suspect.[21] The *J.L.* court noted that *White* was a close case, on the borderline of permissible *Terry* stops. Because the anonymous tip in *J.L.* provided even less corroborating information, the Court held that it crossed over the line into impermissible *Terry* stops.

The *J.L.* court also held that there is no "firearm exception" to the *Terry* stop requirements of indicia of reliability, as contended by the State of Florida. Such an exception, the Court reasoned, would permit any person to "set in motion an intrusive, embarrassing police search of the targeted person simply by placing an anonymous call reporting the target's unlawful carriage of a gun."[22] The Court stated, however, that it was reserving ruling on such stops where the risks are particularly great—for example, where a caller informs the police that a person is carrying a bomb.

anonymous tips Information from an unknown person; could be received in a 911 call or another telephone call.

OBTAINING PHYSICAL EVIDENCE DURING AND AFTER AN ARREST

The Fourth Amendment of the U.S. Constitution requires that probable cause exist for either a law enforcement officer or a private citizen[23] to make an **arrest**. The U.S. Supreme Court pointed out that the "requirement of probable cause has roots that are deep in our history" and that "common rumor or report,

arrest Defined in 1760 by Sir William Blackstone as "the apprehending or restraining of one's person, in order to be forthcoming to answer an alleged or suspected crime."

suspicion, or even 'strong reason to suspect' was not adequate to support a warrant for arrest...."[24]

The famous English lawyer and writer, Sir William Blackstone, defined the legal term "arrest" in his 1760 *Commentaries* as "the apprehending or restraining of one's person, in order to be forthcoming to answer an alleged or suspected crime."

Most traffic stops and all *Terry* stops are not arrests. However, evidence could become available during such stops to support a finding of probable cause to authorize an arrest. Alternatives to an arrest are issuing a citation and ordering the person to appear at a police station or a prosecutor's office. In minor incidents, the person could receive a warning or scolding.

EVIDENCE OBTAINED IN SEARCHES FOLLOWING AN ARREST

A search for weapons and evidence of the crime may be made incident to arrest. The U.S. Supreme Court held that this search could be made "of the arrestee's person and the area 'within his immediate control'—construing that phrase to mean the area from within which he might gain possession of a weapon or destructible evidence."[25]

When the arrested person is in a motor vehicle, the U.S. Supreme Court held that the police "may, as a contemporaneous incident of that arrest, search the passenger compartment of that automobile," and the police "may also examine the contents of any containers found within the passenger compartment."[26]

The cases that permit searches incident to the arrest of persons in automobiles seemed to relate to the possibility that such persons might have weapons or destructible evidence on or near their persons. Both *New York v. Belton* and *Thornton v. United States* (discussed below), however, upheld searches of the interior of an automobile after the occupants had exited the vehicle. These decisions cast some doubt on whether in automobile cases a search incident to a lawful arrest is permitted only if the officers are concerned about weapons or destructible evidence. In the 2007 case of *State v. Gant*,[27] the Arizona Supreme Court held that a search of an automobile after the arrested occupant was handcuffed and placed in a police car was not justified under the search incident to an arrest exception. In 2008 the U.S. Supreme Court took certiorari in *Gant*, stating that the precise question for review was: "Must the police identify a threat to safety or a need to preserve evidence to make a search incident to arrest after vehicle's occupants have been arrested and secured?"[28] A decision is expected in late 2008 or early 2009.

A container could be a box, paper bag, suitcase, briefcase, or anything used to hold objects. The container searched in the *Belton* case was the zipped-up pocket of a black leather jacket belonging to Belton and lying on the backseat. The Supreme Court held that the cocaine found in Belton's leather jacket could be used as evidence to convict Belton of the possession of cocaine.

If during or after an arrest in a home or building there is reason to believe that another person (or persons) may be in a nearby room and may present a security

protective sweep or safety check An investigation of a building or vehicle to determine whether other persons or weapons are present that could jeopardize safety.

risk, a **protective sweep or safety check** is justified. This precaution was described as follows in the case of *United States v. Sheikh:*[29]

> Arresting officers have a right to conduct a quick and cursory check of the arrestee's lodging immediately subsequent to arrest—even if the arrest is near the door but outside the lodging—where they have reasonable grounds to believe that there are other persons present inside who might present a security risk.

EVIDENCE OBTAINED DURING INVENTORY SEARCHES

The U.S. Supreme Court listed the following reasons for inventorying property that is being held by the police:

1. Protection of the owner's property while it remained in police custody
2. Protection of the police against claims or disputes over lost or stolen property
3. Protection of the police from potential danger[30]

inventory searches The procedure that law officers use to account for the property of people who are in their custody.

Inventory searches are therefore not searches for incriminating evidence. They are a common and sensible police procedure to determine what the law enforcement agency is responsible for. They are "not an independent legal concept but rather an incidental administrative step following arrest and preceding incarceration."[31]

In the U.S. Supreme Court case of *Illinois v. Lafayette,*[32] the defendant was arrested for fighting with a theater manager. At the police station, the defendant was told to empty his pockets and the purse-type shoulder bag he was carrying, as part of the established police inventory procedure being used. Ten amphetamine pills were found inside a cigarette package. In holding that the pills could be used as evidence, the Supreme Court stated:

> it is not "unreasonable" for police, as part of the routine procedure incident to incarcerating an arrested person, to search any container or article in his possession, in accordance with established inventory procedure.

OBTAINING EVIDENCE BY POLICE ENTRY INTO PRIVATE PREMISES

The Fourth Amendment of the U.S. Constitution protects the "right of the people to be secure in their persons, houses, papers and effects."[33] The U.S. Supreme Court has held that an illegal or improper police "physical entry of the home is the chief evil against which the wording of the Fourth Amendment is directed."[34]

The right of privacy in the home has deep roots in Anglo-Saxon law. The U.S. Supreme Court quoted the following statement attributed to William Pitt in 1763:

> The poorest man may in his cottage bid defiance to all the forces of the Crown. It may be frail—its roof may shake—the wind may blow through it—the storm may enter—the rain may enter—but the King of England cannot enter—all his force dares not cross the threshold of the ruined tenement![35]

TERRY STOPS AND THE U.S. SUPREME COURT

Cases Where Reasonable Suspicion Authorized *Terry* Stops

Case	Facts That Authorized a *Terry* Stop	Ruling
Terry v. Ohio, 88 S.Ct. 1868 (1968)	A veteran Cleveland detective observed two men who made a dozen trips past a store, looking in and then talking to each other. The officer suspected that the men were "casing" the store for a stickup. The officer approached the men, identified himself, and because he feared for his safety frisked them and seized two pistols.	In affirming the concealed weapons convictions, the Court held "that where a police officer observes unusual conduct which leads him reasonably to conclude in light of his experience that criminal activity may be afoot and that the persons with whom he is dealing may be armed and presently dangerous …" the officer may take protective measures.
Adams v. Williams, 92 S.Ct. 1921 (1972)	A known informant told police that Williams was sitting in a car late at night in a public place and had narcotics and a gun on his person. The tip was corroborated when Williams was seen sitting in the parked car.	After seizing the gun, the police arrested Williams and, in the search incident to the arrest, found the drugs. The Court held: "The purpose of this limited search is not to discover evidence of a crime, but to allow the officer to pursue his investigation without fear of violence." Conviction of two crimes was sustained.
Alabama v. White, 110 S.Ct. 2412 (1990)	An anonymous telephone caller told police that White would be driving a brown Plymouth station wagon with a broken right taillight, from her house to a named motel, carrying cocaine. After the tip was corroborated, when White arrived at the motel, a police *Terry* stop was made.	The Court held that there was sufficient indication of reliability to justify the stop based on reasonable suspicion after police corroborated the tip. White gave the police consent to search her attaché case and gave the police the combination to the lock.
United States v. Sokolow, 109 S.Ct. 1581 (1989)	The defendant bought airline tickets to travel from Honolulu to Miami (20 hours). He stayed in Miami for 48 hours and then returned to Honolulu. He paid $2,100 in cash for his airfare from a big roll of $20 bills and appeared nervous. A drug-detection dog led to the finding of cocaine in Sokolow's luggage.	The Court held that reasonable suspicion existed to make the stop, holding that: "Any one of these factors is not by itself proof of illegal conduct and is quite consistent with innocent travel. But we think that taken together, they amount to reasonable suspicion."

(Continued)

Cases Where Evidence Could Not Be Used

Case	Facts That Did Not Authorize a *Terry* Stop	Ruling
Brown v. Texas, 99 S.Ct. 2637 (1979)	The defendant was stopped in an alley in an area that had a high incidence of drug trafficking. There was no testimony that it was unusual for people to be in the alley.	"The fact that [the defendant] was in a neighborhood frequented by drug users standing alone, is not a basis for concluding that [the defendant] himself was engaged in criminal conduct … [the defendant's] activity was no different from activity of other pedestrians in that neighborhood."
Florida v. Royer, 103 S.Ct. 1319 (1983)	Officers at the Miami airport observed Royer and concluded that he fit the "drug courier profile," but their information did not amount to reasonable suspicion. The officers approached Royer and asked for and examined his plane ticket and driver's license. Without returning the ticket or driver's license, they informed Royer he was suspected of transporting drugs and asked him to come with them to a small police room.	The Court held that the police conduct was such a show of police authority that a reasonable person would not have felt free to leave. Royer's consent to search his luggage was held to be "invalid because [it was] tainted by the unlawful confinement."
Dunaway v. New York, 99 S.Ct. 2248 (1979)	The defendant was picked up on an uncorroborated tip from an informant and taken to a police station for questioning about the murder of a pizza parlor owner. After being given *Miranda* warnings and waiving his rights, the defendant incriminated himself.	The Court ruled that the confession could not be used as evidence because it would allow the police "to violate the Fourth Amendment with impunity, safe in the knowledge that they could wash their hands in the 'procedural safeguards' of the Fifth Amendment."
Davis v. Mississippi, 89 S.Ct. 1394 (1969)	Police rounded up more than twenty young black men for questioning about the rape of a white woman and to seek a match for fingerprints and palm prints found at the scene of the crime. Days later, the defendant was picked up a second time and this time was held overnight and transported to another city, where the defendant's fingerprints were found to match those found at the crime scene.	In reversing the defendant's convictions and holding that the police roundup procedures violated the Fourth Amendment, the Court held: "Nothing is more clear than that the Fourth Amendment was meant to prevent wholesale intrusions upon the personal security of our citizenry, whether those intrusions be termed 'arrests' or 'investigative detentions.'"

Note: Six additional U.S. Supreme Court cases in this area are described in the Problems section at the end of this chapter.

PROBABLE CAUSE: OBJECTIVE OR SUBJECTIVE STANDARD?

As stated earlier in this chapter, before making an arrest, the police must have probable cause to believe that a crime has been committed. If they do, they can make a search incident to that arrest. If physical evidence of criminal activity is found in that search, it is admissible in court.

The following cases illustrate two questions raised about the required probable cause. A common factor is whether the police officer's belief was judged on a subjective or objective basis.

- *May an arrest be upheld if it was made for violation of an offense that didn't exist, but a closely related offense did exist?* In *Devenpeck v. Alford* [125 S.Ct. 588 (2004)], the U.S. Supreme Court held that the subjective intent of the arresting officer does not determine whether probable cause exists. In *Devenpeck*, the police arrested a man and charged him with unlawfully taping a conversation with the police. The police stopped to question the man because he appeared to be impersonating a police officer. They then discovered that the man was taping their conversation, which the officers thought was a criminal violation. The unlawful taping charge was subsequently dismissed because it was not a crime to make such a tape recording. However, probable cause existed to arrest the man for the crime of impersonating a police officer. The Ninth Circuit Court of Appeals held that the arrest was unlawful because probable cause to arrest the man for the "unrelated" offense of impersonating an officer did not cure the lack of probable cause to arrest him for taping the officers' conversation. In reversing the Ninth Circuit Court, the U.S. Supreme Court said that the rule is based on an objective standard; if a reasonable person viewing the facts and circumstances would conclude that probable cause existed to arrest the suspect for a crime, a subsequent arrest is lawful: "[t]he subjective intent of the arresting officer, … is simply no basis for invalidating an arrest. Those are lawfully arrested whom the facts known to the arresting officers gave probable cause to

arrest." The Court therefore remanded the case to determine whether an objective basis for probable cause existed.

- *Must the police intend to make an arrest?* In a case decided after the U.S. Supreme Court's decision in *Devenpeck*, the Wisconsin Supreme Court held that if probable cause to make an arrest exists, judged on an objective basis, then a search conducted by the officers possessing that probable cause is a search incident to a lawful arrest, even if the officers initially had no intent to make an arrest when the search occurred.

  In *State v. Sykes* [695 N.W.2d 277 (2005)], the police were called by a landlord to the landlord's premises because persons had trespassed on his property. The police officer entered the premises and asked those within to identify themselves. The defendant told the officer his wallet was in his jacket, lying on the floor. The officer picked up the jacket, searched the pockets, and found the wallet. Inside the wallet was a bag of crack cocaine. A subsequent search of the apartment found more illegal drugs. The officer arrested the defendant and charged him with illegal drug possession. The defendant moved to suppress the evidence of illegal drug possession, contending that because the officer had no intent to arrest the defendant when he asked to see some identification, but was merely exercising the caretaking function, the search of the wallet could not be incident to a lawful arrest. The lower courts denied his motion to suppress, and the Wisconsin Supreme Court affirmed. The court held, based on the reasoning in *Devenpeck*, that since the officer clearly had probable cause to arrest the defendant for criminal trespass, and the defendant was subsequently arrested, the search was incident to a lawful arrest even though the arrest was for a crime other than the one for which probable cause existed and even though the subjective intent of the officer was not to arrest the defendant when the search took place.

THE THREE TYPES OF POLICE–CITIZEN CONTACTS

Voluntary Conversation and/or Observation/Surveillance

Voluntary conversations may be used for investigative purposes if the person will talk with the officer. Observation and surveillance may be made of persons in public places without a showing of probable cause or reasonable suspicion. [See *Weber v. Cedarburg*, 370 N.W.2d 791 (1985), in which the Supreme Court of Wisconsin affirmed a ruling that the defendant had no civil cause of action for surveillance without reason to suspect wrongdoing. Police followed Weber to bars, sporting events, and so forth and made notes of his activities.]

Investigative Stop, or *Terry* Stop

Police must have reasonable suspicion to make a *Terry* stop (investigative detention). A detention is made and a *Terry* stop has occurred when a "reasonable person would have believed that he was not free to leave" (*United States v. Mendenhall*). The free-to-leave test determines when a police

encounter is no longer a voluntary conversation. The detention, or *Terry* stop, "must be temporary and last no longer than is necessary" (*Florida v. Royer*). In the 1985 case of *United States v. Sharpe*, the Supreme Court held that a 20-minute stop was not unreasonable "when the police have acted diligently and a suspect's actions contributed to the added delay about which he complains" [470 U.S. at 688, 105 S.Ct. at 1576].

Custody or Arrest

Probable cause, also known as reasonable grounds to believe, must exist to hold a person in custody or make an arrest. Incident to a lawful, custodial arrest, a search may be made of the person and the area under the person's immediate control. Under the delayed search exception of *United States v. Edwards*, searches of the arrestee's person may be made at later times. But if police take control of property or a container, they may search it only at the time of the arrest.

As early as 1461, an English court held that it was unlawful for a sheriff to break down the door of a man's house to arrest him in a civil suit for debt or trespass. Sir William Blackstone wrote in 1822 in *4 Blackstone's Commentaries* that "the law of England has [such] … regard to the immunity of a man's house, that it styles it his castle, and will never suffer it to be violated with impunity …" (p. 222).

The home of a person could be worth millions, or it could be a very poor and simple building. It could be an apartment in a large building, or it could be a motel or hotel room. A person could be living alone or with other persons. A tent pitched lawfully on public or private land was held to be a home in the cases of *United States v. Gooch*[36] and *LaDuke v. Nelson*.[37] In whatever form, a person's home is protected by the privacy clause of the Fourth Amendment of the U.S. Constitution.[38]

AUTHORITY NEEDED BY POLICE OFFICERS TO ENTER PRIVATE PREMISES

Probable cause alone does not authorize a law enforcement officer to enter private premises. The general rule is that a search warrant is required to enter and search a

THE FOURTH AMENDMENT

The Fourth Amendment of the U.S. Constitution consists of one long sentence with two clauses:

The Rights (or Privacy) Clause

"The right of the people to be secure in their persons, houses, papers, and effects against unreasonable searches and seizures shall not be violated."

The Warrant Clause

"And no warrant shall issue, but upon probable cause, supported by oath or affirmation, and particularly describing the place to be searched and the persons or things to be seized"

Regarding the Rights Clause, the U.S. Supreme Court Has Held

- "The Fourth Amendment is not a guarantee against all searches and seizures, but only against *unreasonable* searches and seizures"[a]
- "The ultimate standard set forth in the Fourth Amendment is reasonableness"[b]
- The touchstone of the Court's analysis under the Fourth Amendment "is always the reasonableness in all the circumstances of the particular governmental invasion of a citizen's personal security"[c]

Regarding the Warrant Clause, the U.S. Supreme Court Has Held

A basic principle of Fourth Amendment law is "that searches and seizures inside a home without a warrant are presumptively unreasonable"[d]

[a][*United States v. Hensley*, 469 U.S. 221, 105 S.Ct. 675 (1985)].

[b][*Camera v. Municipal Court*, 387 U.S. 523, 87 S.Ct. 1727 (1967)].

[c][*Terry v. Ohio*, 392 U.S. 1, 19, 88 S.Ct. 1868, 1878].

[d][*Payton v. New York*, 445 U.S. at 586, 100 S.Ct. at 1380].

private residence. In the following cases, the U.S. Supreme Court held that the evidence obtained by police officers who entered private premises with only probable cause could not be used in criminal trials.

Vale v. Louisiana

United States Supreme Court, 90 S.Ct. 1969 (1970)

After arresting Vale on the front steps of his house, police had probable cause to believe illegal narcotics were in the house. The narcotics that police seized in the house could not be used as evidence and were suppressed.

Payton v. New York and Riddick v. New York

United States Supreme Court, 100 S.Ct. 1371 (1980)

The Supreme Court combined these cases where police entered private premises to arrest the two defendants without either arrest warrants or search warrants. Police had probable cause to arrest Payton for murder and Riddick for two armed robberies. The Court held that evidence obtained in both cases could not be used in the two criminal trials.

Search warrants and arrest warrants authorize police entry into private premises. However, law enforcement officers who have valid warrants to enter private premises must comply with the rules described next.

arrest warrant An order signed by a judge or magistrate authorizing the arrest of a named person or persons.

search warrant An order signed by a judge or magistrate authorizing the place to be searched and the persons or things to be seized.

An **arrest warrant** "carries with it the limited authority to enter a dwelling in which the suspect lives when there is reason to believe the suspect is within."[39] Police may enter with an arrest warrant under the following limitations:

- Entry is limited to a suspect's *own residence.*
- "There is reason to believe the suspect is within."[40]

If these conditions do not exist, law officers should obtain a **search warrant** in addition to the arrest warrant, or they could wait until the suspect appears in a public place to make an arrest.

Prior to entering private premises with either a search warrant or an arrest warrant, law enforcement officers are obligated to knock, identify themselves, state their purpose, and await a refusal or silence before entering. There are two reasons for imposing these requirements and forbidding unannounced police entries into private premises:

1. *Possibility of mistake*: "[C]ases of mistaken identity are surely not novel in the investigation of crime. The possibility is very real that the police may be misinformed as to the name or address of a suspect, or as to other material information.... Innocent citizens should not suffer the shock, fright or embarrassment attendant upon an unannounced police intrusion."[41]
2. *Protection of the officers*: "[It] is also a safeguard for the police themselves who might be mistaken for prowlers and be shot down by a fearful householder."[42]

Although knock-and-announce entries are the most usual type of police entry, a no-knock entry would be justified if one or more of the following conditions can be shown:

- Such notice would be likely to endanger the life or the safety of the officer or another person.
- Such notice would be likely to result in the evidence subject to seizure being easily and quickly destroyed or disposed of.[43]
- Such notice would be likely to enable the escape of a party to be arrested.
- Such notice would be a useless gesture.

In order to justify a no-knock entry when no prior notice was given, the officer would have to point to evidence that would give the officer the authority to enter without announcement.

Police may detain and prevent owners and occupants from entering private premises while the police are in the process of obtaining a search warrant for the premises. In the 2001 case of *Illinois v. McArthur*,[44] the U.S. Supreme Court held that the police lawfully denied the defendant access to the premises during the 2 hours that it took to obtain a search warrant, unless an officer accompanied the defendant into the building.

In *Michigan v. Summers*,[45] the Supreme Court held that officers executing a search warrant have the authority "to detain the occupants of the premises while a proper search is conducted." The Court noted that a reasonable detention was a "minimal intrusion" compared to the lawful search and served three legitimate law enforcement interests: (1) preventing flight of a suspect,

(2) protecting the officers, and (3) facilitating an orderly completion of the search. In the following 2005 case, the Court considered the scope of the right to detain such occupants.

Muehler v. Mena

United States
Supreme Court, 125
S.Ct. 1465 (2005)

In _Bivens v. Six Unknown Named Agents of the Federal Narcotics Bureau_,[46] the Supreme Court held that the Fourth Amendment created a civil cause of action for damages against police officers who conduct an unreasonable search and seizure. Such causes of action are now brought under 42 U.S.C. section 1983, so-called 1983 actions. Because the basis of these lawsuits is the unreasonableness of a search and seizure, decisions in these civil cases are generally applicable to the same issue when it is raised in a criminal case. _Devenpeck_, discussed previously, is such a case. _Muehler v. Mena_ is another one.

In _Muehler_, the police suspected that a known gang member was residing in Mena's home and that the suspect was armed and dangerous. They obtained a search warrant, and a SWAT team entered the house, woke up Mena, and brought her into the garage. There, they handcuffed her and detained her for 2 to 3 hours. In addition, an INS officer present during the detention asked her questions about her immigration status. After the search was completed, Mena was released. She sued the officers, contending that her detention was in violation of her Fourth Amendment rights and that the questioning by the INS officer was an unlawful seizure because the officer lacked any basis for reasonable suspicion that she was an illegal alien. The jury agreed and awarded her $10,000 in actual damages and $20,000 in punitive damages. The Ninth Circuit Court of Appeals affirmed the verdict.

The U.S. Supreme Court reversed, holding that under _Summers_ the detention was permissible: "An officer's authority to detain incident to a search is categorical; it does not depend on the 'quantum of proof justifying detention or the extent of the intrusion to be imposed by the seizure.'" The Court also stated, "Inherent in _Summers_'s authorization to detain an occupant of the place to be searched is the authority to use reasonable force to effectuate the detention." Finally, the Court held that the questioning by the INS officer was not an independent seizure requiring reasonable suspicion.

EXCEPTIONS TO THE WARRANT REQUIREMENT TO ENTER PRIVATE PREMISES

The Fourth Amendment of the U.S. Constitution forbids "unreasonable searches and seizures" and requires a search warrant unless the government can show that a court-recognized exception to the warrant requirement of the Fourth Amendment exists.

Consent that is voluntarily given by a person who either has sole control of the property or has such mutual use of the premises to have joint access and control of the premises may authorize law enforcement officers to enter the premises.[47] In _Halsema v. State_,[48] the Indiana Supreme Court held that the lessee of an apartment who allowed the defendant to sleep in her bedroom and have the exclusive use of one drawer in her chest of drawers had no authority to give police consent to search that drawer. The illegal drugs discovered in the search were suppressed.

exigent circumstances A court-recognized exception to the warrant requirement of the Fourth Amendment; authorizes entry by not only law enforcement officers but also by firefighters and emergency medical personnel.

Exigent circumstances (or the *emergency search doctrine*) is also a court-recognized exception to the warrant requirement of the Fourth Amendment and authorizes entry by not only law enforcement officers but also firefighters and emergency medical personnel. In 1963, former Chief Justice Warren Burger, while an appeals court judge, wrote about the emergency search doctrine:

> A warrant is not required to break down a door to enter a burning home to rescue occupants or extinguish a fire, to prevent a shooting or to bring emergency aid to an injured person. The need to protect or preserve life or avoid serious injury is justification for what would be otherwise illegal absent an exigency or emergency. Fires or dead bodies are reported to police by cranks where no fires or bodies are to be found. Acting in response to reports of "dead bodies," the police may find the "bodies" to be common drunks, diabetics in shock, or distressed cardiac patients. But the business of policemen and firemen is *to act*, not to speculate or meditate on whether the report is correct. People could well die in emergencies if police tried to act with the calm deliberation associated with the judicial process. Even the apparently dead often are saved by swift police response. A myriad of circumstances could fall within the terms "exigent circumstances"... e.g., smoke coming out a window or under a door, the sound of gunfire in a house, threats from the inside to shoot through the door at police, reasonable grounds to believe an injured or seriously ill person is being held within.[49]

Situations that fall under the exigency, or emergency, search doctrine may be classified as follows:

- When an officer has reason to believe that a life may be in jeopardy
- When an officer is in hot pursuit of a person who has committed a crime, or there is danger of escape by criminals
- Now-or-never situations in which evidence or contraband such as drugs will be destroyed or moved to another place before a search warrant can be obtained

If an entry into premises by a law enforcement officer is lawful and proper, the officer then has the right to be where he or she is. What the officer then sees in plain view (and unexpectedly) comes under the plain view doctrine and can be seized if there is reason to believe it is evidence of a crime.

Brigham City v. Stuart

U.S. Supreme Court, 126 S.Ct. 1943 (2006)

In *Brigham* police officers responding to a call about a loud party, went to a residence, and heard what sounded like a fight inside the residence. They looked in the front window but saw nothing, so they went around to the back of the residence, where they saw two juveniles drinking in the backyard. Through a screened backdoor the officers saw four adults attempting to restrain a juvenile. The officers observed punches being thrown during the altercation. An officer went into the house and announced the police presence. Occupants of the residence were arrested for disorderly conduct, intoxication, and contributing to the delinquency of a minor. At the trial on these charges, the trial court suppressed evidence obtained by the police who entered the residence, and the Utah Supreme Court affirmed the trial court.

The U.S. Supreme Court reversed the Utah Supreme Court, disagreeing on the two reasons given by that court for suppression of the evidence. The first reason was that the police were motivated to enter the residence not to render emergency aid but to arrest the occupants. The Supreme Court held that as long as the officers' actions were objectively reasonable, the Fourth Amendment is not violated. The Court stated:

> It therefore does not matter here—even if [the officers] motives could be so neatly unraveled—whether the officers entered the kitchen to arrest respondents and gather evidence against them or to assist the injured and prevent violence.

The second reason was that the defendants' conduct was not serious enough to justify the police entry into the residence. The Supreme Court held that the ongoing violence was serious enough to justify the police entry, stating that the test is whether entry into the residence was "plainly reasonable under the circumstances." The Court stated:

> Nothing in the Fourth Amendment required [the police] to wait until another blow rendered someone "unconscious" or "semi-conscious" or worse before entering. The role of the police officer includes preventing violence and restoring order, not simply rendering first aid to casualties; an officer is not like a boxing (or hockey) referee, poised to stop a bout only if it becomes one-sided.

OBTAINING EVIDENCE IN TRAFFIC STOPS AND VEHICLE SEARCHES

Studies show that motor vehicles are involved in more than 75 percent of the crimes committed every year in the United States. Vehicles are used as instrumentalities of most crimes; crimes are committed in vehicles; and motor vehicles are the object of criminal efforts because more than a million motor vehicles are stolen every year in the United States. Motor vehicles that are illegally driven cause thousands of deaths and hundreds of thousands of injuries every year.

MAY A POLICE OFFICER STOP A MOTOR VEHICLE FOR NO REASON?

A law enforcement officer may stop a vehicle for many valid reasons: The driver may be speeding or may have violated other sections of the traffic code; there may be an equipment violation, such as a headlight out; or there may be probable cause or reasonable suspicion to arrest or question the driver or a passenger in the vehicle.

But can a vehicle be stopped for no reason? That question was before the U.S. Supreme Court in the 1979 case of *Delaware v. Prouse*.[50] In that case, the officer making the vehicle stop testified, "I saw the car in the area and wasn't answering any complaints, so I decided to pull them off." In holding that such stops are unreasonable under the Fourth Amendment, the Court ruled that:

> [E]xcept in those situations in which there is at least articulable and reasonable suspicion that a motorist is unlicensed or that an automobile is not registered, or that either the vehicle or an occupant is otherwise subject to seizure for violation of law, stopping an automobile and detaining the driver in order to check his driver's license and the registration of the automobile are unreasonable under the Fourth Amendment.

A traffic stop significantly interferes with the freedom of movement of not only the vehicle driver but also the passengers, but, again, most traffic stops are temporary, brief, and public police stops. In the 1984 case of *Berkemer v. McCarty*,[51] the U.S. Supreme Court pointed out the consequences to a motorist of failing to obey a law enforcement officer's signal to stop:

> It must be acknowledged at the outset that a traffic stop significantly curtails the "freedom of action" of the driver and the passengers, if any, of the detained vehicle. Under the law of most States, it is a crime either to ignore a policeman's signal to stop one's car or, once having stopped, to drive away without permission....
>
> ... Certainly few motorists would feel free either to disobey a directive to pull over or to leave the scene of a traffic stop without being told they might do so. Partly for these reasons, we have long acknowledged that "stopping an automobile and detaining its occupants constitute a 'seizure' within the meaning of [the Fourth] Amendmen[t], even though the purpose of the stop is limited and the resulting detention quite brief."[52]

USING PRETEXTUAL STOPS TO OBTAIN EVIDENCE

Thousands of vehicle stops are made every year in the United States. About one-half are made for speeding and about one-fourth for equipment violations. Some of these stops are called *pretextual stops:* On the surface the reason for the stop is some minor violation, but the underlying reason is to obtain evidence of more serious crimes. The officer in a pretextual stop usually suspects the driver (or a passenger) of having committed, or being in the process of committing, a serious crime.

Prior to 1996, a common defense to illegal drug charges and other serious offenses was that the traffic stop was a pretext, and that as a result the evidence obtained should be suppressed. However, in *Whren v. United States*,[53] the U.S. Supreme Court eliminated most of these defenses.

A unanimous court held in *Whren* that, if the traffic stop is objectively supported by probable cause to believe that a traffic violation has occurred, the traffic stop is reasonable under the Fourth Amendment even if the officer's motivation for making the traffic stop was different from enforcement of traffic laws. The Court pointed out that probable cause is an objective standard that is determined by the totality of the circumstances and not by the officer's subjective intent.

OBTAINING EVIDENCE DURING ROUTINE TRAFFIC STOPS

On routine traffic stops, evidence of violations often becomes available as law enforcement officers carry out the following routine:

1. Officers may and do request a driver's license and other required documents.[54] Because operating a motor vehicle on public highways is a privilege rather than a right, it is constitutional to require a lawfully stopped driver to produce a driver's license upon request, the vehicle registration, and other documents required by statute. The information in these documents gives officers important facts to assist them in determining whether they are confronting innocent or criminal conduct. Inconsistencies between documents or between what is found in the documents and what the driver tells the officers may provide clues to criminal behavior that might otherwise be overlooked. Refusal to produce required documents almost universally constitutes criminal behavior

MOST TRAFFIC STOPS ARE TEMPORARY, BRIEF, AND PUBLIC

In pointing out that most traffic stops are temporary, brief, and public, the U.S. Supreme Court stated in footnote 26 of *Berkemer v. McCarty* [104 S.Ct. 3138, 3149 (1984)] that "no state requires that a detained motorist be arrested unless he is accused of a specified serious crime, refuses to promise to appear in court, or demands to be taken before a magistrate."

However, a motorist who fails to furnish satisfactory self-identification or an out-of-state motorist who is unable to post bail or to pay a traffic fine or a citation is likely to be detained until the matter is cleared.

under state statutes. Thus, demand for and examination of required documentation by police officers are sound early steps in investigating a stopped vehicle and its driver.

2. Officers may question the occupants of the vehicle. Police officers gathering information may briefly question a stopped car's driver and other occupants of the car where the car and occupants have been lawfully stopped.[55] The U.S. Supreme Court has made clear that such questioning may take place without any prior *Miranda*-type warnings, so long as the persons questioned have not been placed under arrest or subjected to arrest-type treatment.[56] This is true even where officers may have determined that they have lawful grounds for arrest and have decided to effect such an arrest. Even though no warnings are required, persons being questioned do enjoy a constitutional right not to respond, and although a failure to respond may be taken into consideration as officers assess whether probable cause exists to arrest or search, a person's failure to respond probably cannot constitute in itself a criminal offense, since the person is merely exercising a right guaranteed by the Constitution.

3. Officers sometimes request consent to search. An officer who has lawfully stopped a car may request that the person in lawful control of the car (generally the driver) waive his or her Fourth Amendment rights and give consent to a search of the car.[57] If such a consent is obtained, the officer should be prepared to prove at a later time that the consent was voluntarily given, that the person giving the consent was in lawful control of the items searched, and that the search performed was within the scope of the consent that was given.

4. Officers may make plain view observations of parts of the vehicle exposed to public view.[58] The Fourth Amendment does not require officers who approach a lawfully stopped car to wear blinders. The exterior of a car on a public highway is exposed to the public view, and it is unreasonable for a person to expect that a car's exterior appearance is therefore private. Consequently, an officer's visual inspection of the exterior of a stopped car does not constitute a search for Fourth Amendment purposes. Portions of the interior that are likewise exposed to the public view due to the placement of windows are also not private, and an officer's visual examination of these areas from outside the car is also not a Fourth Amendment search. As a result, officers approaching a lawfully stopped vehicle frequently are exposed to a wealth of information that they may lawfully use for investigative purposes.

WHAT MAY POLICE DO IN ROUTINE TRAFFIC STOPS?

What are the rights of drivers and passengers when police stop a vehicle for a routine traffic violation? In 2007 and 2008 the U.S. Supreme Court discussed two aspects of this question.

In *Brendlin v. California* [127 S.Ct. 2400 (2007)], police officers stopped a vehicle based on invalid registration stickers, even though in fact the sticker on the vehicle was in compliance with the law. The officers observed a passenger drop something out of the passenger door, and after identifying the passenger as a person wanted on a parole violation, they arrested the passenger. A subsequent search by police of the passenger and the vehicle uncovered evidence of illegal drugs. The passenger moved to suppress the evidence, contending that the traffic stop was illegal and was an unlawful seizure of his person.

The California trial court and the California Supreme Court agreed that the traffic stop was not legal because it lacked adequate justification, but refused to suppress any evidence against the passenger. These courts concluded that because the passenger was not "seized" by the stop, the subsequently obtained evidence was not tainted by the illegal stop.

The U.S. Supreme Court reversed, and held that the passenger was "seized" by the traffic stop. The Court held that whether a passenger is seized when the driver of a vehicle is stopped depends on whether the passenger felt "free to leave":

> We resolve this question by asking whether a reasonable person in Brendlin's position when the car stopped would have believed himself free to

"terminate the encounter" between the police and himself. (Citation omitted.) We think that in these circumstances any reasonable passenger would have understood the police officers to be exercising control to the point that no one in the car was free to depart without police permission. [127 S.Ct. at 2406]

In *Virginia v. Moore* [128 S.Ct. 1598 (2008)] police stopped a driver who they knew was driving with a suspended license. Under Virginia state law the officers were authorized to issue a summons for that offense, but were not authorized to make an arrest. The officers nonetheless arrested the driver, and a subsequent search incident to the arrest uncovered crack cocaine on the driver's person. The defendant was convicted of a drug offense, and he appealed, contending that the unauthorized arrest made the resulting search a violation of the Fourth Amendment.

The U.S. Supreme Court disagreed. It noted that the reasonableness of an arrest under the Fourth Amendment has always been upheld if the arresting officer had probable cause to believe a crime was committed in his presence, even a minor crime. That a state decides to make a rule that limits when an officer with such probable cause can actually make an arrest doesn't change the Fourth Amendment analysis, the Court concluded. Thus, because the officer had probable cause to arrest the defendant under Fourth Amendment standards, the resulting custodial search was valid, and the evidence of illegal drugs was properly admitted at his trial.

OBTAINING EVIDENCE IN SEARCHES OF VEHICLES, DRIVERS, AND PASSENGERS

The following two U.S. Supreme Court Cases illustrate the protective measures law enforcement officers may take in traffic stops and while investigating an accident. The U.S. Supreme Court sustained the use of the evidence and affirmed the criminal convictions.

Pennsylvania v. Mimms

United States
Supreme Court, 98
S.Ct. 330 (1977)

Mimms's vehicle was stopped because of an expired license plate. Mimms was asked to step out of the car, and as he did the officer noticed a bulge under his sport coat. The officer reached under the coat and removed a revolver from Mimms's waistband. The Supreme Court sustained the use of the evidence, holding that "In these circumstances, any man of 'reasonable caution' would have conducted the 'pat-down.'"

Michigan v. Long

United States
Supreme Court, 103
S.Ct. 3469 (1983)

Long, the driver, lost control of a speeding car late at night on a country road and crashed in a ditch. Long was the only occupant of the car and appeared to be under the influence of something when officers saw him standing at the rear of the car. When he was asked to show his driver's license, Long began to return to the open door of the car. Before allowing Long into the car, the officers checked the interior of the car for weapons. They found a large hunting knife on the floor of the driver's side of the car. Marijuana was then found in the car, and Long was arrested. The Supreme Court held that officers may make a limited search of the interior of vehicles to locate and control weapons when officers reasonably suspect the presence of weapons.

The next case illustrates the legality of searches incident to the lawful arrest of a driver or passenger of a vehicle.

New York v. Belton

United States
Supreme Court, 101
S.Ct. 2860 (1981)

After a car was stopped for speeding, officers smelled marijuana. The four occupants of the car were directed to get out of the vehicle, and a search incident to the arrest was made. The officers found cocaine in the jacket pocket of Belton's coat, which was on the backseat. Belton was a passenger in the vehicle. The Supreme Court held that the interior of a vehicle, including containers in the vehicle, can be searched even when the arrested person is outside the vehicle.

Subsequently, in the 2004 case of *Thornton v. United States*,[59] the Supreme Court held that a warrantless search of the passenger compartment of a vehicle is a lawful search incident to an arrest, even if the police first initiated contact with the passenger after the passenger had exited the vehicle. The Court rejected the so-called contact initiation rule followed in some jurisdictions, which limits a search of the passenger compartment to cases where contact with the passenger is initiated when the passenger is still inside the vehicle. Stating that such a rule would require arresting officers to make the subjective determination of when they first confronted the suspect, the Court stated:

> This determination would be inherently subjective and highly fact specific, and would require precisely the sort of ad hoc determination on the part of officers in the field and reviewing courts that *Belton* sought to avoid. ... Experience has shown that such a rule is impracticable, and we refuse to adopt it. So long as an arrestee is the sort of "recent occupant" of a vehicle such as petitioner was here, officers may search that vehicle incident to the arrest.[60]

Obtaining Evidence from Motor Vehicles (Including Aircraft, Watercraft, Snowmobiles, Trucks, Buses, and Others)

Authority	Requirements
Plain view observations and smells of vehicles exposed to public view	• The officer is where she or he has a right to be; if the police stop the vehicle, the stop must be lawful. • The contraband is in plain view, and it is "immediately apparent" that the item may be evidence of a crime. • The officer may seize the contraband if the officer has a lawful right of access to the object.
Consent to search	The officer must show that the consent was voluntarily given and that the person giving consent had actual or apparent authority to grant consent.
Reasonable suspicion, which justifies: • An investigative stop • A frisk or search for weapons if there was justifiable concern for safety • A search of the passenger compartment of a vehicle for weapons	To make a *Terry stop*, the officer "must have a particularized and objective basis for suspecting the particular person stopped of criminal activity." The officer has reasonable suspicion that "the suspect is dangerous and the suspect may gain immediate control of weapons" [*Michigan v. Long*, 463 U.S. 1032, 103 S.Ct. 3469 (1983)].
A lawful custodial arrest of the occupant of a motor vehicle	The officer may, at the time of the arrest and the place of the arrest: • Search the "passenger compartment of that automobile" • Search opened or closed containers in the vehicle (Some states have statutes or court rulings that limit this authority.)
The automobile exception (or the *Carroll* rule, or probable cause rule)	There is probable cause to believe that a vehicle contains evidence of a crime. A search of "a lawfully stopped vehicle" can then be made. The search can be "of every part of the vehicle and its contents that may conceal the object of the search" [U.S. Supreme Court in *United States v. Ross* (discussed later)].
Community caretaking function	A community caretaking function is a task or job that has to be done or that should be done in the best interests of the community. The officer is not looking for evidence of a crime but, while he is performing the community caretaking function, comes upon evidence of a crime. For example, an accident blocks traffic lanes on a busy street. To open the street to traffic, an officer gets into one of the cars and moves it to the curb. While in the vehicle, the officer sees contraband. [See the U.S. Supreme Court case of *Cady v. Dombrowski*, 93 S.Ct. 2523 (1973).]

Permissible Searches Under the Motor Vehicle Exception

During the years since motor vehicles were first used as a means of transportation, the courts have consistently noted the constitutional difference between motor vehicles and fixed structures such as homes and other types of buildings.

In the 1976 case of *South Dakota v. Opperman*,[61] the U.S. Supreme Court stated that:

> This Court has traditionally drawn a distinction between automobiles and homes or offices in relation to the Fourth Amendment. Although automobiles are "effects" and thus within the reach of the Fourth Amendment, ... warrantless examinations of automobiles have been upheld in circumstances in which a search of a home or office would not.

The automobile or motor vehicle exception (or the *Carroll* rule, or probable cause rule) is simple. It authorizes a law enforcement officer who has probable cause to believe that a vehicle contains evidence of a crime to search the vehicle and to seize the evidence. Probable cause alone will not get a law enforcement officer into a home to make an arrest or a search for evidence. However, probable cause alone will authorize entry into a vehicle to seize evidence.

The scope of the search of a vehicle is limited by the nature of the probable cause that justified the search. If the search is for a small item, such as a small amount of illegal drugs, the entire vehicle can be searched. If the search is for a large item, like a stolen lawn mower or a large bicycle, only parts of the vehicle where such an item could be located may be searched.

The automobile exception is not limited to ordinary automobiles. In the 1985 case of *California v. Carney*,[62] the U.S. Supreme Court held that a movable motor home, because of its ease of movement, created a lesser expectation of privacy than a regular home or office and was thus subject to the motor vehicle exception:

> Among the factors that might be relevant in determining whether a [search] warrant would be required in such a circumstance is its location, whether the vehicle is readily mobile or instead, for instance, elevated on blocks, whether the vehicle is licensed, whether it is connected to utilities, and whether it has convenient access to a public road.

In an article in the *FBI Law Enforcement Bulletin* of August 2005, entitled "The Motor Vehicle Exception," the author cites cases where the rule has been applied to "trucks, trailers pulled by trucks, boats, house boats, airplanes, and even the sleeping compartments of trains." The rule, which originated during Prohibition in the 1925 case of *Carroll v. United States*, is stated in the following cases.[63]

Carroll v. United States United States Supreme Court, 45 S.Ct. 280 (1925)	Officers had probable cause to believe that Carroll's roadster had gin and whiskey in it, in violation of the National Prohibition Act. The evidence found in the car was held to be lawfully obtained and could be used to sustain Carroll's conviction.
Chambers v. Maroney United States Supreme Court, 90 S.Ct. 1975 (1970)	Four armed robbers were arrested late at night. After the suspects were in a jail cell, officers went out to the robbers' vehicle, which had been moved to the police station, and obtained incriminating evidence that the police had probable cause to believe was in the vehicle. The Supreme Court sustained the use of the evidence, holding that a "careful search [at the place of the arrest] was impractical and perhaps not safe for the officers."

EXCEPTIONS TO THE FOURTH AMENDMENT'S SEARCH WARRANT REQUIREMENT RECOGNIZED BY THE U.S. SUPREME COURT

Exception	Reason for Exception	Requirement of Exception	Other Limitations
Search incident to custodial arrest	1. To protect officers and others 2. To prevent escape 3. To prevent destruction of evidence	1. There must be a lawful, custodial arrest. 2. Search must be made at the time and place of arrest or at a later time. 3. Search can be made only of the area of the arrestee's "immediate presence."	The law of a state or a state court decision may limit any of the listed exceptions.
Automobile exception (includes motor vehicles, watercraft, and aircraft)	The reduced (lesser) right of privacy in these means of transportation as distinguished from homes	There must be probable cause to believe that the vehicle held evidence of a crime or an object that may be seized by a law enforcement officer.	If probable cause justifies the search of a lawfully stopped vehicle, every part of the vehicle that may conceal the object of the search can be searched.
Consent to search	A person may waive his or her right of privacy in a home, vehicle, or object and may waive the Fourth Amendment requirement of probable cause	1. Consent must be given voluntarily and intelligently. 2. It must be shown that the person giving consent had actual or apparent authority to grant consent.	Neither written consent nor *Miranda*-type warnings are required under the federal rule. (However, either or both are helpful in showing that the consent was voluntarily given.)
Protective safety measures • Frisks during investigative stops, and so on • Frisks during execution of search warrants • Protective sweeps	Evidence must show that it is for the safety of law officers or the safety of other persons and that it would be "unreasonable to require … unnecessary risks" [U.S. Sup.Ct. 392 U.S. 1].	1. The officer is where he or she has a right to be. 2. Reasonable suspicion or more exists for the *Terry* stop. 3. Reasonable suspicion or more exists to fear for personal safety or safety of others.	Officer must be able to state justification for his or her action.

Exigency (emergency) searches
• Where there is reason to believe that a life is in danger
• Where there is "hot pursuit"
• "Now-or-never" situations to prevent the loss or destruction of evidence of a crime
	1. Need to protect or preserve life
	2. Need to act immediately to
	  • Prevent escape
	  • Prevent loss or destruction of evidence of a crime
		Reasonable grounds to believe that:
		• A life is endangered
		• A fleeing felon will escape and may arm himself or herself, or may destroy evidence
		• Action must be taken to prevent the loss or destruction of evidence	

United States v. Ross

United States Supreme Court, 102 S.Ct. 2157 (1982)

Police had probable cause to believe that Ross was selling heroin out of the trunk of his car in Washington, DC. After stopping the defendant, the police found a pistol in the glove compartment. The police arrested Ross and took his keys to open the car trunk. They opened a brown paper bag in the trunk and found glassine bags containing white powder. They then took Ross and his car to a police station, where it was determined that the white powder was heroin. A further search of the trunk produced additional evidence. In sustaining the convictions and the use of the evidence, the Supreme Court held that: "If probable cause justifies the search of a lawfully stopped vehicle, it justifies the search of every part of the vehicle and its contents that may conceal the object of the search."

Wyoming v. Houghton

United States Supreme Court, 526 U.S. 295, 302 (1999)

Police had probable cause to believe that an automobile contained illegal drugs, after seeing a hypodermic syringe in the driver's pocket and being told by the driver that he used the syringe to take drugs. The police searched the automobile and found a black container in the backseat that, when opened, was found to contain illegal drugs. The container belonged to Houghton, a passenger in the car. At her trial on the charge of possession of a controlled substance, Houghton argued that the search of her property violated the Fourth Amendment. The Supreme Court held it did not:

> When there is probable cause to search for contraband in a car, it is reasonable for police officers—like customs officials in the Founding era—to examine packages and containers without a showing of individualized probable cause for each one. A passenger's personal belongings, just like the driver's belongings or containers attached to the car like a glove compartment, are "in" the car, and the officer has probable cause to search for contraband *in* the car.

PROFILING AS AN INVESTIGATIVE TOOL

Profiles identify the characteristics and likely conduct of people involved in a given type of criminal activity. There are many types of profiles, such as shoplifting profiles, terrorist profiles, drug courier profiles, and airline hijacker profiles. The Maryland Court of Appeals stated that:

> The use of profiles is simply a means by which the law enforcement team communicates its collective expertise and empirical experience to the officer in the field and by which the officer, in turn, explains the special significance of his observations to the court [*Derricot v. State*, 578 A.2d 791 (1990)].

A profile is not evidence but is an investigative tool. In the 1989 case of *United States v. Sokolow*

[490 U.S. 1, 109 S.Ct. 1581], a DEA agent testified in court to facts that amounted to reasonable suspicion to authorize a detention of Sokolow by the agent. The agent then testified that Sokolow's behavior "had all the classic aspects of a drug courier."

In affirming Sokolow's conviction, the U.S. Supreme Court held that the fact that Sokolow's behavior was consistent with the DEA drug profile did not alter the conclusion that reasonable suspicion existed to make an investigative stop of Sokolow. The Court held that "the fact that these factors may be set forth in a 'profile' does not somehow detract from their evidentiary significance as seen by a trained agent."

(Continued)

Improper Racial Profiling Is Illegal

In 2003 President George W. Bush issued guidelines similar to those used by many states forbidding racial profiling by the seventy federal law enforcement agencies. These guidelines forbid the use of race or ethnicity by law officers in their routine investigations. The following examples were used:[a]

Examples of Forbidden Racial Profiling in Routine Investigations

- Law officers cannot focus on a specific neighborhood only because of its racial makeup.
- A man going into a courthouse passes through a metal detector, which shows nothing suspicious. The man cannot be ordered to undergo a more extensive search "solely because he appears to be of a particular ethnicity."
- An uncorroborated tip states that a man of a certain race will buy an illegal weapon at a bus terminal. Officers cannot use that information to single out men of that race in the terminal because "the information is neither sufficiently reliable nor sufficiently specific."

Examples of the Proper Use of Racial Information

- An all points bulletin (APB) or an AMBER Alert describes a fleeing felon by race, hair color, age, weight, and color of car. Officers may use all these characteristics to decide which drivers to pull over.
- Information exists that terrorists of a particular ethnicity plan to hijack a plane in California in the next week. Officers may subject men of that ethnicity who are boarding planes in California to "heightened security."
- Computer analysis of patterns of drug arrests shows that the majority of drug arrests occur in neighborhoods occupied primarily by people of a single race. Law enforcement operations in these areas may be increased "so long as they are not motivated by racial animus."

[a]Examples and quotations are from "U.S. Justice Department Guidance Regarding the Use of Race by Federal Law Enforcement Agencies" (June 2003).

SUMMARY

The U.S. Supreme Court has repeatedly pointed out that the Fourth Amendment forbids only "unreasonable" searches and seizures. This chapter presents cases and material on lawful searches and seizures that have been held to be "reasonable" under the Fourth Amendment. The following are "reasonable" if done within the guidelines set by the U.S. Supreme Court:

- Investigative detentions
- Protective searches
- Consent searches
- Arrests
- Searches incident to a lawful arrest
- Inventory searches

If police enter private premises, they must be able to show authority under one of the following criteria:

- Consent
- Lawful search warrant
- Life-endangering exigency
- Hot pursuit exigency
- Now-or-never exigency

Vehicle stops must be lawful. To use evidence resulting from the stop, police must demonstrate one of the following:

- Consent
- Plain view seizure
- Result of lawful protective search

- Result of search incident to lawful arrest
- Search under automobile exception
- Inventory search
- Search under community caretaker function

PROBLEMS

All of these problems are from U.S. Supreme Court cases.

1. A police officer patrolling in downtown New York City saw the defendant "continually from the hours of 4:00 P.M. to 12:00 midnight." The officer saw the defendant talking to six or eight people, who the officer knew from experience were narcotic addicts. The officer did not overhear any of the conversations, nor did he see anything pass between the defendant and the people. Later in the evening, the officer saw the defendant enter a restaurant and speak to three more known addicts inside the restaurant. Once again, nothing was overheard and nothing was seen to pass between them. The defendant ordered pie and coffee in the restaurant, and as he was eating, the officer approached him "and told him to come outside." Outside, the officer said to the defendant, "You know what I am after." The defendant "mumbled something and reached into his pocket." The officer also thrust his hand into the same pocket of the defendant and came out with several glassine envelopes, which contained heroin.

   Was the heroin lawfully obtained in an authorized search? Explain. Can the heroin be used as evidence in charging the defendant with possession of heroin? Explain. Should the U.S. Supreme Court affirm the defendant's conviction? [*Sibron v. New York*, 392 U.S. 40, 88 S.Ct. 1899 (1968)]

2. An off-duty police officer was drying himself after a shower in his apartment when he heard a noise at his door. The telephone then rang, however, and he answered it. When he looked out of the peephole in his front door into the hall, he saw two men tiptoeing toward the stairway. The officer called the police, put on some clothes, and armed himself with his service revolver. Looking out of the peephole again, he saw the men continuing to tiptoe. The officer had lived in the apartment building for twelve years but did not recognize either of the men as tenants. Believing that the men were attempting to burglarize an apartment, the officer opened the door, stepped out into the hall, and slammed the door loudly behind him. The men immediately ran down the stairs from the sixth floor. The officer caught defendant Peters between the fourth and fifth floors. With Peters in tow, the officer tried to catch the other man but could not. Peters said he was in the building to visit a girlfriend, but because she was a married woman, he would not give her name. The officer patted down Peters for weapons and discovered a hard object in his pocket. The officer testified that the object did not feel like a gun, but because the object might have been a knife, he removed it from Peters's pocket. It was an opaque plastic envelope containing burglar's tools.

   Was the stop and search lawful and proper? Explain. Did the U.S. Supreme Court permit the use of the evidence in Peters's trial for possessing burglary tools? Why? [*Peters v. New York*, 392 U.S. 40, 88 S.Ct. 1899 (1968)]

3. Detectives first noticed the defendant at a ticket counter in the Miami airport. Their attention was drawn to the defendant because he and his two companions behaved in an unusual manner as they left the counter. The other two men talked to each other but not to the defendant. When one of the men saw the detectives who were following the three men, he turned and talked to the other man. When the second man saw the detectives as the men were getting off an escalator, he turned to the defendant and said, "Let's get out of here." He repeated in a lower voice, "Get out of here." The defendant then saw the detectives. A detective testified that the defendant

attempted to move away, but his "legs were pumping up and down very fast and not covering much ground, but his legs were as if the person were running in place." Finding that he was not leaving the presence of the detectives, the defendant turned to a detective and uttered a vulgar expression.

A detective then showed his badge to the defendant and asked if they might talk. The defendant agreed, and the detective suggested they move a short distance to where the other two men and the other detective stood. Both detectives had identified themselves to all of the men, and as they stood in the public area of the airport, the defendant was asked for identification and if he had an airline ticket. When one of the other men produced a ticket, the officers asked for consent to search the defendant's luggage. The defendant handed the officer a key to the luggage, and three bags of cocaine were found in a suit bag.

Was the procedure used by the officers proper and lawful? Explain. Can the evidence obtained be used in the trial of the three men? Should they be charged with possession with intent to deliver? [*Florida v. Rodriguez*, 469 U.S. 1, 105 S.Ct. 308 (1984)]

4. Police officers were investigating the robbery of a grocery store and other robberies in the Montgomery, Alabama, area. A man held in jail on an unrelated charge told a police officer that "he had heard that Omar Taylor was involved in the [grocery store] robbery." The man did not tell the police where he heard the information, did not provide any details of the crime, and had never provided information to the police before.

Police officers arrested Taylor and, upon arrival at the police station, gave him the *Miranda* warnings. Taylor was fingerprinted, questioned, and placed in a lineup. When victims of the robbery were unable to identify Taylor, he was told that his fingerprints matched those found on objects at the crime scene. After Taylor had a short visit with his girlfriend and a male companion, he signed a

waiver of rights form and executed a written confession. The form and confession were admitted into evidence.

Were the procedures used by the police lawful and proper? Why? Were the form and confession properly used as evidence? Why? Should the Supreme Court affirm the use of the evidence and Taylor's conviction? [*Taylor v. Alabama*, 457 U.S. 687, 102 S.Ct. 2664 (1982)]

5. Portland, Oregon, police officers were investigating the strangulation murder of the defendant's wife in her home. The defendant was not living with his wife and voluntarily came into the police station with an attorney for questioning. The defendant was not arrested, but probable cause to arrest him existed on the following facts:

- The fact that there were no signs of a struggle, break-in, or robbery at the scene of the crime "tended to indicate a killer known to the victim rather than a burglar or other stranger."
- "The decedent's son, the only other person in the house that night, did not have fingernails which could have made the lacerations observed on the victim's throat."
- "The defendant and his deceased wife had a stormy marriage and did not get along well."
- The defendant admitted being at the home of his wife on the night of the murder but claimed that he drove back to central Oregon without entering the house or seeing his wife.
- The defendant "volunteered a great deal of information without being asked, yet expressed no concern or curiosity about his wife."

While the defendant and his attorney were in the police station, officers noticed dark spots on the defendant's finger and under his fingernails. The police asked Murphy if they could take a sample of scraping from under his fingernails. Murphy refused, put his hands in his pockets, and was attempting to clean his nails with objects in his pockets. Was there any way that the police could get samples of scrapings from under Murphy's nails before he destroyed what might be important evidence of the murder? Explain. [*Cupp v. Murphy*, 412 U.S. 291, 93 S.Ct. 2000 (1973)]

6. After overhearing from a public telephone what appeared to be arrangements for a drug transaction, a Florida police officer followed the defendant's car. When Jimeno committed a traffic violation, the officer stopped his car. The officer told Jimeno that he believed that Jimeno was carrying narcotics in his car and asked for consent to search the car. After Jimeno said that he had nothing to hide and gave consent, the officer opened a door on the passenger side and saw a folded brown paper bag on the floor of the car. The officer picked up the bag, opened it, and found cocaine inside. The Supreme Court of Florida held that the consent to search a vehicle does not extend to a closed container found inside the vehicle.

Did the consent to search authorize opening the brown paper bag? Explain. Should the evidence be permitted for use against the defendant? Why or why not? [*Florida v. Jimeno*, 111 S.Ct. 1801 (1991)]

CASE ANALYSIS

Read Appendix B, Finding and Analyzing Cases (p. 427). With these guidelines in mind, please continue with the Case Analysis selections for Chapter 14.

1. Must a search "incident to an arrest" occur after the arrest, or is a search of an automobile made prior to the decision to make an arrest permitted under the rule in *New York v. Belton*? See *United States v. Powell* [451 F.3d 862 (D.C. Cir. 2006)].

2. May the police conduct background checks of passengers during a routine traffic stop? If so, what are the limits on such procedures? Does the *Brendlin* case discussed in this chapter have any bearing on the question? See *People v. Harris* [886 N.E.2d 947 (Ill. 2008)].

3. May the police assist medical personnel in giving a defendant under lawful arrest a laxative to cause him to eliminate a bag of suspected heroin that he had swallowed? What exception to the requirement of a warrant is applicable? See *Winston v. Lee* [470 U.S. 753 (1985)] and *State v. Payano-Roman* [714 N.W.2d 548 (Wis. 2006)].

4. Did a drug-interdiction officer violate the Fourth Amendment when he told bus passengers to leave a bus and claim their luggage, and then he searched a bag in which a canine sniff had alerted to drugs? Does it matter that the defendant initially refused to claim the bag as his property? See *United States v. Ojeda-Ramo* [455 F.3d 1178 (10th Cir. 2006)].

Notes

1. *Terry v. Ohio*, 88 S.Ct. 1868 (1968).
2. Witnesses to crimes or accidents have a civic obligation as good citizens to provide what information they have to law officers who are investigating the incident. If a material witness will not provide his identification, he may be detained and could, if necessary, be taken to a police station and charged. See the box, "Obeying Lawful Police Orders," on page 216 in Chapter 9 of *Criminal Law: Principles and Cases*, 10th ed., by Thomas Gardner and Terry Anderson (Wadsworth, 2009).
3. *Florida v. Royer*, 103 S.Ct. 1319 (1983).
4. Courts will consider the following in determining whether a citizen–police encounter is voluntary or an illegal police seizure:
   • Was there physical contact (touching, holding) by the officer or private security person?

- How many police officers were present (one or ten)? Backup officers should stay in the background unless safety is a problem.
- Were weapons unnecessarily displayed or pointed?
- Did the officers or their vehicle block a clear path for the suspect to leave the area? Was the person free to leave?
- Was the suspect told to go to another location or asked to voluntarily move to another place?
- Were the language and tone of voice intimidating? Was a police badge flashed repeatedly?
- If the police officer examined identification or plane or bus tickets, were they returned promptly? Because a citizen will need his driver's license or bus ticket, he is not free to leave until the item is returned.

See the *FBI Law Enforcement Bulletin* article entitled "Voluntary Encounter or Fourth Amendment Seizure?" (January 1992) for a further discussion and case citations of these factors.

5. *United States v. Mendenhall*, 100 S.Ct. 1870 (1980).
6. *Terry v. Ohio*, 88 S.Ct. 1868 (1968).
7. The U.S. Supreme Court held that reasonable suspicion did exist to authorize the vehicle stop in the *Arvizu* case. The 2002 *FBI Law Enforcement Bulletin* is quoted as follows on the U.S. Supreme Court *Arvizu* decision:

   In *United States v. Arvizu*, the U.S. Supreme Court rejected an attempt by the Court of Appeals for the Ninth Circuit to "describe and delimit" factors that can be used to determine "reasonable suspicion." The Supreme Court reaffirmed its earlier decisions requiring a determination of "reasonable suspicion" be based on a totality of circumstances....

   ... the Supreme Court repudiated the approach taken by the court of appeals and reaffirmed earlier case law requiring courts to use a "totality of circumstances" approach when determining the existence of "reasonable suspicion." Even though when viewed alone some factors may lend themselves to an innocent explanation, they still may be considered along with other more probative factors when reaching a determination of "reasonable suspicion." Applying the "totality of circumstances" approach to the facts presented in Arvizu, the Court concluded that the stop was lawful.

8. 448 U.S. 438 (1980).

9. 561 So.2d 1139 (Fla. 1990).
10. *Snow v. State*, 578 A.2d 816 (Md. App. 1990).
11. *U.S. v. Hernandez-Alvarado*, 891 F.2d 1414 (9th Cir. 1989).
12. *U.S. v. Tapia*, 912 F.2d 1367 (11th Cir. 1990).
13. *U.S. v. Millan*, 912 F.2d 1014 (8th Cir. 1990).
14. 124 S.Ct. 2451 (2004).
15. Nevada Statutes § 171.123.
16. Cited in *FBI Law Enforcement Bulletin*, "Police Intervention Short of Arrest" (November 2006, p. 31).
17. 124 S.Ct. at 2458, citing other cases.
18. *Terry v. Ohio*, 88 S.Ct. 1868 (1968).
19. 113 S.Ct. 2130. A situation similar to *Minnesota v. Dickerson* was before the U.S. Supreme Court in April 2000. In *Bond v. United States* [120 S.Ct. 1462 (2000)], the defendant was a passenger in a public bus. He placed carry-on luggage in a public luggage rack. When the bus properly stopped at a border checkpoint, a border patrol officer entered the bus and verified immigration status. After doing so, the officer "squeezed" soft carry-on luggage in the public bins. He detected a hard, bricklike object in Bond's luggage, which on inspection turned out to be illegal drugs. Bond was convicted over his Fourth Amendment objection to the search of his luggage.

    The Supreme Court reversed, finding that Bond had sought to preserve privacy in his luggage by placing it in the bin above him, and he did not expect the kind of exploratory touching done by the border officer. As a result, Bond's reasonable expectation of privacy was violated without probable cause, and the Fourth Amendment required exclusion of the drugs.

    The rule in *Bond* may have little effect in airline security cases. Passengers who have soft carry-on luggage on airline flights must expect careful scrutiny of such bags, and thus they have no reasonable expectation of privacy.
20. 120 S.Ct. 1375 (2000).
21. Courts to this point have split on the permissibility of stops under these circumstances. Some upheld such stops. See, for example, *United States v. DeBerry* [76 F.3d 884 (7th Cir. 1996)] and *United States v. Clipper* [973 F.2d 944 (C.A.D.C. 1992)]. After *J.L.* it seems likely that state and federal courts will look more closely at the reliability factors in anonymous tips.

22. *J.L.*, 120 S.Ct. at 1379–80.

23. Citizen's arrest goes back to England and early America when law officers were scarce or did not exist in some areas. Under such circumstances, private citizens had to assume the burden of maintaining public order. The common-law doctrine of *private person arrest* usually limits the authority to misdemeanor breaches of the peace committed in the presence of the private person and to felonies committed in the presence of the private person. Check the law of your state before assuming this authority exists.

In some states, the general authority of a private citizen to make a citizen's arrest is set forth in a statute. In most states, the authority to make a citizen's arrest is part of the common law of that state (that is, it is found in the court decisions of that state).

State statutes that give private persons the authority to make arrests include some or all of the following:

- Shoplifting statutes give merchants and their adult employees authority to either arrest or detain a person where there is solid, probable cause to believe the person has shoplifted.
- Statutes that govern railroad and bus employees give them authority.
- Private citizens who are asked or ordered to aid and assist a law officer could be given the "same power as that of a law enforcement officer" [Wisconsin Statute 968.07(2)].
- Surety or extradition statutes could give private citizens authority to make an arrest under circumstances set forth in such statutes.

Law officers who are off duty or out of their jurisdiction (city or state) may have the authority to make a citizen's arrest in another city or state.

24. *Henry v. United States*, 361 U.S. 98 (1959).

25. *Chimel v. California*, 89 S.Ct. 2034 (1969).

26. *New York v. Belton*, 101 S.Ct. 2860 (1981).

27. 162 P.3d 640 (Ariz. 2007).

28. *Arizona v. Gant*, 128 S.Ct. 1443 (2008).

29. 654 F.2d 1057 (5th Cir. 1981), *review denied*, U.S. Supreme Court, 102 S.Ct. 1617 (1982).

30. *Illinois v. Lafayette*, 462 U.S. 640, 103 S.Ct. 2605 (1983).

31. *Id.*

32. *Id.*

33. See Appendix A for relevant sections of the U.S. Constitution.

34. *Payton v. New York*, 445 U.S. 573, 585, 100 S.Ct. 1371–79 (1980).

35. In the 1958 case of *Miller v. United States* [357 U.S. 301, 78 S.Ct. 1190 (1958)], the U.S. Supreme Court quoted from the *Oxford Dictionary of Quotations* (2d ed., 1953), attributing the statement to William Pitt in 1763. The Supreme Court traces the history of the Fourth Amendment in the case of *Stanford v. Texas* [379 U.S. 476, 85 S.Ct. 506 (1965)].

36. 6 F.3d 673 (9th Cir. 1993).

37. 762 F.2d 1318 (9th Cir. 1985).

38. In the 1991 case of *State v. Mooney* [588 A.2d 145 (Conn.)], law officers searched under a highway bridge in a place they knew the defendant regarded as his home. They found additional evidence of the crime for which the defendant had been arrested. The majority of the Supreme Court of Connecticut (three judges dissenting) held that the defendant had a reasonable right and expectation of privacy in the duffel bag and cardboard box from which the officers obtained the evidence. The evidence was suppressed and could not be used against the defendant.

Mobile homes are homes to some people. However, the U.S. Supreme Court has held that mobile motor homes are motor vehicles if they can be quickly driven away. In the 1985 case of *California v. Carney* [471 U.S. 386, 105 S.Ct. 2066], the U.S. Supreme Court held that mobile motor homes have a reduced expectation of privacy and are classified under the law as motor vehicles, where the automobile exception can apply.

39. *Payton v. New York*, 445 U.S. 573, 100 S.Ct. 1371 (1980).

40. *Steagald v. United States*, 451 U.S. 204, 101 S.Ct. 1642 (1981).

41. U.S. Supreme Court in *Ker v. California*, 83 S.Ct. 1623 (1963).

42. U.S. Supreme Court in *Miller v. United States*, 78 S.Ct. 1190 (1958).

43. See *Ker v. California*, 83 S.Ct. 1623 (1963).

44. 531 U.S. 326.

45. 452 U.S. 692 (1981).

46. 403 U.S. 388 (1971).

47. When police receive illegal drug complaints from neighbors and landlords one of the options

available is to knock on the door and talk to the occupant of the suspect's home or apartment. The *FBI Law Enforcement Bulletin* article entitled "Knock and Talk" (November 1991) discusses this option. Consent to search could be requested to check on the validity of the complaint. Because small drug houses have drugs in inventory at only certain times of the day or week, this tactic may or may not work.

48. 823 N.E.2d 668 (2005).

49. *Wayne v. United States*, 318 F.2d 205 (D.C. Cir. 1963), *cert. denied*, 375 U.S. 860 (1963).

50. 440 U.S. 653.

51. 4 S.Ct. 3138.

52. *Delaware v. Prouse*, 440 U.S. 648, 653.

53. 116 S.Ct. 1769.

54. The facts and ruling of the U.S. Supreme Court in the 1986 case of *New York v. Class* [475 U.S. 106, 106 S.Ct. 960] follow: After New York police officers stopped the defendant for exceeding the speed limit and driving with a cracked windshield (both are offenses in New York), one of the officers looked for the VIN (vehicle identification number) on the defendant's car. Because some papers were obscuring the area of the dashboard where the VIN should be located, the officer reached in to move the papers. As he did so, he saw the handle of a gun protruding about an inch from under the driver's seat. The officer seized the gun, and the defendant was arrested. In holding that law enforcement officers making a lawful stop of a vehicle have a right and duty to inspect the VIN, the Court affirmed the defendant's conviction of criminal possession of a gun, ruling that:

We hold that this search was sufficiently unintrusive to be constitutionally permissible in light of the lack of a reasonable expectation of privacy in the VIN and the fact that the officers observed respondent commit two traffic violations. Any other conclusion would expose police officers to potentially grave risks without significantly reducing the intrusiveness of the ultimate conduct —viewing the VIN—which, as we have said, the officers were entitled to do as part of an undoubtedly justified traffic stop.

We note that our holding today does not authorize police officers to enter a vehicle to obtain a dashboard-mounted VIN when the VIN is visible from outside the automobile. If the VIN is in the plain view of someone outside the vehicle, there is no justification for governmental intrusion into the passenger compartment to see it.

55. See *Berkemer v. McCarty*, 468 U.S. 420, 104 S.Ct. 9 (1984).

56. In the 1988 case of *Pennsylvania v. Bruder* [488 U.S. 9, 109 S.Ct. 205], a police officer stopped Bruder, who was driving erratically and ran a red light. Because the officer smelled alcohol and observed Bruder's stumbling movements, he administered field sobriety tests, which included reciting the alphabet and answering questions regarding alcohol. When Bruder failed the sobriety tests, he was placed under arrest and given *Miranda* warnings. Because of Bruder's intoxicated condition, however, waiver or understanding of the warnings could not be shown, and Bruder's answers were suppressed for lack of *Miranda* warnings. The U.S. Supreme Court held that Bruder's answers to the roadside questions were admissible. The Court compared this case to *Berkemer v. McCarty*, holding that:

In Berkemer v McCarty, which involved facts strikingly similar to those in this case, the Court concluded that the "noncoercive aspect of ordinary traffic stops prompts us to hold that persons temporarily detained pursuant to such stops are not 'in custody' for the purposes of Miranda." 468 U.S. at 440.

The Court reasoned that although the stop was unquestionably a seizure within the meaning of the Fourth Amendment, such traffic stops typically are brief, unlike a prolonged station house interrogation. Second, the Court emphasized that traffic stops commonly occur in the "public view," in an atmosphere far "less 'police dominated' than that surrounding the kinds of interrogation at issue in Miranda itself." The detained motorist's "freedom of action [was not] curtailed to 'a degree associated with formal arrest.'" ...

Accordingly, Bruder was not entitled to a recitation of his constitutional rights prior to arrest, and his roadside responses to questioning were admissible.

57. *Schneckloth v. Bustamonte*, 412 U.S. 218, 93 S.Ct. 2041 (1973).

58. In the 1990 case of *Horton v. California* [496 U.S. 128, 110 S.Ct. 2301], the U.S. Supreme Court gave the following requirements for a plain view or open view seizure of evidence by law officers:

• Officers must be in a place where they have a right to be.

- The object or evidence must be in plain or open view and "immediately apparent" to be illegal or evidence of a crime.

- Not only must the officer be lawfully located to see the object, but the officer must also have a lawful right of access to the object. (For example, an officer who is where he or she has a right to be and sees contraband in a home but has no authority to enter the home does not have a lawful right of access to the immediately apparent evidence.)

59. 124 S.Ct. 2127.

60. 124 S.Ct. at 2131.

61. 96 S.Ct. 3092 (1976).

62. 471 U.S. 386.

63. The U.S. Supreme Court has repeatedly held that only probable cause is needed to search an automobile in police custody without a search warrant. A showing of exigent circumstance is not needed, as was held in the 1989 case of *Boyd v. Alabama* [542 So.2d 1276 (Ala.), *review denied*, U.S. Supreme Court, 493 U.S. 883, 110 S.Ct. 219, 46 CrL 3033 (1989)].

64. The U.S. Supreme Court affirmed the criminal convictions of Drayton et al. and held that the evidence showed the bus passengers were free to leave. The Court held:

Law enforcement officers do not violate the Fourth Amendment's prohibition of unreasonable seizures merely by approaching individuals on the street or in other public places and putting questions to them if they are willing to listen.... Even when law enforcement officers have no basis for suspecting a particular individual, they may pose questions, ask for identification, and request consent to search luggage—provided they do not induce cooperation by coercive means. See Florida v. Bostick, 5501 U.S., at 434–435, 111 S.Ct. 2382. (Citations omitted.) If a reasonable person would feel free to terminate the encounter then he or she has not been seized.

... (This) Court has rejected in specific terms the suggestion that police officers must always inform citizens of their right to refuse when seeking permission to conduct a warrantless consent search.... "While knowledge of the right to refuse consent is one factor to be taken into account, the government need not establish such knowledge as the sine qua non of an effective consent." Nor do this Court's decisions suggest that even though there are no per se rules, a presumption of invalidity attaches if a citizen consented without explicit notification that he or she was free to refuse to cooperate. Instead, the Court has repeated that the totality of the circumstances must control, without giving extra weight to the absence of this type of warning.... Although Officer Lang did not inform respondents of their right to refuse the search, he did request permission to search, and the totality of the circumstances indicates that their consent was voluntary, so the searches were reasonable.

In a society based on law, the concept of agreement and consent should be given a weight and dignity of its own. Police officers act in full accord with the law when they ask citizens for consent. It reinforces the rule of law for the citizen to advise the police of his or her wishes and for the police to act in reliance on that understanding. When this exchange takes place, it dispels inferences of coercion.

OBTAINING EVIDENCE FROM COMPUTERS OR BY USE OF SEARCH WARRANTS, WIRETAPPING, OR DOGS TRAINED TO INDICATE AN ALERT

CHAPTER **15**

LEARNING OBJECTIVES

In this chapter we examine other methods of obtaining evidence, including search warrants, electronic surveillance, and canine alerts. The learning objectives for this chapter are:

- Assuming officers are entitled to look at a computer's files, what are the limits on that examination?
- List the various types of search warrants and their requirements.
- List some situations where officers may hear or record statements without the need for a court order.
- State the differences in terms of reliability and the need for a search or arrest warrant between a known informant and an anonymous informant.
- State the rules on the police use of trained dogs to "sniff" a vehicle or luggage.

OBTAINING EVIDENCE FROM COMPUTERS

More than half the homes in the United States, and virtually all the businesses, use computers. Computers store vast amounts of financial and other information and enable us to communicate via e-mail, chat rooms, websites, and the Internet.

Criminals can also put computers to a wide variety of criminal uses. Financial accountings of criminal enterprises, inventories of illegal drugs or contraband, records of money laundering, lists of customers, and records of criminal transactions are just some of the records stored in computers. Communications about pornography are widely seen on computers, and pedophiles (adults who sexually desire children) frequently use computers to communicate with their victims.

Computers thus can be a fertile place for law officers to find evidence of criminal activity. Because people generally have an expectation of privacy in their personal computers, and to a lesser extent in their workplace computers, however, the Fourth Amendment applies to any search of a computer where such an expectation of privacy exists. The following cases and examples illustrate searches of computers:

- *Search warrants*: A search warrant authorizing officers to enter a home or office does not authorize the officers to search a computer found in the premises, unless the search warrant identifies the computer as part of the authorized search. Moreover, even if the search warrant authorizes the officers to search a computer, it does not follow that the officers can open and look at every piece of information stored in the computer.

    Two cases in the Tenth Circuit Court of Appeals illustrate this distinction. In *United States v. Carey*,[1] officers obtained a search warrant that authorized them to search a defendant's computer for evidence of illegal drug trafficking. While looking at the computer files, an officer inadvertently opened a file that contained child pornography images. The officer then conducted a wholesale search of all computer files. The court held that the subsequent general search of the computer files was a violation of the Fourth Amendment.

    By contrast, in *United States v. Walser*,[2] the officer searching a computer pursuant to a search warrant authorizing the search for evidence of illegal drugs immediately stopped the search when he inadvertently opened a file containing child pornographic images. The officer went to a magistrate and, armed with the information gained during his lawful search of the computer, obtained a search warrant to search the computer files for evidence of child pornography. The court said that search was lawful.

- *Consent*: The person who has the sole control and access to a computer can authorize a computer search, if the consent is given voluntarily. If more than one person has such control or access, the search of the computer files cannot extend to files or information accessed only through use of the nonconsenting person's password. The case of *United States v. Block*[3] is often used to illustrate the limits of consent searches. There, the court said that although the "defendant's mother had authority to consent to a search of his room which was located in the home that they shared, ... the mother's authority did not extend to a search of a locked footlocker located within the room."

- *The workplace*: (See the discussion of the *Ortega* case in Chapter 11.) Employers and supervisors have wide authority to make warrantless searches of the offices, desks, files, and computers of private and public employees. However, this authority does not extend to areas where the employee has a legitimate expectation of privacy, such as a purse or personal briefcase.

  In the case of government employees, courts generally hold that the employee has no legitimate expectation of privacy in a computer used in that employment. For example, in the 2004 case of *United States v. Thorn*,[4] a supervisor in a state agency believed Thorn was sending personal e-mails to other employees, a violation of agency policy. The supervisor checked Thorn's computer to determine whether he had sent e-mails as suspected. While looking at the computer files, the supervisor found evidence that Thorn had visited Internet pornography sites. The supervisor turned this information over to the police, who obtained a search warrant and found evidence of child pornography. Thorn was charged with possession of child pornography, and at his trial he moved to suppress all the evidence taken from his computer. His motion was denied, and he was convicted. On appeal, the court held that Thorn had no legitimate expectation of privacy in his computer. The court noted that the state agency had a policy that employees were not to use their computers for personal purposes and that the agency reserved the right to access the computers to determine whether any unauthorized use had occurred. Because Thorn knew these rules, the court said, he could not expect that his use of the computer was private.

- *Plain view*: If a law officer is where he or she is entitled to be, then any evidence the officer sees may be seized under the plain view rule (discussed in Chapter 10). In the case of a computer, that might include information an officer viewed on a monitor screen that showed evidence of a crime.

  For example, in *United States v. Tucker*,[5] police were lawfully in the defendant's home conducting a search for evidence of child pornography. An officer noticed that the defendant's computer was connected to the Internet, to a website called alt.sex.preteen. The officer then seized the computer, and a subsequent search uncovered evidence of child pornography. The court held that the evidence found after the seizure of the computer was admissible because, under the plain view rule, the officer saw sufficient evidence of a crime to seize the computer and conduct a more thorough search.

OBTAINING EVIDENCE FROM THE INTERNET (CYBER EVIDENCE)

Millions of people use the Internet daily. AOL alone has 20 million customers; its permanent staff answers more than a thousand requests each month for information in criminal and civil cases. The most frequently asked questions concern crimes against children, threats, abductions, and pornography, followed by identity theft and computer hacking crimes.

The Internet has become a common avenue for the exchange of child pornography. Attempts to contact and entice children through Internet "chat" rooms occur almost constantly. The *FBI Law Enforcement Bulletin* article titled "Child Pornography Web Sites" (July 2007) estimates that more than 100,000 national and international websites are devoted to child pornography; these sites generate more than $3 billion annually of illegal money. The subtitle of the article, "Techniques Used to Evade Law Enforcement," explains in detail how "savvy pornographers" are able to sell their illegal products worldwide with almost "no fear of capture by law enforcement."

The article also points out that, although illegal child pornography is one of the fastest-growing businesses on the Internet, most of the illegal websites are overseas, and thus neither the websites nor the persons who maintain the websites are within U.S. jurisdiction.

Because those websites that are within U.S. jurisdiction are national in scope, it is difficult for individual states to respond to this growing problem. As a result, the U.S. government has created federal task forces to coordinate the enforcement of state and federal criminal laws that pertain to the Internet. This coordination among federal, state, and local law enforcement is detailed in the December 2007 U.S. Department of Justice publication "Federal Prosecution of Child Exploitation Offenders" (NCJ 219412). That report states:

- All fifty-six FBI field offices have specialized units that investigate crimes against children.
- The Cyber Tipline, part of the National Center for Missing and Exploited Children, coordinates tips from the public on the sexual exploitation of children on the Internet.
- There are currently fifty-six Internet Crimes Against Children (ICAC) task forces composed of federal, state, and local law enforcement agencies located in all fifty states.
- Child-sex tours and child pornography networks are targeted by Homeland Security's Operation Predator. This project acts as a clearinghouse of seized images that can be used to assist in identifying and locating child victims.
- Prosecution of child sex exploitation is emphasized and maximized in the Department of Justice's "Project Safe Childhood."

OBTAINING EVIDENCE FROM OTHER PERSONAL ELECTRONIC DEVICES

Many electronic devices have electronic storage capability; laptop computers, cellular telephones, pagers, flash drives, MP3 players, and personal digital assistants (PDAs) are just some of these devices. Evidence of criminal activity may be stored in these devices, and law enforcement officers want access to the stored information. Law enforcement can obtain access through search warrants based on probable cause or through consent searches, as is often done with computer files. An article in the 2007 *FBI Law Enforcement Bulletin* titled "Search Incident to Arrest in the Age of Personal Electronics" points out that many persons lawfully arrested have on their persons one or more of these electronic devices. Courts have held that these devices may be searched under the search incident to a lawful arrest exception to the requirement of a search warrant.[6] The article notes that although courts have often upheld searches of wallets, purses, briefcases, and other containers in the possession of a person lawfully arrested, the legality of a search incident to arrest when applied to electronic devices is "dubious." Such searches must be reasonable under the Fourth

Amendment, and the massive amount of data that can be stored in these devices raises doubts about such searches.[7]

The *FBI Law Enforcement Bulletin* article also suggests that searches of electronic devices discovered on the person of a suspect arrested without a search warrant may be a problem for two reasons: (1) Federal law forbids "intentionally intercepting ... any wire, oral or electronic communication" without a court order.[8] However, the law also states that "electronic communication" does not include electronic storage.[9] (2) States may have statutory or court-made rules restricting or limiting such searches.

SEARCH WARRANTS

The Fourth Amendment to the U.S. Constitution states that "no Warrant shall issue, but upon probable cause supported by Oath, or affirmation, and particularly describing the place to be searched and the persons or things to be seized" (see Appendix A). One of the most hated practices of the British officers in Colonial America was the general warrant. Pursuant to these warrants, Crown officers conducted searches and seizures of colonial homes with no limits on their actions. The Framers of the Constitution had those general warrants in mind when they wrote the Fourth Amendment. As a result, U.S. Supreme Court cases have established "the basic principle of Fourth Amendment law that searches and seizures inside a home without a warrant are presumptively unreasonable."[10]

When evidence is obtained without a search warrant, the burden is on the government to show that the evidence was obtained under one of the "established and well-delineated exceptions" to the search warrant requirement. The U.S. Supreme Court pointed out that the exceptions to the search warrant requirement are "jealously and carefully drawn."[11]

A search warrant must be issued by a neutral and detached judge or magistrate who determines that probable cause exists to issue the search or arrest warrant.[12] The oath or affirmation supporting the search warrant is in most instances made by a law enforcement officer, based on information known to that officer. Typically, the facts that support the issuance of a search warrant show that the officer has probable cause to believe that the premises to be searched contain evidence of a crime, such as contraband, or instruments used in a crime, such as weapons, or fruits of a crime, such as stolen property.

The search warrant must particularly describe the place to be searched and the persons or things to be seized. If a search warrant does not contain such particular description, it is invalid, even if in fact the officer who obtained the search warrant had probable cause, and even if the search that was made was limited in scope. The following case illustrates the "particular description" requirement.

Groh v. Ramirez

United States Supreme Court, 540 U.S. 551 (2004)

Federal and county officers were told by a reliable informant that the Ramirezes had illegal automatic weapons at their ranch in Montana. Based on an affidavit that recited these facts, a search warrant was issued by a magistrate. The search warrant was on a form used by the officers and stated in the box where the "person or property to be seized" was to be listed only the address and location of the Ramirez house. The warrant did not mention the stockpile of weapons, nor did it incorporate the affidavit of the officers supporting the warrant.

The U.S. Supreme Court held that the search warrant violated the Fourth Amendment, even though the affidavit supporting the warrant recited probable cause and described particularly the place to be searched. In rejecting the officers' argument that the presence of specific descriptions in the affidavit of the "things to be seized" saved the search warrant, the Court stated:

> The fact that the application adequately described the "things to be seized" does not save the warrant from its facial invalidity. The Fourth Amendment by its terms requires particularity in the warrant, not in the supporting documents.... (citations omitted) ... "The presence of a search warrant serves a high function," (citation omitted), and that function is not necessarily vindicated when some other document, somewhere, says something about the objects of the search, but the contents of that document are neither known to the person whose home is being searched nor available for her inspection.

The Court noted that although a search warrant can incorporate other documents, such documents must be attached to the search warrant and available for inspection. That was not the case here. The Court also held that the facts that the magistrate actually knew of the specific things to be seized and that the search was limited to a search for those things did not save the search warrant. Moreover, the error in the search warrant was obvious on its face, and not a mere technical mistake or typographical error. As a result, the Court said, the good faith exception (see Chapter 10) was inapplicable.

Luggage or a package may be detained to obtain a search warrant where probable cause exists to believe that the package or luggage contains evidence of a crime. In the U.S. Supreme Court case of *United States v. Van Leeuwen*,[13] a package was held up in the U.S. mail for 29 hours, and in the case of *State v. Morrison*,[14] the delay was 3 hours. Both delays were held to be reasonable and necessary under the existing circumstances.

TYPES OF SEARCH WARRANTS

Nighttime Search Warrants Most states and the federal government have statutes requiring that search warrants be served and executed during daylight hours. However, such laws permit a magistrate or judge to authorize a nighttime search. Federal Rule of Criminal Procedure 41(e) permits the authorization of a nighttime search when "there be cause for carrying on the unusual nighttime ... search ... upon a showing (that) convinces the magistrate that it is reasonable."

In suspected illegal drug cases, the possibility that the defendant will destroy the illegal drugs before officers can conduct the search is frequently used as the justification for a nighttime search. In *United States v. Kotoa*,[15] police officers obtained a search warrant to search the defendant's home for illegal drugs. The affidavit asked for no-knock and nighttime authorization, and the application was presented to a state district court judge on that basis. However, the warrant issued actually authorized a search "in the daytime with unannounced authority." A police SWAT team executed the search warrant at night and found illegal drugs. During the search, the officers discovered the mistaken omission of "nighttime" from the warrant. They called the district court judge who issued the warrant, and he instructed them to write in "nighttime" in the warrant and said that he would subsequently sign the warrant authorizing the change, which he did. The defendant moved to suppress the evidence found during the search, contending that a night-time search under a daytime warrant violated the Fourth Amendment. The district court refused to suppress the evidence, and the defendant entered a conditional guilty plea, reserving his right to appeal the suppression ruling.

The court of appeals affirmed the conviction, holding that the mistake in the warrant was cured by the telephone call to the issuing judge. The court distinguished the case from the Supreme Court's decision in *Groh* (discussed previously), noting that because the Fourth Amendment does not explicitly require the warrant to indicate the time of day or night, the holding in *Groh*—that the absence of "the things to be seized" made the warrant invalid—did not apply. The court held that the general reasonableness requirement determined that the search was valid and on that question held that the telephone call to the issuing judge that corrected the defect in the warrant made the search reasonable.

The Fourth Circuit Court of Appeals held in the 2006 case of *United States v. Rizzi*[16] that 21 United States Code, section 879, which applies to search warrants in illegal drug cases and authorizes daytime or nighttime executions of the search warrant, "trumps" Rule 41(e). Thus, even though the search warrant in *Rizzi* authorizing a search for illegal drugs failed to state that a nighttime search was permitted, section 879 did not require that specific statement, the court concluded.

No-Knock or Unannounced Entries   Law enforcement officers must knock, identify themselves, state their purpose, and await a refusal or silence before they enter private premises. An unannounced or no-knock entry can be made if it is specifically authorized by the search warrant or if the officers can show that notice by knocking would be likely to:

- Endanger the safety of the officers or another person
- Result in the evidence subject to seizure being easily and quickly destroyed or disposed of
- Enable the party to be arrested or searched to escape
- Be a useless gesture

When officers knock and identify themselves, they are permitted to forcibly enter the premises under certain circumstances. The following U.S. Supreme Court case discusses the rules that determine when an officer may use force in entering premises to conduct a search.

United States v. Banks United States Supreme Court, 540 U.S. 31 (2003)	Police officers obtained a search warrant to search Banks's apartment for evidence of cocaine and drug dealing. At two o'clock in the afternoon, officers went to Banks's apartment, knocked loudly on his door, and after a wait of 15 to 20 seconds with no response from inside, broke down Banks's door with a battering ram. In fact, Banks was in the shower and did not hear the police announcing their presence. The search yielded evidence of drug dealing, which Banks moved to suppress. The district court denied the motion, but on appeal the Ninth Circuit Court of Appeals reversed, holding that waiting only 15 to 20 seconds before breaking down the apartment door was unreasonable, and thus violated the Fourth Amendment. The Supreme Court reversed, finding the decision to make the forced entry reasonable under the circumstances known to the officers. In doing so, the Court reviewed the rules

courts use to determine the reasonableness of the manner in which a search warrant is executed. The Court said:

> The Fourth Amendment says nothing specific about formalities in exercising a warrant's authorization, speaking to the manner of searching as well as the legitimacy of searching at all simply in terms of the right to be "secure ... against unreasonable searches and seizures." Although the notion of reasonable execution must therefore be fleshed out, we have done that case by case, largely avoiding categories and protocols for searches.... We have, however, pointed out factual considerations of unusual, albeit not dispositive, significance.

One such factual consideration, the Court noted, was the presence of exigent circumstances that led the officers to believe that knocking or waiting to enter might result in the destruction of evidence. Where those circumstances are reasonable and expected in the warrant application, a magistrate is justified in authorizing a no-knock warrant: "And even when executing a warrant silent about that, if circumstances support a reasonable suspicion of exigency when the officers arrive at the door, they may go straight in." Under that reasoning, the Court stated, when the exigent circumstances became known to the officers in this case, after knocking and announcing, they could do the same.

The Court concluded that although "this call is a close one," given the nature of the criminal evidence, cocaine, and the ease of its disposal, the officers acted reasonably in waiting only 15 to 20 seconds before making a forced entry. The Court also held that 18 United States Code, section 3109, which permits forced entry "if, after notice of his authority and purpose, [an officer] is refused admittance," is subject to the "exigent circumstances" exception. (See Chapter 9 for *Hudson v. Michigan*, the Supreme Court case on the "knock-and-announce" rule and its relationship to the exclusionary rule.)

Anticipatory Search Warrants   On occasion, law enforcement officers have information that evidence—usually illegal drugs—will be at a particular place at a future time. For example, police might have specific, reliable information that a large shipment of drugs will come into a city to a specific address in the next few days. However, the officers might not have reliable information about where the drugs are presently located, what day and time the drugs will arrive, and how they are being transported.

Because most stocks of illegal drugs are dispersed rapidly due to the danger of a police raid or a snatching by a rival gang, an anticipatory search warrant solves the problem law enforcement officers face in such situations. The police may obtain a search warrant directed at the person and place where it is reliably anticipated the illegal drugs will be located.

In these warrants, the affidavits accompanying the application for the search warrant commonly describe the basis for the officer's belief that some illegal contraband or other evidence of a crime will be located at some specific place in the future. An anticipatory search warrant may be directed toward the search of a person, or it may be used for a "controlled delivery,"[17] as in the following case.

United States v. Grubbs

United States Supreme Court, 547 U.S. 90 (2006)

The defendant Grubbs purchased a child pornography videotape online from a website operated by an undercover postal inspector. The videotape was mailed to Grubbs, and Postal Inspection Service officers obtained an anticipatory search warrant from a federal magistrate in California to search Grubbs's residence after the video arrived. An affidavit accompanying the application for the search warrant stated that execution of the warrant would not occur unless the videotape was received by someone at Grubbs's residence and taken inside the residence. The magistrate issued the warrant, but the "triggering" condition set forth in the affidavit was not incorporated into the warrant.

The video was delivered, and Grubbs's wife took delivery and brought the package into the residence. The police then executed the search warrant and discovered evidence of child pornography in the residence. Grubbs was charged with one count of receiving a visual depiction of a minor engaged in sexually explicit conduct, and he moved to suppress the videotape because the search warrant did not contain the "triggering" condition language. As a result, Grubbs argued, on its face the warrant was a violation of the Fourth Amendment. The district court denied the motion, and Grubbs pleaded guilty, reserving the right to contest the Fourth Amendment claim. The Ninth Circuit Court of Appeals reversed, holding that the absence of the affidavit language in the search warrant rendered the warrant "inoperative." The U.S. Supreme Court granted certiorari and reversed the Ninth Circuit.

The Supreme Court first considered whether "anticipatory search warrants are categorically unconstitutional." The argument against such warrants, the Court said, is that because at the time the search warrant is issued probable cause to suspect that a crime had occurred or contraband was located at a particular place did not exist, anticipatory search warrants violate the Fourth Amendment's requirement that "no Warrants shall issue, but upon probable cause." The Court said, "We reject this view, as has every Court of Appeals to confront the issue."[18]

The Court stated that the probable cause requirement looks to whether probable cause exists to believe evidence will be found when the search is conducted. As a result, the Court said, "all warrants are, in a sense, 'anticipatory'. In the typical case … the Magistrate's determination that there is probable cause for the search amounts to a prediction that the item will still be there when the warrant is executed."[19] An anticipatory warrant is no different from an ordinary warrant, the Court concluded, because based on the "triggering" condition, the magistrate can determine that probable cause exists to believe the contraband will be on the described property when the search warrant is executed. Probable cause in anticipatory search warrants requires only that supporting affidavits provide the issuing magistrate with sufficient information to show that, if the "triggering" condition occurs, contraband or evidence of a crime will be found at the designated place, and it is probable that the "triggering" condition will occur. Here, the Court said, such probable cause existed.

The Court also rejected the Ninth Circuit's conclusion that the search warrant was defective because it failed to explicitly specify the "triggering" condition in the search warrant. The Supreme Court noted that there is no requirement in the Fourth Amendment that the search warrant specify the basis for the warrant's issuance, but only "the place to be searched" and "the persons or things to be seized." "The language of the Fourth Amendment is likewise decisive here; its particularity requirement does not include the conditions precedent to execution of the warrant."[20] As a result, the Supreme Court reversed the Ninth Circuit and upheld the search warrant.

WHEN IN DOUBT, GET A SEARCH WARRANT

The most basic constitutional rule in this area is that "searches conducted outside the judicial process, without prior approval by judge or magistrate, are per se unreasonable under the Fourth Amendment—subject only to a few specifically established and well-delineated exceptions." The exceptions are "jealously and carefully drawn," and there must be "a showing by those who seek exemption ... that the exigencies of the situation made that course imperative.... [T]he burden is on those seeking the exemption to show the need for it" [*Coolidge v. New Hampshire,* 403 U.S. 443, 91 S.Ct. 2022 (1971)].

When a search warrant is obtained, the judge's determination that probable cause exists is given great deference, and the burden shifts to those challenging a search or arrest warrant to prove that it is invalid.

Sneak-and-Peek Entry Warrants   Sneak-and-peek warrants permit law officers to enter premises for various reasons. In the 1993 case of *United States v. Pangburn,* the entry was made to photograph the contents of a suspected clandestine methamphetamine lab.[21]

Law officers may enter private premises to plant listening devices, as was done in the Waco, Texas, Branch Davidian case and also the Arlington, Virginia, home of Aldrich Ames, a high-ranking officer of the CIA who was arrested in 1994 for spying against the United States for the Russians.

In the 1979 U.S. Supreme Court case of *Dalia v. United States,*[22] a search warrant was issued to implant a listening device in a business office. Three weeks later, another entry was made to remove the device. The U.S. Supreme Court affirmed the defendant's conviction, holding that:

> Nothing in the language of the Constitution or in this Court's decisions ... suggest that ... search warrants ... must include a specification of the precise manner in which they are to be executed.... It is generally left to the discretion of the executing officers to determine the details of how best to proceed with the performance of a search authorized by warrant—subject of course to the general Fourth Amendment protection "against unreasonable searches and seizures."

Searches of Computers, Other Electronic Devices, and Documentary Sources
As mentioned at the start of this chapter, computers and other places where records are stored can be important sources of evidence. If consent cannot be obtained but probable cause exists, a search warrant may be obtained to make such searches.

Search warrants are subject to attack if their language is too broad or they fail to specify, with particularity, the items to be seized. In the case of *United States v. Hall,*[23] the search warrant authorized the seizure of image files that contained child pornography. The defendant had taken his computer to a repair shop, and during the repairs, the child pornography was observed. The FBI was called, and the defendant was charged with possession of child pornography. The court found no Fourth Amendment violation.

The Privacy Protection Act of 1980[24] gives special protection to documentary material prepared or gathered for dissemination to the public (newspapers, magazines, and so forth), and a subpoena rather than a search warrant must be used unless one of the exceptions in the Privacy Protection Act permits the use of a search warrant.

Administrative Search Warrants   Under most state laws, fire, health, building, and food inspectors, as well as many other state administrative agencies, may obtain administrative search warrants to determine whether a person or business is violating state laws designed to protect the public. These include health regulation violations, fire hazards, food services, and structural concerns in buildings open to the public.

A lower standard of probable cause than in the traditional probable cause search warrant requirement applies to administrative search warrants. In *Camara v. Municipal Court*,[25] the U.S. Supreme Court held that "(if) a valid public interest justifies the intrusion contemplated, then there is probable cause to issue a suitable restricted search warrant."

Health and food inspectors have the authority to close a restaurant or food processing facility that is in serious violation of the health and sanitation codes of a city or state. For lesser violations, health, fire, and building and housing inspectors generally issue summons or warnings directing the violator to cure the violations.

The New York City Fire Department conducts about 300,000 inspections each year for compliance with fire codes, and each month it issues about 900 summonses for violations. Most offenders answer the summons by appearing in court and providing evidence of efforts to comply with the regulations violated. In 2008, however, *The New York Times*[26] reported that a backlog of about 4,000 persons and businesses had not appeared in court to address fire code violations. More than 200 arrests were made by mid-2008 for the misdemeanor of failing to appear, and more arrest warrants have been issued.

WIRETAPPING AND ELECTRONIC SURVEILLANCE

wiretapping
According to the U.S. Supreme Court [*Dalia v. United States*, 99 S.Ct. 1682 (1979)], "interception of communication by telephone and telegraph."

Prior to 1968 the United States did not have any laws governing **wiretapping** and **electronic surveillance**. However, the 1967 case of *Katz v. United States*[27] caused the U.S. Congress to act. In the *Katz* case, FBI agents attached an electronic listening and recording device to the outside of a public telephone booth that Katz was using to lay off Los Angeles gambling bets in Miami, Florida. The U.S. Supreme Court held that the FBI violated Katz's Fourth Amendment privacy rights and that the evidence obtained could not be used to obtain Katz's criminal gambling conviction.

In 1968 Congress enacted the Federal Wiretapping and Electronic Surveillance Act.[28] Most states followed by enacting similar state laws making the following changes in the laws on electronic surveillance:

- The laws authorize court orders permitting wiretapping and/or electronic surveillance by law enforcement officers in much the same manner as search warrants are issued.[29]

- The act makes wiretapping and electronic surveillance done in violation of the act a felony. The distribution, possession, and advertising of mechanical and electronic devices used for wiretapping and electronic surveillance are also made a felony (section 2513).

THERMAL-IMAGING DEVICES

electronic surveillance
Secret interception of communications by wiretapping or bugging, which "typically is accomplished by installation of a small microphone in the room (or vehicle) to be bugged" [*Dalia v. United States*, 99 S.Ct. 1682 (1979)].

Advances in technology now make it possible to obtain information about activities that occur in houses, cars, and other places. The question of whether police may use such technological advances in investigations of crimes without traditional search warrants has been before the Supreme Court many times. In some cases technology opens what were once private spaces to public, and hence official, observation. For example, in *California v. Ciraolo*,[30] the Court held that the uncovered portions of a house and its curtilage have become open to general observation by air travel and are thus no longer private for purposes of the Fourth Amendment.

To what extent may police use technological advances that enable an observer to sense what is inside a private place, like a house? An Internet website maintained by the National Law Enforcement and Corrections Technology Center (www.nlectc.org/technproj) describes radar and ultrasound devices that enable an observer to detect individuals through interior walls. The Supreme Court considered one of these kinds of devices, thermal-imaging, in the following case.

Kyllo v. United States

United States Supreme Court, 533 U.S. 27 (2001)

Federal agents suspected that Kyllo was growing marijuana in his home. Using a thermal-imaging device, which detects infrared radiation and converts it to a colored image based on the intensity of the radiation, the police believed that Kyllo was using high-intensity lamps to grow marijuana. Based on this and other evidence, the police obtained a search warrant and searched Kyllo's home, discovering more than a hundred marijuana plants. At his trial for the illegal manufacture of marijuana, Kyllo moved to suppress the evidence seized from his home. The trial court and the court of appeals upheld the validity of the search warrant, holding that it did not expose any intimate details of Kyllo's life but only "hot spots" on the roof and exterior walls.

The Supreme Court reversed, holding that use of the thermal-imaging device constituted a search of Kyllo's house and could not be used without a search warrant:

> We think that obtaining by sense-enhancing technology any information regarding the interior of the home that could not otherwise have been obtained without physical "intrusion into a constitutionally protected area" ... constitutes a search—at least where (as here) the technology in question is not in general public use.

TECHNIQUES OF LAWFUL ELECTRONIC SURVEILLANCE

Not only are telecommunications corporations required by federal law to cooperate in conducting lawfully authorized electronic surveillances, but they are also required to modify their equipment, facilities, and services to ensure that lawful electronic surveillance actually can be performed. The primary techniques of electronic surveillance available to law enforcement agencies are pen registers, trap and trace devices, and interception of the content of the message.

- Pen registers and trap and trace devices are the most frequently used surveillance techniques. They identify calling numbers or dialed numbers (outgoing or incoming). They can trap or lock lines when threatening or harassing calls are made, if necessary.
- Another form of lawful electronic surveillance is identification of outgoing and incoming calls and also the content of messages. The federal government and forty-five states permit this technique but only in investigations to obtain evidence of felony offenses, such as kidnapping, extortion, murder, illegal drug trafficking, organized crime, terrorism, and national security matters. Court authorization is granted only when it is shown that the needed evidence cannot be obtained by other means or it is too dangerous to obtain by other means.

ELECTRONIC SURVEILLANCE AND THE USA PATRIOT ACT

Following the terrorist attacks of 9/11, Congress passed the USA PATRIOT Act. This act has far-reaching provisions that affect both foreign and domestic criminal investigations. It made many changes in the way electronic surveillance is permitted and conducted in such investigations. Although some sections of the act relating to electronic surveillance had a "sunset" provision of December 31, 2005, at which time the sections would terminate, this "sunset" provision has been extended. It is therefore likely that many of the provisions regulating electronic surveillance will stay in force for some time. What follows is a brief summary of the federal laws that regulated electronic surveillance prior to the USA PATRIOT Act and the changes the act made to those laws.

Wiretapping   The 1968 federal wiretap law, discussed earlier in this chapter, originally prohibited only the intentional interception of wire (telephone) and oral communications. That law gave various federal officials the power to obtain judicial authorization to conduct wiretaps as part of the investigation of designated crimes. The authorization required a showing that the wiretap was likely to produce information relating to the criminal investigation, that other methods for obtaining the information had failed or were too dangerous, and that the location where the communications were being intercepted was being used in the commission of the crime.

Cell Phones   In 1986 the Electronic Communications Privacy Act amended the Federal Wiretapping and Electronic Surveillance Act to make its prohibitions applicable to cellular phones, although it exempted the broadcast portion of cellular conversations. This was changed in 1994 when the Communications Assistance for Law Enforcement Act made the wiretap law's rules applicable to the broadcast portion of cellular phone conversations. (These amended statutes appeared as 18 United States Code, section 2510(1).)

E-Mail   The 1986 act also extended the prohibition against interceptions to e-mail, though with slightly different rules. For one thing, the statutory exclusionary rule for unlawfully intercepted telephone conversations does not apply to e-mail. Also, an e-mail may be intercepted as part of the investigation of any federal felony and may be procured by a wider range of federal officials. Parts of the 1986 act, generally referred to as the Stored Communications Act, governed law enforcement access to e-mail stored for the recipient in an Internet service provider (ISP). To access a stored e-mail message less than six months old, the government must obtain a search warrant. For older messages, the ISP may be forced to provide access through a subpoena or court order. Under these provisions, it was generally easier for the government to gain access to stored e-mail than to intercept it during transmission.

Other Surveillance   It was not clear whether voice-mail was covered by the provisions of the amended wiretap act or the more relaxed provisions of the Stored Communications Act. The 1986 act placed some limitations on the use by law enforcement officers of pen registers and trap and trace devices. The U.S. Supreme Court held in *Smith v. Maryland*[31] that the use of these devices does not constitute violation of either the wiretap law or the Fourth Amendment because the devices disclose only the number dialed or received, and a person has no expectation of privacy in such numbers. The 1986 act's limitations on the use of these devices were thus minimal: All that was needed was a court authorization based on a claim by the state or federal official that the information obtained was relevant to an ongoing criminal investigation.[32]

USA PATRIOT Act Changes   The PATRIOT Act made several changes to these laws:[33]

- Section 202 of the act adds violations of the Computer Fraud and Abuse Act to the list of crimes for which interceptions of telephone calls or e-mail may be authorized.
- Section 209 makes it clear that the lesser requirements of the Stored Communications Act apply to government requests to access voice-mail.
- Section 210 amends existing law to permit law enforcement officers to use subpoenas to acquire information about persons' Internet use. Previously, such access had been limited to telephone company records.
- Section 212 permits an Internet service provider to volunteer information about a subscriber's communications if the ISP discovers information about an immediate risk of death or serious physical injury.
- Section 216 makes it clear that law enforcement officers may use pen registers or trap and trace devices to obtain certain information from e-mail, such as Internet addresses. It also authorizes the national use of such devices in large-scale investigations, which means law enforcement officers need not seek multiple court orders to use these devices.
- Section 217 allows an ISP to enlist law enforcement help in dealing with a "computer trespasser." Law enforcement officers are permitted to monitor communications to or from the trespasser, but not those of authorized users.

TACTICS USED BY SUSPECTS TO AVOID ELECTRONIC SURVEILLANCE

To avoid having conversations regarding criminal activities intercepted and used as evidence against them, suspects who are aware of government electronic surveillance try the following tactics:

- *"Walk and talk" meetings to avoid bugged rooms, vehicles, and other types of electronic surveillance:* The suspect talks in the middle of a busy city street with trucks, buses, and cars coming dangerously close on either side. This tactic makes the use of a parabolic directional mike more difficult, and the surrounding noise level interferes with reception to a wire planted on a person cooperating with the government.

- *Use of a series of public or private telephones:* To counteract this tactic, the U.S. Congress enacted in 1986 a federal statute authorizing "roving wiretaps,"[34] which permit authorized law officers to anticipate and follow a suspect using a series of public or private telephones.

SITUATIONS WHERE COURT ORDERS ARE NOT REQUIRED

Overheard Conversations (Plain Hearing) Law enforcement officers may use artificial means of aiding their vision, such as bifocals, binoculars, or telescopes, but they may not use mechanical or electronic listening devices that intrude and violate the privacy of another person without a court order.

People who are talking about criminal activity sometimes become careless and do not exercise a right of privacy. We have all been in restaurants, hotel rooms, taverns, airplanes, or other places where we have overheard conversations. If law enforcement officers are where they have a right to be,[35] they may testify in court about statements that they overheard or heard inadvertently. The following cases illustrate.

Examples
- Law enforcement officers were invited into an apartment where they could hear the defendant talking in a loud voice in the next apartment about illegal drug transactions. The conversations were heard without the use of anything but the human ear. Based on this information, the officers obtained a wiretap warrant and then a search warrant. In affirming the defendant's convictions in the 1988 case of *State v. Benton*,[36] the Court held:

  > ... It has widely been recognized, in cases involving apartments and hotel or motel rooms, that ... overhearing of statements does not constitute a search under the Fourth Amendment. This view has been consistently upheld regardless of whether the eavesdropper was positioned in a common hallway of an apartment building, motel or hotel, or in an adjoining motel or hotel room. These cases do not hinge upon the single fact that the defendant is within the confines of his dwelling, but rather rely for their determination upon the conjunction of various facts, including especially the lack of sensory enhancement, the fact that the eavesdropping government agent was lawfully in position to overhear the statements, and that the presence of a person in that place could reasonably be anticipated.

- Law enforcement officers rented the motel room next to the defendants and listened to their conversations as the defendants were having a party and talking in loud voices.[37]
- A federal narcotics agent stood in the hall of an apartment and listened to the loud voices of the defendants within the apartment. Because the apartment door was hanging imperfectly, the officer could also see the defendants through a small crack in the door. The court held that such evidence was admissible because the "conversations [were] knowingly exposed to the public."[38]

- Testimony of what an officer heard coming from a motel room as the officer stood in the motel parking lot was held to be admissible as evidence.[39]
- The defendant's yelling during a telephone conversation was overheard by a law enforcement officer.[40]

Undercover Officers May Testify About What Was Said in Their Presence   All witnesses, including undercover officers, may testify about what was said in their presence unless a privilege exists (husband–wife, and so on). The following two U.S. Supreme Court cases illustrate this type of testimony.

Lewis v. United States

United States Supreme Court, 385 U.S. 206, 87 S.Ct. 424 (1966)

An undercover federal narcotics officer was invited into the defendant's home, where the defendant sold narcotics to the officer. In affirming the defendant's conviction and in holding that testimony about what the defendant said and did was properly used as evidence, the U.S. Supreme Court ruled:

A government agent, in the same manner as a private person, may accept an invitation to do business and may enter upon the premises for the very purposes contemplated by the occupant. Of course, this does not mean that, whenever entry is obtained by invitation and the locus is characterized as a place of business, an agent is authorized to conduct a general search for incriminating materials.

Hoffa v. United States

United States Supreme Court, 385 U.S. 293, 87 S.Ct. 408 (1966)

The former union official, James Hoffa, made incriminating statements in the presence of a paid government informer. Testimony about what Hoffa said was permitted as evidence in Hoffa's trial on criminal charges. The U.S. Supreme Court affirmed the defendant's conviction, holding that no violation occurred of Hoffa's Sixth Amendment right to confer privately with his attorneys out of the presence of government agents and informers.

Use of Pocket Tape Recorders and the Crime of Bribery   The availability of inexpensive pocket tape recorders makes it easy to secretly record conversations. *The Wall Street Journal* reports that secret recordings of conversations are on the increase in the United States.[41]

Federal law allows such secret taping as long as one of the parties to a conversation knows about it. In more than a dozen states, however, the law requires that *all* the parties to a conversation must know about the recording in order to use it as evidence in a civil or criminal trial if no prior court order has been obtained.

Bribery has always presented a problem for law enforcement investigators, whether the case involves a government official seeking to bribe a private citizen or vice versa. The offender will likely deny the wrongdoing, and unless corroborating evidence is available, the word of the victim standing alone may be insufficient evidence to sustain a conviction. The following U.S. Supreme Court case illustrates the usual solution to the problem.

United States v. Caceres

United States Supreme Court, 440 U.S. 741, 99 S.Ct. 1465 (1979)

The defendant was having federal tax problems and offered to bribe a federal tax agent to fix his tax audits. Unknown to the defendant, three of his face-to-face conversations with the IRS agent were recorded by means of a radio transmitter concealed on the agent's person. However, IRS regulation required that prior authorization be obtained before taping, and the tax agent did not obtain the required permission. The U.S. Supreme Court held that the evidence was admissible despite the IRS requirement. The Court referred to and quoted a similar case (*Lopez v. United States*) and stated:

> Nor does the Constitution protect the privacy of individuals in respondent's position. In Lopez v. United States, 373 U.S. 427, 439, 83 S.Ct. 1381, 1388, 10 L.Ed.2d 462, we held that the Fourth Amendment provided no protection to an individual against the recording of his statements by the IRS agent to whom he was speaking. In doing so, we repudiated any suggestion that the defendant had a "constitutional right to rely on possible flaws in the agent's memory, or to challenge the agent's credibility without being beset by corroborating evidence that is not susceptible of impeachment," concluding instead that "the risk that petitioner took in offering a bribe to [the IRS agent] fairly included the risk that the offer would be accurately reproduced in court, whether by faultless memory or mechanical recording."

Do Suspects Have a Right of Privacy in Conversations Held in Police Vehicles, Jails, or Other Police Buildings? Suspects and other people do *not* have a right of privacy in police vehicles, jails, or police or sheriff stations. An article in the September 1993 issue of the *FBI Law Enforcement Bulletin* titled "Surreptitious Recording of Suspects' Conversations" points out that the "effective investigative technique" of surreptitiously recording conversations of suspects in such places will be admissible as evidence if the following points are followed:

> (1) Because the technique does not amount to "interrogation" for purposes of *Miranda*, it is not necessary to advise suspects of their constitutional rights and obtain a waiver prior to using this technique.... (2) To avoid a Sixth Amendment problem, this technique should not be used following the filing of formal charges or the initial appearance in court, unless the conversation does not involve a government actor, the conversation involves a government actor who has assumed the role of a "listening post," or the conversation pertains to a crime other than the one with which the suspect has been charged. (3) ... suspects should not be given any specific assurances that their conversations are private.

In the following cases, either the recordings of conversations were held to be admissible or a witness was permitted to testify about what was said:

- Two robbery suspects were arrested, placed in the backseat of a squad car, and left unattended. Before leaving, one of the officers activated a tape recorder on the front seat of the car. Unaware that their conversation was being recorded, the suspects engaged in an extremely incriminating conversation that was used in their criminal trial.[42]

- Perkins was in jail for aggravated assault. Because he was suspected of a murder unrelated to the assault, an undercover officer was placed in the cell with him. During the planning of a prison break, the undercover officer asked Perkins whether he had ever "done" anyone. Perkins then described in detail

TAPE RECORDING AND WIRETAPPING CASES THAT MADE NATIONAL NEWS

- *Tape recordings that led to the impeachment of a U.S. president:* Linda Tripp, a friend of Monica Lewinski, used a tape recorder to tape more than 20 hours of telephone conversations with Lewinski, in which the White House intern claimed she had an affair with President Bill Clinton. Tripp gave these tapes to independent counsel Kenneth Starr, and the information became public. President Clinton was impeached by the House of Representatives but was acquitted by the Senate. Tripp was charged with a felony under Maryland state law for illegally taping a telephone conversation without the other party's permission, and she received a minor penalty.

- *The crime of dissemination (passing on information about the contents of illegal wiretaps or tapes):* A Florida couple illegally recorded a telephone conversation between two members of the U.S. Congress concerning the problems of then—Speaker of the House Newt Gingrich. The couple then gave the recording to a ranking Democratic congressman, who in turn leaked the recording to newspapers. The Florida couple pleaded guilty to violation of the federal wiretapping law and were fined $500 each. In a related civil suit, in 2007 the Democratic congressman, Jim McDermott, was ordered to pay the Republican congressman, John Boehner, more than $800,000 in damages for leaking the illegal recording to the press.

- *Tapings of public statements by public figures that did not violate privacy laws:* A Wisconsin district attorney bragged to employees about a sexual encounter he had with a woman (not his wife) in his office. One of his employees secretly taped the statements and subsequently used them in an election campaign against his old boss. Both the assistant district attorney and his former employee lost the election, and another lawyer was elected district attorney. In another incident, which occurred in a campaign for U.S. senator in Iowa, the opposition party held a strategic planning meeting of 750 people who supported the election bid of a U.S. congressman. Two men openly attended the meeting and secretly taped what was said. Despite appeals to both state and federal prosecutors for criminal charges against the men, none were brought. Both men were fired, however.

- *A California criminal wiretapping trial:* Anthony Pellicano, a private detective known in the national media as "Hollywood's Mr. Fixit," was convicted in August 2008 of federal wiretapping crimes. Pellicano secretly and illegally taped the conversations of many Hollywood celebrities, including Sylvester Stallone and Garry Shandling, for use by his clients in various lawsuits. It is estimated that more than 150,000 documents and recordings were produced and used by witnesses in these suits. Pellicano faces a prison sentence of up to ten years and a fine of as much as $500,000. *The New York Times* noted, in an article about the case titled "In Pellicano Case Lessons in Wiretaping" (May 5, 2008), that illegal wiretapping can easily be done with $50 in equipment from RadioShack.

the murder-for-hire killing he had committed. The testimony of the officer was held admissible by the U.S. Supreme Court.[43]

- An informer was placed in a jail cell with instructions to just listen and not to question his cellmate. The cellmate, who was formally charged with a crime, made incriminating statements. The U.S. Supreme Court affirmed the defendant's conviction, holding that "the defendant must demonstrate that the police and their informant took some action, beyond merely listening."[44]

- A juvenile who was arrested for murder asked to speak with his mother after being given the *Miranda* warnings. The defendant and his mother talked alone in an interrogation room with the door closed. The juvenile admitted his part in the murder, not knowing the conversation was being recorded. In holding that the recording could be used as evidence, the Court held that "no representations or inquiries were made as to privacy or confidentiality" and that "walls have ears."[45]
- During an investigative stop on reasonable suspicion, the police were given consent to search the suspect's car. The two suspects were asked to sit in the back of a police car while the officers searched the car. Not knowing that a tape recorder was turned on, the two suspects made incriminating statements in their conversation while being left alone in the police car. The court held that the statements could be used as evidence against them.[46]

When One Party to a Telephone Conversation Consents to the Police Listening to and/or Recording the Conversation   The Federal Wiretapping Act of 1968 provides that a person who is a party to a wire, oral, or electronic communication may intercept such conversation "unless [the interception] is ... for the purpose of committing any crime or tortious act."[47]

Therefore, one of the parties to a telephone call may consent to a law enforcement officer listening to or recording the call without disclosing this fact to the other party. Most states follow this rule, although a few states require a court order for this procedure. The following cases illustrate the use of this investigative technique.

Examples
- In a drug investigation, law enforcement officers recorded telephone conversations with the consent of one of the parties to the conversations. The use of the evidence and the conviction were affirmed.[48]
- A cooperative witness consented to the tape recording of telephone conversations with a murder suspect. The tape recording along with the testimony of an Illinois assistant state's attorney who had listened to the defendant's confession in the telephone conversations were held to be properly admitted as evidence.[49]
- In a tax fraud investigation, evidence of the tax fraud was obtained by tape recording a telephone conversation with the consent of one of the parties to the conversations.[50]
- An interpreter listened from an extension telephone while an informant talked in Spanish with a suspected drug dealer. The Supreme Court of Nevada held that the resulting evidence was admissible.[51]

Obtaining Evidence by Use of the Confrontational Telephone Call   If the victim of a crime or a witness is cooperative, law enforcement officers may ask the person to telephone a suspect in a *confrontational call*. Such telephone calls must be made before criminal charging. The following cases illustrate situations in which this technique was used successfully.

Examples
- A minor victim of sexual abuse telephoned her stepfather, who made incriminating admissions while unaware that the conversation was being recorded and a law

officer was listening. The stepfather's admission corroborated the victim's accusations and led to criminal charging and conviction.[52]

- In a child molestation case, the child's mother telephoned the defendant, who admitted that he had fondled the child. The defendant was charged with child molestation, and the tape recording of the telephone call was used as evidence to obtain a conviction.[53]
- A woman who participated in the armed robberies of convenience stores agreed to telephone Walton, who made incriminating statements not knowing that the conversation was being recorded and that a police officer was listening.[54]
- Minnesota officers investigating a murder went to Wisconsin to talk to a woman who was being used as an alibi. After the woman admitted she was being paid $1,000 for her story, she agreed to telephone the two defendants, who made incriminating statements in conversations that were recorded. The defendants were then charged with murder and convicted in Minnesota. Because Wisconsin is one of the few states where evidence obtained in this manner is not admissible unless a prior court order is obtained, the question before the Minnesota courts was whether Wisconsin law or Minnesota law should be used. The Minnesota Supreme Court affirmed the murder convictions, holding that Minnesota law would be used in a Minnesota murder trial.[55]

Defendants who have been charged with a crime have the right to an attorney, however, and the use of a confrontational call after a defendant has been charged with a crime violates the *Massiah* limitation in most instances (see Chapter 12). The following case is an exception.

Jenkins v. Leonardo

Second Circuit Court of Appeals, 991 F.2d 1033 (1993)

After the defendant was charged with rape and was represented by an attorney, he began calling the victim to harass her. The victim contacted the police, who provided her with recording equipment and encouraged her to have the defendant talk about the facts of the crime.

During the next telephone call, the recorder was activated, and the defendant made incriminating statements, unaware that his statements were being recorded. The victim testified about the statements, and the recording was used as evidence in the trial, which resulted in the defendant's conviction. The court of appeals held that the defendant waived his right to an attorney when he made such telephone calls to harass the rape victim.

Using Body Wires or Radio Transmitters   Undercover officers, informants, or other people are sometimes fitted with "body wires" or radio transmitters for any or all of the following reasons:

- To alert backup officers if the undercover officer or the police agent is in danger or needs assistance
- To keep nearby officers informed about what is being said and the events that are occurring (with informants, this is a method of controlling the informant and preventing double dealing)
- To enable the listening officers to testify in court about what they heard

Federal law permits the use of radio transmitters as demonstrated by the following U.S. Supreme Court cases. Most states follow the federal rule, but in some states a prior court order must be obtained to permit the use of such evidence in a criminal trial.

On Lee v. United States

United States
Supreme Court, 343 U.S.
747, 72 S.Ct. 967 (1952)

Federal narcotics agents wired an undercover agent with a small microphone and radio transmitter. The agent then purchased a pound of opium from the defendant after having conversations with the defendant in his laundry and on the streets in New York City. The undercover agent did not testify at the defendant's trial, but one of the federal narcotics agents who overheard the conversations by means of the radio transmitter was permitted to testify about what he heard and saw. In affirming the defendant's conviction and the use of this evidence, the Supreme Court held: "No good reason of public policy occurs to us why the Government should be deprived of the benefit of On Lee's admissions because he made them to a confidante of shady character."

United States v. White

United States
Supreme Court, 401 U.S.
745, 91 S.Ct. 1122
(1971)

A government informant made a drug buy while federal drug agents listened to the conversations between the informant and the defendant by means of a concealed radio transmitter worn by the informant. At the time of the defendant's trial, the informer could not be located to testify, and the narcotics agents were permitted to testify about what they heard. The Supreme Court affirmed the defendant's conviction and the use of the officers' testimony as evidence, holding that:

> Concededly a police agent who conceals his police connections may write down for official use his conversations with a defendant and testify concerning them, without a warrant authorizing his encounters with the defendant and without otherwise violating the latter's Fourth Amendment rights.... For constitutional purposes, no different result is required if the agent instead of immediately reporting and transcribing his conversations with defendant, either (1) simultaneously records them with electronic equipment which he is carrying on his person, ... (2) or carries radio equipment which simultaneously transmits the conversations either to recording equipment located elsewhere or to other agents monitoring the transmitting frequency. On *Lee v. United States*.... If the conduct and revelations of an agent operating without electronic equipment do not invade the defendant's constitutionally justifiable expectations of privacy, neither does a simultaneous recording of the same conversations made by the agent or by others from transmissions received from the agent to whom the defendant is talking and whose trustworthiness the defendant necessarily risks.

May One Family Member Wiretap and Record Telephone Calls of Another Family Member?   Electronic surveillance and wiretapping are governed by Title III of the 1968 Omnibus Crime Control and Safe Streets Act.[56] The act makes it unlawful for any person to intercept or attempt to intercept any wire, oral, or electronic communication "except as otherwise specifically permitted" by the act. Willful disclosure of the contents of communications by a person who knows or has reason to know that the information was obtained through an unlawful interception is also forbidden.[57] No exception in federal law permits electronic surveillance or wiretapping by one family member on another. The following cases illustrate.

OBTAINING EVIDENCE BY OVERHEARING, MONITORING, AND/OR RECORDING STATEMENTS OR CONVERSATIONS

Law enforcement officers sometimes hear or record highly incriminating statements, or private citizens overhear or otherwise monitor conversations. If statements made in such monitored conversations are admitted as evidence in criminal cases, they can have a powerful effect on the judge or jury finding the facts, since the defendant's own words can be used to incriminate him, without the presence of the police. The following examples present the circumstances under which such evidence may be admitted in criminal cases:

Evidence Obtained	Requirements	Evidence Inadmissible
Overheard conversations (plain hearing) in a public or private place	The officer must be where he or she has a right to be and cannot use any mechanical or electronic listening device.	Evidence is not admissible if there is a violation of a right to privacy or a trespass—for example, by going on another person's property to listen to a conversation.
Statements made to undercover officers or others in their presence	The suspect may not already have been charged with a crime and the questions relate to that crime. (See the *Massiah* rule, Chapter 12.)	Some states have laws prohibiting the use of tape recordings of such conversations.
Tape recordings where the suspect has no expectation of privacy (police vehicles, jail cells, etc.)	See the *Massiah* rule (Chapter 12), where statements are made in response to questions after crime has been charged.	Assuring suspects that conversations are private can render statements inadmissible.
Consent by one party to a telephone conversation to the police recording or listening to the conversation	Consent by one party is sufficient, but the *Massiah* rule prohibits the police from using the conversation to ask questions about crimes charged.	This is permitted under federal law, but some states require consent by all parties to a conversation (e.g., Conn. Gen. Stat. § 55-570(d)).
"Confrontational" telephone call or face-to-face meeting with a suspect	If the call or meeting is made by the police, the *Massiah* rule applies.	Such a call or meeting is not permitted in states that require both parties' consent to record telephone conversations.

Examples

- In the 1992 case of *Heggy v. Heggy*,[58] a woman sued her former husband and won a money award against him for recording her telephone conversations.
- After a mother used a microcassette device attached to an extension telephone and recorded conversations between her son and a drug dealer, she turned the recordings over to the police. The recordings were used to obtain a search warrant. In holding that the search warrant was invalid, the North Carolina court cited *Rickenbaker v. Rickenbaker.*[59]
- A California man recorded telephone conversations between his wife and her lover. The husband was then murdered, and his wife and her lover were convicted of the murder with the telephone recordings being used as evidence. The California Supreme Court reversed the convictions following the majority rule, holding that because the recordings were unlawful, they could not be used as evidence.[60]

In discussing listening in on an extension telephone and wiretapping, the Supreme Court of California said:

> The differences between casually overhearing part of a conversation on an extension phone and intentionally wiretapping all incoming and outgoing calls are substantial;

ADMISSIBLE EVIDENCE RESULTING FROM INFORMANTS' TIPS

Informants come from all walks of life. Private citizens may contact the police or call 911 with information regarding a crime. Informants are also persons who could be involved in crime and are providing information for money or to avoid a long prison term.

Some informants are known to law officers and have provided reliable information in the past. Other callers remain anonymous. A caller who is reporting drug or other criminal activity by a neighbor may fear retaliation if his or her identity is disclosed. Some anonymous calls are maliciously made to harm another person or to harass the police. Police must respond to 911 calls, however, because as the court in the case of *United States v. Holloway* [290 F.3d 1331, at 1339, *cert. denied,* 123 S.Ct. 966 (2003)] stated, "If law enforcement could not rely on information conveyed by anonymous 911 callers, their ability to respond effectively to emergency situations would be severely curtailed."

Much of the information from informants is of no or little value to a law enforcement agency. Some information, however, could start an investigation that results in curtailing serious criminal activity. Other information could establish reasonable suspicion to make an investigative stop of a person or vehicle. Information from an informant could also establish probable cause to make an arrest or to obtain a search warrant.

Tips from Known Informants

Case and Crime	Type of Tip	Additional Information and Action by Law Officers
Draper v. United States, 79 S.Ct. 329 (1959), drug peddler	Known paid informer who had provided accurate and reliable information in the past	Detailed information corroborated by federal agents, justified arrest
McCray v. Illinois, 87 S.Ct. 1056 (1967), drug trafficking	Specific information from known, reliable informant	"Officers did rely in good faith upon credible information by a reliable informant," justified arrest
Adams v. Williams, 92 S.Ct. 1921 (1972), concealed weapon and possession of drugs	"Given in person by known informant who had provided information in the past"	"Carried sufficient indicia of reliability to justify a forcible stop." Protective search revealed illegal weapon; search incident to arrest resulted in finding illegal drugs

Anonymous Tips

In two of the following U.S. Supreme Court cases, the Court stated that:

... Unlike a tip from a known informant whose reputation can be assessed and who can be held responsible if her allegations turn out to be fabricated, an anonymous tip alone seldom demonstrates the informant's basis of knowledge or veracity. [110 S.Ct. 2412 and 146 L.Ed. 260]

Case and Crime	Type of Tip	Was Sufficient Indicia of Reliability Shown?
Illinois v. Gates, 103 S.Ct. 2317 (1983), trafficking in drugs	An Illinois police department received a handwritten letter telling how Mr. and Mrs. Gates (address given) were buying and selling drugs out of their home. The letter stated detailed facts and information.	Yes, extensive police investigation corroborated major portions of the letter, causing an Illinois judge to issue a search warrant for the Gates's home and car, where drugs were found. Convictions affirmed.

(Continued)

Case and Crime	Type of Tip	Additional Information and Action by Law Officers
Alabama v. White, 110 S.Ct. 2412 (1990), possession of cocaine and marijuana	"Police received an anonymous tip asserting that a woman was carrying cocaine and predicting that she would leave an apartment building at a specific time, get into a car matching a particular description, and drive to a named motel." [146 L.Ed.2d at 260]	Yes, the Court held that "(k)nowledge about a person's future movements indicates some familiarity with the person's affairs, but having such knowledge does not necessarily imply that the informant knows, in particular, whether that person is carrying contraband. We accordingly classified White as a 'close case.'"
Florida v. J.L., 120 S.Ct. 1375 (2000), illegal possession of a firearm (minor)	"An anonymous caller reported to the (police) that a young black male standing at a particular bus stop and wearing a plaid shirt was carrying a gun." Six minutes later, officers arrived at the bus stop and saw J.L. but did not see a firearm. "J.L. made no threatening or otherwise unusual movements." A frisk revealed a concealed weapon.	No, the Court held that "all the police had to go on in this case was the bare report of an unknown, unaccountable informant who neither explained how he knew about the gun nor supplied any basis for believing he had inside information about J.L."

Tips Warning of Possible Great Danger

Because public safety requires police to respond quickly to tips about great public danger, justices of the U.S. Supreme Court made the following statements in the case of *Florida v. J.L.*:

Justice Ginsburg for the majority of the court

We do not say, for example, that a report of a person carrying a bomb need bear the indicia of reliability we demand for a report of a person carrying a firearm before the police can constitutionally conduct a frisk. Nor do we hold that public safety officers in quarters where the reasonable expectation of privacy is diminished, such as airports and schools, cannot conduct protective searches on the basis of information insufficient to justify searches elsewhere.

Justice Kennedy and Chief Justice Rehnquist

There are many indicia of reliability respecting anonymous tips that we have yet to explore in our cases…. One such feature, as the Court recognizes, is that the tip predicts future conduct of the alleged criminal. There may be others….

Justice Kennedy then uses the example of three similar calls by a voice that sounds the same each time; he states that this situation "ought not to be treated automatically like the tip in the case now before us." Justice Kennedy also points out that because the police have instant caller identification, police cars can be sent to the location used by the informant. Since it is a crime to make false reports to the police, the identity of the informant might then be "a factor which lends reliability…."

the former requires the physical presence of the eavesdropper, which inherently limits the extent and frequency of the invasion; the latter, by contrast, requires no supervision, is of potentially unlimited duration, and is wholly indiscriminate…. Whatever Congress might have intended concerning the occasional use of an extension phone by a parent, we find no evidence of a legislative intent to create a wholesale exception for systematic interspousal wiretapping.

In sum, we follow a majority of the courts in declining to read into Title III an exception for interspousal or domestic wiretapping. Neither the text, the history nor the purposes of Title III permit the conclusion that defendants' conversations were lawfully intercepted.

Appraising the Reliability of Informants' Tips

The December 2003 issue of the *FBI Law Enforcement Bulletin* includes an article titled "When an Informant's Tip Gives Officers Probable Cause to Arrest Drug Traffickers." The article's author provides standards for police officers to use in appraising the reliability of information obtained from informants.

- *The concerned citizen:* "If a concerned citizen is known to the police, he [or she] is presumed credible." "To be considered a concerned citizen informant by the courts, an informant must not be involved in the criminal milieu [environment or setting]." This standard does not apply to the credibility of statements like "The bank was just robbed." Such statements should be investigated immediately to determine the accuracy of the statement.

- *Corroboration of information:* "Once an officer corroborates innocent future conduct of the suspect as predicted by the informant, it would be reasonable for the officer to conclude that the informant is being accurate regarding the suspect's involvement in the alleged crime."

- *Information given to seek a benefit or made against the penal interest of the informant:* "An informant could be considered credible even if he [or she] does not have a track record for reliability, if he [or she] made a statement against his [or her] penal interest, or if it can be established that he has a strong motive to be truthful. It is reasonable to believe that an informant has a motive to be truthful when he [or she] is expecting some leniency for pending [criminal] charges and the circumstances suggest that any benefit expected by him [or her] would only inure to him if the information supplied is accurate." An example of a statement against penal interest is: "Joe Smith is a crack dealer. I buy crack from him every day, including last night." Because the statement exposes the speaker to criminal prosecution, which could result in a prison sentence, it is against his penal interest. The fact that he nonetheless made the statement is a sign of its truthfulness.

- *How much corroborating evidence is needed?* "The degree of corroboration necessary to establish probable cause is dependent on the credibility and basis of knowledge of the informant." The "basis of knowledge" looks to how the informant acquired the information the informant provides to an officer. Was the informant a party to the crime? Was he a witness to the crime? Is it firsthand knowledge or hearsay? Is it "hearsay on hearsay," just "street talk," or a rumor? Depending on the basis for an informant's information, an officer may or may not have probable cause to take additional action.

OBTAINING EVIDENCE BY THE USE OF DOGS TRAINED TO INDICATE AN ALERT

Dogs have a sense of smell that is reported to be several thousand times stronger than the average human's. For years, dogs have been used to pursue fugitives, locate escaped convicts, find missing persons, detect drugs and explosives, and in recent years identify suspects in a lineup.

The article "Detection Dog Lineup" in the January 1996 *FBI Law Enforcement Bulletin* tells of a Colorado bloodhound named Yogi who tracked the scent of a kidnapped 5-year-old girl for 7 hours over a 14-mile trail. After the girl's body was found, Yogi led officers to the suspect in a nearby apartment complex. Yogi has been used in 4 kidnapping cases, 45 homicide cases, and 350 other criminal cases.

The article reports that Yogi has been used in more than twenty-five detection dog lineups and describes the methods for using detection dogs to identify suspects in lineups. Three appellate court cases are cited where detection dog lineup evidence was used to obtain criminal convictions.[61]

DRUG AND BOMB DETECTION DOGS

Drug and bomb detection dogs have become a common and very effective tool used by law enforcement agencies throughout the United States. In a 1983 ruling, the U.S. Supreme Court held that luggage exposed to a trained drug detection dog in a public place "did not constitute a search within the meaning of the Fourth Amendment."[62]

Dogs trained to "alert" when they smell illegal drugs are used by U.S. Customs agents to search for such drugs in containers brought across U.S. borders. The use of dog detection evidence in court is dependent on up-to-date records verifying the dog's reliability.

An January 2000 *FBI Law Enforcement Bulletin* article titled "Drug Detection Dogs: Legal Considerations" observes that drug detection dogs "have proven highly effective and reliable in detecting illegal narcotics" and that the U.S. Supreme Court and "most lower courts have granted particular deference to the olfactory abilities of police drug detection dogs." In reviewing the court rulings of the 1990s, the article concludes:

- "The use of drug detection dogs has met with few real challenges in the courts."
- "A dog's positive alert alone generally constitutes probable cause to search a vehicle...."
- "As long as the [motor] vehicle is not detained beyond the time necessary to accomplish the purposes of the traffic stop ... the exterior of the vehicle is available for a sniff."

In the following 2005 case, the U.S. Supreme Court considered the constitutionality of dog sniffs during a routine traffic stop.

Illinois v. Caballes

United States Supreme Court, 125 S.Ct. 834 (2005)

An Illinois state trooper stopped Caballes for speeding on an interstate highway. When the trooper called in to report the stop, an officer in the Illinois State Police Drug Interdiction Team overheard the call and went to the scene with his drug detection dog. While Caballes sat in the first trooper's car, the dog sniffed the exterior of his vehicle and alerted at its trunk. The entire stop and sniff lasted about 10 minutes. A subsequent search turned up marijuana in the trunk, and Caballes was arrested and charged with drug violations. At his trial, he moved to suppress the drugs, contending that the dog sniff and resulting search were unconstitutional. The trial court denied the motion, and Caballes was convicted. On appeal, the Illinois Supreme Court reversed, holding that because the dog sniff was based on no "specific and articulable facts" suggesting illegal drug activity, the use of the dog was unjustified. The U.S. Supreme Court granted certiorari on the precise question "Whether the Fourth Amendment requires reasonable, articulable suspicion to justify using a drug detection dog to sniff a vehicle during a legitimate traffic stop."

The Court answered that question in the negative. After noting that the total duration of the traffic stop and dog sniff was less than 10 minutes, the Court concluded that the detention of Caballes was lawful. In response to the opinion of the Illinois Supreme Court that the dog sniff turned the detention into an unlawful drug investigation without articulable, reasonable suspicion, the Court said:

> In our view, conducting a dog sniff would not change the character of a traffic stop that is lawful at its inception and otherwise executed in a reasonable manner, unless the dog sniff itself infringed respondent's constitutionally protected interest in privacy. Our cases hold that it did not.

The Court noted that in *United States v. Place* (discussed in note 62 of this chapter) it held that because the alert of a well-trained drug detection dog discloses only illegal contraband, no legitimate expectation of privacy is violated. In contrast, devices like the thermal-imaging device held to be an unlawful search in *Kyllo v. United States* (discussed earlier in this chapter) had the potential to disclose "intimate details in the home," the Court reasoned. Since the traffic stop was lawful and the detention pursuant to that stop reasonable, conducting the dog sniff did not itself infringe on any constitutionally protected privacy interest: "a dog sniff conducted during a concededly lawful traffic stop that reveals no information other than the location of a substance that no individual has any right to possess does not violate the Fourth Amendment."

Justice Souter dissented, contending that the assumption upon which *Place* was based was wrong. He noted that since *Place* was decided, studies have shown that even experienced drug detection dogs give false positives. He cited K. Garner et al., *Duty Cycle of the Detector Dog: A Baseline Study* (April 2001), which stated that the error rate for dog alerts is from 12 to 60 percent, depending on the length of the search. That being so, Justice Souter was of the opinion that using such dogs incident to a simple traffic stop was an unauthorized search.

When dog detection evidence is used in criminal courts, keeping and maintaining updated records on the dog and its handler are essential because the dog's reliability is generally challenged in court. When presenting drug cases where dogs have alerted to the presence of the illegal drugs, dog detection handlers should be prepared to establish the reliability of the dog by testimony regarding:

- The training that the dog received to detect the odors for particular drugs
- The dog's success rate in detecting these drugs
- The method used to train the dog to indicate an alert
- Whether the dog alerted in the proper manner
- Proof of the dog's certification
- Proof that the dog has continued to meet certification requirements and has continued to receive necessary training on a regular basis[63]

SUMMARY

Search warrants have always been an important tool to obtain evidence during the investigation of a criminal case. When a search warrant is issued, the determination by the judge or magistrate issuing the warrant is given great deference, and the burden of proving that probable cause did not exist shifts to persons who are challenging the warrant.

Today, telecommunications systems have become the cornerstones of everyday life. Dependence on computers, data services, and mobile communications has become increasingly important for business and personal use. To cope with the many changes, law enforcement must, on occasion, obtain authority to use electronic surveillance to obtain evidence when dealing with terrorism, organized crime, or sophisticated illegal drug trafficking.

Detection dogs are another important tool law enforcement uses on occasion to obtain evidence or to find missing persons, locate illegal drugs, or detect bombs.

CASE ANALYSIS

Read Appendix B, Finding and Analyzing Cases (p. 427). With these guidelines in mind, please continue with the Case Analysis selections for Chapter 15.

When the police use searches or surveillance techniques that raise Fourth Amendment concerns, an initial question that must be answered is: Did the person claiming the protection of the Fourth Amendment have an expectation of privacy that was invaded by the police actions? The following cases involve determinations of that expectation of privacy in marginal cases.

1. If you are a short-term guest at a friend's home, do you have an expectation of privacy,

such that a warrantless entry by the police into that home violates your Fourth Amendment rights? In the case of *In re welfare of B.R.K.* [658 N.W.2d 565 (2003) (No. C7-01-1466)], the Minnesota Supreme Court said a guest at a party given by the homeowner had such an expectation of privacy. Do you agree?

2. Can one have an expectation of privacy in a public place? Drug deals and other crimes sometimes take place in public restrooms. As a result, police often have officers conduct surveillance of such restrooms. May the police look into a restroom stall to observe a crime being committed? In *State v. Orta* [663 N.W.2d 358 (Wisc. App. 2003) (02–1008-CR)] the court said they could. What are the rules for determining the expectation of privacy in a public restroom?

3. Assuming the police may bring a dog to "sniff" a vehicle stopped for a routine traffic violation without "reasonable suspicion" that illegal drugs are present in the vehicle, may the police detain the vehicle and its passengers beyond the time needed to handle the traffic stop without "reasonable suspicion"? Compare *United States v. Alexander* [448 F.3d 1014 (8th Cir. 2006)] with *State v. Louthan* [744 N.W.2d 454 (2008)].

4. When federal officers in Wisconsin obtained a telephonic search warrant to look for illegal drugs at a "stash" house, Federal Rule of Criminal Procedure 41(e)(3)(A) required that both the officers and the judge issuing the warrant make a written copy of the authorization for the search. Because this was one of the only times the officers had applied for electronic warrants, and the first time for the issuing judge, neither made a written record of the issuance of the search warrant. Is that a violation of the Federal Rule and the Fourth Amendment? If so, should any evidence obtained in the search be excluded? See *United States v. Cazares-Olivas* [515 F.3d 726 (7th Cir. 2008)].

Notes

1. 172 F.3d 1268 (10th Cir. 1999).
2. 275 F.3d 981 (10th Cir. 2001).
3. 590 F.2d 535 (4th Cir. 1978).
4. 375 F.3d 679 (8th Cir. 2004).
5. 305 F.3d 1193 (10th Cir. 2002).
6. See *United States v. Finley*, 477 F.3d 250 (5th Cir. 2007), regarding cell phones.
7. See, for example, *United States v. Park*, 2007 WL 1521573 (N.D. Cal 2007).
8. 18 U.S.C. § 2510–22.
9. 18 U.S.C. § 2510(1).
10. *Payton v. New York*, 445 U.S. 573 (1980).
11. The U.S. Supreme Court has repeatedly held that searches "without prior approval by a judge ... are per se unreasonable under the Fourth Amendment—subject only to a few specifically established and well-delineated exceptions" [*Coolidge v. New Hampshire*, 91 S.Ct. 2022 (1971)]. Therefore, evidence obtained as a result of an unreasonable search is suppressed and may not be used.
12. The U.S. Supreme Court held in the case of *United States v. Leon* [104 S.Ct. 3405 (1984)]

that "the courts must also insist that the magistrate purport to perform his neutral and detached function and not serve merely as a rubber stamp for the police."

13. 90 S.Ct. 1029 (1970).
14. 500 N.W.2d 547 (Nebr. 1993).
15. 379 F.3d 1203 (10th Cir. 2004), *cert. denied,* 125 S.Ct. 1390 (2005).
16. 434 F.3d 669 (4th Cir. 2006), *cert. denied,* 127 S.Ct. 2286 (2007).
17. The U.S. Supreme Court defined "controlled delivery" in the 1983 case of *Illinois v. Andreas* [463 U.S. 765, 103 S.Ct. 3319] and affirmed the manner in which the law enforcement officers acted:

Controlled deliveries of contraband apparently serve a useful function in law enforcement. They most ordinarily occur when a carrier, usually an airline, unexpectedly discovers what seems to be contraband while inspecting luggage to learn the identity of its owner, or when the contraband falls out of a broken or damaged piece of luggage, or when the carrier exercises its inspection privilege because some suspicious circumstance has caused concern that it may unwittingly be transporting contraband. Frequently, after such a discovery, law enforcement agents restore the contraband to its container, then close or reseal the container, and authorize the carrier to deliver the container to its owner. When the owner appears to take delivery he is arrested and the container with the contraband is seized and then searched a second time for the contraband known to be there.

18. 547 U.S. at 95; citations omitted.

19. *Id.*

20. 547 U.S. at 97–98.

21. Federal Rule of Criminal Procedure 41 requires that a covert entry under a sneak-and-peek warrant be followed within seven days by notice to the person whose property has been entered. However, cases where this was not done include *United States v. Pangburn* [983 F.2d 449, 52 CrL 1417 (2d Cir. 1993)] and *United States v. Freitas* [800 F.2d 1451 (9th Cir. 1986)].

22. 441 U.S. 238, 99 S.Ct. 1682.

23. 142 F.3d 988 (7th Cir. 1998).

24. 42 U.S.C. § 2000(a)(a). In addition, the federal "Adam Walsh Child Protection and Safety Act" (18 U.S.C. § 2241) requires that because of the nature of child pornography, pornographic materials seized as evidence in a criminal case must be kept in a secure government facility, and examined only by members of a defense team, and may not be copied. The act, named after the murdered son of John Walsh, host of the television program *America's Most Wanted*, states that "... every instance of viewing images of child pornography represents a renewed violation of the privacy of the victims and a repetition of their abuse."

Viewing the images might relate to the two basic defenses to a child pornography charge: (1) the images were not placed in the computer by the defendant, and (2) the images are not of real children but generated by computer simulation.

25. 389 U.S. 523 (1967).

26. See "Crackdown on Violations of Fire Code: Arresting New Yorkers Who Ignore Citations" (June 11, 2008).

27. 88 S.Ct. 507.

28. Title 18, Chapter 119 of the Omnibus Crime Control and Safe Streets Act of 1968 (18 U.S.C. § 2510).

29. In footnote 1 of the case of *Dalia v. United States* [441 U.S. 238, 99 S.Ct. 1682 (1979)], the U.S.

Supreme Court stated the difference between wiretapping and bugging:

All types of electronic surveillance have the same purpose and effect: the secret interception of communications. As the Court set forth in *Berger v. New York*, 388 U.S. 41, (1967), however, this surveillance is performed in two quite different ways. Some surveillance is performed by "wiretapping," which is confined to the interception of communication by telephone and telegraph and generally may be performed from outside the premises to be monitored.... At issue in the present case is the form of surveillance commonly known as "bugging," which includes the interception of all oral communication in a given location. Unlike wiretapping, this interception typically is accomplished by installation of a small microphone in the room to be bugged and transmission to some nearby receiver.

The issue before the U.S. Supreme Court in *Dalia* was whether a separate court order was necessary to authorize the FBI to enter an office building to place a listening device and then, several weeks later, to enter again at night to remove the device. The majority held that court orders were not necessary.

30. 476 U.S. 207 (1986).

31. 442 U.S. 735 (1979).

32. 18 U.S.C. § 3123(a)(2000).

33. A detailed discussion of these changes is found in Robert A. Pikowsky, *An Overview of the Law of Electronic Surveillance Post September 11*, 94 Law Libr. J. 601 (2002).

34. 18 U.S.C.A. § 2518 (11).

35. The word *eavesdropping* is an old English word meaning "to sneak under the eaves of a home and listen to conversations within the home." This conduct was forbidden under old English law and is forbidden under present law. See the case of *State of Texas v. Gonzales* [388 F.2d 145 (5th Cir. 1968)], where law officers sneaked into the defendant's yard at night and listened to conversations in the house. Because the defendant's Fourth Amendment right of privacy was violated, the evidence obtained was suppressed.

36. 10 Conn. App. 7, 521 A.2d 204 (1987), *review denied*, 486 U.S. 1056, 108 S.Ct. 2823.

37. *United States v. Fisch*, 474 F.2d 1071 (9th Cir. 1973), *review denied*, 412 U.S. 921, 93 S.Ct. 2742 (1973); *United States v. Jackson*, 588 F.2d 1046 (5th Cir. 1979).

38. *United States v. Llanes*, 398 F.2d 880 (2d Cir. 1968).

39. *Ponce v. Craven*, 409 F.2d 621 (9th Cir. 1969).

40. *Pappas v. Municipality of Anchorage*, 698 P.2d 1236 (Alaska App. 1985).

41. See the article "Secret Taping of Supervisors Is on the Rise, Lawyers Say" (November 3, 1992), p. B1. The article points out that labor lawyers report an increase in secret taping of supervisors by employees seeking to protect their jobs in a tight labor market.

42. *Stanley v. Wainwright*, 604 F.2d 379 (5th Cir. 1979), *review denied*, 100 S.Ct. 3019 (1980).

43. *Illinois v. Perkins*, 496 U.S. 292, 110 S.Ct. 2394 (1990).

44. *Kuhlmann v. Wilson*, 477 U.S. 436, 106 S.Ct. 2616 (1986).

45. *Ahmad A. v. Superior Court*, 263 Cal. Rptr. 747 (1989), *review denied*, 498 U.S. 834, 111 S.Ct. 102 (1990).

46. *State v. Fedorchenko*, 630 So.2d 213 (Fla. App. 1993).

47. 18 U.S.C.A. § 2511(2)(d).

48. *State v. Kedoranian*, 828 P.2d 45 (Wash. App. 1992).

49. *People v. Griffin*, 592 N.E.2d 930 (Ill. App. 1992). Illinois law requires a prior court order for one-party consent to the monitoring of a private conversation through the use of an eavesdropping device.

   While investigating an arson, Illinois police officers listened to a telephone conversation between Shinkle (one of the wrongdoers) and a man who admitted to committing the arson and who allowed the police to listen to the conversation. The police officer picked up an extension phone and placed his hand over the mouthpiece. Shinkle made incriminating statements that were used to convict him. The Illinois Supreme Court held that the extension phone did not become an eavesdropping device because the officer cupped his hand over the mouthpiece in the 1989 case of *People v. Shinkle* [539 N.E.2d 1238, 45 CrL 2211].

50. *United States v. Dale*, 991 F.2d 819 (D.C. Cir. 1993).

51. *State v. Reyes*, 808 P.2d 544 (Nev. 1991).

52. *State v. Allgood*, 831 P.2d 1290 (Ariz. App. 1992).

53. *Lawrence v. State*, 393 S.E.2d 475 (Ga. App. 1990).

54. *State v. Walton*, 809 P.2d 81 (Ore. 1991).

55. *State v. Lucas*, 372 N.W.2d 731 (Minn. 1985).

56. 18 U.S.C.A. § 2510–21.

57. 18 U.S.C.A. § 2511(1)(c).

58. 944 F.2d 1537 (10th Cir.), *review denied*, 112 S.Ct. 1574 (1992).

59. *State v. Shaw*, 404 S.E.2d 887, 49 CrL 1340 (N.C. App. 1991); *Rickenbaker v. Rickenbaker*, 226 S.E.2d 347 (N.C. 1976).

60. *People v. Otto*, 831 P.2d 1178 (Calif. 1992), *review denied*, U.S. 113 S.Ct. 414 (1992).

61. See *Ramos v. State*, 4966 So.2d 121 (Fla. 1986); *United States v. McNiece*, 558 F.Supp. 612 (E.D.N.Y. 1983); *State v. Roscoe*, 700 P.2d 1312 (Ariz. 1984), *cert. denied*, 417 U.S. 1094.

62. In the case of *United States v. Place* [462 U.S. 696], the U.S. Supreme Court pointed out that a dog's sniff is nonintrusive and reveals only the presence of illegal drugs. Place was not required to open his luggage and expose his personal belongings to public view. The Supreme Court, however, reversed Place's conviction not because of the dog sniff but because the 90-minute wait for the arrival of the dog at the airport was held to be too long to be reasonable; the officers did not act with due diligence.

   A 90-minute detention based on reasonable suspicion has been held to be reasonable in cases where officers acted with due diligence to get a dog to the scene. In the case of *United States v. $64,765.00* [786 F.Supp. 906 (Ore. 1991)], the officers' efforts and diligence in getting a dog to the scene caused the court to rule that the delay was reasonable under the circumstances.

63. *Id.* at 32.

THE CRIME SCENE, THE CHAIN OF CUSTODY REQUIREMENT, AND THE USE OF FINGERPRINTS AND TRACE EVIDENCE

CHAPTER 16

LEARNING OBJECTIVES

In this chapter we examine the rules that permit law enforcement officers to obtain evidence from crime scenes and arrests, and how that evidence must be maintained—the "chain of custody" requirement. The learning objectives for this chapter are:

- Identify the requirements for a warrantless search under the "exigent circumstances" exception.
- Identify the requirements for a warrantless search under the "protective sweep" and "emergency aid" exceptions.
- State when, if ever, passengers have "standing" to object to searches of automobiles in which they are passengers.
- State what a defendant must show to raise a "chain of custody" argument.

CHAPTER CONTENTS

OBTAINING EVIDENCE FROM A CRIME SCENE

Crimes occur in both public and private places. If a crime occurs on a street or sidewalk or in premises, such as a tavern or store, open to the public, law officers do not have to show authority such as consent, a search warrant, or an exigency to justify their entry.

When a crime occurs in a private place, such as a home, apartment, office, or factory, law enforcement officers most often enter with the consent of victims, family members, or someone who has control of the premises. Two other situations also confer authority to enter:

- Exigency is where a person's life or safety is endangered: where there is concern for an elderly person or some other person, or where a shooting, fire, or explosion has occurred. (See Chapter 14 for cases and the law about exigent entry into private premises.)
- Search warrants are usually necessary to enter premises where there is probable cause to believe that nonemergency crimes have occurred or are occurring (such as drug houses or places where nonviolent crimes are believed to be taking place).

crime scene A location where an illegal act took place and from which law enforcement personnel collect physical evidence.

Law enforcement officers may stay in a **crime scene** for a reasonable period of time to perform whatever tasks they are obligated to do. The question of how long officers may stay on the premises was addressed in the following 1978 case, where the U.S. Supreme Court held that there was no "murder scene exception" to the Fourth Amendment of the U.S. Constitution.

Mincey v. Arizona

United States Supreme Court, 437 U.S. 385, 98 S.Ct. 2408 (1978)

In a drug raid of the defendant's apartment in Tucson, Arizona, Officer Headricks was shot and later died. Police officers seized the apartment and held it for four days. The U.S. Supreme Court described the police search as follows:

> Their search lasted four days, during which period the entire apartment was searched, photographed, and diagrammed. The officers opened drawers, closets, and cupboards, and inspected their contents; they emptied clothing pockets; they dug bullet fragments out of the walls and floors; they pulled up sections of the carpet and removed them for examination. Every item in the apartment was closely examined and inventoried, and 200 to 300 objects were seized. In short, Mincey's apartment was subjected to an exhaustive and intrusive search. No warrant was ever obtained.

In reversing the defendant's convictions and ordering a new trial, the Court held:

> In sum, we hold that the "murder scene exception" created by the Arizona Supreme Court is inconsistent with the Fourth and Fourteenth Amendments—that the warrantless search of Mincey's apartment was not constitutionally permissible simply because a homicide had recently occurred there.

WHAT CAN POLICE SEARCH FOR IN PREMISES WHERE A SERIOUS CRIME HAS RECENTLY OCCURRED?

In the *Mincey* case, the U.S. Supreme Court also decided what police may search for in premises where a serious crime has recently occurred. The Court held that law enforcement officers may make "warrantless entries and searches when they

emergency situation A serious and often dangerous situation that requires immediate action, such as "hot pursuit," now or never, and emergency aid.

reasonably believe that a person within is in need of immediate aid" (**emergency situations**). The Court stated:

- Law officers "may make a prompt warrantless search of the area to see if there are other victims or if a killer is still on the premises...."
- The police "may seize any evidence that is in plain view during the course of their legitimate emergency activities...."[1]

In holding that the police search in the *Mincey* case went too far and exceeded the limits of "emergency activities," the Court held:[2]

> But a warrantless search must be "strictly circumscribed by the exigencies which justify its initiation," *Terry v. Ohio*, 392 U.S., at 25–26, 88 S.Ct., at 1882, and it simply cannot be contended that this search was justified by any emergency threatening life or limb. All the persons in Mincey's apartment had been located before the investigating homicide officers arrived there and began their search. And a four-day search that included opening dresser drawers and ripping up carpets can hardly be rationalized in terms of the legitimate concerns that justify an emergency search.

WHEN CAN POLICE SEARCH PREMISES THEY HAVE ENTERED LAWFULLY?

In *Maryland v. Buie*,[3] the U.S. Supreme Court identified three circumstances where officers may make warrantless searches of premises. First, incident to a lawful arrest, police officers may search the area into which the arrestee might reach in order to grab a weapon or destroy evidence. Second, officers may make a cursory search of the immediate area near the site of the arrest for places a person might be hiding. Third, officers who have lawfully entered a residence may conduct a "protective sweep" of the residence if they reasonably believe that a person posing a threat to the police is on the premises. Any evidence found in plain view during such a sweep is admissible. Athough the sweep must be limited in location and duration, courts do not require that police have any specific reason to fear that a particular person remains inside the premises. For example, in the 2008 case of *United States v. Mata*,[4] the court upheld a protective search of a repair shop where illegal drugs were known to be stored. Although the police had no reason to expect that a particular person was hiding in the shop, the sweep was justified on the grounds that the police knew that a large amount of illegal drugs had just gone into the shop and that the people there were "keeping an eye out" for law enforcement officers.

OBTAINING EVIDENCE AFTER A "HOT-PURSUIT" ENTRY INTO PRIVATE PREMISES

The following U.S. Supreme Court cases state the law about the admissibility of evidence obtained by police in lawful "hot-pursuit" entries into homes.[5]

Warden, Md. Penitentiary v. Hayden

United States Supreme Court, 387 U.S. 294, 87 S.Ct. 1642 (1967)

Immediately after the defendant robbed a Baltimore cab company, his flight was observed by two cab drivers, who reported that he entered a nearby home. Within minutes, police arrived at the home. Having been given a description of the defendant, they requested entrance, and when Mrs. Hayden offered no objections, the police began a search of the home for the defendant. Before the police found Hayden in the home, they found a pistol in a toilet flush tank that was running, and ammunition for the pistol was found under the mattress of Hayden's bed. A shotgun was found, and ammunition for it was found in a bureau drawer. Clothing similar to the type worn by the fleeing felon was found in a washing machine. All the seized items were used as evidence. In affirming the use of the evidence and the conviction of the defendant, the Court held:

> They [the police] acted reasonably when they entered the house and began to search for a man of the description they had been given and for weapons which he had used in the robbery or might be used against them. The Fourth Amendment does not require police officers to delay in the course of an investigation if to do so would gravely endanger their lives or the lives of others. Speed here was essential, and only a thorough search of the house for persons and weapons could have insured that Hayden was the only man present and that the police had control of all weapons which could be used against them or to effect an escape....
>
> ...The permissible scope of search must, therefore, at the least, be as broad as may reasonably be necessary to prevent the dangers that the suspect at large in the house may resist or escape.

United States v. Santana

United States Supreme Court, 427 U.S. 38, 96 S.Ct. 2406 (1976)

In a "buy-and-bust" operation, a police informant bought heroin from Santana and paid for it in marked money. Police officers then had probable cause to arrest Santana. The officers went to Santana's home and identified themselves to the defendant as she stood in her doorway. When the defendant retreated into the house, the officers pursued her and caught her in the vestibule of the home. In a subsequent search, police found additional evidence of illegal drug transactions. Santana successfully moved to suppress the evidence found in the search, contending that the entry into her home was not justified. In holding that the arrest and the evidence obtained in the search incident to the arrest were lawful, the Supreme Court reversed the lower court's ruling suppressing that evidence and held:

> The only remaining question is whether her act of retreating into her house could thwart an otherwise proper arrest. We hold that it could not. In *Warden v. Hayden*, 387 U.S. 294, 87 S.Ct. 1642 (1967), we recognized the right of police, who had probable cause to believe that an armed robber had entered a house a few minutes before, to make a warrantless entry to arrest the robber and to search for weapons. This case, involving a true "hot pursuit," is clearly governed by Warden; the need to act quickly here is even greater than in that case while the intrusion is much less. The District Court was correct in concluding that "hot pursuit" means some sort of a chase, but it need not be an extended hue and cry "in and about [the] public streets." The fact that the pursuit here ended almost as soon as it began did not render it any the less a "hot pursuit" sufficient to justify the warrantless entry into Santana's house. Once Santana saw the police, there was likewise a realistic expectation that any delay would result in destruction of evidence.... Once she had been arrested the search, incident to that arrest, which produced the drugs and money was clearly justified.
>
> We thus conclude that a suspect may not defeat an arrest which has been set in motion in a public place, and is therefore proper under *Watson v. United States*, 96 S.Ct. 820 (1976), by the expedient of escaping to a private place.

OBTAINING EVIDENCE IN NOW-OR-NEVER EXIGENCY SITUATIONS

An exigency exists if law officers have no time to obtain a search warrant and have probable cause to believe that evidence will be destroyed or moved to an unknown place. The burden is on the law officers to show that a now-or-never situation exists; that is, the police must show that they needed to act immediately or else they would lose the opportunity to seize the evidence because it would be destroyed or moved to an unknown place.

In the 1966 case of *Schmerber v. California*,[6] the defendant was involved in a car accident where both he and others were injured. Police had probable cause to believe that Schmerber was driving while intoxicated. Because the human body quickly destroys evidence of intoxication and the police did not have time to obtain a search warrant for intoxication evidence within Schmerber's body, a now-or-never situation existed.

Because of the compelling public interest in highway safety, the U.S. Supreme Court held in both the *Schmerber* case and the 1983 case of *South Dakota v. Neville*[7] that, because there was no time to obtain a search warrant, immediate action was required by law officers to obtain and preserve evidence of intoxication by obtaining blood or breath for testing and use as evidence. All states have now passed an implied consent law: Drivers who use the highways imply their consent to such tests if probable cause exists to believe that the driver is operating a motor vehicle while intoxicated. Failure to consent to testing under such circumstances is a crime.

In the following case, the U.S. Supreme Court held that a now-or-never entry into an apartment was lawful to seize illegal drugs as evidence.

Ker v. California

United States Supreme Court, 374 U.S. 23, 83 S.Ct. 1623 (1963)

Law enforcement officers observed Ker make a large illegal drug buy from a drug dealer. They followed Ker's car but lost it in traffic when Ker made a sudden turn. Believing that Ker knew that he was being followed, the officers then obtained the address of Ker's apartment from his automobile license number. When Ker's car was found parked at his apartment, the officers obtained a key to his apartment from the apartment manager. Believing that evidence would be destroyed if they made an entry by knocking, the officers used the key to make a no-knock entry into Ker's apartment. In holding that the officers' testimony sustained an exception to the California "knock" requirement, the Supreme Court affirmed the defendant's conviction and the use of the narcotics seized as evidence in Ker's trial, holding:

> Here ... the criteria under California law clearly include an exception to the notice requirement where exigent circumstances are present....
>
> ... Here justification for the officers' failure to give notice is uniquely present. In addition to the officers' belief that Ker was in possession of narcotics, which could be quickly and easily destroyed, Ker's furtive conduct in eluding them shortly before the arrest was ground for the belief that he might well have been expecting the police. We therefore hold that in the particular circumstances of this case the officers' method of entry, sanctioned by the law of California, was not unreasonable under the standards of the Fourth Amendment as applied to the States through the Fourteenth Amendment.

OBTAINING EVIDENCE IN EMERGENCY AID SITUATIONS

Thousands of emergency aid cases have come before U.S. courts.[8] Evidence found when police are responding to an emergency may be used in criminal trials. The courts sustained police action in the following examples:

Examples

- To aid physicians who are treating a person suffering from a drug overdose, police may search for the substance the person took and seize it to assist in the person's treatment. In the case of *State v. Follett*,[9] police arrested a driver who was under the influence of some substance. Police could search for and seize the substance the person took (cocaine) to aid the treating physician and to use as evidence. This also has been done in attempted suicides.
- The Supreme Court of Delaware held that when police receive a report indicating that emergency aid might be needed, "it was the duty of the police to act forthwith upon the report of the emergency—not to speculate upon the accuracy of the report or upon legal technicalities regarding search warrants...."[10]
- An injured driver left the scene of a vehicle accident and was traced by a police officer to his home. When the officer observed the man through a window lying on a bed unconscious and bleeding, an emergency entry into the home was authorized. Evidence of drunk driving was then lawfully obtained.[11]
- Police had reasonable suspicion to stop cars leaving an area where shots were heard. In the 1993 case of *United States v. Reedy*,[12] a citizen told the police of the gunshots; in the 1992 case of *Williamson v. United States*,[13] a police officer heard the shots fired. Evidence obtained in the car stops could be used.

OBTAINING SCENT EVIDENCE FROM THE CRIME SCENE

Crime scenes differ greatly, depending on the type of crime committed and the setting in which the crime occurred. Some crime scenes, such as the location of a drive-by shooting, may yield little physical evidence, while others, like a residential or rural setting of homicide or rape, might yield many types of physical evidence.

DNA evidence is reported to be available in only about 10 percent of the scenes of violent felonies, and where that evidence is available, other kinds of physical evidence, such as fingerprints, blood spatters, and other bodily fluids, are also likely to be found. In a large number of crime scenes, however, these kinds of evidence are not present, which makes the identification of the perpetrator more difficult.

One method of identifying a suspect is through the use of scent evidence. Although scent evidence is not always available, if the crime scene holds clothing a suspect has touched or worn, particularly if worn close to the body, or if blood or other bodily fluids are found, then a trained tracking dog can be used to follow the scent of a suspect and lead law enforcement officers to the suspect.

An example of the use of scent evidence is found in the 2007 case of *State v. St. John*.[14] There, a convenience store was robbed at gunpoint by a masked man wearing a knit cap. The robber was seen running from the store and taking off his mask and cap. Police quickly arrived at the store with a tracking dog, which sniffed the scent from the cap and followed the scent to a location about a mile away where the police had detained a suspect. A witness from the store observed the suspect in a showup and stated that she was "pretty" sure he was the robber. At the man's trial, the tracking dog's trainer testified that the dog went directly from the store to the defendant, the dog following the scent the whole way, and when the dog approached the defendant, the dog jumped on the defendant's chest, as the dog was trained to do to indicate the source of the scent. This evidence corroborated the identification evidence, and the defendant was convicted of armed robbery.

A trained dog can use scent evidence to:

1. Follow the trail of a suspect from the crime scene, where objects dropped might be found, footprints or tire tracks discovered, or witnesses found who may have seen the fleeing suspect.

2. Identify a suspect in a "scent" lineup. In the 2006 case of *Risher v. State*,[15] a trained bloodhound used a "scent pad" from a brick of cocaine discarded by the driver of a car during a police chase to identify the driver in a scent lineup as the person who had touched the cocaine. Evidence showed that the dog had participated in seventy-four scent lineups and had identified the person whose scent was on a scent pad in sixty-three cases. The dog had never made a false identification.

3. Place a suspect at or near the scene of the crime.

4. Establish probable cause to make an arrest or obtain a search warrant. In the 2004 case of *Fitzgerald v. State*,[16] the Maryland Supreme Court held that an alert outside a defendant's apartment by a dog trained to sniff marijuana was sufficient probable cause to obtain a search warrant.

5. Locate a missing person, who might be a hostage or dead. Specially trained "cadaver" dogs can be used to find a body or confirm that a body was once at a particular location. In the 2007 case of *Trejos v. State*,[17] evidence that two trained cadaver dogs alerted to a spot where a body of a murder victim that had never been found but had been buried and later moved was admitted to corroborate other evidence that the defendant had murdered the victim.

DEFENDANTS MUST HAVE STANDING TO CHALLENGE THE USE OF EVIDENCE OBTAINED FROM CRIME SCENES

To have *standing* and challenge the manner in which police obtained evidence from a crime scene, a defendant must show that he or she had a legitimate expectation of privacy in the crime scene.

A burglar who illegally entered a home has no legitimate expectation or right of privacy in the home and therefore no standing to challenge evidence against him that police obtained from the home. The following cases illustrate:

Examples

- Michael Perry was convicted of five murders and sentenced to death. Among the murder victims were his mother and father, who had their own home which the defendant could not enter without the consent of his parents and in which he had no belongings. In the 1986 case of *State v. Perry*,[18] the Supreme Court of Louisiana held that: "There was no living person who had a privacy interest in the house at 810 Seventh Street. (Defendant had killed all of the occupants of the house.) Therefore the entries of the house were not in violation of anyone's privacy interest."
- The defendant's girlfriend was murdered in a house that the defendant had built for her, to which he possessed a key and in which he occasionally stayed overnight. The defendant lived elsewhere, however, and the victim paid for the building

supplies used to build the home. The defendant was charged with the murder and challenged the evidence the police had obtained from the victim's home, which was going to be used against him. The Tennessee courts held that the defendant did not have standing to challenge the use of the evidence because he was only a casual visitor who had no right to exclude others from the premises and he had insufficient interest to object to the search that turned up the evidence.[19]

PROTECTING AND SEARCHING A CRIME SCENE

Testimony of a trained law enforcement officer about the observations and findings from a crime scene is vitally important in many criminal cases. Improper protection of a crime scene could result in the contamination, loss, or unnecessary movement of physical evidence.[20] Therefore, the first officer to arrive at the scene of the crime automatically incurs the serious and critical responsibility of securing the crime scene from unauthorized intrusions. Even though the officer who arrives first will also search it for physical evidence, it is most important that the officer immediately take precautions to protect the scene.

To prove that evidence is genuine and authentic and to show that the object is what it is claimed to be, a witness in court must be able to:

- Testify about where and how the object was obtained.
- Identify the object by a serial number if a serial number is on the object. For example, a handgun probably has a serial number, and the gun would be identified in this manner.
- Identify the object based on personal knowledge and observations. This could be done by an officer scratching his or her initials and the date on the object to make it readily identifiable.[21] A *chain of custody* (see below) is not needed if the object is positively identified at trial and the evidence is not susceptible to tampering, contamination, substitution, or mistake.[22]
- Testify about the chain of custody. "If the evidence is not readily identifiable or is susceptible to alteration by tampering, substitution, or contamination, the party must establish a chain of custody; in this event, the chain of custody must be of sufficient completeness to render it improbable that the evidence has been tampered with or substituted."[23]

CRIME SCENES ARE NO PLACE FOR A CROWD

A Michigan forensic scientist asked many of his fellow technicians to name the biggest problem on the job. The same answer came from technicians around the country: "crime scenes contaminated by curious officers, detectives, and supervisors."[24] The technician wrote the following description of the problems caused by "pointless tourism":

Lost Evidence, Lost Opportunities
Widespread trampling of crime scenes can prove very damaging to investigations. Often, it results in several of the more sensitive forensic techniques—such as trace analysis, bloodspatter interpretation, and DNA comparison—not being used to their fullest potential. Crime scene technicians know the futility of collecting hair or fiber samples after a roomful of officers have shed all over the scene. Footwear and tire track

AUTOMOBILE COMPARTMENTS AND "STANDING"

In Fourth Amendment cases, "standing" is short-hand for the expectation-of-privacy analysis. If no such expectation exists, then a defendant charged with a crime based on evidence obtained in an illegal search may not have the evidence suppressed. Thus, in the crime scene cases discussed above, even if the police found evidence in an unreasonable search of the crime scene, a defendant without standing cannot object to the admission of such evidence. This rule can have consequences in automobile stops, detentions, and searches, as the following 2005 case illustrates.

United States v. Pulliam
Ninth Circuit Court of Appeals, 405 F.3d 782 (2005), *cert. denied*, 127 S.Ct. 379 (2006)

Police officers observed the defendant near a known gang headquarters building and had a "hunch" he was "up to no good." When they later saw him riding as a passenger in a car, the officers followed the car and pulled it over because of a broken taillight. They immediately pulled the driver and the defendant out of the car, handcuffed them, and searched the car. The officers found a gun in the search and charged the defendant, the passenger, with violation of firearm laws. The defendant moved to suppress the evidence found in the search of the car, claiming that the detention and search violated his Fourth Amendment rights.

The prosecution conceded that the officers lacked the reasonable suspicion necessary to detain the defendant or search the car. As a result, the driver of the car could have objected to the use of any evidence found in the search against him, had he been charged. However,

the prosecution argued, the defendant as a passenger had no standing to object to the search of the car, and the unconstitutional detention of the defendant bore no relationship to that search.

The court of appeals agreed with the prosecution. Although the defendant could object to the admissibility of any evidence arising out of his illegal detention, such as items found on his person, the illegal detention did not lead to the discovery of the items in the automobile. Since a passenger "with no possessory interest in a vehicle usually cannot object to its continued detention," the court concluded that the defendant had no standing to object to the search of the vehicle.

The court distinguished cases cited by the defendant where passengers were permitted to object to searches of vehicles when the police unlawfully stopped the vehicle. In those cases, the unlawful search of the car could be shown to follow from unlawful actions taken against the passengers as well as the owner of the car. (As noted in Chapter 14, in *Brendlin v. California,* the U.S. Supreme Court held that a passenger was "seized" under the Fourth Amendment and could object to the lawfulness of a traffic stop in which the passenger was present.)

Here, the court said, the police had probable cause to stop the vehicle because of the taillight violation, which made the initial stop of the vehicle lawful. As a result, the search of the car in a lawful stop did not follow from any illegal actions taken against the passenger. The dissenting judge contended that the result in this case would encourage police to make lawful stops of vehicles, and then conduct illegal searches in the hope of finding evidence that could be used against passengers in the car.

evidence is rarely recognized as valuable in departments where officers routinely wander unimpeded through crime scenes. On occasion, this can seriously hamper investigations.

Not long ago, a sheriff's department was forced to conduct a mass fingerprinting of its detective unit after a particularly sensational homicide crime scene became overrun with curious personnel. Considerable time and effort went into eliminating officers' fingerprints from the pool of legitimate prints. In another case involving a different agency, a set of crime scene photographs showed supervisory personnel standing on a blood-soaked carpet.

THE CHAIN OF CUSTODY REQUIREMENT

To use physical evidence in a criminal or civil trial, the party offering the evidence has the burden of proving that the evidence is genuine and authentic. This requires testimony establishing an adequate foundation about where and how the object was obtained and that the object offered in evidence is the object that it is claimed to be.

chain of custody
The set of procedures that accounts for the integrity of evidence by tracking its handling and storage from the time it was obtained to the time it is offered at trial.

If the evidence (such as fingerprints or illegal drugs) could be subject to alteration by tampering, substitution, or contamination, a **chain of custody** must be shown. All persons who had possession of the evidence must appear as witnesses to testify that the fingerprints or illegal drugs have not been tampered with, substituted, or contaminated while each witness had custody and control of the evidence. For evidence that requires a chain of custody, it is therefore best that as few people as possible come in contact with the evidence.

Besides illegal drugs and fingerprints (regular and DNA), courts have held that chains of custody must be presented for the use of the following as evidence: videotapes,[25] a crack pipe,[26] a suitcase full of marijuana,[27] forensic evidence,[28] a shell casing,[29] blood samples,[30] a note found next to the murder victim,[31] human hair and fibers from carpet,[32] semen and blood,[33] a forged check,[34] specimens from a human body,[35] and the body of the murder victim.[36]

FAILING TO SHOW A SUFFICIENT CHAIN OF CUSTODY

To use evidence that could be subject to tampering, substitution, or contamination, the state must, by the use of witnesses, establish a chain of custody to "show a reasonable probability that the [evidence] was not tampered with."[37] In the following examples, the state did *not* prove a sufficient chain of custody for critical evidence in criminal cases.[38]

Examples
- A rape victim identified her panties and blouse in the criminal trial. The semen and blood stains on the panties and the wool fiber on the blouse seriously incriminated the defendant, but there was no showing about where the clothing was during the time between the commission of the crime and the trial. The Supreme Court of Virginia reversed the defendant's conviction of rape and remanded for a new trial in the case of *Robinson v. Commonwealth*.[39]
- The court reversed and remanded for a new trial because the state did not show where the cocaine used as evidence was or how it was kept for a period of 20 days.[40]
- A gap in the chain of custody between the seizure of drugs and the vouching for them at the police station caused reversal for a new trial in the 1993 case of *People v. Rivera*.[41]

WAS THE CRIME SCENE SEARCH LAWFUL?

Thompson v. Louisiana
United States Supreme Court, 105 S.Ct. 409 (1984)

A despondent woman decided to end her life. She shot her husband of many years, wrote a suicide note, and then took an overdose of sleeping pills. While waiting to die, she changed her mind and called her daughter for help.

The daughter quickly notified the sheriff's office and rushed to her parents' home. When sheriff's deputies arrived at the home, the daughter admitted them to the scene of the homicide and the attempted suicide. The unconscious woman was taken to a hospital, and after searching the house for other victims or suspects, the officers secured the house.

Thirty-five minutes later, homicide investigators arrived and went into the house to begin a "general exploratory search for evidence of a crime." Every room in the house was examined during a 2-hour search. Three important items of evidence were seized: a pistol found in a chest of drawers, a torn note found in a bathroom wastepaper basket, and a suicide note tucked inside a Christmas card on top of a chest of drawers.

The detectives had neither consent nor a search warrant for their search. Was their search within the scope of the emergency that had existed in this home? Can the three pieces of evidence be used against the woman who survived and was charged with the second-degree murder of her husband?[a]

[a]The U.S. Supreme Court's ruling is given in note 82 at the end of this chapter.

- Failure of the drug-testing laboratory to complete the chain of custody form for a urine sample caused reversal for a new trial.[42]

SITUATIONS THAT DO NOT REQUIRE A CHAIN OF CUSTODY

A chain of custody is *not* required if the object to be used as evidence is not subject to alteration by tampering, substitution, or contamination.

Examples
- A chain of custody is not required in most shoplifting and theft cases. The Supreme Court of Nebraska held that a chain of custody was not required in the shoplifting case of *State v. Sexton*.[43]
- A pistol was held to be admissible without showing a chain of custody (no fingerprint or ballistics testimony) in the 1991 case of *Outland v. State*.[44]
- Twenty-two silver dollars stolen from a pawn shop were admitted for use in evidence, although the victim could not specifically identify them as the silver dollars stolen. In affirming the defendant's conviction, the court in the 1991 case of *State v. Simmons*[45] stated:

The court does not need a positive and indisputable description of the object in order to admit it into evidence. *Gresham v. State*, 456 P.2d 119 (Okla. 1969). Lack of positive identification goes to weight, not admissibility. See also *State v. Amaya-Ruiz*, 166 Ariz. 152, 800 P.2d 1260 (1990), *cert. denied*, 111 S.Ct. 2044, 114 L.Ed.2d 129 (1991); *State v. Skelton*, 129 Ariz. 181, 629 P.2d 1017 (App. 1981); *State v. Baker*, 219 Kan. 854, 549 P.2d 911 (1976); *Young v. State*, 701

P.2d 415 (Okla. 1985); *State v. Mitchell*, 56 Wash. App. 610, 784 P.2d 568 (1990). Further, because of the physical nature of coins and currency, to sufficiently identify the money to make it admissible as relevant evidence, it is not necessary that the witness identify each bill or coin separately, rather, the witness may testify that the money appears to be the same money alleged to have been stolen after considering its amount, denomination, packaging, and general appearance.

FINGERPRINTS AS EVIDENCE

Historians believe that the Chinese used thumbprints to sign important documents before the birth of Christ. But it was not until the 1870s that a British civil servant in India used fingerprints to record persons on pensions and prisoners in jail. Police in Argentina were reportedly the first law officers to use fingerprinting in 1891.

latent fingerprints
Fingerprints left by a person on a surface other than one designed for recording fingerprints.

A criminal who carelessly leaves fingerprints at the scene of a crime leaves what are called **latent fingerprints**. Latent fingerprints taken from a crime scene can be compared with fingerprints on file in local, state, and FBI files. The FBI has millions of fingerprints on file and receives more than 20,000 fingerprints a day from law enforcement agencies throughout the country.

> Fingerprints are perhaps the most common form of physical evidence, and certainly one of the most valuable. They relate directly to the ultimate objective of every criminal investigation ... the identification of the offender.... Since a print of one finger has never been known to exactly duplicate another fingerprint, even of the same person or identical twin, it is possible to identify an individual with just one impression ... a person's fingerprints have never been known to change. The unchanging pattern thus provides a permanent record of the individual throughout life.[46]

The U.S. Supreme Court stated in the case of *Davis v. Mississippi*[47] that "fingerprinting is an inherently more reliable and effective crime-solving tool than eyewitness identification or confessions and is not subject to such abuses as the improper lineup and the 'third-degree.'"

Because of the serious problems of forged, stolen, or lost driver's licenses, passports, and other forms of identification, law enforcement officers are taking increased security measures to identify persons using their fingerprints. Not only are police cars equipped to take the fingerprints of persons detained on the street, but those same fingerprints can be transmitted electronically to police headquarters for a prompt positive identification of the person detained.

In 2008 Interpol (International Criminal Police Organization) reported that more than 6 million passports have been lost or stolen in recent years. U.S. officers are now testing new biometric systems of identification that can, in less than a minute, record all ten fingerprints of a person entering this country at one of its 311 air and sea entry points.[48]

Another innovation in fingerprint analysis introduced in 2008 is equipment that can analyze fingerprints and not only identify the person leaving the fingerprints but also determine whether that person has touched drugs, explosives, poisons, or other substances. This equipment, which costs about $60,000 per machine, was developed during efforts to build a new surgical tool that could test body tissues for the presence of cancer cells.[49]

A crime scene examiner dusts for fingerprints on shields that had been used to reflect light on marijuana plants. Fingerprints are a highly reliable form of physical evidence because each person's fingerprints are unique and unchanging.

OBTAINING FINGERPRINTS

Persons in lawful police custody are routinely fingerprinted and photographed. Persons who have served in the military have their fingerprints on file, as do many government employees and people who receive licenses for such occupations as bartending, taxicab driving, private security, or jobs that require government security clearance.

People can also consent to having their fingerprints taken, as occurred in the Gainesville, Florida, area in 1990 when five college students were slain in a two-month period. Law officers focused on persons on foot, mopeds, bicycles, and motorcycles. If any question arose concerning why the person was in the area, a voluntary stop was made, and the individual was asked to consent to fingerprinting. In 1994 the killer was apprehended and confessed to the killings.

Several states have statutes that authorize juvenile judges to order a juvenile who is not arrested or in custody to submit to fingerprinting when probable cause does not exist. The Supreme Court of Colorado[50] and the Supreme Court of Ohio[51] found such statutes constitutional.

The U.S. Supreme Court held in the cases of *Davis v. Mississippi*[52] and *Hayes v. Florida*[53] that courts may order fingerprinting "under narrowly defined circumstances ... found to comply with the Fourth Amendment even though there is no probable cause in the traditional sense." Rapes had occurred in both the *Davis* and *Hayes* cases, where the police had fingerprints of the offenders but could not match them up with and identify the defendants, who were not in custody.

PROVING THAT FINGERPRINTS WERE IMPRESSED AT THE TIME OF THE CRIME

Fingerprints are circumstantial evidence from which inferences must be drawn. It is "impossible ... to determine the age of [a] latent print" because the print could have been on an object for a long time before the crime was committed.

As a general rule, the prosecution must first introduce fingerprint evidence by use of an expert witness and then show a chain of custody to prove that the evidence is authentic and genuine and has not been tampered with. The government must then show that the fingerprints "could only have been impressed at the time when the crime was committed." The U.S. Department of Justice work entitled *Crime Scene Search and Physical Evidence Handbook* (note 20) states that: "It is impossible ... to determine the age of a latent print ... to determine the age or sex of the person leaving the print ... to identify the race of the suspect, nor the occupation (unless they are a bricklayer)...."[54]

To prove that fingerprints were impressed at the time of the crime, the following evidence may be used:

- Testimony of the victim or a witness that the defendant touched or handled the object on which the fingerprints were found (rape, assault, theft, or robbery cases where the victim or witness was present at the time of the crime and is available as a witness)
- Testimony that the surface had been washed or cleaned just prior to the crime
- Fingerprints found in a home or an area to which the defendant did not have access (burglary, theft, and sometimes homicide cases)

However, a murder conviction was reversed in the 1991 California case of *Mikes v. Borg*.[55] The court held that the mere fact that the defendant's fingerprints were found on the murder weapon was not sufficient to prove that the defendant was the murderer. The court stated: "[T]he prosecution introduced no evidence placing the defendant at the scene of the crime—either on the day of the murder or on any other occasion."[56]

AUTOMATED FINGERPRINT IDENTIFICATION SYSTEMS

For years, fingerprints found at a crime scene had to be compared manually with cards on file—one card at a time. The search was a slow, time-consuming process, limiting fingerprint searches in most cities to only the most serious crimes. Victims of burglaries were often shocked to find that burglary was not considered serious enough to qualify in most instances.

In 1985 the Automated Fingerprint Identification System (AFIS) for the Los Angeles Police Department was activated. The AFIS uses a computer with a large database to compare latent fingerprints electronically.

The first assignment given to the Los Angeles AFIS was fingerprints found at the scene of one of the killings by the "Night Stalker," who had terrorized Los Angeles for months. Within 3 minutes, AFIS identified a suspect.

In Los Angeles, like other large American cities, thousands of people are arrested each month. Comparing fingerprints from these people to fingerprints found at the scenes of crimes and fingerprints of suspects on wanted lists would be an impossible task without AFIS. The largest database in the United States is at the FBI, with 41 million fingerprint files and 24 million crime history records.

Today, all states and all large cities have their own databases (or have access to a database) that can electronically identify fingerprints lifted at a crime scene—often within hours. AFIS also processes fingerprints found in old cases. With fingerprint and other circumstantial evidence, states have been taking cases into criminal courts that have been unsolved for months and years.

FINGERPRINTS AND THE *DAUBERT* TEST

Prior to 1993, defense lawyers rarely attacked fingerprint evidence, unless there was a break or weakness in the chain of custody foundation necessary to qualify the fingerprints as admissible evidence. This is because the two basic assumptions underlying fingerprint identifications—that every person's fingerprint is unique and that an expert can distinguish between two persons' fingerprints—were accepted as true.

In the 1993 case of *Daubert v. Merrill Dow Pharmaceuticals Co.*[57] (discussed in Chapter 18), the U.S. Supreme Court said there are no certainties in science, only probabilistic results. Scientific assumptions must be demonstrated as being reliable, not simply assumed. The theory of forensic fingerprint identification evidence then came under attack, and courts began requiring fingerprint experts to demonstrate that the procedures used were reliable and that test results had a high probability of accuracy.

Since 1993, higher standards for fingerprint technicians and experts have been established. New proficiency testing and new qualitative and quantitative analyses have been established. Fingerprint science has had to "reconstruct itself." Where these standards have been followed, most courts have concluded that fingerprint evidence is reliable and admissible.[58] Where the testimony of the fingerprint expert is based on a comparison of rolled fingerprints rather than a comparison of a latent print to a rolled print, the evidence has been found to be especially reliable. An FBI study discussed in *United States v. Sanchez-Birruetta*[59] found that in a comparison of 50,000 rolled fingerprints, not one false-positive identification was made.

TRACE EVIDENCE: THE SMALLEST THINGS CAN MAKE THE BIGGEST DIFFERENCE

trace evidence
Small amounts of material that a suspect leaves or acquires when he or she comes in contact with another object.

When two objects come in contact, small amounts of material are often transferred from one to the other. This is nearly always the case when fabrics come in contact with a rough surface. Therefore, when a suspect comes in contact with the victim and objects at the crime scene, he frequently leaves behind traces of himself and takes with him traces of the things he has touched. Materials transferred in this way are normally referred to as **trace evidence**.

The term *trace evidence* is usually very loosely defined; however, it most often is applied to minute or microscopic bits of materials that are not immediately apparent to even a trained investigator. Thus, trace evidence is usually in the hard-to-find category. Because trace materials resulting from exchanges are less likely to excite the attention of the criminal, or even to be apparent to him, there is far less probability that the criminal will deliberately eliminate these materials than is the case with larger items of evidence or latent fingerprints.

The following hypothetical situation illustrates the potential for the exchange of physical evidence during fairly typical criminal actions.

The criminal crosses the back porch of a residence and steps on a brown paper bag lying on the floor. To gain entry, he breaks a small glass pane in the backdoor and reaches in to unlock the door. After gaining entry, he is surprised by the home-owner and a struggle follows. During the struggle, the victim's nose begins to bleed. The suspect flees the scene.

In this situation, the following exchanges of materials are entirely possible:

- The suspect's shoe print to the brown paper bag on the back porch
- Fibers from the suspect's clothing to the edge of the broken pane of glass in the backdoor (or blood on the glass from a cut on the suspect's arm)
- Fingerprints to the glass on the backdoor and possibly to other surfaces along the suspect's route of entry
- Fibers from the suspect's clothing to the victim's clothing during the struggle, and vice versa

The following (transferred) evidence may be found on or in possession of the suspect:

- Glass fragments or small paint chips on the outer garments of the suspect from the backdoor window pane and frame
- Blood or hair from the victim on the suspect's clothing
- Bruises or lacerations on the suspect from the struggle with the victim
- Fibers from the rug or furniture at the crime scene on the shoes or garments of the suspect

It is apparent from this example that the possibilities for exchanges of trace materials are great. Even if the shoe prints and fingerprints are excluded from the potential array of physical evidence, there are still abundant opportunities to link the suspect with the crime scene, if proper collections are made at the scene and from the person of the suspect.

THE EXAMPLE OF THE MISSING 5-YEAR-OLD IN VIRGINIA

The following example of the use of trace evidence is from a May 2002 publication of the U.S. Department of Justice (NCJ 191717). A 5-year-old girl disappeared from a Christmas party in Virginia in 1989. Witness tips authorized police to take a maintenance man into custody. The man worked in the building where the child lived. When found, he was washing his jacket and shoes and a sheath from a knife.

The man never denied that he abducted the child, but he challenged the police to prove it. After learning what clothes the girl wore at the time of the abduction, the police found that only a limited number of suits like the one the girl wore had been made and were sold through JCPenney. Fliers were sent out, and a man who had bought one of the outfits for his granddaughter donated the outfit to the investigation.

Several blue acrylic fibers were recovered from the suspect's car that were consistent with the fabric of the outfit the girl had been wearing when she disappeared. In addition, fibers that matched a black, dyed, rabbit-hair coat the girl's mother had been wearing the night of the abduction were found in the suspect's car. It could be inferred that the rabbit-hair fiber transferred from the mother to the little girl and then transferred to the suspect's vehicle.

The little girl's body was never recovered. The man was convicted based on the trace evidence, which corroborated his incriminating statements and the observations of witnesses placing him at the time and place of the abduction.

OBTAINING EVIDENCE FROM TRACKING DEVICES

Global Positioning System (GPS) devices have been in commercial and private use for years. Rental vehicles have them installed both for the convenience of their customers and to enable the rental company to locate and monitor the vehicles. Employers use them to track company equipment and their employees, and parents use them to monitor their children, particularly in family vehicles. Law enforcement officials have found that GPS devices can be very useful tools in investigating both major and minor crimes and also for locating missing persons and investigating employee misconduct.

In December 2006 the Federal Rules of Criminal Procedure, which serve as guidelines for federal law enforcement officers conducting criminal investigations, were revised on procedures for the installation and use of tracking devices, including GPS devices. The revised rules follow:

- Rule 41(b)(4). Who can issue a warrant for installation? A federal district court magistrate judge.
- Rule 41(e)(2)(B). Contents of the warrant. Must identify the person or property to be tracked, not to exceed 45 days unless extended for good cause.
- Rule 41(f)(2). Return on warrant. Within 10 days after use ended.
- Rule 41(f)(3). Delay in return. Available upon request.

An article in the February 2007 issue of the *FBI Law Enforcement Bulletin* titled "Legal Brief" states:

> The new rule does not address whether law enforcement officers need a warrant to install or monitor a tracking device. Whether a warrant is required to install a tracking device, or track a vehicle or other object, revolves around expectations of privacy. If an intrusion into an area where there is a privacy expectation is necessary to install the device, or the vehicle or object will be tracked in an area where one has a privacy expectation, a warrant is required. If there is no such intrusion or tracking the device will not infringe on privacy, a warrant is not required.

The revised federal rules are in compliance with the U.S. Supreme Court's decisions in *United States v. Knotts*[60] and *United States v. Karo*,[61] where the Court held that attaching a device to a vehicle while used on public roads did not require a warrant, but a warrant is required when a vehicle is in a garage or other private place. Thus, in *United States v. McIver*,[62] the court upheld placing a tracking device in the undercarriage of a vehicle while it was in a public place, which produced evidence of illegal growing of marijuana. Going into a private garage to place the device, or otherwise intruding into a vehicle, would require a warrant, as was the case in the California murder trial of Scott Peterson.

OTHER TYPES OF EVIDENCE

PALM PRINTS AND LIP PRINTS AS EVIDENCE

Palm prints are considered part of fingerprinting and in some cases are found at crime scenes or on victims of crimes. Cases where palm prints were important evidence in obtaining criminal convictions are the murder case of *State v. Inman*,[63] the armed robbery of a post office in the case of *United States v. Moore*,[64] and the rape and robbery case of *Yelder v. State*.[65]

In the 2005 case of *Barber v. State*,[66] the Alabama Court of Criminal Appeals upheld the admissibility of testimony of a fingerprint expert who testified that a bloody palm print found on the wall in a murder victim's house was made by the defendant.

In an article entitled "Focus on Forensics: Lip Prints," published in the November 1992 issue of the *FBI Law Enforcement Bulletin*, the author reported that studies of lip prints indicate that "every individual has unique lip prints—no two were identical in any case." Although lip print cases are rare, at least one state appellate court has determined that lip print identification evidence is reliable and admissible. In the case of *People v. Davis*,[67] the defendant was charged with robbery and murder. Duct tape used to bind the victim contained lip prints of the person who used the duct tape. Experts for the prosecution were permitted to testify that the lip prints on the duct tape were made by the defendant, and the defendant was convicted of murder. On appeal, the court held that lip print identification was sufficiently reliable to be admitted. The court accepted the prosecution expert's statement that "[t]he basis for identification of impression evidence is that everything is unique if looked at in sufficient detail, and if two things are sufficiently similar, they must have come from the same source."

FOOTPRINTS AND SHOE PRINTS AS EVIDENCE

There are very few footprint cases because the majority of criminals wear shoes! One of the more notable cases is the 1984 murder case of *State v. Bullard*,[68] where the Supreme Court of North Carolina discussed the art of footprint identification in affirming the defendant's conviction.

In many cases, however, shoe prints provide important identification evidence. Shoe prints are obtained from surfaces covered with snow, mud, dust, dirt, paint, or other substances in which an imprint can be made. Identification testimony must include enough characteristics—such as size, length, width, type, wear patterns, and individual characteristics such as nicks, cuts, and scratches—to establish a match between the print or prints left at the crime scene and the defendant's shoes.

In the 1992 home burglary case of *People v. Campbell*,[69] the Supreme Court of Illinois held that "shoe-print evidence, standing alone, is sufficient to convict." The court pointed out that shoe-print evidence, like fingerprint evidence, is circumstantial evidence. Supporting the evidence of the shoe prints was further evidence that the defendant had the opportunity to commit the burglary as well as evidence of flight.

In the 1990 murder case of *State v. Jells,*[70] the Supreme Court of Ohio affirmed the defendant's conviction and permitted a lay witness (a police officer) to testify as to the similarities between the prints and the defendant's shoes. The Supreme Court of Nebraska affirmed the attempted sexual assault conviction in the 1989 case of *State v. Rhodes,*[71] where shoe-print evidence was used. Burglary convictions that were affirmed on shoe-print evidence include *State v. Tincher,*[72] *State v. Ingold,*[73] and *State v. Johnson.*[74]

BITE MARKS AS EVIDENCE

To use bite-mark evidence, a chain of custody must be shown and an expert witness must be used, such as a dentist with training and experience as a forensic odontologist.

Bite marks could result from fighting; they could be sexual, attacking, or sadistic. In the 1990 case of *Commonwealth v. Henry,*[75] the Supreme Court of Pennsylvania stated:

> The essence of the distinction is that fighting bite marks are less well defined because they are done carelessly and quickly, whereas attacking or sadistic bite marks are made slowly and produce a clearer pattern. According to Dr. Asen, the sadistic bite mark is one of the most well-defined. Sexual bite marks are also well defined, but usually have a red center, produced by sucking tissue into the mouth. The dentist testified that the bite marks produced in this case were extremely well-defined, and were attacking or sadistic in nature. The legal significance of this testimony is that it might have been considered by the jury as part of their determination that the homicide was committed by means of torture.

In 1986 a Wisconsin Court of Appeals found that no state "has rejected the admission of [bite marks]."[76] Bite-mark evidence is probably used primarily in criminal homicide cases in which police need to establish the identity of the defendant. Examples of such murder cases are *State v. Richards*[77] and *People v. Marsh.*[78]

TIRE TRACKS AS EVIDENCE

In the 1974 U.S. Supreme Court case of *Cardwell v. Lewis,*[79] the defendant parked his car in a commercial parking lot and then went into a police building for questioning regarding a murder. After the police arrested the defendant for the murder, they took his car keys and, without a court order or warrant, had his car towed to a police lot, where tire prints and paint scrapings were taken. This evidence was used to obtain the murder conviction of the defendant.

The U.S. Supreme Court affirmed the conviction and held that no right of privacy was violated, saying:

> In the present case, nothing from the interior of the car and no personal effects, which the Fourth Amendment traditionally has been deemed to protect, were searched or seized and introduced in evidence. With the "search" limited to the examination of

the tire on the wheel and the taking of paint scrapings from the exterior of the vehicle left in the public lot, we fail to comprehend what expectation of privacy was infringed.

Under circumstances such as these, where probable cause exists, a warrantless examination of the exterior of a car is not unreasonable under the Fourth and Fourteenth Amendments.[80]

In the 1991 case of *State v. Tillman*,[81] the manager of a Goodyear tire store was held to have sufficient training and experience in tire tread patterns to testify as an expert witness on tire tracks. The witness testified as to the similarities between tire tracks found at the scene of a murder and tires on the defendant's car. The defendant's conviction for murder was affirmed.

SUMMARY

To use physical, or real, evidence in a criminal trial, the government must show:

- That the evidence was obtained under the authority of a search warrant, or that the evidence was obtained under one of the "established and well-delineated exceptions" to the search warrant requirement
- That the evidence is genuine and authentic, and the object is what the government claims it is

- That all persons who had custody or access to evidence that could be altered, tampered with, or substituted have testified that the evidence is genuine and authentic (proof of a chain of custody)

Higher standards requiring rigorous testing and organized skepticism have been established for scientific evidence such as fingerprinting and trace evidence under the *Daubert* case by the U.S. Supreme Court.

CASE ANALYSIS

Read Appendix B, Finding and Analyzing Cases (p. 427). With these guidelines in mind, please continue with the Case Analysis selections for Chapter 16.

1. In *People v. Cowan* [782 N.E.2d 779 (Ill. App. 2002)], the court held that the state failed to show the required chain of custody of a controlled substance. What did the state do wrong? What should the police do to avoid this result?

2. The case of *State v. Carter* [544 S.E.2d 835 (S.C. 2001)] illustrates some of the chain of custody issues that have arisen when DNA evidence is used in a trial that takes place many years after a crime was committed. When such evidence is stored and moved around during those years, the possibility of contamination or a mistake is greater.

3. *Kirk v. Louisiana* [536 U.S. 635 (2002)] is a case in which the U.S. Supreme Court reversed a state appeals court that permitted the introduction of evidence taken from a person arrested for illegal drugs. What did the police officers do wrong, and what arguments should the prosecution have made? On remand, were those arguments successful? See *State v. Kirk* [833 So.2d 418 (La. App. 2002)].

4. One problem with evidence such as fingerprints, palm prints, or bite marks is showing not only that evidence found at the scene matches the defendant but also that the evidence was left there when the crime occurred. That proved to be a problem for the prosecution in *Buffkin v. State* [207 S.W.3d 779 (Tex. Crim. App. 2007)]. What precisely was the issue in that case?

Notes

1. To seize evidence in plain view, it must be "immediately apparent" to the law officer that the object is evidence of a crime. In the U.S. Supreme Court case of *Arizona v. Hicks* [107 S.Ct. 1149 (1987)], police officers were in an apartment building because a man was wounded when a bullet came through the ceiling of his apartment. The police immediately went into Hicks's apartment, where the bullet came from, to search "for the shooter, for other victims, and weapons."

   While they were lawfully in Hicks's apartment, police saw expensive stereo equipment that they suspected was stolen property. To determine whether the stereo equipment was stolen, an officer picked up stereo parts to read and record the serial numbers, which he called in to the stolen property division. The U.S. Supreme Court held that as it was not "immediately apparent" that the equipment was stolen; thus, the seizure was unlawful and the evidence could not be used against Hicks on the criminal charge of possession of stolen property.

2. An example of a state case in which the police exceeded the limits of an emergency search is *People v. Williams* [557 P.2d 399 (Colo. 1976)]. After Claudine Longet (Mrs. Andy Williams) shot her lover, professional skier "Spider" Sabich, police were in the couple's home after the body was removed. The gun used in the shooting had been seized, and photographs of the crime scene had been taken. The police then went into dresser drawers, where they found Longet's diary, which they seized. The Colorado Supreme Court held that the diary could not be used as evidence in the homicide case because it was seized without consent or a search warrant.

   Can the police cordon off and maintain control of major crime scenes so that they may reenter without consent or a search warrant? This issue was before a number of California courts. In the 1991 case of *People v. Boragno* [49 CrL 1394], police officers continued to enter a murder scene for 13 hours after the apartment was cordoned off and the police retained exclusive control of the apartment. The police continued to take photographs and search for blood and hair samples. The California Court of Appeals held that searches after the first sweep of the apartment were invalid. But the valid and good evidence against the defendant was so overwhelming that "it is not reasonably probable a result more favorable to [the defendant] would have occurred."

   In the case of *People v. Neulist* [43 A.D.2d 150, 350 N.Y.S.2d 178 (1973)], medical examiners first said that the death of a woman in her home was from natural causes. The police still posted a guard at the room where the body was found. However, a physician then discovered that a murder had occurred. The police returned to the crime scene within an hour, and the highest court in New York held that the evidence obtained could be used against the defendant.

3. 494 U.S. 325 (1990).

4. 517 F.3d 279 (5th Cir. 2008).

5. Most (if not all) states authorize "hot-pursuit" entries into private premises for misdemeanor crimes, such as drunk driving, that threaten public safety. However, "hot pursuit" of a person who had committed a civil offense is not justified. The U.S. Supreme Court reversed the conviction in *Welsh v. Wisconsin* [104 S.Ct. 2091 (1984)], holding that, at the time of Welsh's arrest for first-offense drunk driving, the offense was a civil offense punishable in civil court. No imprisonment was possible for the noncriminal, civil forfeiture offense. At the time, Wisconsin was the only state that made first-offense drunk driving a civil offense.

6. 86 S.Ct. 1826.

7. 103 S.Ct. 916.

8. The U.S. Supreme Court held in two cases that when law enforcement officers make a lawful entry into private premises because of an emergency, they may not make a second entry after the emergency no longer exists without a search warrant or consent. In the case of *Michigan v. Tyler* [98 S.Ct. 1942 (1978)], the Supreme Court held that an entry 27 days after a fire to obtain evidence of arson was not a lawful entry. The Court held: "... we hold that an entry to fight a fire requires no warrant, and that once in the building, officials may remain there for a reasonable time to investigate the cause of the blaze. Thereafter, additional entries to investigate the cause of the fire must be made pursuant to the warrant procedures governing administrative searches...."

9. 840 P.2d 1298 (Ore. App.).

10. *Patrick v. State*, 227 A.2d 486 (Del. 1967).

11. *City of Troy v. Oblinger*, 475 N.W.2d 54, 50 CrL 1006 (Mich. 1991).

12. 990 F.2d 167 (4th Cir.).

13. 607 A.2d 471 (D.C. App.).

14. 919 A.2d 452 (Conn. 2007).

15. 227 S.W.3d 133 (Tex. App. 2006).

16. 864 A.2d 1006 (Md. 2004).

17. 243 S.W.3d 30 (Tex. App. 2007).

18. 502 So.2d 453 (La.), *cert. denied,* 108 S.Ct. 205 (1987).

19. *State v. Vann*, 1990 WL 51763, 49 CrL 3042 (Tenn. Crim. App. 1990), *cert. denied,* 111 S.Ct. 2015 (1991).

20. Much of the following material in this section is taken from U.S. Department of Justice Law Enforcement Assistance Administration book entitled *Crime Scene Search and Physical Evidence Handbook* (Government Printing Office, 1973).

21. Police training manuals and directives recommend that objects likely to be used as evidence be identified by having the collecting officer scratch his initials or name and date on the object if practical. The officer can then readily identify the object as the evidence recovered at the crime scene or other place. Firearms, spent cartridges, bullets, clothing, currency, and many other objects have been identified and authenticated as genuine in this manner. Weapons used in the commission of a felony are ordinarily identified not only by the serial number but also by initials and date scratched on the object by a law enforcement officer.

If the weapon is also to be used as the basis for evidence, such as fingerprints or ballistics reports, a chain of custody must then be established and used to show that the evidence has not been altered or tampered with.

22. See *State v. Gustin*, 826 S.W.2d 409 (Mo. App., 1991); *People v. Winters*, 422 N.E.2d 972 (Ill. App. 1981); and *United States v. Clonts*, 966 F.2d 1366 (10th Cir. 1992).

23. *People v. Kabalia*, 587 N.E.2d 1210 (Ill. App. 1992).

24. D.H. Garrison, Jr., "Sound Off: Protecting the Crime Scene," *FBI Law Enforcement Bulletin* (September 1994). Although this problem was noted in 1994, there is reason to believe that it continues today (hopefully, to a lesser degree).

25. *Schultz v. State*, 811 P.2d 1322 (Okla. Crim. App. 1991).

26. *Hunter v. State*, 805 S.W.2d 918 (Tex. App. 1991).

27. *United States v. Clonts*, 966 F.2d 1366 (10th Cir. 1992).

28. *United States v. Gilliam*, 975 F.2d 1050 (4th Cir. 1992).

29. *Van Pelt v. State*, 816 S.W.2d 607 (Ark. 1991); *State v. Clay*, 817 S.W.2d 565 (Mo. App. 1991).

30. *Moorman v. State*, 574 So.2d 953 (Ala. Crim. App. 1990).

31. *English v. State*, 575 N.E.2d 14 (Ind. 1991).

32. *Kennedy v. State*, 578 N.E.2d 633 (Ind. 1991); *Davasher v. State*, 823 S.W.2d 863 (Ark. 1992).

33. *State v. Jackson*, 821 P.2d 1374 (Ariz. App. 1991).

34. *Turner v. State*, 610 S.2d 1198 (Ala. Crim. App. 1992).

35. *Snowden v. State*, 574 So.2d 960 (Ala. Crim. App. 1990).

36. *Holder v. State*, 584 So.2d 872 (Ala. Crim. App. 1991).

37. *Bell v. State*, 339 So.2d 96 (Ala. Crim. App. 1976).

38. One of the authors sat on a jury in 1999 where the defendant was charged criminally for dealing rock cocaine. Because two adjournments had already been granted in the case, the trial judge announced in open court that both parties and the court had agreed that no further adjournments would be granted.

After the rock cocaine was legally seized by the police under the authority of a search warrant, it was delivered to a young lab technician at the state crime lab. The lab technician testified that she received the evidence, she performed two different tests on the substance, and both tests showed that the substance was rock cocaine. After testifying that the rock cocaine was stored in a secured locker, the lab technician was asked whether the storage area was locked at all times and who had a key to the locker. The lab technician answered that the storage area was locked at all times and that she and her two supervisors all had keys to the storage locker. Because the two supervisors who had access to the storage locker were not in court to testify and show a sufficient chain of custody, the charges against the defendant were dismissed, and the state could not file new criminal charges because of the doctrine of double jeopardy.

When a defendant appeals a criminal conviction and wins a reversal of the conviction, as in the cases cited and used in this section, the state may retry the case. The prosecutors in those cases had another chance to prove the chain of custody for the critical evidence. Today, prosecutors in busy criminal courts had better do a good job at the first trial, or they are going to lose cases because they fail to prove a chain of custody for evidence that can be falsified or tampered with.

39. 183 S.E.2d 179 (Va. 1971).

40. *Laws v. State,* 562 So.2d 305 (Ala. Crim. App. 1990).

41. 184 A.D.2d 153 (N.Y.A.D.).

42. *Byerly v. Ashley,* 825 S.W.2d 286 (Ky. App. 1991).

43. 482 N.W.2d 567 (Nebr. 1992).

44. 810 S.W.2d 474 (Tex. App.).

45. 818 P.2d 787 (Idaho App.).

46. *Crime Scene Search and Physical Evidence Handbook,* 47.

47. 394 U.S. 721 (1969).

48. See "At Airport, 2 Fingerprints Are Not Enough," *The New York Times* (March 26, 2008).

49. See "Fingerprint Test Shows Not Only Who, But What," *The New York Times* (August 8, 2008).

50. *People v. Madson,* 638 P.2d 18 (Colo. 1981).

51. *In re Order Requiring Fingerprinting of a Juvenile,* 537 N.E.2d 1286, 45 CrL 2164 (1989).

52. 89 S.Ct. 1394 (1969).

53. 105 S.Ct. 1643 (1985).

54. See the 1992 case of *State v. Hamilton* [827 P.2d 232], where the Supreme Court of Utah reviewed many cases from throughout the United States concerning the general approaches to the weight that may be afforded fingerprint evidence.

55. 947 F.2d 353 (9th Cir.), *review denied,* 112 S.Ct. 3055 (1992).

56. Cases where the state was able to obtain convictions by proving that fingerprints of the defendant were made at the time of the crime (or created a strong inference to that effect) include: murder and theft case of *Commonwealth v. Servich* [602 A.2d 1338 (Pa. Super. 1992)], where a glass touched by the defendant was washed on the morning of the murder; *Commonwealth v. Hall* [590 N.E.2d 1177 (Mass. App. 1992)], where the robber touched a lavatory doorknob while forcing a witness into a room; *State v. Jackson* [582 So.2d 915 (La. App. 1991)], a case of theft from a supermarket where the general public did not have access to the area and the defendant was not an employee of the store and had never been seen in the store before; a home burglary case of *Tyler v. State* [402 S.E.2d 780 (Ga. App. 1991)], where the defendant testified that he had never been in the home and did not know where it was located, but his fingerprints were found in the home; the burglary of an auto sales and repair business in *Commonwealth v. Baptista* [585 N.E.2d 335 (Mass. App. 1992)], where fingerprints found inside a closed, locked Pepsi vending machine justified the inference that the defendant had cut the lock and entered the machine; a home burglary case of *Jones v. State* [825 S.W.2d 529 (Tex. App. 1992)], where fingerprints on a kitchen window screen and mud marks showed that the screen was laid in the mud; the home burglary case of *State v. Evans* [392 S.E.2d 441 (N.C. App. 1990)], where the defendant's fingerprints were found on a piece of glass from the window broken to gain entry; a car theft case of *In the Interest of N.R.* [402 S.E.2d 120 (Ga. App. 1991)], where juvenile fingerprints were found on the inside of the driver's window of a recently stolen car; the burglary case of *Brown v. State* [837 S.W.2d 457 (Ark. 1992)], where fingerprints were found inside the broken glass door of a home; the murder case of *Hanson v. Commonwealth* [416 S.E.2d 14 (Va. App. 1992)], where police went into the murder victim's trash and found the defendant's fingerprints on envelopes, which were used to show his presence at the crime scene; the murder case of *Cavazos v. State* [779 P.2d 987 (Okla. Crim. App. 1989)], where the defendant's fingerprints were found on the victim's unclothed back; the rape and robbery case of *People v. Himmelein* [442 N.W.2d 667 (Mich. App. 1989)], where the defendant's fingerprints were found on a yardstick used to strike a rape victim.

57. 509 U.S. 579 (1993). See *United States v. Plaza* [188 F.Supp.2d 549 (2002)] for a discussion on fingerprinting.

58. See, for example, *United States v. Crisp* [3242 F.3d 261 (4th Cir. 2003), *cert. denied,* 124 S.Ct. 220 (2003)].

59. 128 Fed. Appx. 571 (9th Cir. 2005).

60. 460 U.S. 276 (1983).
61. 468 U.S. 705 (1984).
62. 186 F.3d 1119 (9th Cir. 1999).
63. 350 A.2d 528 (Maine 1976).
64. 936 F.2d 1508 (7th Cir. 1991).
65. 575 So.2d 131 (Ala. Crim. App. 1990).
66. 2005 WL 125745 (Ala. Crim. App.).
67. 710 N.E.2d 1251 (Ill. App. 1999), *review denied*, 720 N.E.2d 1251 (1999).
68. 322 S.E.2d 370 (N.C.).
69. 586 N.E.2d 1261 (Ill.).
70. 559 N.E.2d 464 (Ohio).
71. 445 N.W.2d 622 (Nebr.).
72. 797 S.W.2d 794 (Mo. App. 1990).
73. 450 N.W.2d 344 (Minn. App. 1990).
74. 464 N.W.2d 167 (Nebr. 1991).
75. 569 A.2d 929.
76. *State v. Stinson*, 397 N.W.2d 137.
77. 804 P.2d 109 (Ariz. App. 1990).
78. 441 N.W.2d 33 (Mich. App. 1989).
79. 417 U.S. 583, 94 S.Ct. 2464.
80. 417 U.S. at 592, 94 S.Ct. at 2470.
81. 405 S.E.2d 607 (S.C. App.).
82. There was no exigency (emergency) when the detectives arrived at the defendant's home because the unconscious woman had been taken to the hospital and the house had been secured. A search warrant should have been obtained because the daughter did not have such control of the premises that she could have given consent to search the home of her parents. The case was remanded, and the State of Louisiana could try the defendant again but without the use of the three important (and probably critical) pieces of evidence obtained during the improper search.

VIDEOTAPES, PHOTOGRAPHS, DOCUMENTS, AND WRITINGS AS EVIDENCE

CHAPTER **17**

LEARNING OBJECTIVES

In this chapter we discuss when and how recordings, photographs, and copies of things or events may be introduced as evidence. The learning objectives for this chapter are:

- State when search warrants are required or not for electronic surveillance.
- State the requirements for the introduction into evidence of videotapes, photographs, and other electronic records.
- Explain the "best evidence" rule.
- Explain how the Fifth Amendment applies to documents.

PHOTOS AND VIDEOTAPES AS EVIDENCE

Public surveillance cameras, videocameras, and cell phone cameras are everywhere in the United States. Thousands of people carry cell phones equipped with cameras, and thousands more possess videocameras. Banks, stores, private businesses, schools, and apartment buildings have installed cameras as part of security systems. Some squad cars and buses have them. They are commonly used in drunk-driving cases as well as traffic and investigative stops by the police. Videocameras have filmed murders, armed robberies, shoplifting, and other crimes (see Federal Rule of Evidence 1001 in Appendix C).

Since the "Zapruder" film of the assassination of President John F. Kennedy in 1963, and later the video of the Los Angeles beatings of Rodney King and Reginald Denny, videotapes have brought street events to the American public and evidence into criminal trials. Fixed surveillance cameras and handheld videocameras regularly provide information to law officers for the identification and arrest of offenders.

If the filming is done in a public place where a defendant does not have a right of privacy and if a witness verifies that the tape is a reliable reproduction of the events that occurred, the tape is ordinarily admissible as evidence. The following examples illustrate the thousands of cases where photos and videotapes are used as evidence each year.

Examples

- When Winona Ryder walked out of the Hollywood Saks Fifth Avenue store with $5,560 worth of stolen merchandise, she was unaware that closed-circuit cameras had recorded the felony shoplifting. Photo evidence and the testimony of two security officers caused the jury to convict her in November 2002.
- In the 1990 case of *Pennsylvania v. Muniz*,[1] the U.S. Supreme Court held that a videotape of the defendant's answers to routine booking questions at a police station were admissible as evidence. The tape showing the defendant's slurred speech, his poor performance on sobriety tests, and his unsolicited incriminating statements was used in evidence, which resulted in his conviction. The tape was held not to violate his *Miranda* rights, except for the incriminating statement when the defendant was asked for the year of his sixth birthday.
- The Florida Supreme Court pointed out that either the person taping a street arrest can be ordered to appear as a witness or the tape can be ordered to be produced in the 1991 case of *CBS, Inc. v. Jackson*.[2] Television news reporters do not enjoy a First Amendment privilege when they are eyewitness observers to an event that is relevant in a criminal trial.
- A murder victim's videotaped dying declaration was held admissible in the 1992 murder case of *Grayson v. State*.[3] The victim's physician withheld all pain medication prior to the videotaping, and the victim responded to most questions by nodding his head and sometimes motioning with his hands.
- An undercover officer's videotape of a drug buy and the videotape of a controlled drug buy were used as evidence in the cases of *Hall v. State*[4] and *Edwards v. State*.[5]
- A videotape of the defendant cultivating marijuana in a field was used as evidence in the 1992 case of *Pfaff v. State*.[6]
- A defendant, while being booked on an assault charge, became disruptive and was also charged with disorderly conduct. The videotape of the scene was admitted as evidence in the 1991 case of *State v. Warmsbecker*.[7]

- Surveillance evidence is important in civil personal injury trials as well as in criminal cases. For example, if an insurance company suspects that a personal injury claim is fraudulent, it might use a videocamera to conduct surveillance of the claimant in public places to determine whether injuries are faked or exaggerated. For interesting insights into this practice, see the article titled "Disclosing Surveillance Evidence: 'I've Got a Secret'" in *Wisconsin Lawyer* (September 2006).
- Videotapes of the defendant refusing to submit to blood alcohol testing and refusing to perform field sobriety tests while in police custody were admissible as evidence to obtain a criminal conviction in the 1991 case of *Commonwealth v. McConnell.*[8]
- A videotape of the defendant's arrest and a search of the immediate premises were admissible in the 1991 case of *People v. Schaaefer.*[9]
- A videotape simulation of a highway accident by the Minnesota Highway Patrol was held admissible in the 1990 case of *State v. Rasinski.*[10] In reconstructing the accident, the state stayed within the objective evidence (measurements, placement of the skid marks, and the final resting place of the vehicles at the accident). But video reenactment of a fight at a jail was held inadmissible because the version was biased in favor of what the state believed had occurred (*State v. Hopperstad*).[11]
- When the defendant approached a man with regard to committing an armed robbery, the man went to the police. A videotape then captured the defendant soliciting a police informant for armed robbery. The authenticated videotape was used in evidence, resulting in the defendant's conviction (*Powell v. State*).[12]
- Store security videotapes and apartment lobby videotapes were held admissible for use as evidence in the cases of *MacFarland v. State*[13] and *Smith v. United States.*[14]
- Videotapes of drug dealers, prostitutes, and car thieves taken by people living in the neighborhood are sometimes turned over to local police.

WHEN IS A WARRANT NEEDED TO INSTALL AND CONDUCT VIDEOTAPE SURVEILLANCE?

videotape surveillance
Close observation by use of videocameras.

Search warrants must be obtained to conduct **videotape surveillance** when a suspect has a right of privacy in the place where the videotape surveillance is to be conducted (for instance, the suspect's home, apartment, or office).

Examples
- Law enforcement officers obtained a warrant to install a hidden microphone and videocamera in a hotel room that the officers had rented. The defendant came to the room and offered to buy 185 pounds of marijuana for $121,000. The defendant was arrested when he returned with the money and bought the marijuana. Because the defendant did not have a right of privacy in the hotel room rented by the law officers, the Supreme Court of Massachusetts held that the defendant did not have standing in court to challenge the use of the surveillance tapes as evidence against him (*Commonwealth v. Price*).[15]
- As a general rule, a search warrant is not necessary to search a public employee's workplace (desk, files, and so on) to investigate work-related misconduct under the U.S. Supreme Court case of *O'Connor v. Ortega.*[16]

  In the 1991 case of *United States v. Taketa,*[17] federal agents suspected Taketa (a law officer) of improper wiretapping. The federal agents entered Taketa's office at night to investigate possible work-related misconduct. This was lawful without a warrant under *O'Connor v. Ortega*, but the federal agents also placed a hidden videocamera in the office without a warrant. Their failure to obtain a warrant for the video surveillance spoiled the evidence obtained by the camera.

- A hidden video surveillance camera was installed in the employee break room of a Hawaii post office, where it operated for a year. The camera picked up evidence of illegal gambling against the defendant. The Supreme Court of Hawaii held that the postal employees had a reasonable expectation of privacy in the break room, which was neither a public place nor open to public view or hearing. Because the offense was not related to postal work, it was held not to fall under *O'Connor v. Ortega* (*State v. Bonnell*).[18]

- In 1992 Secret Service agents permitted a CBS camera crew to go with them in the search of a New York home under the authority of a search warrant. The agents had the authority to search for illegal credit cards; however, they had no authority under a search warrant to permit private citizens to accompany them. Only a woman and her 4-year-old son were present in the home, and no evidence of any crime was found. A civil lawsuit against CBS and the federal government was settled by damage payments to the family. The trial judge, in the case of *Ayeni v. CBS et al.*,[19] stated that "CBS had no greater right than that of a thief to be in the home.... [T]he television crew took from the home, for the purpose of broadcasting them to the world at large, pictures of intimate secrets of the household, including sequences of a cowering mother and child resisting the videotaping."

WHERE CAN VIDEOTAPING BE DONE WITHOUT A WARRANT?

Videotaping may be conducted in places where the people being filmed do not have a reasonable expectation of privacy. The following cases further illustrate.

McCray v. State

Maryland Court of Special Appeals, 84 Md. App. 513, 581 A.2d 45 (1990)

The defendant was suspected of being involved in a scheme to provide false driver's licenses for money. Investigating officers videotaped him walking from his home across the public street to the motor vehicle office. This tape was used as evidence in a trial that resulted in the defendant's conviction. In holding that a court order or search warrant was not needed, the court held that:

> ... one walking along a public sidewalk or standing in a public park cannot reasonably expect that his activity will be immune from the public eye or from observation by the police.... Consequently, any justified expectation of privacy is not violated by the videotaping of activity occurring in full public view....
>
> Thus, the videotape surveillance of McCray, in public view, walking across the street to the MVA poses no Fourth Amendment problem. Clearly, the videotape of McCray was captured in a public place and in public view. Consequently, McCray had no reasonable expectation of privacy when he walked on public sidewalks, streets and parking lots, since he voluntarily exposed to anyone interested the fact that he was traveling to a particular destination and meeting a particular individual in a public place. See *Sponick v. City of Detroit Police Dept.*, 49 Mich. App. 162, 211 N.W.2d 674 (1973) (where police officer videotaped in a bar talking with known criminals did not have a "reasonable expectation of privacy" because the observations occurred in a public place).

Here, the police officers were engaged in a legitimate investigation, and upon first utilizing various investigative activities to ferret out this licensing scheme, the police officers then chose to record their own visual observations with a video camera rather than with a note pad. The officers were observing a public place and positioned the video camera to observe the activities in this public place. As such, any visual observations were not an intrusion into an area where appellant possessed a "reasonable expectation of privacy." The videotape surveillance did not, therefore, constitute a search in violation of the Fourth Amendment. The videotaping of that which is lawfully observed is not more invasive or unreasonable than personal observation and is just as lawful. Consequently, neither a court order nor a search warrant was required. The trial court, therefore, did not err in admitting into evidence the videotapes.

People v. Lynch

Michigan Court of Appeals, 445 N.W.2d 803 (1989)

Because of unlawful homosexual activity taking place in a men's public restroom on a public highway, police obtained a search warrant to install videocameras in the ceiling above the toilet stalls because a person in a toilet stall with the door closed has a right of privacy. The defendant was convicted of two counts of gross indecency between males in the common area (the open area a person walks into from outside) of the public restroom, and he appealed, arguing that a right of privacy also exists in the common area. In holding that a warrant was not needed for the common area, the court held:

This was a public bathroom in a public rest area off a public highway. Any member of the public could feel free to enter that restroom. While the structure itself preserves a certain amount of privacy to those using the facilities, it can be presumed that any member of the public would expect that in the common area of the facility their privacy is not absolute and that any activity in that area is open to public examination....

The common area was readily accessible to anyone needing to use the facility. The public's expectation that they were entering a public facility certainly was not extinguished because they had to open two doors rather than one. To the extent that the videotapes were made of activities in the common area of the restroom, we cannot find that they invaded a constitutionally protected expectation of privacy....

As applied to this case, our holding means that the police did not need a warrant to monitor or videotape the common area.

An employee's office can be a place where a reasonable expectation of privacy exists, although the *Ortega* rule discussed in Chapter 11 makes it clear that a public employee's office may generally be searched without the need for a search warrant. Where the intrusion is video surveillance of an employee and the employee's office, courts continue to determine whether a reasonable expectation of privacy exists in relation to the video surveillance. In *Cowells v. State*,[20] the court concluded that a University of Alaska employee had no reasonable expectation of such privacy in her office in the university's ticket office. The court noted that people passing her office could see her desk and other parts of the office and that other employees made frequent and regular entrances to her office. As a result, the court concluded, she could not reasonably expect any privacy for her actions in the public view of her office, including by a hidden videocamera.

© AP Photo/Bedford, N.H. Police Department

A video surveillance camera caught this woman in the act of stealing. Such cameras can provide information that leads to the identification and arrest of suspects. Videotapes are admissible as evidence in court if the incident occurred where the defendant had no right to privacy and if a witness can verify that the tape is a reliable reproduction of the events. Without a witness, the videotape must meet defined standards in order to be admitted as evidence in court.

USING PHOTOGRAPHS AS EVIDENCE

demonstrative evidence
Evidence that portrays objects, persons, or events not in the courtroom—for example, photographs and videotapes.

Photographs and videotapes are **demonstrative evidence** because they portray (demonstrate) objects, persons, or events not in the courtroom. Videotapes present many pictures of an event or object, whereas a photo presents only one picture. Diagrams, maps, drawings, models, and sketches are also demonstrative evidence in that they present information needed to understand events, places, or objects relevant to a case. A Texas court of appeals made the following statement regarding the use of photographs as evidence:

> Photographs are admissible in evidence on the theory that they are pictorial communications of a witness who uses them instead of, or in addition to, some other method of communication. Thus, they are admissible on the same grounds and for the same purposes as are diagrams, maps, and drawings of objects or places, and the same rules of admissibility applicable to objects connected with the crime apply to photographs of such objects. This is true whether they are originals or copies, black and white or colored. So, a photograph, proved to be a true representation of the person, place, or thing which it purports to represent, is competent evidence of those things of which it is material and relevant for a witness to give a verbal description.[21]

INTRODUCING PHOTOGRAPHS AND VIDEOTAPES INTO EVIDENCE

Photographs and videotapes are admissible into evidence to explain or illustrate anything that a witness could testify to or describe in words. It is not necessary to have the person who has taken the photo or video introduce the picture or pictures into evidence. Any witness who can testify from firsthand knowledge that the photograph or video accurately portrays and represents the object, place, person, or event may introduce the photo or video. In many instances, the person who took the photo or video introduces it into evidence, but this is not necessary.

The extent to which the verifying witness must testify about the accuracy of a photograph varies, depending on the importance of each photograph to the issues before the court. Some photographs might be admitted by stipulation (agreement between the parties) or with no challenge, whereas other photographs might be sharply contested and challenged. A photograph that incriminates a defendant is more likely to be contested and therefore requires more testimony about verification. Conversely, minimal proof of accuracy may be sufficient for a photograph that illustrates something not seriously contested.

All evidence sought to be admitted for use in criminal or civil trials must be relevant to at least one of the issues before that court. In determining the admissibility of a photograph or videotape, the trial judge must determine whether the photo or video has probative, or evidentiary, value and tends to prove or disprove some issue in dispute. The Supreme Court of Minnesota stated: "Photographs are admissible if they accurately portray what a witness would be permitted to describe or if they aid a description, provided they are relevant. *State v. De Zeler*, 230 Minn. 39, 46–47, 41 N.W.2d 313, 319 (1950)."[22]

After verifying the accuracy of a photograph, the officer may be asked to state how he or she knows that the photograph is the one the officer took. The witness may identify the photograph by testimony showing any one or more of the following:

- Sole continuous possession of the photograph between the time the photo was taken and its presentation in court.
- The chain of possession for the time between the taking of the photograph and the presentation in court.
- The presence of an identifiable object in the picture that the officer placed at the scene before taking the photograph. The identifiable object could be an information data board or a measuring device with the initials of the officer and the date and place that the photograph was taken.

GRUESOME PHOTOGRAPHS AND VIDEOTAPES

gruesome photographs
Photographs that are shocking and repulsive.

Photographs of some crime scenes and victims are shocking and horrible. Such videotapes or **gruesome photographs** may be used as evidence if they are relevant to some issue before the court. The trial judge has a great deal of discretion in determining whether such photos are needed and how many photos may be shown. In the case of *Young v. State*,[23] a Florida Court of Appeals held as follows:

The fact that the photographs are offensive to our senses and might tend to inflame the jury is insufficient by itself to constitute reversible error, but the admission of such

THE "SILENT WITNESS" METHOD FOR INTRODUCING VIDEOTAPES

When the prosecution plans to introduce a videotape as evidence in a criminal trial, it must lay the proper foundation for its admission. Federal Rule of Evidence 901(A), applicable in federal courts and adopted by many states, requires that all evidence must be "authenticated" before it can be admitted and then presents a nonexclusive list of how such authentication can occur.

In the case of videotape evidence, two methods of authentication have developed in the federal and state courts. The first is generally called the "pictorial-communication" method. Under this method, a live witness must testify that the videotape accurately depicts an event that the witness actually saw. If such a witness can be found, no other authentication of the videotape is required, although the chain of custody requirements discussed in this section may be applicable.

In many situations a live witness may not be available for this kind of authentication. For example, videocameras may be placed in a location and programmed to film events that occur at that location, without a person operating the video recorder. Where videotapes of this type are offered as evidence, they are authenticated through the "silent witness" method. The following case illustrates this second method of authentication.

Straughn v. State
Court of Criminal Appeals of Alabama, 876 So.2d 492 (2003)

Police officers discovered a marijuana field, and in an effort to identify the persons cultivating the marijuana, they set up video recorders near the field to record persons using the road leading to the field and inside the field. The cameras were programmed to begin recording when motion was detected. The cameras subsequently recorded the defendant stopping on the road leading to the field, entering the field, and working on the marijuana plants. At his trial for unlawful possession of marijuana, the defendant moved to suppress the videotapes, contending that they were not properly authenticated. The trial court admitted the videotapes, and the defendant was convicted. On appeal, the court held that the admission of the videotapes was proper under the "silent witness" method.

Under the "silent witness" theory, a witness must explain how the process or mechanism that created the item works and how the process or mechanism ensures reliability.

The court stated that the standards for admission of a videotape under the "silent witness" method were:

1. A showing that the device that produced the videotape was capable of recording what a witness would have seen had a witness been present
2. A showing that the operator of the videocamera was competent
3. A showing that the resulting videotape was correct and authentic
4. A showing that no changes or deletions had been made
5. A showing of the manner the videotapes were preserved
6. An identification of the persons depicted in the videotapes
7. If statements are made in the recording, a showing that such statements were made voluntarily

The court held that because a police officer was able to provide the appropriate testimony meeting the standards set forth above, the videotape was properly admitted into evidence.

photographs, particularly in large numbers must have some relevancy, either independently or as corroborative of other evidence....

The very number of photographs of the victim in evidence here, especially those taken away from the scene of the crime, cannot but have had an inflammatory influence on the normal fact-finding process of the jury. The number of inflammatory photographs and resulting effect thereof was totally unnecessary to a full and complete presentation of the state's case. The same information could have been presented to the jury by use of the less offensive photographs whenever possible and by careful selection and use of a limited number of the more gruesome ones relevant to the issues before the jury.

The Supreme Court of North Carolina gave reasons why photographs of a victim's body could be admitted as evidence in the 1990 case of *State v. Robinson*:[24]

Photographs are usually competent to explain or illustrate anything that is competent for a witness to describe in words ... and properly authenticated photographs of a homicide victim may be introduced into evidence under the trial court's instructions that their use is to be limited to illustrating the witness's testimony....

Thus, photographs of the victim's body may be used to illustrate testimony as to the cause of death... . Photographs may also be introduced in a murder trial to illustrate testimony regarding the manner of killing so as to prove circumstantially the elements of murder in the first degree ... and for this reason such evidence is not precluded by a defendant's stipulation as to the cause of death.... Photographs of a homicide victim may be introduced even if they are gory, gruesome, horrible or revolting, so long as they are used for illustrative purposes and so long as their excessive or repetitious use is not aimed solely at arousing the passions of the jury....

This Court has recognized, however, that when the use of the photographs that have inflammatory potential is excessive or repetitious, the probative value of such evidence is eclipsed by its tendency to prejudice the jury.

X-RAY FILMS AS EVIDENCE

Rule 1001(2) of the Federal Rules of Evidence (see Appendix C) defines photographs as including still photographs, X-ray films, videotapes, and motion pictures. Therefore, X-ray films, videotapes, and motion pictures are introduced into evidence on the same basis and principles as still photographs. X-ray films—radiographs, roentgenograms, and skiagrams—are different from ordinary photographs in the following respects:

- An untrained person may take a photograph, but a trained technician or a physician must take an X-ray. Therefore, the photographer of the X-ray must testify in court unless the defense stipulates or agrees to the admission of the X-ray film.
- Unlike most photographs, X-ray films require an expert to explain and interpret them. Therefore, in most situations a licensed physician who has had experience with X-rays must be qualified as an expert witness to testify about the content of the X-ray film.
- Because no witness is capable of testifying to actually seeing the injury depicted by the X-ray, the picture must be admitted as original evidence in order to provide the basis for the opinion of the expert trained in the interpretation of X-rays.

USING DOCUMENTS AND WRITINGS AS EVIDENCE

document A
piece of written or
printed matter that
provides informa-
tion or evidence or
that serves as an
official record.

Documents and writings are involved in almost all civil cases and in many criminal cases. Generally, anything that conveys a message is a **document**. In criminal cases, documents could include such things as written confessions, bad checks, drug records and accounts, written evidence of fraud, business and hospital records, betting slips, altered prescriptions, incriminating statements found in notes and letters, demand notes used in kidnapping and robbery cases, and computer printouts relating to a criminal case.

The party seeking to use documents (or writings) as evidence must show that the document or writing is not only relevant and material but also genuine and authentic. Some documents and writings can prove their own authenticity. A prosecutor or defense attorney seeking to use a public record, whether sealed or not, or a newspaper or periodical as evidence may use a state rule of evidence similar to Federal Rule of Evidence 902 (self-authentication; see Appendix C). Authenticity may also be agreed upon by a stipulation between the parties that the document is genuine and authentic, leaving only the question whether the document is relevant and material.

Although a document or writing may be shown to be authentic and genuine, this is not proof about statements and assertions made in the document or writing. For example, a newspaper may be shown to be genuine and authentic and accepted for use in evidence as such. However, a jury or judge could find that statements made in the newspaper are not true.

USING DIRECT EVIDENCE TO PROVE THAT DOCUMENTS ARE AUTHENTIC AND GENUINE

Documents and writings may be proven genuine and authentic by any of the following forms of direct evidence:

- Testimony of a witness who observed the signing or the writing of the document—for example, an officer who observed the defendant writing or signing a consent form or a confession.
- Testimony of the person who wrote or signed the document acknowledging that the writing is genuine and authentic.
- Regularly kept business records that are authenticated by witnesses who are custodians or supervisors of such records and who can testify that the writing offered for use in evidence is actually part of the records of the business. In such cases, the custodian or supervisor may not have actually seen the writing or document written or signed. However, the trustworthiness of the writing may be established with testimony that the writing was a regularly kept business record. The *regularly kept business record exception* is also sometimes referred to as the *shop book rule* or the *business record exception*. (See Chapter 8 on "regularly kept records" as a major exception to the hearsay rule.)
- Testimony establishing proof of handwriting by an expert witness who is qualified to testify as to the identity of the writer of the document or writing.

For example, an expert could testify about the identity of the writer of a check, a demand note in a robbery case, or a threat found in a writing sent to a victim.

- Testimony of a person who is not a handwriting expert but is well acquainted with the handwriting of the signer or writer of the document or writing. This could be a member of the family, a friend, or another person who has seen the handwriting of the writer frequently.[25]
- The contents of the document or writing—for example, a demand note or a check may be easily recognized by the contents and form of the writing.[26]

USING CIRCUMSTANTIAL EVIDENCE TO PROVE THAT DOCUMENTS ARE AUTHENTIC AND GENUINE

The majority of documents and writings introduced for use as evidence in criminal trials are proven authentic and genuine by direct evidence or by the contents of the document or writing itself. If the document or writing cannot be proven authentic and genuine by direct evidence or by its contents, then *circumstantial evidence* may be used. The following types of circumstantial evidence may be used:

- Circumstantial evidence such as the fact that the writing was in the custody of the defendant, the victim,[27] or the deceased; or that the defendant, victim, or deceased acted in response to the writing; or that the defendant, victim, or deceased referred to the document or writing in oral or written communications with other persons; or that the document or writing did not appear to be forged or have any other suspicious appearance.

ancient document rule The rule that a piece of written or printed matter may be deemed authentic and genuine without a witness to attest to the circumstances of its creation because its age suggests that it is unlikely to have been falsified.

- The **ancient document rule**, which permits the use of circumstantial evidence where the document has been in existence for a number of years [20 years or more under Federal Rule of Evidence 901(8); see Appendix C].
- Circumstantial evidence derived from the fact that the document or writing was in the custody of a public official. Statements made in a will, an income tax return, a bill of sale, or a deed may be used in evidence. If there is any question about the authenticity or genuineness of such documents, circumstantial evidence may be used.
- The reply doctrine, which permits the use of circumstantial evidence to show that a writing was in response to other communication. Writings in response to other communications often indicate this in their contents. The following case illustrates a situation in which the writing was shown to be a reply communication.

Winel v. United States

Eighth Circuit Court of Appeals, 365 F.2d 646 (1966)

In holding that a postcard was properly admitted for use in evidence in a mail fraud case, the court held:

> It has long been recognized that one of the principal situations where the authenticity of a letter is provable by circumstantial evidence arising out of the letter's context, other than proof of handwriting or the business records exception, is where it can be shown that the letter was sent in reply to a previous communication....

... In the instant case the inherent nature of the communication makes it absolutely certain that it is a reply communication. The only question that can then arise with respect to its admissibility would be whether there was proof of its mailing and receipt. This is clearly answered by the record....

... It is not necessary that there be direct testimony of placing in the mails or removing from the mails if there is a full showing of the customs and usage relating to this type of communication.

REGULARLY KEPT RECORDS

All large businesses, hospitals, law enforcement agencies, and other organizations have regularly kept records. More than 300 years ago, English courts recognized the shop book rule, which is now a well-recognized exception to the hearsay rule. A writing is in most instances recognized as authentic and genuine if it is shown to be a regularly kept record.

Police reports and police records meet the requirements of regularly kept records. Records of illegal sales and shipments of drugs have been held to fall within the hearsay exception.[28] In recognizing computer printouts as a regularly kept business record, the Superior Court of New Jersey held:

We hold that as long as a proper foundation is laid, a computer printout is admissible on the same basis as any other business record....

Computerized bookkeeping has become commonplace. Because the business records exception is intended to bring the realities of the business world into the courtroom, a record kept on computer in the ordinary course of business qualifies as competent evidence. This result is in accordance with that reached in other jurisdictions.... Of course, if the computer printout at issue here is admitted at trial, it will constitute only prima facie evidence of an account stated. Defendant will have the opportunity to refute plaintiff's evidence.[29]

THE BEST EVIDENCE, OR ORIGINAL DOCUMENT, RULE

best evidence rule (original document rule)
The rule of evidence that requires the original of a writing, photograph, or other document to prove the content, unless the original is unavailable.

The famous English lawyer and writer, Sir William Blackstone, wrote in the 1760s that "the best evidence the nature of the case will admit of shall always be required, if possible to be had; but if not possible then the best evidence that can be had shall be allowed."[30]

Federal Rules of Evidence 1002–1006 state the **best evidence rule (original document rule)** used today in federal courts and most state courts (see Appendix C). Rule 1002 provides that the best evidence rule applies to "writing(s), recording(s), or photograph(s)" and requires the original unless "(1) Originals lost or destroyed.... (2) Original not obtainable.... (3) Original in possession of opponent.... (4) ... the writing, recording, or photograph is not closely related to a controlling issue" (Rule 1004).

Carbon or photographic copies of an original document or writing are secondary evidence of the original. The requirement that the original be offered as evidence is an ancient requirement that originated in English law prior to the American Revolution. Some writers state that the reason for the rule was to

THE USE OF WRITINGS OR DOCUMENTS AS EVIDENCE

Documents and writings may be admissible for use as evidence if:

- The document or writing is shown to be genuine and authentic.
- The evidence contained in the document or writing is relevant, material, and competent.
- The document or writing does not contain inadmissible hearsay. (Part of a writing may be held to be inadmissible for this reason.)
- The requirements of the best evidence or original document rule are met.

After the writing or document has been admitted for use as evidence, the jury or judge as fact finder then determines:

- The author and person who wrote the writing, if this question and issue are unresolved
- The truth and credibility of the statements and assertions made in the document or writing
- The weight to be given to the statements and assertions made in the document or writing
- The issue of guilt or innocence of each charge made against the defendant

prevent fraud. Most modern writers, however, state that the primary purpose of the rule was to ensure the most accurate written version, which is the original document or writing.

The rule requires that the best evidence available be used. This preference for the original of any document or writing is a commonsense attempt to minimize the possibilities of errors or fraud in seeking the truth. Possibilities of errors certainly existed years ago when all copies of original documents were made by hand. With modern copy machines, the margin of error has been minimized but still exists. The rule, which originated centuries ago, continues to require that the best available evidence be used.

If a particular state follows the federal best evidence rule, the rule applies only to writings, recordings, or photographs (Rule 1002). In the following case, the Supreme Court of Georgia held that the best evidence rule applies only to writings and not to other evidence.

Munsford v. State

Supreme Court of Georgia, 235 Ga. 38, 218 S.E.2d 792 (1975)

The defendants were convicted of armed robbery. A police officer appeared as one of the witnesses in the case and testified that a track shoe print found at the scene of the crime matched the tennis shoe of one of the defendants. A photograph of the shoe print was admitted into evidence, but the tennis shoe was not used in evidence. The Supreme Court of Georgia held that the procedure did not violate the best evidence rule, quoting an earlier Georgia case holding: "The [best evidence] rule has nothing to do with evidence generally, but is restricted to writing alone."[31]

Failure to comply with the best evidence rule could create problems unless one of the reasons listed in Rule 1004 is shown. The following case illustrates.

FAST BOATS, GPS DEVICES, AND THE BEST EVIDENCE RULE

Illegal drug smugglers frequently use specially built speedboats to bring drugs into the United States. When federal or state officers suspect that a boat is engaged in drug smuggling, several questions arise if the officers stop the boat and search it for drugs. Some of these questions, such as the degree of suspicion needed to stop the boat and search it and the permitted extent of a border search, are discussed in other chapters of this book. Other questions also might arise, some involving the best evidence rule, as the following case illustrates.

United States v. Bennett

Ninth Circuit Court of Appeals, 363 F.3d 947 (2004), *cert. denied,* 125 S.Ct. 363 (2004)

U.S. Customs agents intercepted the defendant's boat in U.S. waters as it was docking in San Diego. A subsequent search of the boat, which included drilling holes in the boat's sides and taking X-rays of the boat's structure, uncovered 1,500 pounds of marijuana. The defendant was charged with possession of marijuana and illegal importation of marijuana from a foreign country, Mexico. At his trial he moved to suppress the marijuana seized in the search of his boat, alleging that the search violated his Fourth Amendment rights. He also moved to exclude the testimony of a customs agent who testified about the boat's travel path based on information taken from a GPS device located in the boat. Both motions were overruled, and the defendant was convicted of possession of marijuana and illegal importing of marijuana.

On appeal, the circuit court affirmed the possession conviction, finding that the search of the defendant's boat was lawful. The court held that the officers reasonably believed the boat entered U.S. waters from international waters, thus making the search at the San Diego dock the equivalent of a border search. The officers were thus justified in conducting a border search under the rule of the 2004 case of *United States v. Flores-Montano* [541 U.S. 149] (discussed in Chapter 11). Moreover, the court held, even if the kind of search conducted by the customs officers was so intrusive or destructive as to require reasonable suspicion under *Flores-Montano*, the fact that the boat was riding low in the water and had an unusual space configuration gave the officers the necessary reasonable suspicion to make the search.

The court reversed the defendant's conviction for illegal importation of marijuana, holding that the customs officer's testimony based on the boat's GPS device should have been excluded under the best evidence rule. The officer testified he used the device's "backtrack" program to produce a graph of the boat's progress, which showed that it traveled from Mexico to the United States. The officer did not produce the graph and did not actually see the boat traveling in the water, but simply testified what he saw when he looked at the backtrack graph. The court held that Federal Rule of Evidence 1002, the best evidence rule, applied to the officer's testimony. Because the officer did not observe the boat's progress, the GPS display seen by the officer was being used to prove the path the boat took, not simply to confirm the perception of the officer testifying. As a result, according to Rule 1002, the GPS data from the device onboard the boat were required, the court concluded. The court also held that Rule 1004, which makes the best evidence rule inapplicable if the original document is lost or destroyed, did not apply because it was possible for the government to download data from the boat's GPS device into a Geographical Information System software application. The court remanded the case for re-sentencing on the possession conviction alone.

Commonwealth v. Lewis

Pennsylvania Superior Court, 623 A.2d 355 (1993)

A shoplifting was recorded by a videocamera in a Sears retail store. At the trial, a police officer who had not viewed the theft testified about what he observed on the store videotape, but the videotape was not introduced for use as evidence.

A store security guard testified that he was unable "to locate the videotape of [defendant's] action." The court held that this explanation was unsatisfactory and reversed the conviction for a new trial, holding that: "whatever knowledge [the police officer] possessed was gained from his viewing of the videotape. Thus, the original tape should have been produced."

THE FOURTH AMENDMENT PROTECTION OF WRITINGS, RECORDS, AND DOCUMENTS

The Fourth Amendment provides that "The right of the people to be secure in their persons, houses, papers and effects, against unreasonable searches and seizures, shall not be violated." Therefore, law enforcement officers and other governmental officials cannot intrude into a "zone of privacy" of a person to seize documents, writings, or records without a showing of proper authority.

The plain view and public view doctrines apply to documents and writings as follows:

- *Plain view:* If officers are where they have a right to be and they see a document or writing in plain view that is immediately apparent to be evidence of a crime, they may seize the document or writing.
- *Public view:* Handwriting, like the tone of a person's voice, is constantly exposed to public view, and therefore samples may be compelled by court or grand jury order.

In addition, the business records of banks, stock brokerage houses, and other financial institutions are available to governmental authorities because such records are not private papers of individual investors and account holders. The following U.S. Supreme Court cases state the law concerning this.

United States v. Dionisio

United States Supreme Court, 410 U.S. 1, 93 S.Ct. 764 (1973)

The Supreme Court held that handwriting, like speech, is a characteristic that is continually on display to the public, and people can have no greater expectation of privacy to their writings than to the tone quality of their voices. A grand jury can therefore order people to submit samples of their handwriting, just as a person can be requested to talk for identification purposes.[32]

United States v. Miller

United States Supreme Court, 425 U.S. 435, 96 S.Ct. 1619 (1976)

The defendant was charged with various federal offenses. The government obtained microfilms of checks, deposit slips, and other records by means of subpoenas duces tecum served upon officials of two banks where the defendant had accounts. The Supreme Court held that these documents and records were properly used as evidence in the defendant's trial because:

- The evidence was business records of the banks and was not private papers of the defendant.

- The defendant had no legitimate expectation of privacy in the original checks and deposit slips because these writings were not confidential communications but negotiable instruments used in commercial transactions.

The Court ruled that:

> The depositor takes the risk, in revealing his affairs to another, that the information will be conveyed by that person to the government…. This Court has held repeatedly that the Fourth Amendment does not prohibit the obtaining of information revealed to a third party and conveyed by him to government authorities, even if the information is revealed on the assumption that it will be used only for a limited purpose and the confidence placed in the third party will not be betrayed.

THE FIFTH AMENDMENT PROTECTION OF WRITINGS, RECORDS, AND DOCUMENTS

The Fifth Amendment provides that "No person shall … be compelled in any criminal case to be a witness against himself." The Fifth Amendment therefore forbids demanding that a suspect write out a confession or otherwise incriminate himself by producing a writing. The U.S. Supreme Court stated the Fifth Amendment privilege against self-incrimination as follows:

> [T]he constitutional privilege against self-incrimination … is designed to prevent the use of legal process to force from the lips of the accused individual the evidence necessary to convict him or to force him to produce and authenticate any personal documents or effects that might incriminate him.[33]

Although the government cannot force a suspect to produce a document that incriminates the suspect, this does not mean that the government cannot lawfully seize a document that incriminates the defendant. U.S. Supreme Court Justice Holmes stated this principle of law in 1913: "A party is privileged from producing the evidence but not from its production."[34] The following U.S. Supreme Court case illustrates.

Andresen v. Maryland

United States Supreme Court, 427 U.S. 463, 96 S.Ct. 2737 (1976)

The defendant, an attorney who practiced alone, was convicted of real estate fraud. Business records were obtained from the defendant's office under the authority of a search warrant. The trial court permitted these records to be used as evidence, holding that the defendant had not been compelled to do anything that incriminated himself. At the trial the records were authenticated by prosecution witnesses, not by the defendant. In affirming the defendant's conviction, the Supreme Court held:

> There is no question that the records seized from petitioner's offices and introduced against him were incriminating. Moreover, it is undisputed that some of these business records contain statements made by petitioner….
>
> This case thus falls within the principle stated by Mr. Justice Holmes: "A party is privileged from producing the evidence but not from its production." *Johnson v. United States*, 228 U.S. 457, 458, 33 S.Ct. 572, 57 L.Ed. 919 (1913). This principle recognizes that the protection afforded by the self-incrimination clause of the Fifth Amendment "adheres basically to the person, not to information that may incriminate him." *Couch v. United States*, 409 U.S., at 328, 93 S.Ct. at 611. Thus, although the Fifth Amendment may protect an individual from complying with a subpoena for the production of his personal records in his possession because the very act of production may

TERMS USED IN THE EXAMINATION OF DOCUMENTS AND WRITINGS

- *Questioned document*: A document or writing is questioned when questions are raised about who wrote, typed, or made the writing; whether the document is genuine and authentic; or whether the writing is totally or partially forged or altered.
- *Questioned document examiner*: A person who has the special training and experience necessary to examine questioned documents to determine the author or the genuineness of the document. To make this determination, the questioned document is often compared with one or more other documents.
- *Graphologist*: A person who studies one or more documents written by a known person and, from the writing or penmanship, infers personality traits of the writer of the document. Because courts do not recognize graphology as a reliable science, such evidence is not admissible.

- *Indented writings*: Writing on a sheet of a note pad or telephone pad that is under the paper on which a person originally wrote. Indented writing may provide valuable information in the investigation of a crime.
- *Charred document*: A writing or document that has been partially or completely burned. If the document is left undisturbed or can be preserved, a document examiner can usually determine the written contents.
- *Linguistics analysis*: The study of language usage. Linguistics analysis may be used to determine the genuineness of a document or to determine who wrote a document. The defense in the Patty Hearst case used linguistic evidence of writings and tape recordings in an attempt to prove that Patty did not participate voluntarily in the bank robbery. See *United States v. Hearst* [412 F.Supp. 893 (N.D. Calif. 1976)].

constitute a compulsory authentication of incriminating information, ... a seizure of the same materials by law enforcement officers differs in a crucial respect—the individual against whom the search is directed is not required to aid in the discovery, production, or authentication of incriminating evidence....

Accordingly, we hold that the search of an individual's office for business records, their seizure, and subsequent introduction into evidence does not offend the Fifth Amendment's prescription that "[n]o person ... shall be compelled in any criminal case to be a witness against himself."

SUMMARY

Fixed surveillance cameras, handheld videocameras, closed-circuit cameras, and ordinary cameras are used every day to provide evidence for police and prosecutors to use in criminal and civil cases throughout the United States.

Documents and writings are also important evidence in many criminal cases. It is hard to imagine a civil case that does not use documents as evidence.

This chapter presents cases and the law about the use of photographs, videotapes, and documents as evidence in criminal cases.

CASE ANALYSIS

Read Appendix B, Finding and Analyzing Cases (p. 427). With these guidelines in mind, please continue with the Case Analysis selections for Chapter 17.

Photographs and videotapes can serve the same function as live witnesses; that is, they can show by pictures what a witness might otherwise describe in words. But more dramatically than words, photographs and videotapes have the potential to unfairly influence or prejudice the jury. This is nowhere more apparent than the admission of gruesome photographs. The two Utah Supreme Court decisions in the first case analysis illustrate the rules on the admission of particularly graphic photographs or videos in child abuse cases.

1. In *State v. Bluff* [52 P.3d 1210 (2002) (No. 990808)] the prosecution in the murder trial of a mother offered as evidence postmortem photographs of the young child, who died from child abuse, as well as videos showing the child's mother participating in sadomasochistic sexual acts. The Utah Supreme Court took the opportunity to explain the rules for admissibility of gruesome photographs and determined that those offered were not gruesome. Do you agree? In *State v. Gulbransen* [106 P.3d 734 (2005) (No. 20020779)] the Utah Supreme Court had the occasion to apply the rules announced in the *Bluff* decision. Do you agree with their conclusion?

2. Videotapes and photographs differ in that photographs are normally visible immediately, whereas videotapes must be placed into a video player. This difference can have consequences when a lawful search of a residence turns up both photographs and videos. May the police put the videotapes into a player and watch them to see if they depict criminal activity? In *Lee v. State* [826 N.E.2d 131 (2005) (45A05-0405-CR-267)] , the Indiana Court of Appeals answered no to this question, at least with respect to videotapes not shown by their owner to his girlfriend. In 2005, the Indiana Supreme Court granted transfer of the case to its docket for review. After reading the opinion of the court of appeals, what do you think the Indiana Supreme Court decided on review? To find out, go to *Lee v. State*, 849 N.E.2d 602 (Ind. 2006), *cert. denied*, 127 S.Ct. 1331 (2007).

3. Is the fact that a juror faints when shown photographs of a victim's body sufficient evidence that the photograph is gruesome? See *State v. Green* [48 P.2d 1276 (Kan. 2002) (No. 86,953)].

4. Assume a minor charges another minor with possession of alcohol after a police officer stopped the defendant in his car and observed alcohol in containers. The police officer demanded the driver's license, which showed the defendant to be underage. At his trial, the defendant refused to produce his license. Can the prosecution prove its case by having the officer testify that he saw the driver's license and the defendant's age? See *United States v. Cuesta* [2007 WL2729853 (E.D. Cal. 2007)].

Notes

1. 496 U.S. 582, 110 S.Ct. 2638.
2. 578 So.2d 698, 49 CrL 1169 (Fla.).
3. 611 So.2d 422 (Ala. Crim. App.).
4. 829 S.W.2d 407 (Tex. App. 1992).
5. 583 So.2d 740 (Fla. App. 1991).
6. 830 P.2d 193 (Okla. Crim. App.).
7. 466 N.W.2d 105 (N.D.).
8. 591 A.2d 288 (Pa. Super.).
9. 577 N.E.2d 855 (Ill. App.).
10. 464 N.W.2d 517 (Minn. App.).
11. 367 N.W.2d 546 (Minn. App. 1985).
12. 808 S.W.2d 102 (Tex. App. 1990).
13. 581 So.2d 1249 (Ala. Crim. App. 1991).
14. 561 A.2d 468 (D.C. App. 1989).
15. 562 N.E.2d 1355 (Mass. 1990).
16. 480 U.S. 709, 107 S.Ct. 1492 (1987).

17. 923 F.2d 665 (9th Cir.).

18. 856 P.2d 1265 (Hawaii 1993).

19. 848 F.Supp. 362 (E.D.N.Y. 1994).

20. 23 P.3d 1168 (Alaska 2001).

21. *Terry v. State*, 491 S.W.2d 161 (Tex. Crim. App. 1973).

22. Quoted in *State v. Olson*, 459 N.W.2d 711 (Minn. App. 1990).

23. 234 So.2d 341 (Fla. 1970).

24. 395 S.E.2d 402.

25. See the 1990 case of *State v. Glidden* [459 N.W.2d 136 (Minn. App.)] , where the Minnesota Court of Appeals quoted *McCormick on Evidence*: "generally anyone familiar with the handwriting of a given person may supply authenticating testimony in the form of his opinion that a writing or a signature is the handwriting of that person." In the *Glidden* case, an office manager who was familiar with the defendant's handwriting identified the handwriting on questioned documents as being the defendant's.

26. Records and writings of drug transactions are often found in raids on drug houses and apartments. In the 1991 case of *United States v. Jaramillo-Suarez* [942 F.2d 1412 (9th Cir.)], a "pay/owe" sheet was held admissible; in *United States v. Lai* [934 F.2d 1414 (9th Cir. 1991)], "what appeared to be handwritten and computer summaries of drug transactions" were allowed in evidence; and in *State v. Lewis* [567 So.2d 726 (Fla. App. 1990)], writings of the drug transactions between the defendant and the undercover officers were admitted into evidence.

27. In the 1990 case of *State v. Boppre* [453 N.W.2d 406], a murder victim wrote the defendant's name on the floor and on a door casement as he was dying. The Supreme Court of Nebraska held that the writing was admissible in evidence as both a dying declaration and an excited utterance. In this case, in which the floor and the door could not be brought into court, a photograph of the writings was introduced as evidence.

For cases where the contents of a writing were used as evidence to identify the writer, see *United States v. Sutton* [426 F.2d 1202 (D.C. Cir. 1969)], where four handwritten, unsigned notes found on the body of a murdered woman revealed knowledge identifying and incriminating the defendant of the murder of the woman, and *People v. Faircloth* [599 N.E.2d 1356 (Ill. App. 1992)], where letters signed using a nickname showed that the defendant sold the illegal drugs that caused the death of the victim. The letters were admitted for use as evidence in the case where the defendant was convicted of the drug-induced death of a woman.

28. See *United States v. Grossman*, 614 F.2d 295 (1st Cir. 1980).

29. *Sears, Roebuck & Co. v. Merla*, 361 A.2d 68 (1976).

30. Blackstone, *Commentaries*, 368.

31. Rule 1002 of the Federal Rules of Evidence, which is followed by most states, now requires "the original writing, recording, or photograph."

32. See also *United States v. Mara*, 410 U.S. 19, 93 S.Ct. 774 (1973).

33. *Bellis v. United States*, 417 U.S. at 88, 94 S.Ct. at 2183.

34. *Johnson v. United States*, 228 U.S. 457, 458, 33 S.Ct. 572 (1913).

SCIENTIFIC EVIDENCE

LEARNING OBJECTIVES

In this chapter we examine a particular kind of evidence that is produced by scientific methods and tests. The learning objectives for this chapter are:

- State the requirements for admissibility of scientific evidence under Rule 702 of the Federal Rules of Evidence.
- Explain the difference between the *Frye* test and the *Daubert* test.
- Explain how DNA evidence is used to identify a suspect in a crime.
- State both the logistical and the theoretical problems with ballistic fingerprinting.

CHAPTER CONTENTS

The Importance of Scientific Evidence

The Use of Scientific Evidence

The Admissibility of Scientific Evidence

What Is Scientific Evidence?

The Use of Judicial Notice for Accepted Scientific Techniques

A Few of the Sciences and Scientific Techniques Used in the Criminal Justice System

DNA Genetic Profiling

Determining the Time of Death in Criminal Cases

Ballistic Fingerprinting or Firearm Fingerprinting

Sources of Other Scientific Evidence

THE IMPORTANCE OF SCIENTIFIC EVIDENCE

scientific evidence
Evidence, usually in the form of expert testimony, that relates to scientific theory, experiments, or tests.

The American criminal justice system relies on the knowledge and equipment of many sciences and skills—chemistry, physics, mathematics, medicine, and dentistry, to name just a few. Crime laboratories with sophisticated equipment are used every day; highly skilled arts and specialized training are often required to analyze and support evidence.

In this chapter we examine a variety of kinds of **scientific evidence** and the rules courts use to determine the admissibility of scientific evidence. DNA evidence is discussed in some detail, owing to the frequency and importance of that evidence in criminal prosecutions.

THE USE OF SCIENTIFIC EVIDENCE

Experienced law enforcement officers state that most crimes are solved through the use of common sense and hard work. An officer who is investigating a crime may obtain enough information to identify the perpetrator of the offense but may have insufficient evidence to charge and obtain a conviction. In such situations, scientific techniques may provide the additional evidence necessary to carry the burden of proving guilt beyond a reasonable doubt.

Sometimes an investigating officer may have only the evidence obtained from crime laboratories. When no additional evidence is available, scientific evidence may be the starting point or the link that leads to the solution of the crime.

For these reasons, scientific evidence has become one of the strongest weapons available for the successful prosecution of criminal offenders. Judges and juries may overestimate the reliability of scientific evidence, however. This problem caused the Supreme Judicial Court of Massachusetts to state: "We are aware that scientific

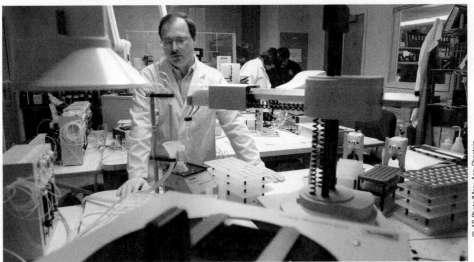

© AP Photo/Mary Ann Chastain

Scientists and technicians in crime laboratories use sophisticated equipment to analyze and provide evidence that can be crucial in solving cases and convicting offenders. Here a toxicologist awaits the results of a lab procedure that extracts drug and poison from biosamples.

"COLD CASE" FILES AND SCIENTIFIC EVIDENCE

There are more than three-quarters of a million law enforcement officers in the United States, working on more than 24 million violent and felony-property crimes that occur each year. Although many crimes are solved soon after they are committed, a significant number of crimes go unsolved. For law enforcement officers, these "cold cases" remain open and are a source of concern. In recent years, the use of scientific techniques and technology has made it possible for investigators to solve many cold cases. The following two cases illustrate how DNA databases and high-tech equipment have led to closure on cold cases:

- *DNA:* In 1988 three people were killed in two separate incidents in northern Virginia. Two of the victims were women who were raped by their murderer. Police were able to collect crime-scene samples that produced a DNA profile of the rapist in each incident, but they were unable to match the DNA to any other DNA sample then stored in a DNA database. In 2000 these DNA samples were entered into the new Virginia DNA database, which quickly showed that the DNA samples from both crime scenes came from the same man. However, the identity of the man was not established. In 2005 California collected DNA samples from all 70,000 inmates in the California Penal System and entered DNA profiles from these samples into the federal DNA database, CODIS (see the discussion of CODIS). In September 2005 the

CODIS database indicated that the DNA sample taken from Alfredo Prieto, a convicted killer on California's death row, matched the DNA taken from the Virginia rapes and murders. Virginia officials began efforts to obtain Prieto's presence in Virginia for trial on those rapes and murders. (*The Washington Post*, September 28, 2005, p. B-1)

- *High-tech equipment:* A young girl was reported missing in Spokane, Washington, in 1999. Extensive searches for the girl or her body came up empty. Although some evidence pointed to the girl's father as a possible suspect in the girl's disappearance, searches of his home and truck produced nothing. When the father picked up his truck after it was searched, police officers said they believed the girl was buried in a shallow grave and that the police would find the body after animals dug it up. Unknown to the father, the police had, pursuant to a court order, placed a global positioning system (GPS) device in his truck. The father then went to the spot where he had buried the girl, dug her body up, and moved it to a new burial site. The police retrieved the GPS device, which showed the movements of the truck. By tracing the truck's movement through the GPS device, officers were able to locate the girl's body. This and other evidence collected from the body resulted in the father's first-degree murder conviction. [*State v. Jackson*, 76 P.3d 217 (Wash. 2003)]

proof may in some instances assume 'a posture of mystic infallibility in the eyes of a jury of laymen.'"[1]

Even though scientific evidence is not infallible, it may contribute to an investigation by:

- Providing a lead or leads to point a criminal investigation in the right direction.
- Providing information that eliminates a suspect as the person who committed the crime being investigated. For example, DNA evidence, regular fingerprinting, or a surveillance videotape could show that the suspect did not commit the crime.

- Providing corpus delicti, or proof that a crime was committed, such as scientific evidence that a fire was intentionally started, as in arson, or that death was caused by poisoning.
- Providing the independent corroborative evidence necessary to support a confession, or to corroborate and support other evidence presented by the prosecutor or the defense attorney.
- Establishing a link between the crime scene and the suspect or between the suspect and the victim of the crime.
- Providing one of the essential elements of the crime being investigated.
- Affirming or disproving an alibi.
- Establishing the innocence of people not involved in the crime.
- Encouraging or inducing a person to make a confession or an incriminating admission when the person is confronted with scientific evidence that incriminates him or her. (If such a person were being held in custody, *Miranda* warnings would have to be given before the confrontation.)
- Providing reasonable suspicion (for an investigative stop), probable cause (to make an arrest, obtain a search warrant, and so on), or sufficient proof beyond a reasonable doubt (necessary for a criminal conviction).
- Building such strong cases against defendants that the number of guilty pleas increases, thus clearing court calendars and permitting faster trials of contested cases.

THE ADMISSIBILITY OF SCIENTIFIC EVIDENCE

WHAT IS SCIENTIFIC EVIDENCE?

Scientific evidence is most often presented in court by an expert witness testifying about expert opinions. When, for example, a person trained in science or technology gives his or her opinion about the chemical or biological composition of a substance, the testimony is scientific evidence. If the scientist has the necessary education, training, and experience to test the substance and if the scientist has conducted suitable tests of the substance, the testimony is usually admissible as expert testimony. Most states have rules identical or similar to Federal Rule of Evidence 702 (see Appendix C), which permits such expert testimony.

Scientific evidence also includes expert testimony that goes beyond science. The scientific expert is frequently called upon to interpret results and draw conclusions about what results mean in the case being tried. This is very common in criminal trials, where experts in a wide variety of scientific disciplines offer comparison testimony linking a defendant to a crime, crime scene, or victim. For example, the fingerprint expert may testify that the defendant's fingerprints match those found on a murder weapon; the ballistics expert may testify that bullets found in the victim were fired from the defendant's pistol; the forensic odontologist may testify that bite marks on the victim's body were made by the defendant's teeth; and a voice identification expert may testify that a recorded voice matches the defendant's voice.

The central issue for this kind of scientific evidence is the reliability of the theory and testing on which the conclusions are based. If the scientific theory is flawed or the tests unpredictable, then the conclusions are unreliable and should not be admitted as evidence.

Some scientific theories and tests are so widely accepted and verified that they are virtually beyond criticism. The theory that each person's fingerprints are unique, for example, has universal acceptance. Similarly, tests used to link bullets to the gun that fired them are rarely questioned.

Other scientific theories have been rejected as unreliable. Voice-print comparisons, for example, have been found inadmissible on both theoretical and testing grounds.[2] Many courts have rejected the theory that voice prints are unique and also the tests by which experts match voice spectrograms.

Thus, an important question in the admissibility of scientific evidence is the theoretical and experimental basis of the scientific expert's testimony. Courts traditionally use one of the following three rules for the admissibility of scientific evidence.

The *Frye* Test   In *Frye v. United States*,[3] the U.S. Court of Appeals refused to admit the results of a lie detector test given to a defendant in a murder trial. In rejecting the scientific basis for lie detector results, the court formulated what has become known as the *general acceptance test*:

> Just when a scientific principle or discovery crosses the line between the experimental and demonstrable stages is difficult to define. Somewhere in this twilight zone the evidential force of the principle must be recognized, and while courts will go a long way in admitting expert testimony deduced from a well-recognized scientific principle or discovery, the thing from which the deduction is made must be sufficiently established to have gained general acceptance in the particular field in which it belongs.[4]

Frye test
The general acceptance test: scientific evidence presented to the court must result from tests and theories that are generally accepted by a meaningful segment of the associated scientific community.

Prior to 1993, when the U.S. Supreme Court decided *Daubert v. Merrill Dow Pharmaceuticals*,[5] the federal courts and most state courts applied the *Frye* test to determine the admissibility of scientific evidence. The *Frye* general acceptance test was subject to significant criticisms. Some thought the test was too broad because it permitted expert scientific testimony in areas where no real scientific methods had been followed. For example, in *Commonwealth v. Lykus*,[6] the Massachusetts Supreme Judicial Court admitted voice spectrographic identification evidence, stating "the requirement of the *Frye* rule of general acceptance is satisfied, in our opinion, if the principle is generally accepted by those who would be expected to be familiar with its use."[7] As critics observed, the only people "familiar with the use" of voice-print analysis are the voice-print experts themselves.

The *Frye* test was also criticized as too narrow because otherwise reliable scientific evidence might be inadmissible even though it had sound theoretical and experimental foundations. Indeed, some courts rejected *Frye* for this reason. In *State v. Hall*,[8] the Iowa Supreme Court permitted an expert witness to testify about blood-spatter analysis. In this analysis the expert reached conclusions about the direction, force, and other physical characteristics of the crime based on the pattern of the victim's blood spatter. Although such evidence is not generally accepted, the Iowa court permitted the evidence because it was otherwise shown to be reliable.

The *Frye* Plus Test   When in the 1980s prosecutors begin using DNA test results to link defendants to crime scenes, some courts modified the *Frye* test by adding other requirements to it. In the leading case of *People v. Castro*,[9] the New York Supreme Court held that DNA evidence[10] is admissible if (1) the theory is generally accepted, (2) procedures for testing the theory are generally accepted, and (3) the testing is shown to have followed those procedures.

In the case of DNA evidence, the theory is generally accepted. Most courts and scientists agree that the DNA chain of an individual can be analyzed and compared with the DNA chain found in crime-scene evidence.[11] Moreover, there is general acceptance for some, but not all, procedures for testing DNA. The RFLP test (see the discussion below) has general acceptance.[12] The PCR test has not been generally accepted by some courts.[13]

In courts that use the *Frye* Plus test, the admissibility question frequently turns on how accurately and faithfully the testing laboratory followed accepted procedures.

The *Daubert* Test   The U.S. Supreme Court decision in *Daubert v. Merrill Dow Pharmaceuticals Co.*[14] rejected the *Frye* test and held that Federal Rule of Evidence 702 created its own standard for the introduction of scientific evidence. Under Rule 702, scientific evidence is admissible if:

> … the expert is proposing to testify to (1) scientific knowledge that (2) will assist the trier of fact to understand or determine a fact in issue. This entails a preliminary assessment of whether the reasoning or methodology underlying the testimony is scientifically valid and of whether that reasoning or methodology properly can be applied to the facts in issue.[15]

The *Daubert* Court suggested that the trial court consider various factors in assessing scientific validity: (1) Has the theory been tested? (2) Has the theory been subjected to peer review by other scientists? (3) What is the theory's or technique's known or potential rate of error? (4) Do standards controlling the application of the theory or technique exist? (5) Is the theory or technique generally accepted?

Daubert test
The principle that scientific evidence presented to the court must result from tests and theories that are testable, have been reviewed by peers, have high reliability rates, and are generally accepted by the associated scientific community.

In 1999 the U.S. Supreme Court held that the **Daubert** test was applicable to technical as well as scientific evidence. In *Kumho Tire Co. v. Carmichael*,[16] the Court held that an engineer's testimony concerning a tire failure was inadmissible under the *Daubert* test.

Kumho and *Daubert* are decisions that interpret Federal Rule of Evidence 702 and are binding only in federal prosecutions. Because most states have adopted a rule similar to Rule 702, *Daubert* and *Kumho* are influential in state cases. In 1998,[17] it was reported that thirty-three states had adopted *Daubert*, seventeen states continued to use *Frye* or *Frye* Plus, and ten had announced no final decision.[18] However, a 2006 study published by the American Bar Association Committee on Continuing Legal Education notes that many states use parts of the *Daubert* test but have not adopted the complete test.[19]

As pointed out in Chapter 16, fingerprint science has reconstructed itself in recent years. New proficiency testing and new qualitative and quantitative analyses have been established. These changes can be attributed to *Daubert*, which emphasizes rigorous testing and organized skepticism and points out that there are no certainties in science, only probabilistic results. Although it is still widely accepted that no two people have the same fingerprints, it is now known that the same finger does not produce the same print twice in a row and that the impression of a small area of a fingerprint may match any number of different fingers.

In 2000 Federal Rule of Evidence 702 (see Appendix C) was amended to incorporate reliability tests mandated by *Daubert*. Many of the states that have adopted the *Daubert* decision will likely make similar amendments to their evidence rules. The amendment to Rule 702 has already resulted in changes in how scientific evidence is received. For example, the horizontal gaze nystagmus (HGN) sobriety test (discussed below) was once such well-regarded scientific evidence that courts took judicial notice of its reliability.[20] Since the amendments to Rule 702, however, courts have taken a more cautious approach to that test. In *United States v. Horn*,[21] the court refused to take judicial notice of the reliability of the HGN test and permitted the introduction of test results only as evidence of probable cause for arrest, not as proof of intoxication.

THE USE OF JUDICIAL NOTICE FOR ACCEPTED SCIENTIFIC TECHNIQUES

After a scientific technique has been found by the highest court to be reliable under Rule 702 or the standard required in a specific state, judicial notice can be made of that court's ruling. As a result, the reliability of the technique itself need not be established, although its application in the case at issue could be attacked.

In the 1993 case of *United States v. Jakobetz*,[22] a woman was abducted from a rest area along Interstate 91 in Vermont. After she was repeatedly raped, the woman was released in New York. The federal trial court used Rule 702 in admitting DNA evidence in the trial of the defendant. In holding that the scientific technique was reliable and did not unfairly prejudice the defendant's case, the Second Circuit Court of Appeals stated:

> [I]t appears that in future cases with a similar evidentiary issue, a court could properly *take judicial notice of the general acceptability of the general theory and the use of these specific techniques.* Beyond such judicial notice, the threshold for admissibility should require only a preliminary showing of reliability of the particular data to be offered, i.e., some indication of how the laboratory work was done and what analysis and assumptions underlie the probability calculations.... *Affidavits should normally suffice to provide a sufficient basis for admissibility.* (emphasis added)

The extent to which judicial notice of a scientific theory is taken can change. For example, the science of handwriting analysis has been the subject of judicial notice.[23] However, as a result of the *Daubert* case and independent handwriting analysis studies,[24] handwriting expert testimony has come under attack. One court concluded that handwriting analysis is not scientific knowledge at all but only technical knowledge.[25] After the *Kumho* decision, which made *Daubert*'s rules applicable to technical evidence, expert handwriting testimony has to meet the *Daubert* reliability tests. The following case illustrates how expert handwriting evidence can satisfy the *Daubert* reliability test.

United States v. Crisp

Fourth Circuit Court of Appeals, 324 F.3d 261 (2003), *cert. denied*, 124 S.Ct. 220 (2003)

Crisp was charged with bank robbery with a dangerous weapon. Part of the evidence against him included the note used by the robber during the bank robbery. The prosecution produced a handwriting expert, who had examined both the note and a sample of Crisp's handwriting given for purposes of the examination. Over Crisp's objection under *Daubert*, the expert was permitted to testify. Crisp was convicted and on appeal contended that the trial court was wrong in admitting the handwriting expert's testimony:

> Crisp contends that, like fingerprinting identifications, the basic premise behind handwriting analysis is that no two persons write alike, and thus that forensic document examiners can reliably determine authorship of a particular document by comparing it with known samples. He maintains that these basic premises have not been tested, nor has any error rate been established. In addition, he asserts that handwriting experts have no numerical standards to govern their analyses and that they have not subjected themselves and their science to critical self-examination and study.

The court rejected these contentions. It noted that the expert, Officer Currin, had 24 years of experience with the North Carolina State Bureau of Investigation. Currin testified that every questioned document was first examined by a "questioned document examiner" and then reviewed by another examiner. He testified that he had passed numerous proficiency tests in handwriting analysis and that document examiners followed a "consistent methodology of handwriting examination." He also testified that studies existed showing that experienced document examiners consistently scored higher on identification of handwriting than laypersons.

Based on this testimony, the court concluded that handwriting analysis was reliable scientific knowledge and admissible. It also noted that every circuit court of appeals that addressed the question after the *Daubert* decision had reached the same conclusion.

The court gave the following description of Currin's tests of the handwriting samples, and the reasons given by him for his expert opinion:

> At trial, Currin drew the jury's attention to similarities between Crisp's known handwriting exemplars and the writing on the Note. Among the similarities that he pointed out were the overall size and spacing of the letters and words in the documents; the unique shaping of the capital letter "L" in the name "Lamont"; the spacing between the capital letter "L" and the rest of the word; a peculiar shaping to the letters "o" and "n" when used in conjunction with one another; the v-like formation of the letter "u" in the word "you"; and the shape of the letter "t", including the horizontal stroke. Currin also noted that the word "tomorrow" was misspelled in the same manner on both the known exemplar and the Note.

The court affirmed the defendant's conviction.

A FEW OF THE SCIENCES AND SCIENTIFIC TECHNIQUES USED IN THE CRIMINAL JUSTICE SYSTEM

Scientific evidence covers a range of evidence that varies widely in probative value, weight, and persuasiveness. Some sciences permit the formulation of an opinion with almost mathematical certainty, whereas others are less precise and become more of an art than a science. For example, polygraph testing is widely used in the United States, yet very few state courts permit the results of lie detector tests to be used as evidence because of the reasons stated in Chapter 12.

A scientific theory that was novel only a few years ago but is now widely accepted by the scientific, legal, and law enforcement community is the DNA test

Providing paternity testing is only one of the services that private DNA companies offer. A number of DNA profile companies also provide information about a person's ancestry and the risks of developing certain genetic diseases. It is reported that the price of this service was reduced to $399 in 2008 by one company. (See "DNA Profile Provider Is Cutting Its Prices," *New York Times*, September 9, 2008.)

and technique. DNA easily passes the *Daubert* test. It is reported that DNA was first used as evidence in a criminal court in 1987, and the FBI first began analyzing DNA in casework in 1996.

DNA GENETIC PROFILING

forensic
Belonging to or connected with a court; for example, forensic fingerprints are fingerprints used as evidence in a civil or criminal trial.

DNA genetic profiling
A method for identifying individuals by the unique structure of their DNA; used for both identifying the person who committed a crime and clearing innocent suspects.

locus points
A point in the sequence of base pairs in human DNA where individual DNA chains vary.

Deoxyribonucleic acid (DNA) testing has become an important **forensic** tool for linking suspects to a crime. Equally important, DNA testing has made it possible to eliminate a suspect in a crime, sometimes even after the suspect has been convicted of that crime.[26] **DNA genetic profiling** has received such wide acceptance among criminal justice professionals that it is frequently called *genetic fingerprinting*.

DNA testing is in many ways similar to fingerprint testing. In both, samples found at the crime scene or on the victim are collected and stored. In the crime of rape, where DNA testing is widely used, most police departments or hospitals have a "rape kit," in which blood or semen samples from the victim are collected and stored. This procedure begins a proper chain of custody, a vital ingredient in any DNA evidence.

Two major tests are used on DNA: polymerase chain reaction (PCR) (see the figure) and restriction fragment length polymorphism (RFLP) analysis. Although these tests are conducted differently, they have a common goal: to identify the genetic code in the crime-scene sample and compare it with the genetic code in the suspect's (and victim's) samples.

The human body consists of billions of cells, most of which carry chromosomal DNA. Human genetic information is encoded in the DNA found in chromosomes. The DNA in chromosomes is arranged in a sequence of paired organic bases, called base pairs, which form the well-known twisted double-helix DNA chain. A set of chromosomes (one from the mother, one from the father) might contain 3 billion of these base pairs arranged in sequences on the DNA chain. Knowledge about these sequences in chromosomes makes DNA matching possible.

If we compare DNA chains from two people who are not identical twins, we discover two things. First, the chains, or sequences of base pairs, are identical for more than 99 percent of the base pairs. Humans are, after all, more alike than different. Second, at certain identifiable sites, called **locus points**, base pairs vary from one

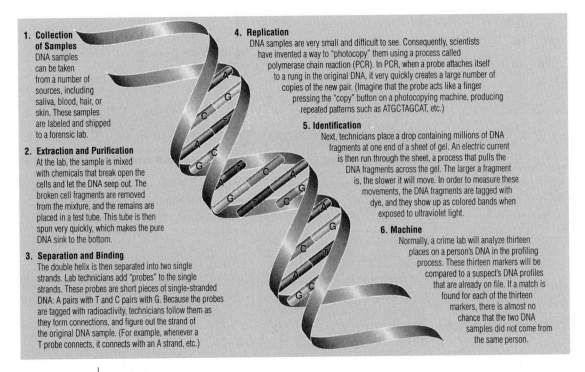

1. Collection of Samples
DNA samples can be taken from a number of sources, including saliva, blood, hair, or skin. These samples are labeled and shipped to a forensic lab.

2. Extraction and Purification
At the lab, the sample is mixed with chemicals that break open the cells and let the DNA seep out. The broken cell fragments are removed from the mixture, and the remains are placed in a test tube. This tube is then spun very quickly, which makes the pure DNA sink to the bottom.

3. Separation and Binding
The double helix is then separated into two single strands. Lab technicians add "probes" to the single strands. These probes are short pieces of single-stranded DNA: A pairs with T and C pairs with G. Because the probes are tagged with radioactivity, technicians follow them as they form connections, and figure out the strand of the original DNA sample. (For example, whenever a T probe connects, it connects with an A strand, etc.)

4. Replication
DNA samples are very small and difficult to see. Consequently, scientists have invented a way to "photocopy" them using a process called polymerase chain reaction (PCR). In PCR, when a probe attaches itself to a rung in the original DNA, it very quickly creates a large number of copies of the new pair. (Imagine that the probe acts like a finger pressing the "copy" button on a photocopying machine, producing repeated patterns such as ATGCTAGCAT, etc.)

5. Identification
Next, technicians place a drop containing millions of DNA fragments at one end of a sheet of gel. An electric current is then run through the sheet, a process that pulls the DNA fragments across the gel. The larger a fragment is, the slower it will move. In order to measure these movements, the DNA fragments are tagged with dye, and they show up as colored bands when exposed to ultraviolet light.

6. Machine
Normally, a crime lab will analyze thirteen places on a person's DNA in the profiling process. These thirteen markers will be compared to a suspect's DNA profiles that are already on file. If a match is found for each of the thirteen markers, there is almost no chance that the two DNA samples did not come from the same person.

FIGURE 18.1 | THE POLYMERASE CHAIN REACTION

Source: L. Gaines and R. Miller, *Criminal Justice in Action,* 4th ed. (Belmont, CA: Wadsworth, 2002).

individual to another. At such a locus, for example, where eye color is determined, base pairs join in a sequence that is repeated; measuring the size of a repetitive sequence of base pairs at many such locations gives a fingerprint-like picture of the DNA chain, since at these locations the sequence of base pairs varies among different individuals. Thus, like fingerprints, if we have a picture of enough of these locations where human DNA varies, then we have an individual's genetic fingerprint.

When a suspect's DNA profile matches the crime-scene sample's DNA profile, it means that the two profiles appear the same at several key points in the DNA chain where individual differences occur. Because databases do not have millions of individual DNA profiles on file, one cannot simply search a database and see whether another person's DNA profile matches the suspect's. Instead, DNA profiles taken from a selected sample of the population are compared with the suspect's profile. Based on the number of times at each of the locus points tested a match in the selected sample is found, a probability estimate can be made.

Experts who perform DNA tests and later testify to test results and meaning usually give probability estimates, taking into account different population samples, as the following example demonstrates:

Deoxyribonucleic acid (DNA) profiles for [the specific sites tested] were developed from specimens obtained from the crime scene, from the victim, and from the suspect. Based on these results, the DNA profiles from the crime scene match those of the suspect. The

DNA is the hereditary material that contains instructions to build a human being. DNA can be collected from very small amounts of blood, mouth (cheek) scrapings, hair roots, or other samples. There are two kinds of DNA in the body: nuclear DNA and mitochondrial DNA. Both kinds of DNA can be used for DNA identification.

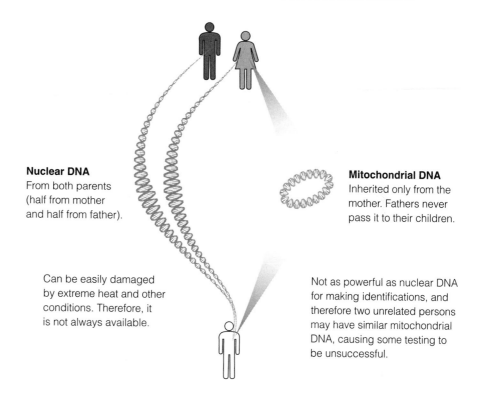

Nuclear DNA
From both parents (half from mother and half from father).

Can be easily damaged by extreme heat and other conditions. Therefore, it is not always available.

Mitochondrial DNA
Inherited only from the mother. Fathers never pass it to their children.

Not as powerful as nuclear DNA for making identifications, and therefore two unrelated persons may have similar mitochondrial DNA, causing some testing to be unsuccessful.

Sources of other DNA samples include bone marrow, biopsy samples, and toothbrush and hairbrush samples. (Urine samples will not work.)

FIGURE 18.2 | TYPES AND SOURCES OF DNA

Source: NCJ 209493, *Identifying Victims Using DNA* (2005).

probability of selecting at random from the population an unrelated individual having a DNA profile matching the suspect's is approximately 1 in 200,000 in Blacks, 1 in 200,000 in Whites, and 1 in 100,000 in Hispanics.[27]

At present, DNA profiles have a wide variety of uses:

- To identify air crash victims and other dead people from bits of bones or charred flesh. For example, casualties from Operation Desert Storm and the Vietnam War have been identified by obtaining DNA samples from family members. Bones thought to be from former Russian Czar Nicholas II and his family, who were executed in 1917, were proven to be the remains of the Russian royal family through blood donated by British Prince Philip, who is a distant relative of the former Russian royalty.[28]

Cases Where DNA Evidence Did Not Carry the Burden of Proof

DNA evidence has had a remarkable record of success since it was first used in 1987. It must be remembered, however, that DNA is available in only about 10 percent of crimes committed because sweat, saliva, skin, blood, or some other bodily substance must be found on the victim or at the crime scene in order to create a DNA "fingerprint." Moreover, even where DNA evidence is available, it still is subject to burden of proof requirements, as the following two situations demonstrate:

- In the O.J. Simpson murder trial, investigators stated they had never seen as much blood at a crime scene as was found near the bodies of Nicole Simpson and Ronald Goldman. Both victims resisted the knife attack, and their blood covered the crime scene. A third person's blood was also found at the scene, and DNA tests showed that the blood came from Simpson. Simpson's attorneys did not attack the DNA evidence itself, but rather the way in which investigators collected the evidence. Simpson was found not guilty by a jury in the criminal trial, but subsequently the Goldman family obtained a multimillion-dollar civil judgment against Simpson. The Goldmans have collected little of that judgment. Simpson was convicted in 2008 on charges of robbery and kidnapping; in December 2008 he was sentenced to 16 years in prison. In

2002 a private company hired by the California Department of Justice donated its DNA papers on the 100 items of bloodstained evidence taken in the murder case to the Smithsonian Institution's anthropological archives, where they will join the museum's extensive collection of forensic material. [See "Simpson's Papers Go to Smithsonian," *The New York Times* (May 18, 2002).]

- In 1975 former Teamsters Union president James (Jimmy) Hoffa disappeared from the parking lot of an exclusive restaurant during the lunch hour. Because of Hoffa's reputed connection to organized crime, many persons believed he was the subject of a mafia "hit." In 2002 FBI scientists, using new technology, were able to match the DNA from Hoffa's hair to a strand of hair found in a vehicle owned by a reputed mafia family. On the day of Hoffa's disappearance, the car had been loaned to a friend of Hoffa to make a delivery, which placed the friend and the car in the vicinity of the restaurant where Hoffa disappeared. The prosecutors concluded that after 27 years, there was not enough evidence to bring criminal charges. [See "Hoffa DNA Evidence Not Enough for State Charges," *Milwaukee Journal-Sentinel* (August 20, 2002).]

- To identify offenders from blood, semen, and hair left at the scene of a crime. The FBI reports that more than 80 percent of the DNA samples they receive from state and local police are from rape cases.
- To clear suspects who are innocent. The FBI reports that in 20–25 percent of the cases sent to them, the suspect is cleared. An FBI official stated that in one case the standard blood tests did not eliminate the suspect and two victims of a serial rapist had identified the suspect, with "one of them fairly positive. He certainly would have gone to trial and probably would have been convicted, but the DNA evidence eliminated him as a suspect."[29]
- To establish proof of corpus delicti, which is proof that a crime was committed. Missing persons are a problem in every American city. To charge murder, the state must prove that the missing person is dead and was killed by the defendant. In the 1991 case of *State v. Davis*,[30] a woman was missing. She was

last seen going to work, but her body was never found. However, DNA from dried blood, skull bone fragments, and blood-encrusted tissue was compared with DNA from her children and husband and showed that the woman had been murdered. The conviction of her husband was affirmed.

- To identify missing persons. More than 88,000 U.S. people who served in the Vietnam War, the Korean War, and World War II are still missing. The military services are asking family members of people listed as missing to submit DNA samples to aid in identifying the remains found. Each service has its own casualty office. The telephone number for the U.S. Army office is 800-892-2490.

The armed forces of the United States are building a DNA database by collecting blood and saliva from all service personnel. The reason for this databank is that military dog tags can be lost, switched, or counterfeited and fingerprinting and dental records are not always reliable.

The creation of DNA databases also affects statutes of limitation. Many states are abolishing, extending, or amending their statutes of limitation for rape; in other states, prosecutors are issuing John Doe criminal complaints or obtaining John Doe indictments when it is determined that they have probable cause based on DNA evidence. New York prosecutors obtained rape indictments against an unknown serial rapist known as the "East Side Rapist" in March 2000. In October 1999 Wisconsin prosecutors filed three rape charges against a man known only by his DNA code, to avoid the expiration of the Wisconsin statute of limitations, and in 1991 Kansas prosecutors filed one rape charge based only on DNA evidence.

DNA Forensic Laboratories and the Work They Do   There are now hundreds of state, federal, and private DNA laboratories in the United States, many of which do only forensic work for law enforcement agencies. The work of these forensic DNA labs is generally of two types: (1) casework on pending criminal cases and (2) classification of DNA samples taken from persons convicted of certain serious offenses.

In addition to fingerprinting, it is now standard practice for state and federal officers to take blood samples from felons who have been convicted of serious offenses, such as rape, homicide, or sexual assault, and those who are serving prison terms for such offenses. These samples are then stored in state and federal databanks. Pursuant to federal statute,[31] the FBI maintains a national DNA database, the Combined DNA Index System (CODIS). Many states maintain similar systems. Blood samples taken from convicted felons are analyzed and classified according to the samples' DNA. The samples' DNA can then be compared with any DNA evidence found in prior or subsequent crimes and help law enforcement officers identify suspects.

The U.S. Circuit Courts of Appeals have all sustained attacks against CODIS and the mandatory collection of blood samples under the federal statute. For example, in the 2004 case of *United States v. Kincade*,[32] the full Ninth Circuit Court of Appeals sitting *en banc* vacated a decision of a Ninth Circuit Court panel that found unconstitutional the mandatory collection of blood samples under the federal statute. In *Kincade*, a paroled felon refused to give a blood sample when requested to do so as a condition of his parole. He was accordingly sentenced to serve additional prison time, and the period of his supervised release was extended. He appealed, alleging that the mandatory blood sample statute violated his Fourth Amendment rights because it amounted to a search without any showing of an "individualized suspicion" that a crime had occurred. The

OTHER WAYS OF USING DNA EVIDENCE TO IDENTIFY SUSPECTS

DNA Source or Technique	**Use of DNA Evidence**
Using a close DNA match as an investigative lead	Not all persons who commit violent crimes have DNA samples in either state or national databases, and as a result the DNA found at a crime scene may not have a perfect "match" in a DNA database. However, that DNA might be a close match to the DNA of a person who is in a database. Because close relatives have closely matching DNA profiles, investigators who find a close match may then concentrate their investigation on relatives of the person in the DNA database.
Using surreptitious sampling	When the DNA of a suspect or a person of interest is not in a national or state databank, police sometimes attempt "surreptitious sampling" to obtain the biological material necessary for a DNA profile. A minute amount of saliva, sweat, or other bodily fluid is sufficient for a laboratory to project a full DNA profile, which may clear or incriminate the person. Objects that are thrown away, abandoned, or left behind may possibly provide sufficient genetic material. The "abandoned" material could be a discarded tissue, cigarette butt, soda can, coffee cup, straw, fork, or napkin with a minute amount of biological material. Lower courts have generally held that persons who discard such genetic material have no subjective expectation of privacy in the material object.
	In a 2007 Washington State case, Seattle police sent a murder suspect a fictitious letter inviting him to join a class-action lawsuit with a return envelope. The DNA on the return envelope (sealed by the suspect) matched the DNA in the semen found at the scene of the 1982 rape and murder of a 13-year-old Seattle girl.
	In Buffalo, New York, police waited until a person of interest left a restaurant and then obtained the suspect's glass. The DNA profile was used as evidence to convict the suspect of the murder of three women.
Using animal DNA to link a suspect to a crime scene or to a victim of a crime	Animals also have distinct DNA fingerprints. Because animals constantly shed hair, animal hair is found at crime scenes where animals have been kept. The hair is on furniture, rugs, carpets, and the clothing of persons in the home.
	A criminal coming onto the property could pick up not only hair on his clothing and shoes but also saliva, feces, or animal blood, which could be critical evidence in linking him to the crime scene and victim.

Ninth Circuit Court panel that first heard his appeal agreed, finding that because taking a blood sample constitutes a search, there must be some degree of reasonable suspicion of criminal activity before the blood sample could be required.[33]

On rehearing before the full Ninth Circuit Court, the decision of the panel was vacated, and the statute was upheld. The court stated that the blood sample requirement could be sustained on either of two bases: (1) the "search was reasonable" under the Fourth Amendment rules, and (2) "special needs" justified the search without any "individualized suspicion." Because a convicted felon or parolee has a diminished expectation of privacy and can be required to keep the government informed of his identity and location, the court held that the mandatory blood sample requirement met the reasonableness requirement of the Fourth Amendment. The court noted that other federal courts had upheld the statute under the "special needs" analysis, finding that the interest the government has in maintaining knowledge about the identity of convicted criminals was a "special need" that justified the statute.[34] State statutes requiring such procedures have also been sustained by state courts when challenged.[35]

DNA evidence has been an important development in criminal investigations. In the 2005 case of *United States v. Sczubelek*,[36] the court made the following comments about the role and importance of DNA testing:

> DNA testing has changed the criminal justice system. All 50 states and the federal government have enacted DNA collection and database statutes. To date, 143 people have been exonerated by DNA evidence, thirteen of whom were sentenced to death. 38 states have enacted some form of a DNA statute, allowing for post-conviction DNA testing, compensation for wrongful conviction, or preservation of evidence. In 2003 the House of Representatives passed the Advancing Justice Through DNA Technology Act (HR3214), a federal statute which would give prisoners the right to petition for DNA testing in support of a claim of innocence.

An example of how a DNA database was used to aid law enforcement officers in solving a crime is a 2002 bank robbery that occurred in Milwaukee, Wisconsin. The bank robbery was well planned and well executed, leaving little evidence for the police. However, one of the bank robbers left gloves that he wore during the robbery in a car stolen for that robbery. Sweat residue from the robber's hands remained in the gloves, enabling investigators to conduct DNA tests. The test results were compared with DNA samples stored in a DNA database, and a match was found. The police arrested the man identified in the database, and after the police showed him the DNA results and offered him a plea bargain, he pled guilty and identified the other robber, who also pled guilty.[37]

In addition to DNA forensic evidence work, crime labs do work in many other scientific fields to produce evidence for law enforcement agencies. The U.S. Department of Justice (NCJ 191191) lists the following kinds of work done by crime labs, in the order of most to least evidence handled:

1. Controlled substance evidence
2. Firearm/tool mark/footwear/tire print evidence
3. Fire debris for arson analysis
4. Crime-scene material
5. Latent fingerprints
6. Blood alcohol evidence
7. Serology (analysis of blood spattering, rape kits, etc.)
8. Explosive residue
9. Toxicology (fluid analysis, such as blood, saliva, semen, etc.)
10. Questioned documents (see Chapter 17)
11. Computer crime investigations
12. Others

DETERMINING THE TIME OF DEATH IN CRIMINAL CASES

When law enforcement officers arrive at a crime scene where a dead person has been found, it is important to the investigation that the officers determine the time the death occurred. Witnesses might be available to provide information about the victim's movements, or an estimate might be made at the crime scene based on the lividity of the body or the advance of rigor mortis.

Lividity and Rigor Mortis   *Lividity* is the process of blood settlement within a body after death. Within 30 minutes of death, gravity causes the blood in the body to settle in the lowest part. A body found on its back will have blood gathered in the body's back surfaces. By looking at the state of lividity, investigators can sometimes determine how long the victim has been dead and in what position he or she died.

Rigor mortis is the stiffening of the body's muscles that occurs after death. Human bodies produce a substance called adenosine triphosphate, which enables energy to flow to the muscles. At death, this substance is no longer produced, and as a result the muscles begin to stiffen. This process affects the small muscles, such as those in the face or neck, first and becomes noticeable within about 2 hours of death. By looking at the extent to which rigor mortis has set in, investigators can sometimes determine how long the victim has been dead.

Investigators at the crime scene must determine whether the death was accidental, by natural causes, or a homicide, and knowing the time of death is critical to that determination. Where neither lividity nor rigor mortis can accurately determine the time of death, investigators may look to forensic entomology to estimate the time of death.

forensic entomology
The study of insects to provide scientific evidence to aid legal investigations.

Forensic Entomology   Entomology is the study of insects. **Forensic entomology** is used to determine the amount of time that has passed since a person's death and also other facts surrounding the death, such as location, placement, movement of the body, and the manner of death.

Because insects can be present on a cadaver for as long as two and a half years, entomological analysis can provide useful information (evidence) concerning the cause and manner of death as well as the approximate time of death when bodies are found or missing persons are found dead.

Extensive studies and experiments have identified five stages in the decomposition process of human corpses and animal remains:

1. *Fresh stage:* In warm temperatures, blowflies can arrive within 10 minutes of death.
2. *Bloated stage:* The body inflates as the result of the release of gas from bacterial composition in the body.
3. *Decay stage:* The odors of decomposition are overwhelming.
4. *Post-decay stage:* Insects such as cloth moths and hide beetles are present.
5. *Skeletal stage:* Insects are usually gone except for wasps and spiders; animals such as mice, foxes, and dogs gnaw on and scatter bones.

The presence of insects in a body can provide information to investigators about many circumstances surrounding the body and the crime scene in which the body was found. Investigators can learn about the time of death and the movement of the body:

- *Time of death (postmortem interval, or PMI):* From controlled laboratory studies, it can be determined exactly, at various temperatures, how long it takes a fly's eggs to hatch, a maggot to grow through its three larval stages, or a fly pupa to mature into an adult. By observing the presence of these insects and the body's stage of decomposition, investigators can establish the length of the decomposition process. They can then reach a close approximation of the time of death.
- *Movement of the body:* It is important in a homicide investigation to determine whether a body has been moved after death has occurred. Entomologists can assist in this determination by identifying the habitat of insects present in the body. Forest, meadow, swamp, farm field, and water-based insects are normally not found in urban areas. The presence of these insects in a body found on a city street, for example, might indicate that the body was moved from another place. Also, the presence of some insects in the body could indicate the time of year the crime took place. Because some insects that have fed on a corpse, such as maggots, retain traces of chemicals taken from the corpse, testing for chemicals in the insects can assist investigators in determining whether those chemicals were present in the corpse.

Entomological evidence is widely accepted as scientific evidence in courts. A May 2002 U.S. Department of Justice publication (NCJ 191717) used the following example to illustrate. An Oklahoma woman's claim about when she last saw her husband was disproved by the third-stage maggot accumulation on his body. The analysis included critical climatological data, the time delay from death until colonization, the effect of the maggot mass temperature on development, and the nocturnal absence of blowflies. The woman was eventually convicted of murdering her husband.

Forensic examination and forensic entomology can provide information that aids investigators in identifying unidentified bodies that are found. Assistance in identifying bodies can also be obtained from the Forensic Anthropology Computer Enhancement Service (FACES) laboratory, which can construct a clay model of what the victim's face may have looked like. Photographs of the clay model and any clothing, jewelry, or available personal belongings are then shown on the FBI website at http://www.fbi.gov/mostwant/seekinfo/seek.htm. Identity can be confirmed by DNA testing.

BALLISTIC FINGERPRINTING OR FIREARM FINGERPRINTING

Because 40 percent of criminal homicides go unsolved, identification of the weapons used by the criminal is critical. With 200 million guns in public hands and an estimated 30,000 gangs with 800,000 members, drive-by shootings and other violent crimes have become all too common. It is often vital to an investigation to link the weapon used in a crime to the person who used it. Moreover, rapid identification of a weapon may also permit law enforcement officers to prevent further killings.

In the 2002 sniper shootings near Washington, DC, law enforcement officers, national guard troops, and medical personnel worked together to try to identify the sniper. The victims were hit by .223-caliber bullets moving at about 2,000 miles per hour, which on impact caused the bullet to shatter into fragments inside the victim. Emergency medical workers as well as doctors and nurses at hospitals where the gunshot victims were taken treated the victim as a "crime scene" and attempted to find bullet fragments for transfer to the U.S. Bureau of Alcohol, Firearms, Tobacco and Explosives (ATF) ballistics laboratory in Rockville, Maryland.[38] It was hoped that tests on the bullet fragments could result in a match with data on weapons maintained by state and federal law enforcement agencies.

ballistic fingerprinting Identification of the gun that fired a bullet from an analysis of the unique marks that every gun makes on the bullet it fires and on the shell ejected from it.

These tests, called **ballistic fingerprinting**, can sometimes lead to a match between the bullet fragments and the weapon used to fire the bullet, but there are limitations on the usefulness of such tests. First, in the case of bullet fragments, unless the bullet recovered is substantial, marks on the bullet may match rifling marks in multiple weapons. One observer compared this to finding a shoe print of a size 10 Nike shoe at a crime scene: Too many shoes would match the print to make it worthwhile.

Second, even if a substantial bullet is found at a crime scene, it is helpful only if it can be compared to weapons data maintained by law enforcement agencies. Although a national database that includes rifling data on every new weapon manufactured has been proposed, groups such as the National Rifle Association have fought efforts to create such a database. A few states have compiled a database of guns used in crimes in those states, but no national database exists.[39] In 2003, after conducting about 2,500 bullet-lead tests of bullets recovered from crime scenes, the FBI notified some 300 law enforcement agencies that it was abandoning tests that attempted to identify the chemical composition of a bullet and match it with the gun that fired it.[40]

It is possible to match a shell casing found at a crime scene to the gun that fired it based on "tool" marks impressed on the shell casing. When a gun is fired, expanding gases in the barrel cause the cartridge shell to forcefully strike parts of the rifle. This collision results in tool marks from the rifle being impressed on the shell casing, and then the casing and the rifle can be matched by scientific testing.[41] Like bullet fragment matching, however, a shell casing is helpful only if a database of rifle markings exists. There has been encouragement for a law that creates a national database that would require every gun manufactured to have a microstamp inside the gun that would enable the gun to be matched to a shell casing,[42] but again organizations like the NRA have resisted microstamping.

In 2007 Governor Arnold Schwarzenegger of California signed a law requiring that, beginning in 2010, all new semiautomatic pistols sold in California must be microstamped to permit police to match shell casings to the pistols that fired them. The new law is prospective only and does not require retrofitting for existing guns.

SOURCES OF OTHER SCIENTIFIC EVIDENCE

Almost every known science and sometimes what is called "junk science"[43] have been presented to courts for use as evidence. The U.S. Supreme Court has stressed the obligation of trial judges as gatekeepers to screen expert witnesses so

OBTAINING EVIDENCE FROM DRUG TESTING

A 2002 study by the National Highway Traffic Safety Administration and the Robert Wood Johnson Foundation estimated that 9 million Americans a year drive while under the influence of illegal drugs.

It has been recognized for some time that drunk drivers are detected far more often than drugged drivers, even though both are very serious dangers on American highways. In 2003 only eight states had laws that made it illegal for a person to drive with any measurable amount of illegal drugs in his or her system. In the other states, prosecutors must prove that the illegal drugs caused the reckless conduct for which a driver was stopped. This is very difficult to prove in many cases. The following chart describes samples that may be used for drug testing:

Sample Used for Testing	Advantages	Detection Times	Disadvantages
Urine—privacy intrusion	Is accurate and economical; contains high concentrations of drugs used by person	Hours to days	Cannot indicate blood levels; is easy to falsify
Blood—highly invasive	Indicates the extent of the person's impairment at the time the sample is taken	Variable	Not recommended for use as evidence in court because of the potential for infection
Breath—noninvasive	Indicates ethanol concentrations and the extent of the person's impairment from alcohol (not other drugs)	Hours	Very short time frame for detection; detects only volatile compounds
Hair	Indicates long-term drug use; is difficult to adulterate	Weeks to months	Can be contaminated by external products; has a potential racial bias because dark pigmented hair absorbs drugs more readily than blonde or bleached hair
Sweat—obtained from patches placed on person for days	Is difficult to adulterate	Days to weeks	May be biased because persons differ in manner of sweat production
Saliva—easily obtained	Provides estimates of blood levels and indicates degree of impairment	Hours to days	Can be contaminated by smoking and other substances as well as pH changes

Sources: "Drug Testing in a Drug Court Environment," NCJ 1811103 (May 2000); "Many, Undetected, Use Drugs and Then Drive, Report Says," *The New York Times* (November 15, 2002).

COMPUTER SYSTEMS USED BY LAW ENFORCEMENT

Large American cities have increased their use of computers to perform the functions listed here:[a]

- All large departments use computer-aided dispatch systems.
- Enhanced 911 emergency systems are capable of pinpointing a caller's location automatically.
- Almost all large departments use in-field computers or terminals.
- Almost all have exclusive or shared ownership of an Automated Fingerprint Identification System (AFIS), which matches fingerprints from a crime scene with a known person (if the person's fingerprints are on file) within minutes.
- The National Crime Information Center (NCIC) provides information to police agencies on wanted suspects, stolen firearms, stolen property and securities, unidentified bodies, and computerized criminal histories. Members enter information into the system for use by other law enforcement agencies.

During the twenty-one days in which snipers terrorized the Washington, DC, area, investigators from a dozen law agencies worked together,

sharing ballistics testing information, geographic and criminal profiling, thousands of tips from citizens, and police files and computer information. To coordinate all of this information, an Internet-based system called Coplink was used that allows police agencies to establish links quickly to their own files and to those of other departments. With resources from the military, federal, state, and local departments, Coplink interconnected files through new computer systems.

Will evidence be excluded if computer error is attributed to court officials rather than to a police record-keeping system?

The purpose of the exclusionary rule is to deter police misconduct. The U.S. Supreme Court held in the 1995 case of *Arizona v. Evans* [115 S.Ct. 1185] that the rule does not apply when the mistake is made by employees of a court. Evidence, therefore, can be used under the good faith exception when the police rely on computerized information.

[a]See the U.S. Department of Justice report NCJ 175703 (May 2002).

that unreliable evidence is not presented to juries and judges. Since *Daubert*, the U.S. Supreme Court has issued two additional opinions dealing with the admissibility of scientific evidence.[44]

Other scientific evidence used regularly in courts throughout the United States includes:

- *Tests for alcohol intoxication:* Used in drunk-driving and other cases. It is necessary in most cases to present evidence showing that the officer had probable cause to arrest the defendant for operating under the influence. This is done by having the officer and in some cases witnesses testify about what they saw and smelled. Field tests include performance tests, the horizontal gaze nystagmus (HGN) test,[45] and alcohol screening devices that sample the air around the suspect, including air from the person. Video pictures of the driver or other person may also be used as evidence. If probable cause exists, the driver is then arrested and informed that under the "implied consent" statute

CORRELATING, COORDINATING, AND COLLECTING EVIDENCE

The following agencies, technology, and databases assist law enforcement officials in gathering and analyzing evidence:

- *National Law Enforcement Data Exchange System (N-Dex):* N-Dex correlates data from all major FBI databases. It provides "one-stop shopping," where an initial search provides combined data in about 30 seconds. Information on crimes from different states and cities can identify trends and allow immediate response. FBI Director Robert Mueller said of the new system: It "provides unprecedented access to information allowing us to link cases, solve crimes, and form broader investigative partnerships." N-Dex began operation in 2005.

- *Terrorist Screening Center:* Begun in December 2004 and operating 24 hours a day, 7 days a week, the center maintains the most up-to-date terrorist watch list in the United States and enables federal, state, and local officials to respond quickly where a known or suspected terrorist is encountered during a routine law enforcement stop or in an airport, bus, or train station. The center provides a strong link between the FBI, military, and civil intelligence agencies and state and local law enforcement.

- *Combined DNA Index System (CODIS):* CODIS has been in operation since 1998, and during the first 6 years helped solve or aided in more than 18,000 investigations nationwide. DNA technology has helped solve serial rape cases that were more than 25 years old. Because of CODIS, rapists or killers who travel from state to state can be apprehended more easily.

- *National Gang Threat Assessment and Database:* The database helps coordinate and target efforts against the more than 20,000 active gangs operating in the United States. Gangs are getting bigger, more organized, and more violent. From 1992 through 2003, there were more than 8,000 gang-related criminal homicides in California alone. The database provides information and links that coordinate federal, state, and local law enforcement agencies.

- *Hazardous Devices School:* Located in Redstone Arsenal, Alabama, the school provides training, information, and instruction on the latest tools and techniques for confronting suicide bombers, large vehicle bombs, weapons of mass destruction, and other threats. The FBI trains more than 1,100 students every year at the school and has provided millions of dollars of equipment for more than 400 bomb squads in the United States.

- *Federal Bureau of Investigation (FBI):* The **Laboratory Division** provides technical and scientific response and forensic support to investigations that involve hazardous materials, including weapons of mass destruction. It offers the capability to disrupt explosive devices and perform forensic examination of explosives in postblast situations. The division also provides expertise in processing crime scenes. The **Engineering Research Facility (ERF)** supplies technical support for secure and nonsecure communications, computer hardware and software, and feasibility assessments for proposed command post sites. The **Critical Incident Response Group (CIRG)** provides subject-matter expertise in counterterrorism tactics, crisis management, hostage negotiations, logistics, and behavioral analysis. **FBI Headquarters** offers language specialists, intelligence analysis, and activation of the Strategic Information and Operations Center (SIOC) in support of special events. The **Cyber Division** evaluates emerging cyber threats and performs forensic examinations of digital evidence. The **Counterterrorism Division** provides financial and administrative support.

of that state or jurisdiction, the person is obligated to submit to a breathalyzer test, a blood-alcohol test, or a urine test.

- *Fire and explosive science evidence:* Used in arson and civil lawsuit cases.
- *Forensic pathology:* Used in determining the cause of death, time of death, and identity of the deceased.
- *Chemistry, toxicology, serology, and hematology tests:* Used for identifying blood stains, human blood types, blood spatters, and age of blood stains; for identifying seminal fluid, sperm cells, saliva, fecal matter, and perspiration; for identifying opiates, hallucinogens, barbiturates, and amphetamines; and for determining narcotic addiction.
- *Microanalysis:* Used to identify and compare small objects and particles, including hair, fibers, paint, glass, soil and dust, cosmetics, wood, and trace evidence.
- *Neutron activation analysis (NAA):* Used for testing gunshot residue.
- *Tests used in questioned documents:* Used for handwriting and typing comparisons, analysis of inks, examination of papers and watermarks, and forensic linguistics.
- *Scientific detection of speeding:* By use of radar, VASCAR (Visual Average Speed Computer and Recorder), and other speed detection devices.
- *Forensic odontology:* Used for identification by dental characteristics, bite-mark analysis, and dental comparisons.
- *Accident reconstruction techniques:* By use of skid marks, tire imprints, and scuff marks.
- *Physical anthropology:* Used to determine time of death and age, sex, race, and identification of victim.

SUMMARY

Science has become a very valuable tool for law enforcement. Scientific evidence is used every day in criminal and civil courts throughout the United States.

More than a hundred years ago, the sciences of chemistry and physics were combined to develop photography. Over the years, the science of photography has improved techniques and skills to develop equipment that we now take for granted. DNA testing and technology are among the new sciences used as evidence in courts today. DNA profiling was first used as evidence in a courtroom in 1987.

Scientific evidence can be used effectively to convict the guilty and to exonerate the innocent. The courts and the scientific community have adopted new standards to increase the reliability of scientific evidence used in criminal and civil courts. Specifically, in many jurisdictions the *Daubert* test has supplanted the older *Frye* test for admissibility of scientific evidence.

CASE ANALYSIS

Read Appendix B, Finding and Analyzing Cases (p. 427). With these guidelines in mind, please continue with the Case Analysis selections for Chapter 18.

1. Once a scientific method has been demonstrated to be reliable, does the party that proposes to introduce expert scientific testimony based on that method have to produce expert

testimony to establish the foundation for the method again? In *Hernandez v. State* [116 S.W.2d 26 (Tex. App. 2003)], the court held that a witness testifying about the results of a urinalysis test on a "ADx" testing machine needed to establish the scientific reliability of the machine and the test protocol used. Should the fact that the machine had been demonstrated to yield valid results in other cases permit the court to take judicial notice of its scientific reliability? Does it make sense to require a witness to "invent the wheel" all over again?

2. As the text notes, some states continue to use the *Frye* test for the admissibility of expert scientific evidence. Florida is one of those states. In *Sybers v. State* [841 So.2d 532 (Fla. App. 2003)], a Florida court held that the state's expert should not have been permitted to testify, based on the *Frye* test. What was the problem with the expert's testimony? Would a different result have been reached under the *Daubert* test?

3. How did the defendant in *United States v. Kapp* [419 F.3d 666 (7th Cir. 2005)] attempt to use animal DNA evidence? Is DNA useful for that purpose?

4. In Chapter 6 we discussed the extent to which courts may take judicial notice of a fact, including the reliability of scientific theories. May a court take judicial notice of the reliability of the scientific theory of blood-spatter analysis? At what point does a theory become so accepted as to be capable of judicial notice? See *Holmes v. State* [135 S.W.3d 178 (Tex. App. 2004)].

Notes

1. *Commonwealth v. Lykus*, 327 N.E.2d 671 (Mass. 1975), quoting *United States v. Addison*, 498 F.2d 741 (D.C. Cir. 1974).

2. See, e.g., *State v. Cortarez*, 686 P.2d 1224 (Ariz. 1984), and *Cornet v. State*, 450 N.E.2d 498 (Ind. 1983).

3. 293 Fed. 1013 (D.C. Cir. 1923).

4. 293 Fed. 1013, 1014 (D.C. Cir. 1923).

5. 509 U.S. 579 (1993).

6. 327 N.E.2d 671 (Mass. 1975).

7. *Id.* at 677.

8. 297 N.W.2d 80 (Iowa 1980).

9. 545 N.Y.S.2d 985 (Sup. Ct. 1989).

10. DNA, DNA tests, and probability estimates are discussed on pages 407–413.

11. In *Hayes v. State* [660 So. 2d 257 (Fla. 1995)], the Florida Supreme Court stated that it could take judicial notice of the general theory of DNA. It also held that one testing procedure sometimes used to explain minor variances in DNA results, the bandwidth connection procedure, was not generally accepted.

12. See, e.g., *State v. Cauthron*, 846 P.2d 502 (Wash. 1993).

13. See, e.g., *State v. Carter*, 524 N.W.2d 763 (Neb. 1994). Other courts have found the PCR test generally accepted. See *State v. Russell*, 882 P.2d 742 (Wash. 1994).

14. 509 U.S. 579 (1993).

15. 509 U.S. 592–93.

16. 119 S.Ct. 1167 (1999).

17. Hamilton, *The Movement from Frye to Daubert: Where Do the States Stand,* Jurimetrics J. 38 (1998): 201.

18. *Id.* at 209.

19. See *Daubert in the States,* SLO84 ALI-ABA 273 (2006).

20. See, e.g., *Emerson v. State*, 880 S.W.2d 759 (Tex. Crim. App. 1994).

21. 185 F.Supp.2d 530 (D. Md. 2002).

22. 955 F.2d 786 (2d Cir.).

23. See, e.g., *Greenberg Gallery Inc. v. Bauman*, 817 F.Supp. 167, 172 (D.D.C. 1993).

24. See, for example, M. Kam, G. Fielding, and R. Conn, *Written Identification by Professional Document Examiners,* J. Forensic Sci. 42(1997): 778. The Kam study found that some, but not all, handwriting professionals were superior to laypersons on matching handwriting samples. Those professionals made mistaken matches on 6.5 percent of 144 samples. Laypersons made mistaken matches on 38.3 percent of those same samples.

25. *United States v. Starzecpyzel*, 880 F.Supp. 1027 (S.O.N.Y. 1995).

26. Between 1988 and 1998, fifty-six wrongfully convicted people were exonerated based on DNA tests that showed they could not have committed the crime for which they were charged. Ten of those exonerated were awaiting the death penalty. See L. Gaines, M. Kaune, and R. Miller, *Criminal Justice in Action* (Belmont, CA: Wadsworth, 2000). That number had increased to 143 as of March 2005.

27. J. McKenna, J. Cecil, and P. Coukos, *Reference Manual on Scientific Evidence*, Federal Judicial Center (St. Paul, MN: West, 1994), p. 278.

28. See "Scientists Identify Bones as Those of the Czar," *The New York Times* (July 10, 1993), p. 1.

29. See *National District Attorneys Association Bulletin* (November 1990), 7.

30. 814 S.W.2d 593 (Mo.).

31. 42 U.S.C. § 14135.

32. 379 F.3d 813 (9th Cir. 2004), *cert. denied,* 125 S.Ct. 1638 (2005).

33. 345 F.3d 1095 (2003).

34. See, e.g., *Green v. Berge*, 354 F.3d 675 (7th Cir. 2004).

35. The constitutionality of the federal statute and similar state statutes was questioned after the U.S. Supreme Court decisions in *City of Indianapolis v. Edmonds* [531 U.S. 32 (2000)] (discussed in Chapter 11) and *Ferguson v. Charleston, S.C.* [532 U.S. 67 (2001)]. In *Edmonds,* the Court held that suspicionless roadblocks set up to discover ordinary criminal wrongdoing were unlawful under the Fourth Amendment. In *Ferguson,* the Court held that a state statute requiring pregnant women being treated at a state hospital to submit to a urine test to discover cocaine use was unconstitutional under the Fourth Amendment. In both of those cases, the Court held that the government could not conduct a search without "individualized" suspicion, if the purpose of the search was to discover or investige ordinary criminal wrongdoing. Most state and federal courts have held that *Edmonds* and *Ferguson* do not apply to mandatory DNA testing of convicted felons. For example, the court in *United States v. Reynard* [220 F.Supp.2d 1142 (S.D. Calif. 2002)] held that the primary purpose of the statute was to expand the CODIS database, which is not a law enforcement purpose. In *Groceman v. United States* [2002 WL 1398559 (N.D. Tex. 2002)], the court upheld the statute as applied to federal prison inmates. The court concluded that the diminished rights to privacy afforded to prisoners, as well as the interest of the government in identifying prisoners for the purpose of avoiding recidivism, made the statute constitutional. State courts have reached the same conclusion. See, e.g., *State v. Martinez* [78 P.3d 769 (Kan. 2003)] and *State v. Steele* [802 N.E.2d 1127 (Ohio App. 2003)].

36. 402 F.3d 175, 185 (3d Cir. 2005).

37. "DNA Helps Solve Bank Robbery," *Milwaukee Journal-Sentinel* (July 16, 2002).

38. See the articles "Sniper Case Renews Debate over Firearm Fingerprinting," *The New York Times* (October 18, 2002), and "Doctors Help Gather Evidence," *The Washington Post* (October 23, 2002).

39. See "Technology: Now, 4 States Look to Start Tracing Shells and Bullets," *The New York Times* (October 24, 2002).

40. See "FBI Bullet Tests Found to Be Flawed," *The New York Times* (November 22, 2003).

41. See, e.g., *United States v. Monteiro*, 407 F.Supp.2d 351 (D. Mass. 2006).

42. See "A Crime-Fighting Opportunity," *The New York Times* (February 15, 2008).

43. Some or all of the following could be called junk science depending on who makes the judgment call: narcoanalysis ("truth serum"), hypnosis, voice-stress analysis, polygraph (lie detector), spectrographic voice recognition, and handwriting analysis.

44. The two additional cases are *General Electric v. Joiner* [522 U.S. 136 (1997)] and *Kumho Tire Co. v. Carmichael* [526 U.S. 137 (1999)].

45. When police officers stop a driver who has been drinking beer or most other alcohol, smell will cause the officer to suspect a driving violation. Most illegal drugs do not have a smell, however, and the person's behavior may be tranquil and calm. It is therefore necessary to use the horizontal gaze test. The horizontal gaze nystagmus (HGN) test is a field sobriety test in which a person is requested to follow an object with his eyes. When a person's central nervous system is depressed by alcohol, barbiturates, phencyclidine (PCP), or certain inhalants, rapid

involuntary jerking of the eyeballs occurs as the eyes seek to follow a pencil or finger moved before them. In the 1960s California police observed this involuntary jerking in the eyes of barbiturate users. Later, East Coast law enforcement officers began applying the concept to intoxicated drivers. The HGN test is administered in conjunction with other field sobriety tests such as the one-leg-stand test and the walk-and-turn test. Many state courts have held that HGN test results can be used with other information to establish probable cause.

SECTIONS OF THE U.S. CONSTITUTION

APPLICABLE SECTIONS OF THE U.S. CONSTITUTION, RATIFIED IN 1788

PREAMBLE

We the People of the United States, in Order to form a more perfect Union, establish Justice, insure domestic Tranquility, provide for the common defence, promote the general Welfare, and secure the Blessings of Liberty to ourselves and our Posterity, do ordain and establish this CONSTITUTION for the United States of America.

ARTICLE I

Section 1. All legislative Powers herein granted shall be vested in a Congress of the United States, which shall consist of a Senate and House of Representatives...

ARTICLE II

Section 1. The executive Power shall be vested in a President of the United States of America....

ARTICLE III

Section 1. The judicial Power of the United States, shall be vested in one supreme Court, and in such inferior Courts as the Congress may from time to time ordain and establish....

ARTICLE IV

Section 4. The United States shall guarantee to every State in this Union a Republican Form of Government, and shall protect each of them against Invasion; and on Application of the Legislature, or of the Executive (when the Legislature cannot be convened) against domestic Violence....

ARTICLE VI

This Constitution, and the Laws of the United States which shall be made in Pursuance thereof; and all Treaties made, or which shall be made, under the Authority of the United States, shall be the supreme Law of the Land; and the Judges in every State shall be bound thereby, any Thing in the Constitution or Laws of any State to the Contrary notwithstanding....

AMERICAN BILL OF RIGHTS, RATIFIED 1791

AMENDMENT I

Congress shall make no law respecting an establishment of religion, or prohibiting the free exercise thereof; or abridging the freedom of speech or of the press; or the right of the people peaceably to assemble and to petition the Government for a redress of grievances.

AMENDMENT II

A well-regulated Militia, being necessary to the security of a free State, the right of the people to keep and bear Arms, shall not be infringed.

AMENDMENT III

No Soldier shall, in time of peace be quartered in any house, without the consent of the Owner, nor in time of war, but in a manner to be prescribed by law.

AMENDMENT IV

The right of the people to be secure in their persons, houses, papers, and effects, against unreasonable searches and seizures, shall not be violated, and no Warrants shall issue, but upon probable cause, supported by Oath, or affirmation, and particularly describing the place to be searched and the persons or things to be seized.

AMENDMENT V

No person shall be held to answer for a capital, or otherwise infamous crime, unless on a presentment or indictment of a Grand Jury, except in cases arising in the land or naval forces, or in the Militia, when in actual service in time of War or public danger; nor shall any person be subject for the same offence to be twice put in jeopardy of life or limb; nor shall be compelled in any criminal case to be a witness against himself, nor be deprived of life, liberty, or property, without due process of law; nor shall private property be taken for public use, without just compensation.

AMENDMENT VI

In all criminal prosecutions, the accused shall enjoy the right to a speedy and public trial, by an impartial jury

of the State and district wherein the crime shall have been committed, which district shall have been previously ascertained by law, and to be informed of the nature and cause of the accusation; to be confronted with the witnesses against him; to have compulsory process for obtaining witnesses in his favor, and to have the Assistance of Counsel for his defence.

AMENDMENT VII

In suits at common law, where the value in controversy shall exceed twenty dollars, the right of trial by jury shall be preserved, and no fact tried by jury, shall be otherwise reexamined in any Court of the United States, than according to the rules of the common law.

AMENDMENT VIII

Excessive bail shall not be required, nor excessive fines imposed, nor cruel and unusual punishments inflicted.

AMENDMENT IX

The enumeration in the Constitution, of certain rights, shall not be construed to deny or disparage others retained by the people.

AMENDMENT X

The powers not delegated to the United States by the Constitution, nor prohibited by it to the States, are reserved to the States respectively, or to the people....

AMENDMENT XIV, RATIFIED 1868

Section 1. All persons born or naturalized in the United States, and subject to the jurisdiction thereof, are citizens of the United States and of the State wherein they reside. No State shall make or enforce any law which shall abridge the privileges or immunities of citizens of the United States; nor shall any State deprive any person of life, liberty, or property, without due process of law; nor deny to any person within its jurisdiction the equal protection of the laws....

FINDING AND ANALYZING CASES | APPENDIX B

INFORMATION ON HOW TO SEARCH FINDLAW

FindLaw.com, a free case-law source service offered by Thomson, contains all of the cases that the Case Analysis exercises will ask you to locate. You must create an account (it is free) with FindLaw before you can begin a search. You may do this the first time you search in the FindLaw website.

When you look for a case on FindLaw, first determine the jurisdiction and level of the case you're searching for. Is it a U.S. court of appeals or a state supreme court or an appellate court decision?

To find a federal case from the FindLaw homepage (www.findlaw.com/casecode/) follow these steps:

1. Click on the "Research the Law" section, and then click the "Cases & Codes" link.
2. Scroll down to the "Browse Cases and Codes" section.
3. Click on the appropriate court in which the case was decided if it was a federal court. There is a separate link for U.S. Supreme Court cases. It appears in a box titled "Popular Federal Resources."
4. Fill in a search window with the case's Docket No. or a Party Name, and then click "Search." (*Note:* You may search using the terms in only one window.)

5. Find the case in the search results list, and click on the highlighted PDF link to view the full-text version of the case.

To find a state case from the FindLaw homepage, follow these steps:

1. Click on the "Browse Cases & Codes" link, which is in the "Research the Law" section.
2. Browse the list of states, and click on the state in which the case was decided.
3. Scroll down the page to the "State" section, and click on the "Supreme Court Cases from FindLaw" link. (This is usually the first link listed in the "State" section. Some states have more than one appellate court, and some states call the highest court the "Court of Appeals." The page lists the state's appellate courts.)
4. In the search window, enter the case's Case No. or a Party Name, and click "Search."
5. Find the case in the search results list, and click on the highlighted PDF link to view the full-text version of the case.

CASE ANALYSIS

In the end materials of each chapter in this text we have included citations to (mostly) recent cases in which issues presented in the chapters are discussed in appellate court opinions. Although criminal evidence, like criminal law, includes many statutory rules, court opinions interpreting and applying those rules continue to play a vital role in the development of the law. We therefore believe the time spent reading and analyzing appellate court opinions will be rewarded with a better understanding of the law of criminal evidence. In each of the eighteen chapters, we recommend that the student find the cases cited in the Case Analysis section, read them carefully, and give some thought to the questions posed.

Appellate court cases have both a name and a citation. The name of a case includes the two main parties in the case, usually called the *appellant* and the *appellee*, but sometimes the *petitioner* and the *respondent*. The citation of the case is a reference to a place where the full text of the opinion in the case can be found. For example, the first case in Chapter 1's Case Analysis section is titled *Brogden v. State*. Brogden is the person appealing the decision of a trial court. The citation is 866 A.2d 129 (2005). That means this opinion can be found in the Atlantic Reporter system, which includes opinions from several states in the eastern United States. Other regional reporter systems exist for other parts of the United States. In addition, many states maintain their own reporter system for opinions of appellate courts in that state.

The highest appellate court in most states is called the state supreme court. Some states, such as New York, call the highest appellate court the court of appeals. Many states have more than one level of appellate courts. When a citation is to an opinion of the highest state court, it usually ends with the date of the case and the state's abbreviation. For example, a citation might read "—N.W.2d— (Iowa 2008)." If the citation is to a lower appellate court, "App." is added to the state abbreviation: "—N.W.2d— (Iowa App. 2008).

We recommend the student consider the following aspects of each appellate opinion:

1. What are the relevant facts of the case? In this text, the exclusion or introduction of some evidence in a criminal trial is important, so try to determine the exact evidence that was under consideration.
2. What did the trial court do (or fail to do) that is challenged on appeal? Did it admit evidence over a party's objection? Did it refuse to permit evidence to be admitted?
3. What is the basis for the appellant's (usually the defendant's) claim that the trial court committed reversible error? Is it a constitutional claim? Is it a procedural error?
4. What did the appellate court decide? Did it affirm the trial court, or reverse it? Did it send the case back (called "remand") to the trial court for more hearings? If so, what precise question must be determined on remand?
5. What were the appellate court's reasons for its decision? The appellate court rarely simply affirms or reverses a trial court's decision on guilt or innocence. The reasons given by the appellate court are really the most important part of the decision, at least for our purposes. Once we pin down the reasons for a decision, we can use those reasons to figure what might happen in related cases. This is how court opinions contribute to the development of the law. Sometimes the members of an appellate court cannot agree on a decision. When that happens, the majority of the judges write their opinion, and that becomes the rule of the case. The minority judges may also write a dissenting opinion, which sometimes influences other courts to disagree with the result ordered by the majority. A concurring opinion is an opinion written by a judge who agrees with the result ordered by the majority, but who wants to state different or more detailed reasons for the result.

FEDERAL RULES OF EVIDENCE

ARTICLE I. GENERAL PROVISIONS

RULE 101. SCOPE

These rules govern proceedings in the courts of the United States and before United States bankruptcy judges, to the extent and with the exceptions stated in Rule 1101.

RULE 102. PURPOSE AND CONSTRUCTION

These rules shall be construed to secure fairness in administration, elimination of unjustifiable expense and delay, and promotion of growth and development of the law of evidence to the end that the truth may be ascertained and proceedings justly determined.

RULE 103. RULINGS ON EVIDENCE

a. Effect of erroneous ruling. Error may not be predicated upon a ruling which admits or excludes evidence unless a substantial right of the party is affected, and
    1. Objection. In case the ruling is one admitting evidence, a timely objection or motion to strike appears of record, stating the specific ground of objection, if the specific ground was not apparent from the context; or
    2. Offer of proof. In case the ruling is one excluding evidence, the substance of the evidence was made known to the court by offer

or was apparent from the context within which questions were asked.

b. Record of offer and ruling. The court may add any other or further statement which shows the character of the evidence, the form in which it was offered, the objection made, and the ruling thereon. It may direct the making of an offer in question and answer form.

c. Hearing of jury. In jury cases, proceedings shall be conducted, to the extent practicable, so as to prevent inadmissible evidence from being suggested to the jury by any means, such as making statements or offers of proof or asking questions in the hearing of the jury.

d. Plain error. Nothing in this rule precludes taking notice of plain errors affecting substantial rights although they were not brought to the attention of the court.

RULE 104. PRELIMINARY QUESTIONS

a. Questions of admissibility generally. Preliminary questions concerning the qualification of a person to be a witness, the existence of a privilege, or the admissibility of evidence shall be determined by the court, subject to the provisions of subdivision (b). In making its determination it is not bound by the rules of evidence except those with respect to privileges.

b. Relevancy conditioned on fact. When the relevancy of evidence depends upon the fulfillment of a condition of fact, the court shall admit it upon, or subject to, the introduction of evidence sufficient to support a finding of the fulfillment of the condition.

c. Hearing of jury. Hearings on the admissibility of confessions shall in all cases be conducted out of the hearing of the jury. Hearings on other preliminary matters shall be so conducted when the interests of justice require or, when an accused is a witness and so requests.

d. Testimony by accused. The accused does not, by testifying upon a preliminary matter, become subject to cross-examination as to other issues in the case.

e. Weight and credibility. This rule does not limit the right of a party to introduce before the jury evidence relevant to weight or credibility.

...

ARTICLE II. JUDICIAL NOTICE

RULE 201. JUDICIAL NOTICE OF ADJUDICATIVE FACTS

a. Scope of rule. This rule governs only judicial notice of adjudicative facts.

b. Kinds of facts. A judicially noticed fact must be one not subject to reasonable dispute in that it is either (1) generally known within the territorial jurisdiction of the trial court or (2) capable of accurate and ready determination by resort to sources whose accuracy cannot reasonably be questioned.

c. When discretionary. A court may take judicial notice, whether requested or not.

d. When mandatory. A court shall take judicial notice if requested by a party and supplied with the necessary information.

e. Opportunity to be heard. A party is entitled upon timely request to an opportunity to be heard as to the propriety of taking judicial notice and the tenor of the matter noticed. In the absence of prior notification, the request may be made after judicial notice has been taken.

f. Time of taking notice. Judicial notice may be taken at any stage of the proceeding.

g. Instructing jury. In a civil action or proceeding, the court shall instruct the jury to accept as conclusive any fact judicially noticed. In a criminal case, the court shall instruct the jury that it may, but is not required to, accept as conclusive any fact judicially noticed.

...

ARTICLE III. PRESUMPTIONS IN CIVIL ACTIONS AND PROCEEDINGS

RULE 301. PRESUMPTIONS IN GENERAL IN CIVIL ACTIONS AND PROCEEDINGS

In all civil actions and proceedings not otherwise provided for by Act of Congress or by these rules, a presumption imposes on the party against whom it is directed the burden of going forward with evidence to rebut or meet the presumption, but does not shift to such party the burden of proof in the sense of the risk of nonpersuasion, which remains throughout the trial upon the party on whom it was originally cast.

...

ARTICLE IV. RELEVANCY AND ITS LIMITS

RULE 401. DEFINITION OF "RELEVANT EVIDENCE"

"Relevant evidence" means evidence having any tendency to make the existence of any fact that is of consequence to the determination of the action more probable or less probable than it would be without the evidence.

RULE 402. RELEVANT EVIDENCE GENERALLY ADMISSIBLE; IRRELEVANT EVIDENCE INADMISSIBLE

All relevant evidence is admissible, except as otherwise provided by the Constitution of the United States, by Act of Congress, by these rules, or by other rules prescribed by the Supreme Court pursuant to statutory authority. Evidence which is not relevant is not admissible.

RULE 403. EXCLUSION OF RELEVANT EVIDENCE ON GROUNDS OF PREJUDICE, CONFUSION, OR WASTE OF TIME

Although relevant, evidence may be excluded if its probative value is substantially outweighed by the danger of unfair prejudice, confusion of the issues, or misleading the jury, or by considerations of undue delay, waste of time, or needless presentation of cumulative evidence.

RULE 404. CHARACTER EVIDENCE NOT ADMISSIBLE TO PROVE CONDUCT; EXCEPTIONS; OTHER CRIMES

a. Character evidence generally. Evidence of a person's character or a trait of character is not admissible for the purpose of proving action in conformity therewith on a particular occasion, except:
    1. Character of accused. Evidence of a pertinent trait of character offered by an accused, or by the prosecution to rebut the same;
    2. Character of victim. Evidence of a pertinent trait of character of the victim of the crime offered by an accused, or by the prosecution to rebut the same, or evidence of a character trait of peacefulness of the victim offered by the prosecution in a homicide case to rebut evidence that the victim was the first aggressor;
    3. Character of witness. Evidence of the character of a witness, as provided in rules 607, 608, and 609.

    . . .

b. Other crimes, wrongs, or acts. Evidence of other crimes, wrongs, or acts is not admissible to prove the character of a person in order to show action in conformity therewith. It may, however, be admissible for other purposes, such as proof of motive, opportunity, intent, preparation, plan, knowledge, identity, or absence of mistake or accident, provided that upon request by the accused, the prosecution in a criminal case shall provide reasonable notice in advance of trial, or during trial if the court excuses pretrial notice on good cause shown, or the general nature of any such evidence it intends to introduce at trial.

RULE 405. METHODS OF PROVING CHARACTER

a. Reputation or opinion. In all cases in which evidence of character or a trait of character of a person is admissible, proof may be made by testimony as to reputation or by testimony in the form of an opinion. On cross-examination, inquiry is allowable into relevant specific instances of conduct.
b. Specific instances of conduct. In cases in which character or a trait of character of a person is an essential element of a charge, claim, or defense,

proof may also be made of specific instances of that person's conduct.

RULE 406. HABIT; ROUTINE PRACTICE

Evidence of the habit of a person or the routine practice of an organization, whether corroborated or not and regardless of the presence of eyewitnesses, is relevant to prove that the conduct of the person or organization on a particular occasion was in conformity with the habit or routine practice.

. . .

RULE 410. INADMISSIBILITY OF PLEAS, PLEA DISCUSSIONS, AND RELATED STATEMENTS

Except as otherwise provided in this rule, evidence of the following is not, in any civil or criminal proceeding, admissible against the defendant who made the plea or was a participant in the plea discussions:

1. a plea of guilty which was later withdrawn;
2. a plea of nolo contendere;
3. any statement made in the course of any proceedings under Rule 11 of the Federal Rules of Criminal Procedure or comparable state procedure regarding either of the foregoing pleas; or
4. any statement made in the course of plea discussions with an attorney for the prosecuting authority which do not result in a plea of guilty or which result in a plea of guilty later withdrawn.

However, such a statement is admissible (i) in any proceeding wherein another statement made in the course of the same plea or plea discussions has been introduced and the statement ought in fairness be considered contemporaneously with it, or (ii) in a criminal proceeding for perjury or false statement if the statement was made by the defendant under oath, on the record and in the presence of counsel.

. . .

RULE 412. SEX OFFENSE CASES; RELEVANCE OF ALLEGED VICTIM'S PAST SEXUAL BEHAVIOR OR ALLEGED SEXUAL PREDISPOSITION

a. Evidence generally inadmissible. The following evidence is not admissible in any civil or criminal proceeding involving alleged sexual misconduct except as provided in subdivisions (b) and (c):

1. Evidence offered to prove that any alleged victim engaged in other sexual behavior.
2. Evidence offered to prove any alleged victim's sexual predisposition.

b. Exceptions.
1. In a criminal case, the following evidence is admissible, if otherwise admissible under these rules:
    A. evidence of specific instances of sexual behavior by the alleged victim offered to prove that a person other than the accused was the source of semen, injury or other physical evidence;
    B. evidence of specific instances of sexual behavior by the alleged victim with respect to the person accused of the sexual misconduct offered by the accused to prove consent or by the prosecution; and
    C. evidence the exclusion of which would violate the constitutional rights of the defendant.
2. In a civil case, evidence offered to prove the sexual behavior or sexual predisposition of any alleged victim is admissible if it is otherwise admissible under these rules and its probative value substantially outweighs the danger of harm to any victim and of unfair prejudice to any party. Evidence of an alleged victim's reputation is admissible only if it has been placed in controversy by the alleged victim.

c. Procedure to determine admissibility.
1. A party intending to offer evidence under subdivision (b) must—
    A. file a written motion at least 14 days before trial specifically describing the evidence and stating the purpose for which it is offered unless the court, for good cause requires a different time for filing or permits filing during trial; and
    B. serve the motion on all parties and notify the alleged victim or, when appropriate, the alleged victim's guardian or representative.
2. Before admitting evidence under this rule the court must conduct a hearing in camera and afford the victim and parties a right to attend and be heard. The motion, related papers, and the record of the hearing must be sealed and remain under seal unless the court orders otherwise.

RULE 413. EVIDENCE OF SIMILAR CRIMES IN SEXUAL ASSAULT CASES

a. In a criminal case in which the defendant is accused of an offense of sexual assault, evidence of the defendant's commission of another offense or offenses of sexual assault is admissible, and may be considered for its bearing on any matter to which it is relevant.

b. In a case in which the Government intends to offer evidence under this rule, the attorney for the Government shall disclose the evidence to the defendant, including statements of witnesses or a summary of the substance of any testimony that is expected to be offered, at least fifteen days before the scheduled date of trial or at such later time as the court may allow for good cause.

c. This rule shall not be construed to limit the admission or consideration of evidence under any other rule.

d. For purposes of this rule and Rule 415, "offense of sexual assault" means a crime under Federal law or the law of a State (as defined in section 513 of title 18, United States Code) that involved—
1. any conduct proscribed by chapter 109A of title 18, United States Code;
2. contact, without consent, between any part of the defendant's body or an object and the genitals or anus of another person;
3. contact, without consent, between the genitals or anus of the defendant and any part of another person's body;
4. deriving sexual pleasure or gratification from the infliction of death, bodily injury, or physical pain on another person; or
5. an attempt or conspiracy to engage in conduct described in paragraphs (1)–(4).

RULE 414. EVIDENCE OF SIMILAR CRIMES IN CHILD MOLESTATION CASES

a. In a criminal case in which the defendant is accused of an offense of child molestation, evidence of the defendant's commission of another offense or offenses of child molestation is admissible, and may be considered for its bearing on any matter to which it is relevant.

b. In a case in which the Government intends to offer evidence under this rule, the attorney for the Government shall disclose the evidence to the defendant, including statements of witnesses or a summary of the substance of any testimony that is expected to be offered, at least fifteen days before the scheduled date of trial or at such later time as the court may allow for good cause.

c. This rule shall not be construed to limit the admission or consideration of evidence under any other rule.

d. For purposes of this rule and Rule 415, "child" means a person below the age of fourteen, and "offense of child molestation" means a crime under Federal law or the law of a State (as defined in section 513 of title 18, United States Code) that involved—

1. any conduct proscribed by chapter 109A of title 18, United States Code, that was committed in relation to a child;
2. any conduct proscribed by chapter 110 of title 18, United States Code;
3. contact between any part of the defendant's body or an object and the genitals or anus of a child;
4. contact between the genitals or anus of the defendant and any part of the body of a child;
5. deriving sexual pleasure or gratification from the infliction of death, bodily injury, or physical pain on a child; or
6. an attempt or conspiracy to engage in conduct described in paragraphs (1)–(5).

RULE 415. EVIDENCE OF SIMILAR ACTS IN CIVIL CASES CONCERNING SEXUAL ASSAULT OR CHILD MOLESTATION

a. In a civil case in which a claim for damages or other relief is predicated on a party's alleged commission of conduct constituting an offense of sexual assault or child molestation, evidence of that party's commission of another offense or offenses of sexual assault or child molestation is admissible and may be considered as provided in Rule 413 and Rule 414 of these rules.

b. A party who intends to offer evidence under this Rule shall disclose the evidence to the party against whom it will be offered, including statements of witnesses or a summary of the substance of any testimony that is expected to be offered, at least fifteen days before the scheduled date of trial

or at such later time as the court may allow for good cause.

c. This rule shall not be construed to limit the admission or consideration of evidence under any other rule.

ARTICLE V. PRIVILEGES
RULE 501. GENERAL RULE

Except as otherwise required by the Constitution of the United States or provided by Act of Congress or in rules prescribed by the Supreme Court pursuant to statutory authority, the privilege of a witness, person, government, State, or political subdivision thereof shall be governed by the principles of the common law as they may be interpreted by the courts of the United States in the light of reason and experience. However, in civil actions and proceedings, with respect to an element of a claim or defense as to which State law supplies the rule of decision, the privilege of a witness, person, government, State, or political subdivision thereof shall be determined in accordance with State law.

ARTICLE VI. WITNESSES
RULE 601. GENERAL RULE OF COMPETENCY

Every person is competent to be a witness except as otherwise provided in these rules. However, in civil actions and proceedings, with respect to an element of a claim or defense as to which State law supplies the rule of decision, the competency of a witness shall be determined in accordance with State law.

RULE 602. LACK OF PERSONAL KNOWLEDGE

A witness may not testify to a matter unless evidence is introduced sufficient to support a finding that he has personal knowledge of the matter. Evidence to prove personal knowledge may, but need not, consist of the witness' own testimony. This rule is subject to the provisions of Rule 703, relating to opinion testimony by expert witnesses.

RULE 603. OATH OR AFFIRMATION

Before testifying, every witness shall be required to declare that the witness will testify truthfully, by oath or affirmation administered in a form calculated to awaken his conscience and impress the witness' mind with the duty to do so.

RULE 604. INTERPRETERS

An interpreter is subject to the provisions of these rules relating to qualification as an expert and the administration of an oath or affirmation to make a true translation.

RULE 605. COMPETENCY OF JUDGE AS WITNESS

The judge presiding at the trial may not testify in that trial as a witness. No objection need be made in order to preserve the point.

RULE 606. COMPETENCY OF JUROR AS WITNESS

a. At the trial. A member of the jury may not testify as a witness before that jury in the trial of the case in which the juror is sitting. If the juror is called so to testify, the opposing party shall be afforded an opportunity to object out of the presence of the jury.

b. Inquiry into validity of verdict or indictment. Upon an inquiry into the validity of a verdict or indictment, a juror may not testify as to any matter or statement occurring during the course of the jury's deliberations or to the effect of anything upon that or any other juror's mind or emotions as influencing the juror to assent to or dissent from the verdict or indictment or concerning the juror's mental processes in connection therewith, except that a juror may testify on the question whether extraneous prejudicial information was improperly brought to the jury's attention or whether any outside influence was improperly brought to bear upon any juror. Nor may a juror's affidavit or evidence of any statement by the juror concerning a matter about which the juror would be precluded from testifying be received for these purposes.

RULE 607. WHO MAY IMPEACH

The credibility of a witness may be attacked by any party, including the party calling the witness.

RULE 608. EVIDENCE OF CHARACTER AND CONDUCT OF WITNESS

a. Opinion and reputation evidence of character. The credibility of a witness may be attacked or supported by evidence in the form of opinion or reputation, but subject to these limitations: (1) the evidence may refer only to character for truthfulness or untruthfulness, and (2) evidence of truthful character is admissible only after the character of the witness for truthfulness has been attacked by opinion or reputation evidence or otherwise.

b. Specific instances of conduct. Specific instances of the conduct of a witness, for the purpose of attacking or supporting the witness' credibility, other than conviction of crime as provided in Rule 609, may not be proved by extrinsic evidence. They may, however, in the discretion of the court, if probative of truthfulness or untruthfulness, be inquired into on cross-examination of the witness (1) concerning the witness' character for truthfulness or untruthfulness, or (2) concerning the character for truthfulness or untruthfulness of another witness as to which character the witness being cross-examined has testified.

The giving of testimony, whether by an accused or by any other witness, does not operate as a waiver of the accused's or the witness' privilege against self-incrimination when examined with respect to matters which relate only to credibility.

RULE 609. IMPEACHMENT BY EVIDENCE OF CONVICTION OF CRIME

a. General rule. For the purpose of attacking the credibility of a witness,

1. evidence that a witness other than an accused has been convicted of a crime shall be admitted, subject to Rule 403, if the crime was punishable by death or imprisonment in excess of one year under the law under which the witness was convicted, and evidence that an accused has been convicted of such a crime shall be admitted if the court determines that the probative value of admitting this evidence outweighs its prejudicial effect to the accused; and

2. evidence that any witness has been convicted of a crime shall be admitted if it involved dishonesty or false statement, regardless of the punishment.

b. Time limit. Evidence of a conviction under this rule is not admissible if a period of more than ten years has elapsed since the date of the conviction or of the release of the witness from the confinement imposed for that conviction, whichever is the later date, unless the court determines, in the interests of justice, that the probative value of the conviction supported by specific facts and circumstances substantially outweighs its prejudicial effect. However, evidence of a conviction more than 10 years old as calculated herein, is not admissible unless the proponent gives to the adverse party sufficient advance written notice of intent to use such evidence to provide the adverse party with a fair opportunity to contest the use of such evidence.

c. Effect of pardon, annulment, or certificate of rehabilitation. Evidence of a conviction is not admissible under this rule if (1) the conviction has been the subject of a pardon, annulment, certificate of rehabilitation, or other equivalent procedure based on a finding of the rehabilitation of the person convicted, and that person has not been convicted of a subsequent crime which was punishable by death or imprisonment in excess of one year, or (2) the conviction has been the subject of a pardon, annulment, or other equivalent procedure based on a finding of innocence.

d. Juvenile adjudications. Evidence of juvenile adjudications is generally not admissible under this rule. The court may, however, in a criminal case allow evidence of a juvenile adjudication of a witness other than the accused if conviction of the offense would be admissible to attack the credibility of an adult and the court is satisfied that admission in evidence is necessary for a fair determination of the issue of guilt or innocence.

e. Pendency of appeal. The pendency of an appeal therefrom does not render evidence of a conviction inadmissible. Evidence of the pendency of an appeal is admissible.

RULE 610. RELIGIOUS BELIEFS OR OPINIONS

Evidence of the beliefs or opinions of a witness on matters of religion is not admissible for the purpose of showing that by reason of their nature the witness' credibility is impaired or enhanced.

RULE 611. MODE AND ORDER OF INTERROGATION AND PRESENTATION

a. Control by court. The court shall exercise reasonable control over the mode and order of interrogating witnesses and presenting evidence so as to (1) make the interrogation and presentation effective for the ascertainment of the truth, (2) avoid needless consumption of time, and (3) protect witnesses from harassment or undue embarrassment.

b. Scope of cross-examination. Cross-examination should be limited to the subject matter of the direct examination and matters affecting the credibility of the witness. The court may, in the exercise of discretion, permit inquiry into additional matters as if on direct examination.

c. Leading questions. Leading questions should not be used on the direct examination of a witness except as may be necessary to develop the witness' testimony. Ordinarily leading questions should be permitted on cross-examination. When a party calls a hostile witness, an adverse party, or a witness identified with an adverse party, interrogation may be by leading questions.

RULE 612. WRITING USED TO REFRESH MEMORY

Except as otherwise provided in criminal proceedings by section 3500 of title 18, United States Code, if a witness uses a writing to refresh his memory for the purpose of testifying, either—

1. while testifying, or
2. before testifying, if the court in its discretion determines it is necessary in the interests of justice, an adverse party is entitled to have the writing produced at the hearing, to inspect it, to cross-examine the witness thereon, and to introduce in evidence those portions which relate to the testimony of the witness. If it is claimed that the writing contains matters not related to the subject matter of the testimony the court shall examine the writing in camera, excise any portions not so related, and order delivery of the remainder to the party entitled thereto. Any portion withheld over objections shall be preserved and made available to the appellate court in the event of an appeal. If a writing is not produced or delivered pursuant to order under this rule, the court shall make any order justice requires,

except that in criminal cases when the prosecution elects not to comply, the order shall be one striking the testimony or, if the court in its discretion determines that the interests of justice so require, declaring a mistrial.

RULE 613. PRIOR STATEMENTS OF WITNESSES

a. Examining witness concerning prior statement. In examining a witness concerning a prior statement made by the witness, whether written or not, the statement need not be shown nor its contents disclosed to the witness at that time, but on request the same shall be shown or disclosed to opposing counsel.

b. Extrinsic evidence of prior inconsistent statement of witness. Extrinsic evidence of a prior inconsistent statement by a witness is not admissible unless the witness is afforded an opportunity to explain or deny the same and the opposite party is afforded an opportunity to interrogate the witness thereon, or the interests of justice otherwise require. This provision does not apply to admissions of a party-opponent as defined in Rule 801(d)(2).

RULE 614. CALLING AND INTERROGATION OF WITNESSES BY COURT

a. Calling by court. The court may, on its own motion or at the suggestion of a party, call witnesses, and all parties are entitled to cross-examine witnesses thus called.

b. Interrogation by court. The court may interrogate witnesses, whether called by itself or by a party.

c. Objections. Objections to the calling of witnesses by the court or to interrogation by it may be made at the time or at the next available opportunity when the jury is not present.

RULE 615. EXCLUSION OF WITNESSES

At the request of a party the court shall order witnesses excluded so that they cannot hear the testimony of other witnesses, and it may make the order of its own motion. This rule does not authorize exclusion of (1) party who is a natural person, or (2) an officer or employee of a party which is not a natural person designated as its representative by its attorney, or (3) a person whose presence is shown by a party to be

essential to the presentation of the party's cause, or (4) a person authorized by statute to be present.

ARTICLE VII. OPINIONS AND EXPERT TESTIMONY

RULE 701. OPINION TESTIMONY BY LAY WITNESSES

If the witness is not testifying as an expert, the witness' testimony in the form of opinions or inferences is limited to those opinions or inferences which are (a) rationally based on the perception of the witness and (b) helpful to a clear understanding of the witness' testimony or the determination of a fact in issue.

RULE 702. TESTIMONY BY EXPERTS

If scientific, technical, or other specialized knowledge will assist the trier of fact to understand the evidence or to determine a fact in issue, a witness qualified as an expert by knowledge, skill, experience, training, or education, may testify thereto in the form of an opinion or otherwise.

RULE 703. BASES OF OPINION TESTIMONY BY EXPERTS

The facts or data in the particular case upon which an expert bases an opinion or inference may be those perceived by or made known to the expert at or before the hearing. If of a type reasonably relied upon by experts in the particular field in forming opinions or inferences upon the subject, the facts or data need not be admissible in evidence.

RULE 704. OPINION ON ULTIMATE ISSUE

a. Except as provided in subdivision (b), testimony in the form of an opinion or inference otherwise admissible is not objectionable because it embraces an ultimate issue to be decided by the trier of fact.

b. No expert witness testifying with respect to the mental state or condition of a defendant in a criminal case may state an opinion or inference as to whether the defendant did or did not have the mental state or condition constituting an element of the crime charged or of a defense thereto. Such ultimate issues are matters for the trier of fact alone.

RULE 705. DISCLOSURE OF FACTS OR DATA UNDERLYING EXPERT OPINION

The expert may testify in terms of opinion or inference and give reasons therefore without prior disclosure of the underlying facts or data, unless the court requires otherwise. The expert may in any event be required to disclose the underlying facts or data on cross-examination.

RULE 706. COURT APPOINTED EXPERTS

a.   Appointment. The court may on its own motion or on the motion of any party enter an order to show cause why expert witnesses should not be appointed, and may request the parties to submit nominations. The court may appoint any expert witnesses agreed upon by the parties, and may appoint expert witnesses of its own selection. An expert witness shall not be appointed by the court unless the witness consents to act. A witness so appointed shall be informed of the witness' duties by the court in writing, a copy of which shall be filed with the clerk, or at a conference in which the parties shall have opportunity to participate. A witness so appointed shall advise the parties of the witness' findings, if any; the witness' deposition may be taken by any party; and the witness may be called to testify by the court or any party. The witness shall be subject to cross-examination by each party, including a party calling the witness.

b.   Compensation. Expert witnesses so appointed are entitled to reasonable compensation in whatever sum the court may allow. The compensation thus fixed is payable from funds which may be provided by law in criminal cases and civil actions and proceedings involving just compensation under the fifth amendment. In other civil actions and proceedings the compensation shall be paid by the parties in such proportion and at such time as the court directs, and thereafter charged in like manner as other costs.

c.   Disclosure of appointment. In the exercise of its discretion, the court may authorize disclosure to the jury of the fact that the court appointed the expert witness.

d.   Parties' experts of own selection. Nothing in this rule limits the parties in calling expert witnesses of their own selection.

ARTICLE VIII. HEARSAY

RULE 801. DEFINITIONS

The following definitions apply under this article:

a.   Statement. A "statement" is (1) an oral or written assertion or (2) nonverbal conduct of a person, if it is intended by the person as an assertion.

b.   Declarant. A "declarant" is a person who makes a statement.

c.   Hearsay. "Hearsay" is a statement, other than one made by the declarant while testifying at the trial or hearing, offered in evidence to prove the truth of the matter asserted.

d.   Statements which are not hearsay. A statement is not hearsay if—

   1.   Prior statement by witness. The declarant testifies at the trial or hearing and is subject to cross-examination concerning the statement, and the statement is (A) inconsistent with the declarant's testimony, and was given under oath subject to the penalty of perjury at a trial, hearing, or other proceedings or in a deposition, or (B) consistent with the declarant's testimony and is offered to rebut an express or implied charge against the declarant of recent fabrication or improper influence or motive, or (C) one of identification of a person made after perceiving the person; or

   2.   Admission by party-opponent. The statement is offered against a party and is (A) the party's own statement, in either an individual or a representative capacity or (B) a statement of which the party has manifested an adoption or belief in its truth, or (C) a statement by a person authorized by the party to make a statement concerning the subject, or (D) a statement by the party's agent or servant concerning a matter within the scope of the agency or employment, made during the existence of the relationship, or (E) a statement by a coconspirator of a party during the course and in furtherance of the conspiracy. The contents of the statement shall be considered but are not alone sufficient to establish the declarant's authority under

subdivision (C), the agency or employment relationship and scope thereof under subdivision (D), or the existence of the conspiracy and the participation therein of the declarant and the party against whom the statement is offered under subdivision (E).

RULE 802. HEARSAY RULE

Hearsay is not admissible except as provided by these rules or by other rules prescribed by the Supreme Court pursuant to statutory authority or by Act of Congress.

RULE 803. HEARSAY EXCEPTIONS; AVAILABILITY OF DECLARANT IMMATERIAL

The following are not excluded by the hearsay rule, even though the declarant is available as a witness:

1. Present sense impression. A statement describing or explaining an event or condition made while the declarant was perceiving the event or condition, or immediately thereafter.
2. Excited utterance. A statement relating to a startling event or condition made while the declarant was under the stress of excitement caused by the event or condition.
3. Then existing mental, emotional, or physical condition. A statement of the declarant's then existing state of mind, emotion, sensation, or physical condition (such as intent, plan, motive, design, mental feeling, pain, and bodily health), but not including a statement of memory or belief to prove the fact remembered or believed unless it relates to the execution, revocation, identification, or terms of declarant's will.
4. Statements for purposes of medical diagnosis or treatment. Statements made for purposes of medical diagnosis or treatment and describing medical history, or past or present symptoms, pain, or sensations, or the inception or general character of the cause or external source thereof insofar as reasonably pertinent to diagnosis or treatment.
5. Recorded recollection. A memorandum or record concerning a matter about which a witness once had knowledge but now has insufficient recollection to enable the witness to testify fully and accurately, shown to have been made or adopted by the witness when the matter was fresh in the witness' memory and to reflect that knowledge correctly. If admitted, the memorandum or record may be read into evidence but may not itself be received as an exhibit unless offered by an adverse party.
6. Records of regularly conducted activity. A memorandum, report, record, or data compilation, in any form, of acts, events, conditions, opinions, or diagnoses, made at or near the time by, or from information transmitted by, a person with knowledge, if kept in the course of a regularly conducted business activity, and if it was the regular practice of that business activity to make the memorandum, report, record, or data compilation, all as shown by the testimony of the custodian or other qualified witness, unless the source of information or the method or circumstances of preparation indicate lack of trustworthiness. The term "business" as used in this paragraph includes business, institution, association, profession, occupation, and calling of every kind, whether or not conducted for profit.
7. Absence of entry in records kept in accordance with the provisions of paragraph (6). Evidence that a matter is not included in the memoranda reports, records, or data compilations, in any form, kept in accordance with the provisions of paragraph (6), to prove the nonoccurrence or nonexistence of the matter if the matter was a kind of which a memorandum report, record, or data compilation was regularly made and preserved, unless the sources of information or other circumstances indicate lack of trustworthiness.
8. Public records and reports. Records, reports, statements, or data compilations, in any form of public offices or agencies, setting forth (A) the activities of the office or agency, or (B) matters observed pursuant to duty imposed by law as to which matters there was a duty to report, excluding, however, in criminal cases matters observed by police officers and other law enforcement personnel, or (C) in civil actions and proceedings and against the Government in criminal cases, factual findings resulting from an investigation made pursuant to authority granted by law, unless the sources of information or other circumstances indicate lack of trustworthiness.
9. Records of vital statistics. Records or data compilations, in any form, of births, fetal deaths, deaths, or marriages, if the report thereof was made to a public office pursuant to requirements of law.

10. Absence of public record or entry. To prove the absence of a record, report, statement, or data compilation, in any form, or the nonoccurrence or nonexistence of a matter of which a record, report, statement, or data compilation, in any form, was regularly made and preserved by a public office or agency, evidence in the form of a certification in accordance with Rule 902, or testimony, that diligent search failed to disclose the record, report, statement, or data compilation, or entry.

11. Records of religious organizations. Statements of births, marriages, divorces, deaths, legitimacy, ancestry, relationship by blood or marriage, or other similar facts of personal or family history, contained in a regularly kept record of a religious organization.

12. Marriage, baptismal, and similar certificates. Statements of fact contained in a certificate that the maker performed a marriage or other ceremony or administered a sacrament, made by a clergyman, public official, or other person authorized by the rules or practices of a religious organization or by law to perform the act certified, and purporting to have been issued at the time of the act or within a reasonable time thereafter.

13. Family records. Statements of fact concerning personal or family history contained in family Bibles, genealogies, charts, engravings on rings, inscriptions on family portraits, engravings on urns, crypts, or tombstones, or the like.

14. Records of documents affecting an interest in property. The record of a document purporting to establish or affect an interest in property, as proof of the content of the original recorded document and its execution and delivery by each person by whom it purports to have been executed, if the record is a record of a public office and an applicable statute authorizes the recording of documents of that kind in that office.

15. Statements in documents affecting an interest in property. A statement contained in a document purporting to establish or affect an interest in property if the matter stated was relevant to the purpose of the document, unless dealings with the property since the document was made have been inconsistent with the truth of the statement or the purport of the document.

16. Statements in ancient documents. Statements in a document in existence twenty years or more the authenticity of which is established.

17. Market reports, commercial publications. Market quotations, tabulations, lists, directories, or other published compilations, generally used and relied upon by the public or by persons in particular occupations.

18. Learned treatises. To the extent called to the attention of an expert witness upon cross-examination or relied upon by the expert witness in direct examination, statements contained in published treatises, periodicals, or pamphlets on a subject of history, medicine, or other science or art, established as a reliable authority by the testimony or admission of the witness or by other expert testimony or by judicial notice. If admitted, the statements may be read into evidence but may not be received as exhibits.

19. Reputation concerning personal or family history. Reputation among members of a person's family by blood, adoption, or marriage, or among a person's associates, or in the community, concerning a person's birth, adoption, marriage, divorce, death, legitimacy, relationship by blood, adoption, or marriage, ancestry, or other similar fact of personal or family history.

20. Reputation concerning boundaries or general history. Reputation in a community, arising before the controversy, as to boundaries of or customs affecting lands in the community, and reputation as to events of general history important to the community or State or nation in which located.

21. Reputation as to character. Reputation of a person's character among associates or in the community.

22. Judgment of previous conviction. Evidence of a final judgment, entered after a trial or upon a plea of guilty (but not upon a plea of nolo contendere), adjudging a person guilty of a crime punishable by death or imprisonment in excess of one year, to prove any fact essential to sustain the judgment, but not including, when offered by the Government in a criminal prosecution for purposes other than impeachment, judgments against persons other than the accused. The pendency of an appeal may be shown but does not affect admissibility.

23. Judgment as to personal, family, or general history, or boundaries. Judgments as proof of matters of personal, family or general history, or boundaries, essential to the judgment, if the same would be provable by evidence of reputation.

24. [Transferred to Rule 807]

Rule 804. Hearsay Exceptions; Declarant Unavailable

a. Definition of unavailability. "Unavailability as a witness" includes situations in which the declarant—

1. is exempted by ruling of the court on the ground of privilege from testifying concerning the subject matter of the declarant's statement; or
2. persists in refusing to testify concerning the subject matter of the declarant's statement despite an order of the court to do so; or
3. testifies to a lack of memory of the subject matter of the declarant's statement; or
4. is unable to be present or to testify at the hearing because of death or then existing physical or mental illness or infirmity; or
5. is absent from the hearing and the proponent of a statement has been unable to procure the declarant's attendance (or in the case of a hearsay exception under subdivision (b)(2), (3), or (4), the declarant's attendance or testimony) by process or other reasonable means.

A declarant is not unavailable as a witness if exemption, refusal, claim of lack of memory, inability, or absence is due to the procurement or wrongdoing of the proponent of a statement for the purpose of preventing the witness from attending or testifying.

b. Hearsay exceptions. The following are not excluded by the hearsay rule if the declarant is unavailable as a witness:

1. Former testimony. Testimony given as a witness at another hearing of the same or a different proceeding, or in a deposition taken in compliance with law in the course of the same or another proceeding, if the party against whom the testimony is now offered, or, in a civil action or proceeding, a predecessor in interest, had an opportunity and similar motive to develop the testimony by direct, cross, or redirect examination.
2. Statement under belief of impending death. In a prosecution for homicide or in a civil action or proceeding, a statement made by a declarant while believing that the declarant's death was imminent, concerning the cause or circumstances of what the declarant believed to be impending death.
3. Statement against interest. A statement which was at the time of its making so far contrary to the declarant's pecuniary or proprietary interest, or so far tended to subject the declarant to civil or criminal liability, or to render invalid a claim by the declarant against another, that a reasonable person in the declarant's position would not have made the statement unless believing it to be true. A statement tending to expose the declarant to criminal liability and offered to exculpate the accused is not admissible unless corroborating circumstances clearly indicate the trustworthiness of the statement.
4. Statement of personal or family history. (A) A statement concerning the declarant's own birth, adoption, marriage, divorce, legitimacy, relationship by blood, adoption, or marriage, ancestry, or other similar fact of personal or family history, even though declarant had no means of acquiring personal knowledge of the matter stated; or (B) a statement concerning the foregoing matters, and death also, of another person, if the declarant was related to the other by blood, adoption, or marriage or was so intimately associated with the other's family as to be likely to have accurate information concerning the matter declared.
5. [Transferred to Rule 807]
6. Forfeiture by wrongdoing. A statement offered against a party that has engaged or acquiesced in wrongdoing that was intended to, and did, procure the unavailability of the declarant as a witness.

Rule 805. Hearsay Within Hearsay

Hearsay included within hearsay is not excluded under the hearsay rule if each part of the combined statements conforms with an exception to the hearsay rule provided in these rules.

Rule 806. Attacking and Supporting Credibility of Declarant

When a hearsay statement, or a statement defined in Rule 801(d)(2)(C), (D), or (E), has been admitted in evidence, the credibility of the declarant may be attacked, and if attacked may be supported, by any evidence which would be admissible for those purposes if declarant had testified as a witness. Evidence of a statement or conduct by the declarant at any time, inconsistent with the declarant's hearsay statement, is not subject to any requirement that the declarant may have been afforded an opportunity to deny or explain. If the party against whom a hearsay statement has been admitted calls the declarant as a witness, the party is entitled to examine the declarant on the statement as if under cross-examination.

Rule 807. Residual Exception

A statement not specifically covered by Rule 803 or 804 but having equivalent circumstantial guarantees of trustworthiness, is not excluded by the hearsay rule, if the court determines that (A) the statement is offered as evidence of a material fact; (B) the statement is more probative on the point for which it is offered than any other evidence which the proponent can procure through reasonable efforts; and (C) the general purposes of these rules and the interests of justice will best be served by admission of the statement into evidence. However, a statement may not be admitted under this exception unless the proponent of it makes known to the adverse party sufficiently in advance of the trial or hearing to provide the adverse party with a fair opportunity to prepare to meet it, the proponent's intention to offer the statement and the particulars of it, including the name and address of the declarant.

ARTICLE IX. AUTHENTICATION AND IDENTIFICATION

Rule 901. Requirement of Authentication or Identification

a. General provision. The requirement of authentication or identification as a condition precedent to admissibility is satisfied by evidence sufficient to support a finding that the matter in question is what its proponent claims.

b. Illustrations. By way of illustration only, and not by way of limitation, the following are examples of authentication or identification conforming with the requirements of this rule:

1. Testimony of witness with knowledge. Testimony that a matter is what it is claimed to be.
2. Nonexpert opinion on handwriting. Nonexpert opinion as to the genuineness of handwriting, based upon familiarity not acquired for purposes of the litigation.
3. Comparison by trier or expert witness. Comparison by the trier of fact or by expert witnesses with specimens which have been authenticated.
4. Distinctive characteristics and the like. Appearance, contents, substance, internal patterns, or other distinctive characteristics, taken in conjunction with circumstances.
5. Voice identification. Identification of a voice, whether heard firsthand or through mechanical or electronic transmission or recording, by opinion based upon hearing the voice at any time under circumstances connecting it with the alleged speaker.
6. Telephone conversations. Telephone conversations, by evidence that a call was made to the number assigned at the time by the telephone company to a particular person or business, if (A) in the case of a person, circumstances, including self-identification, show the person answering to be the one called, or (B) in the case of a business, the call was made to a place of business and the conversation related to business reasonably transacted over the telephone.
7. Public records or reports. Evidence that a writing authorized by law to be recorded or filed and in fact recorded or filed in a public office, or a purported public record, report, statement, or data compilation, in any form, is from the public office where items of this nature are kept.
8. Ancient documents or data compilation. Evidence that a document or data compilation, in any form, (A) is in such condition as to create no suspicion concerning its authenticity, (B) was in a place where it, if authentic, would likely be, and (C) has been in existence 20 years or more at the time it is offered.
9. Process or system. Evidence describing a process or system used to produce a result and showing that the process or system produces an accurate result.
10. Methods provided by statute or rule. Any method of authentication or identification provided by Act of Congress or by other rules prescribed by the Supreme Court pursuant to statutory authority.

RULE 902. SELF-AUTHENTICATION

Extrinsic evidence of authenticity as a condition precedent to admissibility is not required with respect to the following:

1. Domestic public documents under seal. A document bearing a seal purporting to be that of the United States, or of any State, district, Commonwealth, territory, or insular possession thereof, or the Panama Canal Zone, or the Trust Territory of the Pacific Islands, or of a political subdivision, department, officer, or agency thereof, and a signature purporting to be an attestation or execution.
2. Domestic public documents not under seal. A document purporting to bear the signature in the official capacity of an officer or employee of any entity included in paragraph (1) hereof, having no seal, if a public officer having a seal and having official duties in the district or political subdivision of the officer or employee certifies under seal that the signer has the official capacity and that the signature is genuine.
3. Foreign public documents. A document purporting to be executed or attested in an official capacity by a person authorized by the laws of a foreign country to make the execution or attestation, and accompanied by a final certification as to the genuineness of the signature and official position (A) of the executing or attesting person, or (B) of any foreign official whose certificate of genuineness of signature and official position relates to the execution or attestation or is in a chain of certificates of genuineness of signature and official position relating to the execution or attestation. A final certification may be made by a secretary of an embassy or legation, consul general, consul, vice consul, or consular agent of the United States, or a diplomatic or consular official of the foreign country assigned or accredited to the United States. If reasonable opportunity has been given to all parties to investigate the authenticity and accuracy of official documents, the court may, for good cause shown, order that they be treated as presumptively authentic without final certification or permit them to be evidenced by an attested summary with or without final certification.
4. Certified copies of public records. A copy of an official record or report or entry therein, or of a document authorized by law to be recorded or filed and actually recorded or filed in a public office, including data compilations in any form, certified as correct by the custodian or other person authorized to make the certification, by certificate complying with paragraph (1), (2), or (3) of this rule or complying with any Act of Congress or rule prescribed by the Supreme Court pursuant to statutory authority.
5. Official publications. Books, pamphlets, or other publications purporting to be issued by public authority.
6. Newspapers and periodicals. Printed materials purporting to be newspapers or periodicals.
7. Trade inscriptions and the like. Inscriptions, signs, tags, or labels purporting to have been affixed in the course of business and indicating ownership, control, or origin.
8. Acknowledged documents. Documents accompanied by a certificate of acknowledgment executed in the manner provided by law by a notary public or other officer authorized by law to take acknowledgments.
9. Commercial paper and related documents. Commercial paper, signatures thereon, and documents relating thereto to the extent provided by general commercial law.
10. Presumptions under Acts of Congress. Any signature, document, or other matter declared by Act of Congress to be presumptively or prima facie genuine or authentic.

RULE 903. SUBSCRIBING WITNESS' TESTIMONY UNNECESSARY

The testimony of a subscribing witness is not necessary to authenticate a writing unless required by the laws of the jurisdiction whose laws govern the validity of the writing.

ARTICLE X. CONTENTS OF WRITINGS, RECORDINGS, AND PHOTOGRAPHS

RULE 1001. DEFINITIONS

For purposes of this article the following definitions are applicable:

1. Writings and recordings. "Writings" and "recordings" consist of letters, words, or numbers, or their equivalent, set down by handwriting, typewriting, printing, photostating, photographing, magnetic impulse, mechanical or electronic recording, or other form of data compilation.

2. Photographs. "Photographs" include still photographs, X-ray films, video tapes, and motion pictures.
3. Original. An "original" of a writing or recording is the writing or recording itself or any counterpart intended to have the same effect by a person executing or issuing it. An "original" of a photograph includes the negative or any print therefrom. If data are stored in a computer or similar device, any printout or other output readable by sight, shown to reflect the data accurately, is an "original."
4. Duplicate. A "duplicate" is a counterpart produced by the same impression as the original, or from the same matrix, or by means of photography, including enlargements and miniatures, or by mechanical or electronic re-recording, or by chemical reproduction, or by other equivalent techniques which accurately reproduces the original.

RULE 1002. REQUIREMENT OF ORIGINAL

To prove the content of a writing, recording, or photograph, the original writing, recording, or photograph is required, except as otherwise provided in these rules or by Act of Congress.

RULE 1003. ADMISSIBILITY OF DUPLICATES

A duplicate is admissible to the same extent as an original unless (1) a genuine question is raised as to the authenticity of the original or (2) in the circumstances it would be unfair to admit the duplicate in lieu of the original.

RULE 1004. ADMISSIBILITY OF OTHER EVIDENCE OF CONTENTS

The original is not required, and other evidence of the contents of a writing, recording, or photograph is admissible if—
1. Originals lost or destroyed. All originals are lost or have been destroyed, unless the proponent lost or destroyed them in bad faith; or
2. Original not obtainable. No original can be obtained by any available judicial process or procedure; or
3. Original in possession of opponent. At a time when an original was under the control of the party against whom offered, that party was put on notice, by the pleadings or otherwise, that the contents would be a subject of proof at the hearing, and that party does not produce the original at the hearing; or
4. Collateral matters. The writing, recording, or photograph is not closely related to a controlling issue.

RULE 1005. PUBLIC RECORDS

The contents of an official record, or of a document authorized to be recorded or filed and actually recorded or filed, including data compilations in any form, if otherwise admissible, may be proved by copy, certified as correct in accordance with rule 902 or testified to be correct by a witness who has compared it with the original. If a copy which complies with the foregoing cannot be obtained by the exercise of reasonable diligence, then other evidence of the contents may be given.

RULE 1006. SUMMARIES

The contents of voluminous writings, recordings, or photographs which cannot conveniently be examined in court may be presented in the form of a chart, summary, or calculation. The originals, or duplicates, shall be made available for examination or copying, or both, by other parties at reasonable time and place. The court may order that they be produced in court.

RULE 1007. TESTIMONY OR WRITTEN ADMISSION OF PARTY

Contents of writings, recordings, or photographs may be proved by the testimony or deposition of the party against whom offered or by that party's written admission, without accounting for the nonproduction of the original.

RULE 1008. FUNCTIONS OF COURT AND JURY

When the admissibility of other evidence of contents of writings, recordings, or photographs under these rules depends upon the fulfillment of a condition of fact, the question whether the condition has been fulfilled is ordinarily for the court to determine in accordance with the provisions of rule 104. However, when an issue is raised (a) whether the asserted writing ever existed, or (b) whether another writing, recording, or photograph produced at the trial is the original, or (c) whether other evidence of contents correctly reflects the contents, the issue is for the trier of fact to determine as in the case of other issues of fact.

Glossary

abandoned property Property that a person has deserted or thrown away and thereby disclaims interest in it; may be used as evidence against the former owner.

administrative functions Functions such as screening at airports and courthouses and many fire, health, housing, and school services.

adversary system The judicial system in which opposing parties present evidence, and an impartial judge or jury weighs the evidence; contrasts with the inquisitorial system, where the judge actively questions the accused and witnesses.

affirmative defense A defense that admits the defendant committed the crime charged but asserts that the defendant should not be convicted.

Alford guilty plea A guilty plea that permits the accused to maintain innocence.

ancient document rule The rule that a piece of written or printed matter may be deemed authentic and genuine without a witness to attest to the circumstances of its creation because its age suggests that it is unlikely to have been falsified.

anonymous tip Information from an unknown person; could be received in a 911 call or another telephone call.

arraignment The formal proceeding following the indictment or information, where a plea is entered and the case is bound over for trial.

arrest Defined in 1760 by Sir William Blackstone as "the apprehending or restraining of one's person, in order to be forthcoming to answer an alleged or suspected crime."

arrest warrant An order signed by a judge or magistrate authorizing the arrest of a named person or persons.

assertive statement A statement by which a person intends to communicate a thought or belief.

attorney–client privilege The oldest of the privileges.

ballistic fingerprinting Identification of the gun that fired a bullet from an analysis of the unique marks that every gun makes on the bullet it fires and on the shell ejected from it.

best evidence rule (original document rule) The rule of evidence that requires the original of a writing, photograph, or other document to prove the content, unless the original is unavailable.

beyond a reasonable doubt The burden that the prosecution must meet in proving guilt in criminal cases; applies to every element of the crime charged.

Bill of Rights The first ten amendments to the U.S. Constitution.

Brady rule The rule that requires the prosecution to disclose upon request evidence favorable to the accused.

Bruton rule The rule that a criminal trial may not hear a confession or incriminating statement against a defendant that was made by another party to the crime without producing the speaker.

burden of persuasion That part of the burden of proof that requires a party to persuade the jury that a fact exists.

burden of production That part of the burden of proof that requires a party to produce sufficient evidence to establish the fact at issue.

chain of custody The set of procedures that accounts for the integrity of evidence by tracking its handling and storage from the time it was obtained to the time it is offered at trial.

circumstantial evidence Evidence from which proof of the fact in question may be inferred.

closely regulated businesses Businesses that are subject to careful oversight by laws and codes, such as liquor stores, firearms dealers, coal mines, and pharmacies.

common law Legal rules that evolved over many years in English and American court opinions.

444

competent evidence Any evidence that is relevant and reliable and not otherwise excludable. See Chapter 5.

confession A direct acknowledgment of guilt; generally viewed the same as a guilty plea in open court.

Confrontation Clause The clause in the U.S. Constitution that entitles a defendant in a criminal case to demand witnesses to testify against him in his presence.

conspiracy An agreement by two or more people to commit an illegal act.

corpus delicti The body of the crime; the requirement that the government must prove that the crime charged has been committed.

courtroom identification A prescribed series of steps used during a trial to identify the defendant as the person who committed the crime or was a party to the crime charged.

credibility Believability.

crime-fraud exception The exception made to attorney–client privilege when a client consults with an attorney for the purpose of committing a future crime such as perjury; communication and documents relating to this fraud are not protected.

crime scene A location where an illegal act took place and from which law enforcement personnel collect physical evidence.

criminal complaint The formal charge made by the prosecution against a defendant, which begins criminal proceedings; usually found in misdemeanor cases.

criminal indictment The formal charge issued by a grand jury, listing crimes believed to have been committed by the named defendant.

cross-examination Reexamination of a witness by the opposing attorney following the direct examination of the witness.

curtilage The area close to a home where persons have a right of privacy.

custody Under police control, whether or not physically constrained.

Daubert **test** The principle that scientific evidence presented to the court must result from tests and theories that are testable, have been reviewed by peers, have high reliability rates, and are generally accepted by the associated scientific community.

declarant A person who makes a statement, either in or out of court.

demonstrative evidence Evidence that portrays objects, persons, or events not in the courtroom—for example, photographs and videotapes.

derivative evidence rule Another term for the fruit of the poisonous tree doctrine.

direct evidence Evidence that proves or disproves a fact in question with no need for inferences.

direct examination Questioning of a witness by the lawyer who subpoenaed the witness.

discovery Formal procedures used by prosecution and defense attorneys to gather documents, witnesses, and other evidence.

DNA genetic profiling A method for identifying individuals by the unique structure of their DNA; used for both identifying the person who committed a crime and clearing innocent suspects.

document A piece of written or printed matter that provides information or evidence or that serves as an official record.

due process The minimum procedural protections courts must afford those charged with crimes; guaranteed by the Fifth and Fourteenth Amendments to the U.S. Constitution.

dying declaration exception The exception defined by Rule 804(b)(2), making admissible statements made by a victim or other person under the belief of impending death.

electronic surveillance Secret interception of communications by wiretapping or bugging, which "typically is accomplished by installation of a small microphone in the room (or vehicle) to be bugged" [*Dalia v. United States*, 99 S.Ct. 1682 (1979)].

emergency situation A serious and often dangerous situation that requires immediate action, such as "hot pursuit," now or never, and emergency aid.

evidence The means of establishing the truth or untruth of any fact that is alleged.

exclusionary rule A judicial rule that makes evidence obtained in violation of the U.S. Constitution, state or federal laws, or court rules inadmissible.

exigent circumstances A court-recognized exception to the warrant

requirement of the Fourth Amendment; authorizes entry by not only law enforcement officers but also by firefighters and emergency medical personnel.

expert witness A witness who has special knowledge or training in a specialized area.

federalism Division of power between state governments and the federal government, in which the federal government has specified powers delegated to it, with the remaining powers vested in the states.

Federal Rules of Evidence Codification in 1975 of common-law rules of evidence; applicable only in federal courts but the model for most state evidence codes.

forensic Belonging to or connected with a court; for example, forensic fingerprints are fingerprints used as evidence in a civil or criminal trial.

forensic entomology The study of insects to provide scientific evidence to aid legal investigations.

forfeiture by wrongdoing A rule permitting the admission of hearsay evidence as a penalty against a defendant who wrongfully made the declarant unavailable; often used in murder cases.

free-to-leave test The test used to determine whether a conversation between a person and a law officer is voluntary; a reasonable person must believe he is free to leave.

fruit of the poisonous tree Evidence obtained legally through the use of evidence obtained illegally.

Frye **test** The general acceptance test; scientific evidence presented to the court must result from tests and theories that are generally accepted by a meaningful segment of the associated scientific community.

good faith exception The exception that makes admissible evidence that is obtained under a search warrant that has a technical error unknown to the law officers executing the warrant.

grand jury A jury that hears evidence presented by the prosecution and determines whether to charge persons with crimes; used in federal and many state criminal proceedings.

grand jury secrecy requirement The mandate that persons serving on grand juries will not disclose "matters occurring before" the grand jury on which they serve.

gruesome photographs Photographs that are shocking and repulsive.

habeas corpus Latin name of the writ used to compel a government official, such as a prison warden, to show cause why the official is holding a person in custody.

hearsay Secondhand testimony; reports by one person about what another person said.

honest mistake rule The U.S. Supreme Court's ruling that courts must "allow some latitude for honest mistakes that are made by officers in the dangerous and difficult process of making arrests and executing search warrants" [107 S.Ct. 1013].

hypnosis The induction of a sleeplike condition in which a subject obeys many of the suggestions and orders of the hypnotizer.

impeachment Calling into question the truth or accuracy of direct testimony by cross-examination or introduction of contradictory evidence.

impermissible inference An inference a fact finder may not draw; an example is inferring guilt because the defendant does not testify.

incriminating statement "Any statement or conduct from which guilt of the crime can be inferred" [*People v. Stanton*, 158 N.E.2d 47 (Ill. 1959)].

independent source doctrine An exception to the exclusionary rule where evidence obtained lawfully by one source is admissible even though another source (law officers) obtained the same evidence improperly.

indicia of reliability Characteristics of a statement, otherwise inadmissible as hearsay, that courts believe sufficiently establish the statement's reliability so that cross-examination is not required.

inevitable discovery rule An exception to the exclusionary rule where illegally discovered evidence would certainly have been discovered legally.

inferences Conclusions that may be drawn from facts.

informants Persons who provide information to law officers.

initial appearance The first appearance by an accused before a judge or magistrate; a plea is entered and bail is set at this hearing.

insanity plea A plea to a criminal charge of not guilty because of mental disease or defect.

inventory searches The procedure that law officers use to account for the property of people who are in their custody.

judgment NOV A posttrial judgment made by a judge changing or reversing the jury decision; literally, *non obstante veredicto* ("notwithstanding the verdict").

judicial notice The doctrine that evidence of well-accepted facts may be introduced in court without proof; a judicial shortcut.

latent fingerprints Fingerprints left by a person on a surface other than one designed for recording fingerprints.

lineups An identification procedure in which six or more persons are shown to witnesses or the victim of a crime.

locus point A point in the sequence of base pairs in human DNA where individual DNA chains vary.

Magna Carta The Great Charter signed by King John of England and his barons in 1215; created the first standards for arresting and imprisoning those accused of crimes.

Massiah **limitation** The holding that, after a person has been charged with a crime, law officers cannot question the person regarding that crime without the person's attorney present.

material evidence Evidence that will affect the result of a trial.

Miranda **requirements** The procedural safeguards established by the U.S. Supreme Court in 1966.

motion to suppress evidence A written or oral request to a judge to keep out evidence at a trial or hearing, often made when a party believes the evidence was unlawfully obtained.

news reporter's privilege A privilege that does not exist in common law; created by statutes in many states.

no contest or nolo contendere plea A plea in which the accused neither contests nor admits the charges against him; treated as a guilty plea.

nonverbal communication Acts that do not involve words or speech but that may be assertive and therefore hearsay.

objections Formal statements made by attorneys during trials, objecting to the form or substance of a question or to the answer given by a witness to a question.

open fields An unoccupied or undeveloped area outside of the curtilage; objects found there may be used as evidence.

ordeals A medieval method of proof that was an appeal to God to determine guilt or innocence.

ordinary witness A witness who has firsthand information about a fact gained by personal observation.

partner-in-crime exception The exception to the marital privilege if a husband and wife commit a crime together.

passage of time rule (attenuation) An exception to the exclusionary rule where the "taint" from the improper conduct is dissipated over a significant period of time after the improper conduct.

permissible inferences Inferences made from proof of facts that a fact finder may, but need not, draw.

photographic array A group of photographs shown to witnesses or the victim of a crime for identification purposes.

physical evidence (real evidence) Physical objects, such as weapons, drugs, and clothing.

physician–patient privilege The privilege created, not by common law, but by state law for state courts; belongs to the patient and may be waived by the patient.

plain view or open view doctrine The principle that if a law officer is where he or she has a right to be and sees evidence or contraband in plain view, then the evidence may be seized and used in a criminal trial.

plea bargaining Agreement to enter a guilty plea in return for a reduction in the charge or sentence. For example, first-offense shoplifters are often given the opportunity to plea to disorderly conduct in a municipal court instead of going to trial for a theft charge. First-offense drunk drivers are often permitted to enter a guilty plea in return for the dropping of one of the three or four criminal charges that they face.

preliminary hearing Full adversarial hearing with a lawyer present; the judge determines whether probable cause exists to try the accused for the crime charged.

presentment juries English forerunners to grand juries; gave information that crimes had been committed.

prima facie case A civil or criminal case that is so strong that the opponent must respond with rebutting evidence to avoid losing the case.

private search A search by a private person that is not subject to the exclusionary rule.

privilege A benefit or right enjoyed by a person; for example, the privilege of a witness not to answer a question might be based on the privilege against self-incrimination or the marital privilege.

probable cause The quantum (amount) of evidence required by the Fourth Amendment to make an arrest or to issue a search warrant; greater than reasonable suspicion but can be less than proof or reasonable doubt.

proof The result of evidence; evidence is the means of attaining proof.

protective search A search limited to discovering threatening weapons.

protective sweep or safety check An investigation of a building or vehicle to determine whether other persons or weapons are present that could jeopardize safety.

psychotherapist–patient privilege A privilege created by statute in many states.

reasonable doubt standard The standard for evidence that fact finders (juries or judges) must use in criminal cases to find a defendant guilty of the crime charged.

reasonable suspicion The amount of evidence a law enforcement officer needs to make an investigative stop (a *Terry* stop); less than probable cause but more than a hunch or mere suspicion.

regularly kept records exception The exception defined by Rule 803, which allows the use of regularly kept business records and public, religious, and family records.

relevant evidence Evidence that has a tendency to make a material issue that is before the court more or less probable; see Chapter 5.

reliable evidence Evidence that possesses a sufficient degree of likelihood that it is true and accurate.

reversible errors Errors that occur in a trial court that might have a bearing on the outcome of the trial; an error is not sufficient for reversal if the outcome would have been the same without the error.

scientific evidence Evidence, usually in the form of expert testimony, that relates to scientific theory, experiments, or tests.

search warrant An order signed by a judge or magistrate authorizing the place to be searched and the persons or things to be seized.

sexual assault counselor's privilege The privilege for counselors of victims of sexual assault and crimes of violence; also applies to records and testimony by counselors without the consent of the victim or patient.

showups An identification procedure in which only one subject is shown to witnesses or the victim of a crime.

sketches Drawings by an artist or with an Identi-Kit for use in identification.

"special needs" of government The basic government requirements of safety, health, education, and concern for the well-being of the society as a whole.

spectrograms or voiceprints Voice graphs made on a spectrograph, which analyzes voice recordings based on intensity, frequency, and time gaps.

standing Possession of the necessary relationship to an issue to be permitted to raise that issue in a court of law.

statement against-penal-interest exception The exception defined by Rule 804 (b)(3) making admissible a statement that exposes the speaker to criminal liability.

statements for purposes of medical diagnosis or treatment exception The exception defined by Rule 803(4); for example, statements by doctors and nurses are admissible in child abuse cases.

subpoena duces tecum A subpoena that not only requires the appearance of a witness but also requires the witness to bring relevant and competent documents or writings that may be in his or her possession.

subpoena An order compelling a person to appear as a witness; defense lawyers and prosecutors may have subpoenas issued for witnesses needed in either criminal or civil cases.

sufficiency-of-evidence requirement The demand for a reasonably substantial foundation of evidence to support a verdict or finding.

***Terry* stop** An investigative street detention named after the 1968 U.S. Supreme Court case of *Terry v. Ohio*.

then existing mental, emotional, or physical condition exception The exception defined by Rule 803(3); for example, testimony that the victim stated that she was going to visit her boyfriend is admissible under this exception to show intent.

totality of the circumstances test The test that looks at the whole picture—all factors—in determining whether a confession, incriminating statement, or consent was freely and voluntarily given.

trace evidence Small amounts of material that a suspect leaves or acquires when he or she comes in contact with another object.

truth of the matter asserted The subject to be proved in an assertive statement.

videotape surveillance Close observation by use of video cameras.

voir dire The preliminary examination of a prospective juror or a child who is going to be a witness to determine qualifications.

voluntariness test The requirement that confessions, incriminating statements, and consent be voluntary and freely given and not obtained by means that overwhelmed the will of the accused or another person.

wiretapping According to the U.S. Supreme Court [*Dalia v. United States*, 99 S.Ct. 1682 (1979)], "interception of communication by telephone and telegraph."

witnesses Persons who appear and testify under oath or affirmation before civil and criminal courts and other hearings.

work-related searches A search of a worker's desk and workstation for necessary records or equipment so that another employee can fill in for the absent worker or the employer can check for theft or fraud.

writ of certiorari Formal notice by the U.S. Supreme Court to a lower federal or state court that a case will be reviewed by the Supreme Court.

CASE INDEX

Subject Index